McGraw-Hill

Mathematics

Answer Key

- Practice
- Reteach
- Enrich
- Daily Homework

5

Macmillan
McGraw-Hill
New York Farmington

The **Answer Key** provides answers for the Practice, Reteach, Enrich, and Daily Homework blackline masters that accompany lessons in the Student Book. Each page in the **Answer Key** contains the blackline masters that support one lesson.

Macmillan/McGraw-Hill

A Division of The McGraw-Hill Companies

Macmillan/McGraw-Hill
Two Penn Plaza
New York, New York 10121-2298

ISBN 0-02-100422-6
2 3 4 5 6 7 8 9 024 04 03 02 01

Chapter 1 ~ Lesson 1

Practice

Place Value Through Billions

P 1-1 PRACTICE

Name the place and value of each underlined digit.

1. 2,3<u>4</u>6 tens; 40
2. 6<u>5</u>,893 thousands; 5,000
3. 7<u>6</u>3,406,594 ten millions; 60,000,000
4. 40<u>7</u>,356,138,920 billions; 7,000,000,000
5. 64,<u>3</u>21,008 hundred thousands; 300,000
6. 1<u>1</u>7,927,724,417 ten billions; 10,000,000,000
7. 903,00<u>4</u>,200,006 millions; 4,000,000

Complete the table.

	Standard Form	Short Word Name	Expanded Form
8.	3,125	3 thousand, 125	3,000 + 100 + 20 + 5
9.	52,040	52 thousand, 40	50,000 + 2,000 + 40
10.	7,450,693	7 million, 450 thousand, 693	7,000,000 + 400,000 + 50,000 + 600 + 90 + 3
11.	200,080,009	200 million, 80 thousand, 9	200,000,000 + 80,000 + 9
12.	81,245,000,870	81 billion, 245 million, 870	80,000,000,000 + 1,000,000,000 + 200,000,000 + 40,000,000 + 5,000,000 + 800 + 70
13.	9,000,000,006	9 billion, 6	9,000,000,000 + 6
14.	452,370,000,000	452 billion, 370 million	400,000,000,000 + 50,000,000,000 + 2,000,000,000 + 300,000,000 + 70,000,000

Problem Solving

15. Mercury is the closest planet to the Sun. When nearest the Sun, it is 28 million, 600 thousand miles away. How many miles is this in standard form?

28,600,000 miles

16. Pluto is the farthest planet from the Sun. When farthest from the Sun, it is 4 billion, 551 million, 400 thousand miles away. How many miles is this in standard form?

4,551,400,000 miles

Use with Grade 5, Chapter 1, Lesson 1, pages 2–3. (1)

Reteach

Place Value Through Billions

R 1-1 RETEACH

You can use a place-value chart to help read greater numbers. Say the number in each period followed by the period name, except for "ones."

Billions Period			Millions Period			Thousands Period			Ones Period		
H	T	O	H	T	O	H	T	O	H	T	O
	4	7	3	0	2	0	1	6	2	9	4

Standard form: 47,302,016,294

Short word name: 47 **billion**, 302 **million**, 16 **thousand**, 294

Read: forty-seven billion, three hundred two million, sixteen thousand, two hundred ninety-four

Expanded form: 40,000,000,000 + 7,000,000,000 + 300,000,000 + 2,000,000 + 10,000 + 6,000 + 200 + 90 + 4

Write the short word name and the expanded form of each number. Use a place-value chart to help.

1.

Billions Period			Millions Period			Thousands Period			Ones Period		
H	T	O	H	T	O	H	T	O	H	T	O
				2	7	0	0	6	5	9	3

Standard form: 27,006,593

Short word name: 27 million, 6 thousand, 593

Expanded form: 20,000,000 + 7,000,000 + 6,000 + 500 + 90 + 3

2.

Billions Period			Millions Period			Thousands Period			Ones Period		
H	T	O	H	T	O	H	T	O	H	T	O
3	0	0	0	0	0	4	2	0	0	0	7

Standard form: 300,000,420,007

Short word name: 300 billion, 420 thousand, 7

Expanded form: 300,000,000,000 + 400,000 + 20,000 + 7

3. Standard form: 6,020,700,510

Short word name: 6 billion, 20 million, 700 thousand, 510

Expanded form: 6,000,000,000 + 20,000,000 + 700,000 + 500 + 10

Use with Grade 5, Chapter 1, Lesson 1, pages 2–3. (2)

Enrich

Place Value Through Billions

E 1-1 ENRICH

Cross-Number Puzzle

This puzzle is similar to a crossword puzzle. Instead of writing letters in the boxes, write one digit in each box to form numbers. Use the clues below.

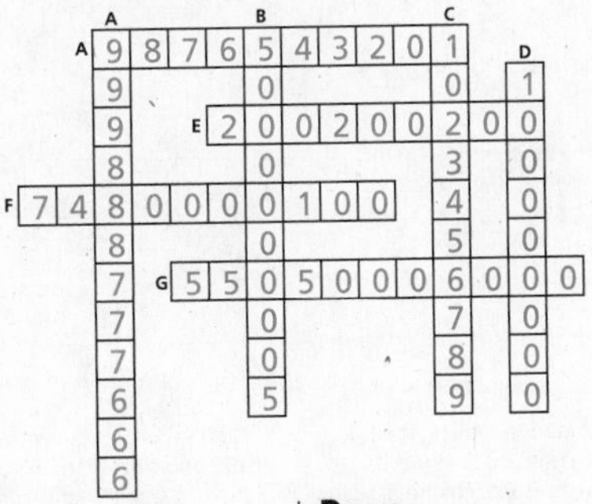

Across

A. the greatest possible number using each of the digits 0–9 once with a zero in the tens place

E. the least possible 9-digit number with a 2 in the hundred millions, hundred thousands, and hundreds places

F. 10 million more than 7 billion, 470 million, 100

G. 1 thousand more than 55 billion, 50 million, 5 thousand

Down

A. the greatest possible 12-digit number using an equal number of 6s, 7s, 8s, and 9s

B. the least possible 10-digit number using 5 as the first and last digit

C. the least possible number using each of the digits 0–9 once

D. 1 million more than 99 million

Look at the clue and number you wrote for B Down. Write two different clues for the same number.

Answers may vary. Possible answer: 5 more than 5 billion; 1 less than 5 billion, 6

Use with Grade 5, Chapter 1, Lesson 1, pages 2–3. (3)

Daily Homework

1-1 Place Value Through Billions

Name the place and value of each underlined digit.

1. 1,2<u>4</u>9 tens; 40
2. 1<u>4</u>,191 thousands; 4,000
3. <u>3</u>,475, 222,892 billions; 3,000,000,000
4. 10,4<u>2</u>6,865 ten thousands; 20,000
5. 8<u>8</u>,776,554 millions; 8,000,000
6. 30,1<u>2</u>3,548,004 ten millions; 20,000,000

Write each number in standard form.

7. 23 million, 864 thousand, 200 23,864,200
8. 212 billion, 804 million, 34 thousand, 401 212,804,034,401

Write the numbers in expanded form.

9. 42,800 40,000 + 2,000 + 800
10. 2,354,476 2,000,000 + 300,000 + 50,000 + 4,000 + 400 + 70 + 6

Problem Solving

11. China's population is 1,246,871,951. How do you read that number?

one billion, two hundred forty-six million, eight hundred seventy-one thousand, nine hundred fifty-one

12. China's total land area is 3,705,392 square miles. Russia's total land area is 6,592,745 square miles. How much more land does Russia have than China?

2,887,353 square miles

Source: *The New York Times Almanac 2000*

Spiral Review

Write each number in standard form.

13. 12 million, 785 thousand, 324 12,785,324
14. 29 billion, 487 million, 123 thousand, 973 29,487,123,973

Grade 5, Chapter 1, Lesson 1, Cluster A 1

Chapter 1 ~ Lesson 2

Practice

Explore Decimal Place Value

P 1-2 PRACTICE

Write the decimal and the fraction for the shaded part.
Each 10-by-10 grid represents 1.

1.
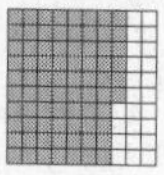

0.76; $\frac{76}{100}$

2.
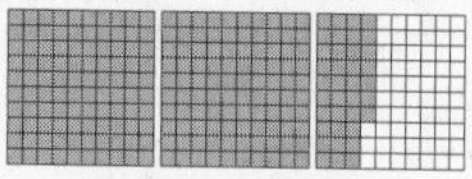

2.37; $2\frac{37}{100}$

3.
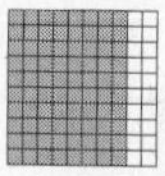

0.80, or 0.8; $\frac{80}{100}$, or $\frac{8}{10}$

4.
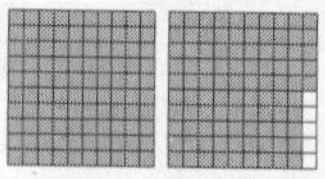

1.95; $1\frac{95}{100}$

5.
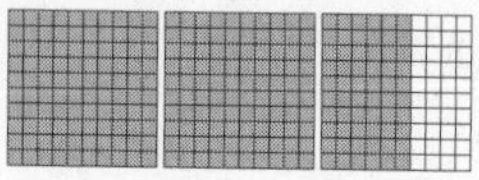

2.60, or 2.6; $2\frac{60}{100}$, or $2\frac{6}{10}$

6.
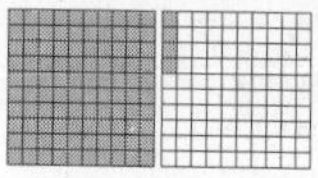

1.04; $1\frac{4}{100}$

Problem Solving

7. In a survey of 100 people, 57 named pepperoni as their favorite pizza topping. What decimal and fraction describe the part of those surveyed who named pepperoni?

0.57; $\frac{57}{100}$

8. In another survey of 100 people, 70 said they eat pizza once a week. What decimal and fraction describe the part of those surveyed who eat pizza once a week?

0.70, or 0.7; $\frac{70}{100}$, or $\frac{7}{10}$

Reteach

Explore Decimal Place Value

R 1-2 RETEACH

You can use 10-by-10 grids to model decimals.

Each completely shaded grid represents 1.

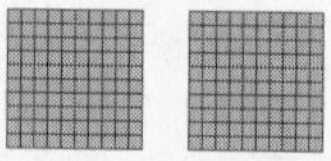

2 ones, or 2

Each small shaded square represents 1 hundredth, or 0.01.

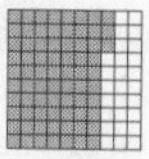

73 hundredths, or 0.73

2.73

Write a decimal to tell how much is shaded.

1.
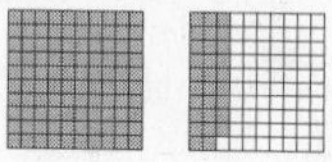

1 0.29

1 . 29

2.
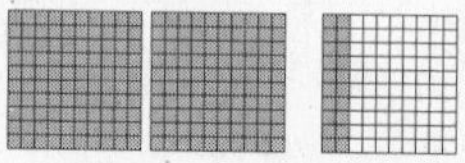

2 0.20, or 0.2

2 . 20, or 2

3.
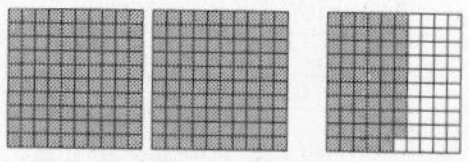

2.59

4.
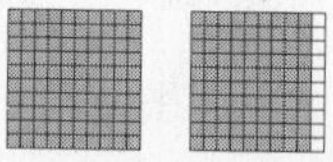

1.90, or 1.9

5.
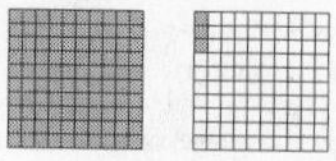

1.03

6.
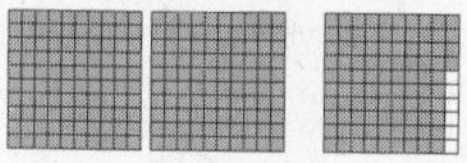

2.94

Enrich

Explore Decimal Place Value

E 1-2 ENRICH

Decimal Designs

Use three colors to make a design on each 10-by-10 grid.
Each 10-by-10 grid represents 1. Color the grids completely.

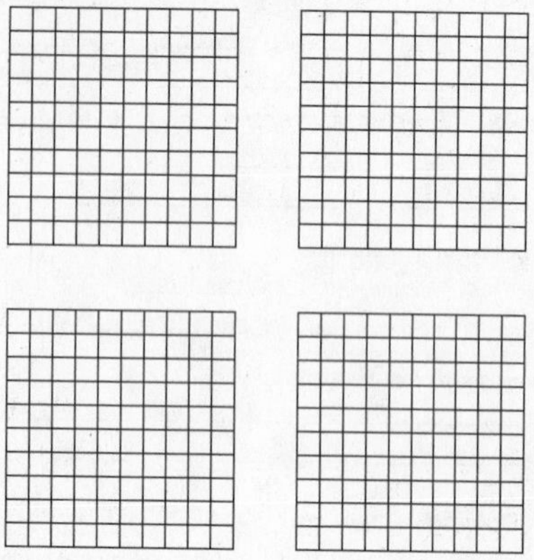

Write a decimal and a fraction to tell how much you shaded with each color.

Answers may vary with designs.

Color	Decimal	Fraction

When was it necessary to write a decimal and a fraction that included a whole number?

I included a whole number when I colored more than 99 squares with the same color.

Daily Homework

1-2 Explore Decimal Place Value

Write the decimal and the fraction.

1.
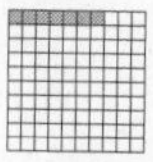

0.07, $\frac{7}{100}$

2.
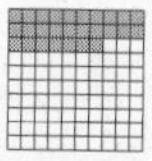

0.27, $\frac{27}{100}$

3.
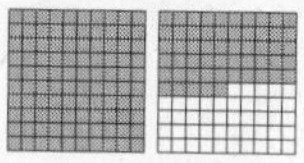

1.55, $1\frac{55}{100}$

4.
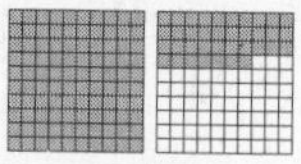

1.37, $1\frac{37}{100}$

Solve.

5. Lola and Mark are planting a vegetable garden. They want to plant lettuce in 0.25 of the garden. Use the grid below to model how much of the garden will be lettuce. Then write the decimal as a fraction.

$\frac{25}{100}$

6. Sue has a coin collection. She has 100 coins in all and 56 of them are nickels. Use the grid to model the number of nickels Sue has. Then write a decimal and a fraction to represent the number of nickels she has.

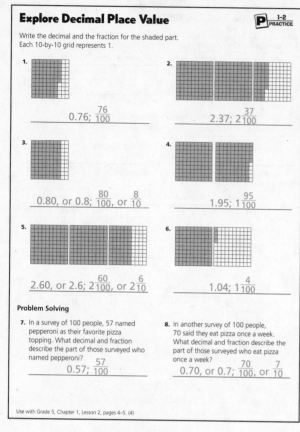

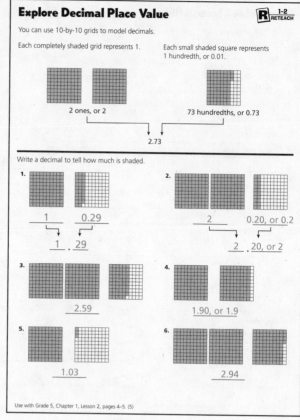

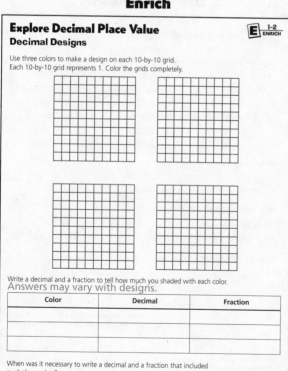

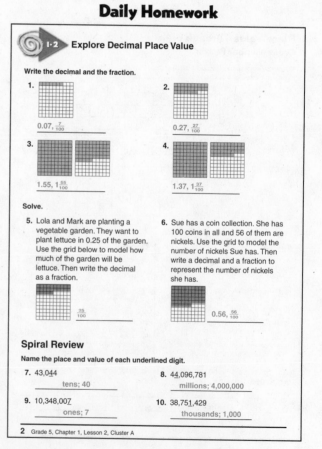

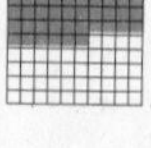

0.56, $\frac{56}{100}$

Spiral Review

Name the place and value of each underlined digit.

7. 43,0<u>4</u>4

tens; 40

8. 4<u>4</u>,096,781

millions; 4,000,000

9. 10,348,00<u>7</u>

ones; 7

10. 38,75<u>1</u>,429

thousands; 1,000

Chapter 1 ~ Lesson 3

Practice

Decimal Place Value

P 1-3 PRACTICE

Name the place of the underlined digit.

1. 7.81 tenths
2. 0.126 hundredths
3. 14.6005 ten-thousandths
4. 20.903 tenths
5. 5.078 thousandths
6. 0.5094 hundredths
7. 9.1576 hundredths
8. 7.6815 ten-thousandths

Complete the table.

	Standard Form	Short Word Name	Expanded Form
9.	4.16	4 and 16 hundredths	4 + 0.1 + 0.06
10.	13.078	13 and 78 thousandths	10 + 3 + 0.07 + 0.008
11.	0.93	93 hundredths	0.9 + 0.03
12.	20.007	20 and 7 thousandths	20 + 0.007
13.	0.1392	1,392 ten-thousandths	0.1 + 0.03 + 0.009 + 0.0002
14.	2.0608	2 and 608 ten-thousandths	2 + 0.06 + 0.0008

Name an equivalent decimal. Answers may vary. Possible answers are given.

15. 0.3 0.30
16. 1.400 1.4
17. 5.00 5.000
18. 3.10 3.1
19. 2.7 2.70
20. 4.75 4.750
21. 16.53 16.530
22. 9.5100 9.51
23. 87.05 87.050

Problem Solving

24. The fifth grade at Highland School is cleaning up 3 and 45 hundredths miles of the banks of Sugar Creek. How many miles is this in standard form?
3.45 miles

25. On one Saturday the fifth graders picked up 30 and 58 thousandths kilograms of trash. How many kilograms is this in standard form?
30.058 kilograms

Use with Grade 5, Chapter 1, Lesson 3, pages 6–9. (7)

Reteach

Decimal Place Value

R 1-3 RETEACH

You can use a place-value chart to help read decimals. Read the whole number part of the number. Say "and" for the decimal point. Read the decimal part of the number, followed by the name of the last place.

Tens	Ones	.	Tenths	Hundredths	Thousandths	Ten-Thousandths
1	2	.	0	9	5	6

Standard form: 12.0956
Short word name: 12 and 956 ten-thousandths
Expanded form: 10 + 2 + 0.09 + 0.005 + 0.0006
Read: twelve and nine hundred fifty-six ten-thousandths

Write the word name and the expanded form of each number. Use a place-value chart to help.

1.

Tens	Ones	.	Tenths	Hundredths	Thousandths	Ten-Thousandths
	3	.	0	7	5	

Standard form: 3.075
Short word name: 3 and 75 thousandths
Expanded form: 3 + 0.07 + 0.005

2.

Tens	Ones	.	Tenths	Hundredths	Thousandths	Ten-Thousandths
1	4	.	9	0	0	6

Standard form: 14.9006
Short word name: 14 and 9,006 ten-thousandths
Expanded form: 10 + 4 + 0.9 + 0.0006

3.

Tens	Ones	.	Tenths	Hundredths	Thousandths	Ten-Thousandths
2	4	.	0	0	1	9

Standard form: 24.0019
Short word name: 24 and 19 ten-thousandths
Expanded form: 20 + 4 + 0.001 + 0.0009

Use with Grade 5, Chapter 1, Lesson 3, pages 6–9. (8)

Enrich

Decimal Place Value

E 1-3 ENRICH

Number Riddle

Write each decimal by writing one digit on each answer line. Look carefully at the position of the decimal point. Circle the digit in the hundredths place.

A. the greatest possible decimal using each of the digits 5–9 once
9 8 7 . 6 (5)

C. the least possible decimal using each of the digits 5–9 once
5 6 . 7 (8) 9

E. the greatest possible decimal using each of the digits 0–5 once
5 4 . 3 (2) 1 0

I. the least possible decimal using each of the digits 0–5 once
1 0 2 . 3 (4) 5

L. the least possible decimal greater than zero
0 . 0 (0) 1

M. the greatest possible decimal
9 . 9 (9) 9 9

N. the decimal with one more tenth than 15.237
1 5 . 3 (3) 7

O. the decimal with one fewer thousandth than 6.3118
6 . 3 (1) 0 8

P. a decimal equivalent to 3.4600
3 . 4 (6) 0

T. a decimal equivalent to 0.7770
0 . 7 (7) 7

Find each circled digit in the riddle below. Write the letter of the clue above the matching digit to answer the riddle.

On what mountain would you expect to find a mathematician?

On D	E	C	I	M	A	L	P	O	I	N	T
	2	8	4	9	5	0	6	1	4	3	7

Look at the clue for I. How did you find out the least possible decimal?
Explanations may vary. Possible explanation: I wrote the least digit, except for zero, in the greatest place. I wrote zero in the next place. I continued working to the right, writing the next lower digit in the greatest place remaining.

Use with Grade 5, Chapter 1, Lesson 3, pages 6–9. (9)

Daily Homework

1-3 Decimal Place Value

Name the place of the underlined digit.

1. 1.23 tenths
2. 3.146 hundredths
3. 8.654 thousandths
4. 0.0163 ten thousandths
5. 2,726.78 hundreds
6. 47.513 thousandths

Write in standard form.

7. seven and 8 tenths 7.8
8. fourteen and 75 hundredths 14.75

Write the word name and expanded form.

9. 4.70 four and seven tenths, 4 + 0.7
10. 34.045 thirty four and forty-five thousandths, 30 + 4 + 0.04 + 0.005

Name an equivalent decimal. Answers may vary.

11. 0.8 0.80
12. 2.14 2.140
13. 210.06 210.060

Problem Solving

14. In 1992, Quincy Watts of the United States won the 400-meter track event with a time of forty-three and five tenths seconds. Write this number.
43.5 seconds
Source: The World Almanac and Book of Facts 2000

15. In 1994 Al Unser, Jr., reached a speed of 160.872 miles per hour in the Indianapolis 500 automobile race. Write an equivalent decimal for this number.
Possible answer: 160.8720

Spiral Review

Name the place and the value of each underlined digit.

16. 3,673 hundreds; 600
17. 78,133 thousands; 8,000
18. 88,114,567 millions; 8,000,000

Grade 5, Chapter 1, Lesson 3, Cluster A 3

Chapter 1 ~ Lesson 4

Practice

Compare and Order Whole Numbers and Decimals

P 1-4 PRACTICE

Compare. Write >, <, or =.

1. 3,976 (<) 4,007
2. 89,001 (<) 89,100
3. 126,698 (>) 126,689
4. 1,435,052 (>) 145,052
5. 19,463,674 (<) 29,436,764
6. 4,303,259,087 (>) 4,033,259,807
7. 328,574,000,256 (<) 328,574,010,256
8. 2.7 (<) 2.82
9. 6.030 (=) 6.03
10. 7.89 (>) 7.189
11. 12.54 (>) 1.254
12. 0.981 (<) 2.3
13. 0.004 (<) 0.040

Order from least to greatest.

14. 17,639; 3,828; 45,947 ___3,828; 17,639; 45,947___
15. 890,409; 890,904; 809,904 ___809,904; 890,409; 890,904___
16. 21,997; 29,979; 219,997; 21,797 ___21,797; 21,997; 29,979; 219,997___
17. 5,630,168; 5,036,168; 6,530,168; 563,168 ___563,168; 5,036,168; 5,630,168; 6,530,168___
18. 8.26; 8.02; 8.6 ___8.02; 8.26; 8.6___
19. 58.50; 5.085; 5.85; 5.805 ___5.085; 5.805; 5.85; 58.50___
20. 0.186; 0.1; 0.86; 0.168 ___0.1; 0.168; 0.186; 0.86___
21. 5.309; 5.003; 0.53; 0.9 ___0.53; 0.9; 5.003; 5.309___

Problem Solving

22. In January, the average low temperature in Montreal, Canada, is 5.2°F, and the average low temperature in Cape Town, South Africa, is 60.3°F. Which city is warmer in January?
    ___Cape Town___

23. In one year Seattle, Washington, recorded 0.24 in. of snow, Chicago, Illinois, recorded 30.9 in. of snow, and Birmingham, Alabama, recorded 1 in. of snow. Write these amounts in order from least to greatest.
    ___0.24 in., 1 in., 30.9 in.___

Use with Grade 5, Chapter 1, Lesson 4, pages 10–13. (10)

Reteach

Compare and Order Whole Numbers and Decimals

R 1-4 RETEACH

You can write numbers in expanded form to compare them.

Compare 43,058 and 48,503.

Write the numbers in expanded form.
43,058 = 40,000 + 3,000 + 50 + 8
48,503 = 40,000 + 8,000 + 500 + 3

Compare the numbers, starting with the greatest place.
40,000 = 40,000 3,000 < 8,000
So, 43,058 < 48,503.

Compare 12.106 and 9.837.

If the numbers have a different number of digits, be sure to line them up correctly.
12.106 = 10 + 2 + 0.1 + 0.006
9.837 = 9 + 0.8 + 0.03 + 0.007

Only 12.106 has a digit in the tens place.
So, 12.106 > 9.837.

Write the numbers in expanded form to compare. Write >, <, or =.

1. 3,505 = ___3,000 + 500 + 5___
   3,055 = ___3,000 + 50 + 5___
   3,505 (>) 3,055
2. 7.15 = ___7 + 0.1 + 0.05___
   17.5 = ___10 + 7 + 0.5___
   7.15 (<) 17.5
3. 42.8 = ___40 + 2 + 0.8___
   42.80 = ___40 + 2 + 0.8___
   42.8 (=) 42.80
4. 0.025 = ___0.02 + 0.005___
   0.250 = ___0.2 + 0.05___
   0.025 (<) 0.250
5. 8,296 = ___8,000 + 200 + 90 + 6___
   596 = ___500 + 90 + 6___
   8,296 (>) 596
6. 4,000,976 = ___4,000,000 + 900 + 70 + 6___
   4,009,076 = ___4,000,000 + 9,000 + 70 + 6___
   4,000,976 (<) 4,009,076

Use with Grade 5, Chapter 1, Lesson 4, pages 10–13. (11)

Enrich

Compare and Order Whole Numbers and Decimals

E 1-4 ENRICH

Orderly Stars

Each star below has a number. Find the stars with numbers greater than 5 tenths and less than 100 million. Connect them in order from least to greatest.

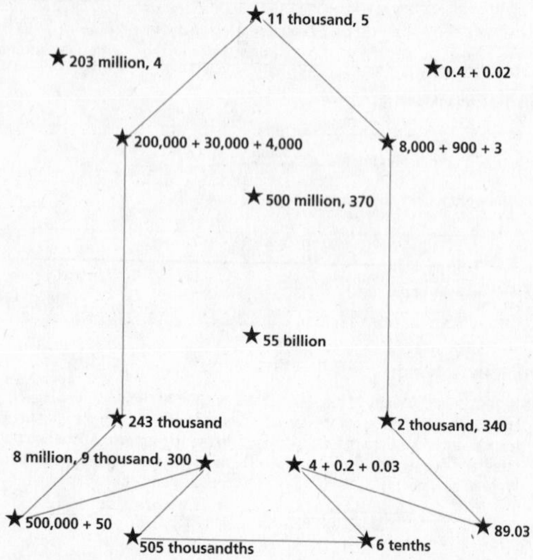

What could you do to make it easier to connect the stars in order?

___Answers may vary. Possible answer: First write each number in standard form.___

Use with Grade 5, Chapter 1, Lesson 4, pages 10–13. (12)

Daily Homework

1-4 Compare and Order Whole Numbers and Decimals

Compare. Write >, <, or =.

1. 1,722 ___<___ 1,723
2. 12,444,832 ___>___ 9,457,998
3. 212,783,806 ___<___ 212,793,806
4. 1.7 ___>___ 1.67
5. 4.560 ___>___ 4.506
6. 35.800 ___=___ 35.8

Order from least to greatest.

7. 413,540; 9,912; 84,127
   ___9,912; 84,127; 413,540___
8. 218,521; 218,512; 218,512.7
   ___218,512; 218,512.7; 218,521___
9. 6.347; 6.437; 6.4; 6.34; 6
   ___6, 6.34, 6.347, 6.4, 6.437___
10. 0.67; 0.671; 0.608; 0.655; 0.635
   ___0.608, 0.635, 0.655, 0.67, 0.671___

Find two numbers between the numbers given.

11. 23.3 and 23.8 ___Possible answers: 23.4 and 23.5___
12. 6,841 and 6,846 ___Possible answers: 6,842 and 6,843___

Problem Solving

13. Philips Arena in Atlanta seats 20,000. The Charlotte Coliseum seats 24,042. The United Center in Chicago seats 21,711. Which is the largest stadium?
    Source: *The World Almanac and Book of Facts 2000*
    ___Charlotte Coliseum___

14. Frankie runs on his school's track team. The top 3 records set by his teammates are 15.02 seconds, 15.09 seconds, and 15.11 seconds. What is the slowest time Frankie can have to be in first place?
    ___15.01 seconds___

Spiral Review

Name the place of the underlined digit.

15. 17.680 ___hundredths___
16. 8.0177 ___thousandths___
17. 18.114 ___tenths___

4 Grade 5, Chapter 1, Lesson 4, Cluster A

Practice

Problem Solving: Reading for Math
Use the Four-Step Process

1-5 PRACTICE — Reading Skill

Solve. Use the four-step process.

1. The highest point in Maine is Mount Katahdin, with an elevation of 5,267 feet. Taum Sauk Mountain has an elevation of 1,772 feet. It is the highest point in Missouri. The highest point in New Jersey has an elevation of 1,803 feet. It is even called High Point. List the highest points by name from greatest to least.
   Mount Katahdin, High Point, Taum Sauk Mountain

2. Black Mountain, Kentucky, is the state's highest point with an elevation of 4,139 feet. At 4,039 feet, Mount Sunflower is the highest point in Kansas. List these elevations and Mount Katahdin from least to greatest by name.
   Mount Sunflower, Black Mountain, Mount Katahdin

3. Mount Mansfield, Vermont, has an elevation of 4,393 feet. It is the highest point in Vermont. Which is greater, the highest point in Vermont or the highest point in Kentucky?
   Vermont

4. Of all the elevations listed above, which two places have elevations of about 2,000 feet?
   Taum Sauk Mountain and High Point

5. Of all the mountains listed above, which has the greatest elevation?
   Mount Katahdin

6. Sassafras Mountain is the highest point in South Carolina. Its elevation is 3,560 feet. If you list all of the elevations above in order from least to greatest, between the elevations of which two places would Sassafras Mountain lie?
   High Point and Mount Sunflower

Use with Grade 5, Chapter 1, Lesson 5, pages 14–15. (13)

Practice

Problem Solving: Reading for Math
Use the Four-Step Process

1-5 PRACTICE — Math Skills Test Prep

Choose the best answer.

The Amoco Building in Chicago is 1,136 feet tall. The First Interstate World Center in Los Angeles is 1,018 feet tall. The CN Tower in Toronto, Ontario, Canada is 1,821 feet tall.

1. Which of the following statements is false?
   - A The Amoco Building is taller than the First Interstate World Center.
   - (B) The First Interstate World Center is taller than the CN Tower.
   - C The CN Tower is taller than the Amoco Building.
   - D The Amoco Building is not as tall as the CN Tower.

2. According to the four-step process, what should you do after solving the problem?
   - F Identify what you need to find out.
   - G Make a plan.
   - H Follow your plan.
   - (J) Look back to see that your answer relates to the question.

The Delaware Memorial Bridge has a span of 2,150 feet. The Bronx-Whitestone Bridge has a span of 2,300 feet. Which bridge spans the greater distance?

3. According to the four-step process, what should you do after making a plan?
   - A Note the information in the problem.
   - B Decide what actions you will take.
   - C Choose to see that the answer is reasonable.
   - (D) Solve the problem.

4. Which of the following statements is true?
   - (F) The Bronx-Whitestone Bridge has the greater span.
   - G The Delaware Memorial Bridge has the greater span.
   - H The Delaware Memorial Bridge spans less than 2,000 feet.
   - J The Bronx-Whitestone Bridge spans about 3,000 feet.

Petronas Tower I, in Kuala Lumpur, Malaysia, is 1,483 feet tall. Petronas Tower II, also in Kuala Lumpur, is as tall as Petronas Tower I. In New York City, One World Trade Center is 1,368 feet tall and Two World Trade Center is 1,362 feet tall.

5. Which of the following statements is true?
   - A Petronas Tower I is taller than Petronas Tower II.
   - (B) One World Trade Center is taller than Two World Trade Center.
   - C One World Trade Center is taller than Petronas Tower I.
   - D Two World Trade Center is taller than Petronas Tower II.

6. According to the four-step process, what should you do when you read the problem?
   - F Make a plan.
   - G Follow your plan.
   - (H) Note the information given in the problem.
   - J Look back to see that your answer relates to the problem.

Use with Grade 5, Chapter 1, Lesson 5, pages 14–15. (14)

Practice

Problem Solving: Reading for Math
Use the Four-Step Process

1-5 PRACTICE — Math Skills Test Prep

Choose the best answer.

The Sumner Tunnel in Boston, Massachusetts, is 5,653 feet long. The Callahan Tunnel, also in Boston, is 5,070 feet long. A third Boston tunnel, the Ted Williams Tunnel, is 8,448 feet long.

7. Which of the following statements is *not* true?
   - A The Callahan Tunnel is the shortest.
   - B The Sumner Tunnel is not as long as the Ted Williams Tunnel.
   - (C) The Callahan Tunnel is longer than the Sumner Tunnel.
   - D The Sumner Tunnel is longer than the Callahan Tunnel.

8. According to the four-step process, what is the first thing you should do to make a plan?
   - F Read the problem.
   - G Identify what you need to find out.
   - H Note information in tables or diagrams.
   - (J) Decide what actions you will take and how you will carry them out.

Solve.

9. Hoover Dam, in the United States, is 221 meters high. Ertan Dam, in China, is 245 meters high. In Canada, Mica Dam is 242 meters high. List the dams by height from least to greatest.
   Hoover, Mica, Ertan

10. The Tacoma Narrows Bridge in Washington has a span of 2,800 feet. The span of the Mackinac Straits Bridge in Missouri is 1,000 feet longer than the Tacoma Narrows Bridge. What is the span of the Mackinac Straits Bridge?
    3,800 feet

Use data from the table for problems 11–14.

Highest Altitudes

State	Name	Elevation (feet)
Alabama	Cheaha Mountain	2,405
Colorado	Mount Elbert	14,433
Montana	Granite Peak	12,799
Texas	Gualalupe Peak	8,749
Wisconsin	Timms Hill	1,951

11. Which state has the highest elevation?
    Colorado

12. List the highest points by name in Alabama, Texas, and Wisconsin, in order from least to greatest.
    Timms Hill, Cheaha Mountain, Guadalupe Peak

13. Which states have elevations greater than 10,000 feet?
    Colorado and Montana

14. Which has a greater elevation: Guadalupe Peak or Cheaha Mountain?
    Guadalupe Peak

Use with Grade 5, Chapter 1, Lesson 5, pages 14–15. (15)

Daily Homework

1-5 Problem Solving: Reading for Math
Use the Four-Step Process

Solve. Use the four-step process.

The Verrazano-Narrows Bridge in New York is 4,260 feet long. The Williamsburg Bridge across the East River is 1,600 feet long and the Brooklyn Bridge, across the same river, is 1,595 feet long. Other suspension bridges include the Oakland Bay Bridge in San Francisco, California, 2,310 feet long; the Golden Gate Bridge in San Francisco, 4,200 feet long; and the Seaway Skyway in Ogdensburg, New York, which is 2,150 feet long.

1. Which bridge is the shortest? Brooklyn Bridge
2. List the three longest bridges in order from greatest to least.
   Verrazano-Narrows, Golden Gate, Oakland Bay

Use data from the table for problems 3–4.

Underwater Vehicular Tunnels

Tunnel Name (Year Built)	Location	Waterway	Length (ft)
Ted Williams (1995)	Boston, MA	Boston Harbor	8,448
Queens Midtown (1940)	New York, NY	East River	6,414
Brooklyn-Battery (1950)	New York, NY	East River	9,117
Holland (1927)	New York, NY	Hudson River	8,557
Baltimore Harbor (1957)	Baltimore, MD	Baltimore Harbor	7,392

Source: *The World Almanac and Book of Facts 2000*

3. Which tunnel was built the earliest? Holland Tunnel
4. List the three longest tunnels in order from greatest to least.
   Brooklyn-Battery Tunnel, Holland Tunnel, Ted Williams Tunnel

Spiral Review

Compare. Write <, >, or =.

5. 28,234,688 > 28,204,669
6. 11,404,687 < 11,405,687

Grade 5, Chapter 1, Lesson 5, Cluster A 5

Practice

ÍAdd and Subtract Whole Numbers and Decimals

P 1-6 PRACTICE

Add or subtract.

1. 9,868 + 6,329 = 16,197
2. 3,136 − 473 = 2,663
3. 0.87 + 6.12 = 6.99
4. 4.45 − 1.02 = 3.43
5. 3,007 − 1,980 = 1,027
6. 4.672 + 15.31 = 19.982
7. 31,043 + 56,691 = 87,734
8. 2.85 − 0.58 = 2.27
9. 4.609 − 2.81 = 1.799
10. 124,543 + 96,883 = 221,426
11. 12.974 + 4.734 = 17.708
12. 20,431 − 17,642 = 2,789
13. 5.8 + 4.289 = 10.089
14. 30,048 − 9,338 = 20,710
15. $1.09 − 0.65 = $0.44
16. 76,509 + 120,306 = 196,815
17. 321,658,400 − 197,369,250 = 124,289,150
18. 3,472,196 + 7,810,984 = 11,283,180
19. 3.65 − 0.824 = 2.826
20. $28.99 + 1.75 = $30.74

21. 34,504 + 5,712 = 40,216
22. 1.265 + 8.77 = 10.035
23. 9.54 − 4.883 = 4.657
24. 2,980 + 135,618 = 138,598
25. $44.65 − $2.19 = $42.46
26. 78,327 − 59,912 = 18,415
27. $0.33 + $5.79 = $6.12
28. 210,336 − 89,481 = 120,855

Problem Solving

29. Gasoline prices are given to the nearest thousandth of a dollar. If gasoline rises in price from $1.499 to $1.589, what is the amount of the increase?
$0.09

30. The area of Texas is 695,676 square kilometers. That is 525,368 more square kilometers than Florida. What is the area of Florida in square kilometers?
170,308 sq km

Reteach

Add and Subtract Whole Numbers and Decimals

R 1-6 RETEACH

You can use a place-value chart to help you add and subtract whole numbers and decimals.

Add 2.87 + 1.6.

Step 1
Line up the decimal points. Write an equivalent decimal if necessary.

Ones	.	Tenths	Hundredths
2 + 1	. .	8 6	7 **0**

Step 2
Add the hundredths. Regroup if necessary.

Ones	.	Tenths	Hundredths
2 + 1	. .	8 6	7 0
			7

Step 3
Add the tenths. Regroup if necessary.

Ones	.	Tenths	Hundredths
1 2 + 1	. .	8 6	7 0
		4	7

Step 4
Add the ones. Regroup if necessary. Write the decimal point in the answer.

Ones	.	Tenths	Hundredths
1 2 + 1	. .	8 6	7 0
4	**.**	4	7

Add or subtract. Use a place-value chart to help.

1. 4.69 + 8.056 = 12.746
2. 491,394 + 17,698 = 509,092
3. 32,681 − 4,095 = 28,586
4. 4.98 − 3.1 = 1.88

5. 67,430 + 25,875 = 93,305
6. 7,043 + 39,605 = 46,648
7. 80,000 − 18,550 = 61,450
8. 40,000 − 398 = 39,602
9. 0.163 + 13.9 = 14.063
10. 8.2 + 6.79 = 14.99
11. 7.25 − 1.6 = 5.65
12. 3 − 0.45 = 2.55

Enrich

Add and Subtract Whole Numbers and Decimals

E 1-6 ENRICH

Palindromes

A math palindrome is a number that reads the same when it is reversed. Use the flowchart to make palindromes.

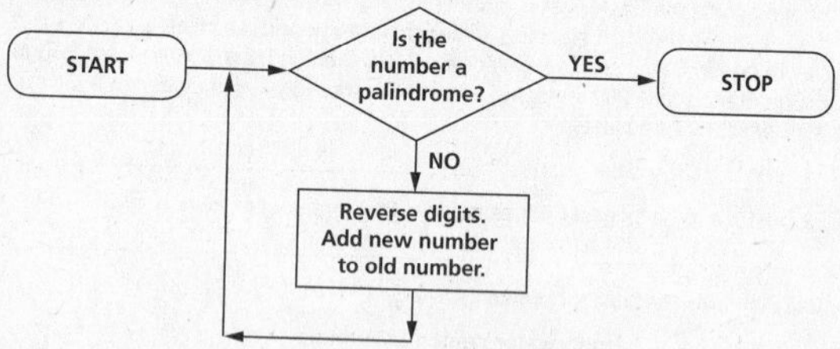

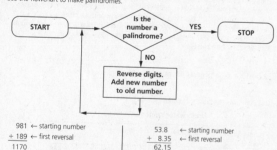

981 ← starting number
+ 189 ← first reversal
1170
+ 0711 ← second reversal
1881 ← palindrome

53.8 ← starting number
+ 8.35 ← first reversal
62.15
+ 51.26 ← second reversal
113.41
+ 14.311 ← third reversal
127.721 ← palindrome

Find the palindrome for each number. Record your process.

1. 5,382 69,696
2. 3,136 9,449
3. 8,096 55,055
4. 15,682 77,677
5. 26,853 258,852
6. 234,567 999,999
7. 2.46 66.66
8. 4.29 96.69
9. 2.9 13.31
10. 4.73 73.37
11. 8.301 213.312
12. 9.8 73.37

Look back at the regrouping you did as you added in exercises 1–12. When will the sum of a number and its reversal result in a palindrome?
A palindrome results when no regrouping is needed.

Daily Homework

1-6 Add and Subtract Whole Numbers and Decimals

Add or subtract.

1. 21,125 − 11,465 = 9,660
2. 32,444 + 29,088 = 61,532
3. 148,809 + 58,911 = 207,720
4. 5,074 − 1,837 = 3,237
5. 56,396 − 39,989 = 16,407
6. 71.475 + 52.364 = 123.839
7. 388.56 − 97.68 = 290.88
8. 92.06 + 19.45 = 111.51
9. 42.706 − 0.844 = 41.862
10. $573.38 + 48.98 = $622.36
11. 614,782,596 + 368,425,491 = 983,208,087
12. 466.724 − 73.968 = 392.756
13. 48,763.612 − 9,483.713 = 39,279.899

Choose the sum that is greater.

14. A. 3,680 + 308
B. 3,670 + 385 *
15. A. 470,000 + 180,000
B. 490,000 + 220,000 *
16. A. 1.346 + 0.318
B. 1.664 + 0.98 *
17. A. 41.650 + 8.48 *
B. 44.580 + 2.561

Problem Solving

18. In 1996, the United States women's 400-meter relay team beat its own 1992 record by 0.16 second. The 1992 time was 42.11 seconds. What was its record time in 1996?
41.95 seconds
Source: *The Time Almanac 2000*

19. If adult tickets to an Olympic event cost $25.50 and a child's ticket costs $20.75, how much will a family of 2 adults and 2 children pay for tickets to the event?
$92.50

Spiral Review

Compare. Write >, <, or =.

20. 21.47 < 21.5
21. 27.17 > 2.710
22. 4.086 < 4.10
23. 75.600 = 75.6
24. 59.218 > 59.208
25. 689.2 < 6,892

Chapter 1 ~ Lesson 7

Practice

Estimate Sums and Differences

P 1-7 PRACTICE

Round to the underlined place.

1. 2,741 3,000
2. 8.37 8
3. $315.95 $316
4. 34,098 34,000
5. 79.437 79
6. 58.164 58.2

Round to the indicated place.

7. 653 (ten) 650
8. 2.468 (hundredth) 2.47
9. $105.49 (dollar) $105
10. 39,281.7 (hundred) 39,300
11. 46.275 (tenth) 46.3
12. $1.6195 (cent) $1.62

Estimates may vary. Possible estimates are shown.

Estimate the sum or difference. Show how you rounded.

13. 317 + 288 → 300 + 300 = 600
14. 0.88 + 6.336 → 1 + 6 = 7
15. 1,642 − 381 → 1,600 − 400 = 1,200
16. 3.09 − 2.98 → 3 − 3 = 0
17. 6.461 − 3.1085 6 − 3 = 3
18. 38 + 504 + 81 0 + 500 + 100 = 600
19. 5,319 − 1,999 5,000 − 2,000 = 3,000
20. $13.77 + $9.95 $10 + $10 = $20
21. 3,498 − 734 3,000 − 1,000 = 2,000
22. $76.08 − $61.97 $80 − $60 = $20

Problem Solving

23. The driving distance from Los Angeles to Chicago is 2,054 mi. The distance from Chicago to Boston is 983 mi. About how many miles is the drive from Los Angeles to Boston through Chicago? about 3,000 mi
24. Rita paid for a $2.95 sandwich and a $1.19 drink with a $10 bill. About how much did her lunch cost? About how much did she receive as change? about $4; about $6

Use with Grade 5, Chapter 1, Lesson 7, pages 22–25. (19)

Reteach

Estimate Sums and Differences

R 1-7 RETEACH

To estimate a sum or difference, you can round the numbers to make it easier to add or subtract mentally.

Method 1

Round to the greatest place in the greater number.

Find the greater number. Circle the number in the greatest place. Round each number to that place. Then add or subtract.

2,732 → 3,000; + 941 → + 1,000; = 4,000

18.7 → 20; − 4.2 → − 0; = 20

Method 2

Round to the greatest place in the lesser number.

Find the lesser number. Circle the number in the greatest place. Round each number to that place. Then add or subtract.

2,732 → 2,700; + 941 → + 900; = 3,600

18.7 → 19; − 4.2 → − 4; = 15

Round to the greatest place in the greater number to estimate each sum or difference.

1. 4,204 → 4,000; + 2,779 → + 3,000; = 7,000
2. $189 → $200; − 53 → − 100; = $100
3. 4,567 → 5,000; − 788 → − 1,000; = 4,000
4. $31.53 → $30; + 2.07 → + 0; = $30
5. 15.497 → 20; + 8.38 → + 10; = 30
6. 47.1 → 50; − 11.66 → − 10; = 40

Round to the greatest place in the lesser number to estimate each sum or difference.

7. 5,087 → 5,100; + 615 → + 600; = 5,700
8. 794 → 800; + 3,157 → + 3,200; = 4,000
9. 4,780 → 4,800; − 103 → − 100; = 4,700
10. $42.469 → $42; + 8.23 → + 8; = $50
11. 58.9 → 59; − 7.1 → − 7; = 52
12. 32.78 → 33; − 6.6 → − 7; = 26

Use with Grade 5, Chapter 1, Lesson 7, pages 22–25. (20)

Enrich

Estimate Sums and Differences

E 1-7 ENRICH

Estimation Point

Cut out the number cards and the decimal-point cards below.

- Arrange the cards to show two decimal numbers. They can have up to three decimal places. Estimate the sum of the two numbers.
- Now move each decimal-point card left or right. Try to make the greatest possible change in your sum. Estimate the new sum.

Repeat with subtraction.

Round 1

1.236 + 78.594

123.6 + 7,859.4

Round 2

9.824 − 3.157

982.4 − 315.7

0	1	2	3	4	5
6	7	8	9	.	.

Use with Grade 5, Chapter 1, Lesson 7, pages 22–25. (21)

Daily Homework

1-7 Estimate Sums and Differences

Round to the underlined place.

1. 2,864 3,000
2. 57,787 57,790
3. 84.53 84.5
4. 36,807 36,810
5. 54.694 54.69
6. 34.75 34.8
7. 74,577,048 74,577,000
8. 2.0036 2.004
9. 3,897 3,900
10. 149.98 150

Round to the place indicated.

11. 848 (hundreds) 800
12. 5,742 (thousands) 6,000
13. 1,875 (tens) 1,880

Estimate each sum or difference. Show your work. Answers may vary. Possible answers are given.

14. 5.37 + 0.08 5.4 + 0.1 = 5.5
15. 0.86 + 3.077 0.9 + 3.1 = 4
16. 45.29 − 10.742 45 − 11 = 34

Problem Solving

17. A well-known television actor makes $44,775 per episode on a weekly television show. About how much does he earn for a 13-week series? about $585,000
18. In 1999, there were 356 different species of animals on the endangered list and 578 species of plants. Estimate these numbers to the nearest ten. Then find the total number of endangered species to the nearest hundred. 360 animals, 580 plants; 1,000 in all

Source: *The New York Times Almanac 2000*

Spiral Review

Write two equivalent decimals for each. Answers may vary.

19. 5.8 5.80, 5.800
20. 0.7 0.70, 0.700
21. 8.05 8.050, 8.0500

Grade 5, Chapter 1, Lesson 7, Cluster B 7

Chapter 1 ~ Lesson 8

Practice

Problem Solving: Strategy
Find a Pattern

P 1-8 PRACTICE

Find a pattern to solve.

1. A student just learning the high jump starts with the bar at 3 feet. The pole is raised 0.4 inch after each successful jump. How high will the bar be after 5 successful jumps?

   3 feet 2 inches

2. A beginning pole vaulter raises the bar 0.5 inch after each successful vault. The bar begins at 4 feet 5 inches. How high will the bar be after 3 successful attempts?

   4 feet 6.5 inches

3. **Art** A designer is making a tile mosaic. The first row of the mosaic has 1 red tile in the center. If the designer increases the number of red tiles in the center of each row by 4, how many red tiles will be in the center of the fifth row?

   17 tiles

4. **Health** Brian has started an exercise program in which he walks daily. He plans to increase the distance that he walks by 0.25 mile each week. He walks 2.25 miles everyday the first week. How many miles will he be walking each day during the fifth week?

   3.25 miles

Mixed Strategy Review

Solve. Use any strategy.

5. **Number Sense** The sum of two whole numbers between 20 and 40 is 58. The difference of the two numbers is 12. What are the two numbers?

   23 and 35

   Strategy: Guess and Check

6. Ramon has $3.50. He buys two pens that cost $0.75 each and a pencil that costs $0.40. How much money does Ramon have left?

   $1.60

   Strategy: Solve multistep problems

7. Denise earns $25 delivering papers each week. She saved $2.00 the first week. She decides to save $3.00 more each week than she saved the previous week until she is saving $20.00 every week. In how many weeks will she save her first $20?

   7 weeks

   Strategy: Find a Pattern

8. **Create a problem** for which you could find a pattern to solve. Share it with others.

   Check students' problems.

Use with Grade 5, Chapter 1, Lesson 8, pages 26–27. (22)

Reteach

Problem Solving: Strategy
Find a Pattern

R 1-8 RETEACH

Page 27, Problem 1

A high school student practices the high jump, starting the bar at 3 feet 4 inches, and raising the bar 0.5 inch after each successful jump. How high will the bar be after 4 successful jumps?

Step 1 Read

Be sure you understand the problem.
Read carefully.

What do you know?

- The student starts the bar at 3 feet 4 inches.
- The student raises the bar 0.5 inch after each successful jump.

What do you need to find?

- You need to find how high the bar will be after 4 jumps.

Step 2 Plan

- Find a Pattern
- Guess and Check
- Work Backward
- Make a Graph
- Make a Table
- Write an Equation
- Make an Organized List
- Draw a Diagram
- Solve a Simpler Problem
- Logical Reasoning

Make a plan.
Choose a strategy.

Using a pattern will help you solve the problem.

Organize the information in a chart.

Find the pattern shown by the first, second, and third successful jumps.

Continue the pattern to find how high the bar will be after the fourth successful jump.

Use with Grade 5, Chapter 1, Lesson 8, pages 26–27. (23)

Reteach

Problem Solving: Strategy
Find a Pattern

R 1-8 RETEACH

Step 3 Solve

Carry out your plan.

Make a chart. Look for a pattern in the chart.

Jump Number	1	2	3	4	5
Bar Height	3 feet 4 inches	3 feet 4.5 inches	3 feet 5 inches	3 feet 5.5 inches	

Look at the chart to find the pattern.

What is the pattern?

The height increases by 0.5 inch.

Continue the pattern to predict the height for the fifth jump.

Jump 5: 3 feet 5.5 inches + 0.5 inch = 3 feet 6 inches

Using the pattern, you can expect that the bar will be set at 3 feet 6 inches for the fifth jump.

Step 4 Look Back

Is the solution reasonable?
Reread the problem.

Have you answered the question? Yes

Does your answer make sense? Yes

Did you find a pattern and continue it? Yes

Practice

1. The first day of the craft fair, 200 people attend. Each day, 150 more people attend the fair than the previous day. The craft fair lasts for five days. How many people attended the fair on the last day?

   800 people

2. A pole vaulter raises the bar 1 inch after each successful vault. The bar begins at 6 feet 3 inches. How high will the bar be after 4 successful attempts?

   6 feet 7 inches

Use with Grade 5, Chapter 1, Lesson 8, pages 26–27. (24)

Daily Homework

1-8 **Problem Solving: Strategy**
Find a Pattern

Find a pattern to solve.

1. A high school student begins practicing the high jump with the bar set at 3 feet 5 inches and raises the bar 0.5 inch after each successful jump. How high will the bar be after 4 successful jumps? 3 feet 7 inches

2. A high school pole vaulter raises the bar for her vaults each time she makes a successful jump. If the bar is set at 9 feet 6 inches and she raises the bar 1.5 inches after each jump, how high will the bar be after 6 successful jumps? 10 feet 3 inches

3. Velma jogs 1 lap around the track each day for two weeks. In the third and fourth weeks, she jogs 3 laps each day around the track. During the next two weeks, she runs 6 laps each day. During the fifth and sixth weeks, her goal is to jog 10 laps each day. If this pattern continues, how many laps will she run each day during the seventh and eighth weeks? 15 laps

Mixed Strategy Review

4. In the 1996 Olympic 200-meter run, a United States runner won with a 19.32 seconds. In the 1992 200-meter run, the record time was 20.01 seconds. By how much did the record improve from 1992 to 1996?

   by 0.69 second

5. The longest women's throws for the javelin in the Olympics are 68.40 meters, 74.66 meters, and 69.56 meters. Write these lengths in order from least to greatest.

   68.40, 69.56, 74.66

Source for both: *The New York Times Almanac 2000*

Spiral Review

Compare. Write <, >, =.

6. 21,455,876 < 21,456,900

7. 234,859,102 > 234,857,404

Chapter 1 ~ Lesson 9

Practice

Properties of Addition

P 1-9 PRACTICE

Identify the addition property used to rewrite each problem.

1. 59 + 83 = 83 + 59 Commutative Property
2. 0 + 426 = 426 Identity Property
3. (33 + 42) + 17 = 33 + (42 + 17) Associative Property
4. 66 + 27 + 24 = 66 + 24 + 27 Commutative Property
5. 3.09 + 0 = 3.09 Identity Property
6. 3.1 + (7.2 + 0.6) = (3.1 + 7.2) + 0.6 Associative Property

Add or subtract mentally. Describe your method for each. Strategies may vary. Check students' answers.

7. 3 + 9 + 7 = 19
8. 14 + 11 + 56 = 81
9. 97 + 74 = 171
10. 76 − 18 = 58
11. \$2.25 + \$5.75 = \$8.00
12. 12 + 194 + 88 = 294
13. 568 − 29 = 539
14. 2.41 + 3.6 = 6.01
15. 249 + 98 = 347
16. 6 + 3 + 2 + 4 + 7 = 22
17. \$234 − \$96 = \$138
18. 27 + 42 = 69
19. 196 − 21 = 175
20. \$3.60 + \$5.40 = \$9.00
21. 1 + 53 + 9 + 7 = 70
22. 9 + (127 + 13) = 149
23. 624 − 302 = 322
24. 3.78 + 1.04 = 4.82
25. 396 + 504 = 900
26. 3.72 − 1.97 = 1.75
27. 247 + (47 + 53) = 347
28. (0.092 + 0.008) − 0.1 = 0

Problem Solving

29. Brandon's lunch order totaled \$3.94. He gave the cashier \$10.00. How much money should he get back? \$6.06

30. To get home from school, Kara has to walk 4 minutes to the bus, ride the bus for 28 minutes, and then walk 6 minutes to her house. How long is her trip? 38 minutes

Use with Grade 5, Chapter 1, Lesson 9, pages 28–31. (25)

Reteach

Properties of Addition

R 1-9 RETEACH

Sometimes you can use compensation to add or subtract mentally.

Add 18 + 23.

Add a number to one addend to make a ten. Then subtract the same number from the other addend. The sum stays the same.

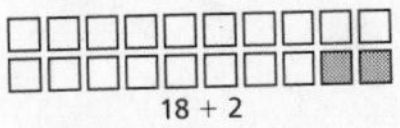

18 + 2

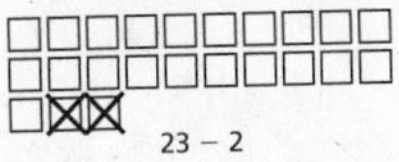

23 − 2

18 + 23 → (+ 2, − 2) → 20 + 21 = 41

Subtract 3.2 − 1.7.

Make the number you are subtracting a whole number by adding a decimal to it. Add the same decimal to the other number. The difference stays the same.

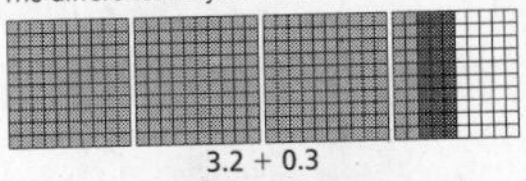

3.2 + 0.3

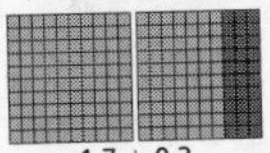

1.7 + 0.3

3.2 − 1.7 → (+ 0.3, + 0.3) → 3.5 − 2.0 = 1.5

Use compensation to add or subtract mentally.

1. 47 + 25 → (+ 3, − 3) → 50 + 22 = 72
2. 87 − 39 → (+ 1, + 1) → 88 − 40 = 48
3. 296 + 138 → (+ 4, − 4) → 300 + 134 = 434
4. 758 − 395 → (+ 5, + 5) → 763 − 400 = 363
5. 13.8 + 2.6 → (+ 0.2, − 0.2) → 14.0 + 2.4 = 16.4
6. 39.1 − 4.75 → (+ 0.25, + 0.25) → 39.35 − 5 = 34.35
7. 237 + 494 → (− 6, + 6) → 231 + 500 = 731
8. 428 − 197 → (+ 3, + 3) → 431 − 200 = 231
9. 12.7 − 5.8 → (+ 0.2, + 0.2) → 12.9 − 6 = 6.9
10. 701 − 98 = 603
11. 653 + 296 = 949
12. 13.8 + 0.65 = 14.45

Use with Grade 5, Chapter 1, Lesson 9, pages 28–31. (26)

Enrich

Properties of Addition

E 1-9 ENRICH

Strategy Jigsaw

Cut out the squares below and rearrange them in a 4 × 4 square so that every problem is adjacent to its solution. Try to use mental math strategies.

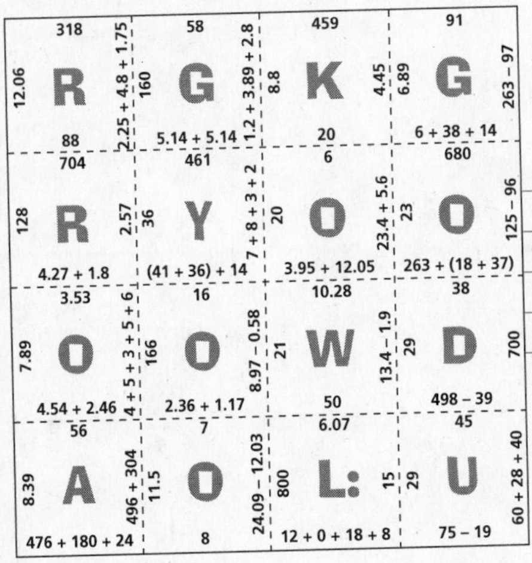

Y	O	U	R
G	O	A	L:
G	O	O	D
W	O	R	K

What message did you find? YOUR GOAL: GOOD WORK

How did you use compensation to find 13.4 − 1.9 in W?
Add 0.1 to 1.9 to make 2. Add 0.1 to 13.4 to make 13.5.
Subtract 2 from 13.5 to get 11.5.

Use with Grade 5, Chapter 1, Lesson 9, pages 28–31. (27)

Daily Homework

1-9 Properties of Addition

Identify the addition property used to rewrite each problem.

1. 8 + 47 + 23 = 47 + 8 + 23 Commutative
2. (3 + 1.73) + 0.37 = 3 + (1.73 + 0.37) Associative
3. 32 + (18 + 28) = (32 + 18) + 28 Associative
4. 336 + 884 = 884 + 336 Commutative
5. 472 + 0 = 472 Identity
6. 47 + 82 + 75 = 82 + 47 + 75 Commutative
7. 25 + 87 + 54 = 25 + 54 + 87 Commutative
8. 2 + 7 + 8 + 3 = (2 + 8) + (7 + 3) Commutative and Associative

Add or subtract. Describe your work. Strategies may vary. Check students' answers.

9. 54 + 22 = 76
10. 683 + 87 = 770
11. 296 + 104 = 400
12. 529 − 371 = 158
13. 304 − 289 = 15
14. \$512 − \$36 = \$476
15. 423 + 78 = 501
16. 276 − 193 = 83
17. 338 + 248 = 586

Problem Solving

18. The loudness of a whisper is measured at 20 decibels. The sound of a jet plane is measured at 140 decibels. How much louder is the plane than the whisper? 120 decibels louder

19. A turtle moves at a speed of about 0.17 mile per hour. A sloth moves at about 0.15 mile per hour, while a snail has a speed of only 0.03 mile per hour. How much faster is a turtle than a snail? 0.14 mile per hour faster

Spiral Review

Order from least to greatest.

20. 0.27, 0.43, 0.05, 1.15 — 0.05, 0.27, 0.43, 1.15
21. 0.125, 0.625, 0.375 — 0.125, 0.375, 0.625
22. 93,909; 87,100; 78,997 — 78,997; 87,100; 93,909

Grade 5, Chapter 1, Lesson 9, Cluster B 9

Chapter 1 ~ Lesson 10

Part A Worksheet

Problem Solving: Application
Applying Addition and Subtraction

Part A 1-10 WORKSHEET Decision Making

Record your data about the expenses for the trip.

T-shirts	Meals	Transportation	Hotel

Your Decision

Where do you recommend that the Greens stay in Weston? Will they stay within their budget? Explain.

Answers may vary.

Use with Grade 5, Chapter 1, Lesson 10, pages 32–33. (28)

Part B Worksheet

Problem Solving: Application
How *fast* are you?

Part B 1-10 WORKSHEET Math & Science

Record your data in the table below.

Try	Starting Mark	Finishing Mark	Difference	Reaction Time
1	50 cm			
2	50 cm			
3	50 cm			

1. Do you think your reaction time would improve if you try the experiment a second time? Explain.

Answers may vary. Possible answer: Yes, because I will know what to expect this time.

2. Repeat the experiment. Record your data in the table below.

Try	Starting Mark	Finishing Mark	Difference	Reaction Time
4	50 cm			
5	50 cm			
6	50 cm			

3. What was your fastest reaction time in each experiment? Did your fastest time improve in the second experiment?

Answers may vary.

Use with Grade 5, Chapter 1, Lesson 10, pages 34–35. (29)

Part B Worksheet

Problem Solving: Application
How *fast* are you?

Part B 1-10 WORKSHEET Math & Science

4. Did your partner's reaction time improve in the second experiment? Explain.

Answers may vary.

5. Compare all of your reaction times. Do they differ by a little or a lot? Do they differ by less in the second experiment than in the first experiment?

Answers may vary.

6. Do you notice any pattern in your reaction times? Explain.

Answers may vary.

7. Do you think your reaction time would improve if you practiced with the meterstick? Explain.

Answers may vary. Possible answer: Yes, because I would be able to anticipate it better.

8. Do you think the reaction time of a child in first grade would differ much from your reaction time? Explain.

Answers may vary. Possible answer: Yes, I think my reaction time would be better since I am older.

9. What are some activities in which a quick reaction time is important?

Answers may vary. Possible answer: Most sports, especially those that involve a ball. Other examples might include jumping rope or playing on monkey bars.

Use with Grade 5, Chapter 1, Lesson 10, pages 34–35. (30)

Chapter 2 ~ Lesson 1

Practice

Patterns of Multiplication

P 2-1 PRACTICE

Complete.

1. 8 × 2 = 16
   8 × 20 = 160
   8 × 200 = 1,600
   8 × 2,000 = 16,000
2. 6 × 4 = 24
   6 × 40 = 240
   6 × 400 = 2,400
   6 × 4,000 = 24,000
3. 4 × 5 = 20
   4 × 50 = 200
   4 × 500 = 2,000
   4 × 5,000 = 20,000
4. 3 × 80 = 240
   30 × 80 = 2,400
   300 × 80 = 24,000
   3,000 × 80 = 240,000
5. 5 × 60 = 300
   50 × 60 = 3,000
   500 × 60 = 30,000
   5,000 × 60 = 300,000
6. 9 × $70 = $630
   90 × $70 = $6,300
   900 × $70 = $63,000
   9,000 × $70 = $630,000
7. 4 × $11 = $44
   40 × $11 = $440
   400 × $11 = $4,400
   4,000 × $11 = $44,000
8. 7 × 8 = 56
   70 × 8 = 560
   700 × 8 = 5,600
   7,000 × 8 = 56,000
9. 2 × $5 = $10
   20 × $5 = $100
   200 × $5 = $1,000
   2,000 × $5 = $10,000

Multiply.

10. 90 × 3 = 270
11. 7 × $4,000 = $28,000
12. 200 × 6 = 1,200
13. 30 × 40 = 1,200
14. 600 × 70 = 42,000
15. 40 × 800 = 32,000
16. 4 × $1,000 = $4,000
17. 500 × 80 = 40,000
18. 70 × 100 = 7,000
19. 3 × 30 = 90
20. 5 × 1,000 = 5,000
21. 7 × $900 = $6,300
22. 50 × 80 = 4,000
23. 100 × 80 = 8,000
24. 50 × 20 = 1,000

Problem Solving

25. The 9 members of a music club in Indianapolis want to fly to New York to see several musicals. The cost of a round trip ticket is $300. How much would the total cost of the airfare be?
    $2,700
26. During one week, an airport shop sold 70 New York City travel guides for $9 each. How much was the total received for the guides?
    $630

Use with Grade 5, Chapter 2, Lesson 1, pages 50–51. (31)

Reteach

Patterns of Multiplication

R 2-1 RETEACH

To multiply by multiples of 10, 100, and 1,000, you can use basic facts and patterns.

Multiply 40 × 800.

Start with the basic fact.	4 × 8 = 32
Count the number of zeros in each factor and find their sum.	40 × 800 ↑ ↑ 1 zero + 2 zeros = 3 zeros
Write the zeros in the product.	40 × 800 = 32,000

Multiply 50 × 80.

Start with the basic fact.	5 × 8 = 40
Count the number of zeros in each factor and find their sum.	50 × 80 ↑ ↑ 1 zero + 1 zero = 2 zeros
Write the zeros in the product.	50 × 80 = 4,000

Complete.

1. 20 × 60
   Basic fact: 2 × 6 = 12
   Number of zeros in each factor:
   1 + 1 = 2
   Product: 20 × 60 = 1,200
2. 9 × 80
   Basic fact: 9 × 8 = 72
   Number of zeros in each factor:
   0 + 1 = 1
   Product: 9 × 80 = 720

Complete the pattern.

3. 5 × 9 = 45
   5 × 90 = 450
   5 × 900 = 4,500
   5 × 9,000 = 45,000
4. 3 × 6 = 18
   3 × 60 = 180
   3 × 600 = 1,800
   3 × 6,000 = 18,000
5. 4 × 12 = 48
   40 × 12 = 480
   400 × 12 = 4,800
   4,000 × 12 = 48,000
6. 6 × 60 = 360
   60 × 60 = 3,600
   600 × 60 = 36,000
   6,000 × 60 = 360,000
7. 7 × $3 = $21
   70 × $3 = $210
   700 × $3 = $2,100
   7,000 × $3 = $21,000
8. 5 × 40 = 200
   50 × 40 = 2,000
   500 × 40 = 20,000
   5,000 × 40 = 200,000

Use with Grade 5, Chapter 2, Lesson 1, pages 50–51. (32)

Enrich

Patterns of Multiplication

Amazing Animal Facts

E 2-1 ENRICH

Multiply each product shown in parentheses to complete these facts.

1. Adult great white sharks weigh about (2 × 800) 1,600 pounds and may grow about (4 × 5) 20 feet long.
2. The smallest mammal, a pygmy shrew, is only about (3 × 1) 3 inches long from head to tail.
3. The largest mammal is the blue whale. Newborn calves weigh about (20 × 300) 6,000 pounds. The heaviest adult ever caught weighed more than (50 × 7,000) 350,000 pounds.
4. The bat with the largest wingspan is the Bismarck flying fox. Its wingspan may be about (10 × 6) 60 inches long.
5. The largest carnivore, the polar bear, may weigh about (30 × 40) 1,200 pounds and have a nose-to-tail length of about (5 × 20) 100 inches long.
6. The fastest recorded speed of a kangaroo is (8 × 5) 40 miles per hour.
7. In the 1950s, an Arctic tern flew the longest distance ever recorded for a bird, (700 × 20) 14,000 miles.
8. In 1989, scientists recorded an elephant seal diving about (7 × 700) 4,900 feet.
9. The largest game preserve in the world is Etosha National Park in Namibia. It covers about (50 × 800) 40,000 square miles.
10. The Monterey Bay Aquarium in California has over (600 × 600) 360,000 specimens of animals and plants.

Use with Grade 5, Chapter 2, Lesson 1, pages 50–51. (33)

Daily Homework

2-1 Patterns of Multiplication

Copy and complete.

1. 2 × 3 = 6
   2 × 30 = 60
   2 × 300 = n
   2 × 3,000 = n
   600; 6,000
2. 3 × 5 = 15
   3 × 50 = x
   3 × 500 = 1,500
   3 × 5,000 = x
   150; 15,000
3. 6 × 30 = 180
   60 × 30 = s
   600 × 30 = 18,000
   6,000 × 300 = s
   1,800; 1,800,000
4. 1 × $40 = $40
   10 × $40 = $400
   100 × $40 = m
   1,000 × $40 = m
   $4,000; $40,000
5. 3 × 7 = d
   30 × 7 = 210
   300 × 7 = d
   3,000 × 7 = d
   21; 2,100; 21,000
6. 4 × 6 = p
   4 × 60 = 240
   4 × 600 = p
   4 × 6,000 = p
   24; 2,400; 24,000

Multiply.

7. 8 × 40 = 320
8. 5 × 1,000 = 5,000
9. 200 × 9 = 1,800
10. 10 × 60 = 600
11. 120 × 20 = 2,400
12. 60 × 300 = 18,000
13. 800 × 7 = 5,600
14. 700 × 40 = 28,000
15. 2,600 × 100 = 260,000

Problem Solving

16. Marcus is reading a book about Spain. He usually reads an average of 15 pages a day. He has 7 days to finish his book. How many pages can he read in that time? He has 100 pages left. Will he be able to finish the book in that time?
    105 pages; yes, 100 < 105, so Marcus will finish on time.
17. Spain has a land area of about 195,000 square miles. If there are about 200 people per square mile, how many people are there in Spain?
    39,000,000 people

Spiral Review

Identify the addition property used to rewrite each problem.

18. 9 + 73 + 13 = 9 + 13 + 73 Commutative
19. (2.1 + 1.7) + 3.6 = 2.1 + (1.7 + 3.6) Associative

10 Grade 5, Chapter 2, Lesson 1, Cluster A

Chapter 2 ~ Lesson 2

Practice

Explore the Distributive Property

P 2-2 PRACTICE

Multiply.

1. 7 × 19 = 133
2. 6 × 22 = 132
3. 8 × 58 = 464
4. 5 × 13 = 65
5. 4 × 76 = 304
6. 2 × 27 = 54
7. 9 × 56 = 504
8. 3 × 71 = 213
9. 7 × 33 = 231
10. 8 × 34 = 272
11. 4 × 83 = 332
12. 3 × 27 = 81
13. 6 × 88 = 528
14. 9 × 98 = 882
15. 5 × 65 = 325
16. 5 × 36 = 180
17. 3 × 98 = 294
18. 2 × 97 = 194

Rewrite each problem using the Distributive Property.

19. 3 × 13 (3 × 10) + (3 × 3)
20. 8 × 68 (8 × 60) + (8 × 8)
21. 7 × 32 (7 × 30) + (7 × 2)
22. 9 × 35 (9 × 30) + (9 × 5)
23. 8 × 17 (8 × 10) + (8 × 7)
24. 4 × 71 (4 × 70) + (4 × 1)
25. 5 × 25 (5 × 20) + (5 × 5)
26. 6 × 84 (6 × 80) + (6 × 4)

Problem Solving

27. Each of 6 hikers were allowed to bring 24 pounds of gear on a cross-country hike. How many pounds of gear was that altogether? 144 lb
28. The hikers plan to travel an average of 12 miles each day for 9 days. How many miles do they plan to travel in all? 108 mi

Use with Grade 5, Chapter 2, Lesson 2, pages 52–53. (34)

Reteach

Explore the Distributive Property

R 2-2 RETEACH

You can use place-value models to show the Distributive Property.

Multiply 3 × 26. Multiply and add (3 × 20) + (3 × 6).

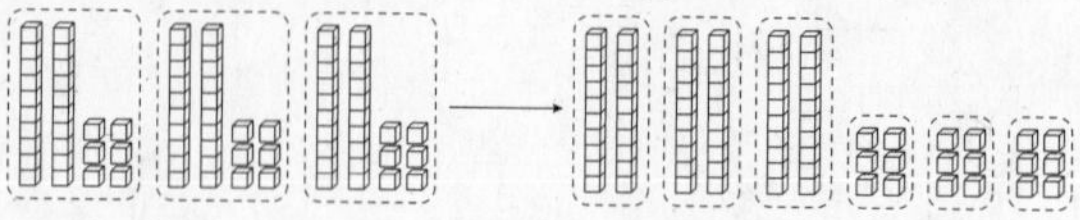

3 × 26 = 3 × (20 + 6) (3 × 20) (3 × 6)

3 × 26 = 3 × (20 + 6)
= (3 × 20) + (3 × 6)
= 60 + 18
= 78

Find each product. You can draw place-value models to help you multiply.

1. 5 × 39 = 5 × (30 + 9)
= (5 × 30) + (5 × 9)
= 150 + 45
= 195

2. 8 × 46 = 8 × (40 + 6)
= (8 × 40) + (8 × 6)
= 320 + 48
= 368

3. 3 × 54 = 3 × (50 + 4)
= (3 × 50) + (3 × 4)
= 150 + 12
= 162

4. 6 × 64 = 6 × (60 + 4)
= (6 × 60) + (6 × 4)
= 360 + 24
= 384

5. 2 × 48 = 96
6. 4 × 72 = 288
7. 9 × 27 = 243
8. 7 × 45 = 315
9. 8 × 19 = 152
10. 3 × 88 = 264

Use with Grade 5, Chapter 2, Lesson 2, pages 52–53. (35)

Enrich

Explore the Distributive Property
Complex Computation

E 2-2 ENRICH

Compute. The symbol ◆ means to add the numbers and then multiply the sum by 3.

Example: 4 ◆ 5 = (4 + 5) × 3 = 27

1. 2 ◆ 9 33
2. 4 ◆ 4 24
3. 1 ◆ 6 21
4. 7 ◆ 4 33
5. 9 ◆ 8 51
6. 5 ◆ 9 42

Compute. The symbol ❤ means to subtract the numbers and then multiply the difference by 2.

Example: 6 ❤ 2 = (6 − 2) × 2 = 8

7. 8 ❤ 3 10
8. 9 ❤ 4 10
9. 6 ❤ 5 2
10. 7 ❤ 3 8
11. 8 ❤ 2 12
12. 5 ❤ 4 2

Compute. The symbol ♣ means to multiply the numbers and then add the first number to the product.

Example: 3 ♣ 5 = (3 × 5) + 3 = 18

13. 2 ♣ 8 18
14. 7 ♣ 2 21
15. 5 ♣ 9 50
16. 8 ♣ 1 16
17. 1 ♣ 5 6
18. 6 ♣ 7 48

Compute. The symbol ▲ means to multiply the numbers and then subtract the first number from the product.

Example: 6 ▲ 7 = (6 × 7) − 6 = 36

19. 6 ▲ 3 12
20. 4 ▲ 8 28
21. 5 ▲ 2 5
22. 9 ▲ 5 36
23. 3 ▲ 7 18
24. 8 ▲ 9 64

25. Study these examples. What does the symbol ♠ mean?
9 ♠ 3 = 24 5 ♠ 8 = 32 6 ♠ 7 = 35
Multiply the numbers and then subtract the second number from the product.

Use with Grade 5, Chapter 2, Lesson 2, pages 52–53. (36)

Daily Homework

2-2 Explore the Distributive Property

Multiply.

1. 8 × 38 = 304
2. 7 × 28 = 196
3. 9 × 31 = 279
4. 5 × 39 = 195
5. 4 × 98 = 392
6. 7 × 297 = 2,079
7. 32 × 8 = 256
8. 99 × 9 = 891
9. 796 × 6 = 4,776

Rewrite each problem using the Distributive Property.

10. 5 × 58 (5 × 50) + (5 × 8)
11. 8 × 29 (8 × 20) + (8 × 9)
12. 7 × 19 (7×10) + (7 × 9)
13. 2 × 37 (2× 30) + (2× 7)
14. 9 × 28 (9 ×20) + (9 × 8)
15. 4 × 49 (4 × 40) + (4 ×9)

Solve.

16. Junius has 4 tulip beds. Each bed has 48 tulip plants. How many tulips in all does Junius have in his garden? 192 tulips
17. Nora is on a committee for a school party. There will be 4 party favors for each guest. If 198 guests have been invited, how many favors should Nora order? 792 favors

Spiral Review

Round each number to the underlined place.

18. 56.6648 56.665
19. 6.787 6.8
20. 428.062 428.1

Chapter 2 ~ Lesson 3

Practice

Multiply Whole Numbers

P 2-3 PRACTICE

Multiply.

1. 3 × 5,012 = 15,036
2. 7 × 2,436 = 17,052
3. 4 × 12,261 = 49,044
4. 43 × $65 = $2,795
5. 458 × 26 = 11,908
6. 329 × 72 = 23,688
7. 58 × 1,036 = 60,088
8. 94 × 5,425 = 509,950
9. 33 × 24,918 = 822,294
10. 328 × 142 = 46,576
11. 179 × 212 = 37,948
12. 826 × $507 = $418,782

13. 371 × 4 = 1,484
14. $507 × 7 = $3,549
15. 7,693 × 8 = 61,544
16. 29,148 × 3 = 87,444
17. 345 × 42 = 14,490
18. $740 × 16 = $11,840
19. 3,006 × 28 = 84,168
20. 26,308 × 25 = 657,700
21. 449 × 515 = 231,235
22. 762 × 108 = 82,296

Compare. Write >, <, or =.

23. 63 × 25 (<) 31 × 78
24. 5 × 5,026 (>) 52 × 189
25. 5 × 123 (=) 15 × 41
26. 835 × 95 (>) 83 × 803
27. 47 × 6,351 (<) 64 × 11,382
28. 597 × 13 (<) 24 × 806
29. 48 × 212 (<) 5,227 × 4,968
30. 43 × 321 (>) 98 × 65
31. 4 × 49 × 7 (>) 9 × 65 × 2
32. 12 × 58 × 29 (<) 37 × 37 × 42

Problem Solving

33. A basketball player scored an average of 23 points per game. He played 82 games during the season. How many points did he score that season? 1,886 points

34. A basketball arena has 36 sections of seats. Each section contains 784 seats. How many people can the arena seat? 28,224 people

Use with Grade 5, Chapter 2, Lesson 3, pages 54–57. (37)

Reteach

Multiply Whole Numbers

R 2-3 RETEACH

You can use the expanded form of factors to help you multiply.

Multiply 4 × 562.

562 = 500 + 60 + 2

```
   500 + 60 + 2
×             4
          8 ← 4 × 2
        240 ← 4 × 60
    + 2,000 ← 4 × 500
      2,248
```

Multiply 27 × 43.

43 = 40 + 3
27 = 20 + 7

```
    40 + 3
  × 20 + 7
        21 ← 7 × 3
       280 ← 7 × 40
        60 ← 20 × 3
     + 800 ← 20 × 40
     1,161
```

Find each product.

1. 439 × 7 = 3,073
2. 152 × 9 = 1,368
3. 2,473 × 9 = 22,257
4. 4,508 × 5 = 22,540
5. $72,417 × 8 = $579,336
6. 68 × 34 = 2,312
7. 25 × 25 = 625
8. 82 × 58 = 4,756
9. 93 × 37 = 3,441
10. 81 × 93 = 7,533
11. $364 × 87 = $31,668
12. 617 × 62 = 38,254
13. 703 × 29 = 20,387
14. 548 × 95 = 52,060
15. 277 × 38 = 10,526
16. 1,228 × 46 = 56,488
17. $6,229 × 12 = $74,748
18. 42,576 × 27 = 1,149,552
19. 326 × 145 = 47,270
20. $449 × 365 = $163,885

Use with Grade 5, Chapter 2, Lesson 3, pages 54–57. (38)

Enrich

Multiply Whole Numbers

E 2-3 ENRICH

Multiplication Game

- Play this game with a partner.
- Choose a number from a circle and a number from a square. Use the numbers to write a number sentence to fit each description. Then find the product.
- Try to finish all ten exercises as fast as possible. Your partner records the amount of time you used to finish the exercise.
- Switch roles. The player that uses less time wins the game.

Circles: 83, 57, 9, 28, 6, 72, 45

Squares: 532, 2,178, 357, 921, 7,059, 42,133, 26,401

1. the least product: 6 × 357 = 2,142
2. the greatest product: 83 × 42,133 = 3,497,039
3. two different products with a zero in the ones place: 45 × 532 = 23,940; 45 × 2,178 = 98,010
4. the greatest product with an 8 in the ones place: 28 × 26,401 = 739,228
5. the least product with a 9 in the ones place: 9 × 921 = 8,289
6. the product with a 3 as the first and last digit: 9 × 357 = 3,213
7. two different products between 30,000 and 40,000: 57 × 532 = 30,324; 72 × 532 = 38,304
8. the product closest to 60,000: 28 × 2,178 = 60,984
9. the product closest to 300,000: 45 × 7,059 = 317,655
10. the product closest to 2 million: 72 × 26,401 = 1,900,872

Your time ________ Your partner's time ________

Use with Grade 5, Chapter 2, Lesson 3, pages 54–57. (39)

Daily Homework

2-3 Multiply Whole Numbers

Multiply.

1. 475 × 3 = 1425
2. 62 × 43 = 2,666
3. 137 × 46 = 6,302
4. 59 × 8 = 472
5. 86 × 82 = 7,052
6. 1,206 × 23 = 27,738
7. 3,465 × 18 = 62,370
8. 704 × 7 = 4,928
9. 654 × 68 = 44,472
10. 245 × 6 = 1,470
11. 333 × 16 = 5,328
12. 36 × 48 = 1,728
13. 498 × 92 = 45,816
14. 3,542 × 48 = 170,016
15. 10,772 × 8 = 86,176
16. 44,333 × 5 = 221,665
17. 2,168 × 88 = 190,784

Compare. Write >, <, or =.

18. 6 × 48 < 9 × 56
19. 8 × 82 > 6 × 96
20. 65 × 174 > 46 × 208
21. 28 × 345 > 32 × 298
22. 92 × 28 = 184 × 14
23. 399 × 46 < 466 × 50

Problem Solving

24. If it costs $1,155 to fly from New York City to Uganda round trip, how much would it cost for 6 round-trip tickets? $6,930

25. Mt. Kilimanjaro in Tanzania is 19,340 feet high. Mt. Margherita in Uganda is 16,750 feet high. How much higher is Mt. Kilimanjaro than Mt. Margherita? 2,590 feet higher

Spiral Review

26. 19.82 + 9.7 = 29.52
27. 27.176 – 18.72 = 8.456
28. 31.2 – 8.8 = 22.4
29. 181.56 + 28.1 = 209.66

12 Grade 5, Chapter 2, Lesson 3, Cluster A

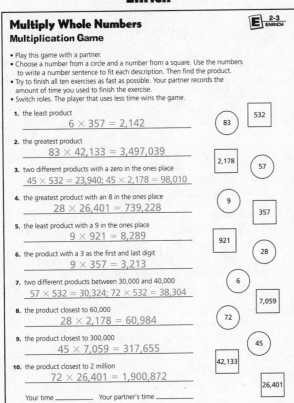

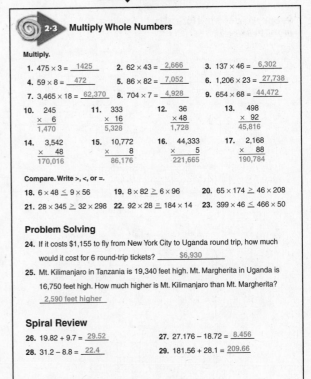

Chapter 2 ~ Lesson 4

Practice

Properties of Multiplication

P 2-4 PRACTICE

Identify the multiplication property used to rewrite each problem.

1. 49 × 0 = 0
Zero Property

2. 3 × 8 = 8 × 3
Commutative Property

3. 1 × 67 = 67
Identity Property

4. 7 × (56 − 3) = (7 × 56) − (7 × 3)
Distributive Property

5. 2 × (36 + 93) = (2 × 36) + (2 × 93)
Distributive Property

6. 2 × (9 × 8) = (2 × 9) × 8
Associative Property

7. 1.41 × 12 = 12 × 1.41
Commutative Property

8. 0 × 5.4 = 0
Zero Property

9. (7 × 5) × 8 = 7 × (5 × 8)
Associative Property

10. 74 × 1 = 74
Identity Property

Multiply. Name the property you used. Choices of properties may vary.

11. 7 × 28 = 196
12. 5 × 25 = 125
13. 0 × 96 = 0
14. 1 × 36 = 36
15. 8 × 72 = 576
16. 6 × 34 = 204
17. 4 × 53 = 212
18. 11 × 11 = 121
19. 50 × 102 = 5,100

Find the number that makes each sentence true.

20. 6 × (2 + 8) = (6 × 2) + (6 × 8)
21. 1 × 7.8 = 7.8
22. 0 × 65 = 0
23. (2.1 × 0.9) × 8.6 = 2.1 × (0.9 × 8.6)
24. 7.6 × 6.4 = 6.4 × 7.6
25. 54 × 1 = 54
26. 53 × (18 × 9) = (53 × 18) × 9
27. 75 × 83 = 83 × 75
28. 7.1 × 0 = 0
29. 1.01 × (8.5 − 5.3) = (1.01 × 8.5) − (1.01 × 5.3)

Problem Solving

30. Tony displayed his model race cars in 3 rows of 11 cars each. How else could Tony have displayed his cars in equal rows?
in 11 rows of 3 cars each

31. Sarah displayed her collection of animal statues on 2 shelves. Each shelf contains 2 rows of 9 statues each. How many statues does Sarah have?
36 statues

Use with Grade 5, Chapter 2, Lesson 4, pages 58–61. (40)

Reteach

Properties of Multiplication

R 2-4 RETEACH

These are properties of multiplication.

Commutative Property of Multiplication
Changing the order of the factors does not affect the product.

6 × 3 × 20 = **3 × 6** × 20
18 × 20 = 18 × 20
360 = 360

Associative Property of Multiplication
Changing the grouping of the factors does not change the product.

(**6 × 3**) × 20 = 6 × (**3 × 20**)
18 × 20 = 6 × 60
360 = 360

Identity Property of Multiplication
Multiplying a factor by one equals the factor.

20 × 1 = 20

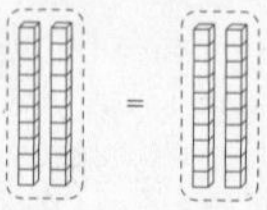

Zero Property
Multiplying a factor by zero equals zero.

35 × 0 = 0

Distributive Property of Multiplication over Addition

2 × (10 + 4) = (2 × 10) + (2 × 4)

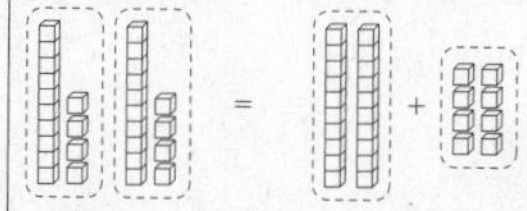

Distributive Property of Multiplication over Subtraction

2 × (10 − 4) = (2 × 10) − (2 × 4)

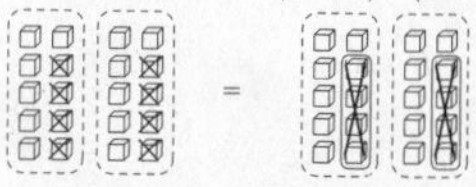

Multiply.

1. 4 × 35 = 140
2. 3 × 29 = 87
3. 6 × 51 = 306
4. 2 × 25 × 5 = 250
5. 16 × 0 × 93 = 0
6. 12 × 1 × 10 = 120
7. 5 × 8 × 20 = 800
8. 7 × 15 × 1 = 105
9. 25 × 3 × 4 = 300
10. 2 × 6 × 50 = 600
11. 13 × 0 × 10 = 0
12. 2 × 4 × 30 = 240

Use with Grade 5, Chapter 2, Lesson 4, pages 58–61. (41)

Enrich

Properties of Multiplication
Visual Properties

E 2-4 ENRICH

Write two number sentences to show the Commutative Property of Multiplication. Then shade the grids to show the number sentences you wrote.

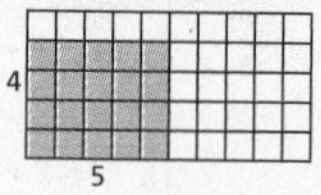

4 × 5 = 20

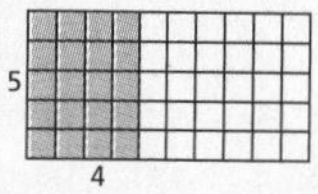

5 × 4 = 20

Write a number sentence to show the Identity Property of Multiplication. Then shade the grid to show the number sentence you wrote.

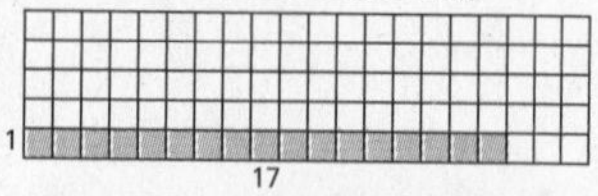

1 × 17 = 17 or 17 × 1 = 17

Write a number sentence to show the Distributive Property of Multiplication over Addition. Then shade the grid to show the number sentence you wrote.

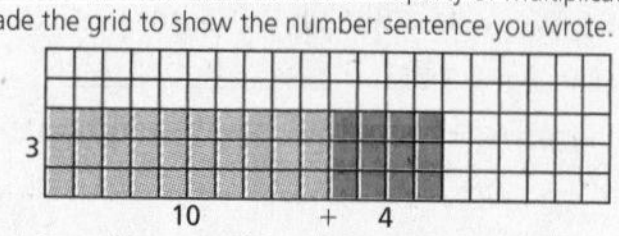

3 × 14 = (3 × 10) + (3 × 4) = 30 + 12 = 42

Write a number sentence to show the Distributive Property of Multiplication over Subtraction. Then shade the grid to show the number sentence you wrote.

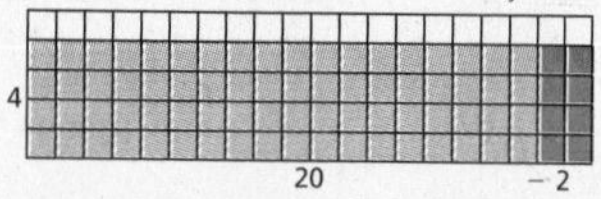

4 × 18 = (4 × 20) − (4 × 2) = 80 − 8 = 72

Use with Grade 5, Chapter 2, Lesson 4, pages 58–61. (42)

Daily Homework

2-4 Properties of Multiplication

Multiply. Name the property you used. Choices of properties may vary. Sample answers given.

1. 5 × 37 = 185
Distributive Property of Multiplication over Subtraction

2. 1 × 97 = 97
Identity Property of Multiplication

3. 6 × 55 × 5 = 1,650
Commutative Property of Multiplication

4. 7 × 297 = 2,079
Distributive Property of Multiplication over Subtraction

5. 21,888 × 0 = 0
Zero Property of Multiplication

6. 12,005 × 4 = 48,020
Distributive Property of Multiplication over Addition

Problem Solving

7. The population of New Zealand is 3,662,265. What is that number rounded to the nearest hundred thousand? 3,700,000

8. The population of Auckland, New Zealand, is 997,940. The population of Wellington is 335,468. How much greater is the population of Auckland than that of Wellington? 662,472

Spiral Review

Compare. Write >, <, or =.

9. 2.1 > 2.01
10. 0.430 = 0.4300
11. 0.807 > 0.087
12. 3.15 > 3.1

Grade 5, Chapter 2, Lesson 4, Cluster A 13

Practice

Estimate Products of Whole Numbers and Decimals

P 2-5 PRACTICE

Estimate by rounding. Possible estimates are given.

1. 3.4 × 10 30
2. 59 × 32 1,800
3. 446 × 682 280,000
4. 816 × 1.04 800
5. 4.27 × 82 320
6. 83 × 303 24,000
7. 21 × 663 14,000
8. 98 × 32 3,000
9. 91 × 3.2 270
10. 3.34 × 847 2,400
11. 9.29 × 0.8 9
12. 43 × 58 2,400
13. 8.9 × 4.5 45
14. 13.1 × 0.6 13
15. 87.2 × 65.8 6,300
16. 186 × 92 18,000
17. 342 × 86 27,000
18. 396 × 23 8,000
19. 631 × 465 300,000
20. 0.863 × 89.24 90
21. 605 × 7.235 4,200
22. 85.47 × 83.6 = 7,200
23. 603 × 29 = 18,000
24. 408 × 46 = 20,000
25. 3,045 × 38 = 120,000
26. 6.34 × 6 = 36
27. 0.8 × 5.2 = 5
28. 27.43 × 8 = 240
29. 8.5 × 38 = 360
30. 5.13 × 24 = 100
31. 3,498 × 5.7 = 18,000

Estimate by clustering. Possible estimates are given.

32. 236 + 186 + 209 600
33. 42.8 + 36.9 + 41.9 120
34. 5,497 + 4,623 + 4,802 15,000
35. 9.07 + 8.7 + 9.45 27
36. 739 + 662 + 720 2,100
37. 11.4 + 9.68 + 10.5 30

Problem Solving Possible estimates are given.

38. Mia bought 2.5 lb of sliced turkey to make sandwiches for a picnic. The turkey cost \$5.89 per pound. About how much did Mia pay for the turkey? about \$18

39. Mia also bought a package of sliced cheese that weighed 2.38 lb. The cheese cost \$4.25 per pound. About how much did Mia pay for the cheese? about \$8

Use with Grade 5, Chapter 2, Lesson 5, pages 62–65. (43)

Reteach

Estimate Products of Whole Numbers and Decimals

R 2-5 RETEACH

To estimate a product, round each number. Then use a basic fact and a multiplication pattern to multiply mentally.

	Estimate 27 × 643.	Estimate 54.3 × 7.6.
Round each number to its greatest place.	27 × 643 ↓ ↓	54.3 × 7.6 ↓ ↓
Write the basic fact. Then, write the same number of zeros in the product as are in both factors.	**3**0 × **6**00 = **18**,000 (1 zero + 2 zeros → 3 zeros)	**5**0 × **8** = **4**00 (1 zero → 1 zero)

Estimate each product. Round each factor. Then multiply.

1. 54 × 68 → 50 × 70 = 3,500
2. 61 × 239 → 60 × 200 = 12,000
3. 6.97 × 4.3 → 7 × 4 = 28
4. 36.4 × 2.8 → 40 × 3 = 120

Estimate the product by rounding. Show how you rounded. Estimates may vary. Possible estimates are given.

5. 8 × 674 — 8 × 700 = 5,600
6. 9 × 45.8 — 9 × 50 = 450
7. 43 × 104 — 40 × 100 = 4,000
8. 1.9 × 74 — 2 × 70 = 140
9. 84 × 13 — 80 × 10 = 800
10. 21 × 663 — 20 × 700 = 14,000
11. 38 × 573 — 40 × 600 = 24,000
12. 18 × 26.4 — 20 × 30 = 600
13. 1.84 × 4.8 — 2 × 5 = 10
14. 2.6 × 9.04 — 3 × 9 = 27

Use with Grade 5, Chapter 2, Lesson 5, pages 62–65. (44)

Enrich

Estimate Products of Whole Numbers and Decimals

E 2-5 ENRICH

Estimation Riddle

Find each estimated product in the box. Write the matching letter next to the multiplication exercise. Read the letters from top to bottom to answer this riddle:

Which Englishman discovered the circle?

1. 68 × 49 S
2. 18.7 × 5.6 I
3. 3.61 × 0.8 R
4. 9.3 × 0.75 C
5. 36.09 × 3.8 U
6. 82 × 17 M
7. 712 × 43.9 F
8. 361 × 59 E
9. 7.05 × 9.765 R
10. 558.6 × 6.3 E
11. 39 × 7.64 N
12. 407 × 9.56 C
13. 250.47 × 18 E

Letter	Product
I	120
U	160
S	3,500
F	28,000
R	70
C	9
E	3,600
R	4
M	1,600
C	4,000
E	6,000
N	320
E	24,000

Explain how you estimated the product of 558.6 × 6.3.

Possible answer: I rounded 558.6 to the nearest hundred: 600. I rounded 6.3 to the nearest one: 6. I used mental math to multiply 600 × 6 = 3,600.

Use with Grade 5, Chapter 2, Lesson 5, pages 62–65. (45)

Daily Homework

2-5 Estimate Products of Whole Numbers and Decimals

Estimate by rounding. Possible estimates are given.

1. 9.2 × 10 90
2. 11 × 63 600
3. 132 × 43 5,200
4. 212 × 82 16,000
5. 61 × 39 2,400
6. 2,029 × 42 80,000
7. 8.7 × 11.1 99
8. 129.4 × 40 5,200
9. 8.22 × 490 4,000
10. 1.78 × 27 = 60
11. 874 × 9 = 8,100
12. 368 × 488 = 200,000
13. 8.3 × 78 = 640

Estimate by clustering. Possible estimates are given.

14. 387 + 372 + 416 1,200
15. 82.8 + 79.2 + 77 240
16. 1,100 + 1,205 + 1,212 3,600
17. 897 + 912 + 889 2,700
18. 1,490 + 1,398 + 1,421 4,300
19. 3.79 + 4.16 + 4.21 12

Estimate by rounding. Write > or <.

20. 37.92 × 1.8 < 78.76
21. 58.89 × 21.07 < 1,600
22. \$340 > \$80.45 × 3.7
23. 78.6 × 4.2 > 92 + 89 + 88

Problem Solving

24. Milagros bought a toy for \$14.99, two postcards for \$2.15 each, and a poster for \$8.99. She gave the clerk \$30. Estimate her change, if there is no sales tax. \$2.00

25. The population of Greenland was estimated to be fify-nine thousand, eight hundred twenty-seven. Write that number in expanded form. 50,000 + 9,000 + 800 + 20 + 7

Spiral Review

Find the number that makes each sentence true.

26. 72 + 8 + 3 = (72 + 3) + 8
27. 376 + 0 = 376
28. 6 × (43 + 7) = (6 × 43) + (6 × 7)
29. 184 + 754 = 754 + 184

14 Grade 5, Chapter 2, Lesson 5, Cluster A

Chapter 2 ~ Lesson 6

Practice

Problem Solving: Reading for Math
Estimate or exact answer

P 2-6 PRACTICE Reading Skill

Solve. State whether the problem requires an estimate or an exact answer.

1. Students at Oak Ridge Elementary School were asked to bring in a new or gently-used book for a community service project. There are 18 classes with about 23 students in each class. About how many books will they collect for the project? about 400; estimate since you do not know the exact number of students in each class

2. Allison and Jake are in charge of a bake sale for their school. They want each fifth grader to bring 6 cookies for the sale. There are 52 fifth graders at the school. How many cookies will they have to sell?
312; exact answer

3. Washington Elementary School is looking for student volunteers to vote on new library books. Five students from each of the classes in the school can participate. There are 22 classes at the elementary school. How many students can volunteer?
110; exact answer

4. A bookstore has just received a new shipment of 15 boxes of books. If each box contains approximately 30 books, how many books are in the shipment?
about 450; estimate since the number of books in each box is an estimate

5. Students at Saddlebrook Elementary School are collecting canned food for a local food bank. They hope to collect 50 pounds of food from each class. There are 17 classes at Saddlebrook Elementary School. If the students meet their goal, how many pounds of food will be collected?
850 pounds; exact answer

6. Mollie is going to a movie. The movie starts at 4:15 P.M. and lasts for about 1 hour 55 minutes. What time should her mother pick her up after the movie?
about 6:15 P.M.; estimate since the length of the movie is approximate

7. A National Forest covers 500 square miles of land. Do you think this number is exact or an estimate? Explain.
Estimate since it would be difficult to measure the size exactly and it does not seem likely that it would be a multiple of 100.

Use with Grade 5, Chapter 2, Lesson 6, pages 66–67. (46)

Practice

Problem Solving: Reading for Math
Estimate or exact answer

P 2-6 PRACTICE Math Skills Test Prep

Choose the correct answer.

A girl scout camp can host 5 troops at a time. Each troop can bring 18 scouts. So, about 100 scouts can stay at the camp.

1. Which of the following statements is true?
   - A The camp can hold 18 troops at one time.
   - (B) A total of 5 troops can stay at the camp at the same time.
   - C Exactly 100 girls can stay at the camp.
   - D Each troop can have 5 girls.

2. When you find an exact answer to solve a problem, you
   - (F) identify the actual numbers you need for the problem.
   - G ignore all facts given in the problem.
   - H round numbers to solve.
   - J guess.

The Natural History Museum allows 8 busloads of children to visit the museum at once. Each bus carries 42 children. The museum estimates that 320 children will be visiting the museum.

3. Which of the following statements is NOT true?
   - A Each bus carries 42 children.
   - B About 320 children will be in the museum at once.
   - C The museum allows 8 busloads of children.
   - (D) 300 students would be a better estimate of the total.

4. You would NOT estimate the answer to a problem when
   - F the numbers in the problem are rounded.
   - G *approximately* is used in the problem.
   - H *about* is used in the problem.
   - (J) you need to know the exact answer.

Jefferson School District has 9 elementary schools. Each school has about 75 fifth graders. In order to have enough history books, the district estimates that it will need 720 textbooks for the fifth grade.

5. Which of the following statements is true?
   - A There are 75 students at each school.
   - (B) The school district should have extra history textbooks.
   - C There are 9 classes in each school.
   - D There are exactly 720 fifth graders in the Jefferson School District.

6. If the numbers in a problem appear to be rounded, you can
   - (F) estimate the answer.
   - G ignore the numbers in the problem.
   - H find an exact answer.
   - J check your answer.

Use with Grade 5, Chapter 2, Lesson 6, pages 66–67. (47)

Practice

Problem Solving: Reading for Math
Estimate or exact answer

P 2-6 PRACTICE Math Skills Test Prep

Choose the correct answer.

The hiking club has 7 groups of students. There are 21 students in each group. The club leaders estimate there are 140 student members in all.

7. Which of the following statements is true?
   - (A) There are 7 groups of students.
   - B There are exactly 140 club members.
   - C There are 21 groups of students.
   - D There are 7 students in each group.

8. If you see the words *about* or *approximately* in a problem, you can
   - F find an exact answer.
   - (G) estimate the answer.
   - H guess.
   - J ignore the facts given in the problem.

Solve. State whether the problem requires an estimate or an exact answer.

9. A restaurant usually sells 48 desserts each night. The restaurant is open 5 days a week. About how many desserts does the restaurant sell in one week?
about 250 desserts; estimate

10. This year about 60 of the 368 students at the elementary school moved. How many students were return students?
about 300 students; estimate

11. Fifth graders at Holmes Elementary School took a survey at their school. Of the 374 students at the school, 195 speak a second language. How many students speak only one language?
179 students; exact

12. Dan and Bev are planning a 10-mile hike to Lake Solitude. They think they can hike about 2 miles an hour. If they start their hike at 8 A.M., what time will they reach the lake?
about 1 P.M.; estimate

13. The ski team has 4 vans. Each van holds 9 team members. If the team has just enough room for the team members, how many members are there?
36 team members; exact

14. The ski team has a race at 9 A.M. The race is 100 miles away. They leave at 6 A.M. and drive 55 miles each hour. Will they arrive at the race on time?
Yes, they will arrive in about 2 hours; estimate.

Use with Grade 5, Chapter 2, Lesson 6, pages 66–67. (48)

Daily Homework

2-6 **Problem Solving: Reading for Math**
Estimate or Exact Answer

Solve. State whether the problem requires an estimate or an exact answer.

1. Marina plans to visit Uruguay next summer. She knows that there are approximately 49 people per square mile in that country. If the land area is 68,000 square miles, how many people live in Uruguay?
about 3,500,000 people; estimate

2. About 91 out of every 100 people live in the cities of Uruguay. Express that number as a decimal and as a fraction.
0.91, $\frac{91}{100}$; exact answer

3. Students in the United States paid a customs fee of $108 to send boxes of English-language books to Uruguay. If the cost was $4.50 per box of books, how many boxes did they send?
24 boxes; exact answer

4. The population of Asunción, the capital of Paraguay, is estimated to be 546,600. The population of Montevideo, the capital of Uruguay, is about 1,303,200. How many more people live in Montevideo than live in Asunción?
756,600; exact answer

5. The border shared by Paraguay and Brazil is 1,290 kilometers in length. If a traveler were to drive 250 kilometers each day, about how many days would it take to start from one end and end at the other?
about 5 days; estimate

6. Tourism in Uruguay brings in about eight hundred ninety-five million dollars each year. Write that number in standard form.
$895,000,000; exact answer

Spiral Review

Estimate by rounding.

7. 9.8×19.9 200
8. 41.8×3.12 120
9. 62.1×7.23 420

Grade 5, Chapter 2, Lesson 6, Cluster A 15

Chapter 2 ~ Lesson 7

Practice

Multiply Whole Numbers by Decimals

P 2-7 PRACTICE

Multiply.

1. 1.6 × 8 = 12.8
2. 2.83 × 7 = 19.81
3. 14.7 × 24 = 352.8
4. 3.75 × 100 = 375
5. 2.09 × 8 = 16.72
6. 12.8 × 10 = 128
7. 2.55 × 42 = 107.1
8. 4.7 × 85 = 399.5
9. $34.99 × 4 = $139.96
10. 147.4 × 2 = 294.8

11. 0.8 × 5 = 4.0 or 4
12. 1.67 × 4 = 6.68
13. 6 × $1.79 = $10.74
14. 2.46 × 10 = 24.6
15. 4.2 × 22 = 92.4
16. 10.4 × 1,000 = 10,400
17. 2.3 × 38 = 87.4
18. 57 × 5.18 = 295.26

Find the multiple of 10 that makes each statement true.

19. 6.1 × 100 = 610
20. 10 × 11.84 = 118.4
21. $24.95 × 10 = $249.50
22. 526.7 × 1,000 = 526,700
23. 0.2687 × 1,000 = 268.7
24. 0.46 × 100 = 46
25. 100 × 32.05 = 3,205
26. 0.012 × 10 = 0.12

Problem Solving

27. Each Sunday during his nine-week summer vacation, Ray buys a newspaper for his family. The Sunday paper costs $1.85. How much does he pay for the Sunday newspapers during the summer? $16.65

28. One Sunday, Ray weighed the newspaper and found that it weighed 2.7 lb. If each Sunday newspaper weighs the same, how many pounds of newspaper will Ray's family recycle if they buy the Sunday paper for 50 weeks? 135 lb

Use with Grade 5, Chapter 2, Lesson 7, pages 70–73. (49)

Reteach

Multiply Whole Numbers by Decimals

R 2-7 RETEACH

To multiply a whole number by a decimal, multiply as you would with whole numbers. Then count the number of decimal places in each factor. Write the same number of decimal places in the product.

Multiply 7 × 3.28.
Estimate: 7 × 3 = 21

3.28 ← 2 decimal places
× 7
22.**96** ← 2 decimal places

Compare the product and the estimate.
22.96 is close to 21,
so 22.96 is a reasonable answer.

Multiply 3 × 0.09.
Estimate: 3 × 0 = 0

0.09 ← 2 decimal places
× 3
0.**27** ← 2 decimal places

Compare the product and the estimate.
0.27 is close to 0,
so 0.27 is a reasonable answer.

Write the number of decimal places. Multiply. Estimate to check if your answer is reasonable.

1. 0.9 ← 1 decimal place(s); × 9; 8.1 ← 1 decimal place(s)
2. $3.92 ← 2 decimal place(s); × 5; $19.60 ← 2 decimal place(s)
3. 3.79 ← 2 decimal place(s); × 8; 30.32 ← 2 decimal place(s)
4. 21.8 ← 1 decimal place(s); × 4; 87.2 ← 1 decimal place(s)

Multiply. Estimate to check if your answer is reasonable.

5. 7.2 × 6 = 43.2
6. 0.67 × 2 = 1.34
7. $1.75 × 7 = $12.25
8. 68.7 × 4 = 274.8
9. 98.5 × 8 = 788
10. 8.5 × 3 = 25.5
11. 1.08 × 9 = 9.72
12. 7.9 × 41 = 323.9
13. 2.6 × 72 = 187.2
14. $23.54 × 5 = $117.70

Use with Grade 5, Chapter 2, Lesson 7, pages 70–73. (50)

Enrich

Multiply Whole Numbers by Decimals

E 2-7 ENRICH

Magic Square Multiplication

The square shown at the right is a magic square. The sum of each row, column, and diagonal equals 15. If you multiply the numbers in the magic square by the same decimal number, you will get a new magic square.

8	3	4
1	5	9
6	7	2

1. Multiply each number in the magic square by 7.4. Then calculate the new magic sum.

59.2	22.2	29.6
7.4	37	66.6
44.4	51.8	14.8

Magic Sum = 111

2. Multiply each number in the magic square by 0.98. Then calculate the new magic sum.

7.84	2.94	3.92
0.98	4.9	8.82
5.88	6.86	1.96

Magic Sum = 14.7

3. Multiply each number in the magic square by 1.03. Then calculate the new magic sum.

8.24	3.09	4.12
1.03	5.15	9.27
6.18	7.21	2.06

Magic Sum = 15.45

4. Multiply each number in the magic square by 25.6. Then calculate the new magic sum.

204.8	76.8	102.4
25.6	128	230.4
153.6	179.2	51.2

Magic Sum = 384

Look back at the magic sum for each new magic square you found. How could you have found the new magic sums without finding the nine new products?

Possible answer: Multiply 15 by the factor given in each exercise.

Use with Grade 5, Chapter 2, Lesson 7, pages 70–73. (51)

Daily Homework

2-7 Multiply Whole Numbers by Decimals

Multiply.

1. 8.4 × 5 = 42
2. 14.4 × 7 = 100.8
3. 6.73 × 8 = 53.84
4. 39.86 × 9 = 358.74
5. 6.04 × 100 = 604

6. 0.6 × 6 = 3.6
7. $41.86 × 5 = $209.30
8. 4.9 × 11 = 53.9
9. 42.86 × 7 = 300.02
10. 342.6 × 4 = 1,370.4
11. 12.85 × 10 = 128.5
12. 74.85 × 5 = 374.25
13. 61.05 × 3 = 183.15
14. 0.43 × 8 = 3.44

Find the multiple of 10 that makes each statement true.

15. 3.4 × 100 = 340
16. 10 × 2.5 = 25
17. 0.58 × 1,000 = 580
18. 26.4 × 100 = 2,640

Compare. Write <, >, or =.

19. 3.6 × 2 < 0.8 × 10
20. 0.7 × 100 = 3.5 × 20
21. 10.1 × 4 < 8.1 × 5

Problem Solving

22. Suppose that 800 tourists buy gifts at a museum gift shop each day. If each tourist spends an average of $15.50, how much will the gift shop take in per day? $12,400

23. Naomi buys 2 maps of Jordan at $19.95 each and a guide book for $25.50. How much does she spend in all? $65.40

Spiral Review

24. 487.65 + 128.24 + 43.17 = 659.06
25. 64.87 − 8.82 = 56.05
26. 83.66 + 9.77 = 93.43
27. 823.45 − 110.33 = 713.12

Chapter 2 ~ Lesson 8

Practice

Explore Multiplying Decimals by Decimals P 2-8 PRACTICE

Shade 10-by-10 grids to find each product.

1. $0.4 \times 0.7 =$ _0.28_   **2.** $0.7 \times 0.3 =$ _0.21_   **3.** $0.2 \times 0.8 =$ _0.16_

Multiply.

4. $0.8 \times 0.4 =$ _0.32_   **5.** $0.3 \times 0.6 =$ _0.18_   **6.** $0.6 \times 0.9 =$ _0.54_

7. $0.7 \times 0.8 =$ _0.56_   **8.** $0.9 \times 0.5 =$ _0.45_   **9.** $0.5 \times 0.6 =$ _0.30, or 0.3_

10. $0.4 \times 0.4 =$ _0.16_   **11.** $0.7 \times 0.7 =$ _0.49_   **12.** $0.5 \times 0.2 =$ _0.10, or 0.1_

13. $0.3 \times 0.3 =$ _0.09_   **14.** $0.5 \times 0.7 =$ _0.35_   **15.** $0.3 \times 0.9 =$ _0.27_

16. $\begin{array}{r} 0.4 \\ \times\, 0.9 \\ \hline 0.36 \end{array}$	**17.** $\begin{array}{r} 0.5 \\ \times\, 0.5 \\ \hline 0.25 \end{array}$	**18.** $\begin{array}{r} 0.2 \\ \times\, 0.7 \\ \hline 0.14 \end{array}$	**19.** $\begin{array}{r} 0.1 \\ \times\, 0.8 \\ \hline 0.08 \end{array}$	**20.** $\begin{array}{r} 0.8 \\ \times\, 0.6 \\ \hline 0.48 \end{array}$
21. $\begin{array}{r} 0.7 \\ \times\, 0.9 \\ \hline 0.63 \end{array}$	**22.** $\begin{array}{r} 0.9 \\ \times\, 0.8 \\ \hline 0.72 \end{array}$	**23.** $\begin{array}{r} 0.2 \\ \times\, 0.1 \\ \hline 0.02 \end{array}$	**24.** $\begin{array}{r} 0.9 \\ \times\, 0.2 \\ \hline 0.18 \end{array}$	**25.** $\begin{array}{r} 0.7 \\ \times\, 0.6 \\ \hline 0.42 \end{array}$

Problem Solving

26. Van bought a poster for his room that measures 0.6 m by 0.4 m. Shade the grid to find the area of the glass Van needs to cover the poster. What is the area of the glass?

_0.24 sq m_

Use with Grade 5, Chapter 2, Lesson 8, pages 74–75. (52)

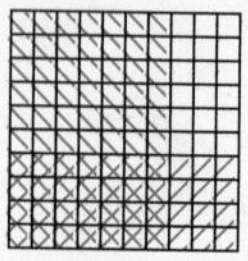

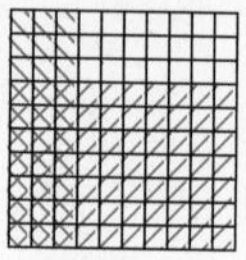

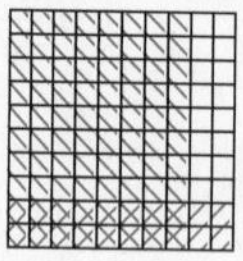

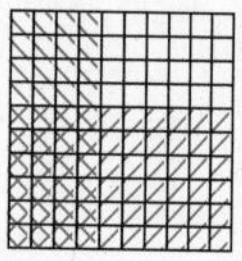

Reteach

Explore Multiplying Decimals by Decimals R 2-8 RETEACH

You can shade parts of a 10-by-10 grid to show the product of two decimals.

Multiply 0.7×0.5.

Shade one row for each tenth in the first factor.

Shade one row for each tenth in the second factor.

Count the total squares that are shaded twice.
Thirty-five squares out of 100, or 0.35, are shaded twice. So, $0.7 \times 0.5 = 0.35$.

Shade 10-by-10 grids to multiply.

1. $0.3 \times 0.7 =$ _0.21_
Shade __3__ columns.
Shade __7__ rows.

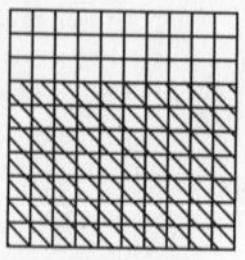

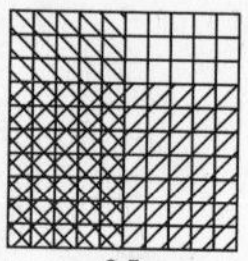

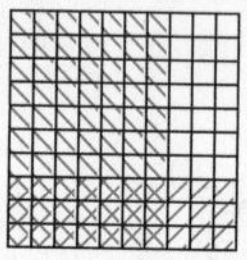

2. $0.6 \times 0.4 =$ _0.24_
Shade __6__ columns.
Shade __4__ rows.

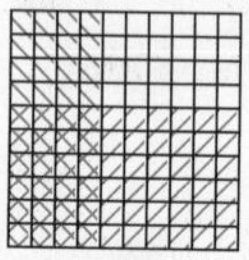

3. $0.4 \times 0.9 =$ _0.36_

4. $0.8 \times 0.6 =$ _0.48_

5. $0.5 \times 0.4 =$ _0.2_   **6.** $0.9 \times 0.1 =$ _0.09_

7. $0.7 \times 0.2 =$ _0.14_   **8.** $0.7 \times 0.9 =$ _0.63_

Use with Grade 5, Chapter 2, Lesson 8, pages 74–75. (53)

Enrich

Explore Multiplying Decimals by Decimals E 2-8 ENRICH
Product to Product

Each dot below has two factors. Find the pairs of factors with products greater than 0.2 and less than 0.7. Connect them in order from least to greatest to find a way of reaching faraway places.

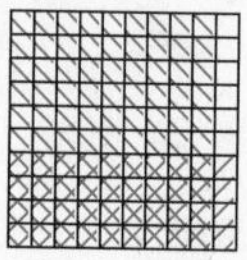

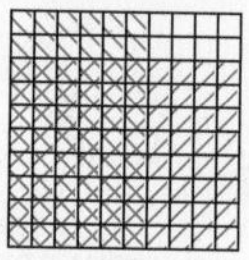

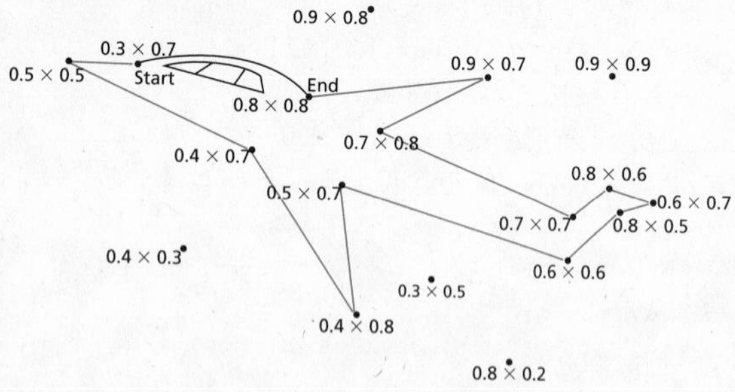

Find the pairs of factors with products greater than 0.4 and less than 0.9. Connect them in order from least to greatest to find a thing you carry when you travel far away.

Use with Grade 5, Chapter 2, Lesson 8, pages 74–75. (54)

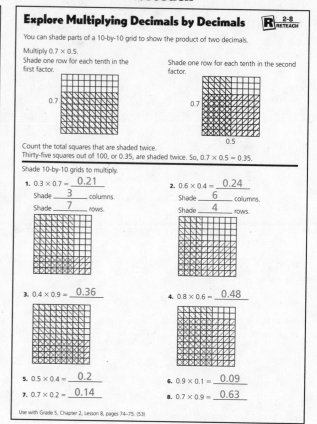

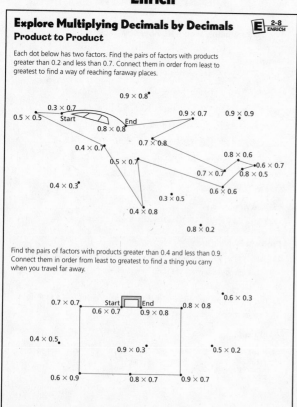

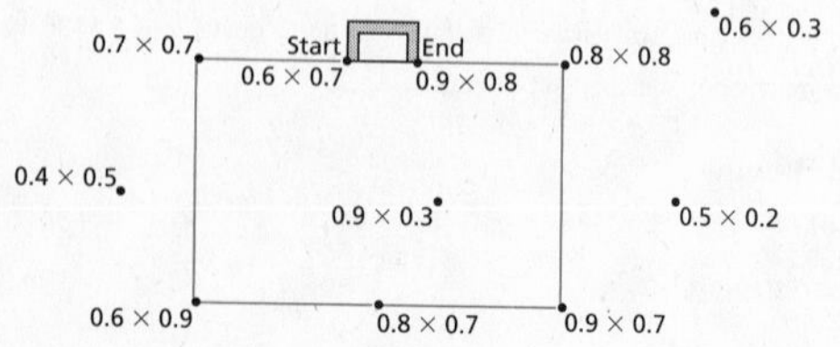

Daily Homework

2·8 Explore Multiplying Decimals by Decimals

Multiply.

1. $0.6 \times 0.4 =$ _0.24_   **2.** $0.3 \times 0.9 =$ _0.27_   **3.** $0.3 \times 0.3 =$ _0.09_

4. $\begin{array}{r} 0.4 \\ \times\, 0.5 \\ \hline 0.2 \end{array}$	**5.** $\begin{array}{r} 0.8 \\ \times\, 0.6 \\ \hline 0.48 \end{array}$	**6.** $\begin{array}{r} 0.7 \\ \times\, 0.5 \\ \hline 0.35 \end{array}$	**7.** $\begin{array}{r} 0.1 \\ \times\, 0.6 \\ \hline 0.06 \end{array}$	**8.** $\begin{array}{r} 0.5 \\ \times\, 0.6 \\ \hline 0.3 \end{array}$

9. $0.7 \times 0.1 =$ _0.07_   **10.** $0.4 \times 0.9 =$ _0.36_   **11.** $0.4 \times 0.8 =$ _0.32_

12. $0.7 \times 0.3 =$ _0.21_   **13.** $0.6 \times 0.6 =$ _0.36_   **14.** $0.9 \times 0.9 =$ _0.81_

15. $0.2 \times 0.1 =$ _0.02_   **16.** $0.3 \times 0.4 =$ _0.12_   **17.** $0.8 \times 0.2 =$ _0.16_

18. $0.4 \times 0.7 =$ _0.28_   **19.** $0.6 \times 0.7 =$ _0.42_   **20.** $0.1 \times 0.1 =$ _0.01_

21. $0.5 \times 0.5 =$ _0.25_   **22.** $0.6 \times 0.3 =$ _0.18_   **23.** $0.4 \times 0.4 =$ _0.16_

Solve.

24. One half, or 0.5, of a box of 24 oranges were eaten. How many oranges were left in the box? _12_

25. One fourth, or 0.25, of the trees in an orchard were flowering. If there were 224 trees in the orchard, how many were in flower? _56_

Spiral Review

26. $7.5 \times 6 =$ _45_   **27.** $8.2 \times 8 =$ _65.6_

28. $4.7 \times 3 =$ _14.1_   **29.** $4 \times 1.8 =$ _7.2_

Practice

Multiply Decimals by Decimals

P 2-9 PRACTICE

Multiply.

1. 0.6 × 0.8 = 0.48	**2.** 0.5 × 0.6 = 0.30, or 0.3	**3.** 1.7 × 0.9 = 1.53	**4.** 2.61 × 0.4 = 1.044	**5.** 2.09 × 0.3 = 0.627
6. 5.18 × 2.7 = 13.986	**7.** 6.09 × 8.6 = 52.374	**8.** 37.24 × 3.1 = 115.444	**9.** 218.7 × 4.8 = 1,049.76	**10.** 432.1 × 1.2 = 518.52

11. 0.9 × 0.7 = 0.63
12. 0.16 × 0.6 = 0.096
13. 7.4 × 0.4 = 2.96
14. 3.47 × 0.9 = 3.123
15. 4.35 × 1.7 = 7.395
16. 58.2 × 6.8 = 395.76
17. 3.06 × 9.1 = 27.846
18. 94.2 × 2.5 = 235.5
19. 17.64 × 3.2 = 56.448
20. 41.38 × 6.3 = 260.694
21. 86.51 × 0.8 = 69.208
22. 0.53 × 9.7 = 5.141

Find the number that makes each problem true.

23. 39.8 × 0.7 = 27.[8]6
24. 46.87 × 0.5 = 23.[4]35
25. 2.3 × 1.8 = [4].14
26. 57.8 × 0.7 = 4[0].46

Problem Solving

27. Beth works as a lifeguard at a city park. She earns $9.50 per hour and works 7.5 hours each day. How much does she earn each day? $71.25

28. The cost of renting a pedal boat at the city park is $6.25 per hour. Jason rented a boat for 1.5 hours. To the nearest cent, how much did the pedal boat rental cost? $9.38

Use with Grade 5, Chapter 2, Lesson 9, pages 76–79. (55)

Reteach

Multiply Decimals by Decimals

R 2-9 RETEACH

To multiply a decimal by a decimal, multiply as you would with whole numbers. Then count the total number of decimal places in both factors. Write the same number of decimal places in the product. Sometimes you have to write zeros to place the decimal in the product.

Multiply 4.7 × 2.63.
Estimate: 5 × 3 = 15

```
    2.63  ← 2 decimal places
  ×  4.7  ← 1 decimal place
    1841
 + 10520
  12.361  ← 3 decimal places
```

Compare the product and the estimate.
12.361 is close to 15,
so 12.361 is a reasonable answer.

Multiply 0.5 × 0.07.

```
   0.07  ← 2 decimal places
 ×  0.5  ← 1 decimal place
  0.035  ← 3 decimal places
   ↑
```

Write a zero to place the decimal in the product.

Write the number of decimal places. Multiply. Estimate to check if your answer is reasonable.

1. 0.9 ← 1 decimal place(s); × 0.5 ← 1 decimal place(s); 0.45 ← 2 decimal place(s)

2. 0.89 ← 2 decimal place(s); × 0.9 ← 1 decimal place(s); 0.801 ← 3 decimal place(s)

3. 1.8 ← 1 decimal place(s); × 3.7 ← 1 decimal place(s); 6.66 ← 2 decimal place(s)

4. 4.14 ← 2 decimal place(s); × 2.8 ← 1 decimal place(s); 11.592 ← 3 decimal place(s)

Multiply. Estimate to check if your answer is reasonable.

5. 0.8 × 0.7 = 0.56	**6.** 2.5 × 0.6 = 1.5	**7.** 3.67 × 0.49 = 1.7983	**8.** 8.73 × 0.5 = 4.365
9. 9.2 × 6.1 = 56.12	**10.** 54.06 × 0.2 = 10.812	**11.** 7.13 × 1.9 = 13.547	**12.** 9.23 × 4.8 = 44.304

Use with Grade 5, Chapter 2, Lesson 9, pages 76–79. (56)

Enrich

Multiply Decimals by Decimals

E 2-9 ENRICH

Sort It Out

Use number sense to sort exercises 1–17 by these rules. When you have finished sorting, multiply to check your answers.

Write **A** if the product is greater than each factor.

Write **B** if the product is less than each factor.

Write **C** if the product is between the two factors.

Letter	Exercise	Product
C	**1.** 0.7 × 5.6 =	3.92
A	**2.** 9.8 × 4.5 =	44.1
C	**3.** 46.9 × 0.5 =	23.45
B	**4.** 0.4 × 0.75 =	0.3
C	**5.** 0.82 × 56.89 =	46.6498
A	**6.** 2.3 × 2.3 =	5.29
B	**7.** 0.39 × 0.24 =	0.0936
A	**8.** 2.5 × 1.01 =	2.525
C	**9.** 0.34 × 23.5 =	7.99
B	**10.** 0.96 × 0.14 =	0.1344
A	**11.** 7.6 × 1.93 =	14.668
C	**12.** 0.4 × 48.129 =	19.2516
C	**13.** 32.8 × 0.56 =	18.368
A	**14.** 52.1 × 73.94 =	3,852.274
A	**15.** 9.06 × 3.75 =	33.975
C	**16.** 67.023 × 0.8 =	53.6184
B	**17.** 0.65 × 0.44 =	0.286

Compare each factor in exercises 1–17 to 1. How could this comparison have helped you sort the exercises? Possible answer: I compared the factors to 1. If each factor is greater than 1, the product is greater than each factor. If each factor is less than 1, the product is less than each factor. If one factor is greater than 1 and one factor is less than 1, the product is between the two factors.

Use with Grade 5, Chapter 2, Lesson 9, pages 76–79. (57)

Daily Homework

2-9 Multiply Decimals by Decimals

Multiply.

1. 3.42 × 0.5 = 1.71	**2.** 72.84 × 6.2 = 451.608	**3.** 10.11 × 0.7 = 7.077	**4.** 2.22 × 3.3 = 7.326	**5.** 4.48 × 5.73 = 25.6704
6. 204.62 × 0.4 = 81.848	**7.** 6.07 × 8.4 = 50.988	**8.** 23.1 × 1.58 = 36.498	**9.** 3.14 × 2.27 = 7.1278	**10.** 1.12 × 1.01 = 1.1312

11. 3.9 × 0.4 = 1.56
12. 4.4 × 0.7 = 3.08
13. 23.5 × 0.5 = 11.75
14. 1.5 × 0.4 = 0.6
15. 14.88 × 2.8 = 41.664
16. 3.08 × 1.4 = 4.312

Compare. Write <, >, or =.

17. 0.86 × 0.258 < 0.300
18. 1.5 × 0.6 = 1.8 × 0.5
19. 0.024 × 7 < 0.141 + 0.18
20. 7.5 × 4 > 3.42 × 8

Problem Solving

21. The number of goats in Nepal is about twice the number of buffalo. If there are about 3,400,000 buffalo, how many goats are there? 6,800,000 goats

22. In Nepal the unit of currency is the rupee. One U.S. dollar is equal to 68.23 rupees. How many rupees would you need to buy three dollars worth of cloth? 204.69 rupees

Spiral Review

23. 44.07 + 2.3 = 46.37
24. 2.4 − 1.58 = 0.82
25. 54.91 − 1.58 = 53.33
26. 43.82 + 3.87 = 47.69

18 Grade 5, Chapter 2, Lesson 9, Cluster B

Chapter 2 ~ Lesson 10

Practice

Problem Solving: Strategy
Guess and Check

P 2-10 PRACTICE

Use the guess and check strategy to solve.

1. **Science** The Bactrian camel has two humps and the Dromedary camel has one hump. In a group of 15 camels, the total number of humps is 21. How many camels of each type are there?
   9 Dromedary and 6 Bactrian

2. The circus is ordering bicycles and unicycles for a new circus act. They order a total of 12 cycles. The cycles will be assembled at the circus and are delivered with 16 tires. How many bicycles and unicycles did they order?
   8 unicycles and 4 bicycles

3. Anja buys a magazine and a pizza while she is out. She spends a total of $8.10. The magazine costs $2.40 less than the pizza. How much does the pizza cost?
   $5.25

4. **Social Studies** A letter to Europe from the United States costs $0.55. Letters within the United States cost $0.33. Nancy mails 5 letters for $2.09, some to Europe and some to the United States. How many letters did she send to Europe?
   2 letters

Mixed Strategy Review

Solve. Use any strategy.

5. Warren spent a total of $8.50 at the store. He spent $2.40 on paper, $0.88 on pencils, and $2.65 on markers. He spent the rest on a notebook. How much did the notebook cost?
   $2.57
   Strategy: Work Backward

6. Ms. Baxter takes a group of 8 children to a concert. Tickets for children 12 years and older cost $3.50. Tickets for children under 12 cost $2.25. She spends a total of $21.75 on tickets for the children. How many children are 12 and older?
   3 children
   Strategy: Guess and Check

7. A cabin has room for 8 campers and 2 counselors. How many cabins are needed for a total of 64 campers and 16 counselors?
   8 cabins
   Strategy: Write an Equation

8. **Create a problem** for which you could guess and check to solve. Share it with others.
   Check students' problems.

Use with Grade 5, Chapter 2, Lesson 10, pages 80–81. (58)

Reteach

Problem Solving: Strategy
Guess and Check

R 2-10 RETEACH

Page 81, Problem 2

After riding on a camel during summer vacation, Sanjay sends letters and postcards to his friends to tell them about his adventure. Letters cost 33¢ each and postcards cost 20¢ to mail. He writes to 8 friends and spends $1.86. How many letters and postcards did he send?

Step 1 Read

Be sure you understand the problem.
Read carefully.

What do you know?

- Letters cost 33¢ each and postcards cost 20¢ each.
- Sanjay writes to 8 friends.
- He spends $1.86.

What do you need to find?

- The number of letters and postcards he sent.

Step 2 Plan

- Do an Experiment
- Guess and Check
- Work Backward
- Make a Graph
- Make a Table
- Write an Equation
- Make an Organized List
- Draw a Diagram
- Solve a Simpler Problem
- Logical Reasoning

Make a plan.
Choose a strategy.

You can solve the problem by making a guess.

Then check the guess.

If it is not the correct answer, adjust the guess and check again until you find the correct answer.

Use with Grade 5, Chapter 2, Lesson 10, pages 80–81. (59)

Reteach

Problem Solving: Strategy
Guess and Check

R 2-10 RETEACH

Step 3 Solve

Carry out your plan.

Make a guess about the number of letters and the number of postcards. Suppose you guess 4 letters and 4 postcards.

Check the amounts for the guess.

Letters: 4 × 33¢ = $1.32
Postcards: 4 × 20¢ = $0.80
Total Cost: $1.32 + $0.80 = $2.12

Does the guess check with the total that Sanjay spent? No

Should you adjust the number of letters up or down? Explain.
Adjust the number of letters down because the total is too much.

Adjust your guess. Check your guess.

Did the guess check? Answers may vary.

If your guess did not check, adjust it again.

How many letters did Sanjay send? 2 letters

How many postcards did Sanjay send? 6 postcards

Answers may vary. Students should guess and check until they find 2 letters ($0.66) and 6 postcards ($1.20). The total cost is $1.86.

Step 4 Look Back

Is the solution reasonable?
Reread the problem.

Have you answered the question? Yes

How can you check your answer? Answers may vary. Possible answer: Check the total cost for the letters and postcards.

Practice

1. Nelson has 7 coins. All of the coins are dimes and quarters. He has a total of $1.15. How many dimes and how many quarters does he have?
   3 quarters and 4 dimes

2. The library charges $0.75 a day for overdue videos and $0.12 a day for overdue books. Emily returns a video and a book and pays a total of $3.48 in late fees. How many days late were her items?
   4 days

Use with Grade 5, Chapter 2, Lesson 10, pages 80–81. (60)

Daily Homework

2-10 **Problem Solving: Strategy**
Guess and Check

Use the guess and check strategy to solve.

1. Franco sees 8 camels and counts 14 humps in all. If all Bactrian camels have two humps and all Dromedary camels have one hump, how many of each type of camel did Franco see?
   6 Bactrian, 2 Dromedary

2. Ronna saw a photograph of a number of Bactrian and Dromedary camels near an oasis. She counted 27 humps in all. How many of each kind of camel were in the photograph?
   9 Bactrian, 9 Dromedary

3. Trisha is on a vacation. She sends letters and postcards to her friends at home. She needs 33¢ in postage for each letter and 20¢ for each postcard. She spends $3.58 in postage. How many letters and postcards did she send?
   6 letters, 8 postcards

Mixed Strategy Review

4. Sam and Gina set up tables for a history club lunch discussion. A square table seats 4 people, one on each side. If they push the tables together end to end, how many tables will they need to seat 16 club members?
   7 tables

5. For a public meeting, the history club spent $37.00 on refreshments, $6.00 for film rentals, and $7.00 for programs. In all, they spent $140 for the meeting. Their only other expense was for rental of the meeting space. How much did they spend on rental?
   $90.00

Spiral Review

Name the place and value of the underlined number.

6. 385,997 — **hundreds; 900**
7. 2,345,007 — **millions; 2,000,000**

Grade 5, Chapter 2, Lesson 10, Cluster B 19

Chapter 2 ~ Lesson 11

Practice

P 2-11 PRACTICE

Exponents

Complete the table.

	Exponent Form	Expanded Form	Standard Form
1.	4^5	4 × 4 × 4 × 4 × 4	1,024
2.	6^2	6 × 6	36
3.	1^7	1 × 1 × 1 × 1 × 1 × 1 × 1	1
4.	5^0		1
5.	6^4	6 × 6 × 6 × 6	1,296
6.	10^2	10 × 10	100
7.	2^6	2 × 2 × 2 × 2 × 2 × 2	64
8.	3^3	3 × 3 × 3	27
9.	8^2	8 × 8	64
10.	4^1	4	4
11.	5^4	5 × 5 × 5 × 5	625
12.	10^6	10 × 10 × 10 × 10 × 10 × 10	1,000,000
13.	7^4	7 × 7 × 7 × 7	2,401
14.	2^3	2 × 2 × 2	8
15.	9^1	9	9
16.	3^0		1

Problem Solving

17. There are 10 boxes of postcards. Each box contains 10 bags. Each bag contains 10 postcards. How many postcards are there? How do you write this number in exponent form?
1,000 postcards; 10^3

18. A school has a telephone chain to let families know about emergency school closings. Three parents are in the first layer of the chain. There are five layers in the chain. Each parent in each layer calls three different parents. How many parents are in the chain?
243 parents

Use with Grade 5, Chapter 2, Lesson 11, pages 82–85. (61)

Reteach

R 2-11 RETEACH

Exponents

Sometimes when you multiply, you use the same number as a factor more than once. You can use exponent form to show this.

$3 \times 3 \times 3 \times 3 \times 3 \times 3 = 3^6$

Write the number of times the factor is used as the *exponent*.
Write the factor as the *base*.

To write 3 × 3 × 3 × 3 × 3 × 3, or 3^6, in standard form, multiply 3 six times.

$3 \times 3 \times 3 \times 3 \times 3 \times 3 = 3^6 = 729$

Write in exponent form and in standard form.

1. 4 × 4 × 4
Exponent Form: 4^3 Standard Form: 64
What is the base? 4
What is the exponent? 3

2. 2 × 2 × 2 × 2 × 2 × 2 × 2
Exponent Form: 2^7 Standard Form: 128
What is the base? 2
What is the exponent? 7

3. 10 × 10 × 10 × 10
Exponent Form: 10^4 Standard Form: 10,000
What is the base? 10
What is the exponent? 4

4. 5 × 5
Exponent Form: 5^2 Standard Form: 25
What is the base? 5
What is the exponent? 2

5. 3 × 3 × 3 × 3 × 3
Exponent Form: 3^5 Standard Form: 243
What is the base? 3
What is the exponent? 5

Use with Grade 5, Chapter 2, Lesson 11, pages 82–85. (62)

Enrich

E 2-11 ENRICH

Exponents
A Powerful Riddle

Write each missing number.

A. 3^2 = 9

C. 7 × 7 × 7 × 7 = 7^4

E. 6^5 = 6 × 6 × 6 × 6 × 6

H. 5^0 = 1

I. 7^1 = 7

L. 2^4 = 16

M. 10^1 = 10

N. 8^2 = 64

T. 5^3 = 125

U. 2^3 = 8

Find each digit you wrote in the riddle below. Write the letter of the exercise above the matching digit to answer the riddle.

At what time would you expect to see an astronaut eating a sandwich?

L	A	U	N	C	H		T	I	M	E
2	9	3	8	4	0		5	7	1	6

What method did you use to find the missing number in exercise T?
Explanations may vary. Possible explanation: I used guess, test, and revise and tried different numbers to find one that when used as a factor 3 times equaled 125.

Use with Grade 5, Chapter 2, Lesson 11, pages 82–85. (63)

Daily Homework

2-11 Exponents

Rewrite using a base and exponent.

1. 3 × 3 × 3 = 3^3
2. 2 × 2 × 2 × 2 × 2 = 2^5
3. 4 × 4 × 4 × 4 × 4 = 4^5
4. 8 × 8 × 8 × 8 × 8 = 8^5
5. 6 × 6 × 6 × 6 × 6 × 6 × 6 = 6^7
6. 9 × 9 × 9 × 9 × 9 × 9 × 9 × 9 = 9^8
7. 7 × 7 × 7 = 7^3
8. 5 × 5 × 5 × 5 × 5 × 5 = 5^6

Write in standard form.

9. 7^2 49
10. 3^4 81
11. 4^6 4,096
12. 2^7 128
13. 9^0 1
14. 3^5 243
15. 11^4 14,641
16. 10^6 1,000,000
17. 18^1 18
18. 8^5 32,768
19. 1^0 1
20. 14^3 2,744
21. $(0.2)^4$ 0.0016
22. $(0.01)^2$ 0.0001
23. $(0.4)^3$ 0.064

Problem Solving

24. If a phone team asks each person to call two people, how many rounds will it take to call 64 people? 6 rounds

25. Members of a tour group take a bus at 8:00 A.M. They travel for 2 hours 35 minutes. They spend 2 hours 45 minutes at their tour site and then return by the same route. What time will they get back to their hotel? 3:55 P.M.

26. A type of bacteria reproduces by splitting in two every thirty minutes. How many bacteria will there be after 4 hours if there are 2 bacteria to begin with? 512

Spiral Review

27. 4.17 × 8.1 = 33.777
28. 1.7 × 0.92 = 1.564
29. 4.2 × 6.2 = 26.04

20 Grade 5, Chapter 2, Lesson 11, Cluster B

Chapter 2 ~ Lesson 12

Part A Worksheet

Problem Solving: Application
Applying Multiplication

Part A 2-12 WORKSHEET Decision Making

Use the table to help you choose an event for the German Club.

Event	Cost	Time Required	Advantages of Event	Projected Profit

Your Decision

What is your recommendation for the German Club? Explain.

Answers may vary. Possible answer: Have a car wash. It is fun, takes the least amount of time, costs the least, and makes the most profit.

Use with Grade 5, Chapter 2, Lesson 12, pages 86–87. (64)

Part B Worksheet

Problem Solving: Application
Build a Model of the Solar System

Part B 2-12 WORKSHEET Math & Science

The solar system covers vast distances. Just how big do you think the solar system is? Make a drawing of the solar system. Put a dot for each planet where you think it will be in relation to the Sun. Use the space below.

Check students' drawings.

Work with a small group.

Complete the table. Multiply the distance from the Sun by 2 to calculate the distance that you will use to make a model of the solar system.

Planet	Distance from the Sun (in astronomical units)	Distance in your model (in centimeters)
Mercury	0.4	0.8
Venus	0.7	1.4
Earth	1	2
Mars	1.5	3
Jupiter	5.2	10.4
Saturn	9.6	19.2
Uranus	19.2	38.4
Neptune	30.1	60.2
Pluto	39.5	79

Use with Grade 5, Chapter 2, Lesson 12, pages 88–89. (65)

Part B Worksheet

Problem Solving: Application
Build a Model of the Solar System

Part B 2-12 WORKSHEET Math & Science

Use the data in the table to make a model of the solar system. You will have to tape some sheets of paper together to include all of the planets.

1. How does the model that you made compare to your drawing? Explain.
   Answers may vary.

2. How accurate were the drawings that other students in your group made to show the solar system?
   Answers may vary.

3. Were you surprised at the size of the model? Explain.
   Answers may vary.

4. Do you think that a textbook can include a scale drawing of the solar system in which you can identify each planet on one page of the textbook? Explain.
   Answers may vary. Possible answer: No, the distances are too large. If you were able to identify each of the planets, the scale would probably be inaccurate.

5. What is another scale that you could choose to make a model of the solar system? What would be some advantages and disadvantages of the scale?
   Answers may vary. Possible answer: Let 1 astronomical unit equal 1 centimeter. Advantages: The greater distances would not be as long in the model. Disadvantages: The planets that are closer to the Sun would be very close together.

Use with Grade 5, Chapter 2, Lesson 12, pages 88–89. (66)

Chapter 3 ~ Lesson 1

Practice

Relate Multiplication and Division

P 3-1 PRACTICE

Divide.

1. 21 ÷ 3 = 7
2. 56 ÷ 7 = 8
3. 50 ÷ 5 = 10
4. 36 ÷ 6 = 6
5. 10 ÷ 2 = 5
6. 25 ÷ 5 = 5
7. 14 ÷ 2 = 7
8. 28 ÷ 4 = 7
9. 72 ÷ 9 = 8
10. 18 ÷ 3 = 6
11. 48 ÷ 8 = 6
12. 36 ÷ 6 = 6
13. 35 ÷ 5 = 7
14. 45 ÷ 9 = 5
15. 70 ÷ 10 = 7
16. 48 ÷ 12 = 4
17. 8)64 = 8
18. 4)32 = 8
19. 9)90 = 10
20. 9)36 = 4
21. 11)99 = 9
22. 3)24 = 8
23. 5)30 = 6
24. 2)18 = 9
25. 9)99 = 11
26. 7)63 = 9
27. 6)42 = 7
28. 8)40 = 5
29. 4)24 = 6
30. 8)32 = 4
31. 6)60 = 10
32. 9)81 = 9
33. 5)40 = 8
34. 10)50 = 5
35. 7)49 = 7
36. 9)45 = 5

Complete the fact family.

37. 4 × 3 = 12
3 × 4 = 12
12 ÷ 3 = 4
12 ÷ 4 = 3

38. 11 × 8 = 88
8 × 11 = 88
88 ÷ 8 = 11
88 ÷ 11 = 8

39. 9 × 6 = 54
6 × 9 = 54
54 ÷ 6 = 9
54 ÷ 9 = 6

Problem Solving

40. Corey has saved 63 files on the hard drive of his computer. He wants to divide them equally among 9 folders. How many files will go in each folder?
7 files

41. Jasmine has 48 computer disks. She has just enough cases to place 8 disks in each case. How many cases does she have?
6 cases

Use with Grade 5, Chapter 3, Lesson 1, pages 104–105. (67)

Reteach

Relate Multiplication and Division

R 3-1 RETEACH

You can use models to help you understand fact families.

This model shows 24 cubes.

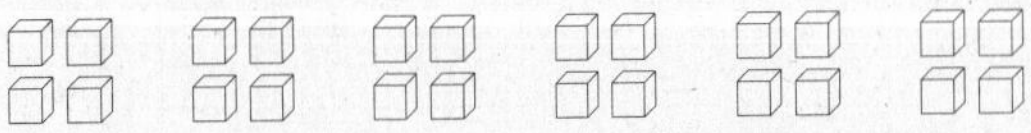

6 groups of 4 cubes each
6 × 4 = 24

24 cubes divided into groups of 4
24 ÷ 4 = 6

This model also shows 24 cubes.

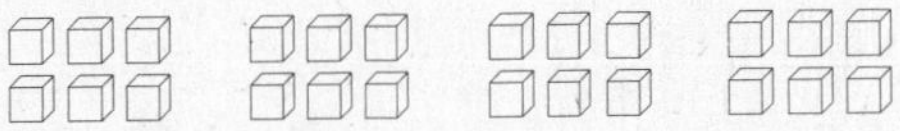

4 groups of 6 cubes each
4 × 6 = 24

24 cubes divided into groups of 6
24 ÷ 6 = 4

These four sentences form a **fact family.**

6 × 4 = 24
4 × 6 = 24
24 ÷ 4 = 6
24 ÷ 6 = 4

Complete each fact family. Draw cubes or counters to help.

1. 7 × 4 = 28; 4 × 7 = 28; 28 ÷ 4 = 7; 28 ÷ 7 = 4
2. 5 × 6 = 30; 6 × 5 = 30; 30 ÷ 6 = 5; 30 ÷ 5 = 6
3. 8 × 3 = 24; 3 × 8 = 24; 24 ÷ 3 = 8; 24 ÷ 8 = 3
4. 7 × 8 = 56; 8 × 7 = 56; 56 ÷ 8 = 7; 56 ÷ 7 = 8

Write the multiplication fact that you can use to help you divide. Then divide and write each quotient.

5. 40 ÷ 8 = 5
8 × 5 = 40 or 5 × 8 = 40
6. 18 ÷ 3 = 6
3 × 6 = 18 or 6 × 3 = 18

Divide.

7. 35 ÷ 5 = 7
8. 18 ÷ 2 = 9
9. 36 ÷ 9 = 4
10. 48 ÷ 6 = 8
11. 3)24 = 8
12. 5)30 = 6
13. 2)18 = 9
14. 9)99 = 11
15. 7)63 = 9

Use with Grade 5, Chapter 3, Lesson 1, pages 104–105. (68)

Enrich

Relate Multiplication and Division
Hidden Facts

E 3-1 ENRICH

Play with a partner.

Player 1 uses red

Player 2 uses blue

Take turns.

To play:

- Player 1 looks for three numbers that form a basic division fact. The player should look across or down. Circle the numbers.
- Player 2 looks for three numbers that form a basic multiplication fact.
- The player with the greater number of circles wins the game.

3	4	12	18	3	6	10	40	8	5
6	4	24	8	3	6	20	5	4	7
18	16	8	4	9	36	10	8	80	36
9	3	3	2	32	24	2	12	4	54
5	5	25	6	8	48	3	6	18	9
45	15	9	12	4	3	18	2	9	6
72	8	9	15	3	5	12	6	2	56
9	9	81	36	20	6	7	42	81	7
8	6	48	6	5	30	9	1	9	8
64	54	9	6	4	24	63	24	9	9

What method did you use to find the division facts?

Answers may vary. Possible answer: I chose a number and looked at the two digits to the right of it or below it to see if they were factors.

Use with Grade 5, Chapter 3, Lesson 1, pages 104–105. (69)

Daily Homework

3-1 Relate Multiplication and Division

Complete the fact family.

1. 4 × 6 = 24
6 × 4 = 24
24 ÷ 6 = 4
24 ÷ 4 = 6

2. 3 × 9 = 27
9 × 3 = 27
27 ÷ 3 = 9
27 ÷ 9 = 3

3. 5 × 6 = 30
6 × 5 = 30
30 ÷ 6 = 5
30 ÷ 5 = 6

4. 9 × 8 = 72
8 × 9 = 72
72 ÷ 9 = 8
72 ÷ 8 = 9

5. 8 × 4 = 32
4 × 8 = 32
32 ÷ 4 = 8
32 ÷ 8 = 4

6. 4 × 12 = 48
12 × 4 = 48
48 ÷ 12 = 4
48 ÷ 4 = 12

Divide.

7. 36 ÷ 9 = 4
8. 49 ÷ 7 = 7
9. 28 ÷ 4 = 7
10. 72 ÷ 8 = 9
11. 21 ÷ 7 = 3
12. 16 ÷ 4 = 4
13. 20 ÷ 4 = 5
14. 56 ÷ 7 = 8
15. 6)48 = 8
16. 12)36 = 3
17. 9)54 = 6
18. 6)42 = 7
19. 2)16 = 8
20. 2)14 = 7
21. 9)81 = 9
22. 12)84 = 7

Problem Solving

23. The duck-billed platypus has a bill about 9 centimeters long. Its body measures about 36 centimeters in length, and its tail is about 18 centimeters long. How many times longer than its bill is the body of the platypus?
4 times as long

24. How many times longer is its body than its tail? 2 times as long

Spiral Review

Rewrite using a base and an exponent.

25. 9 × 9 × 9 9^3
26. 2 × 2 × 2 × 2 2^4
27. 8 × 8 8^2

Grade 5, Chapter 3, Lesson 1, Cluster A 21

Practice

Explore Dividing by 1-Digit Divisors

P 3-2 PRACTICE

Draw place-value models to help you divide.

1. 3)463 — 154 R1

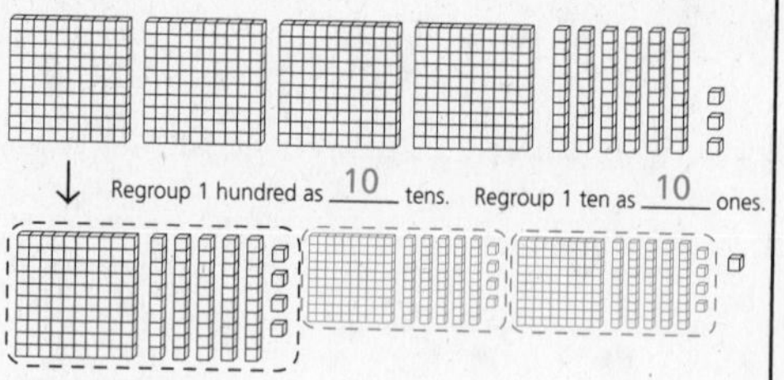

2. 5)123 — 24 R3

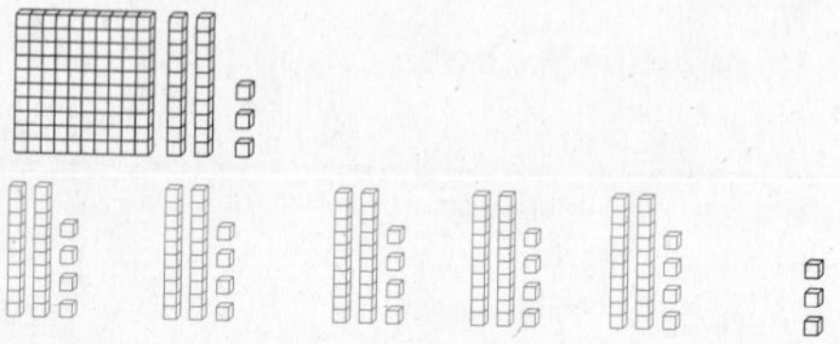

3. 7)226 — 32 R2 — Check students' drawings.

Reteach

Explore Dividing by 1-Digit Divisors

R 3-2 RETEACH

You can think of division as repeated subtraction to help you divide.

Divide 573 ÷ 2.

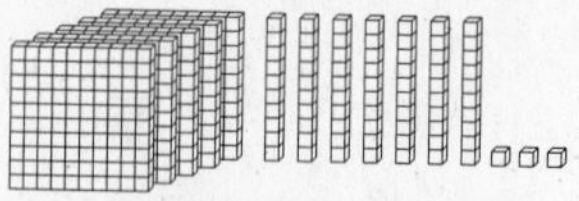

Take away as many groups of 2 hundreds as you can. Change any hundreds that remain to tens.

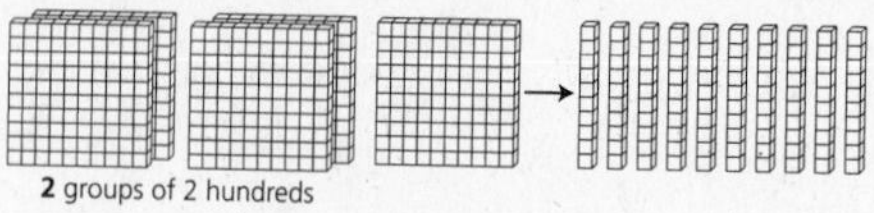

173 remains.

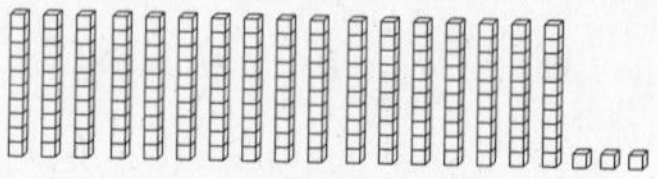

Take away as many groups of 2 tens as you can. Change any that remain to ones.

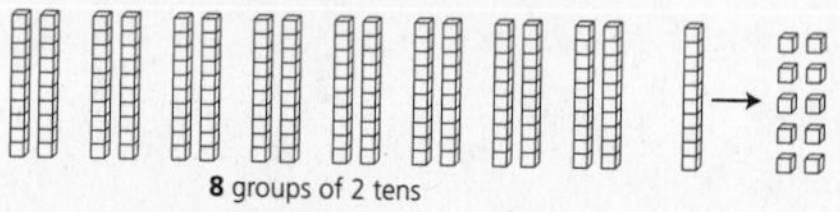

13 remains.

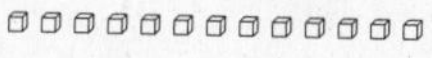

Take away as many groups of 2 ones as you can.

573 ÷ 2 = **286 R1**

Divide. You may show place-value models to help.

1. 725 ÷ 3 = 241 R2
2. 194 ÷ 5 = 38 R4
3. 465 ÷ 6 = 77 R3
4. 8)692 — 86 R4
5. 4)631 — 157 R3
6. 9)237 — 26 R3
7. 7)592 — 84 R4

Enrich

Explore Dividing by 1-Digit Divisors

E 3-2 ENRICH

Dividend Division

Play this game with a partner.

Hint: Remember that you divide the dividend by the divisor to find the quotient.

To play:

- Pick a number from each box.
- Then find the dividend on the game board.
- Write your initials in that space.

Player 1 starts from the upper left or lower right. Player 2 starts from the upper right or lower left. The first player to make a path across the board is the winner.

Divisors		Quotients		Remainders	
6	8	75	65	3	1
7	9	52	81	4	2

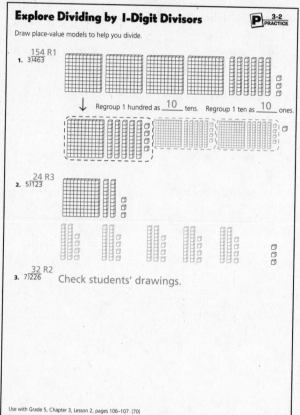

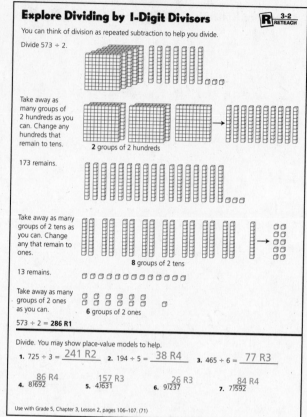

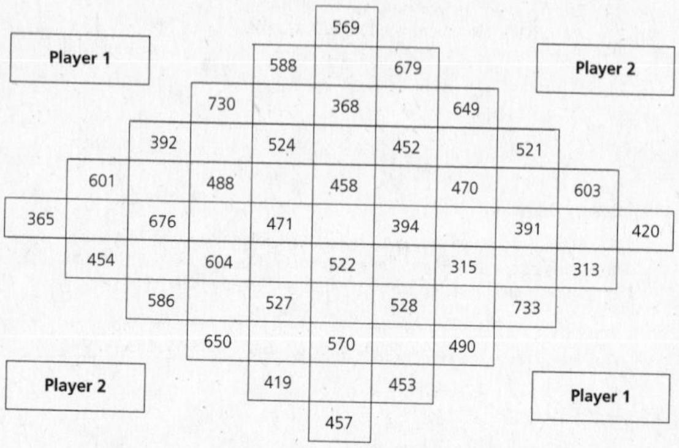

Daily Homework

3-2 Explore Dividing by 1-Digit Divisors

Divide.

1. 4)26 — 6 R2
2. 9)48 — 5 R3
3. 7)32 — 4 R4
4. 8)57 — 7 R1
5. 3)29 — 9 R2
6. 5)108 — 21 R3
7. 8)98 — 12 R2
8. 6)124 — 20 R4
9. 7)64 — 9 R1
10. 6)158 — 26 R2
11. 7)87 — 12 R3
12. 8)196 — 24 R4
13. 6)50 — 8 R2
14. 4)39 — 9 R3
15. 5)56 — 11 R1
16. 4)47 — 11 R3
17. 6)125 — 20 R5
18. 7)93 — 13 R2
19. 3)16 — 5 R1
20. 4)147 — 36 R3
21. 9)83 — 9 R2
22. 4)87 — 21 R3
23. 5)44 — 8 R4
24. 7)120 — 17 R1

Solve.

25. Wanda spent $34.72 on groceries and $18.75 on gasoline. She had $70.00 when she left home. How much money does she have left after her purchases? $16.53
26. Orange juice costs $3.25 a half gallon. How much will 3 half gallons cost? $9.75

Spiral Review

27. (0.04) × (0.2) = 0.008
28. 0.26 × 0.37 = 0.0962
29. 0.83 × 1.25 = 1.0375
30. 0.44 × 4.4 = 1.936
31. 6.4 × 1.8 = 11.52
32. 5.5 × 2.4 = 13.2

Chapter 3 ~ Lesson 3

Practice

Divide by 1-Digit Divisors

P 3-3 PRACTICE

Divide. Check your answers.

1. 3)385 — 218 R1
2. 7)511 — 73
3. 9)179 — 19 R8
4. 5)254 — 50 R4
5. 6)407 — 67 R5
6. 8)167 — 20 R7
7. 4)131 — 32 R3
8. 9)852 — 94 R6
9. 5)1,238 — 247 R3
10. 3)3,049 — 1,524 R1
11. 7)2,242 — 320 R2
12. 9)7,828 — 869 R7
13. 4)2,994 — 748 R2
14. 8)2,077 — 259 R5
15. 5)6,322 — 1,264 R2
16. 3)8,202 — 2,734
17. 5)21,863 — 4,372 R3
18. 3)74,458 — 24,819 R1
19. 9)45,373 — 5,041 R4
20. 7)45,383 — 6,483 R2

21. 463 ÷ 5 = 92 R3
22. 606 ÷ 8 = 75 R6
23. 615 ÷ 2 = 307 R1
24. 103 ÷ 9 = 11 R4
25. 618 ÷ 3 = 206
26. 968 ÷ 6 = 161 R2
27. 1,853 ÷ 2 = 926 R1
28. 5,515 ÷ 4 = 1,378 R3
29. 3,327 ÷ 8 = 415 R7
30. 1,982 ÷ 3 = 660 R2
31. 2,291 ÷ 9 = 254 R5
32. 3,544 ÷ 5 = 708 R4
33. 57,718 ÷ 8 = 7,214 R6
34. 40,125 ÷ 4 = 10,031 R1
35. 32,991 ÷ 6 = 5,498 R3

Problem Solving

36. The driving distance between Dallas, Texas, and New York City is 1,604 miles. You plan to make the drive in 4 days and want to drive the same number of miles each day. How many miles will you have to drive each day?

401 miles

37. The distance from New York to Dallas is 1,604 mi. You will drive from New York to Dallas in July and return in August. Your car gets 25 mi for each gallon of gas it uses. To the nearest gallon, how many gallons will the round trip take?

128 gal

Use with Grade 5, Chapter 3, Lesson 3, pages 108–109. (73)

Reteach

Divide by 1-Digit Divisors

R 3-3 RETEACH

You can think of the dividend in expanded form to help you divide.

Divide 6)394 .

6)394 → 6: Since there are not enough hundreds to be divided by 6, rename 3 hundreds 9 tens as 39 tens. Divide 39 tens by 6. Write the first digit of the quotient above the tens digit of the dividend.

6)394, − 36↓, 34: Multiply: 6 × 6 = 36. Subtract: 39 − 36 = 3. Compare the difference to the divisor: 3 < 6. Bring down the next digit of the dividend.

6)394 = 65 R4; − 36↓, 34, − 30, 4: Divide 34 by 6. Multiply: 5 × 6 = 30. Subtract: 34 − 30 = 4. Compare the difference to the divisor: 4 < 6. Write the remainder.

Check:

65 × 6 = 390 ← Multiply the quotient by the divisor.

390 + 4 ← Add the remainder.

= 394 ← Should equal the dividend.

Divide. Multiply to check.

1. 7)130 = 18 R 4; − 7, 60, − 56, 4. Check: 18 × 7 = 126, + 4 = 130
2. 9)237 = 26 R 3; − 18, 57, − 54, 3. Check: 26 × 9 = 234, + 3 = 237
3. 5)413 = 82 R 3; − 40, 13, − 10, 3. Check: 82 × 5 = 410, + 3 = 413
4. 3)193 — 64 R1
5. 9)4,615 — 512 R7
6. 4)1,374 — 343 R2

Use with Grade 5, Chapter 3, Lesson 3, pages 108–109. (74)

Enrich

Divide by 1-Digit Divisors

A Division Puzzle

E 3-3 ENRICH

Solve each division problem on the shapes. Cut out the shapes. Match the sides with the same quotients to complete the puzzle.

What shape did you make? square

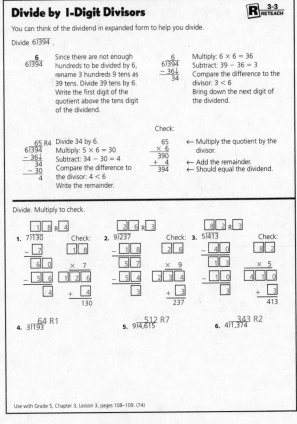

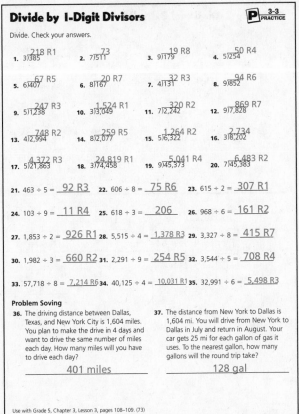

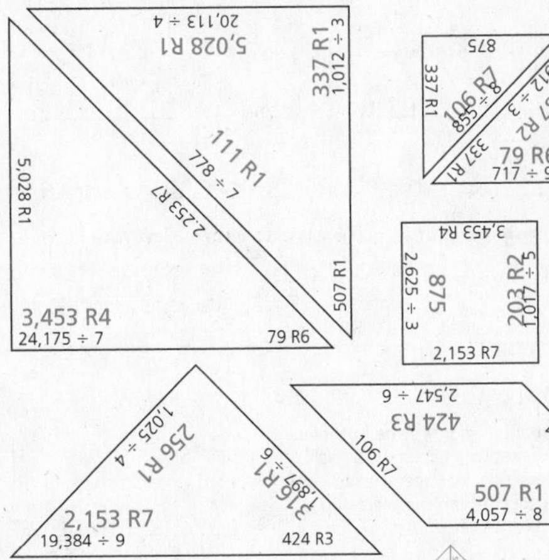

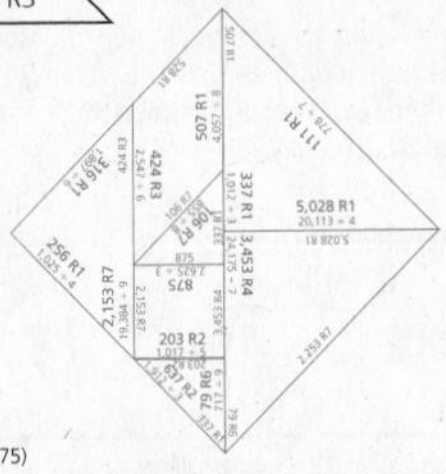

Use with Grade 5, Chapter 3, Lesson 3, pages 108–109. (75)

Daily Homework

3-3 Divide by 1-Digit Divisors

Divide.

1. 4)324 — 81
2. 6)410 — 68 R2
3. 7)256 — 36 R4
4. 8)384 — 48
5. 3)843 — 280 R3
6. 4)850 — 212 R2
7. 8)437 — 54 R5
8. 6)1,743 — 290 R3
9. 8)2,117 — 264 R5
10. 7)2,349 — 335 R4
11. 5)2,443 — 488 R3
12. 3)1,196 — 398 R2
13. 2)1,847 — 923 R1
14. 4)3,870 — 967 R2
15. 5)1,234 — 246 R4
16. 4)5,072 — 1,268
17. 43,064 ÷ 6 = 7,177 R2
18. 13,893 ÷ 6 = 2,315 R3

Problem Solving

19. A marsupial mole has a mass of about 60 grams. The cus cus has a mass about 60 times as great. What is the mass of the cus cus in grams? 3,600 grams

20. A wombat weighs 37,448 grams, a kangaroo weighs 63,582 grams, and a Tasmanian devil weighs 10,854 grams. Estimate their total weight, to the nearest hundred grams. 111,900 grams

Spiral Review

Estimate the sum.

21. 37.4 + 73.6 40 + 70 = 110
22. 1.68 + 0.76 2 + 1 = 3
23. 2,842 + 18 2,840 + 20 = 2,860
24. 1.187 + 4.753 1.2 + 4.8 = 6

Grade 5, Chapter 3, Lesson 3, Cluster A. 23

Chapter 3 ~ Lesson 4

Practice

Divide by 2-Digit and 3-Digit Divisors

P 3-4 PRACTICE

Divide. Multiply to check.

1. 58)1,394 = 24 R2
2. 78)9,161 = 117 R35
3. 23)1,491 = 64 R19
4. 631)2,539 = 4 R15
5. 472)3,390 = 7 R86
6. 255)3,694 = 14 R124
7. 387)5,521 = 14 R103
8. 88)2,755 = 31 R27
9. 646)29,388 = 45 R318
10. 62)9,847 = 158 R51
11. 39)1,998 = 51 R9
12. 188)4,755 = 25 R55
13. 367)23,256 = 63 R135
14. 912)72,096 = 79 R48
15. 132)29,388 = 222 R84

16. 1,204 ÷ 33 = 36 R16
17. 9,649 ÷ 384 = 25 R49
18. 61,129 ÷ 295 = 207 R64
19. 6,720 ÷ 45 = 149 R15
20. 49,201 ÷ 70 = 702 R61
21. 6,639 ÷ 762 = 8 R543
22. 45,488 ÷ 96 = 473 R80
23. 36,289 ÷ 54 = 672 R1
24. 49,205 ÷ 847 = 58 R79
25. 96,878 ÷ 42 = 2,306 R26

Problem Solving

26. Members of the Bladerunners skating club collected $4,320 from car washes, raffles, and donations. They want to buy Ultrablade skates, which are $89 a pair. How many pairs of skates will they be able to buy? 48 pairs

27. A device on Toya's bike shows that the wheels make 773 revolutions during each mile she rides. If the wheels on Toya's bike revolve 11,595 times, how many miles has Toya ridden? 15 miles

Use with Grade 5, Chapter 3, Lesson 4, pages 110–13. (76)

Reteach

Divide by 2-Digit and 3-Digit Divisors

R 3-4 RETEACH

Divide 31)1,671 .

31)1,671 → 5: You cannot divide 1 by 31. You cannot divide 16 by 31. But you can divide 167 by 31. The first digit in the quotient will be in the tens place.

31)1,671, −155↓, 121: 167 ÷ 31 is about 5. Write the 5 above the tens digit of the dividend. Multiply: 5 × 31 = 155

Subtract 167 − 155 = 12. Compare the difference to the divisor: 12 < 31

Bring down the next digit of the dividend.

31)1,671 → 54, −155↓, 121: 121 ÷ 31 is about 4. Multiply 4 × 31 = 124. You cannot subtract because 124 > 121.

31)1,671 → 53 R28, −155↓, 121, −93, 28: Try a lesser number in the divisor. Multiply 3 × 31 = 93. Subtract 121 − 93 = 28. Compare the difference to the divisor: 28 < 31

There are no more digits in the dividend, so write the remainder.

Divide. Multiply to check.

1. 183)8,876 = 48 R92
   − 732, 1556, − 1464, 92
   Check: 48 × 183 = 144 + 3840 + 4800 = 8784; 8784 + 92 = 8,876

2. 38)2,053 = 54 R1
   − 190, 153, − 152, 1
   Check: 54 × 38 = 432 + 1620 = 2052; 2052 + 1 = 2,053

3. 23)1,568 = 68 R4
4. 258)5,750 = 22 R74

Use with Grade 5, Chapter 3, Lesson 4, pages 110–113. (77)

Enrich

Divide by 2-Digit and 3-Digit Divisors

E 3-4 ENRICH

Crossnumber Puzzle

This puzzle is similar to a crossword puzzle. Instead of using letters to form words, you use digits to form numbers. Use the clues below to complete the puzzle.

A 3	2	B 1	■	C 8	D 9	6
4	■	E 3	F 2	7	7	■
G 1	H 2	■	I 1	9	■	J 4
K 4	1	L 1	9	■	M 3	■
■	N 5	3	■	■	O 9	P 4
Q 5	■	6	■	R 3	3	2
S 7	V 3	8	■	T 4	0	6

Across

A. 8,025 ÷ 25
C. 224 × 4
E. 3,604 − 327
G. 696 ÷ 58
I. 7,847 ÷ 413
J. the remainder in 52 ÷ 12
K. 5 × 823 + 4
N. 2,226 ÷ 42
O. 282 ÷ 3
Q. the remainder in 3,821 ÷ 72
R. 83 × 4
S. 99,630 ÷ 135
T. 32,886 ÷ 81

Down

A. 9,030 − 5,616
B. the remainder in 67,867 ÷ 526
C. 1,758 ÷ 2
D. 8,148 ÷ 84
F. 44,457 ÷ 203
H. 1,075 ÷ 5
L. 6 × 12 × 19
M. 131 × 30
P. 71 × 6
Q. 1,881 ÷ 33
R. the remainder in 1,618 ÷ 36

Use with Grade 5, Chapter 3, Lesson 4, pages 110–113. (78)

Daily Homework

3-4 Divide by 2-Digit and 3-Digit Divisors

Divide. Check your answer.

1. 32)4,748 = 148 R12
2. 65)7,512 = 115 R37
3. 27)8,248 = 305 R13
4. 342)2,130 = 6 R78
5. 76)2,498 = 32 R66
6. 54)6,564 = 121 R30
7. 82)9,545 = 116 R33
8. 62)48,136 = 776 R24

9. 32,665 ÷ 62 = 526 R53
10. 23,784 ÷ 44 = 540 R24

Find each dividend.

11. 1,643 ÷ 42 = 39 R5
12. 10,152 ÷ 28 = 362 R16

Decide whether the first digit of the quotient is too high or too low. Then complete.

13. 36)1,304 (4) too high; 36 R8
14. 76)3,214 (3) too low; 42 R22
15. 132)54,400 (5) too high; 412 R16

Problem Solving

16. The whale shark may grow to be 18 meters long. The shortest type of shark may be only 10 centimeters long. How many times longer is the whale shark? Hint: There are 100 centimeters in a meter. 180 times longer

17. It takes Marcia 15 minutes to sew a patch on the sleeve of a club shirt. If she spent 2 hours and 45 minutes sewing patches, how many patches did she sew on? 11 patches

Spiral Review

18. 842.3 + 32.7 = 875.0
19. 0.636 − 0.337 = 0.299
20. 1.78 + 0.48 + 9.22 = 11.48
21. 3.266 − 0.008 = 3.258

24 Grade 5, Chapter 3, Lesson 4, Cluster A

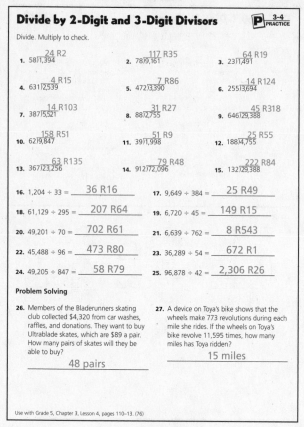

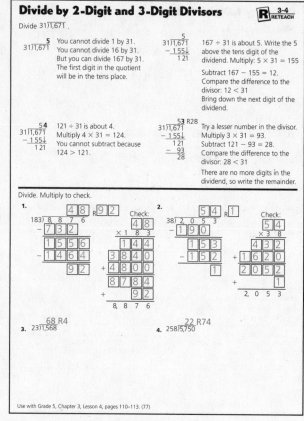

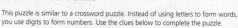

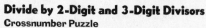

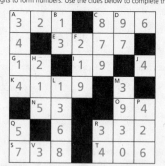

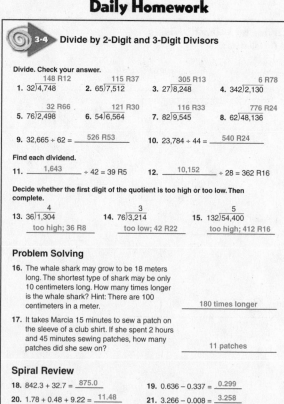

Chapter 3 ~ Lesson 5

Practice

Estimate Quotients

P 3-5 PRACTICE

Estimates may vary. Possible estimates are given.

Complete the pattern.

1. 21 ÷ 7 = 3
   210 ÷ 7 = 30
   2,100 ÷ 7 = 300
   21,000 ÷ 7 = 3,000
2. 48 ÷ 6 = 8
   480 ÷ 6 = 80
   4,800 ÷ 6 = 800
   48,000 ÷ 6 = 8,000
3. 36 ÷ 4 = 9
   360 ÷ 4 = 90
   3,600 ÷ 40 = 90
   36,000 ÷ 40 = 900

Divide.

4. 360 ÷ 6 = 60
5. 45,000 ÷ 5 = 9,000
6. 8,000 ÷ 100 = 80
7. 400,000 ÷ 8 = 50,000
8. 180 ÷ 30 = 6
9. 16,000 ÷ 400 = 40
10. 49,000 ÷ 7 = 7,000
11. 5,400 ÷ 60 = 90
12. 72,000 ÷ 80 = 900

Estimate. Use compatible numbers.

13. 231 ÷ 6 240 ÷ 6 = 40
14. 149 ÷ 4 160 ÷ 4 = 40
15. 4,748 ÷ 7 4,900 ÷ 7 = 700
16. 275 ÷ 44 280 ÷ 40 = 7
17. 314 ÷ 59 300 ÷ 60 = 5
18. 5,603 ÷ 89 5,400 ÷ 90 = 60
19. 8)629 640 ÷ 8 = 80
20. 9)290 270 ÷ 9 = 30
21. 91)342 360 ÷ 90 = 4
22. 52)9,461 10,000 ÷ 50 = 200
23. 78)2,943 3,200 ÷ 80 = 40
24. 73)33,875 35,000 ÷ 70 = 500

Problem Solving Estimates may vary. Possible estimates are given.

25. Each of the 19 parking lots at an automobile plant holds the same number of new cars. If there are 4,134 cars in the lots waiting to be shipped, about how many cars are in each lot?
    about 200 cars
26. A total of 1,652 valves were used for 73 cars as they were being assembled. About how many valves were used for each car?
    about 20 valves

Use with Grade 5, Chapter 3, Lesson 5, pages 114–117. (79)

Reteach

Estimate Quotients

R 3-5 RETEACH

You can use compatible numbers to estimate quotients. Compatible numbers are close to the numbers in a problem, and are easy to divide mentally.

Estimate 4,396 ÷ 68.

Round the divisor to its greatest place.	4,396 ÷ 68 ↓
Circle the first two digits of the dividend and the first digit of the rounded divisor.	(4,3)96 ÷ (7)0
Think of a division fact that is close to 43 ÷ 7.	43 ÷ 7 ↓ 42 ÷ 7
Write zeros in the dividend and the divisor of the basic fact so they have as many digits as the original dividend and divisor.	4,200 ÷ 70
Divide mentally to find the estimated quotient.	**4,2**00 ÷ **7**0 = **6**0

So, 4,396 ÷ 68 is about 60.

Use compatible numbers to estimate each quotient. Estimates may vary. Possible estimates are given.

1. 133 ÷ 42 → 120 ÷ 40 = 3
2. 694 ÷ 78 → 720 ÷ 80 = 9
3. 2,461 ÷ 470 → 2,500 ÷ 500 = 5
4. 1,732 ÷ 59 → 1,800 ÷ 60 = 30
5. 61,191 ÷ 912 → 63,000 ÷ 900 = 70
6. 34,212 ÷ 83 → 32,000 ÷ 80 = 400
7. 1,149 ÷ 173 1,200 ÷ 200 = 6
8. 286 ÷ 45 300 ÷ 50 = 6
9. 592 ÷ 72 560 ÷ 70 = 8
10. 1,359 ÷ 53 1,500 ÷ 50 = 30
11. 43,089 ÷ 796 40,000 ÷ 800 = 50
12. 2,425 ÷ 31 2,400 ÷ 30 = 80
13. 10,126 ÷ 64 12,000 ÷ 60 = 200
14. 29,453 ÷ 36 28,000 ÷ 40 = 700
15. 78,264 ÷ 875 81,000 ÷ 900 = 90

Use with Grade 5, Chapter 3, Lesson 5, pages 114–117. (80)

Enrich

Estimate Quotients

E 3-5 ENRICH

Fast Division

What is the fastest land mammal?

Shade in the boxes below that have estimated quotients from 50 through 500. Use estimation to help you. Follow the path to the answer.

Possible estimates are shown; path leads to Cheetah.

Cheetah	Gazelle			
1,135 ÷ 3 400	5,906 ÷ 9 700	3,802 ÷ 62 60	229 ÷ 3 70	18,377 ÷ 39 500
62,000 ÷ 223 300	1,384 ÷ 78 20	1,723 ÷ 4 400	3,482 ÷ 93 40	21,097 ÷ 77 300
42,613 ÷ 88 500	541,795 ÷ 52 10,000	3,462 ÷ 66 50	103 ÷ 6 20	4,375 ÷ 84 50
5,592 ÷ 83 70	15,820 ÷ 38 400	3,236 ÷ 478 60	7,432 ÷ 8 900	6,443 ÷ 83 80
5,329 ÷ 71 80	192 ÷ 6 30	13,004 ÷ 43 300	66,265 ÷ 68 900	1,432 ÷ 9 200
26,290 ÷ 93 300	324,318 ÷ 48 6,000	4,120 ÷ 75 50	124,316 ÷ 55 2,000	9,434 ÷ 135 90
7,534 ÷ 82 90	1,101 ÷ 5 200	776 ÷ 9 90	4,392 ÷ 7 600	515 ÷ 8 60
			Horse	Start

How did you estimate the quotients?

Answers may vary. Possible answer: I used compatible numbers and division patterns with zeros.

Use with Grade 5, Chapter 3, Lesson 5, pages 114–117. (81)

Daily Homework

3-5 Estimate Quotients

Complete the pattern.

1. 18 ÷ 3 = 6
   180 ÷ 3 = 60
   1,800 ÷ 3 = 600
   18,000 ÷ 3 = 6,000
2. 56 ÷ 7 = 8
   560 ÷ 7 = 80
   5,600 ÷ 7 = 800
   56,000 ÷ 7 = 8,000
   560,000 ÷ 7 = 80,000
3. 24 ÷ 4 = 6
   240 ÷ 40 = 6
   2,400 ÷ 40 = 60
   24,000 ÷ 40 = 600
   240,000 ÷ 40 = 6,000
4. 72 ÷ 12 = 6
   720 ÷ 12 = 60
   7,200 ÷ 120 = 60
   72,000 ÷ 120 = 600
   720,000 ÷ 120 = 6,000

Divide.

5. 350 ÷ 7 = 50
6. 42,000 ÷ 60 = 700
7. 180 ÷ 6 = 30
8. 70,000 ÷ 10 = 7,000
9. 200 ÷ 4 = 50
10. 30,000 ÷ 600 = 50

Estimate. Use compatible numbers. Answers may vary. Possible answers are given.

11. 642 ÷ 9 630 ÷ 9 = 70
12. 552 ÷ 7 560 ÷ 7 = 80
13. 3,574 ÷ 9 3,600 ÷ 9 = 400

Problem Solving

14. Yvonne is reading a book about the animals of Africa. She has 123 pages left to read. If she reads about 20 pages each day, how many days will it take her to finish the book? about 6 days
15. Madagascar has an area of about 226,700 square miles. If there are about 66 people per square mile, estimate the total population.
    70 × 200,000 = 14,000,000 people

Source: *The Time Almanac 2000*

Spiral Review

Compare. Use >, <, or =.

16. 7.23 > 7.19
17. 0.04879 < 0.4879
18. 3.46 < 3.64

Grade 5, Chapter 3, Lesson 5, Cluster A 25

Chapter 3 ~ Lesson 6

Practice

Problem Solving: Reading for Math
Interpreting the Remainder

P 3-6 PRACTICE Reading Skill

Solve. Tell how you interpreted the remainder.

1. Students from four local schools are going to the state science fair. The total number of students and teachers attending is 288. Each bus holds 46 passengers. How many buses will they need?
   7 buses; add 1 to the quotient
2. The group will be sleeping in a college dormitory during the fair. Each room has been set up for 5 people. How many rooms do they need?
   58 rooms; add 1 to the quotient
3. The cafeteria can seat 50 people at a time. How many groups will need to be formed to eat in the cafeteria?
   6 groups; add 1 to the quotient
4. Student presentations last for 7 hours each day. Each student speaks for 9 minutes. How many presentations can there be each day? (Hint: 7 hours = 420 minutes)
   46 presentations; ignore the remainder in this problem
5. A total of 135 students have presentations to give at the fair. If the organizers schedule 40 student presentations each day, how many days will the student presentations take?
   4 days; add 1 to the quotient
6. The electronic display room can hold 25 people at a time. How many groups will need to be formed if 460 people want to see the electronics display?
   19 groups; add 1 to the quotient
7. A young scientist has 50 time-lapse photographs of her experiment. She divides the photos to put them on 4 posters. How many photos will be on each poster?
   12 photos on 2 posters and 13 photos on 2 posters; use the remainder as part of the answer
8. Another young scientist has 70 pieces of litmus paper. He wants to put the litmus paper in packs of 12. How many packs will he be able to make?
   5 packs; ignore the remainder

Use with Grade 5, Chapter 3, Lesson 6, pages 118–119. (82)

Practice

Problem Solving: Reading for Math
Interpreting the Remainder

P 3-6 PRACTICE Math Skills Test Prep

Choose the correct answer.

A chess club has 70 student members. They are going to an out-of-town chess match. Club policy requires one adult to attend for every 8 students.

1. How many adults will be needed to accompany the chess club students to the match?
   - A 8 adults
   - (B) 9 adults
   - C 10 adults
   - D 70 adults
2. When you interpret the remainder, you
   - F guess the answer.
   - (G) determine a reasonable answer.
   - H draw a conclusion from something hinted at.
   - J draw a diagram.

The astronomy club needs to arrange transportation to see an upcoming meteor shower. Each car they are taking can hold 4 club members. The club has 25 members.

3. How many cars does the astronomy club need for transportation to the meteor shower?
   - A 100 cars
   - B 25 cars
   - (C) 7 cars
   - D 6 cars
4. How does an inference help you solve a problem?
   - (F) It helps you draw a conclusion.
   - G It gives you extra information.
   - H It lets you estimate the answer.
   - J It uses information you already know.

The planetarium is showing a special film in an auditorium that can seat 40 people. There are 132 students and teachers coming to see the film on a field trip.

5. How many groups will need to be formed for everyone to view the show?
   - A 3 groups
   - (B) 4 groups
   - C 5 groups
   - D 13 groups
6. When you solve a problem with a remainder, you
   - F always ignore the remainder.
   - G do not use the remainder as part of the answer.
   - (H) sometimes add 1 to the quotient.
   - J estimate the answer.

Use with Grade 5, Chapter 3, Lesson 6, pages 118–119. (83)

Practice

Problem Solving: Reading for Math
Interpreting the Remainder

P 3-6 PRACTICE Math Skills Test Prep

Choose the correct answer.

An amusement park is opening a new log ride. Each log can carry 8 people. As a promotion, the owners have given away 125 free tickets for the ride.

7. How many logs will it take for all the people with free tickets to ride?
   - A 8 logs
   - B 15 logs
   - (C) 16 logs
   - D 25 logs
8. An inference is
   - (F) a conclusion you draw from something known or hinted at.
   - G a reasonable answer to a problem.
   - H extra data that you should ignore.
   - J a guess.

Solve. Tell how you interpreted the remainder.

A garden store received a shipment of flower bulbs. Use data from the table for exercises 9-12.

Flower Bulbs	Number
Iris	248
Daffodil	146
Tulip	330
Assorted	93

9. The garden store sells the iris bulbs in packages of 15. How many packages of iris bulbs can they make?
   16 packages; ignore the remainder
10. A landscaper buys all of the daffodil bulbs. The garden store ships the bulbs in packages of 18. How many packages will they have to make?
    9 packages; add 1 to the quotient
11. The manager wants to divide the assorted bulbs to put into 4 displays. How many bulbs will be in each display?
    23 in 3 displays and 24 in 1 display; use the remainder as part of the answer
12. The manager decides to sell the tulip bulbs in packages of 12. How many packages of tulip bulbs can she make?
    27 packages; ignore the remainder

Use with Grade 5, Chapter 3, Lesson 6, pages 118–119. (84)

Daily Homework

3·6 Problem Solving: Reading for Math
Interpreting the Remainder

Solve. Tell how you interpreted the remainder.

1. On a field trip, 185 students and teachers take buses to a zoological park. If each bus holds 42 persons, how many buses are needed for the trip?
   5 buses; add 1 to the quotient.
2. At the park, there is a special exhibit of exotic insects. No more than 35 persons can go through the exhibit at one time. How many exhibit periods will it take for all the students and teachers to go through the exhibit?
   6 periods; add 1 to the quotient.
3. A special lecture-film show takes 35 minutes. If the park is open for 8 hours each day, how many complete showings will there be during that time? Hint: 8 hours = 480 minutes.
   13 showings; ignore the remainder.
4. The cafeteria at the park has tables that seat 10 people. How many tables will it take to seat these185 persons?
   19 tables; add 1 to the quotient.
5. The students took 58 photographs and plan to display them for their classmates at school. If they can put 10 photographs on each poster, how many posters will they need?
   6 posters; add 1 to the quotient.
6. At the science fair, the students plan to give short talks about their experience at the zoological garden. They can seat only 42 people for their talk. How many times must the students give their talk if they expect 246 students and parents to attend?
   6 times; add 1 to the quotient.

Spiral Review

7. $4\overline{)245}$ = 61 R1
8. $5\overline{)787}$ = 157 R2
9. $8\overline{)116}$ = 14 R4
10. $3\overline{)646}$ = 215 R1

26 Grade 5, Chapter 3, Lesson 6, Cluster A

Chapter 3 ~ Lesson 7

Practice

Problem Solving: Strategy
Work Backward

P 3-7 PRACTICE

Use work backward to solve.

1. Ms. Houston's fifth grade class is going to a dinosaur park. The class raises $68 for the trip. Transportation to the park costs $40. The park sells small fossils for $4 each. How many fossils can they buy with the money they have left?
   7 fossils

2. The outdoors club went on a cross-country ski trip. Rentals for each person cost $4.50. Transportation for the group was $35. The total cost for rentals and transportation was $134. How many rentals did they pay for?
   22 rentals

3. Theresa had $15.65 left after a day at the mall. She spent $35 on a pair of running shoes, $12.50 on a shirt, and $3.85 on lunch. How much money did Theresa have when she arrived at the mall?
   $67

4. **Time** Kusuo's baseball game begins at 5:00 P.M. Kusuo wants to arrive 45 minutes early to warm up. If it takes him $\frac{1}{2}$ hour to get to the baseball field, what time should Kusuo leave his home for the game?
   3:45 P.M.

Mixed Strategy Review

Solve. Use any strategy.

5. A theater seats 44 people. For Friday evening performances, 128 tickets were sold. How many performances were there on Friday evening?
   3 performances
   Strategy: Write an Equation

6. **Science** Many huskies have one brown eye and one blue eye and others have two blue eyes. In a group of 22 huskies, there were 38 blue eyes. How many of the dogs have two blue eyes?
   16 dogs
   Strategy: Guess and Check

7. **Number Sense** Steffy picks a number, subtracts 13, and then multiplies the difference by 2. Finally, she adds 8 to the product. Her final number is 122. What was her starting number?
   70
   Strategy: Work Backward

8. **Create a problem** for which you could work backward to solve. Share it with others.
   Check students' problems.

Use with Grade 5, Chapter 3, Lesson 7, pages 122–123. (85)

Reteach

Problem Solving: Strategy
Work Backward

R 3-7 RETEACH

Page 123, Problem 1

A scientist plans to study exotic birds in the rain forest. A helicopter to fly her round-trip costs $499. Supplies cost $112 for each day. How many days can the scientist stay in the rain forest on a $1,283 budget?

Step 1 Read

Be sure you understand the problem.
Read carefully.

What do you know?

- A helicopter costs $499.
- Supplies cost $112 each day.
- She has a budget of $1,283.

What do you need to find?

- The number of days she can stay in the rain forest.

Step 2 Plan

- Do an Experiment
- Guess and Check
- Work Backward
- Make a Graph
- Make a Table
- Write an Equation
- Make an Organized List
- Draw a Diagram
- Solve a Simpler Problem
- Logical Reasoning

Make a plan.
Choose a strategy.

You can work backward to find the number of days the scientist can stay in the rain forest.

Use math operations to undo each step.

Use with Grade 5, Chapter 3, Lesson 7, pages 122–123. (86)

Reteach

Problem Solving: Strategy
Work Backward

R 3-7 RETEACH

Step 3 Solve

Carry out your plan.
Decide which operation undoes each step.

Undo the addition of the cost of the helicopter.

Which operation undoes addition? subtraction

Subtract the cost of the helicopter from the total budget:
$1,283 − $499 = $784

The scientist has $784 left after she pays for the helicopter.

Undo the multiplication of the number of days she can stay in the rain forest.

Which operation undoes multiplication? division

Divide the amount she has left by the cost of supplies for each day.
$784 ÷ $112 = 7 days

How many days can the scientist stay in the rain forest? 7 days

Step 4 Look Back

Is the solution reasonable?
Reread the problem.
Have you answered the question? yes

How can you check your answer?
Answers may vary. Possible answer: work forward

Practice

1. Ms. Robin's class is planting trees for Arbor Day. They raise a total of $80 to buy trees and supplies. A local nursery has offered to provide trees for $7 each. They spend $17 on supplies. How many trees do they buy?
   9 trees

2. Mr. Stone's class is visiting the aquarium. Mr. Stone has $46 for the trip. The entrance fee for the class is $34. The rest of the money will be used to buy posters for the classroom. Each poster costs $3. How many posters will they be able to buy?
   4 posters

Use with Grade 5, Chapter 3, Lesson 7, pages 122–123. (87)

Daily Homework

3·7 Problem Solving: Strategy
Work Backward

Solve. Use the work-backward strategy.

1. A bird club counts birds in the woods around their town. They see 20 baby birds and count 26 adult female birds. They know that there are an equal number of adult male and adult female birds present. How many birds did the students count in all?
   26 × 2 = 52; 52 + 20 = 72 birds

2. The student council wants to raise money to plant flowers around the school. They decide to sell raffle tickets. They raise $320 in all. The first 20 tickets were sold at $3 each. The rest of the tickets cost $2. How many $2 tickets did they sell?
   $320 – $60 = $260; $260 ÷ 2 = 130 tickets

3. During March, the price of rose bushes tripled. In April, the price dropped $0.75 per bush. By May, the price was cut in half. In June, the price rose $0.25 to $1.75 per bush. What was the price at the beginning of March?
   $1.75 – $0.25 = $1.50 × 2 = $3 + $0.75 = $3.75 ÷ 3 = $1.25

Mixed Strategy Review

4. Mark and Letty play a number game. Mark tells Letty to pick a number, add 19 to it, then multiply the sum by 2, and then subtract 7 from the product. Letty gets 125. What number did she start with? 47

5. A group of 26 people want to sit together at a long table. Each table seats 3 people on a long side and one person on a short side. If they place the short sides end to end, how many tables will it take to seat the group at one long table? 4 tables

Spiral Review

6. 45 × 200 = 9,000
7. 50 × 4,000 = 200,000
8. 80 × 500 = 40,000
9. 70 × 300 = 21,000
10. 25 × 2,000 = 50,000
11. 60 × 600 = 36,000

Grade 5, Chapter 3, Lesson 7, Cluster B 27

Chapter 3 ~ Lesson 8

Practice

Divide Decimals by Whole Numbers

P 3-8 PRACTICE

Divide. Round each quotient to the nearest hundredth if necessary.

1. 3)2.19 = 0.73
2. 6)3.63 = 0.61
3. 5)12 = 2.4
4. 8)18.2 = 2.28
5. 6)22 = 3.67
6. 4)2.06 = 0.52
7. 8)16.8 = 2.1
8. 10)118 = 11.8
9. 6)14.23 = 2.37
10. 23)32.2 = 1.4
11. 62)651 = 10.5
12. 56)13.5 = 0.24
13. 8.01 ÷ 9 = 0.89
14. 6.48 ÷ 40 = 0.16
15. 13.64 ÷ 7 = 1.95
16. 240.5 ÷ 64 = 3.76
17. 627 ÷ 100 = 6.27
18. 26 ÷ 10 = 2.6
19. 30.87 ÷ 4 = 7.72
20. 44.4 ÷ 53 = 0.84

Complete the pattern.

21. 11.7 ÷ 10 = 1.17
11.7 ÷ 100 = 0.117
11.7 ÷ 1,000 = 0.0117

22. 4.2 ÷ 10 = 0.42
4.2 ÷ 100 = 0.042
4.2 ÷ 1,000 = 0.0042

23. 89 ÷ 10 = 8.9
89 ÷ 100 = 0.89
89 ÷ 1000 = 0.089

Problem Solving

24. Twelve students each ordered a different meal from a fast-food restaurant as part of a science project. When they finished eating, they weighed all the packaging. They found that the packaging weighed a total of 2.88 lb. What was the average weight of the packaging from each meal?
0.24 lb

25. Later in the year, the same 12 students repeated the experiment. The total weight of the same order's packaging this time was 2.06 lb. To the nearest hundredth of a pound, what was the new average weight of the packaging?
0.17 lb

Use with Grade 5, Chapter 3, Lesson 8, pages 124–127. (88)

Reteach

Divide Decimals by Whole Numbers

R 3-8 RETEACH

Dividing decimals is similar to dividing whole numbers, except that you don't write a remainder in the quotient. You may have to write one or more zeros in the dividend and keep dividing.

Divide 5.1 ÷ 4.

```
  1.2
4)5.1
 -4↓
  1 1
 -  8
    3
```

Place the decimal point in the quotient. Divide as with whole numbers. The remainder is not 0, so keep dividing.

```
  1.275
4)5.100
 -4↓↓↓
  1 1↓↓
 -  8↓↓
    30↓
   -28↓
     20
    -20
      0
```

Write zeros in the dividend and keep dividing until the remainder is 0

Multiply to check.
1.275 ← quotient
× 4 ← divisor
5.100
5.100 = 5.1 ← dividend

Divide. Multiply to check.

1.
```
   1 5 5
4) 6 . 2 0
  -4 ↓ ↓
   2 2
  -2 0
     2 0
    -2 0
       0
```
Check: 1 5 5 × 4 = 6 2 0

2.
```
   0 2 2 5
8) 1 . 8 0 0
  -1 6 ↓ ↓
     2 0
    -1 6
       4 0
      -4 0
         0
```
Check: 0 2 5 5 × 8 = 1 . 8 0 0

3.
```
   2 4
5) 1 2 . 0
  -1 0 ↓
     2 0
    -2 0
       0
```
Check: 2 4 × 5 = 1 2 . 0

4. 8)45.6 = 5.7
5. 6)21.3 = 3.55
6. 4)18 = 4.5
7. 34)7.82 = 0.23
8. 15)34.65 = 2.31
9. 56)47.6 = 0.85

Use with Grade 5, Chapter 3, Lesson 8, pages 124–127. (89)

Enrich

Divide Decimals by Whole Numbers

E 3-8 ENRICH

Disappearing Divisors

The divisors on this page have mysteriously disappeared. It's your job to find them! Then find each divisor in the box below. Use the code to answer the riddle.

Riddle: What did the remainder say to the decimal?

1. [3])15.18 = 5.06 — I
2. [9])22.5 = 2.5 — S
3. [2])3.56 = 1.78 — E
4. [2])2.5 = 1.25 — E
5. [1 2])60.72 = 5.06 — Y
6. [5])3.56 = 0.712 — O
7. [1 1])5.5 = 0.5 — U
8. [8])3.56 = 0.445 — R
9. [6])36.3 = 6.05 — P
10. [5])25.3 = 5.06 — O
11. [3])2.4 = 0.8 — I
12. [4])24.2 = 6.05 — N
13. [1 0])60.5 = 6.05 — T

1	2	3	4	5	6	7	8	9	10	11	12
A	E	I	N	O	P	Q	R	S	T	U	Y

How were you able to find the missing divisors?

Answers may vary. Possible answer: I used guess, test, and revise. I estimated the quotient of the dividend and the quotient given in the problem. I tested my estimate as the divisor and revised it if necessary.

Use with Grade 5, Chapter 3, Lesson 8, pages 124–127. (90)

Daily Homework

3-8 Divide Decimals by Whole Numbers

Divide. Round each quotient to the nearest hundredth if necessary.

1. 7)9.8 = 1.4
2. 3)3.9 = 1.3
3. 5)6.5 = 1.3
4. 8)65.28 = 8.16
5. 5)3.8 = 0.76
6. 10)4.2 = 0.42
7. 6)9.72 = 1.62
8. 3)24.42 = 8.14
9. 4)1.86 = 0.47
10. 100)482 = 4.82
11. 6)288 = 48
12. 5)78 = 15.6
13. 75.7 ÷ 2 = 37.85
14. 9.25 ÷ 5 = 1.85
15. 22.19 ÷ 7 = 3.17
16. 76 ÷ 6 = 12.67
17. 135 ÷ 4 = 33.75
18. 114 ÷ 10 = 11.4

Complete the pattern.

19. 72.9 ÷ 10 = 7.29
72.9 ÷ 100 = 0.729
72.9 ÷ 1,000 = 0.0729

20. 5.8 ÷ 10 = 0.58
5.8 ÷ 100 = 0.058
5.8 ÷ 1,000 = 0.0058

21. 45 ÷ 10 = 4.5
45 ÷ 100 = 0.45
45 ÷ 1,000 = 0.045

22. 25 ÷ 10 = 2.5
25 ÷ 100 = 0.25
25 ÷ 1,000 = 0.025

23. 46 ÷ 10 = 4.6
46 ÷ 100 = 0.46
46 ÷ 1,000 = 0.046

24. 9.8 ÷ 10 = 0.98
9.8 ÷ 100 = 0.098
9.8 ÷ 1,000 = 0.0098

Problem Solving

25. Lincoln learns from his science textbook that all insects have 6 legs. How many legs would 8,000 insects have?
48,000 legs

26. A millipede having 100 segments is 19.8 centimeters long. How long would each equal segment be? Round to the nearest tenth of a centimeter.
0.2 centimeters

Spiral Review

Express using a base and an exponent.

27. 4 × 4 × 4 × 4 — 4^4
28. 5 × 5 × 5 — 5^3
29. 8 × 8 × 8 × 8 × 8 — 8^5
30. 9 × 9 — 9^2

28 Grade 5, Chapter 3, Lesson 8, Cluster B

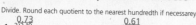

Chapter 3 ~ Lesson 9

Practice

Explore Dividing Decimals by Decimals

P 3-9 PRACTICE

For each problem, shade the grids to show the dividend. Draw lines to show how you could cut apart the shaded areas to find the quotient. Then write the quotient.

1. 2.5 ÷ 0.5 = 5

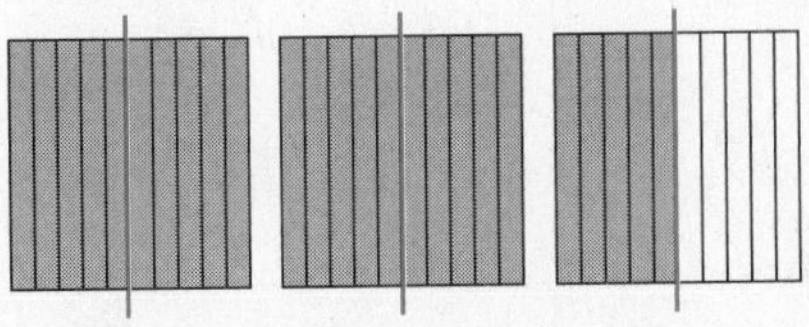

2. 3.9 ÷ 1.3 = 3

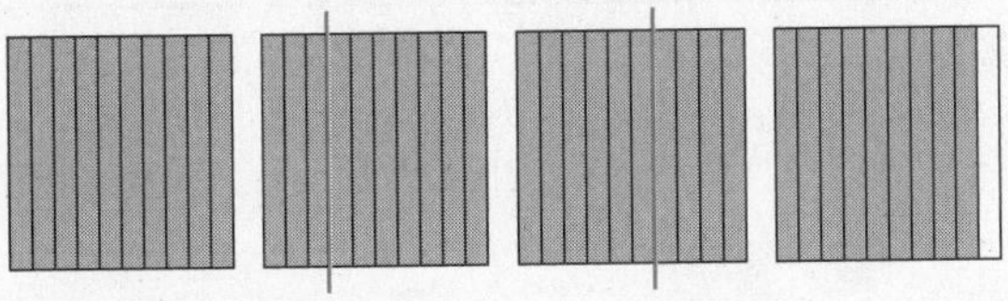

Divide. Use models.

3. 4.8 ÷ 0.8 = 6
4. 4.6 ÷ 2.3 = 2
5. 8.8 ÷ 1.1 = 8
6. 6.5 ÷ 1.3 = 5
7. 7.8 ÷ 2.6 = 3
8. 7.2 ÷ 1.8 = 4

Problem Solving

9. A builder owns a 2.4-acre piece of land. He plans to divide it into 0.6-acre building lots. How many lots can the builder create?

4 lots

10. The builder owns another piece of land that is 4.5 acres. He plans to divide this one into 0.5-acre building lots. How many lots can he create?

9 lots

Use with Grade 5, Chapter 3, Lesson 9, pages 128–129. (91)

Reteach

Explore Dividing Decimals by Decimals

R 3-9 RETEACH

You can use number lines to show division of a decimal by a decimal.

Divide 3.3 ÷ 1.1.

Locate 3.3 on a number line.

Mark groups of 1.1 until you reach 3.3.

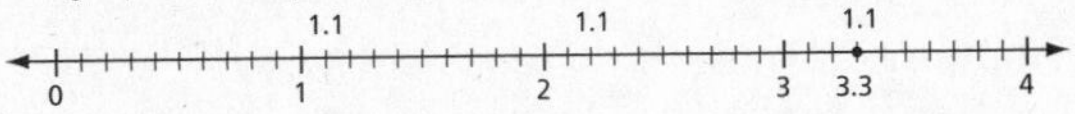

Count the groups of 1.1. There are 3 groups of 1.1 in 3.3, so 3.3 ÷ 1.1 = 3.

Use a number line to find each quotient.

1. 4.5 ÷ 0.9 = 5

2. 4.2 ÷ 1.4 = 3

3. 3.8 ÷ 1.9 = 2

4. 3.6 ÷ 1.2 = 3

Divide. Draw a number line if you need help. Multiply to check.

5. 5.5 ÷ 1.1 = 5
6. 7.2 ÷ 0.8 = 9
7. 5.6 ÷ 0.7 = 8
8. 7.8 ÷ 1.3 = 6
9. 9.2 ÷ 2.3 = 4
10. 4.8 ÷ 1.6 = 3

Use with Grade 5, Chapter 3, Lesson 9, pages 128–129. (92)

Enrich

Explore Dividing Decimals by Decimals

E 3-9 ENRICH

Equation Building

Write as many different division equations as you can using a number from a circle, a triangle, and square.

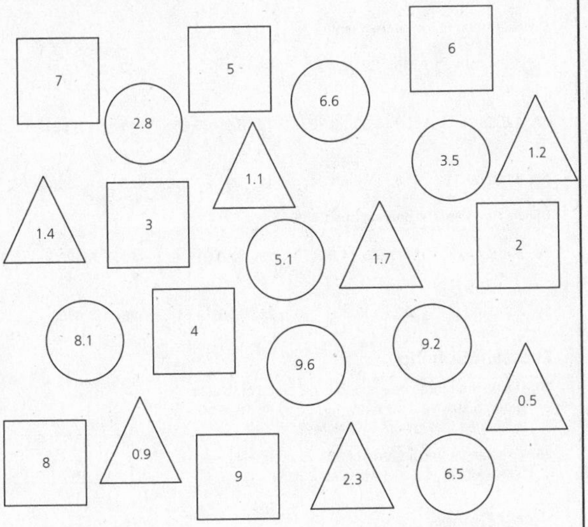

2.8 ÷ 1.4 = 2   5.1 ÷ 1.7 = 3

9.2 ÷ 2.3 = 4   6.5 ÷ 1.3 = 5

6.6 ÷ 1.1 = 6   3.5 ÷ 0.5 = 7

9.6 ÷ 1.2 = 8   8.1 ÷ 0.9 = 9

Use with Grade 5, Chapter 3, Lesson 9, pages 128–129. (93)

Daily Homework

3-9 Explore Dividing Decimals by Decimals

Divide.

1. 5.6 ÷ 0.8 = 7
2. 8.4 ÷ 1.2 = 7
3. 4.5 ÷ 0.9 = 5
4. 6.4 ÷ 0.8 = 8
5. 5.2 ÷ 1.3 = 4
6. 1.6 ÷ 0.4 = 4
7. 9.1 ÷ 0.7 = 13
8. 2.4 ÷ 0.4 = 6
9. 1.4 ÷ 0.2 = 7
10. 1.8 ÷ 0.3 = 6
11. 3.6 ÷ 0.9 = 4
12. 6.5 ÷ 1.3 = 5
13. 7.5 ÷ 0.5 = 15
14. 8.1 ÷ 2.7 = 3
15. 2.1 ÷ 0.3 = 7
16. 5.4 ÷ 0.6 = 9
17. 7.6 ÷ 0.4 = 19
18. 10.5 ÷ 1.5 = 7
19. 14.4 ÷ 1.2 = 12
20. 6.6 ÷ 1.1 = 6
21. 0.64 ÷ 0.08 = 8

Solve.

22. Sara has 30 yards of fabric. She and her friends want to make matching skirts. If it takes 1.5 yards for each skirt, how many skirts can they make from Sara's fabric? 20 skirts

23. Alicia has 5 pennies, 5 quarters, and 5 dimes. Marcus has 18 pennies, 4 quarters, and 6 dimes. Selena has 9 pennies, 8 quarters, and 9 dimes. Order the three students by the amount of money each has, from least to greatest.

Marcus $1.78; Alicia, $1.80; Selena, $2.99

Spiral Review

24. 75 + 139 = 214
25. 308 – 49 = 259
26. 900 × 80 = 72,000
27. 4 × 5 × 18 × 5 = 1,800
28. 36 + 148 = 184
29. 548 – 64 = 484
30. 600 × 50 = 30,000
31. 6 × 4 × 3 × 5 = 360

Grade 5, Chapter 3, Lesson 9, Cluster B 29

Chapter 3 ~ Lesson 10

Practice

Divide Decimals by Decimals

P 3-10 PRACTICE

Divide.

1. 0.9)2.16 — 2.4
2. 4.7)7.52 — 1.6
3. 0.72)313.2 — 435
4. 2.47)9.633 — 3.9
5. 0.513)3.4884 — 6.8
6. 68.9)18.603 — 0.27
7. 1.734 ÷ 0.34 = 5.1
8. 37.128 ÷ 2.38 = 15.6

Divide. Round to the nearest tenth.

9. 5.2)8.36 — 1.6
10. 4.8)13.25 — 2.8
11. 0.36)28.97 — 80.5
12. 7.09)27.9 — 3.9
13. 2.14)37.623 — 17.6
14. 81.6)442.07 — 5.4
15. 80.95 ÷ 4.7 = 17.2
16. 1,194.6 ÷ 63.1 = 18.9

Divide. Round to the nearest hundredth.

17. 9.1)5.24 — 0.58
18. 7.6)13.89 — 1.83
19. 0.38)24.71 — 65.03
20. 4.25)36.2 — 8.52
21. 18.3)7.903 — 0.43
22. 6.08)427.45 — 70.30
23. 8.094 ÷ 0.24 = 33.73
24. 59.286 ÷ 8.71 = 6.81

Problem Solving

25. During a hurricane, 18.6 inches of rain fell in 6.5 hours. To the nearest tenth of an inch, what was the average rainfall per hour? 2.9 inches
26. The eye of a hurricane moved 117.5 miles in 8.25 hours. To the nearest hundredth of a mile, what was the average distance the eye moved per hour? 14.24 miles

Use with Grade 5, Chapter 3, Lesson 10, pages 130–133. (94)

Reteach

Divide Decimals by Decimals

R 3-10 RETEACH

Before you can divide by a decimal, multiply the divisor and dividend by a power of 10 so that the divisor is a whole number. Then you are ready to divide.

Divide 4.2)7.14 .

Count the number of decimal places in the divisor.

4.2)7.14
↓
1 decimal place

Move the decimal point in the divisor and in the dividend that many places to the right.

4.2)7.14

Rewrite the problem and divide.

```
   1.7
42)71.4
  - 42↓
    29 4
  - 29 4
       0
```

Multiply to check. Use the numbers in the original problem.

```
   1.7  ← quotient
 × 4.2  ← divisor
    34
 + 680
  7.14  ← dividend
```

Count the number of decimal places in each divisor. Rewrite each problem and divide. Multiply to check.

1. Number of decimal places: 1

3.6)8.64 → 36)864 = 24

Check: 24 × 36 = 8.64

2. Number of decimal places: 2

0.72)6.552 → 72)6552 = 91

Check: 91 × 0.72 = 6.552

3. Number of decimal places: 2

2.81)9.7788 → 281)97788 = 348

Check: 3.48 × 281 = 9.7788

Use with Grade 5, Chapter 3, Lesson 10, pages 130–133. (95)

Enrich

Divide Decimals by Decimals

A Valuable Riddle

E 3-10 ENRICH

Find each rounded quotient in the box. Write the matching letter next to the division exercise. Read the letters from top to bottom to answer this riddle: What is the value of the moon?

1. 9.84 ÷ 2.7 (to the nearest hundredth) F
2. 1.634 ÷ 7.62 (to the nearest tenth) O
3. 32.85 ÷ 91.7 (to the nearest hundredth) U
4. 0.7723 ÷ 0.48 (to the nearest hundredth) R
5. 376.4 ÷ 80.1 (to the nearest tenth) Q
6. 483.59 ÷ 67.4 (to the nearest hundredth) U
7. 5.248 ÷ 1.85 (to the nearest hundredth) A
8. 25.2 ÷ 0.89 (to the nearest tenth) R
9. 9.316 ÷ 57.6 (to the nearest hundredth) T
10. 301.1 ÷ 4.2 (to the nearest tenth) E
11. 14.21 ÷ 30.4 (to the nearest hundredth) R
12. 102.02 ÷ 6.3 (to the nearest hundredth) S

R	28.3
Q	4.7
L	3.6
U	0.36
T	0.16
O	0.2
R	0.47
R	1.61
U	7.17
F	3.64
A	2.84
S	16.19
E	71.7

Divide. Answer this riddle: How does the moon feel after dinner?

13. 24.389 ÷ 6.7 (to the nearest hundredth) F
14. 24.95 ÷ 3.48 (to the nearest hundredth) U
15. 75 ÷ 20.9 (to the nearest tenth) L
16. 5.4 ÷ 1.5 (to the nearest tenth) L

How could you have solved this riddle without working every division exercise?

Answers may vary. Possible answer: I could have estimated the quotients.

Use with Grade 5, Chapter 3, Lesson 10, pages 130–133. (96)

Daily Homework

3·10 Divide Decimals by Decimals until there is no remainder.

Divide.

1. 1.8 ÷ 0.4 = 4.5
2. 1.47 ÷ 0.7 = 2.1
3. 8.16 ÷ 2.4 = 3.4

Divide. Round to the nearest tenth.

4. 1.6)4.28 — 2.7
5. 4.2)76.25 — 18.2
6. 3.8)82.5 — 21.7
7. 2.6)12.64 — 4.9
8. 1.6)58 — 36.3
9. 0.32)36.36 — 113.6
10. 5.5)485.88 — 88.3
11. 6.2)8,624.6 — 1,391.1
12. 14.62)273.54 — 18.71
13. 1.86)66.24 — 35.61
14. 6.08)77.216 — 12.7
15. 5.12)60.42 — 11.8

Divide. Round to the nearest hundredth.

16. 5.8)20.76 — 3.58
17. 5.5)74.85 — 13.61
18. 10.8)315.4 — 29.20
19. 6.6)123.7 — 18.74
20. 2.44)182.8 — 74.92
21. 0.48)68 — 141.67
22. 0.95)15.55 — 16.37
23. 1.7)675 — 397.06

Problem Solving

24. If a spotted turtle needs about 1.3 acres of land in order to survive, how many turtles could there be in an area that covers 31.2 acres? 24 turtles
25. A rectangle has an area of 534.75 square inches. If its width is 15.5 inches, what is its length? 34.5 inches

Spiral Review

26. 4.7 + 11.4 = 16.1
27. 4.04 × 4.04 = 16.3216
28. 12.6 − 4.56 = 8.04
29. 28.6 + 4.2 = 32.8
30. 3.06 × 8.82 = 26.9892
31. 534.8 − 3.9 = 530.9

30 Grade 5, Chapter 3, Lesson 10, Cluster B

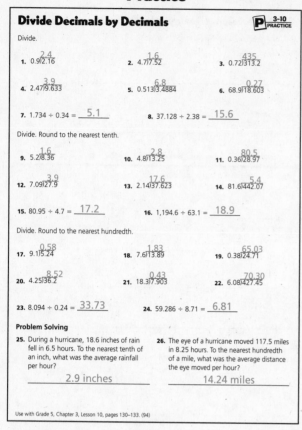

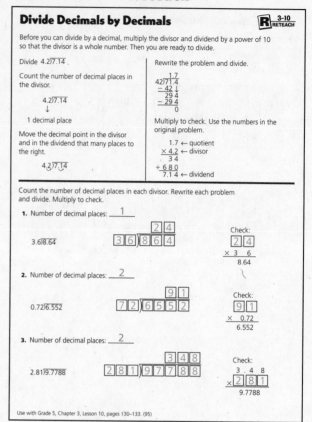

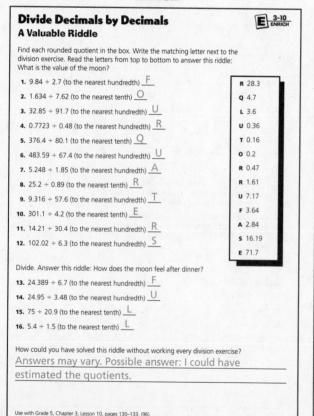

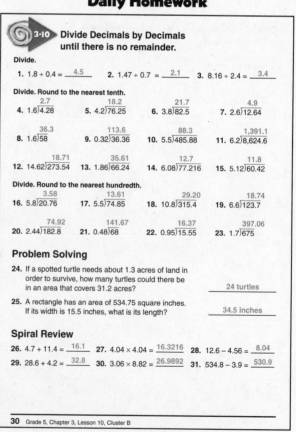

Chapter 3 ~ Lesson 11

Part A Worksheet

Problem Solving: Application
Applying Division

Part A 3-11 WORKSHEET Decision Making

Use the table to help you decide where to buy the CD-ROMs.

Purchase Place	Cost of Each CD-ROM	Other Costs	Total Cost	Cost per Student

Your Decision

What is your recommendation for Ms. Lee's class? Explain.

Answers may vary. Possible answer: Order from the catalog using regular delivery because it costs the least.

Use with Grade 5, Chapter 3, Lesson 11, pages 134–135. (97)

Part B Worksheet

Problem Solving: Application
How much trash do you make each year?

Part B 3-11 WORKSHEET Math & Science

About how many bags of trash do you think you make in one year? Explain.

Answers may vary.

Remember to collect all of your trash throughout the day.

Record your data in the table. Use the amount of trash you collected in one day to predict how much trash you would collect in one week and in one year.

Trash	Number of Bags	Mass of Trash
Each day		
Each week		
Each year		

1. How does the amount of trash you collect each year compare to your estimate? Were you surprised? Explain.

   Answers may vary.

2. Compare your data with the data of some of your classmates. Are your estimates close? Explain why you think there are differences or similarities in the data.

   Answers may vary.

Use with Grade 5, Chapter 3, Lesson 11, pages 136–137. (98)

Part B Worksheet

Problem Solving: Application
How much trash do you make each year?

Part B 3-11 WORKSHEET Math & Science

3. Estimate the mass of the trash your class would make in one year. Explain your estimate.

   Answers may vary.

4. What other types of trash would you have to consider if you were going to try to estimate the amount of trash that your entire school would make?

   Answers may vary. Possible answer: You would have to include papers teachers throw away, old books, and cafeteria trash.

5. Why is it important to be aware of the amount of trash that you make each year?

   Answers may vary. Possible answer: Spaces for trash are limited so we should try to conserve the amount of trash we make. We can try to recycle more and use organic matter for composts.

6. What are some ways that you can reduce the amount of trash that you make each year?

   Answers may vary.

7. What are some ways that you can help your family reduce the amount of trash that they make each year?

   Answers may vary.

Use with Grade 5, Chapter 3, Lesson 11, pages 136–137. (99)

Chapter 4 ~ Lesson 1

Practice

Explore Collecting, Organizing, and Displaying Data

P 4-1 PRACTICE

The Johnson family kept the record of the length of telephone calls they made in one weekend.

8 minutes	6 minutes	4 minutes	10 minutes	4 minutes	8 minutes
7 minutes	8 minutes	8 minutes	7 minutes	9 minutes	8 minutes
3 minutes	9 minutes	7 minutes	8 minutes	4 minutes	6 minutes
9 minutes	8 minutes	7 minutes	9 minutes	7 minutes	

1. Record the results in the frequency table below.

Length of Calls in Minutes	Number of Calls	
	Tally	Frequency
3	/	1
4	///	3
5		0
6	//	2
7	~~////~~	5
8	~~////~~ //	7
9	////	4
10	/	1

2. Make a line plot from the frequency table.

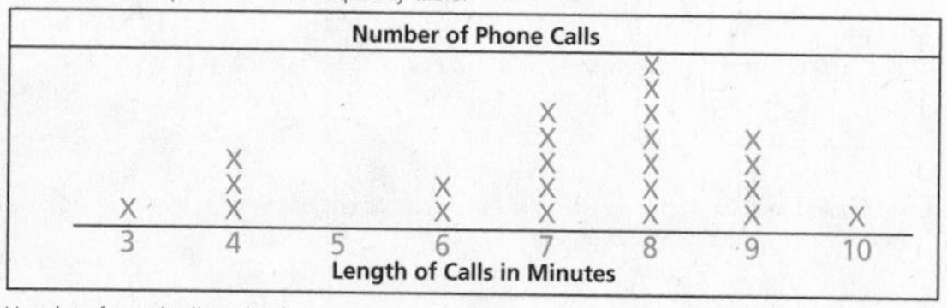

Use data from the line plot for exercises 3–4.

3. Where does most of the data cluster? What does this tell you?
Most of the data clusters from 7 to 9 minutes.
Most of the Johnsons' phone calls were 7 to 9 minutes long.

4. Where is the gap in the line plot? What does this tell you?
There is a gap at 5. No one made a phone call lasting 5 minutes.

Use with Grade 5, Chapter 4, Lesson 1, pages 152–153. (100)

Reteach

Explore Collecting, Organizing, and Displaying Data

R 4-1 RETEACH

Students in one fifth-grade class recorded how many first cousins they each had. Here are the results:

6, 5, 1, 7, 3, 4, 4, 5, 1, 5, 6, 4, 7, 5, 5, 6, 7, 5, 4, 6, 4

Make one tally in the frequency table for each time a particular number of first cousins occurs. Count and record the number of tallies. Display the data in a line plot, making one X for each tally.

Frequency Table

Number of First Cousins	Number of Students	
	Tally	Frequency
1	//	2
2		0
3	/	1
4	~~////~~	5
5	~~////~~ /	6
6	////	4
7	///	3

Line Plot

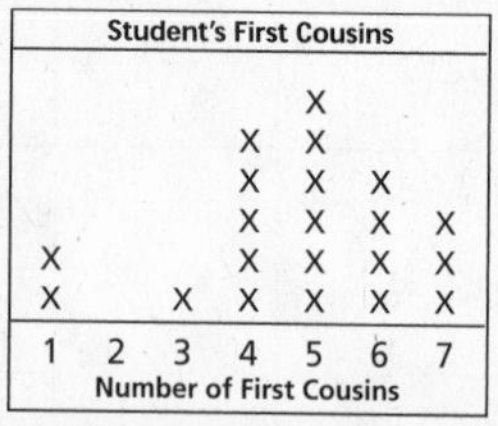

For the next month, the fifth-graders kept a record of how many times they called one of their first cousins on the phone. Here are the results:

2, 0, 2, 1, 1, 3, 4, 2, 2, 3, 4, 3, 6, 0, 3, 2, 1, 2, 3, 1, 2

1. Record the results in the frequency table below.

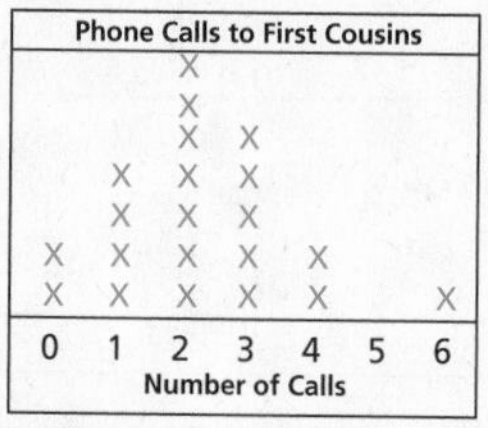

Use the frequency table and line plot for exercises 2–3.

2. How many students made at least one phone call to a first cousin?
19 students

3. Sometimes a gap appears in a line plot because a particular result never occurred. Where is the gap in the line plot? What does this tell you?
There is a gap at 5. No one made 5 phone calls to first cousins.

Use with Grade 5, Chapter 4, Lesson 1, pages 152–153. (101)

Enrich

Explore Collecting, Organizing, and Displaying Data

E 4-1 ENRICH

Count Them Up!

Use a favorite fiction book or story. Count the number of words in each of the first 25 sentences. Record your findings in the frequency table below. Findings may vary.

Number of Words in Sentences

Number of Words	Tally	Frequency
1		
2		
3		
4		
5		
6		
7		
8		
9		
10		
more than 10		

Use your data to make a line plot. Check students' work.

Number of Words in Sentences

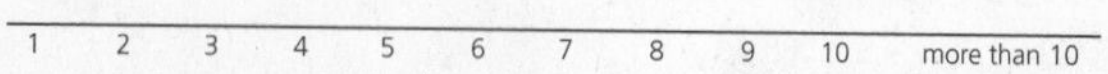

Write a sentence that summarizes your data.
Answers may vary according to the data in the survey.

Use with Grade 5, Chapter 4, Lesson 1, pages 152–153. (102)

Daily Homework

4-1 Explore Collecting, Organizing, and Displaying Data

Use the data in this table to answer the questions that follow.

Candace's Survey		
Telephones at Home	Fifth Graders Surveyed	
	Tally	Frequency
1	~~////~~	5
2	~~////~~ II	7
3	~~////~~ III	8
4	III	3
5	~~////~~	5
6 or more	II	2

1. Fill in the missing data on Candace's table.
2. Make a line plot of Candace's data.

Number of Telephones at Home

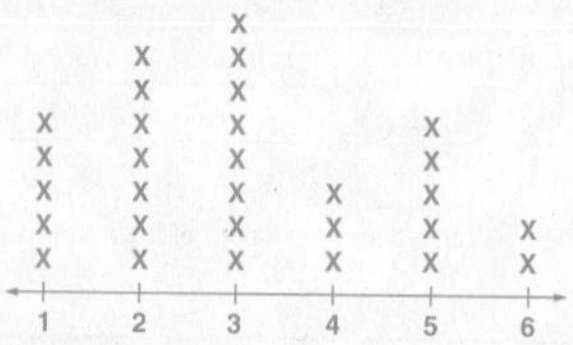

3. Describe the data in the line plot in one sentence.
Most homes have 3 telephones and few have 6 or more.

4. How many fifth-graders were surveyed? 30

Spiral Review

5. 34 × 47 = 1,598
6. 308 × 67 = 20,636
7. 74 × 407 = 30,118
8. 56 × 9,002 = 504,112
9. 30 × 4,200 = 126,000
10. 26 × 512 = 13,312

Grade 5, Chapter 4, Lesson 1, Cluster A 31

Chapter 4 ~ Lesson 2

Practice

Range, Mode, Median, and Mean

P 4-2 PRACTICE

Find the range, mode, median, and mean.

1. 1, 2, 0, 5, 8, 2, 9, 2, 7 range=9; mode=2; median=2; mean=4
2. 9, 4, 7, 9, 3, 10, 8, 6 range=7; mode=9; median=7.5; mean=7
3. 34, 17, 10, 23, 21, 15 range=24; no mode; median= 19; mean=20
4. 67, 67, 98, 49, 98, 89 range=49; mode=67 and 98; median=78; mean=78
5. 27, 31, 76, 59, 33, 48, 24, 58 range=52; no mode; median=40.5; mean=44.5
6. 105, 126, 90, 50, 75, 90, 62, 112 range=76; mode=90; median=90; mean=88.75
7. \$1.50, \$2.50, \$1.50, \$4.00, \$5.00 range=\$3.50; mode=\$1.50; median=\$2.50; mean=\$2.90
8. 1.2, 1.5, 2.1, 1.7, 3.2, 2.4, 2.8, 1.3 range=2; no mode; median=1.9; mean=2.025
9. 20, 12.5, 30, 15.4, 25, 18.6, 17.8 range=17.5; no mode; median=18.6; mean=19.9
10. \$3.35, \$8.50, \$3.35, \$4.35, \$8.25 range=\$5.15; mode=\$3.35; median=\$4.35; mean=\$5.56
11. Find the range, mode, median, and mean.

Student	Ann	Ben	Cara	Fran	Ian	Mike	Kim	Lou
Number of Pets	4	6	0	3	2	5	2	3

range: 6; mode: 2 and 3; median: 3; mean: 3.125

Problem Solving

During the first five basketball games of the season, a player scored 22, 17, 21, 9, and 17 points.

12. What is the mean points scored per game? 17.2 points
13. How many points must the player score in the next game to make the range 15 points? 24 points

Use with Grade 5, Chapter 4, Lesson 2, pages 154–157. (103)

Reteach

Range, Mode, Median, and Mean

R 4-2 RETEACH

You can use the range, mode, median, and mean to describe the numbers of E-mail messages Jon sent.

Day	Sun.	Mon.	Tues.	Wed.	Thur.	Fri.	Sat.
Number of Messages	7	4	6	5	7	5	8

Write the numbers of messages in order from least to greatest. 4, 5, 5, 6, 7, 7, 8.

What you want to know	What you find	How you find it
Is there much difference in the numbers of messages sent?	**range** the difference between the greatest and the least number	8 − 4 = 4 The range of messages is 4.
What is the most common number of messages sent?	**mode** the number that occurs most often	5 and 7 both appear twice. The other numbers appear once. The mode is 5 and 7 messages.
What is the middle number of messages sent?	**median** the middle number	6 is in the middle. The median is 6 messages.
What is the average number of messages sent?	**mean** the sum of the numbers divided by the number of addends	4 + 5 + 5 + 6 + 7 + 7 + 8 = 42 42 ÷ 7 = 6 The mean is 6 messages.

Number of E-mail Messages Jon Received							
Day	Sun.	Mon.	Tues.	Wed.	Thur.	Fri.	Sat.
Number of Messages	3	9	2	5	8	2	6

1. Write the number of messages received in order from least to greatest. 2, 2, 3, 5, 6, 8, 9
2. What is the greatest number of messages received? the least number? 9 messages; 2 messages
3. What is the range of messages received? 7 messages
4. What is the mode of messages received? 2 messages
5. What is the median of messages received? 5 messages
6. What is the mean of messages received? total messages received ÷ number of days messages received = mean
   35 ÷ 7 = 5

Use with Grade 5, Chapter 4, Lesson 2, pages 154–157. (104)

Enrich

Range, Mode, Median, and Mean

E 4-2 ENRICH

Data Game

Use the numbers in the box to complete exercises 1–7. Once you have used a number, cross it out. You may not use it again.

1	2	6	5	1	6	4	7	9	5
10	98	96	79	96	25	75	32	53	50
71	22	81	76	97	44	36	20	72	36
31	40	50	49	18	29	74	96	42	34
198	173	367	379	988	637	724	706	251	600
546	468	809	343	702	706	867	331	828	615

When you have completed exercises 1–7, compare your answers with a classmate. For each of exercises 1–6, give one point to the person who comes closer to the goal. For exercise 7, give one point for each person who finds the mode of the data. Answers may vary with numbers chosen.

1. Choose seven numbers.
   Goal: greatest range
   Numbers: ________
   Range: ________
2. Choose six numbers.
   Goal: least mean
   Numbers: ________
   Mean: ________
3. Choose eight numbers.
   Goal: least median
   Numbers: ________
   Median: ________
4. Choose five numbers.
   Goal: greatest mean
   Numbers: ________
   Mean: ________
5. Choose seven numbers.
   Goal: least range
   Numbers: ________
   Range: ________
6. Choose nine numbers.
   Goal: greatest median
   Numbers: ________
   Median: ________
7. Find the mode of the remaining numbers. ________

Describe one strategy you used in this game.

Answers may vary. Possible answer: For exercise 1, choose the least and greatest numbers you can to get the greatest range.

Use with Grade 5, Chapter 4, Lesson 2, pages 154–157. (105)

Daily Homework

4-2 Range, Mode, Median, and Mean

Find the range, mode, median, and mean.

1. 1, 1, 2, 4, 5, 1, 2, 1, 2, 6, 8
   range: 7, mode: 1, median: 2, mean: 3
2. 1.3, 1.4, 1.5, 1.5, 1.3, 1.4, 1.4, 1.4
   range: 0.2, mode: 1.4, median: 1.4, mean: 1.4
3. 500, 550, 455, 475, 5000, 555, 700, 610, 524
   range:4,545, mode: none, median: 550, mean: 1,041
4. Why is the median so much smaller than the mean in Problem 3?
   The outlier 5000 changes the mean more than the median.

Problem Solving

5. Alexa had the following scores on her math quizzes: 57, 84, 81, 97, 81, 89. She can choose among the mean, the median, or the mode for her quiz grade. Which one should she choose?
   mode = 81, mean = 81.5, median = 82.5. She should pick the median.

Use data in the table for problems 6–7. Round to the nearest tenth.

Ages of Workers in a Fast Food Restaurant												
17	18	17	18	17	19	17	18	18	23	24	25	49

6. What is the mean age of all the workers? 21.5
7. The manager hires a new worker who is 47 years old. What is the new mean age of the entire work crew? 23.4

Spiral Review

8. 2.3 × 45 = 103.5
9. 4.3 × 5.6 = 24.08
10. 1.05 × 24.3 = 25.515

32 Grade 5, Chapter 4, Lesson 2, Cluster A

Practice

Read and Make Pictographs

P 4-3 PRACTICE

The table shows the number of books some members of the Kids Reading Club at Central Library read one summer.

Number of Books Read During Summer	
Reader	Number of Books
Kendra	12
Joel	16
Dan	10
Mae	8
Emily	14

1. Make a pictograph from this data.
Key: Graphs may vary. A sample graph is given.

2. How did you decide what each picture would represent?
Answers may vary. Possible answer: I let each picture represent 4 books because 12, 16, and 8 are divisible by 4, and I could show 10 and 14 using whole and half pictures.

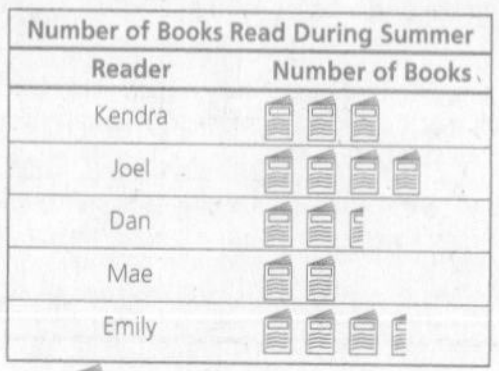

Use data from the pictograph for exercises 3–5.

3. How many more minutes a day does Phil read than Mary?
15 minutes

4. What is the total amount of time the club members spend reading in one day?
170 minutes, or 2 hours 50 minutes

5. How much time does Zach read each week?
140 minutes, or 2 hours 20 minutes

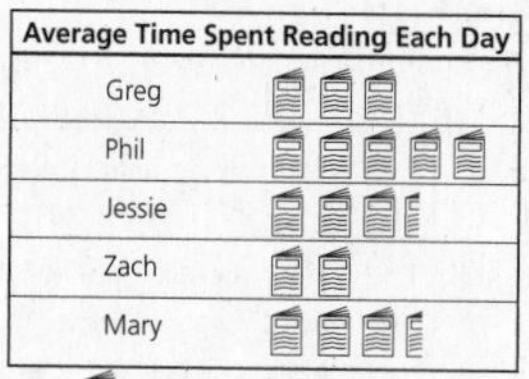

Reteach

Read and Make Pictographs

R 4-3 RETEACH

You can use symbols in a pictograph to display data.

Fifth-Grade Bake Sale

Items	Number Sold
Cupcakes	40
Pies	60
Cookies	15
Cakes	15

First, choose a symbol and decide what it will represent.

Let [cupcake symbol] represent 10 items.

To find how many symbols to draw, divide each piece of data by the number each symbol represents.

Items	Number Sold	Number of Symbols
Cupcakes	40	$40 \div 10 = 4$
Pies	60	$60 \div 10 = 6$
Cookies	15	Think: 5 is half of 10 $15 \div 10 = 1\frac{1}{2}$
Cakes	15	Think: 5 is half of 10 $15 \div 10 = 1\frac{1}{2}$

Now make the pictograph.
Remember to include the key.

The table shows the results of a survey of favorite pizza toppings. Complete the table. Then make a pictograph of the data.

Toppings	Number of People	Number of Symbols
Cheese only	16	$8\overline{)16} = 2$
Pepperoni	40	$8\overline{)40} = 5$
Sausage	20	$8\overline{)20} = 2\frac{1}{2}$
Vegetables	12	$8\overline{)12} = 1\frac{1}{2}$

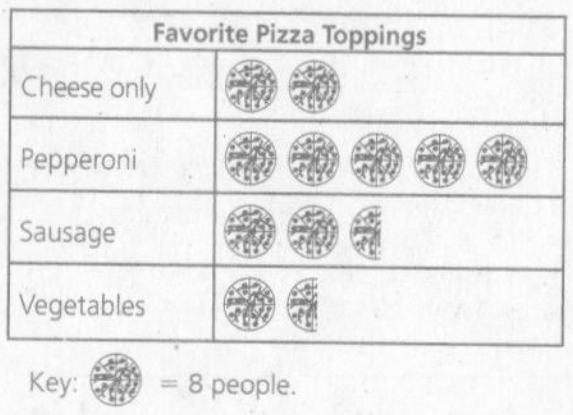

Enrich

Read and Make Pictographs

Complete the Graph

E 4-3 ENRICH

This graph is supposed to show the types and numbers of videotapes in a library. Some parts of the graph are missing. Use the clues to complete the graph.

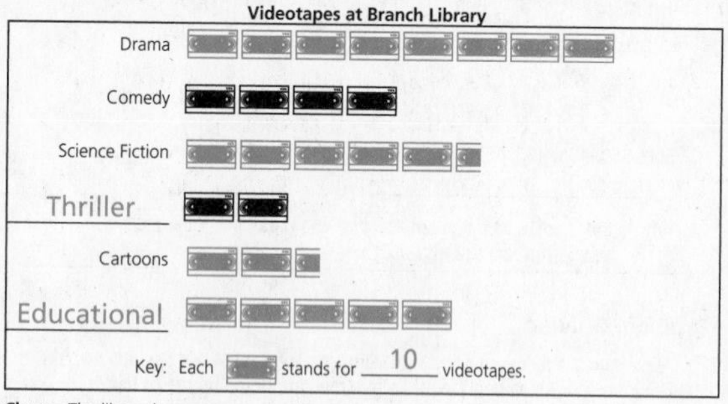

Clues The library has:

- 40 comedy videotapes
- 20 thriller videotapes
- 25 cartoon videotapes
- 10 more educational videotapes than thriller videotapes
- 40 more drama videotapes than comedy videotapes
- a total of 270 videotapes

Use the completed pictograph to find each. Tell how you find each answer.
Answers may vary. Possible answers are given.

Range: 70; Find the difference in the amounts represented by the greatest number of symbols and the least number of symbols and multiply by 10.

Mode: No mode; find which number of symbols, if any, occurs more times than other numbers of symbols, and multiply by 10.

Median: 40; Write the numbers of symbols in order from least to greatest, find the median of the numbers, and multiply by 10.

Mean: 45; Find the mean number of symbols, and multiply by 10.

Daily Homework

4-3 Read and Make Pictographs

Use the pictograph below to answer questions 1–4.

1. Which flavor was most popular?
chocolate chip

2. How many cones of that flavor were sold? 60

3. Rocky Road outsold Butter Crunch by how many cones? 15

4. How many ice cream cones were sold all together? 195

5. Survey your house for books. Count how many books are in each room of your home. Make a frequency table to display the data. Make a pictograph for the data.
Data and tables may vary.

6. The mean number of pages in the books in Janie's bedroom is 252 pages. The mean number of book pages in the kitchen is 1,221 pages, and the mean number of book pages in the living room is 342 pages. What is the mean number of book pages in these three rooms?
605 pages

Spiral Review

Round each number to nearest tenth.

7. 1.34 1.3
8. 1.07 1.1
9. 2.045 2.0

Round each number to nearest hundredth.

10. 1.367 1.37
11. 2.785 2.79
12. 3.8924 3.90

Chapter 4 ~ Lesson 4

Practice

Read and Make Bar Graphs

P 4-4 PRACTICE

1. The table shows the times Ken and Pat rode their bikes each day last week. Make a double-bar graph of the data.

Graphs may vary. Check students' graphs.

Time Spent Riding a Bike (in minutes)

Day	Ken	Pat
Sunday	20	25
Monday	30	40
Tuesday	25	20
Wednesday	5	45
Thursday	20	35
Friday	15	35
Saturday	30	20

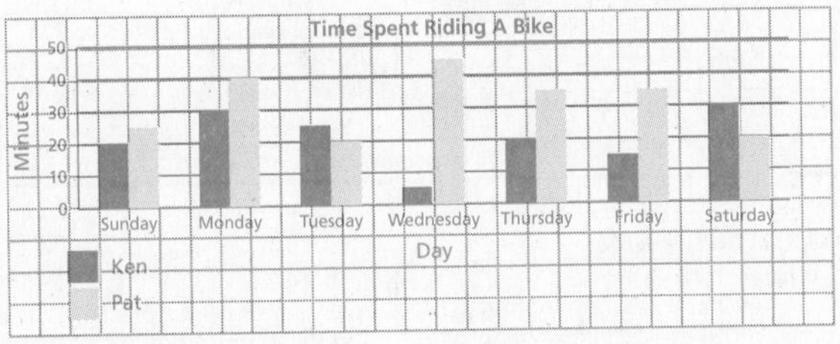

Use data from the graph for exercises 2–4.

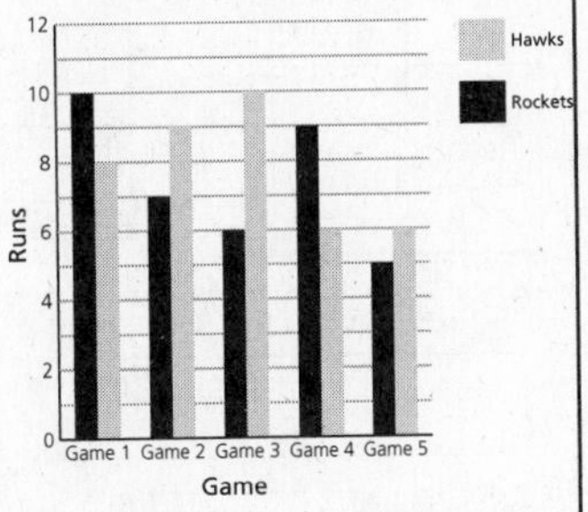

2. What is the mode of the data?
6 points

3. Who won Game 4? By how many runs?
Rockets; 3 runs

4. The team that wins 3 games wins the playoffs. Who won the playoffs?
Hawks

Use with Grade 5, Chapter 4, Lesson 4, pages 160–163. (109)

Reteach

Read and Make Bar Graphs

R 4-4 RETEACH

A double-bar graph is used to compare data for two related groups. You can use this double-bar graph to compare the number of fifth and sixth graders who belong to different clubs at Middlevale School.

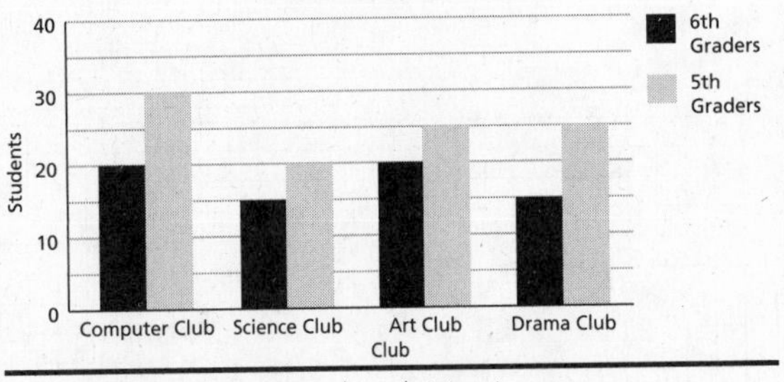

Use the double-bar graph above to complete each statement.

1. The interval of data is the distance between the numbers on an axis. The interval of club members is 10 members.

2. The bar for sixth graders who belong to the Computer Club ends at 20, so 20 sixth graders belong to the Computer Club.

3. The bar for fifth graders who belong to the Art Club ends halfway between 20 and 30, so 25 fifth graders belong to the Art Club.

4. 15 fifth graders and 25 sixth graders belong to the Drama Club. 10 more fifth graders than sixth graders belong to the Drama Club. Altogether 40 students belong to the Drama Club.

5. The tallest bar ends at 30, and the shortest bar ends at 15. So, the range of the data is 15 students.

6. More bars end at 20 than any other number, so the mode of the data is 20 students.

Use with Grade 5, Chapter 4, Lesson 4, pages 160–163. (110)

Enrich

Read and Make Bar Graphs

E 4-4 ENRICH

Graph That Score!

This graph is supposed to show the scores of the eight football games played by the Jaguars in one season. Use the information in the table to complete the graph.

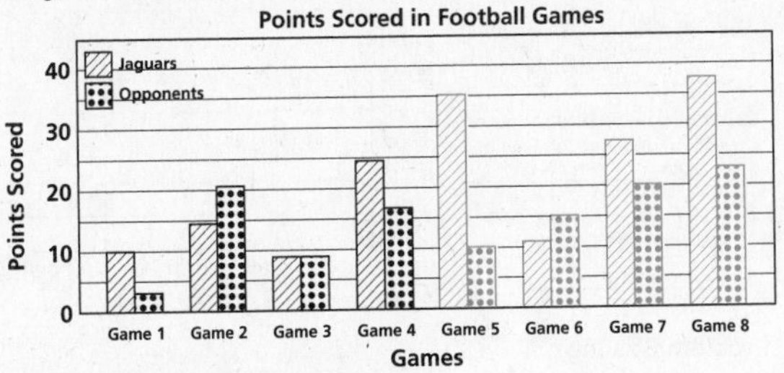

Points Scored in Football Games

Game	Jaguars	Opponents
5	35	10
6	12	15
7	28	20
8	38	23

Use your completed graph to answer these questions.

1. How many games did the Jaguars win?
5 games

2. In which game did the Jaguars win by the most points?
Game 5

3. By how many points did the Jaguars lose in Game 2?
accept answers 6–8 points

4. In how many games did the Jaguars score at least 20 points?
4 games

5. About how many more points altogether did the Jaguars score than their opponents in the 5 games that they won?
about 60 points

Use with Grade 5, Chapter 4, Lesson 4, pages 160–163. (111)

Daily Homework

4-4 Read and Make Bar Graphs

Use data from the graph for problems 1–5.

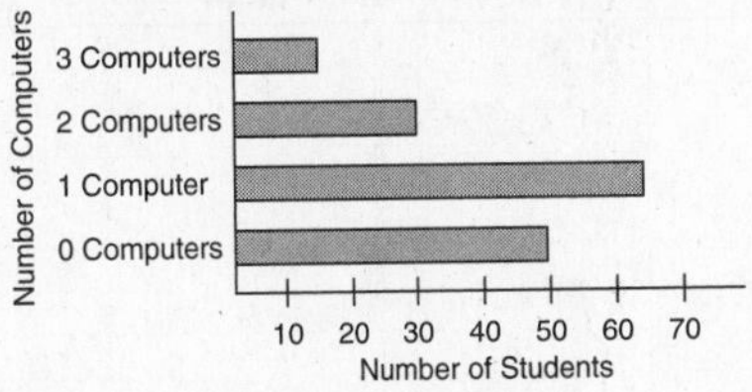

1. How many students have no computer at home? 50
2. How many students have one computer at home? 65
3. What is the range of the data? 50 62
4. How many students were surveyed? 160
5. How many computers are in the homes of all the students surveyed? 170

Problem Solving

Use data from the table for problems 6–7.

Mean January Temperatures (°F)

Honolulu	80
Boston	36
Chicago	29
Miami	75
Houston	

6. Find the range, mode, median, and mean for these temperatures.
range: 51°F, no mode, median: 62°F, mean: 56.4°F

7. Which two cities are closest in mean January temperatures?
Honolulu and Miami

Spiral Review

8. $12 \div 0.3 =$ 40

9. $1.5\overline{)4.5510}$ 3.034

10. $\frac{1.6}{0.8} =$ 2

34 Grade 5, Chapter 4, Lesson 4

Chapter 4 ~ Lesson 5

Practice

Read and Make Histograms

P 4-5 PRACTICE

1. This table shows the distances people rode their bikes on the Riverside Bike Trail one day. Make a histogram to display the data.

Check students' histograms.

Distances Ridden on Trail

Distance in Miles	Number of Cyclists
0–4	9
5–8	16
9–12	24
13–16	14
17–20	6

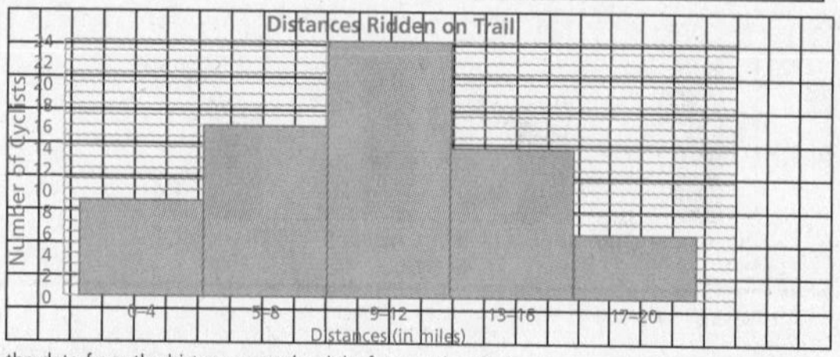

Use the data from the histogram at the right for exercises 2–4.

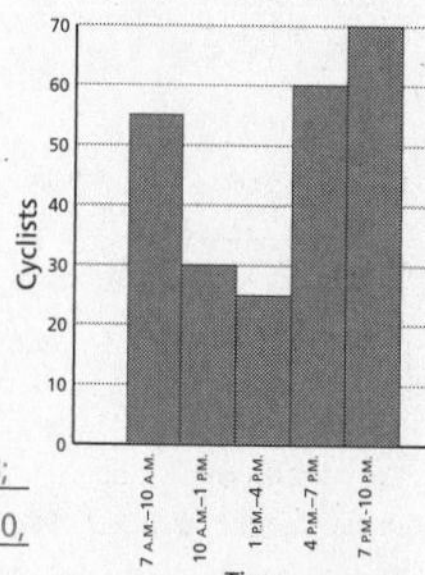

2. During which time period was the trail the most crowded? the least crowded?

7 P.M.–10 P.M.; 1 P.M.–4 P.M.

3. Can you tell how many cyclists were on the trail at 5:00 P.M.? Explain.

No; the histogram shows data for intervals of time, not individual times.

4. On another day, 3 more cyclists were on the trail at 8 A.M., 5 fewer were on at 2:00 P.M., and 10 more were on at 5:30 P.M. How would the histogram for this day be different?

The 7 A.M.–10 A.M. bar would go up to 58; the 1 P.M.–4 P.M. bar would go down to 20, and the 4 P.M.–7 P.M. would go up to 70.

Use with Grade 5, Chapter 4, Lesson 5, pages 164–165. (112)

Reteach

Read and Make Histograms

R 4-5 RETEACH

Histograms are similar to bar graphs. They both use bars to display data, but the bars in a histogram are for intervals of data. There are no gaps between the bars of a histogram.

Hikers at Deer Creek Park

Age of Hikers	Number of Hikers
0–10	20
11–20	15
21–30	30
31–40	40
41–50	35

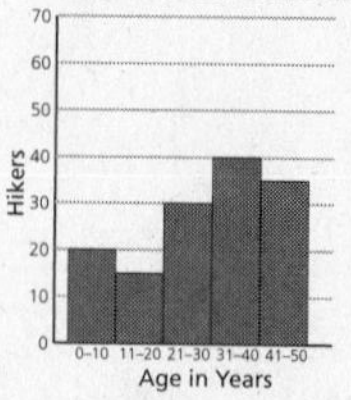

Check students' histograms.

Make a histogram to display the data.

Hikers at Deer Creek Park

Distance in Miles	Number of Hikers
0–3	50
4–6	35
7–9	25
10–12	10
13–15	20

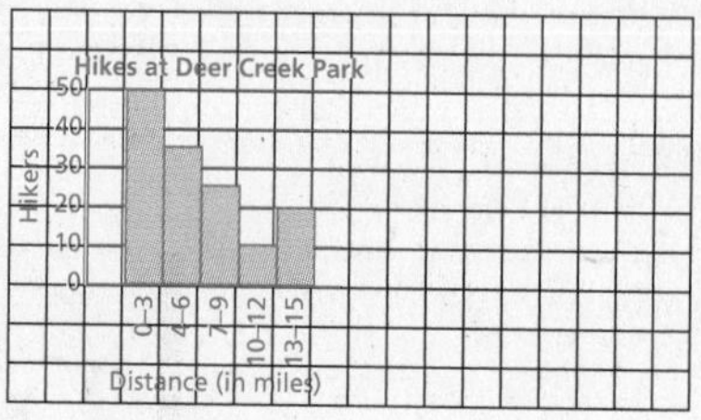

1. What length hike did most hikers take?

0–3 miles

2. How many people hiked 10–12 miles?

10 people

Use with Grade 5, Chapter 4, Lesson 5, pages 164–165. (113)

Enrich

Read and Make Histograms

E 4-5 ENRICH

TV Histogram

Mr. Wong's fifth-grade class recorded this data.

Minutes Spent Watching TV Yesterday

Student	Minutes	Student	Minutes
Jessica	40	Michael	75
Elizabeth	15	Franklin	90
Ben	30	Kara	60
Rosa	75	Lauren	120
Marc	135	Marie	180
Daniel	100	Lashonna	30
Tammy	0	Sean	120
Miguel	90	Corey	90
Jasmine	60	Brent	45
José	90	Ella	75

Complete this frequency table to organize the data above.

Minutes Watching TV Yesterday	Tally	Frequency
0–20	II	2
21–40	III	3
41–60	III	3
61–80	III	3
81–100	~~IIII~~	5
101–120	II	2
121–140	I	1
141–160		0
161–180	I	1

Make a histogram to display the data given in the table.

Check students' work.

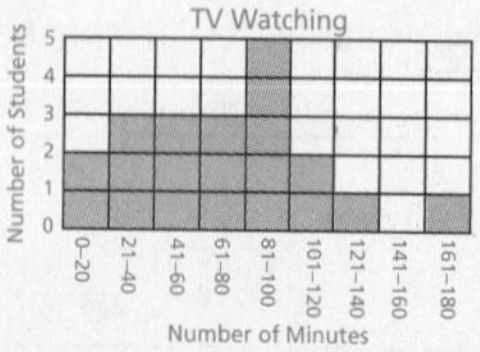

Use with Grade 5, Chapter 4, Lesson 5, pages 164–165. (114)

Daily Homework

4-5 Read and Make Histograms

Use data from the histogram for problems 1–3.

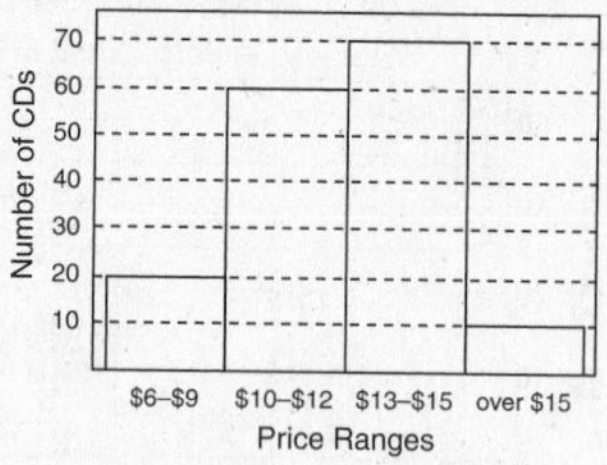

1. What was the most common price range for CDs sold this week? $13–15

2. What was the least common price range for CDs sold this week? over $15

3. How many CDs were sold this week at CD Land? 160

Problem Solving

4. Make a histogram for data in the table.

Ages of people at the park

Age	Number
0–14 years	18
15–29 years	24
30–44 years	6
45–60 years	10

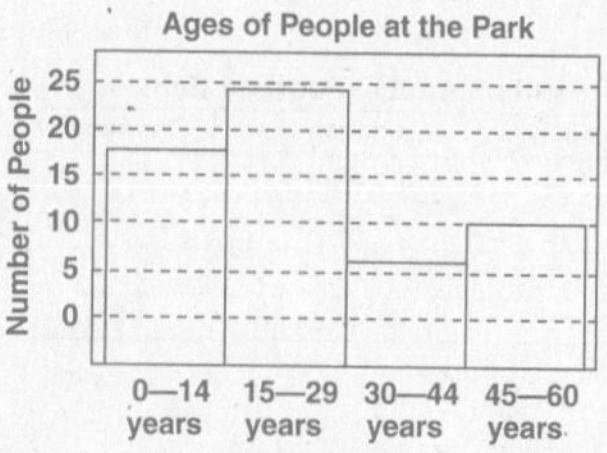

5. Why are the bars in a histogram touching and not separated?

The horizontal axis shows data ranges that are continuous.

Spiral Review

Order from least to greatest

6. 0.345, 3.456, 0.0345, 34.5, 0.3451 — .0345, .345, .3451, 3.456, 34.5

7. 1.01, 1.015, 1.035, 10.35, 0.13, 0.1 — 0.1, 0.13, 1.01, 1.015, 1.035, 10.35

Grade 5, Chapter 4, Lesson 5, Cluster A 35

Chapter 4 ~ Lesson 6

Practice

Read and Make Line Graphs

P 4-6 PRACTICE

Use the coordinate grid to name each ordered pair.

1. A (7, 3) 2. B (1, 8)
3. C (4, 4) 4. D (3, 0)
5. E (6, 5) 6. F (2, 9)

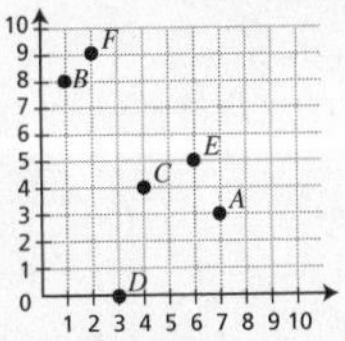

7. Make a line graph to display the data in the table. Graphs may vary. Check students' graphs.

Beth's Airplane Trips

Years	Number of Trips
1995	2
1996	3
1997	7
1998	7
1999	5
2000	6

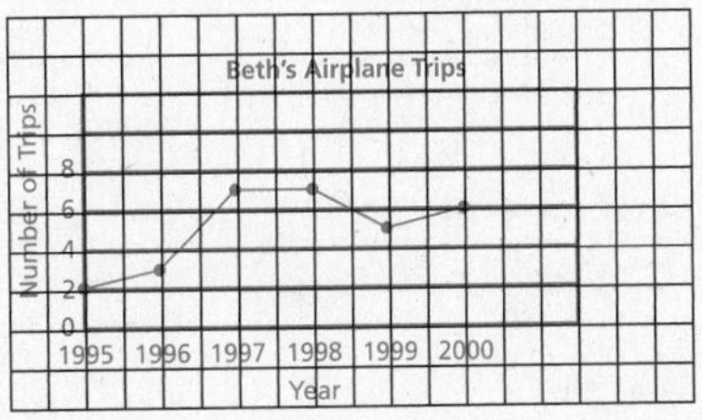

Use the graph at the right for exercises 8–10.

8. During how many years did the Martins travel more than 7 days?
4 years

9. In which years did the number of travel days increase?
1995–1997

10. In which years did the number of travel days decrease?
1998–2000

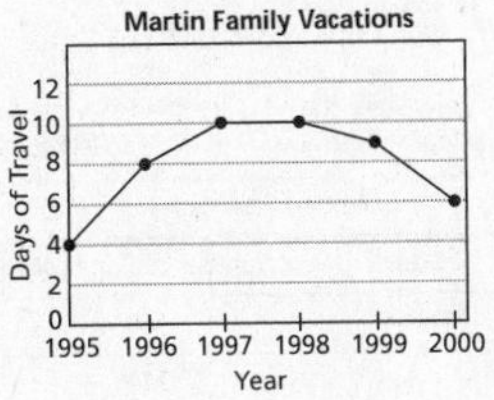

Use with Grade 5, Chapter 4, Lesson 6, pages 166–169. (115)

Reteach

Read and Make Line Graphs

R 4-6 RETEACH

You can use a line graph to show how a quantity changes over time. This graph shows Ricky's height over five years. To make a line graph, plot points to represent the data. Then draw a line to connect the points.

Ricky's Height

Year	Height (in inches)
1996	46
1997	47
1998	49
1999	52
2000	56

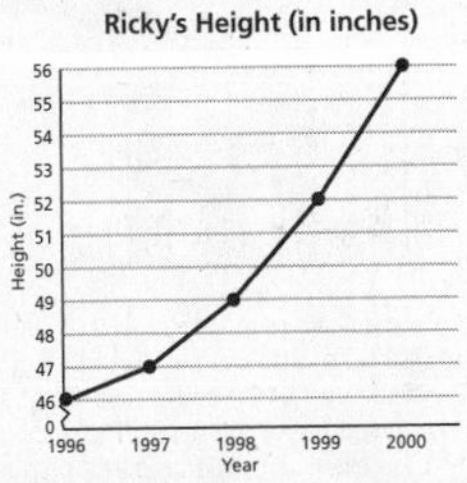

Marie grew pumpkins. The table shows the weight gain in pounds of one pumpkin. Make a line graph to display the data. Use the line graph to solve the problems. Check students' line graphs.

Marie's Pumpkin

Month	Weight (in pounds)
1	$\frac{1}{2}$
2	1
3	3
4	6
5	$8\frac{1}{2}$
6	9
7	9

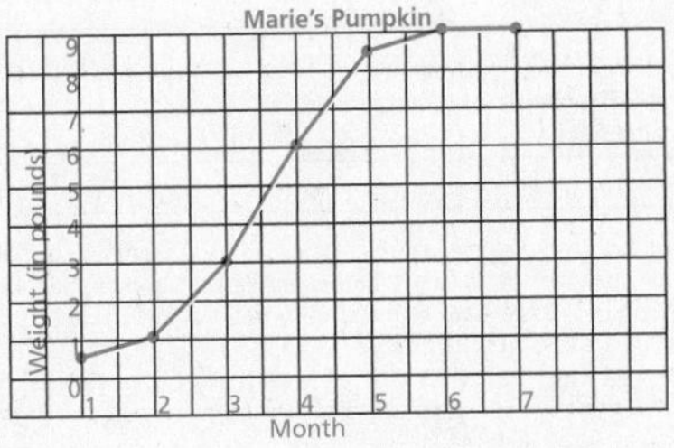

1. On a line graph, a line that rises shows that a quantity is increasing. In which months did Marie's pumpkin gain the most weight?
months 3 and 4

2. On a line graph, a line that is horizontal shows that a quantity stays the same. In which month did the weight of the pumpkin stay the same?
month 7

Use for Grade 5, Chapter 4, Lesson 6, pages 166–169. (116)

Enrich

Read and Make Line Graphs

E 4-6 ENRICH

Weather Week

The ordered pairs show high and low temperatures in degrees Fahrenheit in Amherst, MA, from Sunday through Saturday.

(74, 52) (70, 50) (50, 46) (73, 36) (68, 42) (66, 45) (66, 52)

Make a double-line graph to show this data. Graphs may vary depending upon scale used. Possible graph is shown.

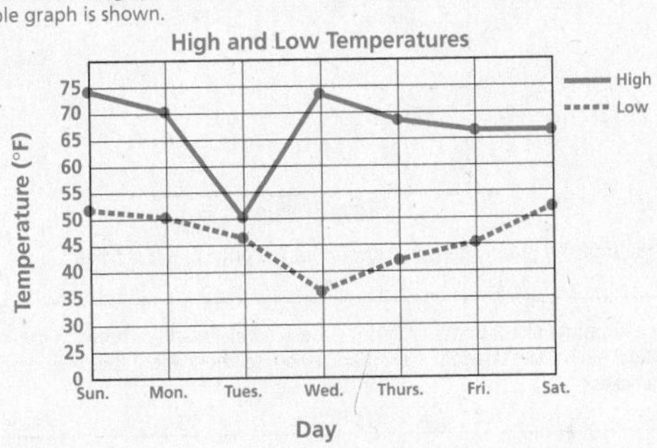

Use your completed graph to answer these questions.

1. Which day had the greatest difference between high and low temperature?
Wednesday

2. Which day had the least difference between the high and low temperature?
Tuesday

3. Write a statement to describe the temperatures for the week.
Answers may vary. Possible answer: The temperature fell, and then it quickly got warmer.

4. When a cold front passes, there is often rain followed by a noticeable drop in temperature. On which day did a cold front pass through Amherst?
Tuesday

Use with Grade 5, Chapter 4, Lesson 6, pages 166–169. (117)

Daily Homework

4-6 Read and Make Line Graphs

Tell how many units to the right and up you would move for each coordinate pair.

1. (6, 3) 6 right, 3 up 2. (5, 2) 5 right, 2 up
3. (4, 6) 4 right, 6 up 4. (0, 3) 0 right, 3 up
5. (6, 0) 6 right, 0 up 6. (8, 8) 8 right, 8 up

Use the coordinates to name each ordered pair.

7. A (2, 1)
8. B (3, 9)
9. C (8, 3)
10. D (3, 5)
11. E (8, 8)
12. F (5, 3)
13. G (6, 6)
14. H (1, 9)

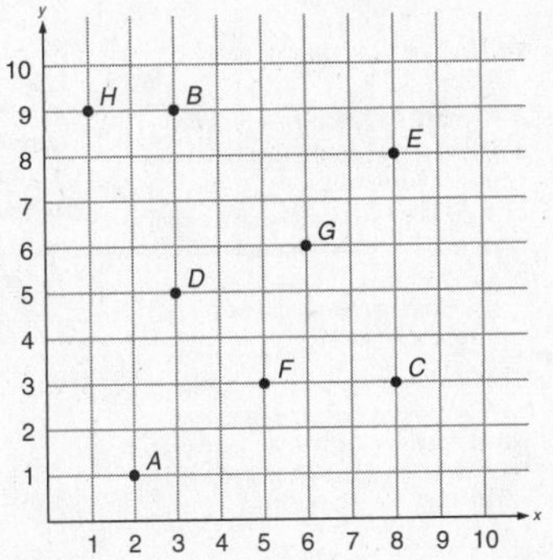

Problem Solving

15. An airplane leaves an airport at (2,7). It lands 6 units east of that point. What are its new coordinates? (8, 7)

16. A pilot leaves an airport at (4, 2) and files to (4, 9). In what direction is she flying? north

Spiral Review

17. 3(6 + 2) = 24 18. 4(7 + 0) = 28
19. 5(4 + 4) = 40 20. 8 (6 + 2) = 64

36 Grade 5, Chapter 4, Lesson 6, Cluster A

Chapter 4 ~ Lesson 7

Practice

Problem Solving: Reading for Math
Change Scales

P 4-7 PRACTICE Reading Skill

Use data from the graphs to solve.

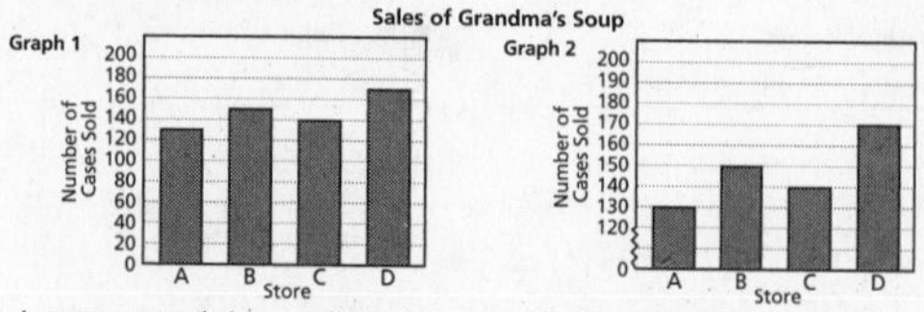

1. A grocery store chain owns Stores A, B, C, and D. The owner of the stores wants to distribute extra cases of Grandma's Soup based on last month's sales. The distributor of the soups says that there are only 100 extra cases available to distribute to the stores. The manager of Store D says that the majority of his clients are older people who purchase a lot of soup. He wants to have 40 extra cases delivered to his store and let the other stores receive 20 extra cases each. Which graph do you think he would show to the owner to convince her to fill the order for his store? Explain.
   Graph 2 because the sales look much greater for Store D.
2. Explain why the two graphs look different although they both show the same data.
   The scales are different. Graph 2 has a broken scale on the vertical axis so that sales look much greater for Store D than for the other stores.
3. The soups were so popular that each store sold its entire stock. All of the store managers want to get more cases. Which graph do you think the manager of Store A would prefer to show the owner to get a more equal share of the extra cases of soup? Explain.
   Graph 1, because sales look about the same at all of the stores.
4. If you were the owner of the stores, how would you distribute the extra cases of soup? Explain.
   Answers may vary. Possible answer: I would use Graph I to make my decision and give each store 25 extra cases since they all sold out.

Use with Grade 5, Chapter 4, Lesson 7, pages 170–171. (118)

Practice

Problem Solving: Reading for Math
Change Scales

P 4-7 PRACTICE Math Skills Test Prep

Choose the best answer.

The graphs show the change in the cost of Grandma's Soup from 1995–2000.

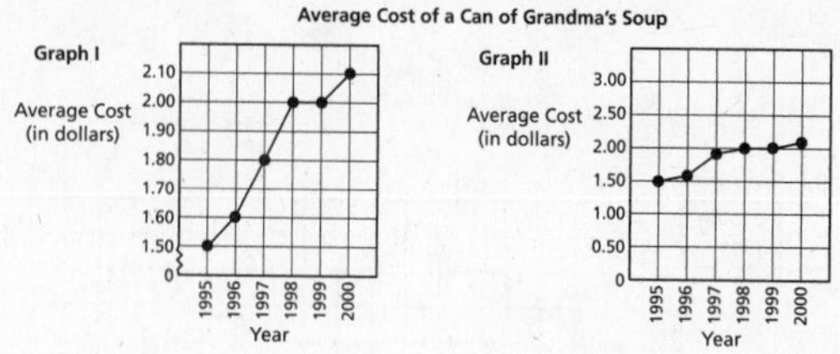

1. Which of the following statements is NOT true?
   - **A** The price of the soup did not change from 1998–1999.
   - **B** Soup prices increased from 1995–1998.
   - **(C)** Prices of the soup rose dramatically from 1995–2000.
   - **D** The average cost of a can of Grandma's soup in 2000 was $2.10.
2. What should you keep in mind when you interpret a graph with a break in the scale?
   - **F** It may be dramatic.
   - **(G)** It may be misleading.
   - **H** It may look convincing.
   - **J** The scale is not important.

A grocery-store chain records the following sales of canned fruit at each of its four stores for a week. They collect the following data.

Canned Fruit Sales	
Store	**Number of Cans Sold**
A	168
B	212
C	188
D	193

3. Suppose you wanted to graph the data. You want to make the number of cans sold at store B seem much greater than the number sold at all the other stores. What could you do to make a convincing bar graph?
   - **A** Use large intervals.
   - **B** Do not emphasize the differences.
   - **(C)** Include a break in the scale.
   - **D** Use intervals of 50.

Use with Grade 5, Chapter 4, Lesson 7, pages 170–171. (119)

Practice

Problem Solving: Reading for Math
Change Scales

P 4-7 PRACTICE Math Skills Test Prep

Choose the best answer.

A bus company records the number of passengers along each route. They are considering adding more buses to each route.

Bus Line	
Route	**Number of Passengers**
Northeast	2,800
Northwest	2,300
North	2,400

4. Which of the following statements is NOT true?
   - **A** At least 2,000 people use each route.
   - **B** More people take the Northeast route than the other routes.
   - **C** About 400 fewer people use the North route than use the Northeast route.
   - **(D)** About 100 more people use the Northwest route than use the North route.
5. Suppose small intervals are used to graph the data about the bus routes. How will the differences in the data appear?
   - **F** Less different.
   - **G** Somewhat different.
   - **H** No different.
   - **(J)** Very different.

Use data from the chart above for problem 6. Graphs will vary. Sample graph:

6. The bus company has ordered six new buses. You think each route should get two new buses. Make a bar graph that will support your argument.

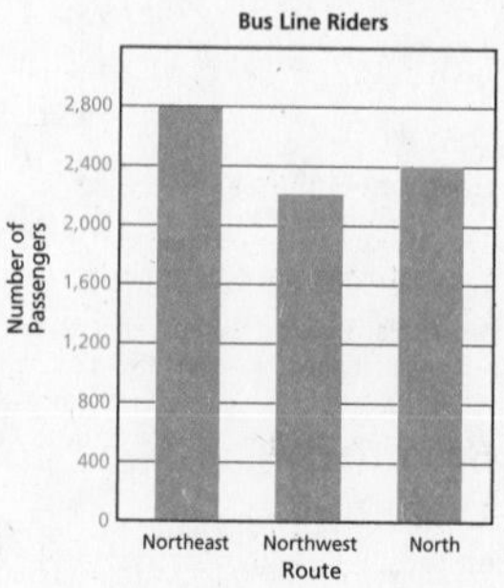

Use your graph for problems 7–8.

7. Explain why your graph supports your argument. Answers may vary. Possible answer: The difference between the number of passengers along each route is not very great.
8. Explain how you made the graph look more convincing. Answers may vary. Possible answer: I used small intervals on the graph.

Use with Grade 5, Chapter 4, Lesson 7, pages 170–171. (120)

Daily Homework

4-7 Problem Solving: Reading for Math
Change Scales

Use data from the graph for problems 1–4.

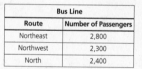

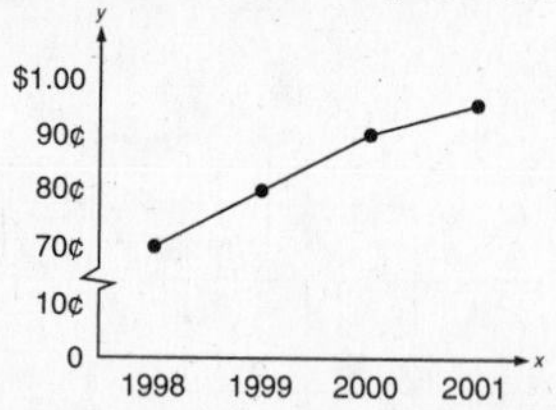

1. What does the graph seem to show about the price of a bus ticket?
   The price seems to have risen sharply from 1998 to 2001.
2. On a separate sheet of paper, redraw the graph without the break in the vertical axis. What does the new graph seem to show about the price of a bus ticket?
   The price rose, but the size of the increase seems relatively smaller.
3. On another sheet of paper, redraw the graph again, keeping the vertical axis interval distance the same but using 5¢ intervals instead of 10¢ intervals. How does this new graph compare with the one you just drew?
   It seems to show an even shaper rise in the bus ticket price.
4. Suppose you wanted to show that the price of a bus ticket hardly changed during 1998–2001. How would you change the vertical axis interval distance of the original graph? You would shorten the interval distance.

Spiral Review

5. 0.36 + 23 = 23.36
6. 2.368 + 4.08 = 6.448
7. 873.7 + 19.48 = 893.18
8. 0.43 + 5 + 4.6 = 10.03

Grade 5, Chapter 4, Lesson 7, Cluster A 37

Chapter 4 ~ Lesson 8

Practice

Problem Solving: Strategy
Make a Graph

P 4-8 PRACTICE

For problems 1–4, choose the graph that best displays the data. Explain.

1. The number of walking shoes, running shoes, tennis shoes, and soccer shoes sold in a shoe store.
   A line graph B bar graph
   B; because the data does not show change over time

2. The types of sports balls men and women buy in a sports store over a three-month period.
   C histogram D double-bar graph
   D; because two related sets of data are compared

3. **Measurement** Daily high and low temperatures recorded for a week.
   A double-line graph
   B double-bar graph
   A; because the data shows a double set of data changing over time

4. **Music** The favorite composers of the members of a music society.
   C pictograph D histogram
   C; because both sets of data are not numerical, so a histogram will not work

Mixed Strategy Review
Solve. Use any strategy.

5. After buying supplies, Enrico has $11 left. He bought 3 boxes of pens for $5 each and 2 boxes of paper for $18 each. He also bought a cartridge that cost $23. How much money did Enrico have before buying the supplies?
   $85
   Strategy: Work Backward

6. **Art** A sculptor has a piece of wood that is 10 feet long. She wants to cut the wood into sections that are 2.5 feet long. How many cuts will she have to make? How many sections will she have?
   3 cuts, 4 sections
   Strategy: Draw a Diagram

7. Julia and Natalie spent a total of $9.75 for lunch. Julia spent $0.75 more than Natalie. How much did each girl spend for lunch?
   Natalie: $4.50, Julia: $5.25
   Strategy: Guess and Check

8. **Create a problem** in which you must choose the graph that best displays a set of data. Share it with others.
   Check students' problems.

Use with Grade 5, Chapter 4, Lesson 8, pages 174–175. (121)

Reteach

Problem Solving: Strategy
Make a Graph

R 4-8 RETEACH

Page 169, Problem 1

Choose the graph that best displays the data: number of paintings by men, number of paintings by women at a museum. Explain.

Step 1 Read

Be sure you understand the problem.
Read carefully.

What do you know?
- Number of paintings by men at the museum.
- Number of paintings by women at the museum.

What do you need to find?
- The graph that best displays the data

Step 2 Plan

- Find a Pattern
- Guess and Check
- Work Backward
- Make a Graph
- Make a Table
- Write an Equation
- Make an Organized List
- Draw a Diagram
- Solve a Simpler Problem
- Logical Reasoning

Make a plan.
Choose a strategy.

Making a graph will help you solve the problem.

Decide which graph best represents the data. Think of the types of graphs with which you are familiar. Choose a bar graph, double-bar graph, histogram, line graph, line plot, or pictograph. Think about how each type of graph is used to display data.

Use with Grade 5, Chapter 4, Lesson 8, pages 174–175. (122)

Reteach

Problem Solving: Strategy
Make a Graph

R 4-8 RETEACH

Step 3 Solve

Carry out your plan.

Since no data exists between dates of the paintings, the data does not show change over time.

So, you can't use a line graph.

You can't use numbers on both axes, so a line plot or a histogram would not be good choices.

The data compares one set of data (the number of paintings by men and the number of paintings by women), so you wouldn't use a double-bar graph.

A good choice for representing the data is a bar graph or pictograph.

Step 4 Look Back

Is the solution reasonable?
Reread the problem.

What other graph could you use to display the data?
pictograph or bar graph

Practice
Choose the graph that best displays the data. Explain.

1. Two schools held book fairs recently. Each book fair lasted four days. Attendance at the fairs was recorded each day for both of the schools.
   A double-bar graph
   B double-line graph
   A; because two related sets of data are compared.

2. A table shows the number of homes and the selling price of homes in a neighborhood.
   C bar graph D histogram
   D; because both sets of data are numerical.

Use with Grade 5, Chapter 4, Lesson 8, pages 174–175. (123)

Daily Homework

4-8 Problem Solving: Strategy
Make a Graph

For problems 1–4, choose the graph that best displays the data. Explain your choice.

1. Hours of sunlight each day for a month
   A. line graph **B.** bar graph
   A; a line graph is a good choice to show change over time.

2. Number of shoes owned by each of five students
   A. line graph **B.** pictograph
   B; a pictograph is a good choice to show numbers of the same kind of item.

3. Number of students of different ages in a middle school
   A. histogram **B.** double bar graph
   A; a histogram is a good choice to show groups in distinct categories.

Mixed Strategy Review

Use data from the table for problems 4–5.

Water Depth at Different Times of Day in Boston Harbor

Time	Water Depth (feet)
12:00	10
1:00	12
2:00	13.5
3:00	15
4:00	17
5:00	20
6:00	21

4. What is the best type of graph to display the data in the table? Explain.
   A line graph is the best way to show changes over time.

5. Does water depth increase at an equal rate?
   No; increase in water depth varies from hour to hour

Spiral Review

6. 8.432 – 2.4 = 6.032
7. 12.62 – 4.354 = 8.266
8. 8 – 2.352 = 5.648
9. 17.863 – 16.9 = 0.963

38 Grade 5, Chapter 4, Lesson 8, Cluster B

Chapter 4 ~ Lesson 9

Practice

Read and Make Stem-and-Leaf Plots

P 4-9 PRACTICE

1. The table shows the amount of milk some fifth graders drank in one day. Show the data in a stem-and-leaf plot.

Amount of Milk We Drink in One Day (in ounces)

Student	Ounces	Student	Ounces
Sam	8	Wendi	36
Keiko	32	Van	28
Tonya	24	Sue	32
Sean	12	Marc	21
Phil	20	Anna	32

Milk Drunk in One Day

Stem	Leaves
0	8
1	2
2	0 1 4 8
3	2 2 2 6

Key: 1 | 2 means 12 ounces

Use data from the stem-and-leaf plot at the right for exercises 2–7.

Stem	Leaves
4	7 8 8 9 9
5	2 4 4 5 7 7 7 8 9 9
6	0 0 1 3

Key: 4 | 7 means 47 inches

2. How many students' heights were measured? 19 students
3. How many students are taller than 56 inches? 10 students
4. What is the height of the tallest student? 63 inches
5. What is the mode of the students' heights? 57 inches
6. What is the range of the students' heights? 16 inches
7. What is the median student height? 57 inches

Use for Grade 5, Chapter 4, Lesson 9, pages 176–177. (124)

Reteach

Read and Make Stem-and-Leaf Plots

R 4-9 RETEACH

In a **stem-and-leaf plot**, each piece of data is listed. The leaves are the ones digits, and the stems are the digits to the left of the ones digits.

Time It Takes Students to Get to School

Stems	Leaves
1	0 2 5 9
2	1 1 2 4 5 5
3	1 2 7 8
4	4

This 3 means 30. → 3 ; 1 2 7 8 ← This 8 means 8.

Key: 3 | 8 means 38 minutes

Use the stem-and-leaf plot above to solve these problems.

1. In a stem-and-leaf plot, there is one leaf for every piece of data. How many students' travel times are displayed? 15 students
2. What times are shown in the stem-and-leaf plot? 10, 12, 15, 19, 21, 21, 22, 24, 25, 25, 31, 32, 37, 38, and 44 minutes
3. How many students take less than 15 minutes to get to school? 2 students
4. How many students take more than 30 minutes to get to school? 5 students
5. To find the range of travel times, find the difference between the greatest and the least times. What is the range of travel times? 34 minutes
6. To find the mode of the travel times, find the time(s) that occur(s) most often. What is the mode of the travel times? 21 and 25 minutes
7. To find the median of the travel times, find the time in the middle. What is the median of the travel times? 24 minutes

Use with Grade 5, Chapter 4, Lesson 9, pages 176–177. (125)

Enrich

Read and Make Stem-and-Leaf Plots
School Days

E 4-9 ENRICH

This table shows how many days students attend Bayside School each month. Make a stem-and-leaf plot to show the data. Remember to write a title and a key.

Number of Days of School Each Month

Month	Days of School
September	17
October	21
November	20
December	15
January	19
February	19
March	18
April	22
May	21
June	8

Number of Days of School Each Month

Stem	Leaves
0	8
1	5 7 8 9 9
2	0 1 1 2

Key: 1|5 means 15 days.

Find the range, mode, median, and mean of the data.

Range: 14 Mode: 19 and 21

Median: 19 Mean: 18

You have learned to display data in pictographs, bar graphs, histograms, and line graphs. Use a piece of grid paper to display the data given in the table and your stem-and-leaf plot in one of these types of graphs. Check students' work.

Which type of graph did you choose? Why? Answers may vary.

Use with Grade 5, Chapter 4, Lesson 9, pages 176–177. (126)

Daily Homework

4-9 Read and Make Stem-and-Leaf Plots

Use data from this stem-and-leaf plot for problems 1–6.

Number of Minutes Spent in a Grocery Store by Shoppers

stems	leaves
3	4 4 6 6 9 9
2	5 5 5 6 8 8 8
1	1 5 7 7 9
0	5 8 9

1. What is the range of time spent in the store? 34 minutes
2. What is the least amount of time spent in the store? 5 minutes
3. How many shoppers are represented in the stem-and-leaf plot? 21 shoppers
4. What is the total number of shopping minutes represented? 504 minutes
5. What was the mean of time spent shopping? 24 minutes
6. What was the median time spent shopping? 25 minutes

Problem Solving

Sunny Days in a Year	
January	8
February	12
March	18
April	16
May	22
June	26
July	27
August	23
September	18
October	21
November	10
December	12

7. On a separate sheet of paper, make a stem-and-leaf plot of the following data. Check students' work.
8. Alice watered her garden twice on every sunny day during the year shown. How many times did she water her garden? 426 times

Spiral Review

Give the range, median, mean, and mode for the following.

9. 12, 15, 13, 15, 11, 10, 8
range: 7, median: 12, mean: 12, mode: 15
10. 7, 4, 6, 12, 4, 4, 6, 7, 8
range: 8, median: 6, mean: 6.4, mode: 4

Grade 5, Chapter 4, Lesson 9, Cluster B 39

Chapter 4 ~ Lesson 10

Practice

Sampling

4-10 PRACTICE

Name each population and sample.

1. Survey all the fifth graders in your school to find how many students in your school watch a certain TV show.
   Population: all students in school Sample: all fifth graders
2. Survey every third fifth grader who enters the school to find the most popular TV actor among fifth graders.
   Population: all fifth graders Sample: every third fifth grader
3. Survey Mr. Myers's class to find how many hours a day most people in town watch TV.
   Population: town Sample: Mr. Myers's class
4. Survey customers in an appliance store to find how many TVs most people in town own.
   Population: town store Sample: customers in appliance store

A researcher wants to find which TV station's news is the most popular in your town. Tell whether or not each sample is a random sample and whether or not each sample is representative.

5. A survey of all people who visit the zoo on one day.
   not random, not representative
6. A survey of every tenth household from the telephone book.
   random; representative
7. A survey of every fifth person who buys a newspaper at a newspaper stand.
   not random, not representative

Problem Solving

Brandon wants to find out how many students in his school must finish their homework before watching TV.

8. He surveys all the students in the cafeteria during his lunch period. Is the sample a random sample? Explain.
   No; only students who have lunch at a certain time are surveyed.
9. Suggest whom Brandon could survey to have a random, representative survey.
   Answers may vary. Possible answer: Ask every fifth student from a list of all students in the school.

Use with Grade 5, Chapter 4, Lesson 10, pages 178–181. (127)

Reteach

Sampling

4-10 RETEACH

Suppose you want to find out what type of movie is the favorite of most students in your school. The **population**, or group you want information about, is the students in your school. Instead of surveying all the students, you could survey a **sample**, or part of the students.

If the sample you survey represents all the students, the sample is representative.

Representative: Every tenth student who enters the school
Some students in each grade are surveyed. Boys and girls are surveyed. Students with different interests are surveyed.

Not representative: All the fifth graders
Only one age of students is surveyed.

If each person in the population has an equal chance of being surveyed, the sample is random.

Random: Every fifth student on an alphabetical list of the school.
Every student has an equal chance of being surveyed.

Not random: All students who went to a movie last weekend.
Students who didn't go to a movie do not have a chance of being surveyed.

Name the population and sample for each. Then answer the question.

1. Lauren wants to know how many students in her school plan to see the new science fiction movie opening this weekend. She surveyed every fifth student as they left school on Friday.
   Population: students in Lauren's school
   Sample: every fifth student leaving the school
   Is this sample representative? Explain.
   Yes; all different ages and types of students are surveyed.
2. Andrew wants to know how many people who saw *Space Travel 3000* liked it. He surveyed every tenth person who came out of one theater after the 8:00 show.
   Population: people who saw *Space Travel 3000*
   Sample: every tenth person who came out of the 8:00 show
   Is this sample random? Explain.
   No; people who saw the movie at other theaters or at different times did not have a chance to be surveyed.

Use with Grade 5, Chapter 4, Lesson 10, pages 178–181. (128)

Enrich

Sampling
Sample Scramble

4-10 ENRICH

Circle the letter of the phrase that describes the population and the letter of the phrase that describes the sample. Unscramble the circled letters to spell a word. Population

1. At a band concert, survey 100 people to find out whether people in your town prefer vocal or instrumental music.

Population	Sample
(P.) people in your town	I. 100 band members
D. 100 concert-goers	G. people in your town
O. band members	(T.) 100 concert-goers

2. Survey 10 band members to find out how long band members practice each day.

Population	Sample
C. 10 band members	U. all band members
Q. all students in school	(O.) 10 band members
(I.) all band members	Y. all students in school

3. Survey every 10th person in a phone directory to find out if adults in one city prefer concerts, plays, or movies.

Population	Sample
W. all adults with phones	(A.) every 10th adult in phone directory
(O.) all adults in one city	L. all adults with phones
H. every 10th person in phone directory	W. all adults in one city

4. During band practice, survey all drummers to find out if fifth graders prefer playing brass, woodwind, string, or percussion instruments.

Population	Sample
I. drummers	C. band members
(B.) band members	T. fifth graders
P. fifth graders	(L.) drummers

5. In a school of 600 students, survey every 5th student entering the cafeteria to find out how many students have attended a concert.

Population	Sample
(U.) 600 students	B. 5 students
F. 5 students	(N.) every 5th student entering the cafeteria
G. every 5th student entering the cafeteria	H. 600 students

Use with Grade 5, Chapter 4, Lesson 10, pages 178–181. (129)

Daily Homework

4-10 Sampling

Name each population and sample.

1. Survey ten players on the soccer team about their favorite shoes.
   population: soccer team; sample: 10 players
2. Survey 100 students out of a school with 633 students.
   population: 633 students in a school; sample: 100 students
3. Survey 20 people in the school band about their favorite music.
   population: band members; sample: 20 people

A researcher wants to find out what type of backpack is the most popular at a school. Tell whether or not each sample is a random sample. Is it a representative sample? Explain.

4. The researcher talks to every tenth student on a list of all the students in the school. Random, representative, every student has an equal chance of being surveyed.
5. The researcher talks to the students who signed up to be interviewed.
   Not random, not representative; only students who signed up are included in the survey.

Problem Solving

6. Jim surveys 64 people. Jill surveys 112 people. How many times more people did Jill survey?
   1.75 times more
7. A survey reveals that 35 students rode their bikes to school in March. In May, 54 students rode their bikes to school. How many more students rode their bikes in May than in March?
   19

Spiral Review

8. $4 - 2.135 =$ 1.865
9. $6.2 \times 7.004 =$ 43.4248
10. $1.3 + 0.794 + 12.005 =$ 14.099
11. $12{,}000 \div 4.8 =$ 2,500

40 Grade 5, Chapter 4, Lesson 10, Cluster B

Chapter 4 ~ Lesson 11

Part A Worksheet

Problem Solving: Application

Make a decision based on information in graphs

Part A 4-11 WORKSHEET Decision Making

Use the table below to help you record your observations from the graphs. Look for patterns or trends in the data. Then use the information to help you make your decision.

Years	Change in the number of museum visitors
1996–1997	down 50
1997–1998	up 100
1998–1999	up 125
1999–2000	up 25

Years	Change in the museum budget
1996–1997	up $3,000
1997–1998	up $2,000
1998–1999	up $3,000
1999–2000	up $2,000

You may use the table below to record any other observations from the graphs that you think will help you make your decision.

Your Decision

As a member of the town council, you must vote to increase the budget for the Oakdale Inventor's Museum by $3,000, decrease the museum's budget by $3,000, or leave the budget the same. How will you vote? Explain.

Answers may vary. Possible answer: I would vote to leave the budget the same because the number of visitors to the museum only increased by 25 over the previous year.

Use with Grade 5, Chapter 4, Lesson 11, pages 182–183. (130)

Part B Worksheet

Problem Solving: Application

Can wind be used to predict the weather?

Part B 4-11 WORKSHEET Math & Science

Reminder:

Wind *direction* means the wind comes from the NORTH, SOUTH, EAST, or WEST. A compass may help you decide the wind direction.

Use the following terms to describe the wind *strength*: NONE, LOW, MEDIUM, STRONG.

Record your data and predictions in the table below.

Day	Wind Direction	Wind Strength	Prediction For Next Day	Actual Weather Today
Monday				
Tuesday				
Wednesday				
Thursday				
Friday				
Monday				
Tuesday				
Wednesday				
Thursday				
Friday				

1. Explain how you decided the direction from which the wind was coming.
   Answers may vary. Possible answer: with a compass.

Use with Grade 5, Chapter 4, Lesson 11, pages 184–185. (131)

Part B Worksheet

Problem Solving: Application

Can wind be used to predict the weather?

Part B 4-11 WORKSHEET Math & Science

2. Explain how you decided to record the wind strength for the day.
   Answers may vary. Possible answer: By checking how the ribbon was fluttering in the wind.
3. Did you make your observations at the same time each day? Do you think it is important to record the data at the same time each day to predict the weather?
   Answers may vary.
4. How many times did you correctly predict the weather? Did your predictions get better as you thought about changing wind directions?
   Answers may vary.
5. Do you think you were reasonably successful at predicting the weather? Explain.
   Answers may vary.
6. Were you able to discover any patterns? Explain.
   Answers may vary.
7. How do your predictions compare to the predictions of your classmates? Who was more successful? Why do you think this is so?
   Answers may vary.
8. Can you predict the weather using wind? Explain.
   Answers may vary.
9. In addition to wind, what other weather phenomena might help you to better predict the weather?
   Answers may vary. Possible answers: temperature, humidity, air pressure

Use with Grade 5, Chapter 4, Lesson 11, pages 184–185. (132)

Chapter 5 ~ Lesson 1

Practice

Divisibility

P 5-1 PRACTICE

Of 2, 3, 5, 6, 9, and 10, list which numbers each number is divisible by.

1. 87 3
2. 96 2, 3, 6
3. 140 2, 5, 10
4. 423 3, 9
5. 824 2
6. 517 none
7. 210 2, 3, 5, 6, 10
8. 675 3, 5, 9
9. 1,293 3
10. 8,340 2, 3, 5, 6, 10
11. 4,095 3, 5, 9
12. 50,006 2
13. 20,304 2, 3, 6, 9
14. 86,420 2, 5, 10
15. 135,952 2
16. 300,480 2, 3, 5, 6, 10
17. 8,550 2, 3, 5, 6, 9, 10
18. 891,235 5
19. 20 2, 5, 10
20. 1,592 2
21. 69,360 2, 3, 5, 6,10
22. 9,999 3, 9
23. 36,521 none
24. 89,745 3, 5
25. 2 2
26. 897,421 none

Problem Solving

27. The school band has 130 members. They can march in rows of 5, 6, or 9 members each. Which should the conductor choose if she wants the same number of members in each row?
rows of 5

28. The school chorus has 80 members. They can stand on the stage in rows of 6, 9, or 10. How should the conductor arrange them to have the same number of members in each row?
rows of 10

Use with Grade 5, Chapter 5, Lesson 1, pages 200–201. (133)

Reteach

Divisibility

R 5-1 RETEACH

A number is divisible by another number if the quotient is a whole number and there is no remainder. You can use rules to find out if one number is divisible by another without actually dividing.

Divisibility Rules

Rule	Example
A whole number is divisible by 2 if its ones digit is 0, 2, 4, 6, or 8.	84 is divisible by 2. The ones digit is 4.
A whole number is divisible by 3 if the sum of its digits is divisible by 3.	207 is divisible by 3. $2 + 0 + 7 = 9$, and 9 is divisible by 3.
A whole number is divisible by 5 if its ones digit is 0 or 5.	1,425 is divisible by 5. The ones digit is 5.
A whole number is divisible by 6 if it is divisible both by 2 and by 3.	726 is divisible by 6. $7 + 2 + 6 = 15$, and 15 is divisible by 3. The ones digit is 6, so 726 is divisible by 2.
A whole number is divisible by 9 if the sum of its digits is divisible by 9.	3,474 is divisible by 9. $3 + 4 + 7 + 4 = 18$, and 18 is divisible by 9.
A whole number is divisible by 10 if its ones digit is 0.	12,340 is divisible by 10. The ones digit is 0.

Look at the digit in the ones place. Tell whether the number is divisible by 2.

1. 78 yes 2. 112 yes 3. 423 no 4. 6,390 yes

Add the digits. Tell whether the number is divisible by 3.

5. 92 no 6. 57 yes 7. 381 yes 8. 5,264 no

Add the digits. Tell whether the number is divisible by 9.

9. 486 yes 10. 109 no 11. 7,677 yes 12. 2,078 no

Of 2, 3, 5, 6, 9, and 10, list which numbers each number is divisible by.

13. 84 2, 3, 6 14. 270 2, 3, 5, 6, 9, 10 15. 412 2
16. 6,225 3, 5 17. 151 none 18. 37,368 2, 3, 6, 9

Use with Grade 5, Chapter 5, Lesson 1, pages 200–201. (134)

Enrich

Divisibility
Missing Digits

E 5-1 ENRICH

Find the missing digit(s) that make each sentence true. Give all possible answers.

1. 3,24▢ is divisible by 5. 0, 5
2. 92▢ is divisible by 6. 4
3. 6,13▢ is divisible by 2. 0, 2, 4, 6, 8
4. 9 is a factor of 7,32▢. 6
5. 10 is a factor of 4,06▢. 0
6. 6,12▢ is divisible by 3. 0, 3, 6, 9
7. 8▢,630 is divisible by 9. 1
8. 2 is a factor of 321,05▢. 0, 2, 4, 6, 8
9. 3 is a factor of 100,3▢3. 2, 5, 8
10. 5 is a factor of 26,1▢0. any digit
11. 50,32▢ is divisible by 5 and 10. 0
12. 6 is a factor of ▢0,566. 1, 4, 7
13. 24,82▢ is divisible by 3 and 6. 2, 8
14. 47,▢18 is divisible by 2 and 3. 1, 4, 7
15. 9 and 10 are factors of 57,2▢0. 4
16. 21,54▢ is divisible by 5 and 6. 0
17. 10 is a factor of 73,▢20. any digit
18. 2 and 5 are factors of 4,35▢. 0
19. 220,36▢ is divisible by 5 and 9. 5
20. 2 and 9 are factors of 306,84▢. 6
21. 6 and 9 are factors of 16,▢34. 4
22. 792,3▢0 is divisible by 3 and 10. 0, 3, 6, 9
23. 3 and 5 are factors of 27,51▢. 0
24. 48,16▢ is divisible by 3 and 5. 5

Use with Grade 5, Chapter 5, Lesson 1, pages 200–201. (135)

Daily Homework

5-1 Divisibility

Of 2, 3, 5, 6, 9, and 10, list which numbers each of these numbers is divisible by.

1. 48 2, 3, 6
2. 72 2, 3, 6, 9
3. 90 2, 3, 5, 6, 9, 10
4. 180 2, 3, 5, 6, 9, 10
5. 200 2, 5, 10
6. 67 none
7. 12,531 3
8. 6,939 3, 9
9. 144 2, 3, 6, 9
10. 1,946 2
11. 4,635 3, 5, 9
12. 9,123 3
13. 2,001 3
14. 546 2, 3, 6
15. 440 2, 5, 10
16. 150 2, 3, 5, 6, 10
17. 720 2, 3, 5, 6, 9, 10
18. 684 2, 3, 6
19. 714 2, 3, 6
20. 406 2

Problem Solving

21. The graduating class at Blaine High School has 328 members. They can sit in rows of 6, 8, or 12 at graduation. Which row size should they choose so that no student is left over? 8

22. Jennifer has baked 24 cookies. She plans to sell them in bags of 2, 3, or 5 cookies. What size bags can she use and not have any cookies left over? 2 or 3

Spiral Review

23. $8 - 2.37 =$ 5.63
24. $5.6 + 7.91 =$ 13.51
25. $12.9 - 4.65 =$ 8.25
26. $18.23 + 7.9 =$ 26.13
27. $3.4 - 0.63 =$ 2.77
28. $5.4 + 8.62 =$ 14.02
29. $29.7 - 3.62 =$ 26.08
30. $94.37 + 4.8 =$ 99.17

Grade 5, Chapter 5, Lesson 1, Cluster A 41

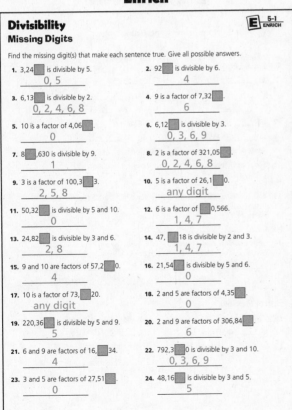

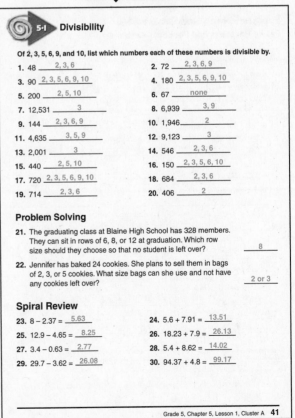

Chapter 5 ~ Lesson 2

Practice

Explore Primes and Composites

P 5-2 PRACTICE

Use a factor tree to find the prime factors of each number.

1. 48

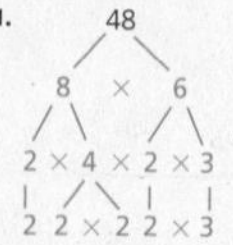

2. 56

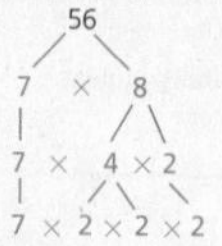

3. 36

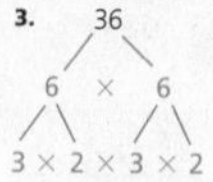

Write a prime factorization for each number. Use exponents. Tell if each number is prime or composite.

4. 64 $64 = 2^6$ composite
5. 45 $45 = 3^2 \times 5$ composite
6. 18 $18 = 3^2 \times 2$ composite
7. 23 $23 = 1 \times 23$ prime
8. 39 $39 = 3 \times 13$ composite
9. 55 $55 = 5 \times 11$ composite
10. 28 $28 = 2^2 \times 7$ composite
11. 79 $79 = 1 \times 79$ prime
12. 62 $62 = 2 \times 31$ composite
13. 97 $97 = 1 \times 97$ prime
14. 88 $88 = 2^3 \times 11$ composite
15. 49 $49 = 7^2$ composite

Problem Solving

16. There are 24 students in Mrs. Green's class. The number of boys and the number of girls are both prime numbers. There are 2 more boys than girls. How many boys and how many girls are in the class?
13 boys and 11 girls

17. There are 27 students in Mr. Lowell's class. The number of boys and the number of girls are both composite numbers. There are 3 more girls than boys. How many girls and how many boys are in the class?
15 girls and 12 boys

Use with Grade 5, Chapter 5, Lesson 2, pages 202–203. (136)

Reteach

Explore Primes and Composites

R 5-2 RETEACH

A **prime number** has exactly two factors, 1 and the number itself. A composite number has more than two factors. You can make a **factor tree** to help you find the prime factors of a composite number, or to tell whether a number is prime or composite.

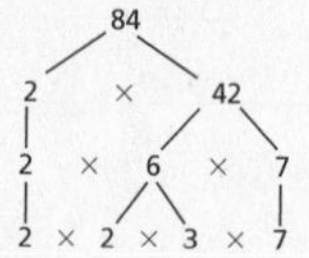

Write the number as a product of any two factors.
If a factor is not a prime number, rewrite it as the product of two factors.
If a factor is a prime number, leave it as it is.
Keep going until all the factors are prime numbers.

You can use exponents to write the prime factorization of a number.
$84 = 2 \times 2 \times 3 \times 7$
$84 = 2^2 \times 3 \times 7$

Complete the factor tree for each number. Then use exponents to write the prime factorization of the number. Factor trees may vary. Possible factor trees are shown.

1. 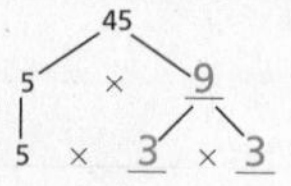
$45 = 5 \times 3^2$

2. 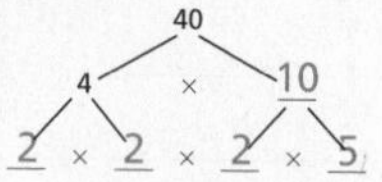
$40 = 2^3 \times 5$

3. 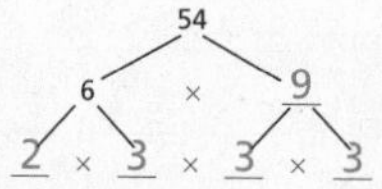
$54 = 2 \times 3^3$

4. 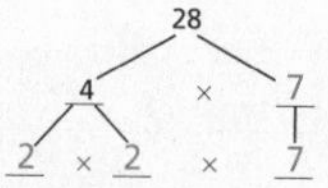
$28 = 2^2 \times 7$

Write the prime factorization for each number. Use exponents.

5. 44 $44 = 2^2 \times 11$
6. 56 $56 = 7 \times 2^3$
7. 75 $75 = 3 \times 5^2$
8. 32 $32 = 2^5$
9. 53 $53 = 1 \times 53$
10. 90 $90 = 2 \times 3^2 \times 5$

Use with Grade 5, Chapter 5, Lesson 2, pages 202–203. (137)

Enrich

Explore Primes and Composites
Prime Patterns and Perfect Numbers

E 5-2 ENRICH

Mathematicians have found interesting patterns among prime and composite numbers. Complete each table. See what pattern you find.

1.

Prime number	11	23	37	41	59	67	73	83	89	97
Remainder when divided by 6	5	5	1	5	5	1	1	5	5	1

2. What do you notice about remainders when prime numbers are divided by 6?
Remainders are either 1 or 5.

3. Try three prime numbers of your choice. Divide by 6. Does the pattern continue? Explain.
Yes; because the remainders are still 1 and 5.

4.

Prime number	11	23	37	41	59	67	73	83	89	97
Remainder when divided by 4	3	3	1	1	3	3	1	3	1	1

5. What do you notice about remainders when prime numbers are divided by 4?
Remainders are either 1 or 3.

6. Try three prime numbers of your choice. Divide by 4. Does the pattern continue? Explain.
Yes; because the remainders are still 1 and 3.

7. Find out if a similar pattern exists when dividing prime numbers by other 1-digit numbers. Make tables like those above to find out what happens when you divide by 3, by 5, by 7, by 8, and by 9. Describe your findings.
A similar pattern only seems to exist for division by 3. However, the remainders 1 and 2 are the only possible remainders when dividing by 3.

A **perfect number** is a composite number whose factors, not including the number itself, add up to the number. 6 is the first perfect number.

The factors of 6 and 1, 2, and 3. $6 = 1 + 2 + 3$

8. Find the next perfect number. Show the number as a sum of its factors.
$28 = 1 + 2 + 4 + 7 + 14$

Use with Grade 5, Chapter 5, Lesson 2, pages 202–203. (138)

Daily Homework

5-2 Explore Primes and Composites

Write a prime factorization for each number. Use exponents if you can. Tell if each number is prime or composite.

1. 20 $2^2 \times 5$; composite
2. 23 1×23; prime
3. 38 2×19; composite
4. 91 7×13; composite
5. 72 $2^3 \times 3^2$; composite
6. 125 5^3; composite
7. 40 $2^3 \times 5$; composite
8. 96 $2^5 \times 3$; composite
9. 53 1×53; prime
10. 54 2×3^3; composite
11. Use a factor tree to show the prime factorization of 60. $2^2 \times 3 \times 5$
12. Use a factor tree to show the prime factorization of 80. $2^4 \times 5$

Solve.

13. Jim is thinking of a number. He says that if he multiplies his number by 2, multiplies it by 2 again, and then multiplies it by 2 one more time, his answer will be 24. What number is he thinking of?
3

14. Frank wants to plant 24 tomato plants in rows of equal numbers of plants. What are three different ways he can plant his tomatoes in equal rows?
Answers may vary; possible answers: 2 rows of 12 plants, 3 rows of 8 plants, and 4 rows of 6 plants.

Spiral Review

15. $4(3 + 5) =$ 32
16. $5(6 +$ 3 $) = 45$
17. $4($ 4 $+ 3) = 28$
18. 8 $(4 + 5) = 72$
19. $6(5 +$ 3 $) = 48$
20. $3(7 + 2) =$ 27

42 Grade 5, Chapter 5, Lesson 2, Cluster A

Chapter 5 ~ Lesson 3

Practice

Common Factors and Greatest Common Factor

P 5-3 PRACTICE

Find the GCF of the numbers.

1. 10 and 15 5
2. 6 and 24 6
3. 16 and 36 4
4. 24 and 30 6
5. 9 and 21 3
6. 12 and 40 4
7. 8 and 28 4
8. 18 and 27 9
9. 12 and 60 12
10. 14 and 18 2
11. 20 and 30 10
12. 24 and 45 3
13. 27 and 30 3
14. 10 and 22 2
15. 12 and 36 12
16. 11 and 15 1
17. 18 and 45 9
18. 21 and 27 3
19. 13 and 25 1
20. 8 and 48 8
21. 16 and 18 2
22. 24 and 36 12
23. 4, 12, and 30 2
24. 12, 18, and 36 6
25. 9, 16, and 25 1
26. 9, 15, and 21 3
27. 12, 15, and 21 3
28. 9, 36, and 45 9
29. 3, 9, and 31 3
30. 15, 30, and 50 5
31. 16, 24, and 30 2
32. 30, 50, and 100 10

Problem Solving

33. Thirty people signed up at the nature center for hiking, and 18 signed up for bird watching. They will be divided up into smaller groups. What is the greatest number of people that can be in each group and have all groups the same size?

6 people

34. Rosa found 8 different wildflowers and 20 different leaves on her hike. She plans to display them in equal rows on a poster. What is the greatest number of flowers or leaves she can put in each row?

4 flowers or leaves

Use with Grade 5, Chapter 5, Lesson 3, pages 204–205. (139)

Reteach

Common Factors and Greatest Common Factor

R 5-3 RETEACH

You can use multiplication facts to find all the factors of a number.

Find the factors of 20.

First find all the multiplication facts for 20. 1 × 20 2 × 10 4 × 5

List the factors in numerical order. 1, 2, 4, 5, 10, 20

Find the factors of 24. 1 × 24 2 × 12 3 × 8 4 × 6

List the factors in numerical order. 1, 2, 3, 4, 6, 8, 12, 24

The GCF (greatest common factor) of two numbers is the greatest number that is a factor of both.

Find the GCF of 20 and 24.

Factors of 20: (1), (2), (4), 5, 10, 20

Factors of 24: (1), (2), 3, (4), 6, 8, 12, and 24

The GCF of 20 and 24 is 4.

List all the factors of each number. Circle the common factors. Then identify the GCF.

1. 8: 1, 2, 4, 8
   32: 1, 2, 4, 8, 16, 32
   GCF: 8
2. 9: 1, 3, 9
   15: 1, 3, 5, 15
   GCF: 3
3. 6: 1, 2, 3, 6
   42: 1, 2, 3, 6, 7, 14, 21, 42
   GCF: 6
4. 7: 1, 7
   11: 1, 11
   GCF: 1

Find the greatest common factor (GCF) of the numbers.

5. 28 and 40 4
6. 10 and 25 5
7. 18 and 24 6
8. 14 and 21 7
9. 35 and 42 7
10. 15, 25, 30 5

Use with Grade 5, Chapter 5, Lesson 3, pages 204–205. (140)

Enrich

Common Factors and Greatest Common Factor

E 5-3 ENRICH

Prime Factors to the Rescue!

You can use the prime factorizations of a pair of numbers to find their GCF.

Find the GCF of 30 and 36.

Make factor trees and write the prime factorizations of 30 and 36.

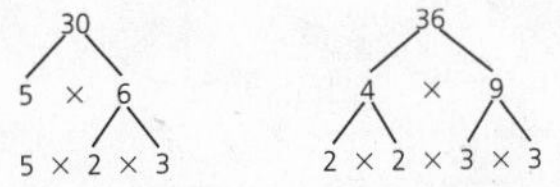

Circle the common factors. 30 = (2) × (3) × 5 36 = (2) × 2 × (3) × 3

Find the product of the common factors. 2 × 3 = 6

6 is the GCF of 30 and 36.

Use the method shown above to find the GCF of each pair of numbers. Check students' work.

1. 18 and 42
   GCF: 6
2. 16 and 72
   GCF: 8
3. 56 and 84
   GCF: 28
4. 45 and 144
   GCF: 9

Which method do you prefer for finding the GCF—the one in which you list all the factors of the numbers and find the greatest common factor, or the one in which you find the prime factorization of the numbers with a factor tree and multiply the common factors?

Answers will vary. Possible answer: I prefer the prime factorization method because I sometimes leave out factors when I am listing all the factors of a greater number.

Use with Grade 5, Chapter 5, Lesson 3, pages 204–205. (141)

Daily Homework

5-3 Common Factors and Greatest Common Factor

Find the GCF of the numbers.

1. 12 and 36 12
2. 16 and 20 4
3. 33 and 55 11
4. 40 and 90 10
5. 18 and 36 18
6. 24 and 54 6
7. 17 and 23 1
8. 18 and 44 2
9. 54 and 81 9
10. 42 and 28 14
11. 56 and 16 8
12. 13 and 39 13
13. 30 and 24 6
14. 35 and 56 7
15. 70 and 55 5
16. 24 and 56 8
17. 18 and 42 6
18. 15 and 50 5
19. 8 and 32 8
20. 28 and 49 7

Problem Solving

21. Tonya and Heather picked flowers in Tonya's garden to sell at the local grocery store. Tonya picked 64 flowers and Heather picked 40. They want to sell the flowers in bunches with an equal number of flowers. What is the greatest number of flowers they can put in a bunch? 8

22. A store sells pencils in packs of six or eight. Mr. Garcia, who teaches one class of 30 students and another class of 24 students, wants to buy pencils for all of his students. What size packs should he buy so that he will have no pencils left over? 6-pencil packs

Spiral Review

Find the mean for each set of numbers.

23. 26, 29, 24, 28, 33 28
24. 40, 42, 39, 46, 50, 47 44
25. 15, 13, 17, 15 15
26. 60, 66, 63, 62, 64 63

Grade 5, Chapter 5, Lesson 3, Cluster A 43

Practice

Fractions

P 5-4 PRACTICE

Name each fraction shown.

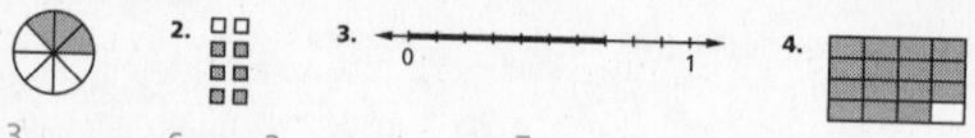

1. $\frac{3}{8}$ 2. $\frac{6}{8}$, or $\frac{3}{4}$ 3. $\frac{7}{10}$ 4. $\frac{15}{16}$

Draw a model to show each fraction. Check students' drawings for accurate representations of numerators and denominators.

5. $\frac{3}{5}$ 6. $\frac{7}{8}$ 7. $\frac{3}{10}$ 8. $\frac{2}{3}$

Write two equivalent fractions for each fraction.

9. $\frac{1}{2}$ Possible answers: $\frac{2}{4}$, $\frac{3}{6}$
10. $\frac{1}{4}$ Possible answers: $\frac{2}{8}$, $\frac{3}{12}$
11. $\frac{2}{5}$ Possible answers: $\frac{4}{10}$, $\frac{6}{15}$
12. $\frac{5}{6}$ Possible answers: $\frac{10}{12}$, $\frac{15}{18}$

Find each missing number.

13. $\frac{1}{4} = \frac{n}{12}$ $n =$ 3
14. $\frac{3}{5} = \frac{a}{10}$ $a =$ 6
15. $\frac{7}{10} = \frac{x}{20}$ $x =$ 14
16. $\frac{8}{12} = \frac{b}{3}$ $b =$ 2
17. $\frac{10}{12} = \frac{y}{6}$ $y =$ 5
18. $\frac{4}{10} = \frac{c}{5}$ $x =$ 2

Problem Solving

19. Van has 12 compact discs in his collection. Of these, 7 are by solo performers. What fraction of Van's compact discs are by solo performers? $\frac{7}{12}$

20. Chris walks $\frac{3}{8}$ mile each day to school. Anna walks $\frac{1}{2}$ mile. Do they walk the same distance to school? Explain. No; $\frac{3}{8}$ and $\frac{1}{2}$ are not equivalent fractions.

Use with Grade 5, Chapter 5, Lesson 4, pages 206–209. (142)

Reteach

Fractions

R 5-4 RETEACH

You can use a fraction to name part of a whole or part of a group. In each of these models, $\frac{6}{8}$ is shaded.

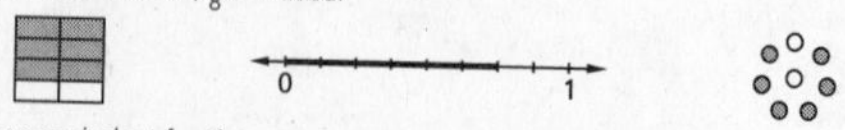

To find an equivalent fraction, you can multiply the numerator and denominator by the same number, or you can divide the numerator and denominator by the same number.

shaded parts → 6 ← numerator
parts in all → 8 ← denominator

Complete: $\frac{6}{8} = \frac{\square}{24}$
Look at the denominators.
8 < 24, so multiply.
Think: 8 × ? = 24
8 × 3 = 24
$\frac{6}{8} = \frac{6 \times 3}{8 \times 3} = \frac{18}{24}$

Complete: $\frac{6}{8} = \frac{3}{\square}$
Look at the numerators.
6 < 3, so divide.
Think: 6 ÷ ? = 3
6 ÷ 2 = 3
$\frac{6}{8} = \frac{6 \div 2}{8 \div 2} = \frac{3}{4}$

Write the fraction for the part that is shaded.

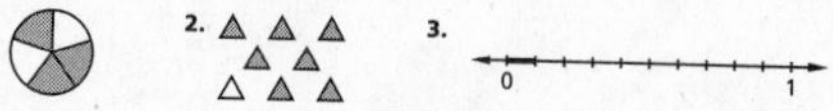

1. $\frac{3}{5}$ 2. $\frac{7}{8}$ 3. $\frac{1}{10}$

Complete each pair of equivalent fractions.

4. $\frac{15}{18} = \frac{15 \div 3}{18 \div 3} = \frac{5}{6}$
5. $\frac{1}{4} = \frac{1 \times 4}{4 \times 4} = \frac{4}{16}$
6. $\frac{75}{100} = \frac{75 \div 25}{100 \div 25} = \frac{3}{4}$
7. $\frac{1}{2} = \frac{6}{12}$
8. $\frac{3}{6} = \frac{1}{2}$
9. $\frac{3}{4} = \frac{15}{20}$
10. $\frac{20}{54} = \frac{10}{27}$
11. $\frac{10}{18} = \frac{5}{9}$
12. $\frac{9}{12} = \frac{3}{4}$
13. $\frac{1}{6} = \frac{2}{12}$
14. $\frac{6}{18} = \frac{1}{3}$

Use with Grade 5, Chapter 5, Lesson 4, pages 206–209. (143)

Enrich

Fractions

Fraction Paths

E 5-4 ENRICH

Find three paths from the top row to the bottom row. Each path must contain fractions equivalent to each other. You can move left, right, down or diagonal. Circle the fraction in each path that is in simplest form.

$\frac{1}{4}$	$\frac{1}{3}$	$\frac{6}{12}$	$\frac{9}{12}$	$\frac{2}{3}$	$\frac{6}{15}$	$\frac{16}{24}$	$\frac{9}{12}$	$\frac{3}{6}$
$\frac{2}{5}$	$\frac{2}{4}$	$\frac{2}{6}$	$\frac{3}{4}$	$\frac{20}{30}$	$\frac{10}{15}$	$\frac{6}{8}$	$\frac{18}{24}$	$\frac{1}{2}$
$\frac{2}{8}$	$\frac{8}{16}$	$\frac{16}{30}$	$\frac{4}{10}$	$\frac{2}{20}$	$\frac{24}{32}$	$\frac{4}{6}$	$\frac{2}{12}$	$\frac{3}{4}$
$\frac{1}{7}$	$\frac{4}{4}$	$\frac{1}{2}$	$\frac{3}{8}$	$\frac{3}{4}$	$\frac{16}{24}$	$\frac{4}{8}$	$\frac{2}{9}$	$\frac{5}{8}$
$\frac{6}{12}$	$\frac{2}{8}$	$\frac{3}{5}$	$\frac{9}{18}$	$\frac{8}{12}$	$\frac{15}{20}$	$\frac{4}{5}$	$\frac{12}{15}$	$\frac{1}{6}$
$\frac{7}{10}$	$\frac{12}{15}$	$\frac{6}{10}$	$\frac{3}{6}$	$\frac{6}{9}$	$\frac{3}{5}$	$\frac{30}{40}$	$\frac{3}{10}$	$\frac{2}{8}$
$\frac{3}{5}$	$\frac{1}{4}$	$\frac{3}{12}$	$\frac{14}{21}$	$\frac{7}{14}$	$\frac{12}{18}$	$\frac{12}{16}$	$\frac{6}{9}$	$\frac{1}{3}$
$\frac{2}{12}$	$\frac{3}{8}$	$\frac{3}{14}$	$\frac{1}{7}$	$\frac{1}{21}$	$\frac{5}{10}$	$\frac{18}{27}$	$\frac{27}{36}$	$\frac{3}{9}$
$\frac{2}{4}$	$\frac{6}{9}$	$\frac{2}{15}$	$\frac{1}{10}$	$\frac{1}{5}$	$\frac{4}{8}$	$\frac{5}{9}$	$\frac{14}{21}$	$\frac{21}{28}$
$\frac{14}{91}$	$\frac{5}{8}$	$\frac{25}{100}$	$\frac{5}{12}$	$\frac{5}{10}$	$\frac{3}{7}$	$\frac{24}{36}$	$\frac{39}{52}$	$\frac{72}{93}$
$\frac{18}{73}$	$\frac{3}{7}$	$\frac{1}{11}$	$\frac{10}{20}$	$\frac{13}{38}$	$\frac{26}{39}$	$\frac{45}{60}$	$\frac{20}{80}$	$\frac{90}{100}$
$\frac{4}{9}$	$\frac{9}{10}$	$\frac{13}{26}$	$\frac{4}{12}$	$\frac{9}{21}$	$\frac{60}{80}$	$\frac{34}{51}$	$\frac{12}{60}$	$\frac{11}{20}$
$\frac{6}{23}$	$\frac{50}{60}$	$\frac{15}{30}$	$\frac{30}{80}$	$\frac{54}{72}$	$\frac{7}{28}$	$\frac{31}{96}$	$\frac{36}{54}$	$\frac{12}{48}$
$\frac{40}{100}$	$\frac{13}{93}$	$\frac{14}{38}$	$\frac{50}{100}$	$\frac{53}{72}$	$\frac{51}{68}$	$\frac{60}{100}$	$\frac{10}{50}$	$\frac{20}{30}$

Explain how you found one path.

Answers may vary. Possible answer: I chose a fraction in the top row. Then I used multiplication and division to find out if any fractions around it were equivalent to it. I found one, so I checked if there was an equivalent fraction I could move to from that one. I continued in this way to the bottom row.

Use with Grade 5, Chapter 5, Lesson 4, pages 206–209. (144)

Daily Homework

5-4 Fractions

Name each fraction shown.

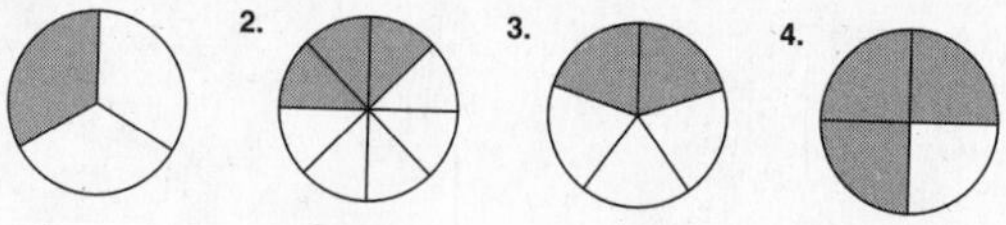

1. $\frac{1}{3}$ 2. $\frac{3}{8}$ 3. $\frac{2}{5}$ 4. $\frac{3}{4}$

Draw a model to show each fraction. Check students' drawings for accurate representation of numerators and denominators.

5. $\frac{2}{3}$ 6. $\frac{1}{8}$ 7. $\frac{3}{5}$

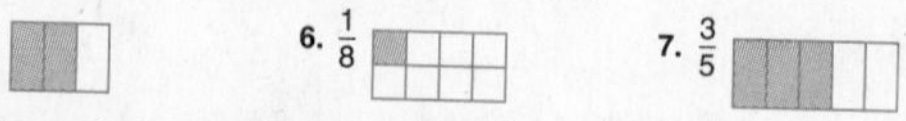

Write two equivalent fractions for each fraction. Answers may vary.

8. $\frac{3}{5}$ Possible answers: $\frac{6}{10}$, $\frac{12}{20}$
9. $\frac{5}{8}$ Possible answers: $\frac{10}{16}$, $\frac{25}{40}$

Problem Solving

10. In a class, four out of 20 students own a pet bird. What fraction of the class own birds? $\frac{1}{5}$

11. Anne has a collection of 30 old coins. Two-fifths of the coins are quarters. How many quarters are there in Anne's coin collection? 12 quarters

Spiral Review

Find the median for each set.

12. 16, 12, 58, 8, 17, 47, 95 17
13. 12, 18, 23, 18, 24 18
14. 18, 52, 48, 86, 50 50
15. 24, 30, 18, 22, 29, 27 25.5

44 Grade 5, Chapter 5, Lesson 4, Cluster A

Practice

Problem Solving: Reading for Math
Extra and Missing Information

P 5-5 PRACTICE Reading Skill

The table shows the number of students who have volunteered to help with the production of the school play. The school has a budget of $800 to produce the play. Tickets for the play will cost $4.00 for adults. Students will be admitted for free. There are 500 students who attend the school.

Activity	Number of Students
Directors	3
Actors	18
Lighting	6
Sound	4
Special effects	3
Set design	8
Costume design	6
Makeup	2

Solve. If there is extra information, identify the extra information. If there is not enough information, write *not enough information.* Then tell what information you would need to solve the problem.

1. What fraction of the students who attend the school have volunteered to help with the play?
   $\frac{50}{500}$ or $\frac{1}{10}$ of the students; extra information: school budget and cost of tickets
2. What fraction of the volunteers are involved in set design and costume design?
   $\frac{14}{50}$ or $\frac{7}{25}$ of the volunteers; Extra information: school budget, cost of tickets, and number of students in the school;
3. If the students sell 300 tickets to the school play, will they have enough money to cover all of the expenses for the play?
   Not enough information; you need to know the total expenses for the play.
4. What fraction of the student volunteers bought tickets for their parents to attend the play?
   Not enough information; you need to know the number of volunteers who bought tickets.

Use with Grade 5, Chapter 5, Lesson 5, pages 210–211. (145)

Practice

Problem Solving: Reading for Math
Extra and Missing Information

P 5-5 PRACTICE Math Skills Test Prep

Choose the correct answer.

Tickets to the karate tournament cost $5.50. There are 45 students in the karate tournament. Of the students, 20 are girls. Of the girls, $\frac{2}{5}$ have brown belts.

1. Which of the following statements is false?
   - A There are 25 boys in the tournament.
   - B Fewer than half of the girls have brown belts.
   - (C) Only 4 girls have brown belts.
   - D Of the students in the tournament, $\frac{4}{9}$ are girls.
2. Which of the following statements is true?
   - F 45 tickets were sold to the tournament.
   - G $\frac{2}{5}$ of the students have brown belts.
   - H $\frac{3}{5}$ of the boys have brown belts.
   - (J) The cost of the tickets is extra information.

A group of 60 students is going on a field trip to the planetarium. The admission fee is $3.50 for each student. The admission fee must be paid in advance. So far, $\frac{3}{10}$ of the students have paid their admission fee.

3. Which of the following statements is true?
   - A More than half of the students have paid their admission fee.
   - B The total cost for all the students will be under $200.
   - (C) There are 42 students who must still pay their admission fee.
   - D At least half of the students have paid their admission fee.
4. If a problem has extra information, you should
   - (F) focus on the information you need to solve the problem.
   - G try to find any missing information.
   - H not solve the problem.
   - J use all of the information to solve the problem.

In a school of 320 students, $\frac{3}{8}$ signed up for an art class. The same number of girls and boys signed up. Supplies for each student cost $5.

5. Which of the following statements is true?
   - A There are 40 students in the class.
   - (B) There are 60 boys in the class.
   - C There are 40 girls in the class.
   - D There are 80 students in the class.
6. Suppose 10 more students sign up for the class. You want to find the fraction of students in the school who are now signed up for the class. Identify the extra information in the problem.
   - F There are 320 students in the school.
   - G Ten more students have signed up for the class.
   - H $\frac{3}{8}$ had already signed up for the class.
   - (J) Supplies for each student cost $5.

Use with Grade 5, Chapter 5, Lesson 5, pages 210–211. (146)

Practice

Problem Solving: Reading for Math
Extra and Missing Information

P 5-5 PRACTICE Math Skills Test Prep

Choose the correct answer.

There are 48 students in a soccer camp. Of the students, 28 are boys. Of the boys, $\frac{3}{4}$ are city residents. Nonresidents must pay a $10 fee to attend the camp.

7. Which of the following statements is *not* true?
   - (A) The total number of girls is less than the number of boys who are nonresidents.
   - B There are 21 boys in the camp who are city residents.
   - C The fees for the boys who are nonresidents will total $70.
   - D There are 20 girls in the camp.
8. Suppose you wanted to find the total fees for the girls who are nonresidents. What information below could you use to solve the problem?
   - F There are fewer nonresident girls than boys who attend the camp.
   - G Of the girls, $\frac{4}{5}$ have attended the camp before.
   - (H) Of the students registered, 11 are nonresidents.
   - J The information is still missing.

Use data from the table for problems 9–14.

A swimming center is offering swimming classes for students ages 6–14. The fee for residents is $35. The fee for nonresidents is $45.

Solve. If there is not enough information, write *not enough information.*

Swimming Lessons	
Class Level	**Students**
Beginner	16
Advanced Beginner	22
Intermediate	28
Advanced	14

9. What fraction of the students signed up for intermediate classes?
   $\frac{7}{20}$
10. What fraction of the students signed up for the beginner classes?
    $\frac{1}{5}$
11. What is the total amount of money the advanced class will raise?
    not enough information
12. What fraction of the students did not sign up for the advanced beginner or intermediate classes?
    $\frac{3}{8}$
13. If $\frac{1}{2}$ of the students in the advanced beginner class are nonresidents, what are their total fees for the class?
    $495
14. Delia and Laura want to take the intermediate class. What fraction of the intermediate class is girls?
    not enough information

Use with Grade 5, Chapter 5, Lesson 5, pages 210–211. (147)

Daily Homework

5-5 Problem Solving: Reading for Math
Extra and Missing Information

Meadville Recreation Center Craft Courses

Courses	Sign-ups	FEES
Pottery	15	**Residents**
Wood Carving	12	$25 per course
Jewelry Making	18	Maximum $100
Flower Arranging	10	**Nonresidents**
Glassblowing	20	$30 per course
		Maximum $125

Solve. If there is not enough information, write *not enough information*.

1. What fraction of all the sign-ups are for glassblowing? $\frac{4}{15}$
2. How many students are taking jewelry making? 18
3. How many different students have signed up for pottery and flower arranging? not enough information
4. Betty wants to take the pottery course. How much will that cost her? not enough information
5. Tina wants to take two courses and has $55. Does she have enough money to pay the fee? not enough information
6. Emily is a resident and wants to take three courses. How much will that cost her? $75

Spiral Review

Write the value of the underlined digit in each number.

7. 3.<u>2</u>65 0.2
8. <u>7</u>48.43 700
9. 12.6<u>8</u>6 0.08
10. 1<u>8</u>5,326 80,000

Grade 5, Chapter 5, Lesson 5, Cluster A 45

Chapter 5 ~ Lesson 6

Practice

Simplify Fractions

P 5-6 PRACTICE

Write each fraction in simplest form.

1. $\frac{4}{28}$ **$\frac{1}{7}$**
2. $\frac{15}{20}$ **$\frac{3}{4}$**
3. $\frac{6}{21}$ **$\frac{2}{7}$**
4. $\frac{30}{35}$ **$\frac{6}{7}$**
5. $\frac{3}{30}$ **$\frac{1}{10}$**
6. $\frac{12}{14}$ **$\frac{6}{7}$**
7. $\frac{9}{24}$ **$\frac{3}{8}$**
8. $\frac{14}{42}$ **$\frac{1}{3}$**
9. $\frac{20}{25}$ **$\frac{4}{5}$**
10. $\frac{14}{21}$ **$\frac{2}{3}$**
11. $\frac{16}{18}$ **$\frac{8}{9}$**
12. $\frac{4}{36}$ **$\frac{1}{9}$**
13. $\frac{8}{14}$ **$\frac{4}{7}$**
14. $\frac{14}{35}$ **$\frac{2}{5}$**
15. $\frac{10}{12}$ **$\frac{5}{6}$**
16. $\frac{24}{40}$ **$\frac{3}{5}$**
17. $\frac{12}{30}$ **$\frac{2}{5}$**
18. $\frac{4}{32}$ **$\frac{1}{8}$**

Write each fraction in simplest form. Write yes if the fraction is already in simplest form.

19. $\frac{16}{20}$ **$\frac{4}{5}$**
20. $\frac{1}{2}$ **yes**
21. $\frac{3}{12}$ **$\frac{1}{4}$**
22. $\frac{2}{5}$ **yes**
23. $\frac{3}{7}$ **yes**
24. $\frac{28}{32}$ **$\frac{7}{8}$**
25. $\frac{40}{48}$ **$\frac{5}{6}$**
26. $\frac{12}{18}$ **$\frac{2}{3}$**
27. $\frac{5}{8}$ **yes**
28. $\frac{15}{36}$ **$\frac{5}{12}$**
29. $\frac{2}{3}$ **yes**
30. $\frac{3}{24}$ **$\frac{1}{8}$**
31. $\frac{12}{16}$ **$\frac{3}{4}$**
32. $\frac{9}{10}$ **yes**
33. $\frac{4}{15}$ **yes**

Problem Solving

34. Of the 27 students in Jarrod's class, 18 receive an allowance each week. What fraction of the students, in simplest form, receive an allowance? **$\frac{2}{3}$**

35. Of the 18 students who receive an allowance, 14 do chores around the house. What fraction of these students, in simplest form, do chores around the house? **$\frac{7}{9}$**

Use with Grade 5, Chapter 5, Lesson 6, pages 214–215. (148)

Reteach

Simplify Fractions

R 5-6 RETEACH

When a fraction is in simplest form, 1 is the only common factor of its numerator and denominator.

Step 1

Write in simplest form: $\frac{16}{40}$

Find the GCF of the numerator and the denominator.

Factors of 16: 1, 2, 4, **8**, 16
Factors of 40: 1, 2, 4, 5, **8**, 10, 20, 40
GCF: 8

Step 2

Divide the numerator and the denominator by their GCF.

$\frac{16}{40} = \frac{16 \div 8}{40 \div 8} = \frac{2}{5}$

Check that $\frac{2}{5}$ is in simplest form.

Factors of 2: 1, 2
Factors of 5: 1, 5

The only common factor of 2 and 5 is 1, so $\frac{2}{5}$ is in simplest form.

Write each fraction in simplest form.

1. $\frac{6}{10}$
Factors of 6: **1, 2, 3, 6**
Factors of 10: **1, 2, 5, 10**
GCF: **2**
$\frac{6}{10} = \frac{6 \div 2}{10 \div 2} = \frac{3}{5}$

2. $\frac{9}{36}$
Factors of 9: **1, 3, 9**
Factors of 36: **1, 2, 3, 4, 6, 9, 12, 18, 36**
GCF: **9**
$\frac{9}{36} = \frac{9 \div 9}{36 \div 9} = \frac{1}{4}$

3. $\frac{12}{30}$
Factors of 12: **1, 2, 3, 4, 6, 12**
Factors of 30: **1, 2, 3, 5, 6, 10, 15, 30**
GCF: **6**
$\frac{12}{30} = \frac{12 \div 6}{30 \div 6} = \frac{2}{5}$

4. $\frac{20}{25}$
Factors of 20: **1, 2, 4, 5, 10, 20**
Factors of 25: **1, 5, 25**
GCF: **5**
$\frac{20}{25} = \frac{20 \div 5}{25 \div 5} = \frac{4}{5}$

5. $\frac{6}{18}$ **$\frac{1}{3}$**
6. $\frac{15}{40}$ **$\frac{3}{8}$**
7. $\frac{8}{30}$ **$\frac{4}{15}$**
8. $\frac{24}{27}$ **$\frac{8}{9}$**
9. $\frac{16}{28}$ **$\frac{4}{7}$**
10. $\frac{30}{48}$ **$\frac{5}{8}$**
11. $\frac{20}{24}$ **$\frac{5}{6}$**
12. $\frac{21}{28}$ **$\frac{3}{4}$**

Use with Grade 5, Chapter 5, Lesson 6, pages 214–215. (149)

Enrich

Simplify Fractions

Fraction Riddles

E 5-6 ENRICH

Solve each riddle. Use logical reasoning to help you find the fraction(s).

1. My simplest form is $\frac{2}{3}$. The GCF of my numerator and denominator is 6. Who am I? **$\frac{12}{18}$**

2. My simplest form is $\frac{1}{2}$. My numerator is a prime number between 30 and 36. Who am I? **$\frac{31}{62}$**

3. My simplest form is $\frac{3}{4}$. My digits are 1, 2, 4, and 8. Who am I? **$\frac{18}{24}$**

4. My numerator and denominator are prime numbers. Their product is 119. Who am I? **$\frac{7}{17}$ or $\frac{17}{7}$**

5. The difference between my numerator and denominator is 16. My simplest form is $\frac{1}{5}$. Who am I? **$\frac{4}{20}$**

6. I am in simplest form. Both my numerator and denominator are 1-digit numbers. My numerator is the GCF of 24 and 30. Who am I? **$\frac{6}{7}$**

7. We are both in simplest form. The product of each of our numerators and denominators is 120. Each of our numerators is a prime number. Who are we? **$\frac{3}{40}$, $\frac{5}{24}$**

8. My numerator is 150 less than my denominator. My denominator is 5 × 100. Who am I? What is my simplest form? **$\frac{350}{500}$; $\frac{7}{10}$**

9. There are four of us. Each of our denominators is a multiple of our numerators. The sum of each of our numerators and denominators is 42. Who are we? What are our simplest forms? **$\frac{2}{40}$, $\frac{3}{39}$, $\frac{6}{36}$, $\frac{14}{28}$; $\frac{1}{20}$, $\frac{1}{13}$, $\frac{1}{6}$, $\frac{1}{2}$**

10. We are a set of triplets. The GCF of each of our numerators and denominators is 1. The sum of each our numerators and denominators is 30. Who are we? **$\frac{7}{23}$, $\frac{11}{19}$, $\frac{13}{17}$ or $\frac{23}{7}$; $\frac{19}{11}$, $\frac{17}{13}$**

Suppose the numerator or denominator of a fraction is a prime number. Is the fraction in simplest form? Explain.

Not necessarily; the numerator could be a prime number and the GCF of the numerator and the denominator. For example, $\frac{13}{39}$ is not in simplest form.

Use with Grade 5, Chapter 5, Lesson 6, pages 214–215. (150)

Daily Homework

5-6 Simplify Fractions

Write each fraction in simplest form

1. $\frac{2}{6}$ **$\frac{1}{3}$**
2. $\frac{3}{9}$ **$\frac{1}{3}$**
3. $\frac{6}{12}$ **$\frac{1}{2}$**
4. $\frac{10}{15}$ **$\frac{2}{3}$**
5. $\frac{16}{20}$ **$\frac{4}{5}$**
6. $\frac{6}{8}$ **$\frac{3}{4}$**
7. $\frac{8}{40}$ **$\frac{1}{5}$**
8. $\frac{24}{30}$ **$\frac{4}{5}$**
9. $\frac{10}{60}$ **$\frac{1}{6}$**
10. $\frac{12}{48}$ **$\frac{1}{4}$**
11. $\frac{24}{36}$ **$\frac{2}{3}$**
12. $\frac{30}{48}$ **$\frac{5}{8}$**
13. $\frac{16}{36}$ **$\frac{4}{9}$**
14. $\frac{6}{30}$ **$\frac{1}{5}$**
15. $\frac{8}{48}$ **$\frac{1}{6}$**
16. $\frac{6}{24}$ **$\frac{1}{4}$**
17. $\frac{18}{24}$ **$\frac{3}{4}$**
18. $\frac{30}{45}$ **$\frac{2}{3}$**

Problem Solving

Use data from the table for problems 19–20.

Class Pets

Pet	Number
dog	10
cat	8
bird	6
fish	4
hamster	2

19. What fraction of all the class pets are fish, in simplest terms? **$\frac{2}{15}$**

20. What fraction of all the class pets are dogs, in simplest terms? **$\frac{1}{3}$**

Spiral Review

Of 2, 3, 5, 6, 9, and 10, list which numbers each of these numbers is divisible by.

21. 48 **2, 3, 6**
22. 56 **2**
23. 64 **2**
24. 67 **none**
25. 24 **2, 3, 6**
26. 30 **2, 3, 5, 6, 10**

46 Grade 5, Chapter 5, Lesson 6, Cluster B

Chapter 5 ~ Lesson 7

Practice

Least Common Multiple and Least Common Denominator

P 5-7 PRACTICE

Find the least common multiple (LCM) of the numbers.

1. 5 and 15 15
2. 2 and 9 18
3. 2 and 11 22
4. 6 and 9 18
5. 4 and 5 20
6. 8 and 12 24
7. 4 and 8 8
8. 10 and 25 50
9. 3 and 4 12
10. 2 and 3 6
11. 8 and 9 72
12. 4 and 10 20
13. 2, 4, and 16 16
14. 3, 5, and 6 30
15. 3, 6, and 8 24

Write equivalent fractions using the LCD.

16. $\frac{7}{10}$ and $\frac{2}{5}$ $\frac{7}{10}$ and $\frac{4}{10}$
17. $\frac{5}{12}$ and $\frac{1}{4}$ $\frac{5}{12}$ and $\frac{3}{12}$
18. $\frac{2}{3}$ and $\frac{3}{8}$ $\frac{16}{24}$ and $\frac{9}{24}$
19. $\frac{3}{5}$ and $\frac{9}{10}$ $\frac{6}{10}$ and $\frac{9}{10}$
20. $\frac{1}{6}$ and $\frac{7}{12}$ $\frac{2}{12}$ and $\frac{7}{12}$
21. $\frac{1}{5}$ and $\frac{2}{3}$ $\frac{3}{15}$ and $\frac{10}{15}$
22. $\frac{5}{8}$ and $\frac{2}{5}$ $\frac{25}{40}$ and $\frac{16}{40}$
23. $\frac{1}{3}$ and $\frac{5}{12}$ $\frac{4}{12}$ and $\frac{5}{12}$
24. $\frac{3}{4}$ and $\frac{13}{16}$ $\frac{12}{16}$ and $\frac{13}{16}$
25. $\frac{3}{10}$ and $\frac{5}{6}$ $\frac{9}{30}$ and $\frac{25}{30}$
26. $\frac{11}{20}$ and $\frac{4}{5}$ $\frac{11}{20}$ and $\frac{16}{20}$
27. $\frac{2}{9}$ and $\frac{1}{8}$ $\frac{16}{72}$ and $\frac{9}{72}$
28. $\frac{3}{8}$ and $\frac{5}{6}$ $\frac{9}{24}$ and $\frac{20}{24}$
29. $\frac{5}{6}$ and $\frac{9}{24}$ $\frac{20}{24}$ and $\frac{9}{24}$

Problem Solving

30. José and Sara are walking around the track at the same time. José walks one lap every 8 minutes. Sara walks a lap every 6 minutes. What is the least amount of time they would both have to walk for them to cross the starting point together?

24 minutes

31. Pamela and David walk on the same track. It takes Pamela 9 minutes and David 6 minutes to walk one lap. If they start walking at the same time, how many laps will each have walked when they cross the starting point together for the first time?

Pamela: 2 laps;
David: 3 laps

Use with Grade 5, Chapter 5, Lesson 7, pages 216–219. (151)

Reteach

Least Common Multiple and Least Common Denominator

R 5-7 RETEACH

To rewrite two fractions with the same denominator, find their LCD (least common denominator). That's the LCM (least common multiple) of their denominators, or the least number that is a multiple of both numbers.

Rewrite $\frac{5}{6}$ and $\frac{4}{9}$ using their LCD.

First find the LCM of 6 and 9.
Write at least the first five multiples of 6: 6, 12, 18, 24, 30
Write multiples of 9 until you find one that is also a multiple of 6: 9, 18
18 is the LCM of 6 and 9.

Now write fractions equivalent to $\frac{5}{6}$ and $\frac{4}{9}$ using their LCD.

$\frac{5}{6} = \frac{5 \times 3}{6 \times 3} = \frac{15}{18}$ $\frac{4}{9} = \frac{4 \times 2}{9 \times 2} = \frac{8}{18}$

Use the LCD to rewrite the fractions.

1. $\frac{3}{5}$ and $\frac{2}{3}$

Multiples of 5: 5, 10, 15, 20, 25
Multiples of 3: 3, 6, 9, 12, 15
LCM of 5 and 3: 15

$\frac{3}{5} = \frac{3 \times 3}{5 \times 3} = \frac{9}{15}$

$\frac{2}{3} = \frac{2 \times 5}{3 \times 5} = \frac{10}{15}$

2. $\frac{1}{2}$ and $\frac{5}{8}$

Multiples of 2: 2, 4, 6, 8, 10
Multiples of 8: 8
LCM of 2 and 8: 8

$\frac{1}{2} = \frac{1 \times 4}{2 \times 4} = \frac{4}{8}$

$\frac{5}{8} = \frac{5}{8}$

3. $\frac{1}{4}$ and $\frac{5}{6}$

Multiples of 4: 4, 8, 12, 16, 20
Multiples of 6: 6, 12
LCM of 4 and 6: 12

$\frac{1}{4} = \frac{1 \times 3}{4 \times 3} = \frac{3}{12}$

$\frac{5}{6} = \frac{5 \times 2}{6 \times 2} = \frac{10}{12}$

4. $\frac{7}{8}$ and $\frac{5}{12}$

Multiples of 8: 8, 16, 24, 32, 40
Multiples of 12: 12, 24
LCM of 8 and 12: 24

$\frac{7}{8} = \frac{7 \times 3}{8 \times 3} = \frac{21}{24}$

$\frac{5}{12} = \frac{5 \times 2}{12 \times 2} = \frac{10}{24}$

5. $\frac{4}{9}$ and $\frac{3}{4}$ $\frac{16}{36}$ and $\frac{27}{36}$

6. $\frac{2}{5}$ and $\frac{7}{10}$ $\frac{4}{10}$ and $\frac{7}{10}$

Use with Grade 5, Chapter 5, Lesson 7, pages 216–219. (152)

Enrich

Least Common Multiple and Least Common Denominator

E 5-7 ENRICH

Camp Ringing Rocks

Camp opens July 1 and runs for the entire month.
Mark the schedule on the calendar.

- Orchestra every day
- Chorus every second day
- Drama every third day
- Pottery every fourth day
- Writing every sixth day

S	M	T	W	T	F	S
1 O	2 O, C	3 O, D	4 O, C, P	5 O	6 O, C, D, W	7 O
8 O, C, P	9 O, D	10 O, C	11 O	12 O, C, D, P, W	13 O	14 O, C
15 O, D	16 O, C, P	17 O	18 O, C D, W	19 O	20 O, C, P	21 O, D
22 O, C	23 O	24 O, C, D P, W	25 O	26 O, C	27 O, D	28 O, C, P
29 O	30 O, C, D, W	31 O				

1. Which activities are available on every fourth day?

orchestra, chorus, pottery

2. On which days will campers have only one activity available?

1st, 5th, 7th, 11th, 13th, 17th, 19th, 23rd, 25th, 29th, 31st

3. Julia's favorite activity is drama. What fractional part of the camp season will she be able to participate in this activity?

orchestra, chorus; orchestra, chorus, pottery

4. How often will campers have orchestra, chorus, drama, and writing available on the same day?

every sixth day, or five times

5. On which days will campers have all five activities available?

12th and 24th

6. Which activities are available on the tenth day? on the twentieth day?

$\frac{10}{31}$

7. A new activity is to be added. When should it be available? Why?

Answers may vary. Possible answer: Offer the activity every other day starting with the first day so at least two different activities will be available each day.

Use with Grade 5, Chapter 5, Lesson 7, pages 216–219. (153)

Daily Homework

5-7 Least Common Multiple and Least Common Denominator

Find the LCM of the numbers.

1. 3 and 6 6
2. 3 and 4 12
3. 7 and 3 21
4. 9 and 5 45
5. 6 and 15 30
6. 6 and 16 48
7. 4 and 5 20
8. 6 and 8 24
9. 6 and 9 36
10. 3 and 10 30
11. 4 and 7 28
12. 5 and 15 15

Find the LCD for each pair of fractions.

13. $\frac{1}{2}$ and $\frac{1}{5}$ 10
14. $\frac{2}{3}$ and $\frac{3}{4}$ 12
15. $\frac{5}{6}$ and $\frac{2}{9}$ 18
16. $\frac{3}{5}$ and $\frac{1}{3}$ 15
17. $\frac{2}{3}$ and $\frac{4}{5}$ 15
18. $\frac{1}{6}$ and $\frac{2}{3}$ 6

Write equivalent fractions using the LCD.

19. $\frac{2}{3}$ and $\frac{3}{4}$ $\frac{8}{12}$ and $\frac{9}{12}$
20. $\frac{2}{5}$ and $\frac{1}{3}$ $\frac{6}{15}$ and $\frac{5}{15}$

Problem Solving

21. Hot dogs are sold in packages of 10. Hot dog rolls are sold in packages of 8. What is the least number of hot dogs Stan can serve at a cookout and not have any hot dogs or hot dog rolls left over? 40

22. Keyshawn is planning his soccer practice and his piano practice for the next 30 days. He plans to practice his piano every third day and to practice soccer every other day. How many days will he practice soccer and piano on the same day? 5

Spiral Review

23. $3.56 \times 8.6 = 30.616$

24. $0.16 \times 0.024 = 0.00384$

25. $12 \div .04 =$ 300

Grade 5, Chapter 5, Lesson 7, Cluster B 47

Chapter 5 ~ Lesson 8

Practice

Compare and Order Fractions

P 5-8 PRACTICE

Compare. Write >, <, or =.

1. $\frac{3}{4}$ (>) $\frac{7}{12}$
2. $\frac{2}{5}$ (<) $\frac{3}{4}$
3. $\frac{1}{6}$ (<) $\frac{1}{3}$
4. $\frac{1}{2}$ (<) $\frac{7}{10}$
5. $\frac{15}{16}$ (>) $\frac{3}{8}$
6. $\frac{3}{8}$ (<) $\frac{5}{6}$
7. $\frac{7}{8}$ (<) $\frac{8}{9}$
8. $\frac{2}{10}$ (=) $\frac{1}{5}$
9. $\frac{11}{12}$ (>) $\frac{5}{8}$
10. $\frac{4}{5}$ (<) $\frac{17}{20}$
11. $\frac{1}{8}$ (<) $\frac{2}{5}$
12. $\frac{2}{3}$ (=) $\frac{4}{6}$
13. $\frac{1}{5}$ (<) $\frac{1}{4}$
14. $\frac{5}{8}$ (>) $\frac{3}{5}$
15. $\frac{1}{6}$ (<) $\frac{4}{18}$

Order from least to greatest.

16. $\frac{2}{5}, \frac{1}{10}, \frac{3}{20}$ — $\frac{1}{10}, \frac{3}{20}, \frac{2}{5}$
17. $\frac{1}{3}, \frac{1}{9}, \frac{1}{12}$ — $\frac{1}{12}, \frac{1}{9}, \frac{1}{3}$
18. $\frac{3}{8}, \frac{3}{4}, \frac{1}{12}$ — $\frac{1}{12}, \frac{3}{8}, \frac{3}{4}$
19. $\frac{2}{5}, \frac{7}{8}, \frac{4}{5}$ — $\frac{2}{5}, \frac{4}{5}, \frac{7}{8}$
20. $\frac{5}{9}, \frac{5}{8}, \frac{5}{6}$ — $\frac{5}{9}, \frac{5}{8}, \frac{5}{6}$
21. $\frac{5}{8}, \frac{7}{10}, \frac{2}{5}$ — $\frac{2}{5}, \frac{5}{8}, \frac{7}{10}$
22. $\frac{2}{5}, \frac{3}{10}, \frac{1}{4}$ — $\frac{1}{4}, \frac{3}{10}, \frac{2}{5}$
23. $\frac{1}{5}, \frac{2}{15}, \frac{4}{9}$ — $\frac{2}{15}, \frac{1}{5}, \frac{4}{9}$
24. $\frac{7}{12}, \frac{5}{8}, \frac{1}{10}$ — $\frac{1}{6}, \frac{7}{12}, \frac{5}{8}$
25. $\frac{3}{4}, \frac{1}{8}, \frac{5}{16}$ — $\frac{1}{8}, \frac{5}{16}, \frac{3}{4}$
26. $\frac{2}{9}, \frac{2}{3}, \frac{1}{2}$ — $\frac{2}{9}, \frac{1}{2}, \frac{2}{3}$
27. $\frac{3}{5}, \frac{3}{15}, \frac{3}{10}$ — $\frac{3}{15}, \frac{3}{10}, \frac{3}{5}$

Problem Solving

28. The members of a play audience were asked to name their favorite type of play. Drama was named by $\frac{1}{4}$ of the audience, comedy was named by $\frac{11}{20}$, and musical was named by $\frac{1}{5}$. What was the audience's least favorite type of play?
musical

29. Visitors to an art museum were asked to name their favorite type of art. Pottery was named by $\frac{9}{40}$ of the visitors, painting was named by $\frac{2}{5}$, and sculpture was named by $\frac{3}{8}$. What was the most visitors' favorite type of art?
painting

Use with Grade 5, Chapter 5, Lesson 8, pages 220–221. (154)

Reteach

Compare and Order Fractions

R 5-8 RETEACH

To order fractions, rewrite them with a common denominator. Then compare the numerators, two at a time to order the numerators.

Order: $\frac{4}{9}, \frac{5}{6}, \frac{7}{18}$

Step 1

Find the LCM of 9, 6, and 18.

Multiples of 9: 9, 18, 27, 36
Multiples of 6: 6, 12, 18
Multiples of 18: 18
LCM: 18

Step 2

Write equivalent fractions.

$\frac{4}{9} = \frac{4 \times 2}{9 \times 2} = \frac{8}{18}$

$\frac{5}{6} = \frac{5 \times 3}{6 \times 3} = \frac{15}{18}$

$\frac{7}{18} = \frac{7}{18}$

Step 3

Compare and order the numerators.

7 < 8 and 8 < 15, so 7 < 8 < 15.

Order least to greatest:

$\frac{7}{18}, \frac{8}{18}, \frac{15}{18}$

↓ ↓ ↓

$\frac{7}{18}, \frac{4}{9}, \frac{5}{6}$

Order from least to greatest.

1. $\frac{3}{4}, \frac{1}{2}, \frac{5}{6}$

Multiples of 4: 4, 8, 12, 16, 20
Multiples of 2: 2, 4, 6, 8, 10, 12
Multiples of 6: 6, 12
LCM: 12
Numerators: 6 < 9 < 10

$\frac{3}{4} = \frac{3 \times 3}{4 \times 3} = \frac{9}{12}$

$\frac{1}{2} = \frac{1 \times 6}{2 \times 6} = \frac{6}{12}$

$\frac{5}{6} = \frac{5 \times 2}{6 \times 2} = \frac{10}{12}$

Fractions from least to greatest: $\frac{1}{2}, \frac{3}{4}, \frac{5}{6}$

2. $\frac{3}{8}, \frac{3}{4}, \frac{1}{3}$

Multiples of 8: 8, 16, 24, 32, 40
Multiples of 4: 4, 8, 12, 16, 20, 24
Multiples of 3: 3, 6, 9, 12, 15, 18, 21, 24
LCM: 24
Numerators: 8 < 9 < 18

$\frac{3}{8} = \frac{3 \times 3}{8 \times 3} = \frac{9}{24}$

$\frac{3}{4} = \frac{3 \times 6}{4 \times 6} = \frac{18}{24}$

$\frac{1}{3} = \frac{1 \times 8}{3 \times 8} = \frac{8}{24}$

Fractions from least to greatest: $\frac{1}{3}, \frac{3}{8}, \frac{3}{4}$

3. $\frac{1}{5}, \frac{1}{6}, \frac{3}{10}$ — $\frac{1}{6}, \frac{1}{5}, \frac{3}{10}$

4. $\frac{9}{10}, \frac{4}{5}, \frac{2}{3}$ — $\frac{2}{3}, \frac{4}{5}, \frac{9}{10}$

Use with Grade 5, Chapter 5, Lesson 8, pages 220–221. (155)

Enrich

Compare and Order Fractions

E 5-8 ENRICH

Come to Order!

Answers may vary. Possible answers are given.

Arrange each set of digits in the boxes to make each statement true.

1. 3, 1, 7, 5 — $\frac{1}{3} < \frac{5}{7}$
2. 1, 8, 4, 2 — $\frac{1}{2} = \frac{4}{8}$
3. 6, 9, 5, 4 — $\frac{4}{6} > \frac{5}{9}$
4. 2, 3, 7, 6 — $\frac{6}{7} > \frac{2}{3}$
5. 8, 3, 1, 5 — $\frac{1}{3} < \frac{5}{8}$
6. 4, 6, 5, 3 — $\frac{3}{5} < \frac{4}{6}$
7. 1, 3, 4, 5, 7, 9 — $\frac{1}{3} < \frac{7}{9} < \frac{4}{5}$
8. 4, 2, 8, 6, 5, 1 — $\frac{1}{8} < \frac{2}{4} < \frac{5}{6}$
9. 7, 1, 8, 3, 2, 9 — $\frac{3}{8} < \frac{1}{2} < \frac{7}{9}$
10. 3, 5, 2, 6, 4, 7 — $\frac{2}{6} < \frac{4}{7} < \frac{3}{5}$

11. How did you solve exercise 10?
Answers may vary. Possible answer: I used two digits to write a fraction less than $\frac{1}{2}$ for the first fraction. I used the other four digits to make two more fractions. I compared them to determine which to write second and third.

Use with Grade 5, Chapter 5, Lesson 8, pages 220–221. (156)

Daily Homework

5•8 Compare and Order Fractions

Compare. Write >, <, or =.

1. $\frac{1}{5}$ < $\frac{1}{3}$
2. $\frac{2}{3}$ < $\frac{3}{4}$
3. $\frac{7}{9}$ > $\frac{3}{5}$
4. $\frac{3}{15}$ = $\frac{1}{5}$
5. $\frac{7}{12}$ > $\frac{3}{9}$
6. $\frac{2}{3}$ = $\frac{8}{12}$

Order from least to greatest.

7. $\frac{1}{2}, \frac{1}{5}, \frac{1}{3}$ — $\frac{1}{5}, \frac{1}{3}, \frac{1}{2}$
8. $\frac{1}{8}, \frac{2}{3}, \frac{1}{4}$ — $\frac{1}{8}, \frac{1}{4}, \frac{2}{3}$
9. $\frac{2}{3}, \frac{2}{5}, \frac{2}{4}$ — $\frac{2}{5}, \frac{2}{4}, \frac{2}{3}$
10. $\frac{3}{8}, \frac{1}{3}, \frac{2}{4}$ — $\frac{1}{3}, \frac{3}{8}, \frac{2}{4}$
11. $\frac{2}{3}, \frac{5}{9}, \frac{7}{8}$ — $\frac{5}{9}, \frac{2}{3}, \frac{7}{8}$
12. $\frac{3}{4}, \frac{8}{12}, \frac{1}{2}$ — $\frac{1}{2}, \frac{8}{12}, \frac{3}{4}$

Problem Solving

13. In Ms. Cruz's class, $\frac{2}{3}$ of the students play only video games, $\frac{3}{5}$ play only board games, and $\frac{7}{8}$ play only outdoor games. Which group has the largest number of students? outdoor game players: $\frac{7}{8}$

14. Fran, Julio, and Doreen have entered a walkathon to raise money for a local community group. After two hours, Julio has walked $\frac{2}{3}$ of the course, Doreen has walked $\frac{7}{9}$ of the course, and Fran has walked $\frac{9}{10}$ of the course. Who is closest to the finish? Fran: $\frac{9}{10}$

Spiral Review

15. 18 × 56.3 = 1,013.4

16. 1,046 × 45 = 47,070

17. 1,800 ÷ 24 = 75

48 Grade 5, Chapter 5, Lesson 8, Cluster B

Chapter 5 ~ Lesson 9

Practice

Relate Fractions and Decimals

P 5-9 PRACTICE

Write each decimal as a fraction in simplest form.

1. 0.3 $\frac{3}{10}$	2. 0.49 $\frac{49}{100}$	3. 0.7 $\frac{7}{10}$	4. 0.50 $\frac{1}{2}$
5. 0.94 $\frac{47}{50}$	6. 0.80 $\frac{4}{5}$	7. 0.72 $\frac{18}{25}$	8. 0.2 $\frac{1}{5}$
9. 0.55 $\frac{11}{20}$	10. 0.1 $\frac{1}{10}$	11. 0.25 $\frac{1}{4}$	12. 0.03 $\frac{3}{100}$
13. 0.77 $\frac{77}{100}$	14. 0.6 $\frac{3}{5}$	15. 0.26 $\frac{13}{50}$	16. 0.99 $\frac{99}{100}$
17. 0.36 $\frac{9}{25}$	18. 0.75 $\frac{3}{4}$	19. 0.70 $\frac{7}{10}$	20. 0.4 $\frac{2}{5}$
21. 0.05 $\frac{1}{20}$	22. 0.35 $\frac{7}{20}$	23. 0.8 $\frac{4}{5}$	24. 0.63 $\frac{63}{100}$

Write each fraction as a decimal.

25. $\frac{2}{5}$ 0.4	26. $\frac{9}{20}$ 0.45	27. $\frac{3}{10}$ 0.3	28. $\frac{7}{25}$ 0.28
29. $\frac{21}{50}$ 0.42	30. $\frac{1}{2}$ 0.5	31. $\frac{89}{100}$ 0.89	32. $\frac{1}{8}$ 0.125
33. $\frac{4}{25}$ 0.16	34. $\frac{3}{5}$ 0.6	35. $\frac{23}{25}$ 0.92	36. $\frac{1}{4}$ 0.25
37. $\frac{17}{20}$ 0.85	38. $\frac{11}{100}$ 0.11	39. $\frac{7}{10}$ 0.7	40. $\frac{3}{8}$ 0.375
41. $\frac{3}{4}$ 0.75	42. $\frac{5}{8}$ 0.625	43. $\frac{1}{5}$ 0.2	44. $\frac{3}{50}$ 0.06
45. $\frac{9}{10}$ 0.9	46. $\frac{4}{5}$ 0.8	47. $\frac{1}{20}$ 0.05	48. $\frac{7}{8}$ 0.875

Problem Solving

49. The largest butterfly in the world is found in Papua, New Guinea. The female of the species weighs about 0.9 ounce. Use a fraction to write the female's weight.

$\frac{9}{10}$ ounce

50. The shortest recorded fish is the dwarf goby found in the Indo-Pacific. The female of this species is about $\frac{7}{20}$ inch long. Use a decimal to write the female's length.

0.35 inch

Use with Grade 5, Chapter 5, Lesson 9, pages 222–223. (157)

Reteach

Relate Fractions and Decimals

R 5-9 RETEACH

You can write a decimal as a fraction. Think of place value. Then simplify the fraction if necessary.

Write 0.12 as a fraction. Think: 12 hundredths

Write: $\frac{12}{100}$

Simplify: $\frac{12}{100} = \frac{12 \div 4}{100 \div 4} = \frac{3}{25}$ So, $0.12 = \frac{3}{25}$.

You can write a fraction as a decimal. Think of the fraction as a division problem.

Write $\frac{3}{5}$ as a decimal. Think: 3 divided by 5

Write: $5\overline{)3.0}$ = 0.6 So, $\frac{3}{5} = 0.6$.

Write each decimal as a fraction in simplest form.

1. 0.65

Think: 65 hundredths

Write: $\frac{65}{100}$

Simplify: $\frac{65}{100} = \frac{65 \div 5}{100 \div 5} = \frac{13}{20}$

2. 0.6

Think: 6 tenths

Write: $\frac{6}{10}$

Simplify: $\frac{6}{10} = \frac{6 \div 2}{10 \div 2} = \frac{3}{5}$

3. 0.86 $\frac{43}{50}$	4. 0.57 $\frac{57}{100}$	5. 0.5 $\frac{1}{2}$	6. 0.68 $\frac{17}{25}$
7. 0.25 $\frac{1}{4}$	8. 0.15 $\frac{3}{20}$	9. 0.40 $\frac{2}{5}$	10. 0.9 $\frac{9}{10}$

Write each fraction as a decimal.

11. $\frac{2}{25}$

Think: 2 divided by 25

Write: $25\overline{)2.00}$ = 0.08

12. $\frac{7}{10}$

Think: 7 divided by 10

Write: $10\overline{)7.0}$ = 0.7

13. $\frac{11}{25}$ 0.44	14. $\frac{31}{100}$ 0.31	15. $\frac{19}{20}$ 0.95	16. $\frac{3}{4}$ 0.75
17. $\frac{3}{10}$ 0.3	18. $\frac{29}{50}$ 0.58	19. $\frac{4}{5}$ 0.8	20. $\frac{5}{8}$ 0.625

Use with Grade 5, Chapter 5, Lesson 9, pages 222–223. (158)

Enrich

Relate Fractions and Decimals

E 5-9 ENRICH

Fraction-Decimal Match Up

Find a decimal in Box B that matches a fraction in Box A.
When you find a match, cross out both numbers and the letters next to them.

Box A

~~M $\frac{29}{50}$~~	F $\frac{1}{25}$
~~H $\frac{7}{10}$~~	~~Y $\frac{7}{25}$~~
R $\frac{2}{5}$	~~B $\frac{37}{50}$~~
~~G $\frac{1}{8}$~~	~~D $\frac{3}{5}$~~
O $\frac{1}{5}$	~~X $\frac{5}{8}$~~
I $\frac{7}{20}$	N $\frac{3}{4}$
~~E $\frac{13}{20}$~~	T $\frac{49}{50}$
~~Z $\frac{24}{25}$~~	~~S $\frac{63}{100}$~~
A $\frac{39}{100}$	C $\frac{13}{25}$
~~W $\frac{1}{4}$~~	~~P $\frac{3}{20}$~~

Box B

~~U 0.28~~	~~R 0.6~~
I 0.07	~~A 0.625~~
P 0.29	~~T 0.15~~
~~C 0.7~~	M 0.12
~~D 0.125~~	~~H 0.63~~
L 0.36	Y 0.62
I 0.18	~~E 0.58~~
~~N 0.65~~	~~K 0.96~~
S 0.5	F 0.48
~~B 0.25~~	~~G 0.74~~

Now write the letters that remain in each box. Unscramble each group of letters to spell a math word.

Box A FRACTION

Box B SIMPLIFY

How did you find the decimal for $\frac{1}{8}$?

Answers may vary. Possible answer: I divided 1 by 8.

Use with Grade 5, Chapter 5, Lesson 9, pages 222–223. (159)

Daily Homework

5-9 Relate Fractions and Decimals

Write each decimal as a fraction in simplest form.

1. 0.25 $\frac{1}{4}$	2. 0.4 $\frac{2}{5}$	3. 0.15 $\frac{3}{20}$
4. 0.75 $\frac{3}{4}$	5. 0.02 $\frac{1}{50}$	6. 0.3 $\frac{3}{10}$

Write each fraction as a decimal.

7. $\frac{1}{2}$ 0.5	8. $\frac{1}{4}$ 0.25	9. $\frac{1}{5}$ 0.2
10. $\frac{1}{8}$ 0.125	11. $\frac{2}{5}$ 0.4	12. $\frac{3}{4}$ 0.75
13. $\frac{4}{5}$ 0.8	14. $\frac{7}{8}$ 0.875	15. $\frac{5}{8}$ 0.625

Is each pair of numbers equivalent? Write *yes* or *no*.

16. $\frac{7}{20}$; 0.35 Yes.

17. $\frac{8}{25}$; 0.36 No.

18. $\frac{17}{50}$; 0.34 Yes.

19. $\frac{3}{4}$; 0.65 No.

Problem Solving

20. The plans for a picnic table call for screws that are each 0.75 inch long. In simplest form, what fraction of an inch is this? $\frac{3}{4}$

21. Jamie's weight at his checkup was $63\frac{1}{4}$ pounds. What is the decimal form of his weight? 63.25

Spiral Review

22. $2.5 \times 6.3 =$ 15.75

23. $9 \div 1.5 =$ 6

24. $7.77 \div 7 =$ 1.11

25. $0.4 \times 1.5 =$ 0.6

Grade 5, Chapter 5, Lesson 9, Cluster B 49

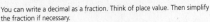

Chapter 5 ~ Lesson 10

Practice

Problem Solving: Strategy
Make a Table

P 5-10 PRACTICE

Use the make-a-table strategy to solve.

A card shop recorded the number of trading card packs sold each week.

Number of Trading Card Packs Sold					
Week	Number	Week	Number	Week	Number
1	28	5	48	9	25
2	32	6	43	10	37
3	38	7	45	11	42
4	44	8	41	12	35

1. In what fraction of the weeks was the number of trading packs sold in the range from 30 to 39? Write the fraction in simplest form. $\frac{1}{3}$

2. In what fraction of the weeks were 40 or more trading packs sold? Write the fraction in simplest form. $\frac{1}{2}$

3. **Literature** A bookstore records 8 months of sales of *The Lion, the Witch, and the Wardrobe*, by C.S. Lewis. In what fraction of the months did the number of copies sold range from 20 to 29? Write the fraction in simplest form. $\frac{1}{4}$

Bookstore Sales			
Month	Copies	Month	Copies
1	26	5	38
2	24	6	19
3	32	7	15
4	18	8	30

Mixed Strategy Review

Solve. Use any strategy. Strategies may vary

4. The number of people who became health club members in May was half as many as the number who became members in June. In July, there were 18 more members than in June. If 76 people became members in July, how many people became members altogether during the three months?
163 people
Strategy: Work backwards

5. There are 86 students in the school band and the school orchestra. There are 62 students in the band and 46 students in the orchestra. Some students play in both the band and the orchestra. How many students play in both the band and the orchestra?
22 students
Strategy: Write an equation

Use with Grade 5, Chapter 5, Lesson 10, pages 224–225. (160)

Reteach

Problem Solving: Strategy
Make a Table

R 5-10 RETEACH

Page 225, Problem 2

The record store kept track of the number of jazz CDs it sold each week. In what fraction of the weeks was the number of CDs sold in the range from 21 to 30? Write the fraction in simplest form.

Number of Jazz CDs Sold					
Week	Number	Week	Number	Week	Number
1	38	6	28	11	17
2	36	7	25	12	15
3	29	8	19	13	18
4	30	9	23	14	21
5	31	10	20	15	23

Step 1 Read

Be sure you understand the problem.
Read carefully.

What do you know?

- The number of CDs sold each week.

What do you need to find?

- The fraction of the weeks the number of CDs sold ranged from 21 to 30.

Step 2 Plan

- Find a Pattern
- Guess and Check
- Work Backward
- Make a Graph
- Make a Table
- Write an Equation
- Make an Organized List
- Draw a Diagram
- Solve a Simpler Problem
- Logical Reasoning

Make a plan.
Choose a strategy.

You can make a table to help you solve the problem.

A table can help you organize the data and make it easier to see the totals for each range.

Organize the data in ranges.

List the number of CDs sold in each range.

Range	Number of CDs Sold	Number of Weeks
11–20	19, 20, 17, 15, 18	5
21–30	29, 30, 28, 25, 23, 21, 23	7
31–40	38, 36, 31	3

Use with Grade 5, Chapter 5, Lesson 10, pages 224–225. (161)

Reteach

Problem Solving: Strategy
Make a Table

R 5-10 RETEACH

Step 3 Solve

Carry out your plan.

Make a table. Find the fraction for each range.

Range		Fraction
11–20	5 of the 15 weeks	$\frac{5}{15} = \frac{1}{3}$
21–30	7 of the 15 weeks	$\frac{7}{15}$
31–40	3 of the 15 weeks	$\frac{3}{15} = \frac{1}{5}$

In what fraction of the weeks was the number of CDs sold in the range from 21 to 30? $\frac{7}{15}$

Step 4 Look Back

Is the solution reasonable?
Reread the problem.

Does your answer make sense? Yes

What other methods could you use to check your answer?
Possible answer: Draw a diagram.

Practice

A meteorologist records the high temperature, in degrees Fahrenheit, each day.

Day	Temperature	Day	Temperature
1	90	6	79
2	86	7	82
3	91	8	76
4	94	9	83
5	88	10	90

1. In what fraction of the days did the temperature range from 80°F to 89°F? Write the fraction in simplest form. $\frac{2}{5}$

2. In what fraction of the days did the temperature range from 70°F to 79°F? Write the fraction in simplest form. $\frac{1}{5}$

Use with Grade 5, Chapter 5, Lesson 10, pages 224–225. (162)

Daily Homework

5-10 Problem Solving: Strategy

Make a Table

Use the make-a-table strategy to solve.

A video store kept track of the number of video games it rented each week.

Number of Video Games Rented

Week	Number	Week	Number	Week	Number
1	39	6	48	11	38
2	47	7	52	12	49
3	52	8	54	13	43
4	53	9	60	14	38
5	37	10	52	15	36

1. In what fraction of the weeks was the number of games rented between 31 and 40? Write the fraction in simplest form. $\frac{1}{3}$

2. In what fraction of the weeks was the number of games rented greater than 50? Write the fraction in simplest form. $\frac{1}{3}$

3. The store manager has discovered a mistake in the records. Week 1 video game rentals were actually 41, not 39. Now, in what fraction of the weeks was the number of games rented between 31 and 40? Write the fraction in simplest form. $\frac{4}{15}$

Mixed Strategy Review

4. By nearly closing time, a CD store's sales for the day were 100 CDs, of which 15 were jazz CDs. Then, one final customer bought 10 jazz CDs. What fraction of the day's total sales were jazz CDs? Write the fraction in simplest form. $\frac{1}{4}$

5. During a one-hour television show, there were 12 minutes of commercials. What fraction of the hour was not commercials? Write the fraction in simplest form. $\frac{4}{5}$

Spiral Review

Find the median.

6. 12, 18, 16, 22, 15 16

7. 21, 3, 5, 8, 13, 24 10.5

50 Grade 5, Chapter 5, Lesson 10, Cluster B

Chapter 5 ~ Lesson 11

Practice

Mixed Numbers

5-11 PRACTICE

Write each mixed number as an improper fraction.

1. $2\frac{3}{4}$ $\frac{11}{4}$ 2. $5\frac{1}{6}$ $\frac{31}{6}$ 3. $8\frac{1}{2}$ $\frac{17}{2}$ 4. $3\frac{2}{3}$ $\frac{11}{3}$

5. $7\frac{2}{5}$ $\frac{37}{5}$ 6. $1\frac{9}{10}$ $\frac{19}{10}$ 7. $4\frac{7}{8}$ $\frac{39}{8}$ 8. $6\frac{5}{7}$ $\frac{47}{7}$

9. $1\frac{8}{9}$ $\frac{17}{9}$ 10. $3\frac{12}{17}$ $\frac{63}{17}$ 11. $2\frac{1}{10}$ $\frac{21}{10}$ 12. $5\frac{5}{13}$ $\frac{70}{13}$

Write each improper fraction as a mixed number, in simplest form.

13. $\frac{18}{12}$ $1\frac{1}{2}$ 14. $\frac{22}{3}$ $7\frac{1}{3}$ 15. $\frac{27}{9}$ 3 16. $\frac{14}{4}$ $3\frac{1}{2}$

17. $\frac{28}{6}$ $4\frac{2}{3}$ 18. $\frac{64}{8}$ 8 19. $\frac{13}{5}$ $2\frac{3}{5}$ 20. $\frac{46}{8}$ $5\frac{3}{4}$

21. $\frac{21}{8}$ $2\frac{5}{8}$ 22. $\frac{64}{35}$ $1\frac{29}{35}$ 23. $\frac{19}{3}$ $6\frac{1}{3}$ 24. $\frac{44}{8}$ $5\frac{1}{2}$

Write each mixed number as a decimal.

25. $3\frac{7}{10}$ 3.7 26. $4\frac{1}{2}$ 4.5 27. $4\frac{1}{10}$ 4.1 28. $5\frac{2}{5}$ 5.4

29. $8\frac{3}{4}$ 8.75 30. $2\frac{3}{5}$ 2.6 31. $5\frac{1}{4}$ 5.25 32. $1\frac{9}{10}$ 1.9

Write each decimal as a mixed number in simplest form.

33. 7.5 $7\frac{1}{2}$ 34. 6.4 $6\frac{2}{5}$ 35. 5.25 $5\frac{1}{4}$ 36. 8.31 $8\frac{31}{100}$

37. 3.72 $3\frac{18}{25}$ 38. 2.75 $2\frac{3}{4}$ 39. 9.6 $9\frac{3}{5}$ 40. 1.9 $1\frac{9}{10}$

41. 5.25 $5\frac{1}{4}$ 42. 3.9 $3\frac{9}{10}$ 43. 9.12 $9\frac{3}{25}$ 44. 6.5 $5\frac{1}{2}$

Problem Solving

45. A shipment of boxes weighs 30 pounds. There are 8 boxes and each weighs the same number of pounds. How much does each box weigh?
$3\frac{3}{4}$ pounds

46. Each box in another shipment weighs $3\frac{1}{6}$ pounds. There are 6 boxes in the shipment. What is the total weight of the shipment?
19 pounds

Use with Grade 5, Chapter 5, Lesson 11, pages 226–229. (163)

Reteach

Mixed Numbers

5-11 RETEACH

Write $\frac{7}{2}$ as a mixed number and as a decimal.

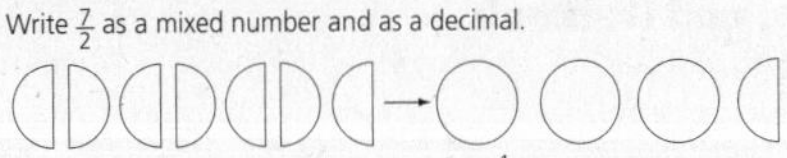

Write $\frac{7}{2}$ as a mixed number.

$\frac{7}{2} = \frac{2}{2} + \frac{2}{2} + \frac{2}{2} + \frac{1}{2}$

$= 3 + \frac{1}{2}$

$= 3\frac{1}{2}$

Write $3\frac{1}{2}$ as a decimal.

$3\frac{1}{2} = 3 + \frac{1}{2}$

$= 3 + 0.5$

$= 3.5$

Write 1.75 as a mixed number and as an improper fraction.

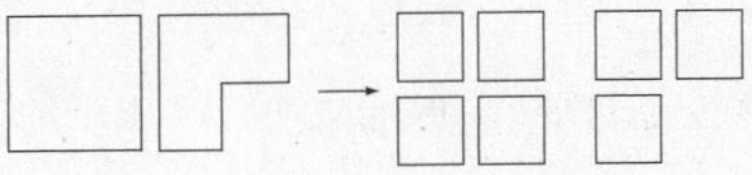

$1.75 = 1 + 0.75$

$= 1 + \frac{3}{4}$

$= 1\frac{3}{4}$

$1\frac{3}{4} = 1 + \frac{3}{4}$

$= \frac{4}{4} + \frac{3}{4}$

$= \frac{7}{4}$

1. Write $\frac{9}{4}$ as a mixed number.

$\frac{9}{4} = \frac{4}{4} + \frac{4}{4} + \frac{1}{4}$

$= 2 + \frac{1}{4}$

$= 2\frac{1}{4}$

Write the mixed number as a decimal.

$2\frac{1}{4} = 2 + \frac{1}{4}$

$= 2 + 0.25$

$= 2.25$

2. Write 2.3 as a mixed number.

$2.3 = 2 + 0.3$

$= 2 + \frac{3}{10}$

$= 2\frac{3}{10}$

Write the mixed number as an improper fraction.

$2\frac{3}{10} = 2 + \frac{3}{10}$

$= \frac{10}{10} + \frac{10}{10} + \frac{3}{10}$

$= \frac{23}{10}$

Use with Grade 5, Chapter 5, Lesson 11, pages 226–229. (164)

Enrich

Mixed Numbers

5-11 ENRICH

A-Maze-ing Mixed Numbers

Find a path through the maze. Shade the spaces that connect two equivalent numbers.

Start

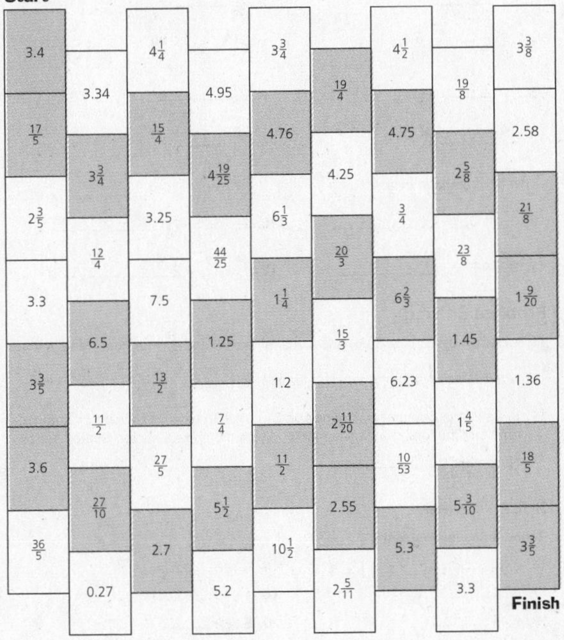

Finish

Use with Grade 5, Chapter 5, Lesson 11, pages 226–229. (165)

Daily Homework

5-11 Mixed Numbers

Write each mixed number as an improper fraction.

1. $2\frac{2}{3}$ $\frac{8}{3}$ 2. $4\frac{3}{5}$ $\frac{23}{5}$ 3. $6\frac{5}{6}$ $\frac{41}{6}$

4. $7\frac{1}{3}$ $\frac{22}{3}$ 5. $5\frac{4}{5}$ $\frac{29}{5}$ 6. $2\frac{3}{4}$ $\frac{11}{4}$

Write each improper fraction as a mixed number, in simplest form.

7. $\frac{7}{2}$ $3\frac{1}{2}$ 8. $\frac{16}{4}$ 4 9. $\frac{17}{3}$ $5\frac{2}{3}$

10. $\frac{18}{2}$ 9 11. $\frac{22}{8}$ $2\frac{3}{4}$ 12. $\frac{21}{9}$ $2\frac{1}{3}$

Write each mixed number as a decimal.

13. $3\frac{1}{2}$ 3.5 14. $4\frac{3}{4}$ 4.75 15. $7\frac{1}{5}$ 7.2

Write each decimal as a mixed number in simplest form.

16. 4.25 $4\frac{1}{4}$ 17. 6.4 $6\frac{2}{5}$ 18. 7.75 $7\frac{3}{4}$

Problem Solving

19. The plans for a kite call for a piece of string 7.75 inches long. What is this measurement expressed as a mixed number in simplest form?
$7\frac{3}{4}$ in.

20. On a space mission, an astronaut spends 10 days and 6 hours in a space station. What is this time period in days, expressed as a mixed number in simplest form?
$10\frac{1}{4}$ days

Spiral Review

21. 5(7 − 3) = 20

22. 4(7 − 2) = 20

23. 6(8 − 5) = 18

24. 8(8 − 4) = 32

Grade 5, Chapter 5, Lesson 11, Cluster B 51

Chapter 5 ~ Lesson 12

Practice

Compare and Order Fractions, Mixed Numbers, and Decimals

P 5-12 PRACTICE

Compare. Write >, <, or =.

1. $3\frac{2}{3}$ (<) $3\frac{3}{4}$
2. 0.75 (=) $\frac{3}{4}$
3. $2\frac{1}{4}$ (<) 2.4
4. $5\frac{3}{4}$ (<) 5.825
5. 4.3 (<) $4\frac{3}{5}$
6. $4\frac{1}{7}$ (>) $2\frac{1}{4}$
7. $5\frac{1}{3}$ (<) 6.7
8. 4.25 (<) $4\frac{1}{3}$
9. 0.4 (>) $\frac{1}{4}$
10. $1\frac{3}{5}$ (<) $5\frac{7}{10}$
11. $3\frac{3}{5}$ (=) 3.6
12. $2\frac{9}{10}$ (<) 2.99
13. $\frac{3}{4}$ (<) 0.9
14. $7\frac{4}{5}$ (>) $7\frac{3}{4}$
15. $\frac{2}{5}$ (>) 0.25
16. 9.5 (=) $9\frac{1}{2}$
17. 0.7 (<) $\frac{4}{5}$
18. $8\frac{11}{12}$ (<) $9\frac{5}{6}$

Order from greatest to least.

19. $\frac{1}{3}$, $\frac{3}{5}$, 0.5 $\frac{3}{5}$, 0.5, $\frac{1}{3}$
20. 0.2, 0.9, $\frac{4}{5}$ 0.9, $\frac{4}{5}$, 0.2
21. $\frac{1}{2}$, 0.4, $\frac{3}{4}$ $\frac{3}{4}$, $\frac{1}{2}$, 0.4
22. 0.6, 5.6, $5\frac{1}{6}$ 5.6, $5\frac{1}{6}$, 0.6
23. 4.2, 4, $4\frac{1}{4}$ $4\frac{1}{4}$, 4.2, 4
24. 2.8, $2\frac{5}{8}$, $2\frac{9}{10}$ $2\frac{9}{10}$, 2.8, $2\frac{5}{8}$
25. 3.85, 4.65, $3\frac{3}{4}$ 4.65, 3.85, $3\frac{3}{4}$
26. $7\frac{1}{8}$, 7.08, 7.18 7.18, $7\frac{1}{8}$, 7.08
27. $4\frac{11}{20}$, 3.5, $4\frac{1}{2}$ $4\frac{11}{20}$, $4\frac{1}{2}$, 3.5
28. $5\frac{1}{4}$, $5\frac{1}{3}$, 5.28 $5\frac{1}{3}$, 5.28, $5\frac{1}{4}$

Problem Solving

29. Martin entered a cross-country race that covered $6\frac{2}{5}$ miles. If Martin runs 6.2 miles, does he complete the race? Explain.

No; $6\frac{2}{5} = 6.4$ and $6.2 < 6.4$

30. Rita tried to break the school high-jump record of $5\frac{3}{4}$ feet. She cleared 5.5 feet. Did she break the record? Explain.

No; $5.5 = 5\frac{1}{2} = 5\frac{2}{4}$ and $5\frac{2}{4} < 5\frac{3}{4}$

Use with Grade 5, Chapter 5, Lesson 12, pages 230–233. (166)

Reteach

Compare and Order Fractions, Mixed Numbers, and Decimals

R 5-12 RETEACH

When you compare and order mixed numbers and decimals greater than 1, always look at the whole numbers first.

Compare $1\frac{3}{4}$ and 2.7. Look at the whole numbers.

$1\frac{3}{4}$ 2.7

$1 < 2$, so $1\frac{3}{4} < 2.7$.

Sometimes the whole numbers are the same. Then you must compare the fraction and decimal parts of the numbers. To do this, write them in the same form.

Compare $1\frac{3}{4}$ and 1.7.

The whole numbers are the same, so compare $\frac{3}{4}$ and 0.7.

Write both numbers as fractions OR Write both numbers as decimals.

$\frac{3}{4}$ ↓ $\frac{3}{4}$ ↓ $\frac{15}{20}$ > $\frac{14}{20}$ ↑ $\frac{7}{10}$ ↑ 0.7

$\frac{3}{4} > 0.7$, so $1\frac{3}{4} > 1.7$.

$\frac{3}{4}$ ↓ 0.75 > 0.7 ↑ 0.7

$\frac{3}{4} > 0.7$, so $1\frac{3}{4} > 1.7$.

Compare. Write >, <, or =.

1. Compare $3\frac{3}{5}$ and 3.5.
The whole numbers are the same, so compare $\frac{3}{5}$ and 0.5.

$\frac{3}{5}$ 0.5 → $\frac{3}{5}$ $\frac{5}{10}$; $\frac{6}{10}$ (>) $\frac{5}{10}$; $3\frac{3}{5}$ (>) 3.5
OR
$\frac{3}{5}$ 0.5 → 0.6 (>) 0.5; $3\frac{3}{5}$ (>) 3.5

2. Compare $1\frac{4}{5}$ and 1.82.
The whole numbers are the same, so compare $\frac{4}{5}$ and 0.82.

$\frac{4}{5}$ 0.82 → $\frac{4}{5}$ $\frac{82}{100}$; $\frac{80}{100}$ (<) $\frac{82}{100}$; $1\frac{4}{5}$ (>) 1.82
OR
$\frac{4}{5}$ 0.82 → 0.8 (<) 0.82; $1\frac{4}{5}$ (<) 1.82

3. $5\frac{3}{4}$ (>) 5.4
4. 0.65 (<) $\frac{4}{5}$
5. 4.2 (<) $4\frac{1}{2}$
6. 3.9 (=) $3\frac{9}{10}$
7. 2.3 (>) $1\frac{1}{3}$
8. 2.88 (>) $2\frac{7}{10}$

Use with Grade 5, Chapter 5, Lesson 12, pages 230–233. (167)

Enrich

Compare and Order Fractions, Mixed Numbers, and Decimals

E 5-12 ENRICH

Make an Orderly Path!

Shade the squares to make a path from Start to Finish. You may move left, right, up, down, or diagonal, but you must move to a square that contains a greater number. Paths may be different. Possible path is given.

Finish

4.9	$5\frac{11}{100}$	5.29	5	$5\frac{7}{20}$	5.5	7.4	$7\frac{7}{10}$	7	$7\frac{7}{8}$
4.75	$4\frac{4}{5}$	$5\frac{3}{10}$	4.1	5.39	$7\frac{1}{20}$	$7\frac{1}{25}$	7.02	7.004	7.78
4.3	vowels in alphabet	$4\frac{3}{10}$	$5\frac{1}{2}$	$5\frac{3}{8}$	$5\frac{2}{5}$	$6\frac{7}{8}$	7.1	$7\frac{1}{20}$	$7\frac{16}{25}$
4	4.35	$4\frac{9}{50}$	4.15	5.55	5.056	days in week	$6\frac{23}{25}$	$7\frac{1}{4}$	7.6
$4\frac{13}{50}$	$4\frac{3}{25}$	$4\frac{1}{5}$	$4\frac{1}{10}$	half dozen	$5\frac{9}{20}$	$6\frac{19}{20}$	$6\frac{5}{8}$	$6\frac{4}{5}$	$7\frac{3}{20}$
4.1	4.04	$4\frac{1}{8}$	4.009	$6\frac{3}{8}$	5.7	$6\frac{3}{10}$	6.88	6.78	6.778
4	$3\frac{19}{20}$	4.08	3.64	3.09	6.38	$6\frac{8}{25}$	6.33	6.8	$6\frac{77}{100}$
$\frac{5}{8}$	3.99	full weeks in a month	$3\frac{7}{10}$	1.7	1.725	$6\frac{2}{5}$	$6\frac{3}{4}$	6.5	$6\frac{39}{50}$
$\frac{1}{8}$	0.28	$\frac{1}{5}$	0.42	1.75	$1\frac{18}{25}$	$6\frac{39}{100}$	6.385	$6\frac{7}{10}$	6.87
$\frac{1}{4}$	0.3	0.45	$1\frac{9}{20}$	1.4	$1\frac{7}{10}$	6.4	$6\frac{3}{8}$	6	6.75

Start

Explain how to compare 1.75 to $1\frac{7}{10}$.

Possible answer: First, compare the whole-number parts: 1 = 1; then compare the decimal part and the fraction part: $0.75 = \frac{75}{100}$, $\frac{7}{10} = \frac{70}{100}$, $\frac{75}{100} > \frac{70}{100}$; so, $0.75 > \frac{7}{10}$; $1.75 > 1\frac{7}{10}$.

Use with Grade 5, Chapter 5, Lesson 12, pages 230–233. (168)

Daily Homework

5-12 Compare and Order Fractions, Mixed Numbers, and Decimals

Compare. Write <, >, or =.

1. $1\frac{1}{4}$ < $1\frac{1}{2}$
2. $2\frac{3}{5}$ > $2\frac{1}{2}$
3. $4\frac{1}{2}$ < $4\frac{6}{10}$
4. $6\frac{1}{3}$ > $\frac{25}{4}$
5. $\frac{19}{4}$ > $4\frac{3}{8}$
6. $8\frac{2}{8}$ = $8\frac{1}{4}$
7. $2\frac{4}{5}$ > $2\frac{3}{4}$
8. $7\frac{2}{3}$ < $7\frac{3}{4}$

Order from greatest to least.

9. $5\frac{2}{3}$, 5.9, $5\frac{3}{4}$ 5.9, $5\frac{3}{4}$, $5\frac{2}{3}$
10. $7\frac{1}{3}$, 7.25, $7\frac{1}{5}$ $7\frac{1}{3}$, 7.25, $7\frac{1}{5}$
11. $9\frac{2}{5}$, $9\frac{3}{4}$, $9\frac{1}{2}$ $9\frac{3}{4}$, $9\frac{1}{2}$, $9\frac{2}{5}$
12. $4\frac{1}{8}$, $4\frac{1}{6}$, 4.2 4.2, $4\frac{1}{6}$, $4\frac{1}{8}$

Problem Solving

13. A certain brand of soap claims to make you "98 and $\frac{64}{100}$ percent clean." What is this mixed number in simplest terms? $98\frac{16}{25}$

14. In Seattle in September, it rained on 24 out of 30 days. In November, it rained on 0.6 of the total days in the month. Which month was rainier, September or November? September

Spiral Review

Round to the nearest tenth.

15. 3.25 3.3
16. 6.143 6.1
17. 8.27 8.3
18. 1.976 2.0
19. 7.44 7.4
20. 5.362 5.4

52 Grade 5, Chapter 5, Lesson 12, Cluster B

Chapter 5 ~ Lesson 13

Part A Worksheet

Problem Solving: Application
Organize the School Orchestra

Part A 5-13 WORKSHEET Decision Making

Use the table to help you decide on the number of musicians for each instrument.

Number of Musicians for Each Instrument			
Instrument	Choice 1	Choice 2	Choice 3
Violin			
Viola			
Cello			
Bass			
Flute			
Oboe			
Clarinet			
Bassoon			
Horns			
Trumpet			
Trombone			
Tuba			
Timpani and Percussion			
Piano			
Total Number of Musicians			

Your Decision

How many of each instrument did you decide to use in your orchestra? Write the answer as a fraction and decimal of the whole orchestra.

Answers may vary. Total number of musicians for each choice should be 100.

What factors did you consider when making your final choice of music and the number of musicians for each instrument? What musical program will you present?

Answers may vary. Total number of musicians for each choice should be 100.

Use with Grade 5, Chapter 5, Lesson 13, pages 234–235. (169)

Part B Worksheet

Problem Solving: Application
What are the properties of matter?

Part B 5-13 WORKSHEET Math & Science

Reminder: You can classify states of matter as solids, liquids, or gases.

Record the state of matter of each object in the table below.

Object	State of matter

Record the data about your observations in the table below.

Property	Fraction
Hold shape	
Fill a container	
Expand in a container	

1. Use your data.

Which states of matter hold their shape? solid

Which states of matter fill a container? liquid

Which states of matter expand in a container? gas

Use with Grade 5, Chapter 5, Lesson 13, pages 236–237. (170)

Part B Worksheet

Problem Solving: Application
What are the properties of matter?

Part B 5-13 WORKSHEET Math & Science

2. Explain how you decided on the state of matter of each object.

Objects that hold their shapes are solids, objects that fill a container are liquids, objects that expand in a container are gases.

3. Define gas, liquid, and solid.

Answers may vary. Possible answer: Gas: A form of matter that can move about freely and does not have a definite shape. Liquid: A form of matter that can flow easily and take the shape of any container into which it is poured. Solid: A form of matter that has shape and hardness.

4. Based on the fractions you found, would you conclude that most objects are solids, liquids, or gases?

Answers may vary.

5. Use data in *Did You Know?* to order gas, liquid, and solid from greatest density to least.

solid, liquid, gas

6. Can you think of any common objects which can be transformed from a solid to a liquid to a gas or a liquid to a gas? Explain. What do you think causes the transformation?

Possible answer: Ice (a solid) melts to become water (a liquid) which can evaporate to become water vapor (a gas). Water vapor can condense to become water which can be frozen to become ice. Heat changes the state.

Use with Grade 5, Chapter 5, Lesson 13, pages 236–237. (171)

Chapter 6 ~ Lesson 1

Practice

Add and Subtract Fractions and Mixed Numbers with Like Denominators

6-1 PRACTICE

Add or subtract. Write your answer in simplest form.

1. $\frac{7}{10} + \frac{1}{10} = \underline{\frac{4}{5}}$ **2.** $\frac{13}{16} - \frac{7}{16} = \underline{\frac{3}{8}}$ **3.** $\frac{4}{5} + \frac{1}{5} = \underline{1}$

4. $\frac{7}{12} - \frac{5}{12} = \underline{\frac{1}{6}}$ **5.** $\frac{4}{5} - \frac{1}{5} = \underline{\frac{3}{5}}$ **6.** $\frac{5}{6} + \frac{5}{6} = \underline{1\frac{2}{3}}$

7. $\frac{3}{8} + \frac{5}{8} = \underline{1}$ **8.** $\frac{9}{10} - \frac{7}{10} = \underline{\frac{1}{5}}$ **9.** $\frac{3}{4} + \frac{3}{4} = \underline{1\frac{1}{2}}$

10. $3\frac{3}{8} + 2\frac{1}{8} = 5\frac{1}{2}$ **11.** $7\frac{2}{3} + 6\frac{1}{3} = 14$ **12.** $9\frac{5}{6} - 5\frac{1}{6} = 4\frac{2}{3}$ **13.** $11\frac{7}{16} - 3\frac{3}{16} = 8\frac{1}{4}$

14. $8\frac{3}{10} + 5\frac{9}{10} = 14\frac{1}{5}$ **15.** $16\frac{7}{8} - 7\frac{7}{8} = 9$ **16.** $4\frac{7}{12} + 7\frac{11}{12} = 12\frac{1}{2}$ **17.** $14\frac{19}{20} - 8\frac{5}{20} = 6\frac{7}{10}$

18. $27\frac{11}{16} + 43\frac{9}{16} = 71\frac{1}{4}$ **19.** $98\frac{9}{10} - 16\frac{1}{10} = 82\frac{4}{5}$ **20.** $52\frac{1}{6} + 35\frac{5}{6} = 88$ **21.** $74\frac{11}{12} - 29\frac{7}{12} = 45\frac{1}{3}$

Algebra & Functions Find each missing number.

22. $\frac{2}{5} + \underline{\frac{4}{5}} = 1\frac{1}{5}$ **23.** $\frac{7}{8} - \underline{\frac{1}{8}} = \frac{3}{4}$ **24.** $\underline{\frac{9}{16}} - \frac{5}{16} = \frac{1}{4}$

25. $r + 2\frac{1}{4} = 4$ $r = \underline{1\frac{3}{4}}$ **26.** $8\frac{1}{6} - b = 7$ $b = \underline{1\frac{1}{6}}$ **27.** $3\frac{11}{12} + h = 6\frac{1}{3}$ $h = \underline{2\frac{5}{12}}$

Problem Solving

28. A stock trading at $\$9\frac{5}{8}$ rose $\$1\frac{5}{8}$ during one day. At what price did the stock close that day?

$\underline{\$11\frac{1}{4}}$

29. A stock opened at $\$18\frac{3}{4}$ and closed at $\$15\frac{1}{4}$. How much did the stock fall during the day?

$\underline{\$3\frac{1}{2}}$

Reteach

Add and Subtract Fractions and Mixed Numbers with Like Denominators

6-1 RETEACH

You can use a number line to help you add and subtract fractions and mixed numbers with like denominators.

Add $1\frac{7}{8} + 2\frac{7}{8}$. Estimate: $2 + 3 = 5$

Locate $1\frac{7}{8}$ on the number line.

Add the fraction, $\frac{7}{8}$.

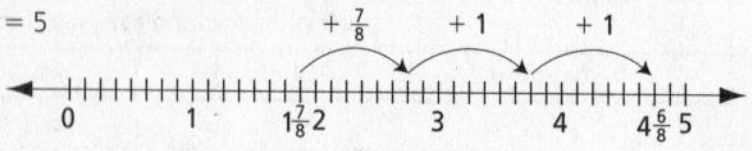

Then add the whole number, 2.

$1\frac{7}{8} + 2\frac{7}{8} = 4\frac{6}{8} = 4\frac{3}{4}$

$4\frac{3}{4}$ is close to 5, so $4\frac{3}{4}$ is reasonable.

Subtract $4\frac{2}{3} - 1\frac{1}{3}$. Estimate: $5 - 1 = 4$

Locate $4\frac{2}{3}$ on the number line.

Subtract the fraction, $\frac{1}{3}$.

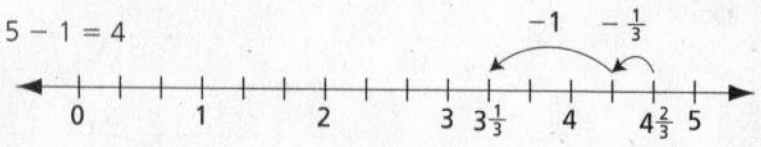

Then subtract the whole number, 1.

$4\frac{2}{3} - 1\frac{1}{3} = 3\frac{1}{3}$

Use the number line to add or subtract. Write your answer in simplest form.

1. $1\frac{7}{10} + 1\frac{9}{10} = \underline{3\frac{3}{5}}$

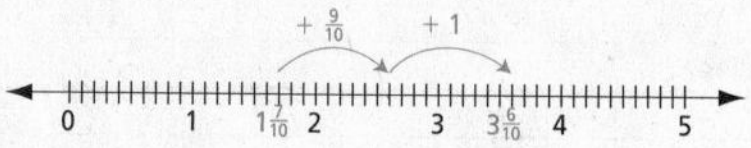

2. $4\frac{4}{5} - 2\frac{3}{5} = \underline{2\frac{1}{5}}$

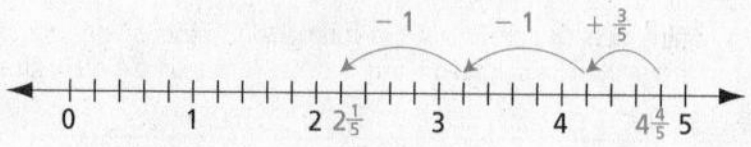

Add or subtract. You may use a number line. Write your answer in simplest form.

3. $6\frac{11}{12} - 4\frac{5}{12} = \underline{2\frac{1}{2}}$ **4.** $4\frac{2}{3} + 4\frac{2}{3} = \underline{9\frac{1}{3}}$ **5.** $2\frac{7}{16} + 1\frac{5}{16} = \underline{3\frac{3}{4}}$

6. $5\frac{7}{10} - 2\frac{1}{10} = \underline{3\frac{3}{5}}$ **7.** $3\frac{1}{6} + 4\frac{5}{6} = \underline{8}$ **8.** $6\frac{7}{8} - 1\frac{3}{8} = \underline{5\frac{1}{2}}$

Enrich

Add and Subtract Fractions and Mixed Numbers with Like Denominators

6-1 ENRICH

Sum and Difference Pair-Up

Find the sums and differences for the exercises in the squares. Shade pairs of adjacent squares that have the same answer to find a path through the maze.

Start

$9\frac{5}{8} - 4\frac{3}{8}$ ($5\frac{1}{4}$)	$6\frac{7}{8} - 2\frac{5}{8}$ ($4\frac{1}{4}$)	$2\frac{1}{8} + 1\frac{1}{8}$ ($3\frac{1}{4}$)	$15\frac{17}{20} - 7\frac{1}{20}$ ($8\frac{4}{5}$)	$3\frac{1}{3} + 3\frac{1}{3}$ ($6\frac{2}{3}$)	$9\frac{7}{8} - 3\frac{1}{8}$ ($6\frac{3}{4}$)	$4\frac{15}{16} + \frac{13}{16}$ ($5\frac{3}{4}$)
$2\frac{1}{16} + 3\frac{3}{16}$ ($5\frac{1}{4}$)	$4\frac{7}{8} + 2\frac{7}{8}$ ($7\frac{3}{4}$)	$6\frac{5}{8} + 1\frac{5}{8}$ ($8\frac{1}{4}$)	$1\frac{7}{8} + 7\frac{3}{8}$ ($9\frac{1}{4}$)	$15\frac{5}{16} - 6\frac{1}{16}$ ($9\frac{1}{4}$)	$15\frac{4}{5} - 8\frac{3}{5}$ ($7\frac{1}{5}$)	$2\frac{1}{16} + 4\frac{11}{16}$ ($6\frac{3}{4}$)
$9\frac{13}{16} - 2\frac{1}{16}$ ($7\frac{3}{4}$)	$3\frac{5}{12} + \frac{5}{12}$ ($3\frac{5}{6}$)	$2\frac{5}{12} + 2\frac{5}{12}$ ($4\frac{5}{6}$)	$3\frac{1}{20} + 2\frac{3}{20}$ ($5\frac{1}{5}$)	$9\frac{5}{8} - 4\frac{3}{8}$ ($5\frac{1}{4}$)	$17\frac{7}{20} - 9\frac{3}{20}$ ($8\frac{1}{5}$)	$5\frac{4}{5} + 2\frac{2}{5}$ ($8\frac{1}{5}$)
$8\frac{19}{20} - 5\frac{3}{20}$ ($3\frac{4}{5}$)	$1\frac{11}{12} + 1\frac{11}{12}$ ($3\frac{5}{6}$)	$7\frac{1}{10} - 2$ ($5\frac{1}{10}$)	$14\frac{9}{10} - 9\frac{7}{10}$ ($5\frac{1}{5}$)	$1\frac{7}{10} + 1\frac{7}{10}$ ($3\frac{2}{5}$)	$2\frac{2}{3} + 3\frac{2}{3}$ ($6\frac{1}{3}$)	$3\frac{11}{12} + 3\frac{11}{12}$ ($7\frac{5}{6}$)
$6\frac{4}{5} - 4\frac{1}{5}$ ($2\frac{3}{5}$)	$\frac{9}{10} + 1\frac{7}{10}$ ($2\frac{3}{5}$)	$3\frac{4}{5} - 2\frac{1}{5}$ ($1\frac{3}{5}$)	$6\frac{1}{4} + 7\frac{1}{4}$ ($13\frac{1}{2}$)	$1\frac{3}{5} + 2\frac{4}{5}$ ($4\frac{2}{5}$)	$13\frac{5}{12} - 7\frac{1}{12}$ ($6\frac{1}{3}$)	$10\frac{2}{3} - 5\frac{1}{3}$ ($5\frac{1}{3}$)
$1\frac{4}{5} + 8\frac{4}{5}$ ($10\frac{3}{5}$)	$5\frac{9}{10} - 4\frac{1}{10}$ ($1\frac{4}{5}$)	$1\frac{13}{16} + 2\frac{13}{16}$ ($4\frac{5}{8}$)	$1\frac{3}{16} + 1\frac{9}{16}$ ($2\frac{3}{4}$)	$8\frac{19}{20} - 4\frac{11}{20}$ ($4\frac{2}{5}$)	$8\frac{1}{2} - 4$ ($4\frac{1}{2}$)	$2\frac{13}{16} + 2\frac{9}{16}$ ($5\frac{3}{8}$)
$3\frac{1}{20} + 1\frac{7}{20}$ ($4\frac{2}{5}$)	$2\frac{1}{2} + 1\frac{1}{2}$ (4)	$4\frac{13}{16} - \frac{3}{16}$ ($4\frac{5}{8}$)	$9\frac{5}{6} - 7\frac{1}{6}$ ($2\frac{2}{3}$)	$1\frac{7}{12} + 1\frac{1}{12}$ ($2\frac{2}{3}$)	$8\frac{11}{12} - 6\frac{7}{12}$ ($2\frac{1}{3}$)	$11\frac{11}{16} - 6\frac{5}{16}$ ($5\frac{3}{8}$)

Finish

Daily Homework

6-1 Add and Subtract Fractions and Mixed Numbers with Like Denominators

Add or subtract. Write your answer in simplest form.

1. $\frac{1}{5} + \frac{2}{5} = \underline{\frac{3}{5}}$ **2.** $3\frac{4}{6} - 2\frac{1}{6} = \underline{1\frac{1}{2}}$ **3.** $5\frac{1}{4} + 2\frac{1}{4} = \underline{7\frac{1}{2}}$

4. $5\frac{2}{7} - 2\frac{1}{7} = \underline{3\frac{1}{7}}$ **5.** $4\frac{4}{9} + 2\frac{2}{9} = \underline{6\frac{2}{3}}$ **6.** $8\frac{7}{12} - 4\frac{3}{12} = \underline{4\frac{1}{3}}$

7. $7\frac{7}{8} - 4\frac{3}{8} = 3\frac{1}{2}$ **8.** $8\frac{5}{9} + 4\frac{1}{9} = 12\frac{2}{3}$ **9.** $6\frac{5}{6} - 2\frac{1}{6} = 4\frac{2}{3}$ **10.** $15\frac{7}{10} - 9\frac{3}{10} = 6\frac{2}{5}$

Problem Solving

11. $16\frac{3}{8} + 12\frac{5}{8} = 29$ **12.** $18\frac{9}{12} - 14\frac{1}{12} = 4\frac{2}{3}$ **13.** $8\frac{5}{8} - 3\frac{1}{8} = 5\frac{1}{2}$ **14.** $29\frac{7}{12} - 22\frac{1}{12} = 7\frac{1}{2}$

15. Jolene needs to cut a piece of ribbon $4\frac{1}{4}$ in. long from a longer piece that is $10\frac{3}{4}$ in. long. How much ribbon will be left after she cuts off the piece she needs? $\underline{6\frac{1}{2}\text{ in.}}$

16. Carl was $52\frac{3}{8}$ in. tall at the start of the school year and $54\frac{7}{8}$ in. tall at the end of the school year. How many inches did Carl grow during the school year? $\underline{2\frac{1}{2}\text{ in.}}$

Spiral Review

Compare. Write <, >, or =.

17. $\frac{1}{10}$ $\underline{=}$ 0.1 **18.** $\frac{2}{9}$ $\underline{<}$ $\frac{3}{8}$ **19.** 4.25 $\underline{<}$ $4\frac{4}{5}$

Chapter 6 ~ Lesson 2

Practice

Problem Solving: Reading for Math
Choosing an Operation

P 6-2 PRACTICE — Reading Skill

Solve. Tell how you chose the operation.

1. Ms. Montoya made $2\frac{3}{4}$ pounds of goat cheese in the morning. In the afternoon, she made $1\frac{1}{4}$ pounds of goat cheese. How much goat cheese did Ms. Montoya make for the day?
   4 lb of goat cheese; You need to find the total amount of cheese made.

2. The Wilsons decided to churn butter for a family project. The boys in the family made $2\frac{1}{2}$ pounds of butter. How much butter did the girls make if the Wilson children made a total of $4\frac{1}{2}$ pounds of butter?
   2 pounds; You need to find the difference, so subtract.

3. Clara picked $4\frac{1}{2}$ bushels of apples. Franz picked $3\frac{1}{2}$ bushels of apples. How many more bushels of apples did Clara pick than Franz?
   1 bushel; The words *how many more* indicate subtraction.

4. Tina has $2\frac{3}{4}$ pounds of raisins. She uses $1\frac{1}{4}$ pounds of raisins to make a fruit salad. How many pounds of raisins does Tina have left?
   $1\frac{1}{2}$ pounds; The words *how many left* indicate subtraction.

5. Miguel picked $3\frac{1}{4}$ pounds of grapes from his vine last week. This week, he picked $2\frac{1}{4}$ pounds of grapes. What is the total number of pounds of grapes Miguel picked last week and this week?
   $5\frac{1}{2}$ pounds; The word *total* indicates addition.

6. At the beginning of the week, there were $2\frac{7}{8}$ pounds of almonds in the jar. By the end of the week, there were $1\frac{5}{8}$ pounds of almonds in the jar. What is the difference in the amount of almonds in the jar from the beginning of the week to the end of the week?
   $1\frac{1}{4}$ pounds; The word *difference* indicates subtraction.

Use with Grade 5, Chapter 6, Lesson 2, pages 256–257. (175)

Practice

Problem Solving: Reading for Math
Choosing an Operation

P 6-2 PRACTICE — Math Skills Test Prep

Choose the correct answer.

Mr. Clark shipped four packages of cheese. Each package contained $1\frac{1}{2}$ pounds of cheese. Mr. Clark shipped a total of 6 pounds of cheese.

1. Which of the following statements is true?
   A Each package held 6 pounds of cheese.
   B Two packages contained 4 pounds of cheese.
   (C) Two packages contained 3 pounds of cheese.
   D Mr. Clark shipped 6 packages of cheese.

2. When you are deciding which operation to use, you should
   F estimate the answer.
   G try addition first.
   H never use subtraction.
   (J) use key words to help you decide.

Kimberly has 3 jars of maple syrup. Each jar contains $1\frac{1}{4}$ pounds of maple syrup. Kimberly ships one jar of the syrup to her brother.

3. Which of the following statements is true?
   A Kimberly has 3 pounds of maple syrup.
   B Kimberly ships $2\frac{1}{2}$ jars of syrup to her brother.
   C Kimberly had $3\frac{1}{2}$ pounds of maple syrup altogether.
   (D) Kimberly has $2\frac{1}{2}$ pounds of maple syrup left.

4. Which of the following is a word that might help you identify subtraction as the operation to solve a problem?
   F total
   (G) difference
   H sum
   J altogether

Alan shipped 3 packages of mushrooms. Each box held $2\frac{1}{8}$ pounds of mushrooms. Alan shipped a total of $6\frac{3}{8}$ pounds of mushrooms.

5. Which of the following statements is NOT true?
   A One box contained $2\frac{1}{8}$ pounds of mushrooms.
   (B) Two boxes contained $3\frac{3}{8}$ pounds of mushrooms.
   C Two packages contained $4\frac{1}{4}$ pounds of mushrooms.
   D Three packages contained $6\frac{3}{8}$ pounds of mushrooms.

6. Which of the following might help you identify addition as the operation to solve a problem?
   F how much less
   G decrease
   H difference
   (J) in all

Use with Grade 5, Chapter 6, Lesson 2, pages 256–257. (176)

Practice

Problem Solving: Reading for Math
Choosing an Operation

P 6-2 PRACTICE — Math Skills Test Prep

Choose the correct answer.

Melissa shipped 4 cans of almonds in 2 packages. Each can contained $1\frac{1}{2}$ pounds of almonds.

7. Which of the following statements is true?
   A Both packages contained 4 cans of almonds.
   B One package contained 6 pounds of almonds.
   (C) Both packages contained 3 pounds of almonds.
   D Each package contained $1\frac{1}{2}$ cans of almonds.

8. To decide which operation to use to solve a problem, you should
   (F) look for clues in the problem.
   G guess the answer.
   H ignore key words.
   J always subtract first.

Solve.

The table shows the pounds of raisins the Taylor family made from their grapes last week. Use data from the table for problems 9–14.

Day	Monday	Tuesday	Wednesday	Thursday	Friday
Pounds of Raisins	$5\frac{3}{8}$	$3\frac{1}{8}$	$4\frac{3}{4}$	$6\frac{7}{8}$	$2\frac{1}{4}$

9. How many pounds of raisins were made on Monday and Tuesday?
   $8\frac{1}{2}$ lb

10. How many more pounds of raisins were made on Thursday than on Tuesday?
   $3\frac{3}{4}$ lb

11. What is the difference in the amount of raisins made on Wednesday and on Friday?
   $2\frac{1}{2}$ lb

12. How many pounds of raisins were made on Wednesday and on Friday altogether?
   7 lb

13. How many more pounds of raisins were made on Thursday than on Monday?
   $1\frac{1}{2}$ lb

14. Estimate the total amount of raisins made during the five days listed.
   about 22 lb

Use with Grade 5, Chapter 6, Lesson 2, pages 256–257. (177)

Daily Homework

6-2 **Problem Solving: Reading for Math**
Choose an Operation

Solve. Tell how you chose the operation.

1. In the first week of January, rainfall totaled $1\frac{1}{16}$ in. In the second week, it totaled $1\frac{7}{16}$ in. How much more rain fell in the second week?
   $\frac{3}{8}$ in. The words *how much more* indicate subtraction.

2. In the first two weeks of March, rainfall totaled $\frac{5}{8}$ in. In the third week, rainfall totaled $2\frac{1}{4}$ in. How much rain fell in all during those three weeks?
   $2\frac{7}{8}$ in. The words *in all* indicate addition.

Use data from the table for problems 3–10.

Rainfall This Year

Month	Inches
January	$2\frac{1}{2}$
February	$2\frac{3}{4}$
March	$4\frac{1}{4}$
April	$4\frac{1}{2}$
May	$2\frac{3}{4}$

3. What was the difference in rainfall between April and May? $1\frac{3}{4}$ in.
4. The record for rainfall in March is $9\frac{1}{2}$ inches. How far from the record was the rainfall this March? $5\frac{1}{4}$ in.
5. What was the total rainfall during January and February? $5\frac{1}{4}$ in.
6. How much more rain fell in April than in January? 2 in.
7. What was the total rainfall during April and May? $7\frac{1}{4}$ in.
8. Estimate the total rainfall for all five months. 18 in.
9. How much rain fell in all during the first three months of the year? $9\frac{1}{2}$ in.
10. How much rain fell in all during February and March? 7 in.

Spiral Review

11. 3.2 + 5.63 = 8.83
12. 8.1 − 2.32 = 5.78
13. 5.65 + 2.4 = 8.05
14. 7 − 2.83 = 4.17

54 Grade 5, Chapter 6, Lesson 2, Cluster A

Chapter 6 ~ Lesson 3

Practice

Explore Adding Fractions with Unlike Denominators

P 6-3 PRACTICE

Write the addition sentence shown by each model.
Write the sum in simplest form.

1.
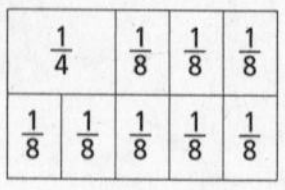

$\frac{1}{4} + \frac{3}{8} = \frac{5}{8}$

2.
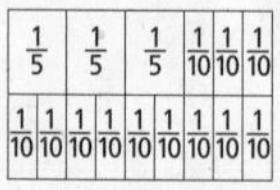

$\frac{3}{5} + \frac{3}{10} = \frac{9}{10}$

3.
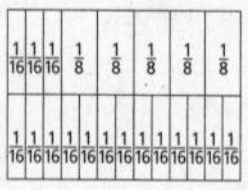

$\frac{3}{16} + \frac{5}{8} = \frac{13}{16}$

4.
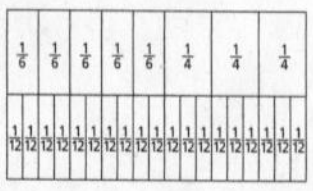

$\frac{5}{6} + \frac{3}{4} = 1\frac{7}{12}$

5.
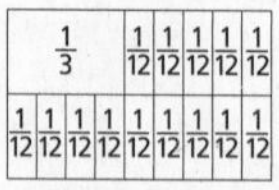

$\frac{1}{3} + \frac{5}{12} = \frac{3}{4}$

6.
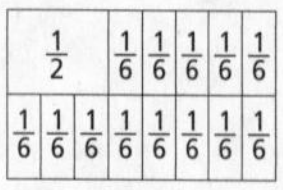

$\frac{1}{2} + \frac{5}{6} = 1\frac{1}{3}$

Add.

7. $\frac{1}{10} + \frac{1}{5} = \frac{3}{10}$
8. $\frac{1}{12} + \frac{1}{6} = \frac{1}{4}$
9. $\frac{5}{16} + \frac{3}{8} = \frac{11}{16}$
10. $\frac{3}{4} + \frac{1}{12} = \frac{5}{6}$
11. $\frac{1}{2} + \frac{3}{8} = \frac{7}{8}$
12. $\frac{2}{3} + \frac{5}{6} = 1\frac{1}{2}$
13. $\frac{3}{8} + \frac{3}{4} = 1\frac{1}{8}$
14. $\frac{1}{2} + \frac{2}{3} = 1\frac{1}{6}$
15. $\frac{4}{5} + \frac{1}{10} = \frac{9}{10}$
16. $\frac{1}{6} + \frac{5}{12} = \frac{7}{12}$
17. $\frac{5}{8} + \frac{7}{16} = 1\frac{1}{16}$
18. $\frac{3}{5} + \frac{1}{2} = 1\frac{1}{10}$

Problem Solving

19. At a park, a picnic shelter covers $\frac{1}{4}$ acre and a playground covers $\frac{5}{8}$ acre. How much area is covered by the picnic shelter and the playground? $\frac{7}{8}$ acre

20. The tropical rain forest at a zoo covers $\frac{3}{4}$ acre, and the desert area covers $\frac{1}{2}$ acre. How much of the zoo is rain forest or desert? $1\frac{1}{4}$ acres

Use with Grade 5, Chapter 6, Lesson 3, pages 258–259. (178)

Reteach

Explore Adding Fractions with Unlike Denominators

R 6-3 RETEACH

You can draw models to help add fractions with unlike denominators.

Add $\frac{7}{12} + \frac{1}{4}$.

Draw models for each addend.

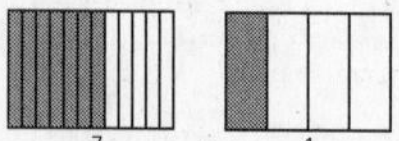

$\frac{7}{12}$ + $\frac{1}{4}$

Find the LCD of the addends.

Multiples of 12: **12**, 24, 36, ...
Multiples of 4: 4, 8, **12**, ...
The LCD of $\frac{7}{12}$ and $\frac{1}{4}$ is 12.

Redraw the models to show twelfths.

Count the twelfths to find the sum.

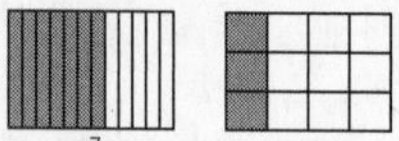

$\frac{7}{12}$ +

$\frac{7}{12} + \frac{3}{12} = \frac{10}{12} = \frac{5}{6}$

Complete each model to help add the fractions. Write your answer in simplest form.

1.
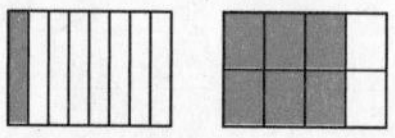

$\frac{1}{8} + \frac{3}{4}$
↓ ↓
$\frac{1}{8} + \frac{6}{8} = \frac{7}{8}$

2.
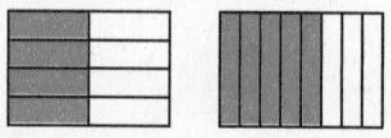

$\frac{1}{2} + \frac{5}{8}$
↓ ↓
$\frac{4}{8} + \frac{5}{8} = 1\frac{1}{8}$

3.
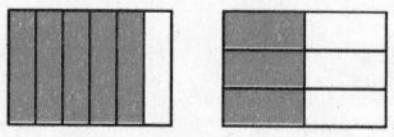

$\frac{5}{6} + \frac{1}{2}$

$\frac{5}{6} + \frac{3}{6} = 1\frac{1}{3}$

4.
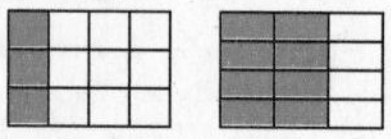

$\frac{1}{4} + \frac{2}{3}$

$\frac{3}{12} + \frac{8}{12} = \frac{11}{12}$

Use with Grade 5, Chapter 6, Lesson 3, pages 258–259. (179)

Enrich

Explore Adding Fractions with Unlike Denominators

E 6-3 ENRICH

Sum Inches

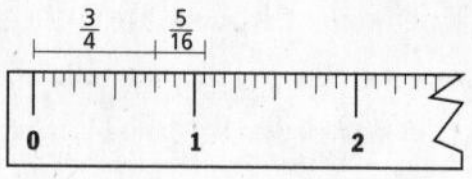

You can use an inch ruler to help you add fractions whose denominators are 2, 4, 8, or 16.

$\frac{3}{4} + \frac{5}{16} = \frac{17}{16} = 1\frac{1}{16}$

Show each addend on the ruler.
Then record the sum. Write your answer in simplest form.

1. $\frac{1}{2} + \frac{3}{4} = 1\frac{1}{4}$

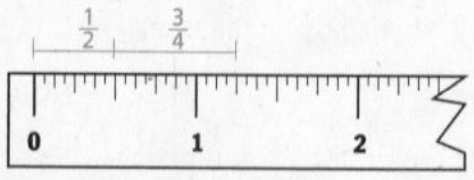

2. $\frac{7}{16} + \frac{3}{8} = \frac{13}{16}$

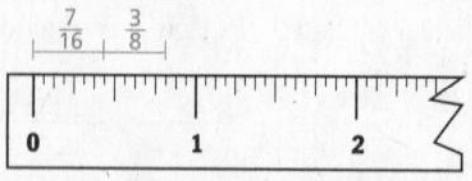

3. $\frac{5}{8} + \frac{3}{4} = 1\frac{3}{8}$

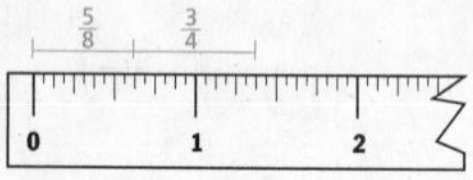

4. $\frac{1}{2} + \frac{7}{8} = 1\frac{3}{8}$

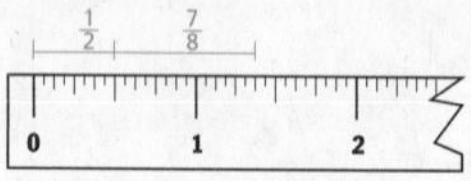

5. $\frac{15}{16} + \frac{1}{4} = 1\frac{3}{16}$

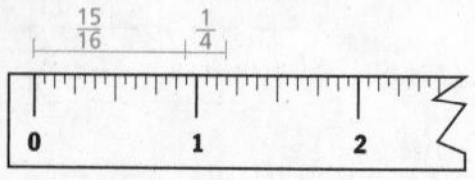

6. $\frac{3}{8} + \frac{1}{2} = \frac{7}{8}$

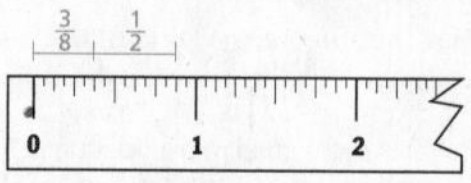

7. $\frac{1}{2} + \frac{13}{16} = 1\frac{5}{16}$

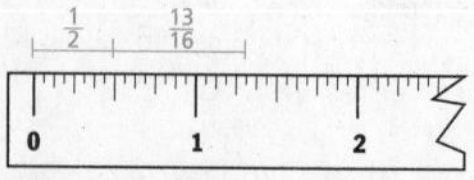

8. $\frac{7}{8} + \frac{9}{16} = 1\frac{7}{16}$

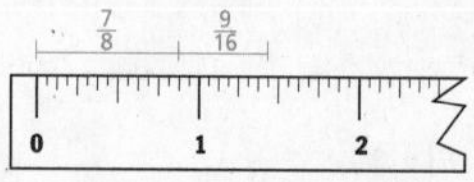

Can you show $\frac{4}{5} + \frac{3}{4}$ on an inch ruler? Explain.

No; on an inch ruler, inches are not divided into fifths.

Use with Grade 5, Chapter 6, Lesson 3, pages 258–259. (180)

Daily Homework

6-3 Explore Adding Fractions with Unlike Denominators

Add.

1. $\frac{1}{2} + \frac{1}{4} = \frac{3}{4}$
2. $\frac{1}{3} + \frac{1}{6} = \frac{1}{2}$
3. $\frac{1}{4} + \frac{1}{6} = \frac{5}{12}$
4. $\frac{3}{10} + \frac{2}{5} = \frac{7}{10}$
5. $\frac{2}{3} + \frac{1}{4} = \frac{11}{12}$
6. $\frac{3}{8} + \frac{1}{4} = \frac{5}{8}$
7. $\frac{2}{5} + \frac{1}{4} = \frac{13}{20}$
8. $\frac{3}{4} + \frac{1}{6} = \frac{11}{12}$
9. $\frac{3}{5} + \frac{3}{10} = \frac{9}{10}$
10. $\frac{3}{4} + \frac{1}{12} = \frac{5}{6}$
11. $\frac{3}{8} + \frac{1}{3} = \frac{17}{24}$
12. $\frac{1}{6} + \frac{1}{5} = \frac{11}{30}$
13. $\frac{3}{5} + \frac{3}{12} = \frac{17}{20}$
14. $\frac{3}{5} + \frac{1}{4} = \frac{17}{20}$
15. $\frac{1}{3} + \frac{1}{4} = \frac{7}{12}$
16. $\frac{3}{8} + \frac{1}{2} = \frac{7}{8}$
17. $\frac{2}{3} + \frac{1}{6} = \frac{5}{6}$
18. $\frac{1}{4} + \frac{1}{8} = \frac{3}{8}$

Solve.

19. On the first day of Lanier's vacation, $\frac{1}{4}$ in. of rain fell. On the second day, $\frac{3}{8}$ in. of rain fell. How much rain fell in all during these two days? Express your answer in inches. $\frac{5}{8}$ in.

20. On Monday, Jayne's stock rose $\frac{3}{8}$ per share. On Tuesday, it rose $\frac{1}{2}$ per share. How much did her stock rise per share in all during the two days? $\frac{7}{8}$

Spiral Review

21. $4.2 \times 10.06 =$ 42.252
22. $1.03 \times 2.74 =$ 2.8222
23. $0.25 \div 5 =$ 0.05
24. $3.2 \div 5 =$ 0.64
25. $5.82 \times 6.3 =$ 36.666
26. $4.8 \div 6 =$ 0.8

Grade 5, Chapter 6, Lesson 3, Cluster A 55

Chapter 6 ~ Lesson 4

Practice

Explore Subtracting Fractions with Unlike Denominators

P 6-4 PRACTICE

Write the subtraction sentence shown by each model. Write the difference in simplest form.

1. 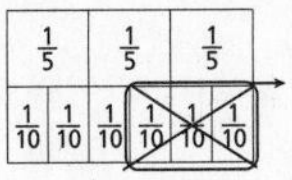

$\frac{3}{5} - \frac{3}{10} = \frac{3}{10}$

2. 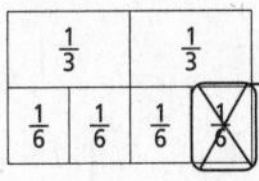

$\frac{2}{3} - \frac{1}{6} = \frac{1}{2}$

3. 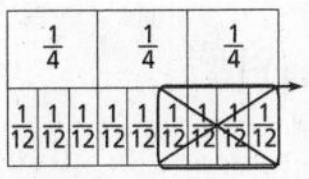

$\frac{7}{8} - \frac{3}{4} = \frac{1}{8}$

4. 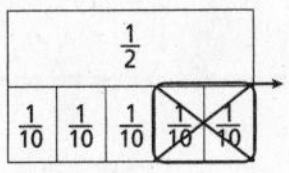

$\frac{1}{2} - \frac{1}{5} = \frac{3}{10}$

5. 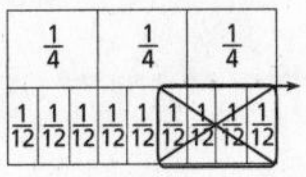

$\frac{3}{4} - \frac{1}{3} = \frac{5}{12}$

6. 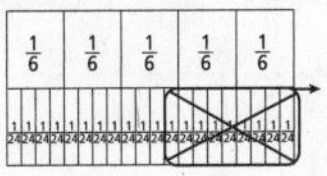

$\frac{5}{6} - \frac{3}{8} = \frac{11}{24}$

Subtract.

7. $\frac{7}{12} - \frac{1}{4} = \frac{1}{3}$
8. $\frac{1}{2} - \frac{1}{3} = \frac{1}{6}$
9. $\frac{9}{10} - \frac{2}{5} = \frac{1}{2}$
10. $\frac{5}{8} - \frac{1}{4} = \frac{3}{8}$
11. $\frac{11}{20} - \frac{3}{10} = \frac{1}{4}$
12. $\frac{11}{12} - \frac{1}{3} = \frac{7}{12}$
13. $\frac{7}{10} - \frac{1}{2} = \frac{1}{5}$
14. $\frac{3}{4} - \frac{2}{3} = \frac{1}{12}$
15. $\frac{5}{6} - \frac{3}{4} = \frac{1}{12}$
16. $\frac{3}{4} - \frac{3}{5} = \frac{3}{20}$
17. $\frac{11}{12} - \frac{1}{4} = \frac{2}{3}$
18. $\frac{4}{5} - \frac{1}{2} = \frac{3}{10}$

Problem Solving

19. The distance around a lily pond is $\frac{7}{10}$ mile. Rocks have been placed for $\frac{1}{4}$ mile along the pond's edge. How much of the edge does not have rocks? $\frac{9}{20}$ mile

20. The first $\frac{1}{5}$ mile of a $\frac{3}{4}$-mile path through a rose garden is paved with bricks. How much of the path is not paved with bricks? $\frac{11}{20}$ mile

Use with Grade 5, Chapter 6, Lesson 4, pages 260–261. (181)

Reteach

Explore Subtracting Fractions with Unlike Denominators

R 6-4 RETEACH

You can draw models to help subtract fractions with unlike denominators.

Subtract $\frac{3}{5} - \frac{1}{4}$.

Draw a model for $\frac{3}{5}$.

$\frac{3}{5}$

Find the LCD of the fractions.

Multiples of 5: 5, 10, 15, **20**, ...
Multiples of 4: 4, 8, 12, 16, **20**, ...
The LCD of $\frac{3}{5}$ and $\frac{1}{4}$ is 20.

Redraw the model to show twentieths.

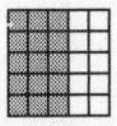

$\frac{3}{5}$ ↓ $\frac{12}{20}$

Count the twentieths left to find the difference.

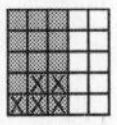

$\frac{3}{5} - \frac{1}{4}$
↓ ↓
$\frac{12}{20} - \frac{5}{20} = \frac{7}{20}$

So, $\frac{3}{5} - \frac{1}{4} = \frac{7}{20}$.

Complete each model to help subtract the fractions. Write your answer in simplest form.

1. 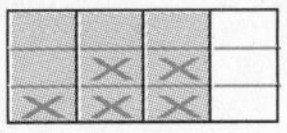

$\frac{3}{4} - \frac{5}{12}$
↓ ↓
$\frac{9}{12} - \frac{5}{12} = \frac{1}{3}$

2. 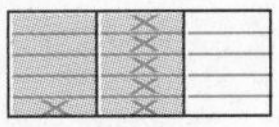

$\frac{2}{3} - \frac{2}{5}$
↓ ↓
$\frac{10}{15} - \frac{6}{15} = \frac{4}{15}$

3. 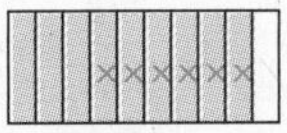

$\frac{9}{10} - \frac{3}{5}$
↓ ↓
$\frac{9}{10} - \frac{6}{10} = \frac{3}{10}$

Subtract. You may draw models. Write your answer in simplest form.

4. $\frac{1}{2} - \frac{3}{8} = \frac{1}{8}$
5. $\frac{5}{6} - \frac{7}{12} = \frac{1}{4}$
6. $\frac{11}{12} - \frac{1}{4} = \frac{2}{3}$
7. $\frac{2}{3} - \frac{1}{2} = \frac{1}{6}$
8. $\frac{9}{20} - \frac{2}{5} = \frac{1}{20}$
9. $\frac{7}{8} - \frac{1}{3} = \frac{13}{24}$

Use with Grade 5, Chapter 6, Lesson 4, pages 260–261. (182)

Enrich

Explore Subtracting Fractions with Unlike Denominators

E 6-4 ENRICH

The Sum of the Differences

Find each difference in the tables below. Write your answers in simplest form in the box below each problem.

$\frac{1}{2} - \frac{3}{8}$	$\frac{7}{12} - \frac{1}{3}$	$\frac{11}{12} - \frac{1}{2}$	$\frac{5}{6} - \frac{3}{8}$	$\frac{5}{6} - \frac{1}{2}$
N $\frac{1}{8}$	**F** $\frac{1}{4}$	**T** $\frac{5}{12}$	**E** $\frac{11}{24}$	**R** $\frac{1}{3}$

$\frac{3}{4} - \frac{3}{8}$	$\frac{11}{12} - \frac{3}{4}$	$\frac{3}{4} - \frac{1}{8}$	$\frac{19}{20} - \frac{1}{5}$	$\frac{2}{3} - \frac{1}{6}$
O $\frac{3}{8}$	**U** $\frac{1}{6}$	**B** $\frac{5}{8}$	**H** $\frac{3}{4}$	**M** $\frac{1}{2}$

What is the sum of the fractions in the boxes with the letters? 4

Check your answer by placing the corresponding letter from each box above its difference below.

T H E   N U M B E R
$\frac{5}{12}$ $\frac{3}{4}$ $\frac{11}{24}$ $\frac{1}{8}$ $\frac{1}{6}$ $\frac{1}{2}$ $\frac{5}{8}$ $\frac{11}{24}$ $\frac{1}{3}$

F O U R
$\frac{1}{4}$ $\frac{3}{8}$ $\frac{1}{6}$ $\frac{1}{3}$

Use with Grade 5, Chapter 6, Lesson 4, pages 260–261. (183)

Daily Homework

6-4 Explore Subtracting Fractions with Unlike Denominators

Subtract.

1. $\frac{7}{8} - \frac{1}{2} = \frac{3}{8}$
2. $\frac{3}{4} - \frac{5}{8} = \frac{1}{8}$
3. $\frac{1}{3} - \frac{1}{6} = \frac{1}{6}$
4. $\frac{2}{3} - \frac{1}{4} = \frac{5}{12}$
5. $\frac{6}{8} - \frac{1}{4} = \frac{1}{2}$
6. $\frac{2}{3} - \frac{3}{8} = \frac{7}{24}$
7. $\frac{5}{6} - \frac{3}{4} = \frac{1}{12}$
8. $\frac{2}{3} - \frac{1}{2} = \frac{1}{6}$
9. $\frac{1}{2} - \frac{1}{8} = \frac{3}{8}$
10. $\frac{3}{4} - \frac{2}{3} = \frac{1}{12}$
11. $\frac{5}{6} - \frac{2}{3} = \frac{1}{6}$
12. $\frac{2}{6} - \frac{1}{8} = \frac{5}{24}$
13. $\frac{11}{20} - \frac{2}{5} = \frac{3}{20}$
14. $\frac{7}{10} - \frac{3}{5} = \frac{1}{10}$
15. $\frac{3}{4} - \frac{3}{8} = \frac{3}{8}$
16. $\frac{5}{6} - \frac{7}{12} = \frac{1}{4}$
17. $\frac{3}{4} - \frac{3}{10} = \frac{9}{20}$
18. $\frac{1}{2} - \frac{3}{10} = \frac{1}{5}$

Solve.

19. Marcia is growing plants for a science project. This week one very young plant grew from $\frac{1}{4}$ in. tall to $\frac{7}{8}$ in. tall. How much did the plant grow this week? $\frac{5}{8}$ in.

20. A repair order calls for $\frac{3}{8}$-inch nails. Fred plans to use $\frac{3}{4}$-inch nails. How much longer are the nails Fred plans to use? $\frac{3}{8}$ in.

Spiral Review

Name the value of the underlined digit.

21. 23.<u>6</u>25 0.6
22. 15.8<u>7</u>3 0.07
23. <u>3</u>2.859 30
24. 15.32<u>5</u> 0.005
25. 6<u>8</u>.523 8
26. 51.<u>5</u>92 0.5

56 Grade 5, Chapter 6, Lesson 4, Cluster A

Chapter 6 ~ Lesson 5

Practice

Add and Subtract Fractions with Unlike Denominators

P 6-5 PRACTICE

Add or subtract. Write your answer in simplest form.

1. $\frac{1}{2} + \frac{1}{5}$ = $\frac{7}{10}$
2. $\frac{2}{5} + \frac{7}{10}$ = $1\frac{1}{10}$
3. $\frac{5}{8} - \frac{3}{16}$ = $\frac{7}{16}$
4. $\frac{3}{5} - \frac{3}{20}$ = $\frac{9}{20}$
5. $\frac{9}{10} + \frac{7}{10}$ = $1\frac{3}{5}$
6. $\frac{7}{12} - \frac{1}{3}$ = $\frac{1}{4}$
7. $\frac{9}{10} - \frac{2}{5}$ = $\frac{1}{2}$
8. $\frac{2}{3} + \frac{3}{8}$ = $1\frac{1}{24}$
9. $\frac{3}{4} - \frac{2}{5}$ = $\frac{7}{20}$
10. $\frac{7}{12} + \frac{3}{4}$ = $1\frac{1}{3}$
11. $\frac{2}{3} - \frac{3}{8}$ = $\frac{7}{24}$
12. $\frac{9}{20} + \frac{3}{5}$ = $1\frac{1}{20}$
13. $\frac{7}{16} + \frac{3}{8} =$ $\frac{13}{16}$
14. $\frac{5}{6} + \frac{7}{12} =$ $1\frac{5}{12}$
15. $\frac{15}{16} - \frac{5}{8} =$ $\frac{5}{16}$
16. $\frac{17}{20} - \frac{3}{4} =$ $\frac{1}{10}$
17. $\frac{1}{4} + \frac{4}{5} =$ $1\frac{1}{20}$
18. $\frac{1}{2} - \frac{1}{5} =$ $\frac{3}{10}$
19. $\frac{5}{8} + \frac{2}{5} =$ $1\frac{1}{40}$
20. $\frac{7}{10} - \frac{1}{2} =$ $\frac{1}{5}$
21. $\frac{5}{6} - \frac{5}{8} =$ $\frac{5}{24}$

Algebra & Functions Find each missing number.

22. $\frac{3}{8}$ $+ \frac{1}{2} = \frac{7}{8}$
23. $\frac{3}{4}$ $- \frac{5}{12} = \frac{1}{3}$
24. $\frac{4}{5} -$ $\frac{1}{10}$ $= \frac{7}{10}$
25. $\frac{1}{4} +$ $\frac{9}{16}$ $= \frac{13}{16}$
26. $\frac{1}{12}$ $+ \frac{3}{4} = \frac{5}{6}$
27. $\frac{3}{5}$ $- \frac{1}{3} = \frac{4}{15}$

Problem Solving

28. After school, Michael walks $\frac{3}{5}$ mile to the park and then walks $\frac{3}{4}$ mile to his house. How far does Michael walk from school to his house?
$1\frac{7}{20}$ miles

29. When Rachel walks to school on the sidewalk, she walks $\frac{7}{10}$ mile. When she takes the shortcut across the field, she walks $\frac{1}{4}$ mile less. How long is the shorter route?
$\frac{9}{20}$ mile

Use with Grade 5, Chapter 6, Lesson 5, pages 262–265. (184)

Reteach

Add and Subtract Fractions with Unlike Denominators

R 6-5 RETEACH

When adding and subtracting fractions with unlike denominators, it helps to write the problems in vertical form.

Add $\frac{7}{8} + \frac{2}{3}$. Subtract $\frac{7}{8} - \frac{2}{3}$.

Step 1

Find the least common denominator (LCD).

Multiples of 3:
3, 6, 9, 12, 15,18, 21, **24**, ...

Multiples of 8: 8, 16, **24**, ...

The LCD is 24.

Step 2

Rename each fraction using the LCD.

$\frac{7}{8} = \frac{21}{24}$

$\frac{2}{3} = \frac{16}{24}$

Step 3

Write the problems in vertical form.

Add.

$\frac{7}{8} = \frac{21}{24}$

$+\frac{2}{3} = +\frac{16}{24}$

$\frac{37}{24} = 1\frac{13}{24}$

Subtract.

$\frac{7}{8} = \frac{21}{24}$

$-\frac{2}{3} = -\frac{16}{24}$

$\frac{5}{24}$

Add or subtract. Write your answer in simplest form.

1. $\frac{3}{8} + \frac{5}{6}$

Multiples of 8: 8, 16, 24, 32, ...

Multiples of 6: 6, 12, 18, 24, ...

LCD: 24

So, $\frac{3}{8} + \frac{5}{6} =$ $\frac{9}{24} + \frac{20}{24} = \frac{29}{24} = 1\frac{5}{24}$.

2. $\frac{11}{12} - \frac{3}{4}$

Multiples of 12: 12, 24, 36, ...

Multiples of 4: 4, 8, 12, ...

LCD: 12

So, $\frac{11}{12} - \frac{3}{4} =$ $\frac{11}{12} - \frac{9}{12} = \frac{2}{12} = \frac{1}{6}$.

3. $\frac{4}{5} - \frac{2}{3} =$ $\frac{2}{15}$
4. $\frac{3}{5} + \frac{9}{10} =$ $\frac{15}{10} = 1\frac{1}{2}$
5. $\frac{9}{10} - \frac{5}{6} =$ $\frac{2}{30} = \frac{1}{15}$
6. $\frac{7}{10} + \frac{3}{4} =$ $1\frac{9}{20}$
7. $\frac{5}{8} - \frac{2}{5} =$ $\frac{9}{40}$
8. $\frac{3}{4} + \frac{5}{6} =$ $1\frac{7}{12}$
9. $\frac{1}{2} - \frac{3}{8} =$ $\frac{1}{8}$
10. $\frac{1}{2} + \frac{3}{8} =$ $\frac{7}{8}$
11. $\frac{3}{5} + \frac{3}{4} =$ $\frac{27}{20} = 1\frac{7}{20}$
12. $\frac{7}{12} - \frac{1}{3} =$ $\frac{1}{4}$
13. $\frac{5}{6} + \frac{5}{8} =$ $\frac{35}{24} = 1\frac{11}{24}$
14. $\frac{7}{10} - \frac{2}{5} =$ $\frac{3}{10}$

Use with Grade 5, Chapter 6, Lesson 5, pages 262–265. (185)

Enrich

Add and Subtract Fractions with Unlike Denominators

E 6-5 ENRICH

Five-in-a Row

Play this game with a partner. You will need a coin.

- The first player selects any two fractions on the game board. Then the player tosses the coin. If the coin lands heads up, the player finds the sum of the fractions. If the coin lands tails up, the player finds the difference.
- The other player checks the first player's sum or difference. If it is correct, the first player writes an X in the boxes containing the fractions added or subtracted.
- Players take turns. The second player writes Os in the boxes.
- The winner is the first player to mark five Xs or five Os in a row. If no more boxes can be marked, the player who marked more boxes is the winner.

$\frac{1}{10}$	$\frac{3}{5}$	$\frac{7}{8}$	$\frac{1}{4}$	$\frac{4}{5}$
$\frac{3}{4}$	$\frac{1}{2}$	$\frac{5}{12}$	$\frac{1}{8}$	$\frac{7}{20}$
$\frac{5}{6}$	$\frac{3}{8}$	$\frac{1}{6}$	$\frac{3}{10}$	$\frac{1}{5}$
$\frac{1}{12}$	$\frac{2}{3}$	$\frac{2}{5}$	$\frac{5}{6}$	$\frac{1}{2}$
$\frac{5}{8}$	$\frac{1}{4}$	$\frac{7}{10}$	$\frac{3}{8}$	$\frac{1}{3}$

Use with Grade 5, Chapter 6, Lesson 5, pages 262–265. (186)

Daily Homework

6•5 Add and Subtract Fractions with Unlike Denominators

Add or subtract. Write your answer in simplest form.

1. $\frac{1}{2} + \frac{1}{3} =$ $\frac{5}{6}$
2. $\frac{3}{5} - \frac{3}{8} =$ $\frac{9}{40}$
3. $\frac{3}{4} - \frac{2}{3} =$ $\frac{1}{12}$
4. $\frac{3}{10} + \frac{1}{4} =$ $\frac{11}{20}$
5. $\frac{1}{2} + \frac{5}{6} =$ $1\frac{1}{3}$
6. $\frac{3}{4} + \frac{1}{2} =$ $1\frac{1}{4}$
7. $\frac{7}{8} - \frac{1}{4} =$ $\frac{5}{8}$
8. $\frac{5}{6} - \frac{7}{12} =$ $\frac{1}{4}$
9. $\frac{5}{6} + \frac{7}{24} =$ $1\frac{1}{8}$
10. $\frac{1}{2} - \frac{1}{5}$ = $\frac{3}{10}$
11. $\frac{2}{3} + \frac{5}{6}$ = $1\frac{1}{2}$
12. $\frac{3}{5} + \frac{7}{10}$ = $1\frac{3}{10}$
13. $\frac{7}{8} - \frac{2}{3}$ = $\frac{5}{24}$

Problem Solving

14. Andy picks a big bag of apples at an orchard. When he gets home, he gives $\frac{1}{2}$ of the apples to his neighbor and another $\frac{1}{4}$ of the apples to his friend. What fraction of his apples does Andy give away? $\frac{3}{4}$

15. It takes Juana $\frac{1}{2}$ hour to drive from her home to Mel's Garage. It takes her another $\frac{1}{6}$ hour to drive from Mel's Garage to Barbara's house. What fraction of an hour does it take for Juana to drive from her home to Barbara's house? $\frac{2}{3}$ hour

Spiral Review

Write whether each number is prime or composite.

16. 43 prime
17. 39 composite
18. 63 composite
19. 54 composite
20. 31 prime
21. 19 prime

Grade 5, Chapter 6, Lesson 5, Cluster A 57

Chapter 6 ~ Lesson 6

Practice

Explore Adding Mixed Numbers with Unlike Denominators

P 6-6 PRACTICE

Write the addition sentence shown by each model. Write the answer in simplest form.

1.

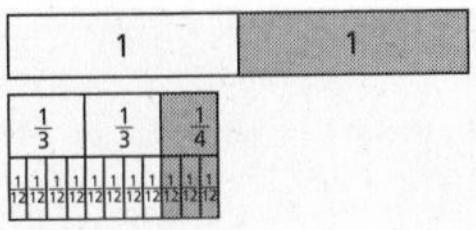

$1\frac{2}{3} + 1\frac{1}{4} = 2\frac{11}{12}$

2.

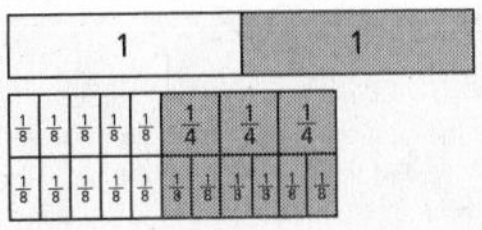

$1\frac{5}{8} + 1\frac{3}{4} = 3\frac{3}{8}$

Add. Write your answer in simplest form.

3. $1\frac{3}{5} + 1\frac{3}{10} = 2\frac{9}{10}$
4. $2\frac{1}{2} + 1\frac{5}{8} = 4\frac{1}{8}$
5. $1\frac{1}{6} + 2\frac{3}{4} = 3\frac{11}{12}$
6. $1\frac{1}{3} + 1\frac{1}{6} = 2\frac{1}{2}$
7. $2\frac{7}{10} + 1\frac{1}{2} = 4\frac{1}{5}$
8. $2\frac{11}{12} + 2\frac{1}{4} = 5\frac{1}{6}$
9. $2\frac{1}{2} + 2\frac{3}{5} = 5\frac{1}{10}$
10. $1\frac{3}{4} + 2\frac{2}{3} = 4\frac{5}{12}$
11. $1\frac{3}{8} + 2\frac{1}{2} = 3\frac{7}{8}$
12. $2\frac{5}{6} + 1\frac{1}{3} = 4\frac{1}{6}$
13. $1\frac{3}{10} + 1\frac{3}{4} = 3\frac{1}{20}$
14. $2\frac{4}{5} + 2\frac{1}{4} = 5\frac{1}{20}$
15. $4\frac{3}{8} + 4\frac{3}{4} = 9\frac{1}{8}$
16. $5\frac{2}{3} + 1\frac{1}{5} = 6\frac{13}{15}$
17. $3\frac{7}{10} + 3\frac{1}{2} = 7\frac{1}{5}$

Problem Solving

18. Every weekend Josh spends $2\frac{1}{4}$ hours at swim practice and $1\frac{1}{2}$ hours practicing his guitar. How many hours does Josh spend swimming and practicing guitar on the weekend?

$3\frac{3}{4}$ hours

19. On Saturday Marie spent $1\frac{3}{4}$ hours mowing the yard and $2\frac{3}{4}$ hours raking leaves. How much time did Marie spend doing yard work on Saturday?

$4\frac{1}{2}$ hours

Use with Grade 5, Chapter 6, Lesson 6, pages 268–269. (187)

Reteach

Explore Adding Mixed Numbers with Unlike Denominators

R 6-6 RETEACH

You can draw models to help add mixed numbers with unlike denominators.

Add $2\frac{7}{8} + 1\frac{1}{2}$.

Draw models for each addend.

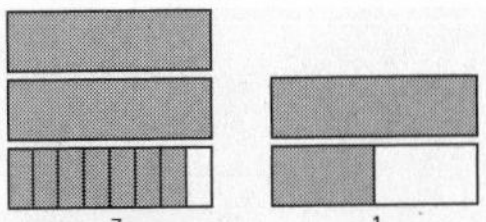

$2\frac{7}{8}$ + $1\frac{1}{2}$

Rename the addends using their LCD.
Redraw the models to show eighths.

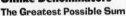

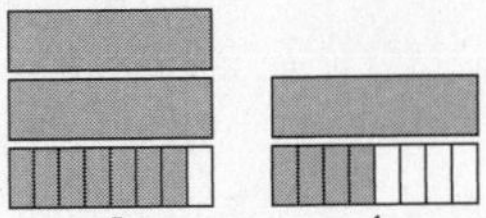

$2\frac{7}{8}$ + $1\frac{1}{2}$
↓ ↓
$2\frac{7}{8}$ + $1\frac{4}{8}$

To find the sum, count the ones.
Then count the eighths.

$2\frac{7}{8} + 1\frac{4}{8} = 3 + \frac{11}{8} = 3 + 1\frac{3}{8} = 4\frac{3}{8}$

Complete. Find each sum. Write your answer in simplest form.

1. $2\frac{5}{8} + 1\frac{3}{4}$
↓ ↓
$2\frac{5}{8} + 1\frac{6}{8} = 3\frac{11}{8} = 4\frac{3}{8}$

2. $1\frac{3}{5} + 2\frac{7}{10}$
↓ ↓
$1\frac{6}{10} + 2\frac{7}{10} = 3\frac{13}{10} = 4\frac{3}{10}$

3. $1\frac{1}{3} + 1\frac{1}{2}$
↓ ↓
$1\frac{2}{6} + 1\frac{3}{6} = 2\frac{5}{6}$

4. $2\frac{5}{6} + 2\frac{1}{4}$
↓ ↓
$2\frac{10}{12} + 2\frac{3}{12} = 5\frac{1}{12}$

Add. You may draw models. Write your answer in simplest form.

5. $1\frac{1}{2} + 2\frac{1}{4} = 3\frac{3}{4}$
6. $2\frac{9}{10} + 2\frac{1}{5} = 5\frac{1}{10}$
7. $2\frac{3}{4} + 1\frac{2}{5} = 4\frac{3}{20}$

Use with Grade 5, Chapter 6, Lesson 6, pages 268–269. (188)

Enrich

Explore Adding Mixed Numbers with Unlike Denominators

E 6-6 ENRICH

The Greatest Possible Sum

Play this game with a partner. Check each other's work.
Try to find two mixed numbers having the greatest possible sum.

- Write two different denominators from the choices given in each exercise.
- Roll a number cube four times. Record the numbers rolled. Write each number rolled as a whole number or numerator in each exercise. Make sure the numerator in each mixed number is less than the denominator.
- Find the sum of each pair of mixed numbers.
- The person with the greater sum scores a point. The person with the greater number of points wins the game.

Answers may vary. Sample answer is given for exercise 1.

1. Numbers rolled: 1, 3, 5, 6 — Your choices of denominators: 2, 4, 8
☐ ☐/☐ + ☐ ☐/☐ = $6\frac{3}{8} + 6\frac{1}{2} = 11\frac{7}{8}$

2. Numbers rolled: ______ — Your choices of denominators: 3, 6, 12
☐ ☐/☐ + ☐ ☐/☐ = ______

3. Numbers rolled: ______ — Your choices of denominators: 2, 5, 10
☐ ☐/☐ + ☐ ☐/☐ = ______

4. Numbers rolled: ______ — Your choices of denominators: 3, 8, 12
☐ ☐/☐ + ☐ ☐/☐ = ______

5. Numbers rolled: ______ — Your choices of denominators: 2, 4, 5
☐ ☐/☐ + ☐ ☐/☐ = ______

Use with Grade 5, Chapter 6, Lesson 6, pages 268–269. (189)

Daily Homework

6-6 Explore Adding Mixed Numbers with Unlike Denominators

Add. Write your answer in simplest form.

1. $2\frac{1}{3} + 4\frac{5}{6} = 7\frac{1}{6}$
2. $6\frac{1}{3} + 4\frac{3}{4} = 11\frac{1}{12}$
3. $7\frac{1}{2} + 3\frac{1}{4} = 10\frac{3}{4}$
4. $2\frac{7}{10} + 4\frac{2}{5} = 7\frac{1}{10}$
5. $5\frac{7}{10} + 8\frac{1}{2} = 14\frac{1}{5}$
6. $10\frac{1}{2} + 2\frac{5}{6} = 13\frac{1}{3}$
7. $11\frac{7}{12} + 15\frac{2}{3} = 27\frac{1}{4}$
8. $13\frac{3}{5} + 3\frac{3}{4} = 17\frac{7}{20}$
9. $17\frac{7}{8} + 6\frac{2}{5} = 24\frac{11}{40}$
10. $19\frac{5}{6} + 8\frac{3}{4} = 28\frac{7}{12}$
11. $13\frac{5}{6} + 18\frac{3}{4} = 32\frac{7}{12}$
12. $22\frac{2}{3} + 26\frac{5}{6} = 49\frac{1}{2}$

Solve.

13. Harold owns stock in an insurance company. On Monday the stock was worth $16\frac{1}{2}$ per share. On Tuesday it rose in value by $4\frac{3}{4}$. What was the stock worth at the end of the day on Tuesday? $21\frac{1}{4}$ per share

14. Fargo, ND, had snowstorms on two days in a row in March. The first storm left $8\frac{3}{4}$ in. of snow, and the second storm left $12\frac{3}{4}$ in. of snow. How many inches of snow did the two storms leave in all? $21\frac{1}{2}$ in.

Spiral Review

15. 4.7 + 2.6 = 7.3
16. 7.5 ÷ 1.5 = 5
17. 3.33 ÷ 3 = 1.11
18. 25 ÷ 2.5 = 10

58 Grade 5, Chapter 6, Lesson 6, Cluster B

Chapter 6 ~ Lesson 7

Practice

Add Mixed Numbers with Unlike Denominators

P 6-7 PRACTICE

Add. Write your answer in simplest form.

1. $5\frac{3}{4} + 4\frac{1}{12} =$ $9\frac{5}{6}$
2. $3\frac{1}{3} + 7\frac{7}{10} =$ $11\frac{1}{30}$
3. $2\frac{11}{12} + 9\frac{5}{8} =$ $12\frac{13}{24}$
4. $7\frac{9}{10} + \frac{3}{5} =$ $8\frac{1}{2}$
5. $6\frac{1}{6} + 6\frac{3}{4} =$ $12\frac{11}{12}$
6. $5\frac{2}{5} + 8\frac{3}{8} =$ $13\frac{31}{40}$
7. $14\frac{7}{16} + 25\frac{3}{4} =$ $40\frac{3}{16}$
8. $38\frac{3}{8} + 19\frac{13}{16} =$ $58\frac{3}{16}$
9. $46 + 37\frac{11}{12} =$ $83\frac{11}{12}$
10. $3\frac{5}{12} + 4\frac{1}{6}$ = $7\frac{7}{12}$
11. $5\frac{1}{2} + 9\frac{3}{8}$ = $14\frac{7}{8}$
12. $7\frac{5}{8} + 2\frac{3}{4}$ = $10\frac{3}{8}$
13. $1\frac{3}{5} + 8\frac{1}{4}$ = $9\frac{17}{20}$
14. $6\frac{1}{4} + 7\frac{9}{10}$ = $14\frac{3}{20}$
15. $\frac{5}{6} + 3\frac{3}{8}$ = $4\frac{5}{24}$
16. $7\frac{2}{3} + 8\frac{3}{5}$ = $16\frac{4}{15}$
17. $5\frac{7}{10} + 6\frac{3}{4}$ = $12\frac{9}{20}$
18. $24\frac{3}{16} + 32\frac{5}{8}$ = $56\frac{13}{16}$
19. $56\frac{13}{20} + 19\frac{4}{5}$ = $76\frac{9}{20}$
20. $37\frac{2}{3} + 45\frac{5}{8}$ = $83\frac{7}{24}$
21. $18\frac{7}{12} + 76\frac{3}{10}$ = $94\frac{53}{60}$

Problem Solving

22. A house is $52\frac{3}{4}$ feet wide. The attached garage is $20\frac{1}{2}$ feet wide. What is the total width of the house? $73\frac{1}{4}$ feet

23. In a family room, a fireplace is $12\frac{5}{6}$ feet wide. The total wall space on the sides of the fireplace is $18\frac{1}{4}$ feet wide. How wide is the family room? $31\frac{1}{12}$ feet

Use with Grade 5, Chapter 6, Lesson 7, pages 270–271. (190)

Reteach

Add Mixed Numbers with Unlike Denominators

R 6-7 RETEACH

When adding mixed numbers with unlike denominators, it helps to write the problems in vertical form.

Add $2\frac{4}{5} + 5\frac{1}{4}$.

Step 1

Find the least common denominator (LCD).

Multiples of 5: 5, 10, 15, 20, …

Multiples of 4: 4, 8, 12, 16, 20, …

The LCD is 20.

Step 2

Rename each mixed number using the LCD.

$2\frac{4}{5} = 2\frac{16}{20}$

$5\frac{1}{4} = 5\frac{5}{20}$

Step 3

Write the problem in vertical form.

Add the fractions. Then add the whole numbers. Write the answer in simplest form.

$2\frac{4}{5} = 2\frac{16}{20}$

$+ 5\frac{1}{4} = + 5\frac{5}{20}$

$7\frac{21}{20} = 8\frac{1}{20}$

Add. Write your answer in simplest form.

1. $4\frac{5}{6} + 3\frac{2}{3}$

Multiples of 6: 6, 12, 18, 24, …

Multiples of 3: 3, 6, 9, …

LCD: 6

So, $4\frac{5}{6} + 3\frac{2}{3} =$

$4\frac{5}{6} + 3\frac{4}{6} = 7\frac{9}{6} = 8\frac{1}{2}$

2. $2\frac{3}{8} + 9\frac{2}{5}$

Multiples of 8: 8, 16, 24, 32, …

Multiples of 5: 5, 10, 15, 20, …

LCD: 40

So, $2\frac{3}{8} + 9\frac{2}{5} =$

$2\frac{15}{40} + 9\frac{16}{40} = 11\frac{31}{40}$

3. $2\frac{1}{2} + 4\frac{4}{5} =$ $7\frac{3}{10}$
4. $6\frac{5}{16} + 8\frac{1}{4} =$ $14\frac{9}{16}$
5. $7\frac{3}{4} + 7\frac{5}{12} =$ $15\frac{1}{6}$
6. $5\frac{1}{3} + 3\frac{3}{5} =$ $8\frac{14}{15}$
7. $9\frac{1}{2} + 4\frac{5}{8} =$ $14\frac{1}{8}$
8. $8\frac{1}{6} + 6\frac{7}{8} =$ $15\frac{1}{24}$
9. $6\frac{2}{3} + 2\frac{5}{8} =$ $9\frac{7}{24}$
10. $1\frac{3}{4} + 4\frac{1}{2} =$ $6\frac{1}{4}$
11. $10\frac{1}{5} + 3\frac{7}{8} =$ $14\frac{1}{40}$
12. $15\frac{2}{3} + 20\frac{3}{4} =$ $36\frac{5}{12}$
13. $35\frac{4}{5} + 18\frac{1}{2} =$ $54\frac{3}{10}$
14. $45\frac{3}{8} + 50\frac{5}{6} =$ $96\frac{5}{24}$

Use with Grade 5, Chapter 6, Lesson 7, pages 270–271. (191)

Enrich

Add Mixed Numbers with Unlike Denominators

E 6-7 ENRICH

Getting to the Soccer Field

The map below shows distances in miles. Find the shortest route from each soccer player's house to the field. Record the length of that route.

Pedro $6\frac{1}{8}$ miles Oscar $5\frac{1}{4}$ miles

Beth $6\frac{1}{4}$ miles Shannon $4\frac{7}{8}$ miles

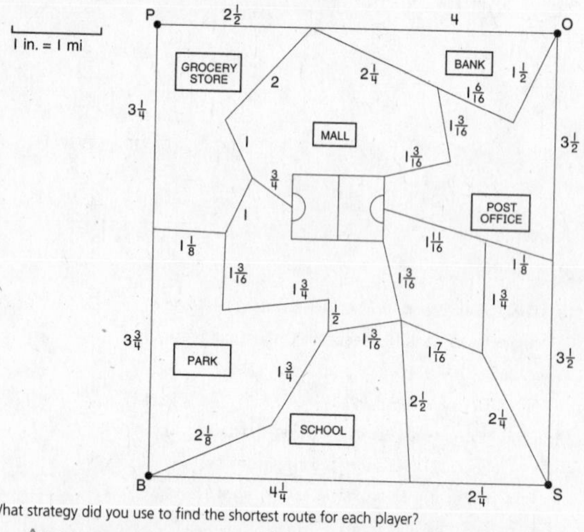

What strategy did you use to find the shortest route for each player?

Answers may vary. Possible answer: I estimated the distances of several routes. When I had decided on the two shorter routes, I used number sense or found the actual sums of the distances and compared them.

Use with Grade 5, Chapter 6, Lesson 7, pages 270–271. (192)

Daily Homework

6-7 Add Mixed Numbers with Unlike Denominators

Add. Write your answer in simplest form.

1. $4\frac{2}{3} + 2\frac{1}{6} =$ $6\frac{5}{6}$
2. $5\frac{3}{4} + 2\frac{1}{2} =$ $8\frac{1}{4}$
3. $8\frac{7}{8} + 4 =$ $12\frac{7}{8}$
4. $6\frac{2}{3} + 4\frac{2}{3} =$ $11\frac{1}{3}$
5. $5\frac{3}{20} + 24\frac{1}{4} =$ $29\frac{2}{5}$
6. $\frac{3}{5} + 4\frac{3}{10} =$ $4\frac{9}{10}$
7. $6\frac{1}{2} + 5\frac{3}{4} =$ $12\frac{1}{4}$
8. $3\frac{7}{12} + 18\frac{3}{4} =$ $22\frac{1}{3}$
9. $4\frac{4}{5} + 3\frac{3}{20} =$ $7\frac{19}{20}$
10. $14\frac{1}{2} + 12\frac{2}{3}$ = $27\frac{1}{6}$
11. $18\frac{5}{6} + 12\frac{2}{3}$ = $31\frac{1}{2}$
12. $35\frac{4}{5} + 19\frac{3}{5}$ = $55\frac{2}{5}$
13. $12\frac{11}{12} + 6\frac{1}{6}$ = $19\frac{1}{12}$

Problem Solving

14. Two boards are being cut into pieces to make a garden border. One is $8\frac{1}{2}$ feet long, and the other is $5\frac{3}{4}$ feet long. If both boards are completely used, how long will the border be? $14\frac{1}{4}$ ft

15. Sally delivers newspapers once a week in the morning before school for $1\frac{1}{2}$ hours and after school for $2\frac{1}{2}$ hours. How long does she work on the day she delivers papers? 4 hours

Spiral Review

Find the LCM for each pair of numbers.

16. 6 and 9 18
17. 5 and 8 40
18. 8 and 12 24
19. 5 and 4 20
20. 9 and 5 45
21. 5 and 6 30

Grade 5, Chapter 6, Lesson 7, Cluster B 59

Chapter 6 ~ Lesson 8

Practice

Properties of Addition

6-8 PRACTICE

Find each missing number. Identify the property you used.

1. $\frac{3}{4} + \boxed{0} = \frac{3}{4}$
   Identity Property

2. $3\frac{1}{8} + (\frac{5}{8} + 1\frac{1}{4}) = (3\frac{1}{8} + \boxed{\frac{5}{8}}) + 1\frac{1}{4}$
   Associative Property

3. $\frac{9}{16} + \frac{1}{4} = \frac{1}{4} + \boxed{\frac{9}{16}}$
   Commutative Property

4. $\frac{1}{10} + (\frac{3}{5} + \boxed{\frac{1}{2}}) = (\frac{1}{10} + \frac{3}{5}) + \frac{1}{2}$
   Associative Property

5. $7\frac{1}{2} = \boxed{7\frac{1}{2}} + 0$
   Identity Property

6. $2\frac{1}{3} + (1\frac{1}{2} + \frac{1}{3}) = 2\frac{1}{3} + (\boxed{\frac{1}{3}} + 1\frac{1}{2})$
   Commutative Property

Use the Associative Property to solve. Show your work.

7. $\frac{1}{4} + (\frac{1}{4} + \frac{1}{5})$
   $(\frac{1}{4} + \frac{1}{4}) + \frac{1}{5} = \frac{1}{2} + \frac{1}{5} = \frac{7}{10}$

8. $(\frac{1}{6} + \frac{3}{8}) + \frac{7}{8}$
   $\frac{1}{6} + (\frac{3}{8} + \frac{7}{8}) = \frac{1}{6} + 1\frac{1}{4} = 1\frac{5}{12}$

9. $(\frac{1}{2} + 4\frac{1}{10}) + \frac{7}{10}$
   $\frac{1}{2} + (4\frac{1}{10} + \frac{7}{10}) = \frac{1}{2} + 4\frac{4}{5} = 5\frac{3}{10}$

10. $\frac{5}{12} + (2\frac{7}{12} + 1\frac{5}{6})$
    $(\frac{5}{12} + 2\frac{7}{12}) + 1\frac{5}{6} = 3 + 1\frac{5}{6} = 4\frac{5}{6}$

11. $(2\frac{5}{8} + 3\frac{1}{2}) + 4\frac{1}{2}$
    $2\frac{5}{8} + (3\frac{1}{2} + 4\frac{1}{2}) = 2\frac{5}{8} + 8 = 10\frac{5}{8}$

12. $3\frac{7}{16} + (1\frac{5}{16} + 3\frac{1}{3})$
    $(3\frac{7}{16} + 1\frac{5}{16}) + 3\frac{1}{3} = 4\frac{3}{4} + 3\frac{1}{3} = 8\frac{1}{12}$

Algebra & Functions Find each missing number.

13. $\frac{3}{8} + \frac{7}{12} = c + \frac{3}{8}$
    $c = \frac{7}{12}$

14. $2\frac{1}{5} = h + 2\frac{1}{5}$
    $h = 0$

15. $3\frac{7}{10} + 0 = 0 + s$
    $s = 3\frac{7}{10}$

Problem Solving

16. During one day at school, Marc spends $4\frac{3}{4}$ hours in class. He also spends $\frac{2}{3}$ hour at lunch and $\frac{3}{4}$ hour at recess. How long is Marc's school day?
    $6\frac{1}{6}$ h

17. One afternoon, Laura spent $\frac{1}{2}$ hour doing math homework, $\frac{3}{4}$ hour doing English homework, and $1\frac{1}{4}$ hours doing science homework. How much time did she spend doing homework that afternoon?
    $2\frac{1}{2}$ h

Use with Grade 5, Chapter 6, Lesson 8, pages 272–273. (193)

Reteach

Properties of Addition

6-8 RETEACH

You can use the properties of addition to help you add fractions.

Commutative Property of Addition

When adding, the order of the addends does not change the sum.

$4\frac{2}{3} + 2\frac{1}{6} = 6\frac{5}{6}$

$2\frac{1}{6} + 4\frac{2}{3} = 6\frac{5}{6}$

So, $4\frac{2}{3} + 2\frac{1}{6} = 2\frac{1}{6} + 4\frac{2}{3}$.

Identity Property of Addition

When a number is added to 0, the sum is that number.

$\frac{4}{5} + 0 = \frac{4}{5}$

$0 + \frac{4}{5} = \frac{4}{5}$

So, $\frac{4}{5} + 0 = 0 + \frac{4}{5}$.

Associative Property of Addition

When adding three addends, the grouping of the addends does not change the sum.

$(\frac{3}{4} + \frac{5}{6}) + \frac{5}{6} = (\frac{9}{12} + \frac{10}{12}) + \frac{5}{6}$
$= 1\frac{7}{12} + \frac{5}{6}$
$= 1\frac{7}{12} + \frac{10}{12}$
$= 2\frac{5}{12}$

$\frac{3}{4} + (\frac{5}{6} + \frac{5}{6}) = \frac{3}{4} + 1\frac{2}{3}$
$= \frac{9}{12} + 1\frac{8}{12}$
$= 2\frac{5}{12}$

So, $(\frac{3}{4} + \frac{5}{6}) + \frac{5}{6} = \frac{3}{4} + (\frac{5}{6} + \frac{5}{6})$.

Complete. Use the properties to find each sum.

1. $\frac{1}{2} + (\frac{7}{8} + \frac{7}{8})$
   $\frac{1}{2} + 1\frac{3}{4} = \frac{2}{4} + 1\frac{3}{4} = 2\frac{1}{4}$

2. $(\frac{3}{4} + \frac{1}{4}) + \frac{5}{8}$
   $1 + \frac{5}{8} = 1\frac{5}{8}$

3. $2\frac{7}{12} + \frac{11}{12} + 1\frac{1}{2}$
   $= (2\frac{7}{12} + \boxed{\frac{11}{12}}) + 1\frac{1}{2}$
   $= \boxed{3\frac{1}{2}} + 1\frac{1}{2}$
   $= \boxed{5}$

4. $3\frac{1}{4} + (2\frac{3}{16} + 0)$
   $= 3\frac{1}{4} + \boxed{2\frac{3}{16}}$
   $= \boxed{5\frac{7}{16}}$

5. $(2\frac{4}{5} + 7\frac{4}{5}) + 0$
   $= \boxed{10\frac{3}{5}} + 0$

6. $4\frac{7}{10} + (3\frac{3}{10} + 1\frac{3}{8})$
   $= (4\frac{7}{10} + 3\frac{3}{10}) + \boxed{1\frac{3}{8}}$

Use with Grade 5, Chapter 6, Lesson 8, pages 272–273. (194)

Enrich

Properties of Addition

Property Match

6-8 ENRICH

For each number sentence, write the letter of the solution that will make it true.

Number sentence	Letter	Solution
1. $(\frac{1}{2} + \frac{1}{6}) + \frac{2}{3} = \square + (\frac{1}{6} + \frac{2}{3})$	R	R. $4\frac{7}{10}$
2. $\frac{2}{3} + \frac{4}{5} = \frac{4}{5} + \square$	D	D. $\frac{2}{3}$
3. $\frac{3}{4} + 2\frac{7}{12} = \square + \frac{3}{4}$	R	O. $\frac{7}{8}$
4. $\frac{3}{4} + 0 = \square$	E	Z. $2\frac{1}{2}$
5. $(2\frac{1}{2} + \frac{3}{8}) + \square = 2\frac{1}{2} + (\frac{3}{8} + \frac{5}{8})$	O	R. $\frac{1}{2}$
6. $1\frac{7}{12} + (\frac{5}{12} + 2\frac{1}{3}) = (1\frac{7}{12} + \square) + 2\frac{1}{3}$	P	U. $\frac{5}{6}$
7. $\square + 0 = 2\frac{1}{2}$	Z	G. $1\frac{3}{8}$
8. $\frac{7}{16} + \square = 4\frac{7}{10} + \frac{7}{16}$	R	E. $\frac{3}{4}$
9. $\frac{9}{20} + \square = \frac{9}{20}$	O	R. $2\frac{7}{12}$
10. $(\square + 1\frac{2}{5}) + 4\frac{7}{10} = 1\frac{3}{8} + (1\frac{2}{5} + 4\frac{7}{10})$	G	O. 0
11. $2\frac{1}{3} = \square + 0$	R	E. $3\frac{5}{6}$
12. $3\frac{5}{6} + 0 = 0 + \square$	E	P. $\frac{5}{12}$
13. $\frac{2}{3} + (\square + \frac{3}{4}) = (\frac{2}{3} + \frac{5}{6}) + \frac{3}{4}$	U	O. $\frac{5}{8}$
14. $\frac{3}{8} + (\frac{2}{5} + \frac{7}{8}) = \frac{3}{8} + (\square + \frac{2}{5})$	O	R. $2\frac{1}{3}$

Write the letter of the solution above the corresponding exercise number to find a word related to the property.

Property					
Identity Property	Z (7)	E (4)	R (11)	O (9)	
Commutative Property	O (14)	R (3)	D (2)	E (12)	R (8)
Associative Property	G (10)	R (1)	O (5)	U (13)	P (6)

Use with Grade 5, Chapter 6, Lesson 8, pages 272–273. (195)

Daily Homework

6-8 Properties of Addition

Find each missing number. Identify the property you used.

1. $14\frac{2}{3} + \underline{0} = 14\frac{2}{3}$ Identity

2. $4\frac{2}{3} + 3\frac{2}{5} = 3\frac{2}{5} + 4\frac{2}{3}$ Commutative

3. $\frac{3}{4} + \left(\frac{2}{5} + \frac{2}{3}\right) = \left(\frac{3}{4} + \frac{2}{5}\right) + \frac{2}{3}$ Associative

4. $4\frac{1}{2} + 7\frac{1}{3} = 7\frac{1}{3} + 4\frac{1}{2}$ Commutative

Use the Associative Property to solve. Show your work.

5. $\frac{1}{4} + \left(\frac{1}{4} + \frac{1}{2}\right) =$
   $\left(\frac{1}{4} + \frac{1}{4}\right) + \frac{1}{2} = \frac{1}{2} + \frac{1}{2} = 1$

6. $2\frac{1}{2} + \left(4\frac{1}{2} + \frac{5}{8}\right) =$
   $\left(2\frac{1}{2} + 4\frac{1}{2}\right) + \frac{5}{8} = 7 + \frac{5}{8} = 7\frac{5}{8}$

7. $\left(\frac{3}{5} + \frac{1}{6}\right) + \frac{5}{6} =$
   $\frac{3}{5} + \left(\frac{1}{6} + \frac{5}{6}\right) = \frac{3}{5} + 1 = 1\frac{3}{5}$

8. $\frac{7}{10} + \left(\frac{3}{10} + \frac{2}{3}\right) =$
   $\left(\frac{7}{10} + \frac{3}{10}\right) + \frac{2}{3} = 1 + \frac{2}{3} = 1\frac{2}{3}$

Problem Solving

9. Carmen has a job walking dogs. On Saturday she worked for $2\frac{1}{2}$ hours, and on Sunday she worked for $3\frac{3}{4}$ hours. How many hours did she work in all during the weekend? $6\frac{1}{4}$ h

10. A gift box needs two lengths of ribbon to be properly wrapped. One length must be $3\frac{1}{2}$ inches long, and the other must be $8\frac{3}{4}$ inches long. What is the total length of ribbon needed to wrap the box? $12\frac{1}{4}$ in.

Spiral Review

11. $4(3 + 5) = \underline{32}$

12. $6(2 + \underline{2}) = 24$

13. $5(\underline{7} - 4) = 15$

14. $\underline{5}(2 + 3) = 25$

60 Grade 5, Chapter 6, Lesson 8, Cluster B

Chapter 6 ~ Lesson 9

Practice

Problem Solving: Strategy
Write an Equation

P 6-9 PRACTICE

Write an equation. Then solve. Equations may vary. Possible equations are given.

1. At the end of the day, a baker has $3\frac{1}{2}$ pounds of rye flour left. How many pounds of rye flour did he use if he started with 15 pounds?
   $15 - \square = 3\frac{1}{2}$; $11\frac{1}{2}$ lb

2. A chef buys 50 pounds of rice. At the end of the week, there are only $12\frac{3}{4}$ pounds of rice left. How much did she use?
   $12\frac{3}{4} + \square = 50$; $37\frac{1}{4}$ lb

3. **Social Studies** Daniel Boone was born in 1734. In 1789, George Washington was elected the first president of the United States. How old was Daniel Boone when Washington was elected President?
   $1734 + \square = 1789$; 55 yr old

4. **Measurement** A carpenter has a piece of wood that is 12 feet long. After cutting the wood into pieces, $3\frac{5}{8}$ feet are left. How much of the wood did the carpenter use?
   $12 - \square = 3\frac{5}{8}$; $8\frac{3}{8}$ ft

Mixed Strategy Review

Solve. Use any strategy.

5. Five students were standing in line in the cafeteria. Beth was first in line. Jeff was 2 places behind Ernesto. Leah was ahead of Peter, who was fifth in line. Who was third in line?
   Leah
   Strategy: Draw a Diagram

6. **Time** Amanda leaves her house at 4:12 P.M. She meets Kyle 6 minutes later and together they walk to the library. If they arrive at the library at 4:35 P.M., how long did Kyle and Amanda walk together?
   17 min
   Strategy: Write an Equation

7. Daniel makes candles. Supplies to make a dozen candles cost \$5.25. How much profit does he make if he sells all the candles for \$4.50 each?
   \$48.75
   Strategy: Solve a Simpler Problem

8. **Create a problem** for which you could write an equation to solve. Share it with others.
   Check students' problems.

Use with Grade 5, Chapter 6, Lesson 9, pages 274–275. (196)

Reteach

Problem Solving: Strategy
Write an Equation

R 6-9 RETEACH

Page 275, Problem 1

A baker buys 20 pounds of butter. At the end of the week, there is only $1\frac{1}{4}$ pounds left. How much did she use?

Step 1
Read

Be sure you understand the problem.
Read carefully.

What do you know?
- A baker buys 20 pounds of butter.
- There is $1\frac{1}{4}$ pounds left.

What do you need to find?
- How much butter she used.

Step 2
Plan

- Do an Experiment
- Guess and Check
- Work Backward
- Make a Graph
- Make a Table
- Write an Equation
- Make an Organized List
- Draw a Diagram
- Solve a Simpler Problem
- Logical Reasoning

Make a plan.
Choose a strategy.

You can write an equation to make it easier to solve the problem.

Then you can use the guess-and-check strategy to find the number that makes the equation true.

Use with Grade 5, Chapter 6, Lesson 9, pages 274–275. (197)

Reteach

Problem Solving: Strategy
Write an Equation

R 6-9 RETEACH

Step 3
Solve

Carry out your plan.
Write an equation to show the problem.
Think:
amount of butter left + amount of butter used = total amount

Equation: $1\frac{1}{4} + \square = 20$

Use the guess-and-check strategy to find the number that makes the equation true. Answers may vary.

Guess: Eventually, correct guess should be $18\frac{3}{4}$.
Check: Answers may vary.

Guess: Answers may vary.
Check: Answers may vary.

Guess: Answers may vary.
Check: Answers may vary.

How many pounds of butter did the baker use? $18\frac{3}{4}$ pounds

Step 4
Look Back

Is the solution reasonable?
Reread the problem.
Have you answered the question? Yes
Is your answer reasonable? Answers may vary. Possible answer: Yes, since $18\frac{3}{4}$ is less than 20.

Practice

1. A deli has $2\frac{1}{4}$ pounds of tuna salad left at the end of the day. How many pounds of tuna salad did they sell if they started with 12 pounds?
   $12 - \square = 2\frac{1}{4}$; $9\frac{3}{4}$ lb

2. A contractor buys 30 pounds of cement. At the end of the week there are only $6\frac{1}{2}$ pounds of cement left. How much cement did he use?
   $6\frac{1}{2} + \square = 30$; $23\frac{1}{2}$ lb

Use with Grade 5, Chapter 6, Lesson 9, pages 274–275. (198)

Daily Homework

6-9 **Problem Solving: Strategy**
Write an Equation

Write an equation, then solve.

1. Jim's stock started the day at $12\frac{3}{8}$ per share and rose to $15\frac{3}{4}$ per share. How much did the stock increase per share?
   $15\frac{3}{4} - 12\frac{3}{8} = 3\frac{3}{8}$

2. One weekend Stu worked $7\frac{1}{2}$ hours on Saturday and $6\frac{3}{4}$ hours on Sunday. How many hours did he work in all during the weekend?
   $7\frac{1}{2} + 6\frac{3}{4} = 14\frac{1}{4}$ h

3. Karen's grandmother gave her a $2\frac{1}{2}$-pound tin of cookies. Karen brought $1\frac{1}{4}$ pounds of cookies to school to share with her class. How many pounds of cookies does that leave?
   $2\frac{1}{2} - 1\frac{1}{4} = 1\frac{1}{4}$ lb

4. Latisha's puppy weighed $3\frac{1}{4}$ pounds when they brought her home. Now the puppy weighs $8\frac{7}{8}$ pounds. How many pounds did the puppy gain?
   $8\frac{7}{8} - 3\frac{1}{4} = 5\frac{5}{8}$ lb

5. At the start of the school year, Jayne was $47\frac{3}{4}$ in. tall. During the year she grew $2\frac{3}{8}$ in. What is her height now?
   $47\frac{3}{4} + 2\frac{3}{8} = 50\frac{1}{8}$ in.

Spiral Review

Find the median.

6. 3, 6, 2, 9, 15 6
7. 12, 18, 22, 8 15
8. 12, 19, 6, 16, 18, 18, 13 16
9. 8, 9, 3, 15, 21, 12 10.5

Grade 5, Chapter 6, Lesson 9, Cluster B 61

Chapter 6 ~ Lesson 10

Practice

Explore Subtracting Mixed Numbers with Unlike Denominators

6-10 PRACTICE

Write the subtraction sentence shown by each model.
Write the answer in simplest form.

1. 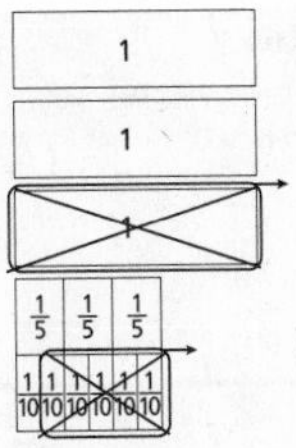

$3\frac{3}{5} - 1\frac{1}{2} = 2\frac{1}{10}$

2. 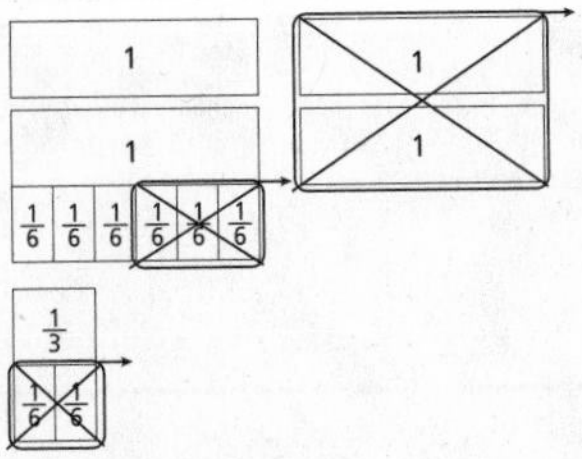

$4\frac{1}{3} - 2\frac{5}{6} = 1\frac{1}{2}$

Subtract. Write your answer in simplest form.

3. $3\frac{7}{8} - 2\frac{1}{4} = 1\frac{5}{8}$
4. $4\frac{5}{6} - 1\frac{1}{3} = 3\frac{1}{2}$
5. $2\frac{9}{10} - 2\frac{3}{5} = \frac{3}{10}$
6. $3\frac{3}{4} - 1\frac{5}{16} = 2\frac{7}{16}$
7. $2\frac{1}{2} - 1\frac{3}{8} = 1\frac{1}{8}$
8. $4\frac{11}{12} - 2\frac{5}{6} = 2\frac{1}{12}$
9. $4\frac{1}{6} - 2\frac{1}{2} = 1\frac{2}{3}$
10. $3\frac{7}{10} - 2\frac{1}{5} = 1\frac{1}{2}$
11. $3\frac{3}{8} - 1\frac{3}{4} = 1\frac{5}{8}$
12. $3\frac{5}{16} - 2\frac{5}{16} = 1$
13. $4\frac{1}{3} - 1\frac{1}{2} = 2\frac{5}{6}$
14. $3\frac{5}{12} - 2\frac{2}{3} = \frac{3}{4}$

Problem Solving

15. A disc jockey has $4\frac{3}{4}$ minutes of radio time to fill with a song and a commercial. If the song lasts $3\frac{1}{2}$ minutes, how much time remains for the commercial? $1\frac{1}{4}$ minutes

16. A listener requests a disc jockey to play a song that lasts $3\frac{3}{4}$ minutes. Only $2\frac{5}{6}$ minutes of time is available. How much before the end of the song will the music have to stop? $\frac{11}{12}$ minute

Reteach

Explore Subtracting Mixed Numbers with Unlike Denominators

6-10 RETEACH

You can draw models to help subtract mixed numbers with unlike denominators.

Subtract $3\frac{3}{4} - 1\frac{5}{8}$.

Draw models for each mixed number.

Find the LCD fractions.
Redraw the model to show eighths.
To find the difference, count the ones, then count the eighths.

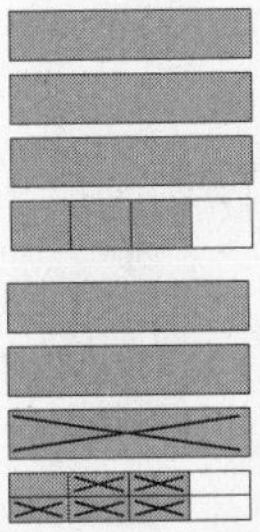

$3\frac{3}{4}$

$3\frac{3}{4} - 1\frac{5}{8}$
↓
$3\frac{6}{8} - 1\frac{5}{8} = 2\frac{1}{8}$

Complete. Find each difference. Write your answer in simplest form.

1. $2\frac{4}{5} - 1\frac{7}{10}$ → $2\frac{8}{10} - 1\frac{7}{10} = 1\frac{1}{10}$
2. $2\frac{5}{8} - 1\frac{1}{4}$ → $2\frac{5}{8} - 1\frac{2}{8} = 1\frac{3}{8}$
3. $3\frac{4}{5} - 1\frac{1}{3}$ → $3\frac{12}{15} - 1\frac{5}{15} = 2\frac{7}{15}$

Subtract. You may draw models. Write your answer in simplest form.

4. $4\frac{7}{16} - 1\frac{1}{4} = 3\frac{3}{16}$
5. $3\frac{1}{2} - 1\frac{3}{10} = 2\frac{1}{5}$
6. $2\frac{5}{6} - 2\frac{3}{4} = \frac{1}{12}$
7. $3\frac{7}{12} - 2\frac{1}{6} = 1\frac{5}{12}$
8. $4\frac{2}{3} - 2\frac{1}{2} = 2\frac{1}{6}$
9. $3\frac{3}{4} - 3\frac{1}{3} = \frac{5}{12}$
10. $4\frac{4}{5} - 1\frac{3}{10} = 3\frac{1}{2}$
11. $6\frac{1}{2} - 6\frac{3}{8} = \frac{1}{8}$
12. $7\frac{2}{3} - 5\frac{1}{5} = 2\frac{7}{15}$

Enrich

Explore Subtracting Mixed Numbers with Unlike Denominators

6-10 ENRICH

Magic Boxes

Each row, column, and diagonal in a magic square has the same sum. Use addition and subtraction of mixed numbers to complete each box. Record the magic sum of each box.

1.

$2\frac{7}{8}$	1	$1\frac{3}{8}$
$\frac{1}{4}$	$1\frac{3}{4}$	$3\frac{1}{4}$
$2\frac{1}{8}$	$2\frac{1}{2}$	$\frac{5}{8}$

Magic Sum: $5\frac{1}{4}$

2.

$1\frac{1}{3}$	6	$2\frac{2}{3}$
$4\frac{2}{3}$	$3\frac{1}{3}$	3
4	$\frac{2}{3}$	$5\frac{1}{3}$

Magic Sum: 10

3.

1	$2\frac{1}{4}$	2
$2\frac{3}{4}$	$1\frac{3}{4}$	$\frac{3}{4}$
$1\frac{1}{2}$	$1\frac{1}{4}$	$2\frac{1}{2}$

Magic Sum: $5\frac{1}{4}$

4.

2	$1\frac{5}{8}$	2
$1\frac{7}{8}$	$1\frac{7}{8}$	$1\frac{7}{8}$
$1\frac{3}{4}$	$2\frac{1}{8}$	$1\frac{3}{4}$

Magic Sum: $5\frac{5}{8}$

5.

$2\frac{1}{2}$	$\frac{5}{6}$	$3\frac{1}{6}$
$2\frac{5}{6}$	$2\frac{1}{6}$	$1\frac{1}{2}$
$1\frac{1}{6}$	$3\frac{1}{2}$	$1\frac{5}{6}$

Magic Sum: $6\frac{1}{2}$

6.

$2\frac{4}{5}$	$2\frac{3}{10}$	$2\frac{2}{5}$
$2\frac{1}{10}$	$2\frac{1}{2}$	$2\frac{9}{10}$
$2\frac{3}{5}$	$2\frac{7}{10}$	$2\frac{1}{5}$

Magic Sum: $7\frac{1}{2}$

Daily Homework

6-10 Explore Subtracting Mixed Numbers with Unlike Denominators

Subtract. Write your answer in simplest form.

1. $7\frac{1}{2} - 3\frac{1}{3} = 4\frac{1}{6}$
2. $4\frac{1}{2} - 1\frac{2}{3} = 2\frac{5}{6}$
3. $5\frac{1}{4} - 4\frac{5}{6} = \frac{5}{12}$
4. $6\frac{3}{8} - 4\frac{5}{6} = 1\frac{13}{24}$
5. $4\frac{1}{2} - 3\frac{1}{2} = 1$
6. $4\frac{2}{3} - 1\frac{7}{8} = 2\frac{19}{24}$
7. $14\frac{3}{4} - 6\frac{1}{2} = 8\frac{1}{4}$
8. $7\frac{7}{16} - 3\frac{1}{4} = 4\frac{3}{16}$
9. $13\frac{3}{8} - 5\frac{3}{4} = 7\frac{5}{8}$
10. $7\frac{1}{2} - 3\frac{5}{6} = 3\frac{2}{3}$
11. $7\frac{2}{3} - 4\frac{2}{3} = 3$
12. $7\frac{1}{4} - 4\frac{1}{2} = 2\frac{3}{4}$
13. $4\frac{2}{3} - 2\frac{3}{4} = 1\frac{11}{12}$
14. $4\frac{3}{4} - 1\frac{3}{4} = 3$
15. $5\frac{1}{3} - 1\frac{5}{6} = 3\frac{1}{2}$
16. $7\frac{2}{3} - 1\frac{1}{4} = 6\frac{5}{12}$

Solve.

17. A can of tuna fish contains $6\frac{1}{2}$ ounces of tuna. Harry used $2\frac{3}{4}$ ounces for his sandwich. How much tuna fish is left? $3\frac{3}{4}$ oz

18. Cory's hat size is $5\frac{1}{2}$. His father's hat size is 8. How much larger is his father's hat size? $2\frac{1}{2}$

Spiral Review

Compare. Write <, >, or =.

19. $1.4 = 1\frac{2}{5}$
20. $2\frac{3}{4} < 2.8$
21. $5.6 > 5\frac{1}{2}$

Chapter 6 ~ Lesson 11

Practice

Subtract Mixed Numbers

P 6-11 PRACTICE

Subtract. Write your answer in simplest form.

1. $7\frac{15}{16} - 2\frac{11}{16} = 5\frac{1}{4}$
2. $11\frac{4}{5} - 4\frac{3}{10} = 7\frac{1}{2}$
3. $12 - 9\frac{1}{3} = 2\frac{2}{3}$
4. $18\frac{1}{6} - 9\frac{5}{6} = 8\frac{1}{3}$
5. $9 - 5\frac{1}{12} = 3\frac{11}{12}$
6. $16\frac{1}{3} - 7\frac{7}{10} = 8\frac{19}{30}$
7. $34\frac{11}{20} - 15 = 19\frac{11}{20}$
8. $64\frac{3}{4} - 37\frac{11}{12} = 26\frac{5}{6}$
9. $51\frac{2}{5} - 25\frac{3}{4} = 25\frac{13}{20}$
10. $46 - 27\frac{3}{4} = 18\frac{1}{4}$
11. $82\frac{4}{5} - 62 = 20\frac{4}{5}$
12. $23\frac{1}{8} - 15\frac{2}{5} = 7\frac{29}{40}$
13. $16 - 7\frac{11}{12} = 8\frac{1}{12}$
14. $35\frac{7}{8} - 21\frac{1}{4} = 14\frac{5}{8}$
15. $97 - 87\frac{4}{5} = 9\frac{1}{5}$
16. $6\frac{11}{12} - 4\frac{5}{12} = 2\frac{1}{2}$
17. $11\frac{2}{3} - 3\frac{2}{5} = 8\frac{4}{15}$
18. $14\frac{7}{8} - 5 = 9\frac{7}{8}$
19. $15\frac{1}{6} - 6\frac{1}{4} = 8\frac{11}{12}$
20. $9\frac{3}{10} - 8\frac{7}{10} = \frac{3}{5}$
21. $12\frac{1}{2} - 3\frac{1}{5} = 9\frac{3}{10}$
22. $44 - 21\frac{13}{16} = 22\frac{3}{16}$
23. $74\frac{3}{8} - 38\frac{3}{5} = 35\frac{31}{40}$
24. $50\frac{1}{2} - 41 = 9\frac{1}{2}$
25. $35\frac{3}{8} - 18\frac{3}{4} = 16\frac{5}{8}$
26. $99\frac{9}{10} - 75\frac{3}{5} = 24\frac{3}{10}$
27. $23 - 14\frac{5}{12} = 8\frac{7}{12}$

Problem Solving

28. A bag for oranges will hold 8 pounds. Kyle already put $3\frac{5}{8}$ pounds of oranges in the bag. How many more pounds of oranges can he put in the bag? $4\frac{3}{8}$ pounds

29. Sara needs $2\frac{1}{2}$ pounds of grapes for a salad. She chose a bag of grapes that weighs $1\frac{7}{8}$ pounds. How many more grapes does she need? $\frac{5}{8}$ pound

Use with Grade 5, Chapter 6, Lesson 11, pages 278–279. (202)

Reteach

Subtract Mixed Numbers

R 6-11 RETEACH

When subtracting mixed numbers, you may have to rename twice. First, you must rename one or both fractions using the LCD. Then you must rename a mixed or whole number so you can subtract the fractions.

Subtract $9\frac{3}{10} - 3\frac{1}{2}$. Estimate: $9 - 4 = 5$

Step 1

Write the problem in vertical form.

Write equivalent fractions using the LCD.

$$\begin{array}{r} 9\frac{3}{10} = 9\frac{3}{10} \\ -\ 3\frac{1}{2} = -\ 3\frac{5}{10} \\ \hline \end{array}$$

Step 2

Rename the mixed number you are subtracting from.

$$9\frac{3}{10} = 8\frac{10}{10} + \frac{3}{10} = 8\frac{13}{10}$$
$$-\ 3\frac{5}{10} = \qquad -\ 3\frac{5}{10}$$

Step 3

Subtract the fractions. Then subtract the whole numbers. Simplify.

$$\begin{array}{r} 8\frac{13}{10} \\ -\ 3\frac{5}{10} \\ \hline 5\frac{8}{10} = 5\frac{4}{5} \end{array}$$

Subtract. Write your answer in simplest form.

1. $7\frac{1}{4} - 4\frac{1}{2} = 2\frac{3}{4}$
2. $8 - 2\frac{4}{5} = 5\frac{1}{5}$
3. $12\frac{7}{10} - 5\frac{4}{5} = 6\frac{9}{10}$
4. $8\frac{5}{12} - 1\frac{2}{3} = 6\frac{3}{4}$
5. $15\frac{3}{8} - 6\frac{3}{4} = 8\frac{5}{8}$
6. $14 - 5\frac{11}{16} = 8\frac{5}{16}$
7. $5\frac{1}{3} - 4\frac{3}{4} = \frac{7}{12}$
8. $10\frac{1}{2} - 3\frac{9}{10} = 6\frac{3}{5}$
9. $13\frac{3}{5} - 7\frac{2}{3} = 5\frac{14}{15}$
10. $14\frac{7}{8} - 5 = 9\frac{7}{8}$
11. $35\frac{7}{8} - 21\frac{1}{4} = 14\frac{5}{8}$
12. $9\frac{3}{10} - 8\frac{7}{10} = \frac{3}{5}$
13. $17 - 7\frac{4}{5} = 9\frac{1}{5}$
14. $11\frac{2}{3} - 3\frac{2}{5} = 8\frac{4}{15}$
15. $46 - 27\frac{1}{5} = 18\frac{1}{4}$
16. $99\frac{9}{10} - 75\frac{3}{5} = 24\frac{3}{10}$
17. $16\frac{3}{8} - 7\frac{3}{5} = 8\frac{1}{12}$

Use with Grade 5, Chapter 6, Lesson 11, pages 278–279. (203)

Enrich

Subtract Mixed Numbers

E 6-11 ENRICH

Target Practice

Play this game with a partner. You will each need a counter.

- Together choose a whole number from 5 through 10. Write it in the square at the bottom right of the game board. Place your counter on Start. Then move it one square in any direction. Find the sum or difference of the numbers in the starting square and the square you moved to. Record it on a separate sheet of paper.
- Players alternate turns. On each turn, move one square. Add or subtract the number in that square to or from your previous sum or difference and record your answer. You cannot return to a square.
- The winner is the first player who reaches the target square with a sum or difference equal to the target number.

Start

$2\frac{1}{2}$	$1\frac{1}{6}$	$3\frac{5}{8}$	$2\frac{1}{8}$	$4\frac{1}{2}$	$1\frac{1}{3}$
$3\frac{1}{4}$	$2\frac{2}{5}$	$1\frac{2}{3}$	$1\frac{1}{4}$	$1\frac{4}{5}$	$2\frac{1}{4}$
$3\frac{2}{3}$	$1\frac{7}{8}$	$3\frac{1}{2}$	$1\frac{7}{10}$	$1\frac{1}{2}$	$2\frac{5}{6}$
$1\frac{3}{4}$	$1\frac{3}{8}$	$\frac{2}{3}$	$\frac{5}{8}$	$\frac{3}{5}$	$\frac{3}{8}$
$1\frac{1}{2}$	$2\frac{3}{10}$	$\frac{1}{4}$	$\frac{1}{5}$	$\frac{1}{2}$	$\frac{3}{4}$
$5\frac{1}{4}$	$2\frac{3}{4}$	$\frac{1}{8}$	$\frac{1}{6}$	$\frac{1}{3}$	Target Number ______

Use with Grade 5, Chapter 6, Lesson 11, pages 278–279. (204)

Daily Homework

6-11 Subtract Mixed Numbers

Subtract. Write your answer in simplest form.

1. $7\frac{1}{8} - 2\frac{3}{4} = 4\frac{3}{8}$
2. $5\frac{1}{2} - 2\frac{5}{6} = 2\frac{2}{3}$
3. $4\frac{2}{3} - 1\frac{5}{6} = 2\frac{5}{6}$
4. $10\frac{1}{3} - 4\frac{7}{10} = 5\frac{19}{30}$
5. $8 - 2\frac{2}{3} = 5\frac{1}{3}$
6. $83\frac{4}{5} - 5\frac{1}{4} = 78\frac{11}{20}$
7. $6\frac{5}{6} - 2\frac{1}{4} = 4\frac{7}{12}$
8. $5\frac{3}{8} - 2\frac{3}{8} = 3$
9. $18\frac{7}{8} - 5\frac{1}{3} = 13\frac{13}{24}$
10. $5\frac{3}{5} - 3 = 2\frac{3}{5}$
11. $9\frac{1}{2} - 4\frac{2}{3} = 4\frac{5}{6}$
12. $7\frac{11}{20} - 2\frac{1}{5} = 5\frac{7}{20}$

Problem Solving

13. Kendra is baking an apple pie. The recipe calls for $3\frac{2}{3}$ pounds of apples. Kendra has a 5-pound bag of apples. How many pounds of apples will be left over? $1\frac{1}{3}$ lb

14. A stock that Matt owns fell in value from $83\frac{3}{8}$ to $77\frac{1}{2}$. How much did the stock fall? $5\frac{7}{8}$

Spiral Review

Simplify each fraction.

15. $\frac{36}{48}$ $\frac{3}{4}$
16. $\frac{40}{56}$ $\frac{5}{7}$
17. $\frac{32}{48}$ $\frac{2}{3}$
18. $\frac{18}{32}$ $\frac{9}{16}$

Grade 5, Chapter 6, Lesson 11, Cluster B 63

Chapter 6 ~ Lesson 12

Practice

Estimate Sums and Differences of Mixed Numbers

P 6-12 PRACTICE

Round to the nearest whole number.

1. $7\frac{3}{4}$ 8
2. $4\frac{1}{6}$ 4
3. $8\frac{3}{10}$ 8
4. $3\frac{1}{2}$ 4
5. $2\frac{9}{16}$ 3
6. $9\frac{4}{5}$ 10
7. $1\frac{7}{8}$ 2
8. $5\frac{5}{12}$ 5

Estimate. Answers may vary. Possible estimates are given.

9. $3\frac{7}{8} + 2\frac{1}{6}$ — $4 + 2 = 6$
10. $8\frac{5}{6} - 3\frac{2}{3}$ — $9 - 4 = 5$
11. $5\frac{1}{8} - 1\frac{7}{8}$ — $5 - 2 = 3$
12. $9\frac{7}{10} + 3\frac{4}{5}$ — $10 + 4 = 14$
13. $6\frac{1}{4} + 7\frac{3}{8}$ — $6 + 7 = 13$
14. $14\frac{1}{5} - 9\frac{3}{5}$ — $14 - 10 = 4$
15. $18\frac{5}{16} - 9\frac{13}{16}$ — $18 - 10 = 8$
16. $6\frac{11}{12} + 4\frac{5}{12}$ — $7 + 4 = 11$
17. $7\frac{1}{3} + 6\frac{7}{12}$ — $7 + 7 = 14$
18. $15\frac{3}{8} - 7\frac{7}{16}$ — $15 - 7 = 8$
19. $9\frac{4}{5} + 6\frac{2}{3}$ — $10 + 7 = 17$
20. $6\frac{11}{12} - 6\frac{1}{5}$ — $7 - 6 = 1$
21. $8\frac{2}{5} + 8\frac{11}{16}$ — $8 + 9 = 17$
22. $17\frac{7}{10} - 9\frac{1}{3}$ — $18 - 9 = 9$
23. $7\frac{1}{2} + 9\frac{3}{8}$ — $8 + 9 = 17$
24. $25\frac{7}{12} + 34\frac{1}{12}$ — $30 + 30 = 60$
25. $58\frac{4}{5} - 29\frac{7}{8}$ — $60 - 30 = 30$
26. $52\frac{1}{3} - 34\frac{5}{16}$ — $50 - 30 = 20$

Problem Solving

27. After walking $10\frac{7}{8}$ miles one week, Beth walked $2\frac{1}{2}$ fewer miles the following week. About how many miles did she walk the second week?
about 8 miles

28. Jon wanted to walk at least 8 miles by the end of the week. He walked $5\frac{3}{4}$ miles by Thursday. If he walks another $2\frac{5}{8}$ miles on Friday, will he have met his goal? Explain.
yes; $5\frac{3}{4} + 2\frac{5}{8} = 8\frac{3}{8}$

Use with Grade 5, Chapter 6, Lesson 12, pages 280–281. (205)

Reteach

Estimate Sums and Differences of Mixed Numbers

R 6-12 RETEACH

You can round mixed numbers to the nearest whole number to estimate sums and differences of mixed numbers. Use number lines to help you.

Estimate $5\frac{5}{8} - 2\frac{1}{5}$.

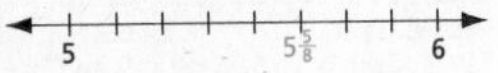

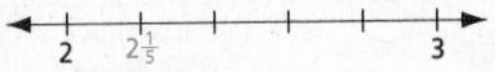

$5\frac{5}{8}$ is closer to 6 than to 5.

$2\frac{1}{5}$ is closer to 2 than to 3.

$5\frac{5}{8} - 2\frac{1}{5}$
↓ ↓
$6 - 2 = 4$ So, $5\frac{5}{8} - 2\frac{1}{5}$ is about 4.

Show each mixed number on a number line. Round each mixed number to the nearest whole number. Then estimate the sum or difference.

1. $3\frac{2}{5} + 4\frac{9}{10}$

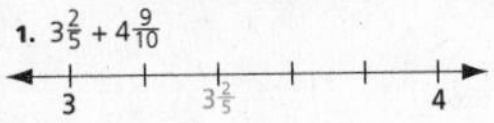

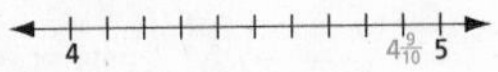

4
$4\frac{9}{10}$
5

$3\frac{2}{5}$ is closer to 3 than to 4.

$4\frac{9}{10}$ is closer to 5 than to 4.

$3\frac{2}{5}$ + $4\frac{9}{10}$
↓ ↓
3 + 5 = 8

2. $10\frac{3}{4} - 3\frac{7}{8}$

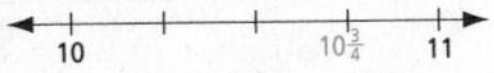

10
$10\frac{3}{4}$
11

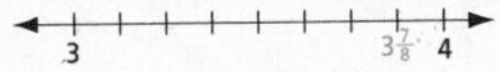

$10\frac{3}{4}$ is closer to 11 than to 10.

$3\frac{7}{8}$ is closer to 4 than to 3.

$10\frac{3}{4}$ − $3\frac{7}{8}$
↓ ↓
11 − 4 = 7

Estimate the sum or difference. You may draw number lines.

3. $8\frac{1}{6} - 3\frac{9}{16}$
↓ ↓
8 – 4 = 4

4. $7\frac{9}{10} + 6\frac{7}{10}$
↓ ↓
8 – 7 = 15

5. $9\frac{7}{12} - 2\frac{3}{8}$
↓ ↓
10 – 3 = 7

Use with Grade 5, Chapter 6, Lesson 12, pages 280–281. (206)

Enrich

Estimate Sums and Differences of Mixed Numbers

E 6-12 ENRICH

Road Rallies

Round each mixed number to the nearest whole number. Then find three paths of four parts each. The estimated sums and differences of the mixed numbers on the paths must match the estimates at the finish lines. Do not use a number more than once.

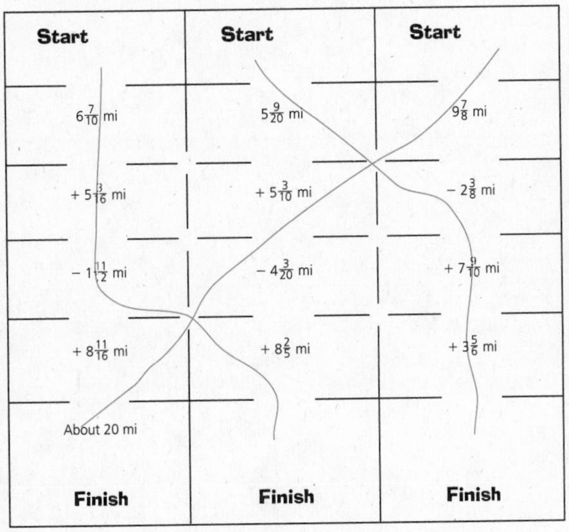

Start
Start
Start
$6\frac{7}{10}$ mi
$5\frac{9}{20}$ mi
$9\frac{7}{8}$ mi
+ $5\frac{3}{16}$ mi
+ $5\frac{3}{10}$ mi
− $2\frac{3}{8}$ mi
− $1\frac{11}{12}$ mi
− $4\frac{3}{20}$ mi
+ $7\frac{9}{10}$ mi
+ $8\frac{11}{16}$ mi
+ $8\frac{2}{5}$ mi
+ $3\frac{5}{6}$ mi
About 20 mi
Finish
Finish
Finish

Use with Grade 5, Chapter 6, Lesson 12, pages 280–281. (207)

Daily Homework

6-12 Estimate Sums and Differences of Mixed Numbers

Round to the nearest whole number.

1. $8\frac{1}{3}$ 8
2. $5\frac{4}{5}$ 6
3. $7\frac{2}{7}$ 7
4. $54\frac{3}{4}$ 55

Estimate. Answers may vary. Possible estimates are given.

5. $4\frac{2}{3} + 7\frac{1}{5}$ — $5 + 7 = 12$
6. $8\frac{2}{3} - 4\frac{1}{4}$ — $9 - 4 = 5$
7. $8\frac{1}{3} + 6\frac{1}{4}$ — $8 + 6 = 14$
8. $9\frac{2}{3} - 8\frac{1}{5}$ — $10 - 8 = 2$
9. $8\frac{1}{4} + 4\frac{7}{8}$ — $8 + 5 = 13$
10. $6\frac{3}{4} - 2\frac{1}{3}$ — $7 - 2 = 5$
11. $9\frac{2}{3} + 8\frac{5}{6}$ — $10 + 9 = 19$
12. $20\frac{1}{5} - 17\frac{3}{8}$ — $20 - 17 = 3$
13. $21\frac{3}{5} - 17\frac{7}{8}$ — $22 - 18 = 4$
14. $9\frac{3}{5} + 8\frac{1}{4}$ — $10 + 8 = 18$
15. $3\frac{1}{4} + 18\frac{2}{9}$ — $3 + 18 = 21$
16. $15\frac{3}{4} - 7\frac{1}{4}$ — $16 - 7 = 9$
17. $18\frac{7}{8} - 4\frac{3}{5}$ — $19 - 5 = 14$
18. $8\frac{9}{15} - 7\frac{1}{20}$ — $9 - 7 = 2$
19. $3\frac{3}{7} + 5\frac{1}{5}$ — $3 + 5 = 8$
20. $19\frac{7}{8} - 15\frac{2}{3}$ — $20 - 16 = 4$

Problem Solving

21. Two pieces of string are needed to tie up a package for mailing. One piece must be $15\frac{7}{8}$ in. long, and the other piece must be $22\frac{1}{4}$ inches long. How much string is needed to tie up the package? $38\frac{1}{8}$ in.

22. One side of a square picture is $5\frac{1}{3}$ inches long. How much framing is needed for all four sides of the picture? $21\frac{1}{3}$ in.

Spiral Review

For each pair of numbers, find the GCF.

23. 24 and 26 2
24. 32 and 24 8
25. 10 and 25 5
26. 16 and 28 4

64 Grade 5, Chapter 6, Lesson 12, Cluster B

Chapter 6 ~ Lesson 13

Part A Worksheet

Problem Solving: Application
Adding and Subtracting Mixed Numbers

Part A 6-13 WORKSHEET Decision Making

Use the tables to help you to decide which store and which border to recommend to the decorator.

Wallpaper City			
Border Pattern	**Total Number of Rolls Needed**	**Total Cost of Wallpaper**	**Total Cost with Paste**
Flowered			
Plaid			
Striped			

Interior Décor Store			
Border Pattern	**Total Number of Rolls Needed**	**Total Cost of Wallpaper**	**Total Cost with Paste**
Flowered			
Plaid			
Striped			

Your Decision

What would you recommend to the decorator? Explain.

Answers may vary. Possible answer: Buy the plaid paper at Wallpaper City to make the greatest profit.

Use with Grade 5, Chapter 6, Lesson 13, pages 282–283. (208)

Part B Worksheet

Problem Solving: Application
How does the size of your body parts relate to your height?

Part B 6-13 WORKSHEET Math & Science

Estimate your height. Answers may vary.

Now look at your feet, hands, and arm span. Estimate:

- the fraction the length of your foot is to your total height. Answers may vary.
- the fraction the length of your hand is to your total height. Answers may vary.
- the fraction the length of your arm span is to your total height. Answers may vary.

Work with a partner. Round each measurement to the nearest centimeter.

Remember: To measure your arm span, measure from fingertip to fingertip, with your arms spread out.

Record your data in the tables. Then find the fraction of your height for each length.

Height:

Length	Fraction of Height
Foot length:	
Hand length:	
Arm span:	

Remember: To find the fraction of each length to your height, write the following fractions using your measurements: foot length/height, hand length/height, and arm span/height.

1. Look at the fractions in your table. Are any of the fractions close to 1?

   Answers may vary. Possible answer: arm span.

Use with Grade 5, Chapter 6, Lesson 13, pages 284–285. (209)

Part B Worksheet

Problem Solving: Application
How does the size of your body parts relate to your height?

Part B 6-13 WORKSHEET Math & Science

Collect data from your classmates. Record the data in the table.

Length	Fraction of Height
Foot length:	
Hand length:	
Arm span:	

2. Do you see any patterns in the data? Explain.

   Answers may vary.

3. How did your estimates compare to your actual measurements? Were you surprised? Explain.

   Answers may vary.

Use with Grade 5, Chapter 6, Lesson 13, pages 284–285. (210)

Chapter 7 ~ Lesson 1

Practice

Multiply a Whole Number by a Fraction

P 7-1 PRACTICE

Multiply.

1. $\frac{1}{5} \times 45 =$ 9
2. $\frac{5}{8} \times 32 =$ 20
3. $\frac{3}{4} \times 40 =$ 30
4. $\frac{1}{2} \times 14 =$ 7
5. $\frac{4}{9} \times 63 =$ 28
6. $\frac{2}{11} \times 33 =$ 6
7. $\frac{3}{10} \times 70 =$ 21
8. $\frac{5}{7} \times 42 =$ 30
9. $\frac{1}{10} \times 20 =$ 2
10. $\frac{2}{5} \times 35 =$ 14
11. $\frac{9}{10} \times 50 =$ 45
12. $\frac{5}{8} \times 24 =$ 15
13. $\frac{1}{12} \times 96 =$ 8
14. $\frac{8}{9} \times 72 =$ 64
15. $\frac{1}{3} \times 18 =$ 6
16. $\frac{7}{9} \times 45 =$ 35
17. $\frac{3}{5} \times 15 =$ 9
18. $\frac{3}{4} \times 48 =$ 36
19. $\frac{7}{10} \times 30 =$ 21
20. $\frac{4}{7} \times 77 =$ 44
21. $\frac{7}{8} \times 64 =$ 56
22. $\frac{2}{3} \times 27 =$ 18
23. $\frac{5}{12} \times 60 =$ 25
24. $\frac{3}{11} \times 88 =$ 24

Algebra & Functions Complete each table.

25. Rule: Multiply by $\frac{1}{4}$

Input	Output
12	3
20	5
32	8
40	10

26. Rule: Multiply by $\frac{5}{6}$

Input	Output
12	10
30	25
42	35
54	45

27. Rule: Multiply by $\frac{7}{12}$

Input	Output
36	21
60	35
96	56
144	84

Problem Solving

28. A basketball that normally sells for \$24 is on sale for $\frac{2}{3}$ of the regular price. What is the sale price of the basketball? \$16

29. Kari received a \$30 gift certificate. After she bought a sweatshirt, she had $\frac{3}{10}$ of the money left. How much money did Kari have left? \$9

Use with Grade 5, Chapter 7, Lesson 1, pages 300–301. (211)

Reteach

Multiply a Whole Number by a Fraction

R 7-1 RETEACH

Multiply $\frac{3}{5} \times 10$.

Divide the whole number by the denominator of the fraction. $10 \div 5 = \mathbf{2}$

Multiply the numerator of the fraction by the quotient. $\mathbf{2} \times 3 = 6$

$\frac{3}{5} \times 10 = 6$

Multiply.

1. $\frac{2}{3} \times 24$
   Divide: $24 \div 3 =$ 8
   Multiply: 8 $\times 2 =$ 16
   $\frac{2}{3} \times 24 =$ 16

2. $\frac{1}{4} \times 12$
   Divide: $12 \div 4 =$ 3
   Multiply: 3 $\times 1 =$ 3
   $\frac{1}{4} \times 12 =$ 3

3. $\frac{5}{6} \times 48$
   Divide: $48 \div 6 =$ 8
   Multiply: 8 $\times 5 =$ 40
   $\frac{5}{6} \times 48 =$ 40

4. $\frac{3}{10} \times 40$
   Divide: 40 $\div$ 10 $=$ 4
   Multiply: 4 $\times$ 3 $=$ 12
   $\frac{3}{10} \times 40 =$ 12

5. $\frac{7}{8} \times 72$
   Divide: 72 $\div$ 8 $=$ 9
   Multiply: 9 $\times$ 7 $=$ 63
   $\frac{7}{8} \times 72 =$ 63

6. $\frac{2}{5} \times 40$
   Divide: 40 $\div$ 5 $=$ 8
   Multiply: 8 $\times$ 2 $=$ 16
   $\frac{2}{5} \times 40 =$ 16

7. $\frac{5}{8} \times 56 =$ 35
8. $\frac{3}{4} \times 16 =$ 12
9. $\frac{9}{10} \times 70 =$ 63
10. $\frac{4}{7} \times 35 =$ 20
11. $\frac{1}{6} \times 30 =$ 5
12. $\frac{5}{12} \times 48 =$ 20
13. $\frac{4}{5} \times 50 =$ 40
14. $\frac{2}{9} \times 81 =$ 18
15. $\frac{3}{8} \times 88 =$ 33
16. $\frac{2}{3} \times 18 =$ 12
17. $\frac{3}{10} \times 50 =$ 15
18. $\frac{7}{12} \times 24 =$ 14

Use with Grade 5, Chapter 7, Lesson 1, pages 300–301. (212)

Enrich

Multiply a Whole Number by a Fraction

E 7-1 ENRICH

Fraction Puzzle

Complete each crossnumber puzzle.

Puzzle A

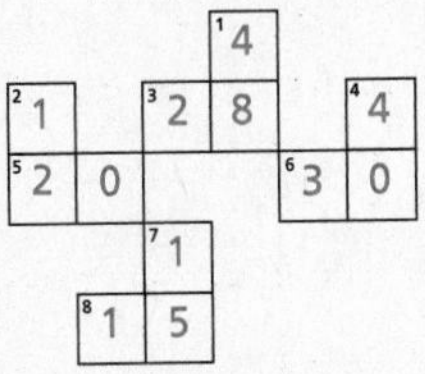

Products Across
3. $42 \times \frac{2}{3}$
5. $24 \times \frac{5}{6}$
6. $54 \times \frac{5}{9}$
8. $40 \times \frac{3}{8}$

Products Down
1. $72 \times \frac{2}{3}$
2. $16 \times \frac{3}{4}$
4. $50 \times \frac{4}{5}$
7. $36 \times \frac{5}{12}$

Puzzle B

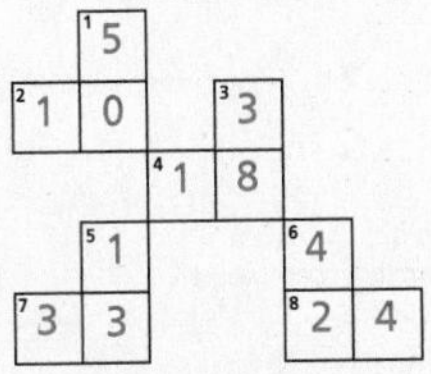

Products Across
2. $15 \times \frac{2}{3}$
4. $36 \times \frac{3}{6}$
7. $99 \times \frac{1}{3}$
8. $88 \times \frac{3}{11}$

Products Down
1. $100 \times \frac{1}{2}$
3. $57 \times \frac{2}{3}$
5. $65 \times \frac{1}{5}$
6. $70 \times \frac{3}{5}$

Puzzle C

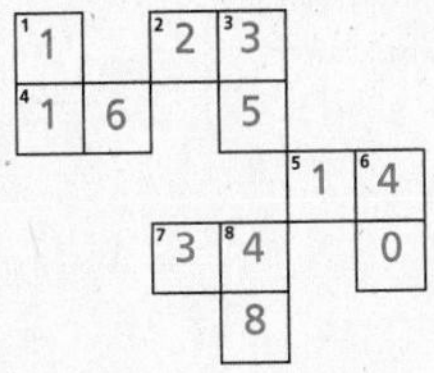

Products Across
2. $92 \times \frac{1}{4}$
4. $64 \times \frac{2}{8}$
5. $70 \times \frac{1}{5}$
7. $68 \times \frac{1}{2}$

Products Down
1. $33 \times \frac{1}{3}$
3. $49 \times \frac{5}{7}$
6. $80 \times \frac{8}{16}$
8. $64 \times \frac{3}{4}$

Use with Grade 5, Chapter 7, Lesson 1, pages 300–301. (213)

Daily Homework

7-1 Multiply a Whole Number by a Fraction

Multiply.

1. $\frac{2}{3} \times 48 =$ 32
2. $\frac{1}{5} \times 20 =$ 4
3. $\frac{3}{4} \times 20 =$ 15
4. $\frac{5}{6} \times 12 =$ 10
5. $\frac{1}{3} \times 33 =$ 11
6. $40 \times \frac{3}{5} =$ 24
7. $\frac{5}{8} \times 16 =$ 10
8. $\frac{9}{10} \times 80 =$ 72
9. $\frac{2}{5} \times 350 =$ 140
10. $\frac{1}{4} \times 24 =$ 6
11. $\frac{2}{3} \times 45 =$ 30
12. $\frac{3}{8} \times 56 =$ 21
13. $\frac{1}{2} \times 38 =$ 19
14. $36 \times \frac{5}{12} =$ 15
15. $\frac{4}{5} \times 35 =$ 28
16. $\frac{7}{10} \times 60 =$ 42
17. $\frac{3}{4} \times 36 =$ 27
18. $\frac{2}{3} \times 24 =$ 16
19. $\frac{3}{8} \times 24 =$ 9
20. $27 \times \frac{2}{9} =$ 6
21. $\frac{3}{8} \times 16 =$ 6

Problem Solving

22. Ben and his family are taking a 450-mile car trip to visit relatives. After they have traveled $\frac{2}{5}$ of the way, they stop for lunch. How many miles have they traveled so far? 180 miles

23. Two-thirds of Paul's class have signed up to play soccer. There are 24 students in the class. How many have signed up for soccer? 16 students

Spiral Review

24. $\frac{2}{3} + \frac{1}{5} =$ $\frac{13}{15}$
25. $4\frac{1}{2} + 2\frac{2}{3} =$ $7\frac{1}{6}$
26. $\frac{5}{6} + \frac{3}{8} =$ $1\frac{5}{24}$
27. $5\frac{1}{3} + 4\frac{1}{12} =$ $9\frac{5}{12}$

Grade 5, Chapter 7, Lesson 1, Cluster A 65

Chapter 7 ~ Lesson 2

Practice

Multiply a Fraction by a Fraction

P 7-2 PRACTICE

Multiply.

1. $\frac{1}{2} \times \frac{3}{8} =$ $\frac{3}{16}$
2. $\frac{7}{12} \times \frac{4}{5} =$ $\frac{7}{15}$
3. $\frac{3}{4} \times \frac{1}{9} =$ $\frac{1}{12}$
4. $\frac{4}{9} \times \frac{5}{6} =$ $\frac{10}{27}$
5. $\frac{3}{4} \times \frac{1}{3} =$ $\frac{1}{4}$
6. $\frac{5}{8} \times \frac{3}{10} =$ $\frac{3}{16}$
7. $\frac{2}{9} \times \frac{1}{2} =$ $\frac{1}{9}$
8. $\frac{3}{5} \times \frac{3}{8} =$ $\frac{9}{40}$
9. $\frac{8}{9} \times \frac{5}{16} =$ $\frac{5}{18}$
10. $\frac{1}{5} \times \frac{7}{12} =$ $\frac{7}{60}$
11. $\frac{3}{10} \times \frac{1}{4} =$ $\frac{3}{40}$
12. $\frac{5}{7} \times \frac{7}{9} =$ $\frac{5}{9}$
13. $\frac{9}{20} \times \frac{2}{3} =$ $\frac{3}{10}$
14. $\frac{3}{5} \times \frac{7}{12} =$ $\frac{7}{20}$
15. $\frac{1}{16} \times \frac{8}{9} =$ $\frac{1}{18}$
16. $\frac{2}{3} \times \frac{3}{5} =$ $\frac{2}{5}$
17. $\frac{2}{7} \times \frac{13}{20} =$ $\frac{13}{70}$
18. $\frac{4}{5} \times \frac{7}{16} =$ $\frac{7}{20}$
19. $\frac{11}{12} \times \frac{6}{7} =$ $\frac{11}{14}$
20. $\frac{2}{3} \times \frac{7}{8} =$ $\frac{7}{12}$
21. $\frac{1}{6} \times \frac{1}{12} =$ $\frac{1}{72}$
22. $\frac{5}{9} \times \frac{3}{20} =$ $\frac{1}{12}$
23. $\frac{9}{16} \times \frac{2}{3} =$ $\frac{3}{8}$
24. $\frac{3}{20} \times \frac{4}{5} =$ $\frac{3}{25}$

Algebra & Functions Find n so that each expression is true.

25. $\frac{1}{6} \times \frac{n}{2} = \frac{1}{12}$ $n =$ 1
26. $\frac{5}{6} \times \frac{n}{8} = \frac{15}{48}$ $n =$ 3
27. $\frac{7}{8} \times \frac{n}{8} = \frac{35}{64}$ $n =$ 5
28. $\frac{2}{3} \times \frac{n}{8} = \frac{7}{12}$ $n =$ 7
29. $\frac{4}{5} \times \frac{n}{4} = \frac{3}{5}$ $n =$ 3
30. $\frac{3}{4} \times \frac{n}{6} = \frac{5}{8}$ $n =$ 5

Problem Solving

31. Each year the Gardners plant $\frac{7}{8}$ of an acre with tomatoes. They sell half of what they grow at a roadside stand. What part of an acre do the Gardners use for the tomatoes they sell?
$\frac{7}{16}$ acre

32. The Wilsons' garden covers $\frac{5}{8}$ acre. One fourth of the garden is planted with flowers. The rest is vegetables. What part of an acre is planted with flowers? with vegetables?
$\frac{5}{32}$ acre; $\frac{15}{32}$ acre

Use with Grade 5, Chapter 7, Lesson 2, pages 302–305. (214)

Reteach

Multiply a Fraction by a Fraction

R 7-2 RETEACH

To multiply a fraction by a fraction, multiply the numerators and the denominators. Then simplify the product.

$$\frac{2}{3} \times \frac{5}{8} = \frac{2 \times 5}{3 \times 8} = \frac{10}{24} = \frac{10 \div 2}{24 \div 2} = \frac{5}{12}$$

When the numerator and denominator of either fraction have a common factor, you can simplify before you multiply. Divide the numerator and the denominator by their GCF (greatest common factor).

Look at the numerator, 2, and the denominator, 8. Their GCF is 2, so divide both 2 and 8 by 2.

$$\frac{2}{3} \times \frac{5}{8} \rightarrow \frac{\not{2}^{1}}{3} \times \frac{5}{\not{8}_{4}}$$

Look at the other numerator, 5, and the other denominator, 3. Their GCF is 1, so dividing won't change the answer.

Now multiply. The product is already in simplest form.

$$\frac{\not{2}^{1}}{3} \times \frac{5}{\not{8}_{4}} = \frac{1 \times 5}{3 \times 4} = \frac{5}{12}$$

Complete. Write the product in simplest form.

1. $\frac{3}{5} \times \frac{1}{4} = \frac{3 \times 1}{5 \times 4} = \frac{3}{20}$
2. $\frac{2}{3} \times \frac{5}{9} = \frac{2 \times 5}{3 \times 9} = \frac{10}{27}$
3. $\frac{3}{\not{4}_{2}} \times \frac{\not{2}^{1}}{5} = \frac{3 \times 1}{2 \times 5} = \frac{3}{10}$
4. $\frac{\not{4}^{2}}{7} \times \frac{5}{\not{6}_{3}} = \frac{2 \times 5}{7 \times 3} = \frac{10}{21}$
5. $\frac{\not{5}^{1}}{\not{6}_{2}} \times \frac{\not{9}^{3}}{\not{10}_{2}} = \frac{1 \times 3}{2 \times 2} = \frac{3}{4}$
6. $\frac{\not{4}^{1}}{\not{5}_{1}} \times \frac{\not{5}^{1}}{\not{8}_{2}} = \frac{1 \times 1}{1 \times 2} = \frac{1}{2}$

Multiply. Write each answer in simplest form.

7. $\frac{1}{2} \times \frac{3}{4} =$ $\frac{3}{8}$
8. $\frac{1}{6} \times \frac{4}{5} =$ $\frac{2}{15}$
9. $\frac{3}{8} \times \frac{5}{6} =$ $\frac{5}{16}$
10. $\frac{2}{9} \times \frac{3}{10} =$ $\frac{1}{15}$
11. $\frac{1}{12} \times \frac{1}{3} =$ $\frac{1}{36}$
12. $\frac{5}{16} \times \frac{2}{5} =$ $\frac{1}{8}$
13. $\frac{2}{5} \times \frac{3}{8} =$ $\frac{3}{20}$
14. $\frac{3}{8} \times \frac{7}{9} =$ $\frac{7}{24}$
15. $\frac{5}{12} \times \frac{3}{25} =$ $\frac{1}{20}$

Use with Grade 5, Chapter 7, Lesson 2, pages 302–305. (215)

Enrich

Multiply a Fraction by a Fraction

E 7-2 ENRICH

Puzzling Pieces

Use the fractions at the right.
Use each fraction once to make true sentences.

$(\frac{1}{3} \times \frac{1}{4}) \times 48 = 4$

$(\frac{7}{9} \times \frac{6}{7}) \times 27 = 18$

$(\frac{1}{2} \times \frac{4}{5}) \times 25 = 10$

$(\frac{5}{7} \times \frac{1}{5}) \times 56 = 8$

$(\frac{4}{9} \times \frac{3}{4}) \times 69 = 23$

$8 = (\frac{5}{9} \times \frac{2}{5}) \times 36$

$5 = (\frac{4}{7} \times \frac{7}{8}) \times 10$

$20 = (\frac{5}{8} \times \frac{8}{9}) \times 36$

$5 = (\frac{2}{3} \times \frac{3}{8}) \times 20$

$3 = (\frac{5}{6} \times \frac{3}{5}) \times 6$

$\frac{8}{9}$	$\frac{7}{9}$
$\frac{5}{9}$	$\frac{5}{7}$
$\frac{1}{3}$	$\frac{3}{5}$
$\frac{6}{7}$	$\frac{1}{2}$
$\frac{1}{5}$	$\frac{4}{7}$
$\frac{4}{5}$	$\frac{1}{4}$
$\frac{3}{4}$	$\frac{2}{5}$
$\frac{2}{3}$	$\frac{5}{6}$
$\frac{4}{9}$	$\frac{7}{8}$
$\frac{5}{8}$	$\frac{3}{8}$

What strategy did you use to complete each sentence?

Answers may vary. Possible answer: I worked backward to find out what the product in the parentheses had to be. Then I used guess, test, and revise to find two fractions that had that product.

Use with Grade 5, Chapter 7, Lesson 2, pages 302–305. (216)

Daily Homework

7-2 Multiply a Fraction by a Fraction

Multiply. Write each answer in simplest form.

1. $\frac{2}{5} \times \frac{1}{4} =$ $\frac{1}{10}$
2. $\frac{3}{5} \times \frac{2}{9} =$ $\frac{2}{15}$
3. $\frac{3}{4} \times \frac{5}{7} =$ $\frac{15}{28}$
4. $\frac{5}{6} \times \frac{3}{10} =$ $\frac{1}{4}$
5. $\frac{2}{3} \times \frac{4}{5} =$ $\frac{8}{15}$
6. $\frac{3}{8} \times \frac{4}{5} =$ $\frac{3}{10}$
7. $\frac{1}{2} \times \frac{3}{5} =$ $\frac{3}{10}$
8. $\frac{3}{16} \times \frac{4}{5} =$ $\frac{3}{20}$
9. $\frac{3}{8} \times \frac{5}{6} =$ $\frac{5}{16}$
10. $\frac{1}{3} \times \frac{1}{6} =$ $\frac{1}{18}$
11. $\frac{2}{3} \times \frac{3}{5} =$ $\frac{2}{5}$
12. $\frac{3}{8} \times \frac{1}{6} =$ $\frac{1}{16}$
13. $\frac{7}{12} \times \frac{3}{5} =$ $\frac{7}{20}$
14. $\frac{3}{8} \times \frac{4}{7} =$ $\frac{3}{14}$
15. $\frac{1}{4} \times \frac{1}{5} =$ $\frac{1}{20}$
16. $\frac{2}{5} \times \frac{3}{8} =$ $\frac{3}{20}$
17. $\frac{3}{4} \times \frac{5}{12} =$ $\frac{5}{16}$
18. $\frac{5}{12} \times \frac{3}{10} =$ $\frac{1}{8}$
19. $\frac{5}{12} \times \frac{3}{5} =$ $\frac{1}{4}$
20. $\frac{5}{8} \times \frac{3}{10} =$ $\frac{3}{16}$
21. $\frac{2}{5} \times \frac{5}{6} =$ $\frac{1}{3}$

Problem Solving

22. One-half of the animals at the Middletown Zoo are mammals. One-sixth of the mammals belong to the cat family. What fraction of the animals at the zoo belong to the cat family? $\frac{1}{12}$

23. Ryan spends $\frac{1}{2}$ of his homework time working on the computer.
He spends $\frac{1}{4}$ of his computer time connected to the Internet.
What fraction of his homework time does he spend connected to the Internet? $\frac{1}{8}$

Spiral Review

Compare. Write <, >, or =.

24. 0.25 > $\frac{1}{5}$
25. $\frac{2}{3}$ > $\frac{3}{5}$
26. 0.6 < $\frac{2}{3}$
27. 0.75 = $\frac{3}{4}$

66 Grade 5, Chapter 7, Lesson 2, Cluster A

Practice

Problem Solving: Reading for Math
Solve Multi-Step Problems

7-3 PRACTICE — Reading Skill

Solve. Use the diagrams below to solve problems 1–5. Write the inference that you made.

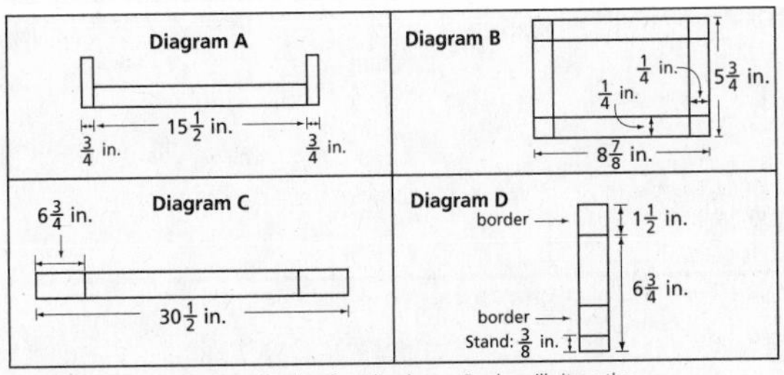

1. Diagram A shows a view of a plan for a bookcase. Books will sit on the interior of the bookcase. What is the length of the bottom of the bookcase?
   17 in.; Each side piece is the same length.
2. Diagram B shows a plan for a rectangular frame. What is the greatest width a picture can have to fit inside the frame?
   $5\frac{1}{4}$ in.; Each corner square is $\frac{1}{4}$ in. by $\frac{1}{4}$ in.
3. Diagram B shows a plan for a rectangular frame. What is the greatest length a picture can have to fit inside the frame?
   $8\frac{3}{8}$ in.; Each corner square is $\frac{1}{4}$ in. by $\frac{1}{4}$ in.
4. Diagram C shows a plan for the design of a folding leaf table. The sections at each end show the leaves that fold down. How long is the table when the leaves are folded down?
   17 in.; Each leaf is the same length.
5. Diagram D shows the plan for a countertop spice rack that sits on a stand. How tall is the spice rack without the stand?
   $7\frac{7}{8}$ in.; The borders are the same height.

Use with Grade 5, Chapter 7, Lesson 3, pages 306–307. (217)

Practice

Problem Solving: Reading for Math
Solve Multistep Problems

7-3 PRACTICE — Math Skills Test Prep

Choose the correct answer.

Kyoko has a piece of fabric that is $45\frac{3}{8}$ inches long. Since she uses equal amounts of fabric to make 3 banners, each banner uses $15\frac{1}{8}$ inches of fabric.

1. Which of the following statements is true?
   - A Kyoko uses $15\frac{1}{8}$ inches of fabric.
   - B Each banner uses $45\frac{3}{8}$ inches of fabric.
   - C Kyoko made 15 banners.
   - (D) Each banner uses $15\frac{1}{8}$ inches of fabric.
2. To solve a multistep problem, you
   - F should always add first.
   - (G) perform a series of actions.
   - H make a good guess at the solution.
   - J use only one operation.

Eduardo has $35\frac{7}{8}$ inches of wood. He cuts off two sections of wood that are each $5\frac{3}{8}$ inches long.

3. Which of the following statements is true?
   - A The piece of wood is $46\frac{5}{8}$ inches long before it is cut.
   - (B) The piece of wood is $25\frac{1}{8}$ inches long after it is cut.
   - C Eduardo cuts the wood into 2 pieces.
   - D After the wood is cut, each piece is $5\frac{3}{8}$ inches long.
4. When you solve a multistep problem, you
   - F never use subtraction.
   - G estimate each step in the problem.
   - (H) use more than one operation to solve the problem.
   - J decide on a single action to solve the problem.

Carrie has $40\frac{5}{8}$ inches of ribbon. She cuts the ribbon into 5 equal lengths of $8\frac{1}{8}$ inches each.

5. Which of the following statements is NOT true?
   - A Each piece of ribbon is $8\frac{1}{8}$ inches long.
   - B There are 5 pieces of ribbon.
   - (C) Before she cuts the ribbon, Carrie has $8\frac{1}{8}$ inches of ribbon.
   - D The combined length of 5 pieces of ribbon is $40\frac{5}{8}$ inches.
6. When you make an inference to solve a problem, you
   - F guess the solution.
   - G are estimating the answer.
   - H do not use information given in the problem.
   - (J) draw a conclusion from information in the problem.

Use with Grade 5, Chapter 7, Lesson 3, pages 306–307. (218)

Practice

Problem Solving: Reading for Math
Solve Multistep Problems

7-3 PRACTICE — Math Skills Test Prep

Choose the correct answer.

Martin has a piece of cord that is $35\frac{7}{8}$ inches long. He cuts $3\frac{3}{8}$ inches off each end of the cord.

7. Which of the following statements is true?
   - A The piece of cord is $32\frac{1}{2}$ inches long after it is cut.
   - B The piece of cord is $39\frac{1}{4}$ inches long after it is cut.
   - (C) Martin cuts $6\frac{3}{4}$ inches of cord off the original length of cord.
   - D Martin cuts the cord into 3 equal pieces.
8. When you solve a multistep problem, you
   - F always make an inference.
   - G always use a diagram.
   - H make a table to organize the data.
   - (J) perform a series of actions.

Solve.

9. Jeff has a piece of wood that is $15\frac{7}{8}$ inches long. He cuts off two sections of wood that are each $6\frac{1}{4}$ inches long. How much wood is left after the cuts?
   $3\frac{3}{8}$ in.
10. Sun has a scarf that is $20\frac{3}{4}$ inches long. She adds fringe that is $3\frac{1}{2}$ inches long to each end of the scarf. What is the total length of the scarf?
    $27\frac{3}{4}$ in.
11. Kevin is assembling a bookshelf with two shelves. Each shelf requires 6 screws at each end to attach to the side boards. How many screws does Kevin need?
    24 screws
12. Mr. Nelson has a $56\frac{3}{8}$-inch tube. He shortens the tube by cutting $4\frac{1}{8}$ inches off each end. How long is the tube after it is shortened?
    $48\frac{1}{8}$ in.
13. Spring can reupholster a pillow with 8 ounces of filling. She has 48 ounces of filling and 8 pillows. How many pillows will Spring not be able to upholster?
    2 pillows
14. A pane of glass is $18\frac{1}{2}$ inches long. The frame along the edge of the glass is $\frac{3}{8}$-inch wide. How long should the window well be for the window and frame to fit?
    $19\frac{1}{4}$ in.

Use with Grade 5, Chapter 7, Lesson 3, pages 306–307. (219)

Daily Homework

7-3 Problem Solving: Reading for Math
Solve Multistep Problems

Solve. Write the inference that you made.

1. What length of molding is needed to make a picture frame that is $4\frac{1}{2}$ in. tall and $8\frac{1}{2}$ in. wide?
   26 in.; the frame is a rectangle with 2 pairs of equal sides.
2. Amanda can walk to the park in $\frac{3}{4}$ of an hour. How long will it take her to walk to the park and back?
   $1\frac{1}{2}$ hours; the trip each way takes the same time.
3. Carrie takes $1\frac{3}{4}$ hours to sew a uniform for a toy soldier. How long will it take her to sew 4 uniforms?
   7 hours; all the uniforms are identical and so take the same time to sew.

Solve.

4. A recipe for a single peach pie calls for $2\frac{3}{4}$ pounds of peaches. How many pounds of peaches are needed to make 5 pies? $13\frac{3}{4}$ pounds
5. Freida uses $2\frac{1}{2}$ yards of cloth to make 2 tablecloths. How many yards of cloth will she need to make 6 tablecloths? $7\frac{1}{2}$ yards
6. Art's pancake recipe calls for $1\frac{3}{4}$ cups of flour to make 3 servings. How much flour will Art need to serve 9 people? $5\frac{1}{4}$ cups

Spiral Review

7. 1.3×2.73 = 3.549
8. $45 \div 0.05$ = 900
9. $3 - 1.634$ = 1.366
10. $100.6 \div 0.02$ = 5,030

Grade 5, Chapter 7, Lesson 3, Cluster A 67

Chapter 7 ~ Lesson 4

Practice

Multiply Mixed Numbers

P 7-4 PRACTICE

Multiply. Write each answer in simplest form.

1. $\frac{3}{4} \times 15 =$ $11\frac{1}{4}$
2. $13 \times \frac{1}{3} =$ $4\frac{1}{3}$
3. $\frac{5}{6} \times 20 =$ $16\frac{2}{3}$
4. $12 \times 1\frac{1}{5} =$ $14\frac{2}{5}$
5. $3\frac{1}{8} \times 18 =$ $56\frac{1}{4}$
6. $21 \times 1\frac{3}{4} =$ $36\frac{3}{4}$
7. $\frac{1}{3} \times 4\frac{1}{2} =$ $1\frac{1}{2}$
8. $7\frac{1}{5} \times \frac{5}{8} =$ $4\frac{1}{2}$
9. $\frac{2}{9} \times 2\frac{2}{3} =$ $\frac{16}{27}$
10. $2\frac{1}{2} \times 3\frac{2}{3} =$ $9\frac{1}{6}$
11. $1\frac{4}{9} \times 1\frac{1}{6} =$ $1\frac{37}{54}$
12. $3\frac{3}{4} \times 2\frac{2}{5} =$ 9
13. $10 \times 5\frac{1}{2} =$ 55
14. $\frac{1}{8} \times 12 =$ $1\frac{1}{2}$
15. $3\frac{1}{6} \times \frac{3}{4} =$ $2\frac{3}{8}$
16. $1\frac{1}{8} \times 1\frac{3}{10} =$ $1\frac{37}{80}$
17. $\frac{5}{12} \times 6\frac{3}{4} =$ $2\frac{13}{16}$
18. $10\frac{1}{2} \times 26 =$ 273
19. $14 \times \frac{3}{10} =$ $4\frac{1}{5}$
20. $6\frac{2}{5} \times 1\frac{1}{6} =$ $7\frac{7}{15}$
21. $\frac{8}{9} \times 3\frac{1}{2} =$ $3\frac{1}{9}$
22. $7\frac{3}{5} \times 2\frac{1}{2} =$ 19
23. $40 \times 7\frac{5}{8} =$ 305
24. $\frac{2}{5} \times 24 =$ $9\frac{3}{5}$
25. $4\frac{5}{8} \times 5\frac{1}{3} =$ $24\frac{2}{3}$
26. $21 \times \frac{7}{8} =$ $18\frac{3}{8}$
27. $\frac{5}{6} \times 4\frac{2}{5} =$ $3\frac{2}{3}$
28. $2\frac{3}{4} \times 32 =$ 88
29. $7\frac{1}{3} \times 3\frac{1}{4} =$ $23\frac{5}{6}$
30. $10\frac{1}{6} \times \frac{3}{8} =$ $3\frac{13}{16}$
31. $16 \times \frac{4}{5} =$ $12\frac{4}{5}$
32. $1\frac{1}{4} \times 8\frac{7}{8} =$ $11\frac{3}{32}$
33. $24 \times 6\frac{2}{3} =$ 160
34. $\frac{1}{3} \times 4\frac{2}{5} =$ $1\frac{7}{15}$
35. $3\frac{7}{8} \times 2\frac{1}{3} =$ $9\frac{1}{24}$
36. $66 \times 1\frac{4}{11} =$ 90

Problem Solving

37. The Parks Department uses $1\frac{3}{4}$ gallons of paint for each picnic shelter. At the end of the first day, the workers had painted $2\frac{1}{2}$ shelters. How much paint had they used that day?

    $4\frac{3}{8}$ gallons

38. While cleaning up around one picnic shelter, the workers filled $6\frac{1}{2}$ plastic bags with trash. If the average weight of a bag was $2\frac{1}{2}$ pounds, how many pounds of trash was collected?

    $16\frac{1}{4}$ pounds

Use with Grade 5, Chapter 7, Lesson 4, pages 310–313. (220)

Reteach

Multiply Mixed Numbers

R 7-4 RETEACH

When you multiply with mixed numbers, fractions, and whole numbers, write the numbers as fractions. Then you can multiply the fractions.

Multiply $2\frac{4}{5} \times 1\frac{2}{3}$.

Write the mixed numbers as fractions.

$2\frac{4}{5} \times 1\frac{2}{3}$
↓ ↓
$\frac{14}{5} \times \frac{5}{3}$
↓ ↓

Divide a numerator and a denominator by their GCF, if possible. Then multiply and simplify the product.

$\frac{14}{\cancel{5}_1} \times \frac{\cancel{5}^1}{3} = \frac{14 \times 1}{1 \times 3} = \frac{14}{3} = 4\frac{2}{3}$

Complete. Find each product. Write the product in simplest form.

1. $\frac{3}{5} \times 14$

   $\frac{3}{5} \times \frac{14}{1} = \frac{3 \times 14}{5 \times 1} = \frac{42}{5} =$ $8\frac{2}{5}$

2. $\frac{5}{6} \times 3\frac{3}{4}$

   $\frac{5}{\cancel{6}_2} \times \frac{\cancel{15}^5}{4} = \frac{5 \times 5}{2 \times 4} = \frac{25}{8} =$ $3\frac{1}{8}$

3. $22 \times 1\frac{3}{4}$

   $\frac{\cancel{22}^{11}}{1} \times \frac{7}{\cancel{4}_2} = \frac{11 \times 7}{1 \times 2} = \frac{77}{2} =$ $38\frac{1}{2}$

4. $3\frac{1}{3} \times 1\frac{5}{6}$

   $\frac{\cancel{10}^5}{3} \times \frac{11}{\cancel{6}_3} = \frac{5 \times 11}{3 \times 3} = \frac{55}{9} =$ $6\frac{1}{9}$

5. $\frac{1}{3} \times 2\frac{5}{8}$

   $\frac{1}{\cancel{3}_1} \times \frac{\cancel{21}^7}{8} = \frac{1 \times 7}{1 \times 8} = \frac{7}{8} =$ $\frac{7}{8}$

6. $1\frac{2}{3} \times 2\frac{1}{4}$

   $\frac{5}{\cancel{3}_1} \times \frac{\cancel{9}^3}{4} = \frac{5 \times 3}{1 \times 4} = \frac{15}{4} =$ $3\frac{3}{4}$

Use with Grade 5, Chapter 7, Lesson 4, pages 310–313. (221)

Enrich

Multiply Mixed Numbers

Number Trick

E 7-4 ENRICH

Try this number trick.

> Choose any whole number except 0.
>
> Multiply it by $2\frac{1}{2}$.
>
> Multiply the product by 4.
>
> Divide by your original number.
>
> Add 100.

1. Follow the steps of the number trick with a number between 0 and 10. Then follow the steps with a number between 10 and 100 and with a number between 100 and 1,000. What conclusion can you draw about your final answer?

   It will always be 110.

2. How could you change the number trick so that the final answer is always 25?

   Answers may vary.
   Possible answer: Instead of adding 100, add 15.

3. How could you change the number trick so that the final answer is always the original answer?

   Answers may vary. Possible answer:
   Instead of dividing by the original number, divide by 10 and do not add 100.

Why does this number trick work?

Answers may vary. Possible answer: Multiplying by $2\frac{1}{2}$ and then by 4 is the same as multiplying by 10. Then, dividing by the original number always results in 10. Finally, adding 100 results in 110.

Invent your own number trick. Tell why your number trick works.

Answers may vary.

Use with Grade 5, Chapter 7, Lesson 4, pages 310–313. (222)

Daily Homework

7·4 Multiply Mixed Numbers

Multiply. Write each answer in simplest form.

1. $6\frac{2}{5} \times 2\frac{3}{8} =$ $15\frac{1}{5}$
2. $4\frac{1}{4} \times 1\frac{1}{3} =$ $5\frac{2}{3}$
3. $4\frac{1}{6} \times 1\frac{4}{5} =$ $7\frac{1}{2}$
4. $8\frac{1}{4} \times 2\frac{2}{3} =$ 22
5. $\frac{2}{3} \times 12\frac{1}{2} =$ $8\frac{1}{3}$
6. $2\frac{1}{2} \times \frac{3}{4} =$ $1\frac{7}{8}$
7. $6\frac{2}{3} \times 2\frac{7}{10} =$ 18
8. $4\frac{1}{3} \times 5\frac{2}{5} =$ $23\frac{2}{5}$
9. $3\frac{1}{3} \times 10 =$ $33\frac{1}{3}$
10. $8\frac{1}{3} \times 4\frac{4}{5} =$ 40
11. $6\frac{1}{2} \times 5\frac{1}{3} =$ $34\frac{2}{3}$
12. $\frac{1}{15} \times 2\frac{1}{2} =$ $\frac{1}{6}$
13. $2\frac{7}{10} \times 3\frac{1}{3} =$ 9
14. $\frac{3}{5} \times 2\frac{1}{6} =$ $1\frac{3}{10}$
15. $7\frac{1}{3} \times 9\frac{1}{2} =$ $69\frac{2}{3}$
16. $12\frac{1}{2} \times 2\frac{1}{2} =$ $31\frac{1}{4}$
17. $4\frac{1}{5} \times 2\frac{1}{7} =$ 9
18. $8\frac{4}{5} \times 2\frac{3}{11} =$ 20
19. $4\frac{1}{2} \times 2\frac{2}{3} =$ 12
20. $7\frac{1}{3} \times 2\frac{5}{11} =$ 18
21. $4\frac{2}{5} \times 3\frac{3}{4} =$ $16\frac{1}{2}$

Problem Solving

22. Kate carves dolls from lengths of plywood. Each doll is $2\frac{3}{4}$ inches tall. How many inches of plywood does she need for 8 dolls? 22 inches

23. Carole measures her height in $4\frac{3}{4}$-inch clothespins. She is $12\frac{1}{2}$ clothespins tall. How many inches tall is she? $59\frac{3}{8}$ in.

Spiral Review

Label as prime or composite.

24. 37 prime
25. 27 composite
26. 57 composite
27. 67 prime

68 Grade 5, Chapter 7, Lesson 4, Cluster B

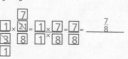

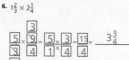

Chapter 7 ~ Lesson 5

Practice

Estimate Products

P 7-5 PRACTICE

Estimate. Estimates may vary. Possible answers are given.

1. $\frac{1}{2} \times 13$ — $\frac{1}{2} \times 12 = 6$
2. $7 \times 3\frac{1}{4}$ — $7 \times 3 = 21$
3. $\frac{4}{7} \times 8\frac{1}{9}$ — $\frac{1}{2} \times 8 = 4$
4. $\frac{5}{6} \times 23$ — $\frac{5}{6} \times 24 = 20$
5. $21\frac{8}{9} \times \frac{5}{12}$ — $22 \times \frac{1}{2} = 11$
6. $17 \times \frac{2}{5}$ — $15 \times \frac{2}{5} = 6$
7. $2\frac{1}{6} \times 9\frac{3}{4}$ — $2 \times 10 = 20$
8. $13\frac{7}{8} \times \frac{3}{8}$ — $14 \times \frac{1}{2} = 7$
9. $6 \times 8\frac{4}{5}$ — $6 \times 9 = 54$
10. $31 \times \frac{2}{3}$ — $30 \times \frac{2}{3} = 20$
11. $\frac{2}{5} \times 24\frac{1}{4}$ — $\frac{2}{5} \times 25 = 10$
12. $3\frac{5}{6} \times 4\frac{2}{3}$ — $4 \times 5 = 20$
13. $\frac{7}{8} \times 62$ — $\frac{7}{8} \times 64 = 56$
14. $1\frac{11}{12} \times 9\frac{1}{5}$ — $2 \times 9 = 18$
15. $34 \times \frac{1}{6}$ — $36 \times \frac{1}{6} = 6$
16. $5\frac{7}{9} \times 4$ — $6 \times 4 = 24$
17. $\frac{5}{12} \times 49$ — $\frac{5}{12} \times 48 = 20$
18. $23\frac{3}{8} \times 42\frac{7}{9}$ — $20 \times 40 = 800$

Estimate to compare. Write >, <, or =.

19. $47 \times \frac{3}{4}$ (>) $59\frac{5}{6} \times \frac{4}{9}$ — $48 \times \frac{3}{4} > 60 \times \frac{1}{2}$
20. $\frac{3}{8} \times 33$ (>) $\frac{5}{8} \times 10\frac{1}{4}$ — $\frac{3}{8} \times 32 > \frac{1}{2} \times 10$
21. $54\frac{1}{2} \times 18\frac{3}{5}$ (<) $37\frac{5}{6} \times 27\frac{1}{3}$ — $50 \times 20 < 40 \times 30$

Problem Solving

22. Teresa rode $6\frac{7}{10}$ miles on her bike in one hour. If she continues at this pace, about how far could she ride in 5 hours?
about 35 miles

23. Chan is riding his bike on a 48-mile cross-country course. He knows that $\frac{2}{5}$ of the course is uphill. About how many miles will Chan have to ride uphill?
about 20 miles

Use with Grade 5, Chapter 7, Lesson 5, pages 314–317. (223)

Reteach

Estimate Products

R 7-5 RETEACH

To estimate a fraction of a whole number or mixed number, you can round the whole number or mixed number to a multiple of the denominator.

Estimate $\frac{5}{6} \times 44$.

Round the whole number to the closest multiple of the denominator. 42 is close to 44.

Think: $\frac{5}{6} \times 42$
$42 \div 6 = 7$
$5 \times 7 = 35$
So, $\frac{5}{6} \times 44$ is about 35.

Estimate $\frac{3}{4} \times 19\frac{1}{2}$.

$19\frac{1}{2}$ is close to 20. (Round to a whole number.)

Think: $\frac{3}{4} \times 20$
$20 \div 4 = 5$
$3 \times 5 = 15$
So, $\frac{3}{4} \times 19\frac{1}{2}$ is about 15.

Estimate each product.

1. $\frac{1}{5} \times 27$
Denominator of fraction: 5
Multiples of denominator: 5, 10, 15, 20, 25, 30
Estimate: $\frac{1}{5} \times$ 25 = 5

2. $30 \times \frac{7}{8}$
Denominator of fraction: 8
Multiples of denominator: 8, 16, 24, 32
Estimate: 32 $\times \frac{7}{8} =$ 28

3. $\frac{2}{3} \times 17$ — $\frac{2}{3} \times 15 = 10$
4. $43 \times \frac{3}{5}$ — $45 \times \frac{3}{5} = 27$
5. $\frac{1}{6} \times 28$ — $\frac{1}{6} \times 30 = 5$
6. $\frac{3}{4} \times 37$ — $\frac{3}{4} \times 36 = 27$
7. $29 \times \frac{3}{8}$ — $32 \times \frac{3}{8} = 12$
8. $\frac{4}{5} \times 34$ — $\frac{4}{5} \times 35 = 28$
9. $\frac{5}{6} \times 43\frac{1}{4}$ — $\frac{5}{6} \times 42 = 35$
10. $\frac{9}{10} \times 28\frac{2}{3}$ — $\frac{9}{10} \times 30 = 27$
11. $39\frac{9}{10} \times \frac{7}{8}$ — $40 \times \frac{7}{8} = 35$

Use with Grade 5, Chapter 7, Lesson 5, pages 314–317. (224)

Enrich

Estimate Products
Product Range Game

E 7-5 ENRICH

- Play with a partner and take turns.
- When it is your turn, choose a factor from the circle and a factor from the square. Cross out the factors in the circle and square so they cannot be used again.
- Estimate their product, and record the pair of factors in the appropriate column. Put your initials beside the pair of factors.

Only five pairs of factors may be recorded in each column. If there is not a line remaining in a column for you to write on, your turn is over.

Continue play until neither player is able to record a pair of factors in a column. The player who recorded the greater number of factor pairs is the winner.

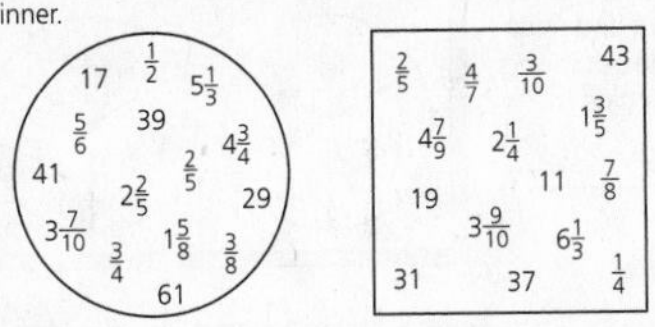

Possible recordings using all factors are shown.

Products: 1–10	Products: 11–20	Products: 21–30
$\frac{2}{5}$ and 11	$\frac{3}{8}$ and 31	61 and $\frac{2}{5}$
$\frac{1}{4}$ and 39	$\frac{5}{6}$ and 19	29 and $\frac{7}{8}$
$\frac{3}{10}$ and 17	$1\frac{5}{8}$ and $6\frac{1}{3}$	41 and $\frac{4}{7}$
$5\frac{1}{3}$ and $1\frac{3}{5}$	$3\frac{7}{10}$ and $4\frac{7}{9}$	$\frac{3}{4}$ and 37
$2\frac{2}{5}$ and $2\frac{1}{4}$	$4\frac{3}{4}$ and $3\frac{9}{10}$	$\frac{1}{2}$ and 43

Describe a strategy you could use in this game. Strategies may vary. Possible strategy is given.

To find factor pairs for the last column, I chose greater numbers and tried pairing them with different fractions to find estimated products of 21 through 30.

Use with Grade 5, Chapter 7, Lesson 5, pages 314–317. (225)

Daily Homework

7-5 Estimate Products

Estimate. Answers may vary. Possible estimates are given.

1. $53 \times \frac{1}{5}$ 10
2. $45\frac{1}{5} \times \frac{3}{4}$ 33
3. $5\frac{3}{5} \times 2\frac{1}{12}$ 12
4. $28\frac{1}{3} \times \frac{2}{3}$ 18
5. $4\frac{4}{5} \times 5\frac{1}{4}$ 25
6. $9\frac{3}{5} \times 2\frac{1}{8}$ 20
7. $8\frac{5}{8} \times \frac{2}{3}$ 6
8. $3\frac{2}{7} \times 2\frac{3}{10}$ 6
9. $31\frac{1}{8} \times \frac{2}{3}$ 20
10. $1\frac{2}{3} \times 4\frac{3}{5}$ 10
11. $7\frac{1}{3} \times 8\frac{1}{6}$ 56
12. $16\frac{5}{7} \times 4$ 68
13. $\frac{2}{3} \times 20\frac{4}{5}$ 14
14. $\frac{1}{5} \times 25\frac{1}{12}$ 5
15. $6\frac{1}{3} \times 2\frac{1}{3}$ 12

Estimate to compare. Write >, <, or =.

16. $4\frac{1}{4} \times 3\frac{1}{8}$ = $3\frac{8}{9} \times 2\frac{5}{6}$
17. $9\frac{2}{7} \times 1\frac{15}{16}$ < $3\frac{2}{9} \times 6\frac{9}{10}$
18. $2\frac{4}{5} \times 5\frac{1}{12}$ < $4\frac{1}{9} \times 3\frac{7}{8}$
19. $8\frac{1}{5} \times 3\frac{7}{8}$ > $4\frac{11}{12} \times 5\frac{2}{3}$

Problem Solving

Estimate the solutions.

20. Kareem delivers newspapers every day. It takes him about $1\frac{3}{4}$ hours per day to do the job. About how many hours a week does he spend delivering papers? about 14 hours

21. Freida makes pots for plants and sells them in sets of three. If each pot weighs $2\frac{1}{8}$ pounds, about how much does a three-pot set weigh? about 6 lb

Spiral Review

Round to the underlined digit.

22. 3.2̲45 3.2
23. 8.67̲6 8.68
24. 8̲.732 9

Grade 5, Chapter 7, Lesson 5, Cluster B 69

Chapter 7 ~ Lesson 6

Practice

Problem Solving: Strategy
Make an Organized List

P 7-6 PRACTICE

Make an organized list to solve.

1. Marsha plays this spinner game. She spins both spinners and finds the product of the fractions. What products can Marsha make?

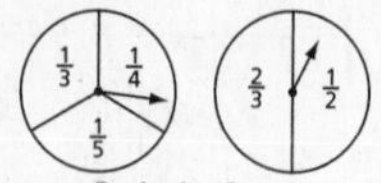

$\frac{2}{9}, \frac{1}{6}, \frac{1}{8}, \frac{2}{15}, \frac{1}{10}$

2. David plays this spinner game. He spins both spinners and finds the product of the fractions and the mixed numbers. What products can David make?

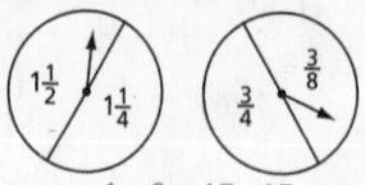

$1\frac{1}{8}, \frac{9}{16}, \frac{15}{16}, \frac{15}{32}$

3. Allie has square beads that are red, blue, and green. She has round beads that are yellow and white. If she chooses one color from each shape of beads, how many combinations of colors can she have?

6 combinations

4. **Health** Ms. Dawson eats a fruit and a vegetable for lunch each day. She selects an apple, a banana, an orange, or a pear for her fruit. She chooses carrot sticks, celery sticks, or green-pepper slices for her vegetable. How many combinations of 1 fruit and 1 vegetable can she make?

12 combinations

Mixed Strategy Review

Solve. Use any strategy.

5. **Time** Mario is making a new recipe for dinner. It takes $1\frac{1}{2}$ hours to prepare and $1\frac{1}{4}$ hours to bake. If he wants to serve dinner at 6:00 P.M., what time should Mario begin preparing the new recipe?

3:15 P.M.

Strategy: Work Backward

6. Greta orders stickers that come with 12 sheets per package. Each sheet has 10 rows of stickers and each row has 8 stickers. How many stickers are in each package?

960 stickers

Strategy: Write an Equation

7. Jamal, Katie, and Marion are standing in a line to buy tickets. In how many different ways can they stand?

6 ways

Strategy: Make an Organized List

8. **Create a problem** for which you could make an organized list to solve. Share it with others.

Check students' problems.

Reteach

Problem Solving: Strategy
Make an Organized List

R 7-6 RETEACH

Page 319, Problem 2

Otto plays this spinner game. He spins both spinners and finds the product of the fractions. What products can Otto make?

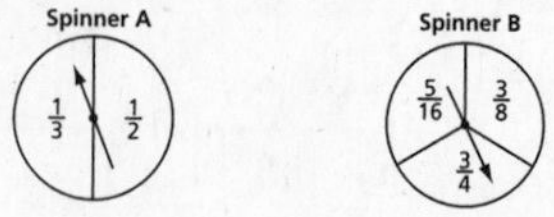

Step 1 Read

Be sure you understand the problem.
Read carefully.

What do you know?

- Spinner A is marked $\frac{1}{3}$ and $\frac{1}{2}$ and Spinner B is marked $\frac{5}{16}, \frac{3}{8}$, and $\frac{3}{4}$

What do you need to find?

- What products Otto can make.

Step 2 Plan

- Do an Experiment
- Guess and Check
- Work Backward
- Make a Graph
- Make a Table
- Write an Equation
- Make an Organized List
- Draw a Diagram
- Solve a Simpler Problem
- Logical Reasoning

Make a plan.
Choose a strategy.

You can make an organized list to solve the problem.

Remember: A product is the answer of a multiplication problem.

Reteach

Problem Solving: Strategy
Make an Organized List

R 7-6 RETEACH

Step 3 Solve

Carry out your plan.
Make a list of all the possible spinner products.
Then find each product.

Spinner A		Spinner B		Product
$\frac{1}{3}$	×	$\frac{5}{16}$	=	$\frac{5}{48}$
$\frac{1}{3}$	×	$\frac{3}{8}$	=	$\frac{1}{8}$
$\frac{1}{3}$	×	$\frac{3}{4}$	=	$\frac{1}{4}$
$\frac{1}{2}$	×	$\frac{5}{16}$	=	$\frac{5}{32}$
$\frac{1}{2}$	×	$\frac{3}{8}$	=	$\frac{3}{16}$
$\frac{1}{2}$	×	$\frac{3}{4}$	=	$\frac{3}{8}$

What products can Otto make? $\frac{5}{48}, \frac{1}{8}, \frac{1}{4}, \frac{5}{32}, \frac{3}{16}, \frac{3}{8}$

Step 4 Look Back

Is the solution reasonable?
Reread the problem.

Have you answered the question? Yes

How can you check your answer? Answers may vary. Possible answer: Check each of the products in the list to make sure each one has a factor from Spinner A and a factor from Spinner B.

Practice

1. A spinner is divided into 3 equal sections that are white, yellow, and green. Another spinner is divided into 3 equal sections that are blue, purple, and red. How many different combinations of colors are possible if you spin each spinner once?

9 combinations

2. Liz has 4 different rings and 3 different bracelets. If she wears one ring and one bracelet, how many different combinations can she have?

12 combinations

Daily Homework

7-6 Problem Solving: Strategy
Make an Organized List

Make an organized list to solve.

1. Kurt and Matthew play darts using the dartboard shown. The numbers indicate the points scored for hitting each area on the board. If Kurt and Matthew each throw one dart and both hit some part of the board, what are their possible combined scores?

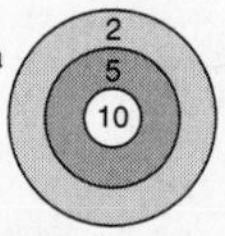

4, 7, 10, 12, 15, 20

2. Francine plays this spinner game. She spins both spinners and finds the products of the mixed numbers. What products can Francine make?

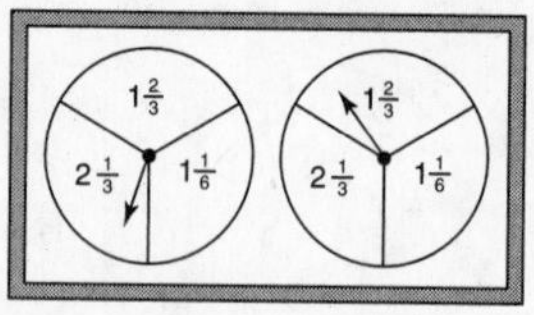

$2\frac{7}{9}, 1\frac{13}{36}, 5\frac{4}{9}, 1\frac{17}{18}, 3\frac{8}{9}, 2\frac{13}{18}$

Mixed Strategy Review

3. Six students stand in line for lunch. Hank is first in line and Gwen is fifth. Keisha is not standing next to Hank or next to Gwen. Latrelle is standing just ahead of Keisha. Janice is not fourth in line. Where in the line is Fred?

Fred is fourth in line.

4. Maria has collected 16 oak leaves and 18 maple leaves. Chuck has collected $\frac{1}{4}$ as many oak leaves and $1\frac{1}{3}$ as many maple leaves. How many leaves has Chuck collected? 28 leaves

Spiral Review

5. $\frac{3}{5} - \frac{1}{10} = \frac{1}{2}$

6. $4 - 2\frac{1}{2} = 1\frac{1}{2}$

7. $5\frac{3}{4} - 2\frac{1}{6} = 3\frac{7}{12}$

8. $7\frac{1}{2} - 3\frac{2}{3} = 3\frac{5}{6}$

Practice

Properties of Multiplication

P 7-7 PRACTICE

Identify each property of multiplication.

1. $\frac{2}{3} \times (\frac{3}{8} \times 1\frac{1}{2}) = (\frac{2}{3} \times \frac{3}{8}) \times 1\frac{1}{2}$ Associative Property
2. $7 \times 2\frac{2}{9} = 2\frac{2}{9} \times 7$ Commutative Property
3. $1 \times 2\frac{3}{4} = 2\frac{3}{4}$ Identity Property
4. $4 \times (3 + \frac{1}{4}) = (4 \times 3) + (4 \times \frac{1}{4})$ Distributive Property
5. $3 \times 5 = 5 \times 3$ Commutative Property
6. $4\frac{1}{6} \times 0 = 0$ Zero Property
7. $(3 + \frac{2}{3}) \times 9 = (3 \times 9) + (\frac{2}{3} \times 9)$ Distributive Property
8. $\frac{5}{6} \times \frac{3}{8} \times 1 = \frac{5}{6} \times \frac{3}{8}$ Identity Property

Use the Associative Property to solve. Show your work.

9. $8 \times (\frac{3}{4} \times \frac{1}{6})$ $(8 \times \frac{3}{4}) \times \frac{1}{6} = 6 \times \frac{1}{6} = 1$
10. $(2\frac{1}{3} \times 1\frac{4}{5}) \times 5$ $2\frac{1}{3} \times (1\frac{4}{5} \times 5) = 2\frac{1}{3} \times 9 = 21$

Use the Distributive Property to solve.

11. $12 \times 4\frac{3}{4}$ $(12 \times 4) + (12 \times \frac{3}{4}) = 48 + 9 = 57$
12. $7\frac{3}{5} \times 10$ $(7 \times 10) + (\frac{3}{5} \times 10) = 70 + 6 = 76$
13. $6\frac{2}{3} \times 9$ $(6 \times 9) + (\frac{2}{3} \times 9) = 54 + 6 = 60$
14. $16 \times 3\frac{5}{8}$ $(16 \times 3) + (16 \times \frac{5}{8}) = 48 + 10 = 58$

Problem Solving

15. Mrs. Miller works $9\frac{1}{2}$ hours each day, 4 days a week. For how many hours does she work each week? Explain.
38 hours; $9\frac{1}{2} \times 4 = (9 \times 4) + (\frac{1}{2} \times 4) = 36 + 2 = 38$

16. Each week Mr. Ortez makes 10 trips of $8\frac{1}{4}$ miles each between his house and work. Half of each trip is on the expressway. How many miles does Mr. Ortez drive on the expressway between home and work each week? Explain.
$41\frac{1}{4}$ miles; $(10 \times 8\frac{1}{4}) \times \frac{1}{2} = (8\frac{1}{4} \times 10) \times \frac{1}{2} = 8\frac{1}{4} \times (10 \times \frac{1}{2}) = 8\frac{1}{4} \times 5 = (8 \times 5) + (\frac{1}{4} \times 5) = 40 + 1\frac{1}{4} = 41\frac{1}{4}$

Use with Grade 5, Chapter 7, Lesson 7, pages 320–321. (229)

Reteach

Properties of Multiplication

R 7-7 RETEACH

Sometimes using the Associative Property makes it easier to multiply because you can use mental math. Remember, the grouping of the factors does not change the product.

Multiply $8 \times (\frac{1}{2} \times \frac{5}{6})$. Regroup.→ $8 \times (\frac{1}{2} \times \frac{5}{6}) = (8 \times \frac{1}{2}) \times \frac{5}{6}$
Multiply.→ $= 4 \times \frac{5}{6}$
$= \frac{20}{6}$
Simplify the product.→ $= 3\frac{2}{6} = 3\frac{1}{3}$

You can also use the Distributive Property and mental math to make some multiplication problems easier. Remember, to multiply a sum by a number, you can multiply each addend by the number and then add the products.

Multiply $6 \times 5\frac{2}{3}$. Write the mixed number as a sum.→ $6 \times 5\frac{2}{3} = 6 \times (5 + \frac{2}{3})$
Use the Distributive Property.→ $= (6 \times 5) + (6 \times \frac{2}{3})$
$= 30 + 4$
$= 34$

Use the Associative Property to solve. Show your work.

1. $(\frac{1}{6} \times \frac{3}{4}) \times 16$ $\frac{1}{6} \times (\frac{3}{4} \times 16) = \frac{1}{6} \times 12 = 2$
2. $10 \times (1\frac{2}{5} \times 1\frac{1}{3})$ $(10 \times 1\frac{2}{5}) \times 1\frac{1}{3} = 14 \times 1\frac{1}{3} = \frac{56}{3} = 18\frac{2}{3}$
3. $5 \times (\frac{3}{5} \times \frac{7}{8})$ $(5 \times \frac{3}{5}) \times \frac{7}{8} = 3 \times \frac{7}{8} = \frac{21}{8} = 2\frac{5}{8}$
4. $(1\frac{1}{4} \times 2\frac{1}{3} \times 9)$ $1\frac{1}{4} \times (2\frac{1}{3} \times 9) = 1\frac{1}{4} \times (\frac{7}{3} \times 9) = 1\frac{1}{4} \times 21 = \frac{105}{4} = 26\frac{1}{4}$

Use the Distributive Property to solve.

5. $12 \times 2\frac{1}{4}$
$= (12 \times$ 2 $) + (12 \times$ $\frac{1}{4}$ $)$
$=$ 24 $+$ 3
$=$ 27

6. $2\frac{5}{6} \times 18$
$= ($ 2 $\times$ 18 $) + ($ $\frac{5}{6}$ $\times$ 18 $)$
$=$ 36 $+$ 15
$=$ 51

7. $9 \times 3\frac{1}{3}$ $(9 \times 3) + (9 \times \frac{1}{3}) = 27 + 3 = 30$
8. $2\frac{4}{5} \times 20$ $(2 \times 20) + (\frac{4}{5} \times 20) = 40 + 16 = 56$

Use with Grade 5, Chapter 7, Lesson 7, pages 320–321. (230)

Enrich

Properties of Multiplication
10-Digit Properties

E 7-7 ENRICH

Use each of the digits 0 through 9 once in each exercise set to make true math sentences.

Set A

1. $3\frac{1}{2} \times 4\frac{2}{3} = 4\frac{4}{[6]} \times 3\frac{1}{2}$
2. $0 \times 6\frac{[7]}{10} = 0$
3. $[1] \times 9\frac{1}{4} = 9\frac{1}{4}$
4. $[8] \times 1\frac{3}{8} = 11$
5. $9 \times (\frac{1}{[3]} \times \frac{2}{5}) = 1\frac{1}{5}$
6. $3\frac{4}{7} \times [0] = 0$
7. $[5]\frac{2}{3} \times 9 = 51$
8. $2\frac{7}{8} \times \frac{[9]}{12} = \frac{3}{4} \times 2\frac{7}{8}$
9. $(\frac{[2]}{9} \times 2\frac{1}{4}) \times 8 = 4$
10. $12 \times 2\frac{3}{[4]} = 33$

Set B

11. $4\frac{1}{3} \times 3\frac{3}{[4]} = 3\frac{3}{4} \times 4\frac{1}{3}$
12. $0 \times 7\frac{[8]}{9} = 0$
13. $6\frac{1}{2} \times [1] = 6\frac{1}{2}$
14. $9 \times 2\frac{[5]}{9} = 23$
15. $[7] \times (\frac{2}{5} \times \frac{3}{4}) = 2\frac{1}{10}$
16. $3\frac{5}{9} \times \frac{5}{10} = \frac{1}{[2]} \times 3\frac{5}{9}$
17. $6\frac{7}{9} \times [0] = 6\frac{7}{9}$
18. $54 \times \frac{2}{[9]} = 12$
19. $(\frac{[3]}{9} \times 2\frac{2}{3}) \times \frac{9}{8} = 1$
20. $8\frac{5}{6} \times 7\frac{3}{4} = 7\frac{3}{4} \times 8\frac{5}{[6]}$

How did you complete exercise 5?

Answers may vary. Possible answer: I used the Associative Property to write $(9 \times \frac{1}{\square}) \times \frac{2}{5} = 1\frac{1}{5}$. Then I worked backward. I thought—what number times $\frac{2}{5}$ equals $1\frac{1}{5}$, or $\frac{6}{5}$. That number is 3, so the product in the parentheses must be 3. Then I thought of what fractional part of 9, 3 is. 3 is $\frac{1}{3}$ of 9, so the missing number is 3.

Use with Grade 5, Chapter 7, Lesson 7, pages 320–321. (231)

Daily Homework

7-7 Properties of Multiplication

Identify each property of multiplication.

1. $4(3 + 5) = 4 \times 3 + 4 \times 5$ Distributive Property
2. $8\frac{1}{3} \times 4\frac{1}{2} = 4\frac{1}{2} \times 8\frac{1}{3}$ Commutative Property
3. $6\frac{2}{3} \times 1 = 6\frac{2}{3}$ Identity Property
4. $18\frac{2}{3} \times 0 = 0$ Zero Property
5. $7\frac{2}{3} \times \left(4\frac{1}{2} \times 6\right) = \left(7\frac{2}{3} \times 4\frac{1}{2}\right) \times 6$ Associative Property
6. $2\frac{2}{3} \times 4\frac{4}{5} = 4\frac{4}{5} \times 2\frac{2}{3}$ Commutative Property

Use a multiplication property to solve. Show your work.

7. $\left(3\frac{1}{2} \times 2\frac{2}{3}\right) \times 6 =$ $3\frac{1}{2} \times \left(2\frac{2}{3} \times 6\right) = 3\frac{1}{2} \times 16 = 56$
8. $7\frac{3}{4} \times 8 =$ $8 \times 7 + 8 \times \frac{3}{4} = 56 + 6 = 62$

Problem Solving

9. Gwen has a three-hour phone card. She uses $1\frac{1}{3}$ hours to call her sister and $\frac{3}{4}$ of an hour to call her aunt. How much time is left on her card?
$\frac{11}{12}$ of an hour, or 55 minutes

10. Ken has 10 pounds of plaster. He plans to make five figurines using $1\frac{3}{4}$ pounds of plaster for each one. How much plaster will Ken have left? $1\frac{1}{4}$ lb

Spiral Review

Order from least to greatest.

11. $3\frac{1}{3}, 3\frac{1}{2}, 3.4$ $3\frac{1}{3}, 3.4, 3\frac{1}{2}$
12. $7.2, 7\frac{1}{4}, 7\frac{1}{10}$ $7\frac{1}{10}, 7.2, 7\frac{1}{4}$

Grade 5, Chapter 7, Lesson 7, Cluster B 71

Chapter 7 ~ Lesson 8

Practice

Explore Dividing Fractions

P 7-8 PRACTICE

Write a division sentence for each model.

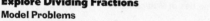

1. 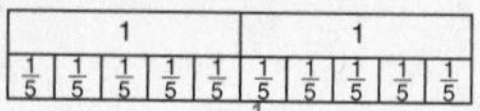
$2 \div \frac{1}{5} = 10$

2. 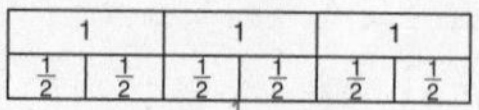
$3 \div \frac{1}{2} = 6$

3. 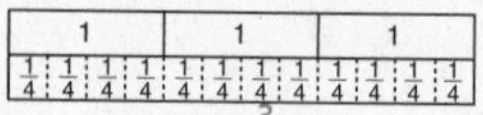
$3 \div \frac{3}{4} = 4$

4. 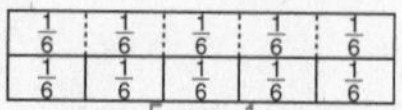
$\frac{5}{6} \div \frac{1}{6} = 5$

5. 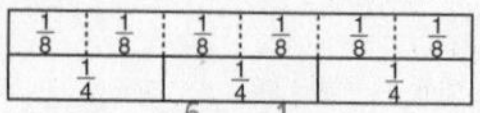
$\frac{6}{8} \div \frac{1}{4} = 3$

6. 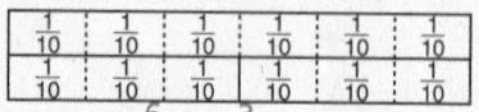
$\frac{6}{10} \div \frac{3}{10} = 2$

Divide. You may use fraction strips.

7. $2 \div \frac{1}{12} =$ 24
8. $5 \div \frac{1}{2} =$ 10
9. $8 \div \frac{1}{4} =$ 32
10. $3 \div \frac{3}{5} =$ 5
11. $4 \div \frac{2}{3} =$ 6
12. $9 \div \frac{3}{4} =$ 12
13. $\frac{5}{8} \div \frac{1}{8} =$ 5
14. $\frac{8}{9} \div \frac{2}{9} =$ 4
15. $\frac{7}{12} \div \frac{1}{12} =$ 7
16. $\frac{4}{6} \div \frac{1}{3} =$ 2
17. $\frac{9}{12} \div \frac{1}{4} =$ 3
18. $\frac{8}{10} \div \frac{1}{5} =$ 4
19. $\frac{6}{8} \div \frac{1}{4} =$ 3
20. $\frac{4}{5} \div \frac{4}{5} =$ 1
21. $\frac{4}{6} \div \frac{1}{3} =$ 2

Problem Solving

22. Lunch in a school cafeteria is served for 2 hours. Lunch periods are for $\frac{1}{3}$ hour. How many different lunch periods are there each day?
6 lunch periods

23. At Janelle's school, classes are held for 6 hours each day. An art class is $\frac{3}{4}$ hour long. How many classes can the art teacher schedule in one day?
8 classes

Use with Grade 5, Chapter 7, Lesson 8, pages 322–323. (232)

Reteach

Explore Dividing Fractions

R 7-8 RETEACH

You can draw a model to help you divide fractions.

Divide $2 \div \frac{1}{4}$.

Draw a model to show how many $\frac{1}{4}$s there are in 2.

First draw a row of 2 units. Then draw a row of $\frac{1}{4}$s as long as the row of units.

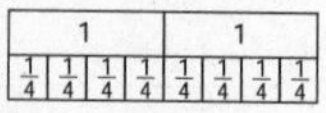

Count how many $\frac{1}{4}$s are drawn.

There are eight $\frac{1}{4}$s, so $2 \div \frac{1}{4} = 8$.

Divide $2 \div \frac{2}{3}$.

Draw a model to show how many $\frac{2}{3}$s there are in 2.

First draw a row of 2 units. Then draw a row of $\frac{2}{3}$s as long as the row of units.

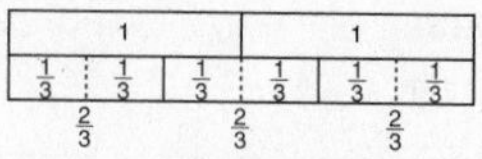

Count how many $\frac{2}{3}$s are drawn.

There are three $\frac{2}{3}$s, so $2 \div \frac{2}{3} = 3$.

Complete the model to find each quotient.

1. $4 \div \frac{1}{2} =$ 8

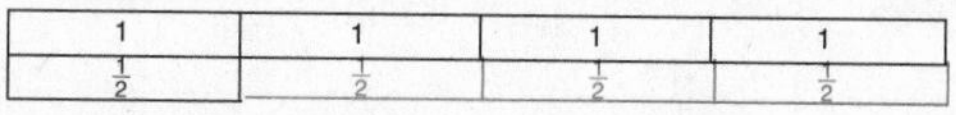

2. $3 \div \frac{3}{8} =$ 8

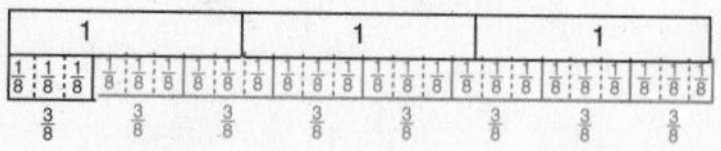

Find each quotient. You may draw a model.

3. $3 \div \frac{1}{8} =$ 24
4. $2 \div \frac{2}{5} =$ 5
5. $\frac{9}{10} \div \frac{3}{10} =$ 3

Use with Grade 5, Chapter 7, Lesson 8, pages 322–323. (233)

Enrich

Explore Dividing Fractions
Model Problems

E 7-8 ENRICH

Sometimes when you divide with fractions, the quotient is a fraction or a mixed number.

$1 \div \frac{3}{4} = 1\frac{1}{3}$

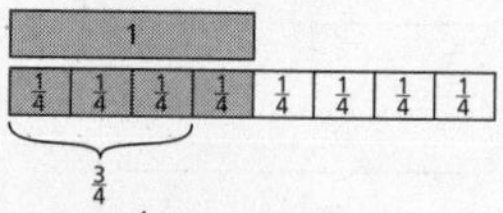

There are $1\frac{1}{3}$ three-fourths in 1.

$\frac{1}{8} \div \frac{3}{8} = \frac{1}{3}$

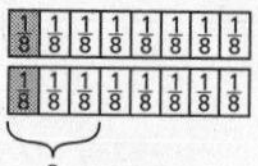

There is $\frac{1}{3}$ of $\frac{3}{8}$ in $\frac{1}{8}$.

Use the models to help you find each quotient.

1. $1 \div \frac{2}{3} =$ $1\frac{1}{2}$

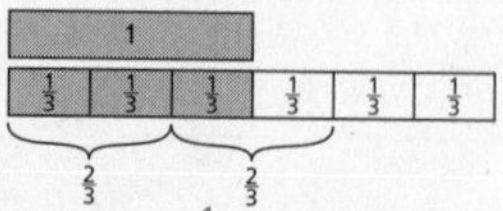

There are $1\frac{1}{2}$ two-thirds in 1.

2. $\frac{3}{4} \div \frac{1}{2} =$ $1\frac{1}{2}$

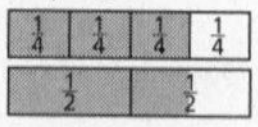

There are $1\frac{1}{2}$ one-halves in $\frac{3}{4}$.

3. $2 \div \frac{3}{8} =$ $5\frac{1}{3}$

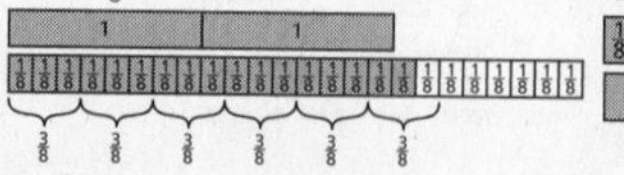

There are $5\frac{1}{3}$ three-eighths in 2.

4. $\frac{7}{8} \div \frac{1}{4} =$ $3\frac{1}{2}$

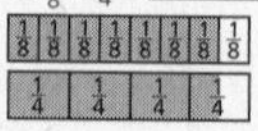

There are $3\frac{1}{2}$ one-fourths in $\frac{7}{8}$.

Divide.

5. $\frac{1}{4} \div \frac{1}{2} =$ $\frac{1}{2}$
6. $\frac{1}{4} \div \frac{5}{8} =$ $\frac{2}{5}$
7. $\frac{2}{3} \div \frac{5}{6} =$ $\frac{4}{5}$
8. $\frac{3}{8} \div \frac{1}{2} =$ $\frac{3}{4}$

Use with Grade 5, Chapter 7, Lesson 8, pages 322–323. (234)

Daily Homework

7·8 Explore Dividing Fractions

Divide.

1. $3 \div \frac{1}{6} =$ 18
2. $5 \div \frac{1}{4} =$ 20
3. $8 \div \frac{1}{3} =$ 24
4. $13 \div \frac{1}{5} =$ 65
5. $4 \div \frac{1}{9} =$ 36
6. $7 \div \frac{1}{7} =$ 49
7. $8 \div \frac{1}{8} =$ 64
8. $2 \div \frac{1}{2} =$ 4
9. $5 \div \frac{1}{3} =$ 15
10. $6 \div \frac{1}{5} =$ 30
11. $6 \div \frac{1}{4} =$ 24
12. $7 \div \frac{1}{8} =$ 56
13. $4 \div \frac{1}{6} =$ 24
14. $3 \div \frac{1}{4} =$ 12
15. $13 \div \frac{1}{3} =$ 39
16. $17 \div \frac{1}{10} =$ 170
17. $8 \div \frac{1}{12} =$ 96
18. $36 \div \frac{1}{10} =$ 360
19. $15 \div \frac{1}{3} =$ 45
20. $6 \div \frac{1}{8} =$ 48
21. $4 \div \frac{1}{12} =$ 48

Solve.

22. Each of Conan's chocolates weighs $\frac{1}{3}$ of an ounce. How many chocolates are there in a 6-ounce box? 18

23. Harry is cutting $\frac{1}{2}$-inch blocks from a 12-inch wooden board. How many blocks can he cut? 24

Spiral Review

Give the GCF.

24. 12, 20 4
25. 24, 30 6
26. 18, 42 6
27. 24, 36 12

72 Grade 5, Chapter 7, Lesson 8, Cluster B

Chapter 7 ~ Lesson 9

Practice

Divide Fractions

P 7-9 PRACTICE

Write the reciprocal of each number.

1. $\frac{2}{3}$ $\frac{3}{2}$
2. $\frac{3}{5}$ $\frac{5}{3}$
3. $\frac{1}{7}$ $\frac{7}{1}$
4. $\frac{5}{6}$ $\frac{6}{5}$
5. 3 $\frac{1}{3}$
6. $\frac{7}{8}$ $\frac{8}{7}$
7. $\frac{1}{4}$ $\frac{4}{1}$
8. $\frac{11}{12}$ $\frac{12}{11}$
9. $1\frac{3}{10}$ $\frac{10}{13}$
10. $3\frac{1}{2}$ $\frac{2}{7}$
11. $5\frac{4}{5}$ $\frac{5}{29}$
12. $2\frac{5}{9}$ $\frac{9}{23}$

Divide. Write each answer in simplest form.

13. $\frac{1}{3} \div \frac{1}{4} =$ $1\frac{1}{3}$
14. $\frac{1}{2} \div \frac{4}{5} =$ $\frac{5}{8}$
15. $\frac{2}{3} \div 8 =$ $\frac{1}{12}$
16. $\frac{7}{10} \div \frac{3}{4} =$ $\frac{14}{15}$
17. $\frac{5}{8} \div \frac{3}{4} =$ $\frac{5}{6}$
18. $\frac{1}{3} \div \frac{5}{6} =$ $\frac{2}{5}$
19. $\frac{5}{6} \div 5 =$ $\frac{1}{6}$
20. $\frac{3}{5} \div \frac{4}{5} =$ $\frac{3}{4}$
21. $\frac{3}{10} \div 9 =$ $\frac{1}{30}$
22. $\frac{2}{3} \div \frac{9}{10} =$ $\frac{20}{27}$
23. $\frac{4}{5} \div 8 =$ $\frac{1}{10}$
24. $\frac{1}{3} \div \frac{2}{3} =$ $\frac{1}{2}$
25. $\frac{3}{8} \div 6 =$ $\frac{1}{16}$
26. $\frac{3}{4} \div \frac{1}{8} =$ 6
27. $\frac{1}{5} \div \frac{2}{5} =$ $\frac{1}{2}$

Algebra & Functions Write × or ÷ to make each number sentence true.

28. $\frac{1}{3}$ (×) $\frac{3}{8} = \frac{1}{8}$
29. $\frac{5}{12}$ (÷) $\frac{5}{6} = \frac{1}{2}$
30. $\frac{1}{5}$ (÷) $3 = \frac{1}{15}$
31. $\frac{3}{10}$ (÷) $\frac{2}{5} = \frac{3}{4}$
32. $\frac{4}{5}$ (×) $6 = 4\frac{4}{5}$
33. $\frac{7}{8}$ (×) $\frac{2}{3} = \frac{7}{12}$

Problem Solving

34. It takes $\frac{7}{8}$ inch of wire to make a small paper clip. How many small paper clips can be made from a piece of wire that is 14 inches long?
16 small paper clips

35. Lewis uses $\frac{1}{2}$ of a container to hold large paper clips. Each large paper clip takes up $\frac{1}{16}$ of the container. How many large paper clips are in the container?
8 large paper clips

Use with Grade 5, Chapter 7, Lesson 9, pages 324–325. (235)

Reteach

Divide Fractions

R 7-9 RETEACH

Dividing by a fraction is the same as multiplying by its **reciprocal**.

Divide $\frac{7}{8} \div \frac{3}{4}$.

Step 1: Find the reciprocal of the divisor. The divisor is $\frac{3}{4}$. The reciprocal of $\frac{3}{4}$ is $\frac{4}{3}$.

Step 2: Multiply by the reciprocal of the divisor. $\frac{7}{8} \times \frac{4}{3} = \frac{7}{6}$

Step 3: Simplify. $\frac{7}{6} = 1\frac{1}{6}$

Divide $\frac{5}{8} \div 3$.

Step 1: Find the reciprocal of the divisor. The divisor is 3, or $\frac{3}{1}$. The reciprocal of $\frac{3}{1}$ is $\frac{1}{3}$.

Step 2: Multiply by the reciprocal of the divisor. $\frac{5}{8} \times \frac{1}{3} = \frac{5}{24}$

Divide. Write each quotient in simplest form.

1. $\frac{3}{4} \div \frac{7}{8}$
$\frac{3}{4} \times \frac{8}{7} = \frac{24}{28} = \frac{6}{7}$

2. $\frac{1}{2} \div \frac{3}{5}$
$\frac{1}{2} \times \frac{5}{3} = \frac{5}{6}$

3. $\frac{2}{3} \div 2$
$\frac{2}{3} \div \frac{2}{1}$
$\frac{2}{3} \times \frac{1}{2} = \frac{1}{3}$

4. $8 \div \frac{1}{3}$
$\frac{8}{1} \div \frac{1}{3}$
$\frac{8}{1} \times \frac{3}{1} = \frac{24}{1} =$ 24

5. $\frac{1}{3} \div \frac{5}{9}$
$\frac{1}{3} \times \frac{9}{5} = \frac{3}{5}$

6. $\frac{5}{8} \div \frac{1}{4}$
$\frac{5}{8} \times \frac{4}{1} = \frac{5}{2} =$ $2\frac{1}{2}$

Use with Grade 5, Chapter 7, Lesson 9, pages 324–325. (236)

Enrich

Divide Fractions

E 7-9 ENRICH

Math Book Riddle

Find each quotient to find out why the math book was so sad.

A. $\frac{5}{8} \div \frac{1}{4} =$ $2\frac{1}{2}$
B. $\frac{4}{9} \div \frac{1}{12} =$ $5\frac{1}{3}$
E. $\frac{2}{3} \div \frac{5}{6} =$ $\frac{4}{5}$
F. $\frac{3}{10} \div \frac{3}{4} =$ $\frac{2}{5}$
I. $\frac{4}{5} \div \frac{2}{5} =$ 2
L. $\frac{1}{4} \div \frac{7}{8} =$ $\frac{2}{7}$
M. $\frac{5}{9} \div 2 =$ $\frac{5}{18}$
O. $\frac{3}{4} \div 6 =$ $\frac{1}{8}$
P. $\frac{1}{8} \div \frac{2}{3} =$ $\frac{3}{16}$
R. $\frac{1}{4} \div 4 =$ $\frac{1}{16}$
S. $\frac{3}{8} \div \frac{3}{4} =$ $\frac{1}{2}$
T. $\frac{1}{5} \div 4 =$ $\frac{1}{20}$
U. $\frac{7}{12} \div 7 =$ $\frac{1}{12}$
W. $\frac{3}{4} \div \frac{1}{4} =$ 3

Write the letter of the exercise above the matching number.

I	T	W	A	S	F	U	L	L
2	$\frac{1}{20}$	3	$2\frac{1}{2}$	$\frac{1}{2}$	$\frac{2}{5}$	$\frac{1}{12}$	$\frac{2}{7}$	$\frac{2}{7}$

O	F	P	R	O	B	L	E	M	S
$\frac{1}{8}$	$\frac{2}{5}$	$\frac{3}{16}$	$\frac{1}{16}$	$\frac{1}{8}$	$5\frac{1}{3}$	$\frac{2}{7}$	$\frac{4}{5}$	$\frac{5}{18}$	$\frac{1}{2}$

Explain how you solved exercise P.
Find the reciprocal and multiply mentally. The answer is already in simplest form.

Explain how you solved exercise U.
Rewrite the whole number as a fraction, find the reciprocal, and multiply. Finally simplify the answer.

Use with Grade 5, Chapter 7, Lesson 9, pages 324–325. (237)

Daily Homework

7-9 Divide Fractions

Write the reciprocal of each number.

1. $\frac{2}{3}$ $\frac{3}{2}$
2. $\frac{5}{6}$ $\frac{6}{5}$
3. 6 $\frac{1}{6}$
4. $2\frac{3}{4}$ $\frac{4}{11}$

Divide. Write each answer in simplest form.

5. $4 \div \frac{2}{3} =$ 6
6. $\frac{1}{6} \div \frac{2}{3} =$ $\frac{1}{4}$
7. $\frac{3}{8} \div \frac{1}{4} =$ $1\frac{1}{2}$
8. $\frac{1}{2} \div \frac{1}{6} =$ 3
9. $\frac{7}{10} \div \frac{3}{5} =$ $1\frac{1}{6}$
10. $\frac{2}{5} \div \frac{3}{8} =$ $1\frac{1}{15}$
11. $\frac{7}{12} \div \frac{3}{4} =$ $\frac{7}{9}$
12. $\frac{8}{15} \div \frac{2}{5} =$ $1\frac{1}{3}$
13. $\frac{3}{5} \div \frac{2}{3} =$ $\frac{9}{10}$
14. $\frac{2}{3} \div \frac{4}{5} =$ $\frac{5}{6}$
15. $\frac{3}{5} \div \frac{3}{5} =$ 1
16. $\frac{1}{4} \div \frac{2}{7} =$ $\frac{7}{8}$

Problem Solving

17. Martina is meeting her friends at the mall. They will meet at a bench located on the mall's $\frac{3}{4}$-mile walker's route. The bench marks the $\frac{1}{3}$ point on the route. If Martina begins at the start of the route, how far must she walk to meet her friends? $\frac{1}{4}$ mile

18. A standard sheet of lined paper is $8\frac{1}{2}$ inches wide. How many $\frac{1}{2}$-inch columns can be drawn on the paper? 17

Spiral Review

Give the LCM.

19. 6, 8 24
20. 3, 6 6
21. 2, 5 10
22. 4, 6 12
23. 4, 3 12
24. 6, 9 18

Grade 5, Chapter 7, Lesson 9, Cluster B 73

Chapter 7 ~ Lesson 10

Practice

Divide Mixed Numbers

P 7-10 PRACTICE

Divide. Write each answer in simplest form.

1. $1\frac{5}{6} \div \frac{1}{5} =$ $9\frac{1}{6}$
2. $4 \div \frac{3}{4} =$ $5\frac{1}{3}$
3. $3\frac{1}{2} \div 9 =$ $\frac{7}{18}$
4. $2\frac{3}{4} \div \frac{1}{2} =$ $5\frac{1}{2}$
5. $5 \div 1\frac{1}{4} =$ 4
6. $2\frac{1}{4} \div \frac{7}{8} =$ $2\frac{4}{7}$
7. $7 \div \frac{3}{5} =$ $11\frac{2}{3}$
8. $\frac{5}{6} \div 1\frac{1}{5} =$ $\frac{25}{36}$
9. $\frac{1}{3} \div 5 =$ $\frac{1}{15}$
10. $3\frac{1}{2} \div 1\frac{1}{2} =$ $2\frac{1}{3}$
11. $3\frac{2}{5} \div \frac{3}{5} =$ $5\frac{2}{3}$
12. $9 \div 3\frac{3}{5} =$ $2\frac{1}{2}$
13. $\frac{4}{5} \div 3 =$ $\frac{4}{15}$
14. $1\frac{1}{2} \div \frac{3}{4} =$ 2
15. $5\frac{3}{4} \div 2\frac{1}{3} =$ $2\frac{13}{28}$
16. $\frac{1}{4} \div 2\frac{5}{8} =$ $\frac{2}{21}$
17. $4\frac{2}{5} \div 2 =$ $2\frac{1}{5}$
18. $4 \div \frac{5}{8} =$ $6\frac{2}{5}$
19. $8 \div 1\frac{5}{8} =$ $4\frac{12}{13}$
20. $3\frac{1}{3} \div \frac{2}{5} =$ $8\frac{1}{3}$
21. $3\frac{1}{2} \div 3\frac{1}{4} =$ $1\frac{1}{13}$
22. $2\frac{1}{8} \div \frac{3}{4} =$ $2\frac{5}{6}$
23. $4\frac{1}{8} \div 2\frac{1}{12} =$ $1\frac{49}{50}$
24. $6\frac{1}{5} \div 3\frac{7}{10} =$ $1\frac{25}{37}$

Solve.

25. $2\frac{1}{10} \div n = 3\frac{1}{2}$ $n =$ $\frac{3}{5}$
26. $3\frac{5}{8} \div n = 4\frac{5}{6}$ $n =$ $\frac{3}{4}$
27. $1 \div n = 4\frac{1}{2}$ $n =$ $\frac{2}{9}$
28. $6 \div n = 16$ $n =$ $\frac{3}{8}$
29. $\frac{7}{8} \div n = 1\frac{5}{16}$ $n =$ $\frac{2}{3}$
30. $3\frac{1}{10} \div n = 2\frac{9}{11}$ $n =$ $1\frac{1}{10}$

Problem Solving

31. Bettina has a 10-foot-long board. She plans to cut bookshelves $2\frac{1}{2}$ feet long from it. How many shelves will she be able to cut?
4 shelves

32. Joel has a $9\frac{1}{2}$-foot-long board. How many $3\frac{1}{4}$-foot shelves could he cut from it?
2 shelves

Use with Grade 5, Chapter 7, Lesson 10, pages 326–327. (238)

Reteach

Divide Mixed Numbers

R 7-10 RETEACH

Divide mixed numbers in the same way as you divide fractions.

Divide $3\frac{1}{2} \div 2$. $3\frac{1}{2} \div 2$
↓ ↓

Step 1: Write the numbers as fractions. $\frac{7}{2} \div \frac{2}{1}$
↓ ↓

Step 2: Multiply by the reciprocal of the divisor. $\frac{7}{2} \times \frac{1}{2} = \frac{7}{4}$

Step 3: Simplify. $\frac{7}{4} = 1\frac{3}{4}$

Divide. Write each quotient in simplest form.

1. $2\frac{3}{4} \div \frac{7}{8}$

$\frac{11}{4} \times \frac{8}{7} = \frac{88}{28} =$ $3\frac{1}{7}$

2. $6 \div \frac{4}{5}$

$\frac{6}{1} \div \frac{4}{5}$

$\frac{6}{1} \times \frac{5}{4} = \frac{30}{4} =$ $7\frac{1}{2}$

3. $\frac{2}{3} \div 4$

$\frac{2}{3} \div \frac{4}{1}$

$\frac{2}{3} \times \frac{1}{4} = \frac{2}{12} =$ $\frac{1}{6}$

4. $2\frac{1}{2} \div 3$

$\frac{5}{2} \div \frac{3}{1}$

$\frac{5}{2} \times \frac{1}{3} = \frac{5}{6} =$ $\frac{5}{6}$

5. $1\frac{2}{5} \div \frac{5}{6}$

$\frac{7}{5} \div \frac{5}{6}$

$\frac{7}{5} \times \frac{6}{5} = \frac{42}{25} =$ $1\frac{17}{25}$

6. $\frac{5}{8} \div 1\frac{1}{4}$

$\frac{5}{8} \div \frac{5}{4}$

$\frac{5}{8} \times \frac{4}{5} = \frac{20}{40} =$ $\frac{1}{2}$

Use with Grade 5, Chapter 7, Lesson 10, pages 326–327. (239)

Enrich

Divide Mixed Numbers

Fraction Riddle

E 7-10 ENRICH

Find each answer. Then solve the riddle below by writing the letter of the exercise above the matching number.

C. $2\frac{1}{4} \div 4$ $\frac{9}{16}$

E. $2\frac{2}{5} \div 1\frac{1}{2}$ $1\frac{3}{5}$

H. $3\frac{1}{2} \div \frac{5}{8}$ $5\frac{3}{5}$

I. $6 \div 1\frac{1}{5}$ 5

L. $3\frac{5}{9} \div 2$ $1\frac{7}{9}$

M. $4\frac{2}{3} \div \frac{2}{3}$ 7

N. $3\frac{1}{8} \div 1\frac{2}{3}$ $1\frac{7}{8}$

O. $3\frac{2}{3} \div \frac{2}{3}$ $5\frac{1}{2}$

S. $5\frac{3}{4} \div 2$ $2\frac{7}{8}$

T. $1\frac{3}{4} \div 2\frac{2}{3}$ $\frac{21}{32}$

W. $7 \div 2\frac{4}{5}$ $2\frac{1}{2}$

Y. $4\frac{1}{3} \div 1\frac{1}{12}$ 4

Why are fish so smart?

T	H	E	Y	S	W	I	M	I	N	S	C	H	O	O	L	S
$\frac{21}{32}$	$5\frac{3}{5}$	$1\frac{3}{5}$	4	$2\frac{7}{8}$	$2\frac{1}{2}$	5	7	5	$1\frac{7}{8}$	$2\frac{7}{8}$	$\frac{9}{16}$	$5\frac{3}{5}$	$5\frac{1}{2}$	$5\frac{1}{2}$	$1\frac{7}{9}$	$2\frac{7}{8}$

How did you solve exercise Y? Write each mixed number as an improper fraction.
Multiply $\frac{13}{3}$ by the reciprocal of $\frac{13}{12}$ and simplify the answer.

Use with Grade 5, Chapter 7, Lesson 10, pages 326–327. (240)

Daily Homework

7·10 Divide Mixed Numbers

Divide. Write each answer in simplest form.

1. $8\frac{1}{4} \div 3\frac{2}{3} =$ $2\frac{1}{4}$
2. $6\frac{2}{3} \div \frac{2}{3} =$ 10
3. $4\frac{1}{2} \div \frac{3}{4} =$ 6
4. $4\frac{3}{4} \div 2 =$ $2\frac{3}{8}$
5. $4\frac{2}{3} \div \frac{7}{12} =$ 8
6. $1\frac{3}{10} \div \frac{1}{2} =$ $2\frac{3}{5}$
7. $7\frac{3}{4} \div 3\frac{1}{2} =$ $2\frac{3}{14}$
8. $3\frac{1}{4} \div 1\frac{3}{10} =$ $2\frac{1}{2}$
9. $3\frac{1}{6} \div 6\frac{1}{3} =$ $\frac{1}{2}$
10. $3\frac{1}{2} \div \frac{14}{15} =$ $3\frac{3}{4}$
11. $9\frac{3}{5} \div 12 =$ $\frac{4}{5}$
12. $\frac{5}{12} \div 3\frac{1}{3} =$ $\frac{1}{8}$
13. $\frac{4}{5} \div 3\frac{1}{10}$ $\frac{8}{31}$
14. $6\frac{1}{3} \div 3 =$ $2\frac{1}{9}$
15. $4\frac{2}{3} \div \frac{1}{6} =$ 28
16. $5\frac{3}{4} \div \frac{7}{8} =$ $6\frac{4}{7}$
17. $1\frac{5}{12} \div \frac{1}{12} =$ 17
18. $10\frac{1}{2} \div 4\frac{2}{3} =$ $2\frac{1}{4}$

Solve.

19. $4\frac{1}{2} \div n = 9$ $\frac{1}{2}$
20. $5\frac{1}{4} \div n = \frac{3}{8}$ 14

Problem Solving

21. Acme clothespins are $3\frac{1}{2}$ inches long. How many wooden clothespins can be cut from a 21-inch piece of stock? 6

22. Gary sells cookies at his school's fund-raiser. Each package of cookies weighs $2\frac{3}{4}$ ounces. How many packages can he make from 22 ounces of cookies? 8

Spiral Review

Find the mean.

23. 4, 6, 3, 11 6
24. 8, 15, 12, 20, 25 16
25. 8, 6, 15, 20 $12\frac{1}{4}$
26. 18, 22, 28, 32, 49 $29\frac{4}{5}$

74 Grade 5, Chapter 7, Lesson 10, Cluster B

Chapter 7 ~ Lesson 11

Part A Worksheet

Part A 7-11 WORKSHEET Decision Making

Problem Solving: Application
Multiplying Fractions

Use the tables to determine how much Brandon will need to spend for each recipe.

Chicken Pasta Salad			
Ingredient	**Amount Needed**	**Cost per Item**	**Total Cost**
		Total cost to make chicken pasta salad:	

German Potato Salad			
Ingredient	**Amount Needed**	**Cost per Item**	**Total Cost**
		Total cost to make German potato salad:	

Your Decision

What is your recommendation for Brandon? Explain.

Answers may vary. Possible answer: Chicken Pasta Salad because the recipe sounds good.

Use with Grade 5, Chapter 7, Lesson 11, pages 328–329. (241)

Part B Worksheet

Part B 7-11 WORKSHEET Math & Science

Problem Solving: Application
What is GOOP?

SAFETY: Do not eat GOOP.

Read the recipe for GOOP. Do you think it is a solid or a liquid? Explain.

Answers may vary.

Work with a group.

Record the increased recipe amounts in the table. Then use the recipe to make the GOOP. There should be enough for everyone in your group to examine its properties.

Recipe	Recipe times 5
$\frac{1}{4}$ cup water	$1\frac{1}{4}$ cup water
$\frac{1}{4}$ cup white glue	$1\frac{1}{4}$ cup white glue
$\frac{1}{4}$ cup warm water	$1\frac{1}{4}$ cup warm water
$\frac{3}{8}$ teaspoon borax	$1\frac{7}{8}$ teaspoon borax

Examine the GOOP. Think about its color, shape, texture, smell, and sounds.

Throw it, drop it, roll it, catch it, squeeze it, and put it in a container. Try as many different things as you can think of.

Record your observations in the table below.

GOOP

Use with Grade 5, Chapter 7, Lesson 11, pages 330–331. (242)

Part B Worksheet

Part B 7-11 WORKSHEET Math & Science

Problem Solving: Application
What is GOOP?

1. Is GOOP a solid or a liquid? Explain.
   Answers may vary.

2. Why is it difficult to classify GOOP as a solid or a liquid?
   Answers may vary.

3. Compare your observations with those of your classmates. Are they similar or different? Explain.
   Answers may vary.

4. Did your classmates reach the same conclusion about GOOP as you did? Explain.
   Answers may vary.

5. What did you like best about the experiment? Explain.
   Answers may vary.

6. Can you think of any other substances that have characteristics similar to GOOP?
   Answers may vary.

Use with Grade 5, Chapter 7, Lesson 11, pages 330–331. (243)

Chapter 8 ~ Lesson 1

Practice

Time

P 8-1 PRACTICE

Complete.

1. 9 min = 540 s
2. 96 h = 4 d
3. 900 y = 9 centuries
4. 15 wk = 105 d
5. 12 h = 720 min
6. 730 d = 2 y
7. 7 decades = 70 y
8. 350 s = 5 min 50 s
9. 58 h = 2 d 10 h
10. 72 mo = 6 y
11. 6 d 9 h = 153 h
12. 60 d = 8 wk 4 d

Find each elapsed time.

13. 3:00 P.M. to 9:45 P.M. 6 h 45 min
14. 7:45 A.M. to 11:03 A.M. 3 h 18 min
15. 2:19 P.M. to 8:38 P.M. 6 h 19 min
16. 11:12 P.M. to 4:05 A.M. 4 h 53 min
17. 8:40 A.M. to 2:56 P.M. 6 h 16 min
18. 7:32 P.M. to 2:26 A.M. 6 h 54 min

Find each time.

19. 2 h 15 min after 1:30 P.M. 3:45 P.M.
20. 5 h 26 min after 10:18 P.M. 3:44 A.M.
21. 3 h 49 min after 6:45 A.M. 10:34 A.M.
22. 8 h 57 min after 9:53 A.M. 6:50 P.M.

Choose the most reasonable unit. Write *s, min, h, d, wk, mo,* or *y*.

23. It usually takes Danielle 30 min to do her math homework.
24. Every 10 y a census is taken to count the population of the United States.
25. You should try to get at least 8 h of sleep every day.

Problem Solving

26. A bus trip from New York City to Boston takes 4 hours 15 minutes. If you must be in Boston by 1:00 P.M., can you take a bus that leaves at 8:40 A.M.? Why or why not?
 yes; 4 h 15 min after 8:40 A.M. is 12:55 P.M.
27. The ride from the bus station to downtown takes 35 minutes by taxicab. If you are meeting a friend at 2:20 P.M., what is the latest you should get into the taxicab?
 1:45 P.M.

Use with Grade 5, Chapter 8, Lesson 1, pages 346–349. (244)

Reteach

Time

R 8-1 RETEACH

You can multiply or divide to change units of time.

Multiply to change larger units to smaller units.
13 wk = ☐ d
Weeks are larger units than days.
1 week = 7 days
So, multiply by 7.
13 × 7 = 91
13 wk = 91 d

Divide to change smaller units to larger units.
250 s = ☐ min ☐ s
Seconds are smaller units than minutes.
60 seconds = 1 minute
So, divide by 60.
250 ÷ 60 = 4 R10
250 s = 4 min 10 s

You can count on from the earlier time to the later time to find elapsed time.
You can count to find the elapsed time from 9:45 A.M. to 1:20 P.M.

15 min	← 9:45 A.M. to 10:00 A.M.
3 h	← 10:00 A.M. to 1:00 P.M.
+ 20 min	← 1:00 P.M. to 1:20 P.M.
3 h 35 min	

Complete.

1. 600 min = 10 h
2. 4 y 7 mo = 55 mo
3. 8 min = 480 s
4. 139 d = 19 wk 6 d
5. 4 h 53 min = 293 min

Find each elapsed time.

6. 7:15 P.M. to 3:05 A.M.
 7:15 P.M. to 8:00 P.M. — 45 min
 8:00 P.M. to 3:00 A.M. — 7 h
 3:00 A.M. to 3:05 A.M. — + 5 min
 7 h 50 min
7. 9:29 P.M. to 6:08 A.M.
 9:29 P.M. to 10:00 P.M. — 31 min
 10:00 P.M. to 6:00 A.M. — 8 h
 6:00 A.M. to 6:08 A.M. — + 8 min
 8 h 39 min

Use with Grade 5, Chapter 8, Lesson 1, pages 346–349. (245)

Enrich

Time
Time Flies!

E 8-1 ENRICH

Choose the best answer for each exercise. Write the letter of your answer above the problem at the bottom of the page to find out about a unit of time.

1. How many seconds are in 3 hours 5 minutes 30 seconds?
 N. 11,130 seconds
 O. 11,100 seconds
 P. 510 seconds
2. One million days is about ☐.
 K. 3,000 months
 L. 19,000 months
 M. 2,700 years
3. One million seconds is about ☐.
 R. 12 hours
 S. 12 days
 T. 12 months
4. One million hours is about ☐.
 Q. 1,114 months
 R. 114 years
 S. 1,114 years
5. Suppose you sleep an average of 9 hours each night. How long would you have slept by the age of 12 years?
 C. 470 weeks
 D. 108 months
 E. $4\frac{1}{2}$ years
6. 4 hours 22 minutes after 6:48 A.M. is ☐.
 I. 11:10 A.M.
 J. 11:00 A.M.
 K. 10:10 A.M.
7. 2 hours 47 minutes after 9:58 P.M. is ☐.
 X. 12:05 A.M.
 Y. 12:45 A.M.
 Z. 12:45 P.M.
8. Which time span is longest?
 A. from 11:05 P.M. to 12:43 A.M.
 B. from 10:37 P.M. to 12:12 A.M.
 C. from 1:48 A.M. to 3:14 A.M.
9. The movie ended at 5:10 in the afternoon. If it lasted 1 hour 47 minutes, at what time did it start?
 S. 4:57 P.M.
 T. 4:23 P.M.
 U. 3:23 P.M.
10. You are 3 years 8 months older than your friend. If your friend is 8 years 6 months old, how old are you?
 J. 11 years 2 months
 K. 11 years 11 months
 L. 12 years 2 months

1,000	Y	E	A	R	S	= 1	M	I	L	L	E	N	N	I	U	M
	7	5	8	4	3		2	6	10	10	5	1	1	6	9	2

Use with Grade 5, Chapter 8, Lesson 1, pages 346–349. (246)

Daily Homework

8-1 Time

Complete.

1. 49 d = 7 w
2. 216 h = 9 d
3. 730 d = 2 y
4. 2 d 5 h = 53 h
5. 1 h 15 min = 75 min
6. 50 mo = 4 y 2 mo
7. 4 d 4 h = 100 h
8. 48 min = 2,880 s
9. 8 decades = 80 y

Find each elapsed time.

10. 2:15 A.M. to 8:00 A.M. 5 h 45 min
11. 9:40 P.M. to 11:05 P.M. 1 h 25 min
12. 11:06 A.M. to 3:15 P.M. 4 h 9 min
13. 5:30 A.M. to 11:04 A.M. 5 h 34 min

Find each time.

14. 1 h 30 min after 7:00 A.M. 8:30 A.M.
15. 3 h 43 min after 10:30 A.M. 2:13 P.M.

Problem Solving

16. Mary starts working in her garden one morning at 10:30 A.M. At 1:15 P.M. she goes inside for lunch. How long does she work in her garden?
 2 h 45 min
17. Carlo plans to walk across town to a friend's house. He figures it will take him $2\frac{1}{2}$ hours to make the trip. If he wants to get there at 2:45 P.M., when should Carlo leave home?
 12:15 P.M.

Spiral Review

18. $16 \times \frac{1}{4} =$ 4
19. $84 \times \frac{1}{12} =$ 7
20. $24 \div \frac{2}{3} =$ 36
21. $30 \div \frac{5}{6} =$ 36

Grade 5, Chapter 8, Lesson 1, Cluster A 75

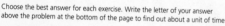

Chapter 8 ~ Lesson 2

Practice

Customary Length

P 8-2 PRACTICE

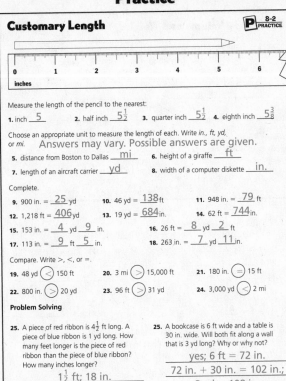

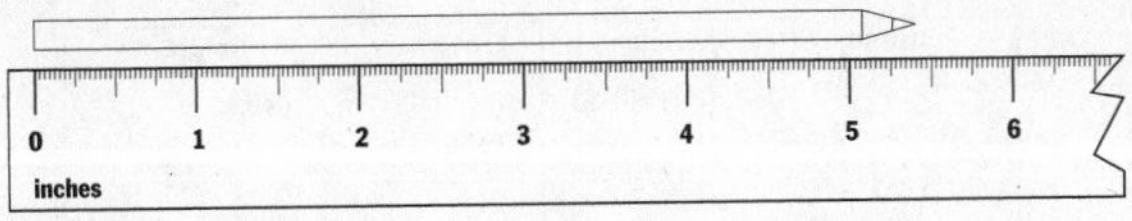

Measure the length of the pencil to the nearest:

1. inch 5
2. half inch $5\frac{1}{2}$
3. quarter inch $5\frac{1}{2}$
4. eighth inch $5\frac{3}{8}$

Choose an appropriate unit to measure the length of each. Write *in., ft, yd,* or *mi.* Answers may vary. Possible answers are given.

5. distance from Boston to Dallas mi
6. height of a giraffe ft
7. length of an aircraft carrier yd
8. width of a computer diskette in.

Complete.

9. 900 in. = 25 yd
10. 46 yd = 138 ft
11. 948 in. = 79 ft
12. 1,218 ft = 406 yd
13. 19 yd = 684 in.
14. 62 ft = 744 in.
15. 153 in. = 4 yd 9 in.
16. 26 ft = 8 yd 2 ft
17. 113 in. = 9 ft 5 in.
18. 263 in. = 7 yd 11 in.

Compare. Write >, <, or =.

19. 48 yd (<) 150 ft
20. 3 mi (>) 15,000 ft
21. 180 in. (=) 15 ft
22. 800 in. (>) 20 yd
23. 96 ft (>) 31 yd
24. 3,000 yd (<) 2 mi

Problem Solving

25. A piece of red ribbon is $4\frac{1}{2}$ ft long. A piece of blue ribbon is 1 yd long. How many feet longer is the piece of red ribbon than the piece of blue ribbon? How many inches longer?
$1\frac{1}{2}$ ft; 18 in.

25. A bookcase is 6 ft wide and a table is 30 in. wide. Will both fit along a wall that is 3 yd long? Why or why not?
yes; 6 ft = 72 in.
72 in. + 30 in. = 102 in.;
3 yd = 108 in.

Use with Grade 5, Chapter 8, Lesson 2, pages 350–353. (247)

Reteach

Customary Length

R 8-2 RETEACH

Customary Units of Length

1 foot (ft) = 12 inches (in.)
1 yard (yd) = 36 in.
1 yard (yd) = 3 ft
1 mile (mi) = 5,280 ft
1 mile (mi) = 1,760 yd

Multiply to change larger units to smaller units.

9 yd = ■ ft
Yards are larger units than feet.
1 yard = 3 feet
So, multiply by 3.
9 × 3 = 27
9 yd = 27 ft

Divide to change smaller units to larger units.

37 ft = ■ yd ■ ft
Feet are smaller units than yards.
3 feet = 1 yard
So, divide by 3.
37 ÷ 3 = 12 R1
37 ft = 12 yd 1 ft

Complete.

1. 7 ft = ■ in.
1 foot = 12 inches
So, multiply by 12.
7 × 12 = 84
7 ft = 84 in.

2. 80 in. = ■ ft ■ in.
12 inches = 1 foot
So, divide by 12.
80 ÷ 12 = 6 R 8
80 in. = 6 ft 8 in.

3. 72 in. = 2 yd
4. 60 yd = 180 ft
5. 96 in. = 8 ft
6. 3 yd = 108 in.
7. 10 ft = 120 in.
8. 60 in. = 5 ft
9. 52 in. = 1 yd 16 in.
10. 79 in. = 6 ft 7 in.
11. 17 ft = 5 yd 2 ft
12. 8 ft. = 2 yd 2 ft

Choose an appropriate unit to measure the length of each. Write *in., ft, yd,* or *mi.* Answers may vary. Possible answers are given.

13. distance a football is thrown yd
14. length of a train ride mi
15. height of your school ft
16. width of your math book in.

Use with Grade 5, Chapter 8, Lesson 2, pages 350–353. (248)

Enrich

Customary Length
Estimated Measure Game

E 8-2 ENRICH

- In Column 1 write each of the whole numbers 1 through 9 in random order.
- In Column 2 write the name of an object in your classroom that you estimate to have the target measurement.
- In Column 3 have your partner record whether he or she thinks each object is actually "Shorter" or "Longer" than the target measurement.
- Work with your partner to measure each object. Record its actual measurement in Column 4.
- Your partner gets a point for each of your estimates he or she evaluated correctly. For each incorrect evaluation, you get a point.

Target Measurement	Item	Shorter or Longer?	Actual Measurement
____ in.			
____ in.			
____ in.			
____ ft			
____ ft			
____ ft			
____ yd			
____ yd			
____ yd			

Scoring Chart

Name	Number of Points

Use with Grade 5, Chapter 8, Lesson 2, pages 350–353. (249)

Daily Homework

8-2 Customary Length

Choose an appropriate unit to measure the length of each. Write *in., ft, yd,* or *mi*.
Answers may vary. Possible answers are given.

1. height of a table ft or in.
2. distance across a baseball field ft or yd
3. width of a book in.
4. distance from New York to Chicago mi

Complete.

5. 4 yd = 144 in.
6. 100 in. = 8 ft 4 in.
7. 18 yd = 54 ft
8. 75 ft = 25 yd
9. 180 in. = 5 yd
10. 30 ft = 10 yd
11. 6 ft = 72 in.
12. 108 ft = 36 yd
13. 3 ft 6 in. = 42 in.
14. 4 ft 10 in. = 58 in.
15. 8 yd = 288 in.

Compare. Write <, >, or =.

16. 9 ft < 4 yd
17. 150 in. > 10 ft
18. 345 ft = 115 yd
19. 180 in. > 5 ft
20. 11 yd < 500 in.
21. 35 in. > 2 ft 10 in.

Problem Solving

22. Kandy's height is 5 feet 1 inch. What is Kandy's height in inches? 61 in.
23. A football field is 100 yards long. How long is this in feet? 300 ft
How long is this in inches? 3,600 in.

Spiral Review

24. $4\frac{1}{2} \times \frac{7}{8} = 3\frac{15}{16}$
25. $5\frac{3}{4} \times 6\frac{2}{3} = 38\frac{1}{3}$
26. $2\frac{5}{8} \times 5\frac{1}{7} = 13\frac{1}{2}$
27. $16 \times 4\frac{7}{8} = 78$

76 Grade 5, Chapter 8, Lesson 2, Cluster A

Chapter 8 ~ Lesson 3

Practice

Customary Volume and Weight

P 8-3 PRACTICE

Choose an appropriate unit to measure the volume of each. Write *fl oz, c, pt, qt,* or *gal.* Answers may vary. Possible answers are given.

1. drinking glass fl oz **2.** kitchen sink gal **3.** shampoo bottle pt

Choose an appropriate unit to measure the weight of each. Write *oz, lb,* or *T.* Answers may vary. Possible answers are given.

4. bowling ball lb **5.** compact disc oz **6.** ocean liner T

Complete.

7. 38 pt = 19 qt **8.** 9 c = 72 fl oz **9.** $4\frac{1}{2}$ T = 9,000 lb

10. 15 pt = 30 c **11.** 64 oz = 4 lb **12.** 32 qt = 8 gal

13. 21 fl oz = 2 c 5 fl oz **14.** 2,450 lb = 1 T 450 lb

15. 26 qt = 6 gal 2 qt **16.** 85 c = 42 pt 1 c

17. 6,500 lb = 3 T 500 lb **18.** 19 pt = 9 qt 1 pt

Compare. Write >, <, or =.

19. 63 c (<) 129 pt **20.** 5 lb (>) 50 oz **21.** 164 pt (>) 82 c

22. 7,000 lb (>) 3 T **23.** 65 gal (>) 256 qt **24.** 60 fl oz (<) 10 c

25. 12 qt 1 pt (=) 25 pt **26.** 55 oz (<) 3 lb 10 oz **27.** 50 qt (>) 12 gal 1 qt

Problem Solving

28. Shannon combines 3 quarts of cranberry juice with 3 pints of apple juice. Does Shannon have at least one gallon of cranapple juice? Why or why not?
yes: 3 pt = $1\frac{1}{2}$ qt; 3 qt + $1\frac{1}{2}$ qt = $4\frac{1}{2}$ qt; 1 gal = 4 qt

29. Mr. Hill's truck weighs $1\frac{1}{2}$ tons. His car weighs 1,600 pounds. Which vehicle weighs more? How much more?
The truck weighs 1,400 pounds more.

Use with Grade 5, Chapter 8, Lesson 3, pages 354–357. (250)

Reteach

Customary Volume and Weight

R 8-3 RETEACH

Customary Units of Volume	Customary Units of Weight
1 cup (c) = 8 fluid ounces (fl oz) 1 pint (pt) = 2 c = 16 fl oz 1 quart (qt) = 2 pt = 32 fl oz 1 gallon (gal) = 4 qt	1 pound (lb) = 16 ounces (oz) 1 ton (T) = 2,000 lb

Multiply to change larger units to smaller units.
8 qt = ▢ pt
Quarts are larger units than pints.
1 quart = 2 pints
So, multiply by 2.
8 × 2 = 16
8 qt = 16 pt

Divide to change smaller units to larger units.
50 oz = ▢ lb ▢ oz
Ounces are smaller units than pounds.
16 ounces = 1 pound
So, divide by 16.
50 ÷ 16 = 3 R2
50 oz = 3 lb 2 oz

Complete.

1. 9 T = ▢ lb
1 ton = 2,000 pounds
So, multiply by 2,000.
9 × 2,000 = 18,000
9 T = 18,000 lb

2. 35 fl oz = ▢ c ▢ fl oz
8 fluid ounces = 1 cup
So, divide by 8.
35 ÷ 8 = 4 R 3
35 fl oz = 4 c 3 fl oz

3. 42 pt = 21 qt **4.** 12 gal = 48 qt **5.** 6 lb = 96 oz

6. 16,000 lb = 8 T **7.** 24 pt = 48 c **8.** 40 oz = 2 lb 8 oz

Choose an appropriate unit to measure the volume of each. Write *fl oz, c, pt, qt,* or *gal.* Answers may vary. Possible answers are given.

9. washing machine gal **10.** medicine bottle fl oz **11.** soup bowl c

Choose an appropriate unit to measure the weight of each. Write *oz, lb,* or *T.* Answers may vary. Possible answers are given.

12. horse lb **13.** blue whale T **14.** robin oz

Use with Grade 5, Chapter 8, Lesson 3, pages 354–357. (251)

Enrich

Customary Volume and Weight
Clueless

E 8-3 ENRICH

Use what you know about customary units for measuring volume and weight to complete the clues.

Across

Number of:
B. gallons in 80 quarts
C. quarts in 62 pints
E. ounces in $5\frac{3}{4}$ pounds
F. quarts in 50 gallons
G. 2 quarts more than 12 gallons
H. cups in 240 fluid ounces
I. fluid ounces in 20 quarts

Down

Number of:
A. fluid ounces in $15\frac{1}{4}$ cups
D. fluid ounces in 1 gallon
E. pounds in $4\frac{1}{2}$ tons
G. pounds in $\frac{1}{4}$ ton
H. ounces in $2\frac{1}{8}$ pounds

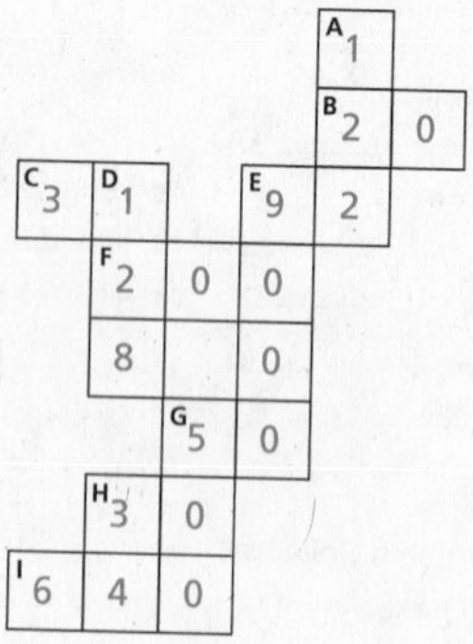

How did you decide what clue to write for I Across?
Answers may vary. Possible answer: I knew that 32 fluid ounces equals 1 quart, so I multiplied 20 by 32. 20 quarts = 640 fluid ounces

Use with Grade 5, Chapter 8, Lesson 3, pages 354–357. (252)

Daily Homework

8-3 Customary Capacity and Weight

Choose an appropriate unit to measure the capacity of each. Write *fl oz, c, pt, qt,* or *gal.* Answers may vary. Possible answers are given.

1. juice box fl oz 2. water pitcher pt or qt
3. home aquarium gal

Choose an appropriate unit to measure the weight of each. Write *oz, lb,* or *T.* Answers may vary. Possible answers are given.

4. newborn kitten oz 5. truck T 6. bag of apples lb

Complete.

7. 3 c = 24 fl oz 8. 20 pt = 40 c
9. 12 pt = 6 qt 10. 30 fl oz = 3 c 6 fl oz
11. 7 gal = 28 qt 12. 6 qt = 12 pt
13. 6 lb = 96 oz 14. $2\frac{1}{2}$ T = 5,000 lb
15. 24 qt = 6 gal 16. 80 oz = 5 lb
17. 80 fl oz = 2 qt 1 pt 18. 10,000 lb = 5 T

Compare. Write >, <, or =.

19. 26 c > 200 fl oz 20. 16 lb = 256 oz 21. 35 pt > 17 qt

Problem Solving

22. A juice box contains 4 fl oz. How many juice boxes of orange juice can be poured into a 1-gallon pitcher? 32

23. Ariel's family is having a cookout. They plan to serve hamburgers. A typical hamburger patty weighs 4 oz. How many patties can be made from a 3-pound package of chopped meat? 12

Spiral Review

Find the LCD.

24. $\frac{1}{6}, \frac{1}{4}$ 12 25. $\frac{4}{5}, \frac{2}{3}$ 15 26. $\frac{3}{8}, \frac{3}{10}$ 40

Grade 5, Chapter 8, Lesson 3, Cluster A 77

Chapter 8 ~ Lesson 4

Practice

Problem Solving: Reading for Math — 8-4 PRACTICE — Reading Skill

Check for Reasonableness

Is each estimate reasonable? Explain.

1. Sandra needs to buy a phone cord that will reach a distance of at least 12 yards. At the store, all of the packages are marked in feet. Sandra estimates that the package with 40 feet of cord will be enough. Is her estimate reasonable?
   Yes, the cord will be long enough since there are 3 ft in 1 yd and $12 \times 3 = 36$.
2. Kyle and Julie are watching a television program on weight lifting. A man is going to lift 210 pounds. Julie comments that he is going to lift 4,000 ounces. Is her estimate reasonable?
   No, since there are 16 oz in 1 lb, the estimate should be about 3,200 oz.
3. Ryan and Tyler are going to the pet shop to buy 12 cans of dog food. They are trying to decide whether they should take their wagon to help carry the dog food home. The cans weigh 15 ounces each. They estimate that the dog food will weigh 10 pounds. Is the estimate reasonable?
   Yes, each can weighs almost 1 pound, so 12 cans would weigh about 12 pounds. The estimate is reasonable.
4. Nicole is trying out a new recipe. The recipe calls for 4 pints of broth. Nicole only has a 1-cup measuring cup. She estimates that she will need 16 cups of broth. Is her estimate reasonable?
   No, there are 2 cups in 1 pint, so her estimate is too large.
5. A scoutmaster needs 10 feet of nylon cord to teach his scouts how to tie different types of knots. The cord is sold in yards. He estimates that he should buy 30 yards of the nylon cord. Is his estimate reasonable?
   No, it is too large; there are 3 ft in 1 yd so he only needs about 4 yards of rope.

Use with Grade 5, Chapter 8, Lesson 4, pages 358–359. (253)

Practice

Problem Solving: Reading for Math — 8-4 PRACTICE — Math Skills Test Prep

Check for Reasonableness

Choose the correct answer.

George has a 1-gallon water bottle. He says that the bottle will hold 2 quarts of water.

1. Which of the following statements is true?
   - A The bottle will hold 1 quart of water.
   - B The bottle will hold 2 quarts of water.
   - **(C)** The bottle will hold 4 quarts of water.
   - D The bottle will hold 4 gallons of water.
2. When you check that an answer is reasonable, you
   - F read the problem carefully.
   - **(G)** compare the answer with what you already know.
   - H divide to check.
   - J guess the answer.

Amy has a piece of cable that is 3 feet long. She says that the cable is 9 inches long.

3. Which of the following statements is true?
   - A The cable is 9 inches long.
   - B The cable is 12 inches long.
   - C The cable is 27 inches long.
   - **(D)** The cable is 36 inches long.
4. Which of the following statements is true?
   - **(F)** The cable is 1 yard long.
   - G The cable is 3 yards long.
   - H The cable is 9 yards long.
   - J The cable is 12 yards long.

A jar of spaghetti sauce weighs 32 ounces. Kenny says that the jar weighs 2 pounds.

5. Which of the following statements is true?
   - **(A)** The jar weighs 2 pounds.
   - B The jar weighs 16 ounces.
   - C The jar weighs 16 pounds.
   - D The jar weighs 64 pounds.
6. Which of the following should you do to check that an answer is reasonable?
   - F Make a good guess.
   - G Check the computations.
   - **(H)** Make sure the answer makes sense.
   - J Try different conversions.

Sonya has 2 quarts of water to take on her hike. She says that this is 8 pints of water.

7. Which of the following statements is true?
   - A Sonya has 1 pint of water.
   - B Sonya has 2 pints of water.
   - **(C)** Sonya has 4 pints of water.
   - D Sonya has 8 pints of water.
8. Which of the following statements is NOT true?
   - F 1 pint = 2 cups
   - G 1 quart = 4 cups
   - H 1 quart = 2 pints
   - **(J)** 1 gallon = 2 quarts

Use with Grade 5, Chapter 8, Lesson 4, pages 358–359. (254)

Practice

Problem Solving: Reading for Math — 8-4 PRACTICE — Math Skills Test Prep

Check for Reasonableness

Choose the correct answer.

A recipe for a pizza calls for 1 cup of tomato sauce. Taylor says that he needs 1 pint of tomato sauce.

9. Which of the following statements is true?
   - **(A)** Taylor needs $\frac{1}{2}$ pint of tomato sauce.
   - B Taylor needs 1 pint of tomato sauce.
   - C Taylor needs 2 pints of tomato sauce.
   - D Taylor needs 1 quart of tomato sauce.
10. Which of the following statements is true?
    - F 1 cup = 4 fluid ounces
    - **(G)** 1 cup = 8 fluid ounces
    - H 1 cup = 12 fluid ounces
    - J 1 cup = 16 fluid ounces

Is each estimate reasonable? Explain.

11. The distance between two fence posts is 6 feet. Kevin says that the distance is 200 inches. Is this distance reasonable?
    No, 200 inches is much more than 6 feet.
12. The height of a flagpole is 12 yards. How many feet is this? Maya says that it is 4 feet. Is her estimate reasonable?
    No, there are 3 feet in 1 yard so the estimate should be greater than 12, not less than 12.
13. Josh wants to recycle 3 quarts of oil. He says that he will need a 12-gallon container to hold the oil. Is his estimate reasonable?
    No, there are 4 quarts in 1 gallon, so a 1-gallon container would hold all of the oil.
14. Cameron's suitcase weighs 325 ounces. She says that it weighs about 20 pounds. Is her estimate reasonable?
    Yes, since there are 16 ounces in 1 pound, 20 pounds is close to 320 ounces.
15. Ms. Smithson needs a container that will hold 8 cups of soup. How many pints is this? Her daughter says it is 16 pints. Is her answer reasonable?
    No, 16 pints is 32 cups. She only needs a container that will hold 4 pints.
16. A deliveryman carries a large package to the door. It weighs 450 ounces. Akil says that the package weighs 7,200 pounds. Is this estimate reasonable?
    No, a person could not carry 7,200 lb.

Use with Grade 5, Chapter 8, Lesson 4, pages 358–359. (255)

Daily Homework

8-4 Problem Solving: Reading for Math

Check for Reasonableness

Is each estimate reasonable? Explain.

1. Jack's family just bought a new car. Jack says it is about 50 feet long.
   No, that would be more than twice the length of a typical car.
2. Jack also says his family's new car weighs about 400 pounds.
   No, in fact about 3,000 might be closer to the real weight.
3. Mary's house is 30 feet wide. She says this is 90 yards.
   No, Mary multiplied by 3 instead of dividing by 3. The actual answer is 10 yards.
4. Karen lives two miles from her school. She says this distance is about 10,000 feet.
   Yes, two miles is exactly 10,560 feet
5. A swimming pool at the town recreation center is about 9 feet deep at one end. Nick says this is about 100 inches.
   Yes, 9 feet is exactly 108 inches.
6. Jan needs 12 feet of rope for a jump rope competition. She asks her mother to buy 36 yards of rope.
   No, Jan multiplied by 3 instead of dividing by 3. She needs only 4 yards of rope.
7. In the owner's manual for his lawn mower, Harry reads that he needs 16 fluid ounces of oil. He buys 1 quart of oil.
   No, Harry needs only half of what he bought. A quart contains 32 fluid ounces.

Spiral Review

Solve.

8. $4(3 + 2) =$ 20
9. $5(6 +$ 3 $) = 45$
10. $7($ 2 $+ 3) = 35$
11. 8 $(4 + 6) = 80$

78 Grade 5, Chapter 8, Lesson 4, Cluster A

Chapter 8 ~ Lesson 5

Practice

Explore Metric Length

P 8-5 PRACTICE

Measure to the nearest centimeter and millimeter.

1. 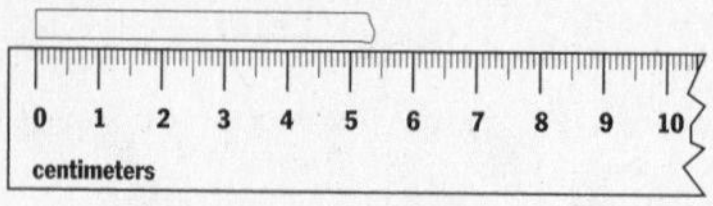

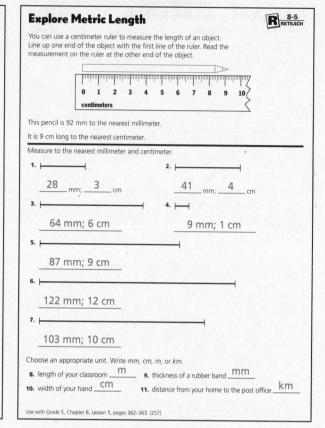

5 cm 54 mm

2. 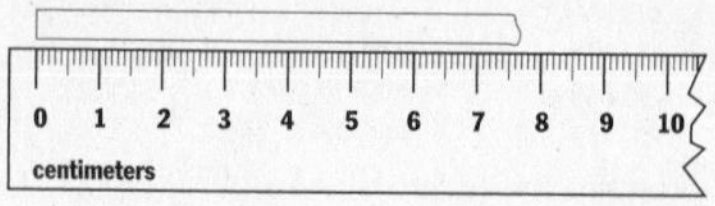

8 cm 77 mm

3. 4 cm 36 mm

4. 6 cm 61 mm

5. 9 cm 92 mm

6. 11 cm 107 mm

Answers may vary. Possible answers are given.

Choose an appropriate unit. Write *mm, cm, m,* or *km.*

7. length of your arm cm
8. thickness of a penny mm
9. length of a bus m
10. height of a mountain m
11. distance from your home to school km
12. length of a shoelace cm
13. length of a canoe m
14. height of a diving board m

Problem Solving

15. Kay is reading a book. Is the book's thickness most likely to be 19 mm or 19 km?

19 mm

16. Scott kicked a football. Is the distance he kicked it most likely to be 35 m or 35 km?

35 m

Use with Grade 5, Chapter 8, Lesson 5, pages 362–363. (256)

Reteach

Explore Metric Length

R 8-5 RETEACH

You can use a centimeter ruler to measure the length of an object. Line up one end of the object with the first line of the ruler. Read the measurement on the ruler at the other end of the object.

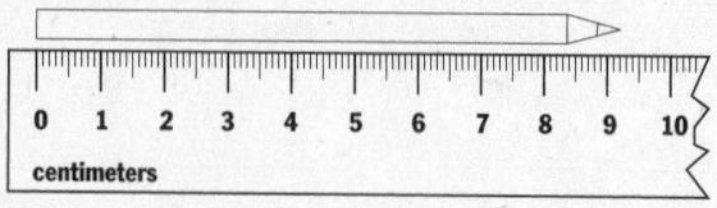

This pencil is 92 mm to the nearest millimeter.

It is 9 cm long to the nearest centimeter.

Measure to the nearest millimeter and centimeter.

1. 28 mm; 3 cm
2. 41 mm; 4 cm
3. 64 mm; 6 cm
4. 9 mm; 1 cm
5. 87 mm; 9 cm
6. 122 mm; 12 cm
7. 103 mm; 10 cm

Choose an appropriate unit. Write *mm, cm, m,* or *km.*

8. length of your classroom m
9. thickness of a rubber band mm
10. width of your hand cm
11. distance from your home to the post office km

Use with Grade 5, Chapter 8, Lesson 5, pages 362–363. (257)

Enrich

Explore Metric Length

E 8-5 ENRICH

Follow the Metric Road

Begin at Start. Move in the directions indicated in order and draw the distances along the grid. Do not lift your pencil off the paper until you finish.

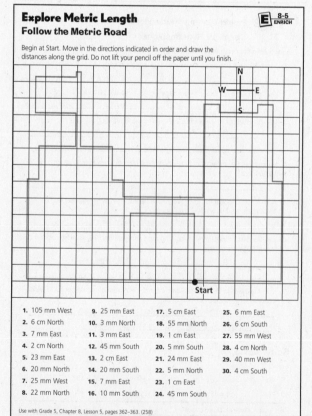

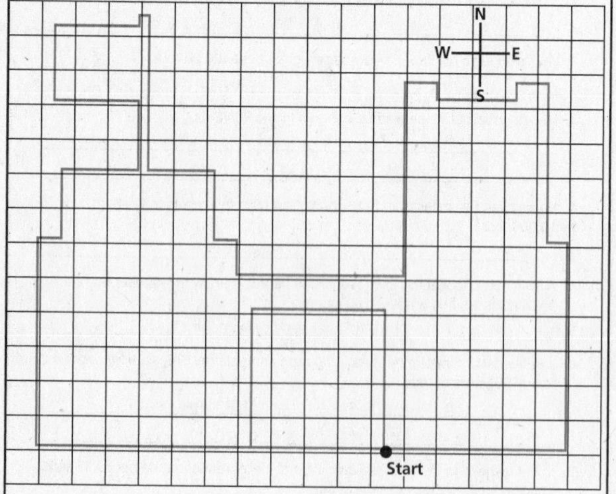

1. 105 mm West
2. 6 cm North
3. 7 mm East
4. 2 cm North
5. 23 mm East
6. 20 mm North
7. 25 mm West
8. 22 mm North
9. 25 mm East
10. 3 mm North
11. 3 mm East
12. 45 mm South
13. 2 cm East
14. 20 mm South
15. 7 mm East
16. 10 mm South
17. 5 cm East
18. 55 mm North
19. 1 cm East
20. 5 mm South
21. 24 mm East
22. 5 mm North
23. 1 cm East
24. 45 mm South
25. 6 mm East
26. 6 cm South
27. 55 mm West
28. 4 cm North
29. 40 mm West
30. 4 cm South

Use with Grade 5, Chapter 8, Lesson 5, pages 362–363. (258)

Daily Homework

8-5 Explore Metric Length

Choose an appropriate unit. Write *mm, cm, m,* or *km.*

1. length of your math book **cm**
2. your height **cm or m**
3. width of your classroom **m**
4. thickness of a crayon **mm or cm**
5. distance from your school to home **m or km**
6. length of the school playground **m**
7. height of the classroom ceiling **m**
8. length of your bed **cm or m**
9. thickness of 10 pieces of paper **mm**
10. length of a dollar bill **cm**
11. width of a quarter **mm or cm**
12. distance across your town **km**

Solve.

13. Would you measure the width of a standard television screen in centimeters or meters? Explain.

Possible answer: The width of a standard television screen is less than a meter. Centimeters are a more appropriate unit of measure.

14. Would you measure the height of your school in meters or kilometers? Explain.

Possible answer: A kilometer is much too large to measure the height of a building. Meters are more appropriate.

Spiral Review

15. $\frac{7}{9} - \frac{1}{3} = \frac{4}{9}$

16. $4 - 2\frac{1}{2} = 1\frac{1}{2}$

17. $6\frac{3}{4} - 5\frac{1}{2} = 1\frac{1}{4}$

Grade 5, Chapter 8, Lesson 5, Cluster B 79

Chapter 8 ~ Lesson 6

Practice

Metric Volume and Mass

P 8-6 PRACTICE

Choose an appropriate unit of volume to measure each. Write *mL* or *L*.

1. water glass <u>mL</u>
2. bath tub <u>L</u>
3. ice cream cone <u>mL</u>
4. baby bottle <u>mL</u>
5. watering can <u>L</u>
6. gasoline can <u>L</u>

Choose an appropriate unit of mass to measure each. Write *mg*, *g*, or *kg*.

7. cat <u>kg</u>
8. sheet of paper <u>mg</u>
9. sandwich <u>g</u>
10. quarter <u>g</u>
11. brick <u>kg</u>
12. feather <u>mg</u>

Circle an appropriate estimate for each.

	A	B	C	D
13. coffee mug	25 mL	(B) 250 mL	25 L	250 L
14. sink	2 L	2 mL	200 mL	(D) 20 L
15. medicine dropper	30 mL	(B) 3 mL	30 L	3 L
16. water bucket	(A) 4 L	40 L	400 L	400 mL
17. dog	(A) 12 kg	120 mg	12 g	120 g
18. nickel	50 mg	5 kg	50 kg	(D) 5 g
19. apple	2 g	20 mg	(C) 200 g	2 kg
20. box of cereal	(A) 350 g	35 g	35 kg	350 mg

Problem Solving

21. Marc was telling his friends about his new baby sister. Is her mass more likely to be 40 mg or 4 kg?
<u>4 kg</u>

22. Kate bought her mother a vase for a present. Is the volume of the vase more likely to be 800 mL or 80 L?
<u>800 mL</u>

23. Lila's class drank a lot of juice at the party. Was the volume of the juice more likely 75 mL or 75 L?
<u>75 L</u>

24. Gavin likes to hold his pet cat, Shadow. Is Shadow's mass more likely to be 6 kg or 6 g?
<u>6 kg</u>

Use with Grade 5, Chapter 8, Lesson 6, pages 364–367. (259)

Reteach

Metric Volume and Mass

R 8-6 RETEACH

Volume tells how much a container can hold. Milliliters (mL), centiliters (cL), and liters (L) are metric units of volume.

Milliliters soup spoon; glass of juice

Centiliters bowl of soup; small can of paint

Liters large juice bottle; wading pool

Mass can be used to tell how heavy an object is. Milligrams (mg), grams (g), and kilograms (kg) are metric units of mass.

Milligrams spider; sheet of paper

Grams sandwich; bird

Kilograms person; car

Choose an appropriate unit of volume to measure each. Write *mL* or *L*.

1. aquarium <u>L</u>
2. teaspoon <u>mL</u>
3. juice box <u>mL</u>
4. city reservoir <u>L</u>
5. cereal bowl <u>mL</u>
6. kitchen sink <u>L</u>

Choose an appropriate unit of mass to measure each. Write *mg*, *g*, or *kg*.

7. encyclopedia <u>kg</u>
8. postage stamp <u>mg</u>
9. bag of popcorn <u>g</u>
10. sunflower seed <u>mg</u>
11. daily newspaper <u>g</u>
12. bear <u>kg</u>

Circle an appropriate estimate for each.

	A	B	C	D
13. shampoo bottle	500 L	5 mL	(C) 500 mL	5 L
14. goldfish	3 mg	(B) 30 g	3 kg	30 kg

Use with Grade 5, Chapter 8, Lesson 6, pages 364–367. (260)

Enrich

Metric Volume and Mass

E 8-6 ENRICH

Metric Race

Play this game with a partner. Use the game board below. Make sure your playing pieces can fit in each box on the game board.

Take turns.

- Toss a number cube and move colored cubes or counters the number of spaces tossed.
- Name an item that should be measured in the unit you landed on. For example, if you roll 5 and land on "kg" you might say "cat" because a cat has a mass of about 5 kilograms.
- If you can't name an item or you name an inappropriate item, you lose your next turn. The winner is the first player to reach the finish line.

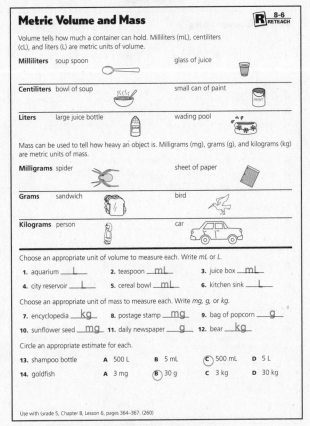

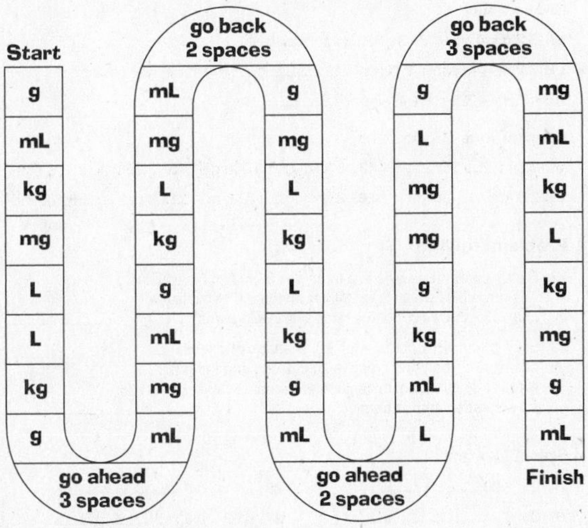

Use with Grade 5, Chapter 8, Lesson 6, pages 364–367. (261)

Daily Homework

8-6 Metric Capacity and Mass

Choose an appropriate unit of capacity to measure each. Write *mL* or *L*.

1. soda bottle <u>mL or L</u>
2. tablespoon <u>mL</u>
3. thermos <u>mL</u>
4. cereal bowl <u>mL</u>
5. car gas tank <u>L</u>
6. bathtub <u>L</u>

Choose an appropriate unit of mass to measure each. Write *mg*, *g*, or *kg*.

7. pencil <u>g</u>
8. computer <u>kg</u>
9. 6 sheets of paper <u>mg</u>
10. bicycle <u>kg</u>

Choose an appropriate estimate for each.

11. small dog <u>C</u>
A 5 grams B 50 grams
C 5 kilograms D 50 kilograms

12. CD <u>C</u>
A 20 milligrams B 200 milligrams
C 20 grams D 200 grams

13. flower vase <u>B</u>
A 10 milliliters B 1 liter
C 20 liters D 100 liters

14. stick of margarine <u>A</u>
A 250 milliliters B 1 liter
C 10 liters D 50 liters

Problem Solving

15. Sean is mailing his cousin two boxes of crayons. Do they weigh about 50 grams or about 50 kilograms? <u>about 50 grams</u>
How do you know? <u>50 kilograms would be too heavy for any child to lift.</u>

16. Curt is filling up his new fish tank. Will he need about 20 milliliters or about 20 liters of water? <u>about 20 liters</u>
How do you know? <u>20 milliliters is a very tiny amount of water.</u>

Spiral Review

Write each fraction in simplest form.

17. $\frac{12}{24}$ <u>$\frac{1}{2}$</u>
18. $\frac{18}{32}$ <u>$\frac{9}{16}$</u>
19. $\frac{65}{100}$ <u>$\frac{13}{20}$</u>
20. $\frac{28}{64}$ <u>$\frac{7}{16}$</u>

80 Grade 5, Chapter 8, Lesson 6, Cluster B

Chapter 8 ~ Lesson 7

Practice

Metric Conversions

P 8-7 PRACTICE

Complete.

1. 26 cm = 260 mm
2. 745 cm = 7.45 m
3. 8.4 km = 8,400 m
4. 350 mL = 0.35 L
5. 93 cL = 930 mL
6. 13.5 L = 13,500 mL
7. 65 kg = 65,000 g
8. 16 g = 0.016 kg
9. 52 mg = 0.052 g
10. 3.07 L = 3,070 mL
11. 0.6 m = 60 cm
12. 44.2 g = 0.0442 kg
13. 62 mL = 6.2 c
14. 6,400 L = 6.4 mL
15. 250 mm = 25 cm
16. 4,500 mm = 4.5 m
17. 7.2 kg = 7,200 g
18. 800 cm = 8,000 mm

Find each sum.

19. 650 g + 2 kg + 195 g = 2.845 kg
20. 36.7 g + 24.8 g + 513 mg = 62.013 g
21. 580 m + 1.2 km + 7 km = 8.78 km
22. 53 cm + 124 cm + 3.4 m = 5.17 m
23. 3.4 L + 16 mL + 297 mL = 3.713 L
24. 6.8 cL + 156 mL + 94 cL = 116.4 cL

Compare. Write >, <, or =.

25. 520.8 cm (=) 5,208 mm
26. 320 m (<) 3.2 km
27. 295 cm (<) 29.5 m
28. 6.34 m (>) 63.4 cm
29. 2,000 mL (>) 20 cL
30. 4.027 L (=) 4,027 mL
31. 129 mL (<) 12.9 L
32. 56.8 cL (=) 568 mL
33. 4,300 g (>) 0.43 kg
34. 0.9 g (=) 900 mg
35. 2.45 kg (>) 245 g
36. 0.384 g (<) 3,840 mg

Problem Solving

37. Jacob has 0.5 L of milk to use in two recipes. Each recipe uses 300 mL. Does he have enough? Explain.
no; 0.5 L = 500 mL;
2 × 300 mL > 500 mL

38. When completed, a tunnel will be 1.3 km long. The workers have already completed 825 m of the tunnel. How many meters more of the tunnel remains to be built?
475 m, or 0.475 km

Use with Grade 5, Chapter 8, Lesson 7, pages 368–371. (262)

Reteach

Metric Conversions

R 8-7 RETEACH

Metric Units of Length	Metric Units of Volume	Metric Units of Mass
1 centimeter (cm) = 10 millimeters (mm) 1 meter (m) = 100 cm = 1,000 mm 1 kilometer (km) = 1,000 m	1 centiliter (cL) = 10 milliliters (mL) 1 metric cup (c) = 250 mL 1 liter (L) = 1,000 mL	1 gram (g) = 1,000 milligrams (mg) 1 kilogram (kg) = 1,000 g

Multiply to change larger units to smaller units.
3.2 m = ▢ cm
Meters are larger units than centimeters.
1 meter = 100 centimeters
So, multiply by 100.
3.2 × 100 = 320
3.2 m = 320 cm

Divide to change smaller units to larger units.
900 g = ▢ kg
Grams are smaller units than kilograms.
1,000 grams = 1 kilogram
So, divide by 1,000.
900 ÷ 1,000 = 0.9
900 g = 0.9 kg

Complete.

1. 42 mm = ▢ cm
10 millimeters = 1 centimeter
So, divide by 10
42 ÷ 10 = 4.2
42 mm = 4.2 cm

2. 5.9 L = ▢ mL
1 liter = 1,000 milliliters
So, multiply by 1,000
5.9 × 1,000 = 5,900
5.9 L = 5,900 mL

3. 23 cm = 230 mm
4. 50 g = 50,000 mg
5. 64 mL = 6.4 cL
6. 348 mg = 0.348 g
7. 0.25 km = 250 m
8. 9,438 g = 9.438 kg
9. 12 cL = 120 mL
10. 375 cm = 3.75 m
11. 40 mL = 0.04 L
12. 6.8 m = 680 cm
13. 2.45 kg = 2,450 g
14. 3 m = 0.003 km
15. 420 cL = 4,200 mL
16. 3 cL = 30 mL
17. 6 cm = 60 mm
18. 35 m = 0.035 km
19. 52 mL = 5.2 cL
20. 738 g = 0.738 kg
21. 2.5 L = 2,500 mL
22. 86.62 kg = 86,620 g
23. 2,250 mL = 225 cL

Use with Grade 5, Chapter 8, Lesson 7, pages 368–371. (263)

Enrich

Metric Conversions
Water Volume

E 8-7 ENRICH

Did you know that 1 hollow centimeter cube will hold 1 milliliter of water?

1 centimeter cube
1 mL of water

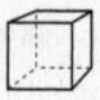

To find out how much water will fit in a container, find out how many centimeter cubes will fit in the container.

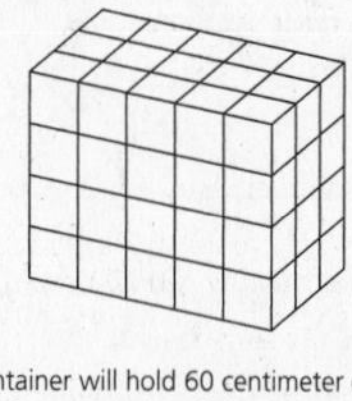

Multiply the number of cubes in each layer times the number of layers.

cubes in one layer	×	number of layers
↓		↓
(5 × 3)	×	4
15	×	4 = 60 cubes

The container will hold 60 centimeter cubes, so it will hold 60 mL of water. It has a capacity of 60 mL.

Find the capacity of each container. Each cube represents a centimeter cube.

1. 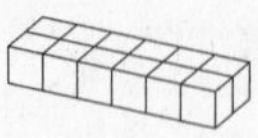
12 mL

2. 
64 mL

3. 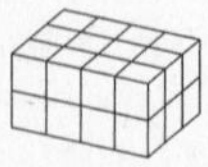
24 mL

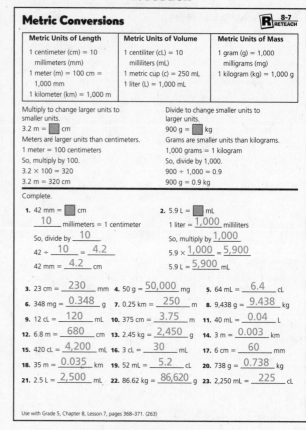

Make a drawing of a container with each capacity. Let each cube in your drawings represent a centimeter cube. Check students' work.

4. 32 mL
Drawing should show a total of 32 cubes.

5. 1 L
Drawing should show a total of 1,000 cubes.

6. 0.2 L
Drawing should show a total of 200 cubes.

How did you decide what to draw for exercise 5?
1 L = 1,000 mL, so I found three numbers whose product is 1,000. I used these numbers for the number of cubes in each row of each layer, the number of rows of cubes in each layer, and the number of layers of cubes.

Use with Grade 5, Chapter 8, Lesson 7, pages 368–371. (264)

Daily Homework

8-7 Metric Conversions

Complete.

1. 380 g = 0.380 kg
2. 180 cm = 1.8 m
3. 2 L = 2,000 mL
4. 1,946 cm = 19.46 m
5. 8 L = 800 cL
6. 13 m = 13,000 mm
7. 295 m = 0.295 km
8. 27.4 g = 0.0274 kg
9. 1,853 mm = 1.853 m
10. 61 cL = 0.61 L
11. 2,115 mg = 2.115 g
12. 6,125 mL = 612.5 cL

Find each sum.

13. 3.2 g + 4 kg + 135.3 g = 4,138.5 g
14. 3.2 m + 4.68 m + 123 cm = 9.11 m
15. 108 m + 225 cm + 4.1 km = 4,210.25 m

Compare. Write <, >, or =.

16. 3.6 m = 360 cm
17. 8.3 kg = 8,300 g
18. 3,685 mL = 3.685 L
19. 3.6 km > 360 m
20. 236 cm < 23.6 m
21. 81 cL < 8,100 mL

Problem Solving

22. Sandy packs three gifts in a large box to mail to his cousins. The three gifts weigh 3 kg, 384 g, and 985 g. What is the total shipping weight of the large box in kilograms? 4.369 kg

23. Lucy is framing a photograph in the shape of a rectangle. One side of the photograph is 20 cm long and the other side is 135 mm long. In centimeters, what is the length of stock needed for this frame? 67 cm

Spiral Review

24. 0.3 × 80 24
25. 2.01 × 0.5 1.005
26. 6 × 3.2 19.2
27. 0.03 × 0.03 0.0009

Grade 5, Chapter 8, Lesson 7, Cluster B 81

Chapter 8 ~ Lesson 8

Practice

Problem Solving: Strategy
Draw a Diagram

P 8-8 PRACTICE

Draw a diagram to solve.

1. For a concert, Ron must set the speakers for a sound system every 10 yards around the walls of a square room. Speakers are not set up in corners of the room. The room is 60 yards long. How many speakers will Ron set up?
   20 speakers
2. Katya makes a 4-by-4 grid. She writes the numbers 0 through 15 in order on the grid, starting with the top left square. What are the four numbers in the right column of the grid?
   3, 7, 11, 15
3. Pine cones are evenly spaced on a circular wreath. The third pine cone is opposite the ninth pine cone. How many pine cones are on the wreath?
   12 pine cones
4. Jason is building a dog run that is 24 feet by 18 feet. He is setting a fence post every 6 feet and one at each corner. How many posts will he need in all?
   14 fence posts

Mixed Strategy Review Strategies may vary. Possible strategies are given.

Solve. Use any strategy.

5. Tami, Evan, and Scott each prefer a different type of music. They listen to rock, rap, and country. Tami does not like country. Evan does not like country or rap. Which type of music does each person like best?
   Evan: rock, Tami: rap,
   Scott: country
   Strategy: Make a Table
6. **Social Studies** The writer F. Scott Fitzgerald was born in St. Paul, Minnesota in 1896. The city of his birth was first called Pig's Eye when it was established 56 years earlier. The name of the city was changed to St. Paul one year after it was established. What year was the city named St. Paul?
   1841
   Strategy: Work Backward
7. **Number Sense** Renaldo paid for a roll and a large glass of juice with 9 coins. If the total cost for both items was \$2.52, which coins did Renaldo use to pay the bill?
   3 half-dollars,
   4 quarters, 2 pennies
   Strategy: Guess and Check
8. **Create a problem** for which you could draw a diagram to solve. Share it with others.
   Check students' work

Use with Grade 5, Chapter 8, Lesson 8, pages 372–373. (265)

Reteach

Problem Solving: Strategy
Draw a Diagram

R 8-8 RETEACH

Page 373, Problem 1

Mark builds a telephone stand. He nails a square piece of wood that is 35 centimeters on each side to a pole. Mark puts a nail every 7 centimeters, including at the corners. How many nails does Mark use?

Step 1 Read

Be sure you understand the problem.
Read carefully.

What do you know?

- The piece of wood is square.
- Each side of the square is 35 cm.
- The nails are every 7 cm.

What do you need to find?

- The number of nails Mark uses.

Step 2 Plan

- Find a Pattern
- Guess and Check
- Work Backward
- Make a Graph
- Make a Table
- Write an Equation
- Make an Organized List
- Draw a Diagram
- Solve a Simpler Problem
- Logical Reasoning

Make a plan.
Choose a strategy.

Drawing a diagram will help you solve the problem.

You can draw a square on graph paper. Label the length of each side of the square. Draw and label dots to represent the nails every 7 centimeters. Then you can count the number of dots on the drawing to find the number of nails Mark uses.

Use with Grade 5, Chapter 8, Lesson 8, pages 372–373. (266)

Reteach

Problem Solving: Strategy
Draw a Diagram

R 8-8 RETEACH

Step 3 Solve

Carry out your plan.
Draw a diagram.

The piece of wood is square, so you should draw a square.

After you draw the diagram, place dots at the 4 corners of the square.

Then, draw a dot every 7 cm on the diagram. Keep in mind the length of each side of the square as you draw in each dot. Use the grid below to draw a diagram.

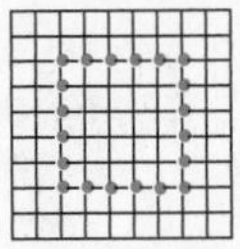

To find the number of nails Mark uses, count the number of dots on the diagram.

How many nails does Mark use? 20 nails

Step 4 Look Back

Is the solution reasonable?
Reread the problem.

Have you answered the question? Yes

How can you check that your answer is reasonable?
Answers may vary. Possible answer: Estimate the answer and check that the answer is close to the estimate.

Practice

1. A table 6 feet wide and 8 feet long is set so that there is a plate every 2 feet, except at the corners. How many plates are on the table?
   10 plates
2. To enclose a garden that is 15 feet long and 12 feet wide, fence posts are set every 3 feet, including the corners. How many posts are needed to enclose the yard?
   18 fence posts

Use with Grade 5, Chapter 8, Lesson 8, pages 372–373. (267)

Daily Homework

8·8 Problem Solving: Strategy
Draw a Diagram

Draw a diagram to solve.

1. LaTonya's father is building a fence for his garden. The garden is 40 feet by 20 feet. The fence will have fence posts at each corner and also at every 4 feet of fence. How many fence posts will be needed? 30
2. Ginny is going to the movies. She has a ticket for seat number 54. At the theater the first row has 10 seats, and the second row has 9 seats The following rows continue to alternate between 10 and 9 seats. In which row is Ginny's seat? 6th row
3. Joanie is taking a walk. She begins by heading north. After a while she turns to her left. Later she turns to the opposite direction. Finally, she turns right and then turns right again. In which direction is she now facing? West
4. Juanita wants to decorate a square picture frame. She wants to put six gold stars on each side, with an additional star at each corner. How many gold stars will she need? 28

Mixed Strategy Review

5. Calvin makes 8 telephone calls on Saturday. This is 4 less than 3 times the number of calls he makes on Sunday. How many telephone calls does Calvin make on Sunday? 4 calls
6. Claire has a piano lesson at 1:15 P.M. The lesson lasts 1 hour 30 minutes. Afterward she reads for 45 minutes, and then she spends 25 minutes doing exercises. At what time does Claire finish doing exercises? 3:55 P.M.

Spiral Review

Find the mean.

7. 13, 6, 12, 79, 15 25
8. 9, 14, 8, 12, 17 12
9. 6, 14, 12, 20, 22, 25 $16\frac{1}{2}$
10. 18, 36, 25, 21, 32, 42, 51 $32\frac{1}{7}$

82 Grade 5, Chapter 8, Lesson 6, Cluster B

Chapter 8 ~ Lesson 9

Practice

Temperature

P 8-9 PRACTICE

Estimate each temperature in °F and °C. Answers may vary. Possible answers are given.

1. comfortable room temperature 70°F; 21°C
2. cup of hot chocolate 140°F; 55°C
3. warm day 80°F; 26°C
4. glass of cold milk 40°F; 5°C
5. icy day 30°F; 0°C
6. boiling water 212°F; 100°C

Estimate each Fahrenheit temperature. Show your work.

7. 3°C ≈ 36 °F
   $2 \times 3 + 30 = 36$
8. 90°C ≈ 210 °F
   $2 \times 90 + 30 = 210$
9. 32°C ≈ 94 °F
   $2 \times 32 + 30 = 94$
10. 66°C ≈ 162 °F
    $2 \times 66 + 30 = 162$
11. 85°C ≈ 200 °F
    $2 \times 85 + 30 = 200$
12. 13°C ≈ 56 °F
    $2 \times 13 + 30 = 56$
13. 20°C ≈ 70 °F
    $2 \times 20 + 30 = 70$
14. 49°C ≈ 128 °F
    $2 \times 49 + 30 = 128$
15. 34°C ≈ 98 °F
    $2 \times 34 + 30 = 98$
16. 23°C ≈ 76 °F
    $2 \times 23 + 30 = 76$
17. 51°C ≈ 132 °F
    $2 \times 51 + 30 = 132$
18. 27°C ≈ 84 °F
    $2 \times 27 + 30 = 84$

Problem Solving

19. A weather forecast predicts that temperatures will fall from a high of 2°C and there will be precipitation. What form do you think the precipitation will take? Explain.
    ice or snow; 2°C is about 34°F. If the temperature falls, it could be cold enough for ice or snow.
20. Yesterday's low temperature was 18°C. The high temperature was 26°C. What was the temperature range in degrees Fahrenheit?
    about 16°F

Use with Grade 5, Chapter 8, Lesson 9, pages 374–375. (268)

Reteach

Temperature

R 8-9 RETEACH

Sometimes temperatures are given in degrees Celsius and sometimes in degrees Fahrenheit. If you are given a temperature in degrees Celsius, you can estimate the temperature in degrees Fahrenheit.

40 °C is about ▢ °F.

Double the Celsius temperature. ↓ 2 × 40   Add 30. ↓ + 30   = 80 + 30 = 110

So, 40°C is about 110°F.

Estimate each Fahrenheit temperature. Show your work.

1. 28°C ≈ ▢ °F
   2 × 28 + 30 = 56 + 30 = 86
   So, 28°C ≈ 86 °F.
2. 11°C = ▢ °F
   2 × 11 + 30 = 22 + 30 = 52
   So, 11 °C ≈ 52 °F.
3. 7°C ≈ ▢ °F
   2 × 7 + 30 = 14 + 30 = 44
   So, 7°C ≈ 44 °F.
4. 80°C ≈ 190 °F
   $2 \times 80 + 30 = 160 + 30 = 190$
5. 14°C ≈ 58 °F
   $2 \times 14 + 30 = 28 + 30 = 58$
6. 4°C ≈ 38 °F
   $2 \times 4 + 30 = 8 + 30 = 38$
7. 37°C ≈ 104 °F
   $2 \times 37 + 30 = 74 + 30 = 104$

Circle the most reasonable temperature for each.

	A	B	C
8. a cool autumn day	A 45°C	(B) 7°C	C 7°F
9. a cold winter day	A 20°C	B 70°F	(C) 20°F
10. cup of hot soup	(A) 140°F	B 310°F	C 140°C

Use with Grade 5, Chapter 8, Lesson 9, pages 374–375. (269)

Enrich

Temperature

E 8-9 ENRICH

Fahrenheit-Celsius Match-Up

Try to find a Fahrenheit temperature in Box B that is a close estimate of each Celsius temperature in Box A. When you find a match, cross out both numbers and the letters next to them.

To convert from Fahrenheit to Celsius, use this formula: $°C = \frac{5}{9}°F - 32$

To convert from Celsius to Fahrenheit, use this formula: $°F = \frac{9}{5}°C + 32$

Box A		Box B	
~~E. 3°C~~	T. 107°C	~~F. 36 °F~~	~~C. 90°F~~
O. 130°C	~~F. 100°C~~	T. 0°F	H. 100°F
~~G. 63°C~~	~~V. 30°C~~	~~S. 114°F~~	~~I. 30°F~~
~~B. 7°C~~	N. 14°C	~~B. 214°F~~	~~D. 156°F~~
~~P. 42°C~~	A. 36°C	~~K. 50°F~~	Y. 20°F
~~W. 10°C~~	~~H. 72°C~~	O. 6°F	~~L. 174°F~~
O. 25°C	~~C. 0°C~~	P. 84°F	~~E. 230°F~~
~~U. 55°C~~	~~S. 18°C~~	~~M. 44°F~~	~~R. 140°F~~
~~M. 92°C~~	R. 120°C	~~G. 200°F~~	O. 126°F
D. 80°C	~~L. 85°C~~	N. 300°F	~~A. 66°F~~

Now write the letters that remain in each box. Unscramble each group of letters to spell a weather word.

Box A T O R N A D O

Box B T Y P H O O N

How did you find a close estimate in degrees Fahrenheit for 42°C?
Answers may vary. Possible answer: $\frac{9}{5}$ is close to 2 and 32 is close to 30, so I multiplied 42 × 2 and added 30.

Use with Grade 5, Chapter 8, Lesson 9, pages 374–375. (270)

Daily Homework

8-9 Temperature

Estimate each temperature in °F and °C.
Answers may vary. Possible answers are given.

1. cool autumn day 50°F, 10°C
2. classroom 68°F, 20°C
3. hot chocolate 160°F, 65°C

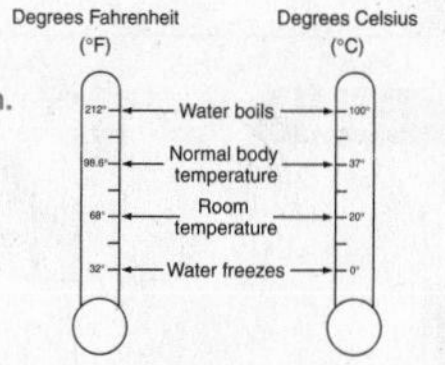

Estimate each Fahrenheit temperature.

4. 15°C = 60 °F
5. 18°C = 66 °F
6. 42°C = 114 °F
7. 70°C = 170 °F
8. 23°C = 76 °F
9. 53°C = 136 °F
10. 76°C = 182 °F
11. 62°C = 154 °F
12. 82°C = 194 °F

Problem Solving

13. In Christy's family's new refrigerator, all the temperature gauges are in Celsius. Christy checks the temperature in the freezer. It is 4°C. Should she adjust it? If so, why?
    Yes, 4°C is above freezing. Unless the temperature is lowered, everything in the freezer will melt.
14. Tricia's school group is traveling to Paris, but she isn't sure what kind of clothes to pack. During the week of the visit, temperatures in Paris are expected to be near 30°C. Should Tricia bring cool clothes or warm clothes? Explain your answer.
    A temperature of 30°C is quite warm to hot. She needs cool clothing.

Spiral Review

15. $4\frac{1}{2} \times 2\frac{2}{3}$ 12
16. $6\frac{1}{8} \div 7$ $\frac{7}{8}$
17. $2\frac{3}{4} \times 1\frac{2}{3}$ $4\frac{7}{12}$
18. $2\frac{2}{5} \div \frac{2}{5}$ 6

Grade 5, Chapter 8, Lesson 9, Cluster B 83

Chapter 8 ~ Lesson 10

Part A Worksheet

Problem Solving: Application

Part A 8-10 WORKSHEET
Decision Making

The table shows the costs for different Internet providers that Adela is considering.

Internet Service Providers			
Company	**Cost per Month**	**Minutes per Month**	**E-mail Messages per Month**
Adelphi	$19.95	500	250
Baretta	$15.00	450	150
Cameo	$20.00	450	No limit
Darden	$10.00	225	100

What do you think are the advantages and disadvantages of each company? Record your opinions in the table below. Answers may vary.

Company	Advantages	Disadvantages
Adelphi		
Baretta		
Cameo		
Darden		

Your Decision

What is your recommendation? Which Internet service provider should Adela choose? Explain.

Answers may vary. Possible answer: Darden, because it costs the least per month.

Use with Grade 5, Chapter 8, Lesson 10, pages 376–377. (271)

Part B Worksheet

Problem Solving: Application

Part B 8-10 WORKSHEET
Math & Science

How does temperature affect how fast salt dissolves?

Remember to wear your goggles when you perform the experiment. Be careful when you work with hot water.

Work with a partner. Decide how you will be able to recognize that the salt has dissolved. Also decide how you will determine if the water is cold, cool, warm, or hot.

You may want to try dissolving salt in some water before you actually time how long it takes so that you are able to recognize when the salt is dissolved in the water.

Collect all the materials that you will need for the experiment. Then put your goggles on before you start. Be careful to measure the same amount of water and the same amount of salt for the different water temperatures. Measure the water temperature to the nearest degree.

Record your data in the table below.

Water	Temperature	Time to Dissolve
Cold		
Cool		
Warm		
Hot		

1. For which temperature of water did the salt dissolve the fastest? the slowest? Explain.
   The salt dissolved fastest in hot water and slowest in cold water.

Use with Grade 5, Chapter 8, Lesson 10, pages 378–379. (272)

Part B Worksheet

Problem Solving: Application

Part B 8-10 WORKSHEET
Math & Science

How does temperature affect how fast salt dissolves?

2. Describe any pattern you see in the data. Is the pattern consistent with your hypothesis? Explain.
   Answers may vary. Possible answer: Salt dissolves more quickly as the water temperature increases. Yes, this is what I thought would happen.
3. Compare your data with the data of some of your classmates. How does the data compare?
   Answers may vary. Possible answer: It is similar.
4. Did everyone record the same water temperature for cold, cool, warm, and hot? Why or why not?
   Answers may vary. Possible answer: No, each label can mean a variety of temperatures.
5. Make a graph to show your data in the space below. Check students' graphs.

   Work Space

6. Compare your graphs with the graphs of some of your classmates. How do the graphs compare?
   Answers may vary. Possible answer: They are similar.

Use with Grade 5, Chapter 8, Lesson 10, pages 378–379. (273)

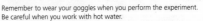

Chapter 9 ~ Lesson 1

Practice

Integers and the Number Line: Comparing and Ordering Integers

P 9-1 PRACTICE

Write an integer to represent each situation.

1. spent $15 -15
2. 11 degrees colder than 0°F -11
3. 8-yard gain in football +8
4. deposit of $25 into bank account +25
5. 10 feet below sea level -10
6. 3-centimeter increase in height +3
7. withdrawal of $50 from bank account -50
8. received $5 allowance +5
9. speed increase of 15 mph +15
10. 30 seconds before liftoff -30

Compare. Write < or >. You may use a number line.

11. -2 (<) 4
12. 3 (>) -7
13. -6 (>) -9
14. -5 (<) 1
15. 6 (>) -8
16. -4 (<) 0
17. -3 (>) -10
18. 6 (>) -6
19. -12 (<) -10
20. 13 (>) -17
21. 0 (>) -17
22. -14 (<) 21

Order the integers from least to greatest.

23. -8, 3, -6 -8, -6, 3
24. -1, 1, -2 -2, -1, 1
25. -5, 0, -2 -5, -2, 0
26. -4, -6, -3 -6, -4, -3
27. 1, 0, -7 -7, 0, 1
28. 9, -8, 8 -8, 8, 9
29. -12, 6, -9 -12, -9, 6
30. -1, -5, 1 -5, -1, 1

Problem Solving

31. The low temperature on Saturday was -5°F. The low temperature on Sunday was -9°F. Which day was colder?

Sunday

32. On one play a football team moved the ball -6 yards. On the next play, they moved the ball exactly the opposite. Did they gain or lose yards on the second play? How many yards?

gain; 6 yd

Use with Grade 5, Chapter 9, Lesson 1, pages 394–397. (274)

Reteach

Integers and the Number Line: Comparing and Ordering Integers

R 9-1 RETEACH

On a number line, numbers become greater as you move from left to right. You can use a number line to compare and order integers.

Compare: -5 ◯ 3

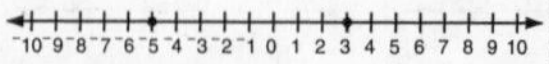

-5 is to the left of 3, so -5 is less than 3.
-5 < 3.

Order from least to greatest: -4, 6, -8

Read the integers from left to right.
The order from least to greatest is -8, -4, 6.

Compare. You may use a number line to help you.

1. -9 is to the left of 7, so -9 (<) 7.
2. 4 is to the right of -4, so 4 (>) -4.
3. -7 is to the right of -8, so -7 (>) -8.
4. -10 is to the left of 0, so -10 (<) 0.

5. 3 (>) -5
6. -6 (<) -4
7. 0 (>) -3
8. 7 (>) -1
9. -7 (<) 2
10. -8 (<) 3
11. -2 (>) -5
12. 6 (>) -6
13. -9 (<) 0
14. -4 (>) -8
15. -6 (<) 10
16. -7 (<) -5

Write the integers in order from least to greatest. You may use a number line to help.

17. 9, -3, -6 -6, -3, 9
18. -8, 5, 0 -8, 0, 5
19. -1, -9, -5 -9, -5, -1
20. 10, -10, 8 -10, 8, 10
21. -4, 3, -2 -4, -2, 3
22. 8, -3, 0 -3, 0, 8
23. 9, -5, -9 -9, -5, 9
24. -7, -3, -8 -8, -7, -3

Use with Grade 5, Chapter 9, Lesson 1, pages 394–397. (275)

Enrich

Integers and the Number Line: Comparing and Ordering Integers

E 9-1 ENRICH

"And" or "Or"?

Think carefully when you read statements that include the words *and* and *or*.

Examples

Graph the integers that are greater than -5 **and** less than 3.

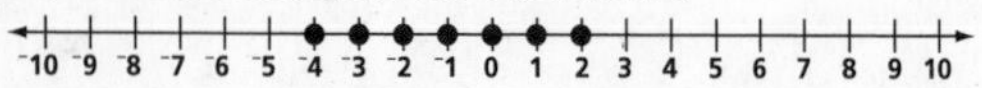

Graph the integers that are greater than 3 **or** less than -5.

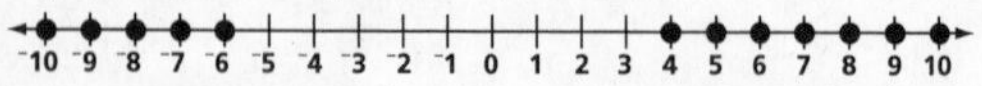

Graph each set of integers.

1. Graph the integers that are greater than -1 and less than 10.

2. Graph the integers that are greater than 0 or less than -3.

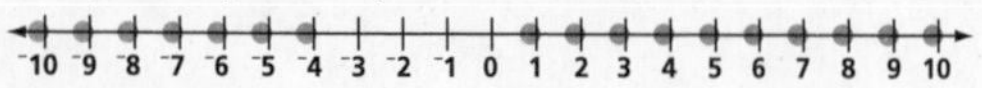

3. Graph the integers that are greater than -9 and less than -2.

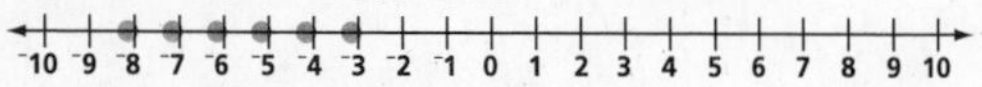

4. Graph the integers that are greater than 4 or less than -4.

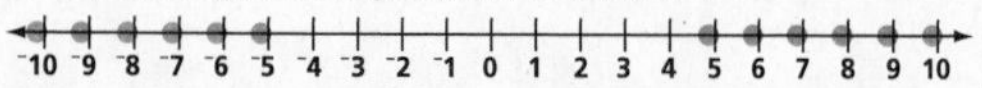

5. Graph the integers that are greater than -6 and less than 6.

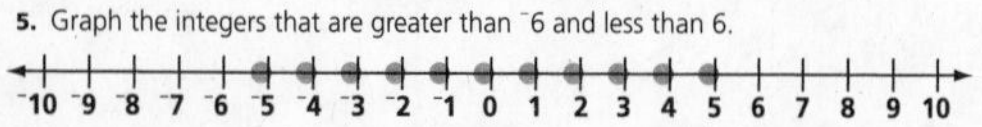

What is another way to describe the integers that are greater than -6 and less than 6?

Answers may vary. Possible answer: The integers between -6 and 6.

Use with Grade 5, Chapter 9, Lesson 1, pages 394–397. (276)

Daily Homework

9-1 Integers and the Number Line: Comparing and Ordering Integers

Write an integer to represent each situation.

1. A hot air balloon descends 300 feet. -300
2. Michele earns $5.00 selling lemonade. +$5
3. Paula took $25.95 out of her bank account. -$25.95
4. An elevator goes from the seventh floor to the third floor. -4

Compare. Write < or >. You may use a number line.

5. 1 > -3
6. -6 < 2
7. -8 < -2
8. -4 < 5
9. 0 > -2
10. -14 < 13
11. -17 < 13
12. 17 > -13

Order the integers from least to greatest.

13. -6, 6, 0 -6, 0, 6
14. 1, -2, 3 -2, 1, 3
15. 5, -4, 3 -4, 3, 5
16. -2, -3, 2 -3, -2, 2
17. 4, 0, -3 -3, 0, 4
18. 1, 0, -3 -3, 0, 1

Problem Solving

19. Marcia and her friends are hiking up a mountain. When they reach the 1,500-foot level, they stop to rest. The next time they stop, they have climbed another 500 feet. How far up the mountain are they when they stop the second time? 2,000 feet

20. At the start of the month Billy has $50.63 in his bank account. During the month he takes out $10.40. What is his account balance at the end of the month? $40.23

Spiral Review

Find the GCF.

21. 12, 20 4
22. 36, 30 6
23. 14, 54 2
24. 9, 6 3

84 Grade 5, Chapter 9, Lesson 1, Cluster A

Chapter 9 ~ Lesson 2

Practice

Explore Adding Integers

P 9-2 PRACTICE

Add.

1. ⊕⊕⊕⊕⊕⊕⊕ ⊖⊖
$7 + (^-2) =$ 5

2. ⊕⊕⊕⊕⊕⊕ ⊖⊖⊖⊖⊖⊖
$6 + (^-6) =$ 0

3. ⊖⊖⊖⊖⊖⊖⊖⊖ ⊕⊕⊕
$^-8 + 3 =$ $^-5$

4. ⊖⊖⊖ ⊖⊖⊖
$^-3 + (^-3) =$ $^-6$

5. ⊕⊕ ⊖⊖⊖⊖⊖⊖
$2 + (^-6) =$ $^-4$

6. ⊖⊖⊖⊖⊖⊖ ⊕⊕⊕⊕⊕⊕⊕⊕
$^-6 + 8 =$ 2

7. $9 + (^-3) =$ 6
8. $4 + (^-9) =$ $^-5$
9. $^-4 + (^-4) =$ $^-8$
10. $^-2 + 5 =$ 3
11. $8 + (^-8) =$ 0
12. $^-7 + 2 =$ $^-5$
13. $^-5 + (^-2) =$ $^-7$
14. $3 + (^-2) =$ 1
15. $^-8 + 10 =$ 2
16. $3 + (^-8) =$ $^-5$
17. $^-6 + (^-6) =$ $^-12$
18. $^-9 + 3 =$ $^-6$
19. $7 + (^-4) =$ 3
20. $^-6 + 5 =$ $^-1$
21. $1 + (^-10) =$ $^-9$
22. $^-2 + (^-7) =$ $^-9$
23. $^-1 + 9 =$ 8
24. $^-7 + 7 =$ 0
25. $^-7 + (^-3) =$ $^-10$
26. $10 + (^-3) =$ 7
27. $^-3 + (^-9) =$ $^-12$
28. $6 + (^-7) =$ $^-1$
29. $^-10 + 4 =$ $^-6$
30. $^-4 + 8 =$ 4

Problem Solving

31. Each week Martin received $8 allowance. He spent $5. How much did Martin have left to put in savings?
$3

32. The low temperature one day was $^-2$°F. The temperature rose 6° during the day. What was the high temperature?
4 °F

Use with Grade 5, Chapter 9, Lesson 2, pages 398–399. (277)

Reteach

Explore Adding Integers

R 9-2 RETEACH

You can draw a diagram to help you add integers.

Add: $3 + {}^-5$

Draw positive and negative signs to show 3 and $^-5$.
3: + + +
$^-5$: − − − − −

Circle pairs of one positive sign and one negative sign.
3: (+)(+)(+)
$^-5$: (−)(−)(−) − −

Count the unpaired signs. ↑ 2 negative signs

$3 + (^-5) = {}^-2$

Draw a diagram to find the total. Check students' diagrams.

1. 4: (+) + + +
$^-1$: (−)
$4 + (^-1) =$ 3

2. $^-5$: (−)(−)(−)(−)(−)
7: (+)(+)(+)(+)(+) + +
$^-5 + 7 =$ 2

3. 3: (+)(+)(+)
$^-3$: (−)(−)(−)
$3 + (^-3) =$ 0

4. $^-2$: − −
$^-2$: − −
$^-2 + (^-2) =$ $^-4$

5. $^-4$: (−) − − −
1: (+)
$^-4 + 1 =$ $^-3$

6. 2: (+)(+)
$^-6$: (−)(−) − − − −
$2 + (^-6) =$ $^-4$

Add. You may draw diagrams.

7. $8 + (^-5) =$ 3
8. $^-3 + (^-3) =$ $^-6$
9. $7 + (^-9) =$ $^-2$
10. $^-4 + 4 =$ 0
11. $^-6 + 7 =$ 1
12. $^-3 + (^-6) =$ $^-9$
13. $^-9 + 4 =$ $^-5$
14. $9 + (^-10) =$ $^-1$
15. $^-6 + 2 =$ $^-4$
16. $4 + (^-7) =$ $^-3$
17. $^-1 + 7 =$ 6
18. $2 + (^-2) =$ 0

Use with Grade 5, Chapter 9, Lesson 2, pages 398–399. (278)

Enrich

Explore Adding Integers
Boating with Integers

E 9-2 ENRICH

Find each sum. You may use counters to help.

W. $^-2 + (^-5) =$ $^-7$
T. $7 + 8 =$ 15
O. $5 + 7 =$ 12
S. $9 + 9 =$ 18
A. $9 + 4 =$ 13
E. $7 + (^-7) =$ 0
E. $2 + (^-6) =$ $^-4$
O. $^-1 + 6 =$ 5
H. $^-5 + (^-9) =$ $^-14$
R. $^-9 + 7 =$ $^-2$
B. $4 + 6 =$ 10
E. $^-3 + (^-9) =$ $^-12$
T. $^-9 + (^-8) =$ $^-17$
W. $(^-1) + 8 =$ 7
R. $^-6 + 9 =$ 3
Y. $^-4 + (^-7) =$ $^-11$

To solve the riddle, write the sums in order from least to greatest under each answer line. Then write the letter of the exercise having that sum above each answer line.

Why were the boats all lined up?

T	H	E	Y		W	E	R	E
$^-17$	$^-14$	$^-12$	$^-11$		$^-7$	$^-4$	$^-2$	0

R	O	W	B	O	A	T	S
3	5	7	10	12	13	15	18

Use with Grade 5, Chapter 9, Lesson 2, pages 398–399. (279)

Daily Homework

9•2 Explore Adding Integers

Add.

1. $5 + 2 =$ 7
2. $^-8 + 3 =$ $^-5$
3. $5 + {}^-2 =$ 3
4. $7 + {}^-8 =$ $^-1$
5. $0 + {}^-3 =$ $^-3$
6. $7 + 4 =$ 11
7. $0 + {}^-9 =$ $^-9$
8. $^-6 + {}^-4 =$ $^-10$
9. $8 + {}^-8 =$ 0
10. $^-6 + 4 =$ $^-2$
11. $5 + {}^-5 =$ 0
12. $^-9 + {}^-2 =$ $^-11$
13. $6 + 4 =$ 10
14. $9 + {}^-3 =$ 6
15. $^-8 + 4 =$ $^-4$
16. $^-12 + 0 =$ $^-12$
17. $^-18 + {}^-3 =$ $^-21$
18. $^-9 + 3 =$ $^-6$
19. $6 + {}^-6 =$ 0
20. $12 - 14 =$ $^-2$
21. $^-8 + {}^-4 =$ $^-12$
22. $^-5 + 6 =$ 1
23. $8 + 3 =$ 11
24. $16 + {}^-9 =$ 7

Solve.

25. On the same day that Sandy withdraws $35 from her bank account, she also deposits a check for $45. Use a signed number to show how her bank account has changed. $^+$$10

26. When Dave reads the thermometer at 4 P.M., the temperature is 63°F. At 6 P.M. the temperature is 58°F. Use a signed number to show how the temperature has changed. $^-5$° F

Spiral Review

27. $2.35 \div 0.05 =$ 47
28. $8.34 \times 0.05 =$ 0.4170
29. $6 - 1.05 =$ 4.95
30. $6.25 + 10.324 =$ 16.574

Grade 5, Chapter 9, Lesson 2, Cluster A 85

Chapter 9 ~ Lesson 3

Practice

Add Integers

P 9-3 PRACTICE

Add.

1. -2 + (-2) = -4
2. 7 + 6 = 13
3. 1 + (-8) = -7
4. -10 + 10 = 0
5. 3 + (-1) = 2
6. -5 + (-6) = -11
7. -7 + 10 = 3
8. -9 + 4 = -5
9. -8 + 9 = 1
10. -3 + (-9) = -12
11. -1 + 8 = 7
12. 3 + (-3) = 0
13. 7 + (-4) = 3
14. -7 + 2 = -5
15. 2 + (-9) = -7
16. 8 + (-8) = 0
17. -16 + 7 = -9
18. 8 + (-2) = 6
19. 4 + (-13) = -9
20. -9 + 18 = 9
21. -5 + 5 = 0
22. 10 + (-4) = 6
23. 5 + (-12) = -7
24. 17 + (-9) = 8
25. 2 + (-3) + 1 = 0
26. 5 + (-6) + (-4) = -5
27. 12 + (-9) + 3 = 6
28. 13 + 5 + (-9) = 9
29. 3 + (-11) + 5 = -3
30. -3 + 14 + (-9) = 2

Complete the function tables.

31. $y = x + 3$

x	y
-8	-5
-6	-3
-3	0
0	3
4	7

32. $y = x + (-7)$

x	y
-9	-16
-4	-11
0	-7
5	-2
9	2

33. $y = x + (-10)$

x	y
-10	-20
-2	-12
0	-10
4	-6
10	0

Problem Solving

34. A diver descends 80 feet below sea level. She rises 15 feet. How far below sea level is she?

65 feet

35. Along the shore line a rock 25 feet tall rises from 8 feet below sea level. How much of the rock is above sea level?

17 feet

Reteach

Add Integers

R 9-3 RETEACH

You can use a number line to add integers.

Add: 2 + (-7)

Find 2. Move to the left to add a negative integer. So, move 7 spaces to the left.

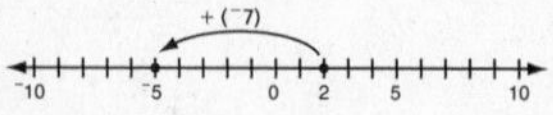

2 + (-7) = -5

Add: -7 + 5

Find -7. Move to the right to add a positive integer. So, move 5 spaces to the right.

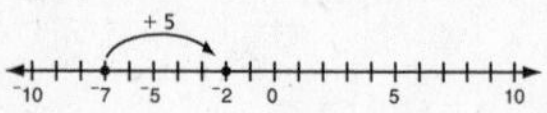

-7 + 5 = -2

Show each sum on the number line. Then record the sum.

1.

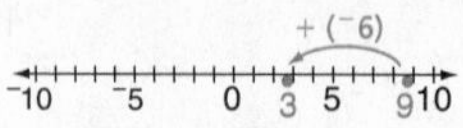

9 + (-6) = 3

2.

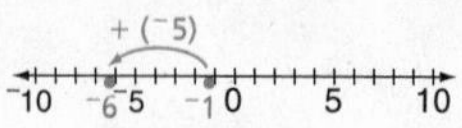

-1 + (-5) = -6

3.

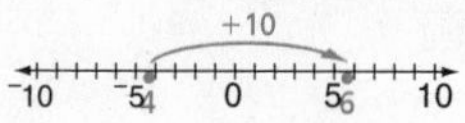

-4 + 10 = 6

4.

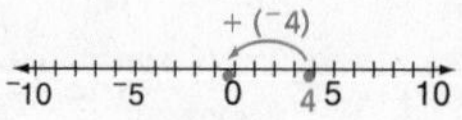

4 + (-4) = 0

5.

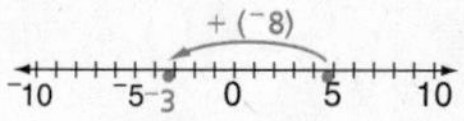

5 + (-8) = -3

6.

-8 + 2 = -6

Add.

7. -8 + (-2) = -10
8. 6 + 3 = 9
9. 3 + -7 = -4
10. 8 + (-7) = 1
11. 5 + (-5) = 0
12. -5 + 9 = 4
13. 2 + (-8) = -6
14. -10 + 3 = -7
15. -4 + (-4) = -8
16. -6 + 6 = 0
17. 7 + (-2) = 5
18. -3 + 8 = 5

Enrich

Add Integers

Target Zero

E 9-3 ENRICH

For each set of digits, write a negative or positive sign in front of each digit to create a set of integers. Then find the sum of the integers. Your goal is to create integers with a sum as close to zero as possible.

Answers may vary. One possible set of signs and sum is shown for each.

1. [+] 8 [-] 2 [-] 2 Sum: 4
2. [-] 1 [-] 7 [+] 5 [+] 6 Sum: 3
3. [-] 9 [-] 4 [-] 2 [+] 8 [+] 8 Sum: 1
4. [-] 6 [-] 5 [+] 9 [-] 8 [+] 3 [+] 7 Sum: 0
5. [-] 3 [-] 6 [+] 9 [-] 3 [-] 2 [+] 4 Sum: -1
6. [+] 7 [-] 4 [+] 1 [+] 8 [-] 3 [-] 7 [-] 2 Sum: 0
7. [-] 1 [+] 5 [-] 3 [+] 6 [+] 7 [-] 3 [-] 6 [-] 4 Sum: 1
8. [+] 6 [-] 1 [+] 2 [+] 5 [-] 2 [+] 9 [-] 7 [-] 8 [-] 3 Sum: 1
9. [-] 5 [-] 7 [-] 3 [+] 8 [+] 6 [-] 4 [+] 2 [+] 1 [-] 8 [+] 9 Sum: -1

Describe the strategy you used to create each set of integers.

Answers may vary. Possible answer: I looked for two digits that were the same or two pairs of digits whose sums were the same. I wrote a positive sign by one and a negative sign by the other because, together, their sums equal zero. Then I used guess, test, and revise with the remaining digits.

Daily Homework

9-3 Add Integers

1. 5 + 7 = 12
2. -7 + 4 = -3
3. 6 + -3 = 3
4. 3 + -7 = -4
5. 0 + -4 = -4
6. 3 + 5 = 8
7. 0 + -8 = -8
8. -5 + -3 = -8
9. 5 + -5 = 0
10. -6 + 8 = 2
11. 7 + -8 = -1
12. -2 + 2 = 0

Complete the function tables.

$y = 2x + ^-3$

	x	y
13.	-6	-15
14.	-3	-9
15.	0	-3
16.	1	-1
17.	3	3

$y = x + ^-4$

	x	y
18.	-5	-9
19.	-2	-6
20.	0	-4
21.	3	-1
22.	6	2

Problem Solving

23. An elevator stops at the 54th floor of a skyscraper. Then it rises 5 floors, then descends 8 floors. On what floor is the elevator now? 51st floor

24. A telephone pole is 30 feet long. It is sunk 6 feet into the ground when it is put into service. How high off the ground is the top of the pole? 24 feet

Spiral Review

25. $4\frac{2}{3} + 5\frac{1}{2} = 10\frac{1}{6}$
26. $7\frac{1}{3} - 2\frac{1}{2} = 4\frac{5}{6}$
27. $\frac{5}{8} + 3\frac{2}{5} = 4\frac{1}{40}$
28. $5 - 2\frac{1}{4} = 2\frac{3}{4}$
29. $6\frac{1}{2} + 5\frac{3}{8} = 11\frac{7}{8}$
30. $12\frac{5}{6} - 7\frac{11}{15} = 5\frac{1}{10}$

Chapter 9 ~ Lesson 4

Practice

Problem Solving: Reading for Math
Check the reasonableness of an answer

P 9-4 PRACTICE — Reading Skill

The table shows temperature data collected over a five-day period.

Day	High Temperature (°F)	Low Temperature (°F)
Monday	18°	$^{-}28$°
Tuesday	14°	$^{-}2$°
Wednesday	8°	$^{-}5$°
Thursday	32°	0°
Friday	16°	$^{-}3$°

Use data from the table.

1. Mike thinks that some of the temperatures were recorded incorrectly when the data was put into the table. He examines the data for the high temperatures over the five-day period recorded in the table. Do any of the temperature entries seem unreasonable? Explain.
   Yes, the entry for Thursday seems too high. It is much higher than the other high temperatures.
2. Mike also examines the data for the low temperatures over the five-day period recorded in the table. Do any of the temperature entries seem unreasonable? Explain.
   Yes, the entry for Monday seems too low. It is much lower than the other low temperatures.
3. Mike considers the high and low temperature recorded for each day. Do any of the differences between the high and low temperatures seem unreasonable? Explain.
   Yes, the temperature differences on Monday and Thursday seem extreme.
4. What if the low temperature on Monday was actually $^{-}1$°F. Does this temperature seem unreasonable compared to the other low temperatures for the five-day period? Explain.
   No, it is in the same range as the other low temperatures.
5. Do you think that a forecast for a high temperature of 60°F on Saturday would be a reasonable temperature forecast? Explain.
   No, it is too high.

Use with Grade 5, Chapter 9, Lesson 4, pages 404–405. (283)

Practice

Problem Solving: Reading for Math
Check the reasonableness of an answer

P 9-4 PRACTICE — Math Skills Test Prep

Choose the correct answer.

At 1 A.M., the air temperature was $^{-}4$°F. By 5 A.M., the temperature had fallen 2°F. The temperature at 5 A.M. was $^{-}6$°F.

1. Which of the following statements is true?
   - A The air temperature was 2°F at 5 A.M.
   - (B) The air temperature fell from 1 A.M. to 5 A.M.
   - C The air temperature fell 2°F every hour.
   - D The air temperature rose from 1 A.M. to 5 A.M.
2. When you check the reasonableness of an answer, you
   - F guess the answer.
   - G look for more than one answer.
   - (H) compare and contrast the answer with what you know.
   - J make sure all your computations are correct.

The low temperature on Monday, recorded at 6 A.M., was 3°F. By 4 P.M., the temperature had risen 19°F to the high temperature of 22°F for the day.

3. Which of the following statements is true?
   - A The air temperature was warmer at 6 A.M. than at 4 P.M.
   - B The air temperature fell 3°F from 6 A.M. to 4 P.M.
   - C The air temperature was 19°F at 4 P.M.
   - (D) The air temperature rose from 6 A.M. to 4 P.M.
4. Which of the following is NOT a reasonable temperature for the temperature at noon?
   - (F) 0°F
   - G 12°F
   - H 18°F
   - J 20°F

A lifeguard is checking the temperature at a swimming pool. At 9 A.M., the temperature is 62°F. After turning the heater on, the temperature rises 8°F by noon.

5. Which of the following statements is true?
   - (A) The water temperature at noon is higher than the water temperature at 9 A.M.
   - B The water temperature at noon is lower than the water temperature at 9 A.M.
   - C The water temperature remains constant.
   - D The water temperature at noon is 8°F.
6. Which of the following should you do to check that an answer is reasonable?
   - F Compare the answer with the data in the problem.
   - G Reverse the order of operations to check the answer.
   - H Solve the problem two different ways.
   - (J) Determine whether the answer makes sense.

Use with Grade 5, Chapter 9, Lesson 4, pages 404–405. (284)

Practice

Problem Solving: Reading for Math
Check the reasonableness of an answer

P 9-4 PRACTICE — Math Skills Test Prep

Choose the correct answer.

The evening temperature of the water in a pond is 42°F. By midnight, the temperature of the pond fell 4°F.

7. Which of the following statements is true?
   - A The temperature of the pond at midnight is 4°F.
   - (B) The temperature of the pond at midnight is 38°F.
   - C The temperature of the pond at midnight is 42°F.
   - D The temperature of the pond at midnight is 46°F.
8. When you check the reasonableness of an answer, you
   - (F) compare the answer with known facts.
   - G try a different strategy to solve.
   - H do all the calculations twice.
   - J guess whether the answer makes sense.

The table shows temperature readings from midnight to noon.

Use data from the table for problems 9–12.

Time	Temperature (°F)
Midnight	$^{-}5$°
3 A.M.	0°
6 A.M.	$^{-}8$°
9 A.M.	6°
Noon	15°

9. Wilma said that the lowest temperature occurred at 6 A.M. Is her statement reasonable? Explain.
   Yes, $^{-}8 < {}^{-}5 < 0 < 6 < 15$
10. Alfred commented that the temperature fell from 6 A.M. to 9 A.M. Is his statement reasonable? Explain.
    No, the temperature rose from 6 A.M. to 9 A.M.
11. Do all the entries in the table seem reasonable? Explain.
    No. Answers may vary. Possible answer: The temperature at 3 A.M. seems unreasonable. It is unlikely that the temperature rose from midnight to 3 A.M. and then fell from 3 A.M. to 6 A.M.
12. Did the temperature change more from 6 A.M. to 9 A.M. or from 9 A.M. to noon? Explain.
    The temperature changed more from 6 a.m. to 9 a.m. since the difference is 14°; the 9 a.m. to noon difference is 9°.

Use with Grade 5, Chapter 9, Lesson 4, pages 404–405. (285)

Daily Homework

9•4 Problem Solving: Reading for Math
Check the Reasonableness of an Answer

Use the data from the graph to answer problems 1–5.

Temperature Readings at Three Locations

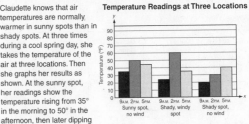

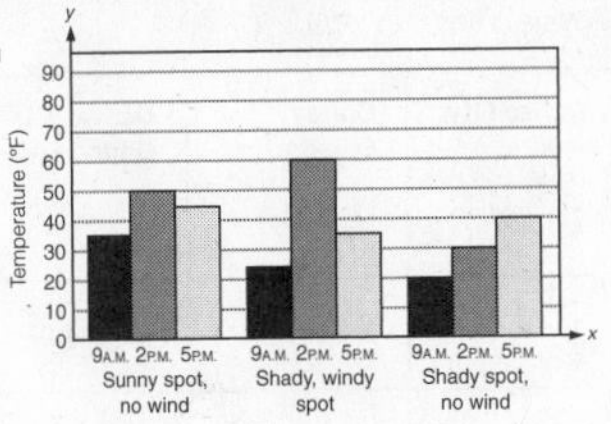

1. Claudette knows that air temperatures are normally warmer in sunny spots than in shady spots. At three times during a cool spring day, she takes the temperature of the air at three locations. Then she graphs her results as shown. At the sunny spot, her readings show the temperature rising from 35° in the morning to 50° in the afternoon, then later dipping to 45°. Is this reasonable?
   Yes; as the sun warms the air, its temperature rises.
2. At the shady, windy spot, her readings show the temperature starting out lower than in the sunny spot, then rising to 60°. Is this reasonable?
   No; the temperature at the sunny spot only reaches 50°, and a shady spot is unlikely to be warmer.
3. At the shady spot with no wind, her readings show the temperature reaching 30° by 2:00 P.M., then rising to 40° by 5:00 P.M. Is this reasonable?
   No; the temperature at the other two locations dropped from 2:00 P.M. to 5:00 P.M. A rise in temperature at the third location is not reasonable.
4. Claudette writes that in the sunny spot, the temperature rose by 15°F between 9:00 A.M. and 2:00 P.M. Is her statement reasonable?
   Yes; 50° − 35° = 15°.

Spiral Review

5. 44 mo = 3 y 8 mo
6. 100 min = 1 h 40 min

Grade 5, Chapter 9, Lesson 4, Cluster A 87

Chapter 9 ~ Lesson 5

Practice

Explore Subtracting Integers

P 9-5 PRACTICE

Subtract.

1. 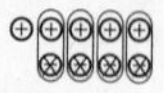
$1 - (^-4) =$ 5

2. 
$^-4 - 4 =$ $^-8$

3. 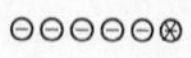
$^-6 - (^-1) =$ $^-5$

4. 
$2 - 3 =$ $^-1$

5. 
$^-1 - (^-3) =$ 2

6. 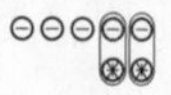
$^-3 - 2 =$ $^-5$

7. $^-2 - 6 =$ $^-8$
8. $^-4 - (^-6) =$ 2
9. $^-7 - (^-5) =$ $^-2$
10. $4 - (^-5) =$ 9
11. $^-2 - (^-7) =$ 5
12. $^-3 - 3 =$ $^-6$
13. $^-5 - (^-5) =$ 0
14. $5 - (^-5) =$ 10
15. $^-1 - (^-9) =$ 8
16. $^-7 - 7 =$ $^-14$
17. $^-6 - (^-9) =$ 3
18. $9 - (^-1) =$ 10
19. $^-5 - 4 =$ $^-9$
20. $6 - 9 =$ $^-3$
21. $^-3 - (^-3) =$ 0
22. $^-9 - (^-4) =$ $^-5$
23. $3 - (^-4) =$ 7
24. $^-8 - 6 =$ $^-14$
25. $7 - (^-10) =$ $^-3$
26. $^-5 - 6 =$ $^-11$
27. $^-10 - (^-7) =$ $^-3$
28. $1 - (^-6) =$ 7
29. $^-8 - (^-2) =$ $^-6$
30. $^-9 - 3 =$ $^-12$

Draw counters to represent the situation. Then solve.

Problem Solving

31. Yesterday's low temperature was $^-2$°F. The high temperature was 8°F. What was the difference between yesterday's high and low temperatures?

10°

Use with Grade 5, Chapter 9, Lesson 5, pages 408–409. (286)

Reteach

Explore Subtracting Integers

R 9-5 RETEACH

You can draw a diagram to help you subtract integers.

Subtract: $^-6 - 5$

Draw negative signs to show $^-6$. — — — — — —

Draw enough pairs of positive and negative signs to have 5 to subtract. — — — — — — 

Subtract 5. — — — — — — 

Count the signs that are not crossed out.

$^-6 - 5 = {}^-11$

11 negative signs are left.

Draw a diagram to find the difference. Check students' diagrams.

1. + +
$2 - (^-3) =$ 5

2. — — —
$^-3 - 1 =$ $^-4$

3. — — — —
$^-4 - (^-4) =$ 0

Subtract. You may draw diagrams.

4. $^-5 - (^-2) =$ $^-3$
5. $^-2 - (^-4) =$ 2
6. $4 - 6 =$ $^-2$
7. $^-2 - 2 =$ $^-4$
8. $5 - (^-1) =$ 6
9. $^-1 - 6 =$ $^-7$
10. $1 - 6 =$ $^-5$
11. $^-5 - (^-3) =$ $^-2$
12. $^-3 - (^-3) =$ 0
13. $^-2 - (^-6) =$ 4
14. $1 - (^-5) =$ 6
15. $3 - 5 =$ $^-2$
16. $^-6 - (^-4) =$ $^-2$
17. $^-1 - (^-4) =$ 3
18. $^-4 - (^-5) =$ 1
19. $^-3 - 4 =$ $^-7$
20. $6 - 7 =$ $^-1$
21. $^-7 - (^-7) =$ 0
22. $4 - (^-3) =$ 7
23. $^-8 - (^-4) =$ $^-4$
24. $^-6 - 2 =$ $^-8$

Use with Grade 5, Chapter 9, Lesson 5, pages 408–409. (287)

Enrich

Explore Subtracting Integers

E 9-5 ENRICH

Altitude Maze

Draw a path through this maze. Starting in the top row, find the square that shows the least difference. Move to the touching square that has the next least difference. You can move horizontally, vertically, or diagonally. Continue until you have reached the greatest difference. You may use counters to help.

Mexico City, Mexico $^-1 - (^-9)$ 8	**Quito, Ecuador** $^-4 - 5$ $^-9$	**Denver, CO United States** $^-2 - {}^-7$ 5	**Bogota, Colombia** $^-3 - (^-7)$ 4	**Jerusalem, Israel** $4 - (^-1)$ 5
$^-2 - 6$ $^-8$	$8 - 14$ $^-6$	$^-7 - (^-14)$ 7	$2 - (^-1)$ 3	$^-2 - (^-8)$ 6
$^-3 - 4$ $^-7$	$7 - 12$ $^-5$	$^-6 - (^-8)$ 2	$^-3 - (^-10)$ 7	$^-1 - 5$ $^-6$
$^-2 - 2$ $^-4$	$3 - (^-1)$ 4	$^-6 - (^-6)$ 0	$6 - (^-2)$ 8	$5 - 12$ $^-7$
$0 - 3$ $^-3$ **Washington, D.C. United States**	$6 - 8$ $^-2$ **Rome, Italy**	$8 - 9$ $^-1$ **Bombay, India**	$^-3 - (^-6)$ 3 **Athens, Greece**	$2 - (^-7)$ 9 **Buenos Aires, Argentina**

Answer each question about the cities named in the maze.

Of these cities, which has the highest altitude, or distance above sea level? Its name is in the square where you started.

Quito, Ecuador

Of these cities, which has the lowest altitude? Its name is in the square where you ended.

Buenos Aires, Argentina

Use with Grade 5, Chapter 9, Lesson 5, pages 408–409. (288)

Daily Homework

9•5 Explore Subtracting Integers

Subtract. You may use counters.

1. $^-8 - {}^-2 =$ $^-6$
2. $5 - {}^-2 =$ 7
3. $8 - {}^-3 =$ 11
4. $6 - {}^-2 =$ 8
5. $^-8 - 3 =$ $^-11$
6. $^-3 - 5 =$ $^-8$
7. $8 - {}^-6 =$ 14
8. $^-13 - 5 =$ $^-18$
9. $7 - {}^-2 =$ 9
10. $^-9 - 5 =$ $^-14$
11. $^-1 - {}^-8 =$ 7
12. $7 - {}^-7 =$ 14
13. $^-2 - 8 =$ $^-10$
14. $^-3 - {}^-7 =$ 4
15. $1 - {}^-9 =$ 10
16. $4 - {}^-2 =$ 6
17. $^-4 - 7 =$ $^-11$
18. $^-6 - {}^-6 =$ 0
19. $^-8 - 4 =$ $^-12$
20. $^-9 - {}^-14 =$ 5
21. $1 - {}^-6 =$ 7
22. $5 - 9 =$ $^-4$
23. $^-2 - {}^-12 =$ 10
24. $7 - 12 =$ $^-5$

Solve.

25. Construction workers are digging the foundation for a skyscraper. On Monday they reach a level 14 feet below the surface. On Tuesday they dig down another 18 feet. How far below the surface are they now? 32 feet

26. Divers swim down to a reef 42 feet below the ocean surface. Then they swim up 16 feet to investigate the top of a rock ledge. How far below the surface are they now? 26 feet

Spiral Review

Tell whether each number is prime or composite.

27. 33 composite
28. 23 prime
29. 63 composite
30. 43 prime
31. 93 composite
32. 83 prime

88 Grade 5, Chapter 9, Lesson 5, Cluster B

Chapter 9 ~ Lesson 6

Practice

Subtract Integers

P 9-6 PRACTICE

Subtract.

1. 7 − (-4) = 11
2. -6 − (-2) = -4
3. 3 − 8 = -5
4. -2 − (-10) = 8
5. -5 − (-5) = 0
6. 13 − (-6) = 19
7. -1 − 7 = -8
8. -3 − 8 = -11
9. -7 − (-4) = -3
10. 32 − (-16) = 48
11. 17 − 23 = -6
12. -12 − (-30) = 18
13. -23 − (-11) = -12
14. -15 − 27 = -42
15. -45 − (-45) = 0

Complete.

16. 5 − 7 = 5 + -7 = -2
17. -6 − 3 = -6 + -3 = -9
18. -4 − (-3) = -4 + 3 = -1
19. 7 − (-6) = 7 + 6 = 13
20. 3 − -9 = 3 + 9 = 12
21. -5 − -7 = -5 + 7 = 2
22. -2 − 8 = -2 + (-8) = -10
23. 6 − 10 = 6 + (-10) = -4

Compare. Write <, >, or =

24. 1 − 7 (<) 7 − 1
25. -6 − 4 (>) -7 − 4
26. 5 − 9 (<) -5 − (-9)
27. -4 − (-8) (=) -9 + 13
28. -5 − 1 (=) -7 − (-1)
29. 7 − 5 (<) 7 − (-5)
30. 6 − (-3) (>) -6 − 3
31. -2 − (-2) (>) -2 − 2
32. -1 − 6 (>) -12 − (-4)
33. -8 − 2 (<) 2 − 8
34. -10 − (-2) (<) 10 − 2
35. -6 − 4 (=) 2 − 12

Problem Solving

36. A sunken ship is located 80 feet below sea level. On his first dive, a diver descends 52 feet. How far is the diver above the sunken ship?
28 feet

37. A coral reef is 56 feet below sea level. A diver standing on a boat's deck is 6 feet above sea level. How far is the diver above the reef?
62 feet

Use with Grade 5, Chapter 9, Lesson 6, pages 410–413. (289)

Reteach

Subtract Integers

R 9-6 RETEACH

You can use a number line to subtract integers.

Subtract: -4 − 2

Find -4. You move to the right to add a positive integer, so move to the left to subtract a positive integer. Move 2 spaces to the left.

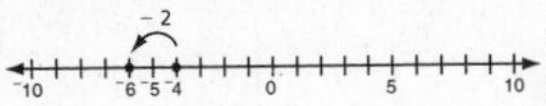

-4 − 2 = -6

Subtract: -5 − (-1)

Find -5. You move to the left to add a negative integer, so move to the right to subtract a negative integer. Move 1 space to the right.

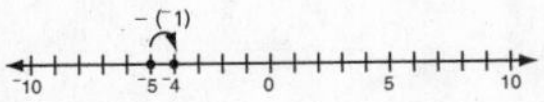

-5 − (-1) = -4

Show each difference on the number line. Then record the difference.

1. 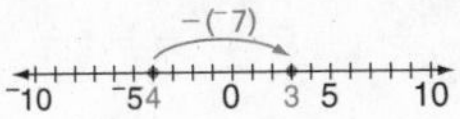
-4 − (-7) = 3

2. 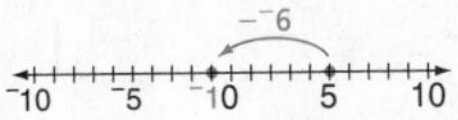
5 − 6 = -1

3. 
-9 − (-5) = -4

4. 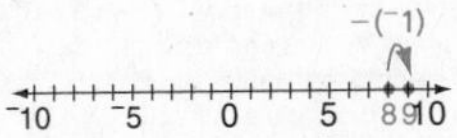
8 − (-1) = 9

5. 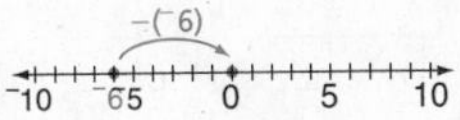
-6 − (-6) = 0

6. 
-7 − 2 = -9

7. 1 − 8 = -7
8. -2 − (-3) = 1
9. 4 − (-4) = 8
10. -4 − (-1) = -3
11. -6 − 4 = -10
12. -3 − (-1) = -2
13. 7 − (-2) = 9
14. -6 − (-8) = 2
15. -7 − 3 = -10
16. -7 − (-7) = 0
17. 3 − 9 = -6
18. -8 − (-3) = -5

Use with Grade 5, Chapter 9, Lesson 6, pages 410–413. (290)

Enrich

Subtract Integers
Order of Operations

E 9-6 ENRICH

You have already studied how to use the order of operations when computing with whole numbers and decimals. You can also use the order of operations with integers.

Find the answer for each exercise.

- Do operations inside the parentheses first.
- Add and subtract from left to right.

1. -5 − (-2 + 6) = -9
   -5 − -2 + 6 = 3
2. (circled) -7 + (1 − 6) = -12
   -7 + 1 − 6 = -12
3. 10 − (7 − 4) = 7
   10 − 7 − 4 = -1
4. (circled) 4 + (-3 − 4) = -3
   4 + -3 − 4 = -3
5. -2 − (6 − 5) = -3
   -2 − 6 − 5 = -13
6. -6 − (-2 + 5) = -9
   -6 − -2 + 5 = 1
7. -8 − (3 + 2) = -13
   -8 − 3 + 2 = -9
8. (circled) 9 + (-4 − -1) = 6
   9 + -4 − -1 = 6
9. (circled) 2 + (-9 + 3) = -4
   2 + -9 + 3 = -4
10. 8 − (4 + 7) = -3
    8 − 4 + 7 = 11
11. 1 − (6 + 2) = -7
    1 − 6 + 2 = -3
12. -5 − (-1 − -8) = -12
    -5 − -1 − -8 = 4

Circle the number of each exercise above whose value did not change when the parentheses were removed. How are these exercises different from an exercise whose value did change?

Answers may vary. Possible answer: In an exercise whose value did not change, the sum or difference in parentheses was added to the first number. In the other exercises, it was subtracted.

Use with Grade 5, Chapter 9, Lesson 6, pages 410–413. (291)

Daily Homework

9-6 Subtract Integers

Subtract.

1. 8 − -3 = 11
2. -3 − -3 = 0
3. -13 − 18 = -31
4. -17 − -8 = -9
5. -8 − -6 = -2
6. 7 − -2 = 9
7. 12 − -5 = 17
8. -15 − -5 = -10
9. 5 − 8 = -3
10. -15 − -6 = -9
11. 83 − -42 = 125
12. -8 − 6 = -14
13. -17 − 12 = -29
14. -48 − -20 = -28
15. -6 − 6 = -12
16. -12 − -15 = 3
17. 13 − -6 = 19
18. -9 + 4 = -5

Complete.

19. -5 − -7 = -5 + 7 = 2
20. 12 − -6 = 12 + 6 = 18
21. 6 − 9 = 6 + -9 = -3
22. 11 − -4 = 11 + 4 = 15

Compare. Write <, >, or =.

23. 8 − -7 = 18 − 3
24. 2 − 6 > -3 − 4
25. -16 − -7 < 2 − 9
26. 7 − 9 > -6 − -3

Problem Solving

27. An elevator is on the second floor of a building and descends 4 floors to a sub-basement. Write an equation to show where it is now located.
2 + -4 = -2 or 2 − 4 = -2

28. Weng has $100.32 in his bank account. He withdraws $7.14. Write an equation to show how much money he has now in his account.
$100.32 + -$7.14 = $93.18 or $100.32 − $7.14 = $93.18

Spiral Review

Write as a prime factorization.

29. 20 $2^2 \times 5$
30. 36 $2^2 \times 3^2$
31. 24 $2^3 \times 3$
32. 30 $2 \times 3 \times 5$

Grade 5, Chapter 9, Lesson 6, Cluster B 89

Chapter 9 ~ Lesson 7

Practice

Problem Solving: Strategy
Alternate Solution Methods Methods chosen will vary.

P 9-7 PRACTICE

Solve using two different methods. Tell which methods you used.

1. There are 4 pizzas at a party. Each pizza has 8 slices. How many slices of pizza are left if the guests eat $2\frac{3}{4}$ pizzas?
   10 slices

2. A certain liquid boils at 225°F. It cools at an average rate of 8° per minute. About how long will it take to cool to 65°F?
   20 minutes

3. A composite material is baked and cured at a temperature of 2,800°F. It cools at an average rate of 260°F per day. About how long will it take to cool to 70°F?
   about 10 days

4. A chef has 12 cups of tomato sauce. He uses $2\frac{2}{3}$ cups for each pan of lasagna. How many cups of tomato sauce will he have left if he makes 4 pans of lasagna?
   $1\frac{1}{3}$ c

Mixed Strategy Review

Solve. Use any strategy. Strategies may vary. Possible strategies are given.

5. **Health** The first week of Manny's fitness program, he runs up the stairs 4 times. He plans to increase the number of times he runs up the stairs by 5 each week. In how many weeks will he be running up the stairs 25 times?
   6 weeks
   Strategy: Make a Table

6. Gayle is making a square quilt. She wants to put a tassel every 6 inches along the edge of the quilt, including the corners. Each side of the quilt is 36 inches long. How many tassels will she need?
   24 tassels
   Strategy: Draw a Diagram

7. **Music** The school choir has 6 sopranos, 8 altos, and 5 tenors. Including the basses, there are 23 people in the choir. How many basses are in the choir?
   4 basses
   Strategy: Work Backward

8. **Create a problem** for which you could use different solution methods to solve. Share it with others.
   Check students' problems.

Use with Grade 5, Chapter 9, Lesson 7, pages 414–415. (292)

Reteach

Problem Solving: Strategy
Alternate Solution Methods

R 9-7 RETEACH

Page 415, Problem 2

Donna has $4\frac{3}{4}$ cups of sugar. She plans to make cookies that take $1\frac{2}{3}$ cups of sugar per pan. If she makes 2 pans of cookies, how much sugar will she have left over?

Step 1 Read

Be sure you understand the problem.
Read carefully.

What do you know?
- Donna has $4\frac{3}{4}$ cups of sugar.
- She plans to make 2 pans of cookies that take $1\frac{2}{3}$ cups of sugar per pan.

What do you need to find?
- The amount of sugar left over.

Step 2 Plan

- Find a Pattern
- Guess and Check
- Work Backward
- Make a Graph
- Make a Table
- Write an Equation
- Make an Organized List
- Draw a Diagram
- Solve a Simpler Problem
- Logical Reasoning

Make a plan.
Choose a strategy.

Some problems can be solved using more than one strategy.

Method 1 To solve the problem, you can make a table.

Method 2 To solve the problem, you can also write an equation.

Use with Grade 5, Chapter 9, Lesson 7, pages 414–415. (293)

Reteach

Problem Solving: Strategy
Alternate Solution Methods

R 9-7 RETEACH

Step 3 Solve

Carry out your plan.

Method 1 Make a Table

Pans	Sugar	Sugar Used	Sugar Left Over
1	$4\frac{3}{4}$	$1\frac{2}{3}$	$3\frac{1}{12}$
2	$3\frac{1}{12}$	$1\frac{2}{3}$	$1\frac{5}{12}$

So, Donna will have $1\frac{5}{12}$ cups of sugar left over.

Method 2 Write an Equation

You can multiply to find the number of cups of sugar for 2 pans.

$2 \times 1\frac{2}{3} = 3\frac{1}{3}$

Now, subtract to find the amount of sugar left over.

$4\frac{3}{4} - 3\frac{1}{3} = 1\frac{5}{12}$

How much sugar will Donna have left over? $1\frac{5}{12}$ c

Step 4 Look Back

Is the solution reasonable?
Reread the problem.

Have you answered the question? Yes

How can an alternate strategy help you solve the problem?
Answers may vary. Possible answer: You can use an alternate strategy to check the answer.

Practice

1. A recipe that serves 8 people calls for 3 cups of pasta, 2 tablespoons of parsley, and 4 ounces of olive oil. How much of each ingredient will Monica need to prepare enough for 40 people?
   15 c of pasta, 10 tbsp of parsley, 20 oz of olive oil

2. A bookstore is having a sale: buy 2 books for $5.50 and get a third book for free. Carter spent $22 on books. How many books did he get?
   12 books

Use with Grade 5, Chapter 9, Lesson 7, pages 414–415. (294)

Daily Homework

9-7 Problem Solving: Strategy
Alternate Solution Methods

Solve using two different methods. Tell which methods you used.
Methods chosen will vary. Answers are given.

1. A fence surrounds a square garden. Each side of the garden is 12 yards long. How long is the fence in feet? 48 feet
2. Amy is helping her parents seed their yard. Two bags of grass seed will cover about 500 square feet of yard. Amy's yard is about 1,250 square feet. How many bags will she need? 5 bags
3. Kerry can sell her handmade bracelets to a local craft store for $2.50 each. How many will she have to sell to afford a new CD that costs $15.99? 7 bracelets
4. Lamont has a collection of 486 baseball cards. His friend Manuel has a third as many. How many baseball cards do they have in all? 648 cards

Mixed Strategy Review

Use data from the graph for problems 5–6.

Average Daily High Temperatures by Month at Centerville

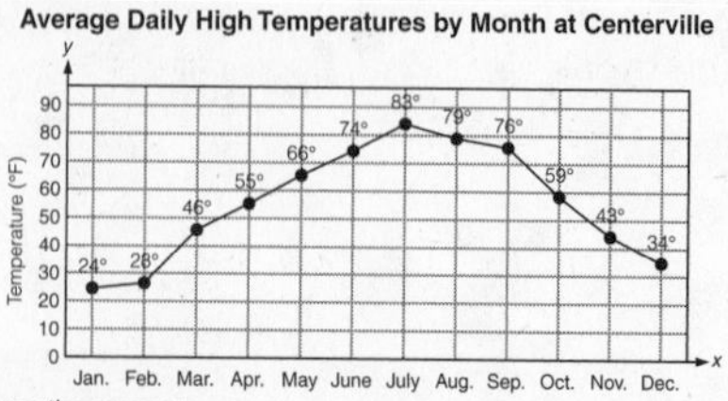

5. Which month had the lowest average daily high temperature? January
   What was that temperature? 24°F
6. How much lower was the average daily high temperature in February than in August? 51°F

Spiral Review

7. 3 m = 3,000 mm
8. 125 cm = 1.25 m
9. 4,900 g = 4.9 kg
10. 83 L = 8,300 mL

90 Grade 5, Chapter 9, Lesson 7, Cluster B

Chapter 9 ~ Lesson 8

Part A Worksheet

Problem Solving: Application

Part A 9-8 WORKSHEET Decision Making

Use the table to record expenses and income for the Science Club to decide how to balance their budget.

	Expenses	Income
First Semester		
Totals		
Second Semester		
Totals		

Use the table below to record expenses and income that you think are necessary for the Science Club to balance their budget.

	Expenses	Income
First Semester		
Totals		
Second Semester		
Totals		

Your Decision

What is your recommendation for how the Science Club can balance its budget so that the club takes in more than it earns? Explain.

Answers may vary.

Use with Grade 5, Chapter 9, Lesson 8, pages 416–417. (295)

Part B Worksheet

Problem Solving: Application

Is it easier to memorize positive or negative integers?

Part B 9-8 WORKSHEET Math & Science

Hypothesis Do you think it will be easier to memorize negative or positive numbers (or neither)? Explain.

Answers may vary.

1. Work with a partner. Take turns.
2. Make up number sequences and record them in the table. Include number sequences that are both positive and negative.
3. Study the first number sequence until you think you have it memorized.
4. Cover the sequence and recite it to your partner.
5. Record whether you knew the sequence perfectly or not.
6. Switch. Let you partner memorize the next sequence.
7. Continue taking turns until you complete all your sequences.

Sequence	Positive or Negative?	Perfect (yes or no)?
1		
2		
3		
4		
5		
6		
7		
8		
9		
10		

Use with Grade 5, Chapter 9, Lesson 8, pages 418–419. (296)

Part B Worksheet

Problem Solving: Application

Is it easier to memorize positive or negative integers?

Part B 9-8 WORKSHEET Math & Science

1. How many numbers were in the shortest sequence?
   Answers may vary.
2. How many numbers were in the longest sequence?
   Answers may vary.
3. Which did you and your partner memorize perfectly, more short sequences or more long sequences?
   Answers may vary.
4. Was it easier to memorize short sequences or long sequences?
   Answers may vary.
5. How many positive sequences did you and your partner memorize perfectly?
   Answers may vary.
6. Was it easier to memorize short positive sequences or long positive sequences?
   Answers may vary.
7. How many negative sequences did you and your partner memorize perfectly?
   Answers may vary.
8. Was it easier to memorize short negative sequences or long negative sequences?
   Answers may vary.
9. Which type of sequence was easiest to memorize, a short positive sequence, a long positive sequence, a short negative sequence, or a long negative sequence?
   Answers may vary.
10. Was it easier to memorize positive or negative sequences (or neither)? How does your answer compare with your answer to the hypothesis?
    Answers may vary.
11. Compare your answer with your classmates. Which type of sequence did the class as a whole find easiest to memorize?
    Answers may vary.

Use with Grade 5, Chapter 9, Lesson 8, pages 418–419. (297)

Chapter 10 ~ Lesson 1

Practice

Explore Addition and Subtraction Expressions

1. A scout troop planted bushes in a park. They planted 3 fewer lilac bushes than rose bushes. How many lilac bushes did they plant?

Draw □ to show the number of lilac bushes planted when certain numbers of rose bushes are planted. Let each □ represent 1 lilac bush.

□	□ □	□ □	□ □ □	□ □ □
□	□	□ □	□ □	□ □ □
5 rose bushes	6 rose bushes	7 rose bushes	8 rose bushes	9 rose bushes

Use your drawing to complete the table.

Number of Rose Bushes	5	6	7	8	9
Number of Lilac Bushes	2	3	4	5	6

2. Write an expression for the relationship between the number of lilac bushes and rose bushes. Use the variable, r, to represent the number of rose bushes.

$r - 3$

3. Suppose the troop planted 12 rose bushes. How many lilac bushes did they plant? Evaluate the expression you wrote for $r = 12$. Show your work.

$12 - 3 = 9$

Write an expression for each situation.

4. John worked x hours planting bushes. Kim worked 2 more hours than John. How many hours did Kim work?

$x + 2$

5. A rose bush costs x dollars. A lilac bush costs \$2.50 less than a rose bush. How much does a lilac bush cost, in dollars?

$x - 2.50$

6. The lilac bush is x feet tall now. By next year, it should be $2\frac{1}{2}$ feet taller. How tall will the lilac bush be then, in feet?

$x + 2\frac{1}{2}$

7. The troop has x bushes to plant. They have already planted 8 bushes. How many bushes do they still have to plant?

$x - 8$

Problem Solving

8. This year the troop planted 15 more bushes than last year. Write an expression for the number planted this year. Let y represent the number planted last year.

$y + 15$

9. Last year the troop planted 12 bushes. Evaluate the expression you wrote in problem 8 to find how many bushes they planted this year.

$12 + 15 = 27$

Reteach

Explore Addition and Subtraction Expressions

A box contains some baseballs. There are 2 baseballs on the ground. How many baseballs are there altogether?

You can draw models to show the total number of baseballs if the box contains certain numbers of baseballs.

| 5 baseballs | 6 baseballs | 7 baseballs | 8 baseballs |

You can also write an algebraic expression to represent the total number of baseballs.
- The number of baseballs in the box changes, so represent it with the variable, b.
- The number of baseballs on the ground stays the same: 2.
- Add the number of baseballs in the box and the number on the ground to find the number of baseballs altogether.

So, $b + 2$ represents the total number of baseballs.

Suppose there are 9 baseballs in the box. $b = 9$
You can find the total number of baseballs $b + 2$
by evaluating the expression. $9 + 2 = 11$ baseballs

Complete the steps to write and evaluate an expression for the situation.

1. Laura had 5 more hits than Susan. How many hits did Laura have?

   What number changes? ____ hits Susan had

   Write a variable to represent the number that changes. ____ s

   What number stays the same? ____ more hits Laura had than Susan

   Write the number that stays the same. ____ 5

   What operation do you need to use to find the number of hits Laura had? ____ addition

   Write an expression to represent the number of hits Laura had. ____ $s + 5$

   Suppose Susan had 2 hits. Evaluate the expression for $s = 2$. ____ $2 + 5 = 7$ hits

2. The Mustangs scored m runs in the softball game. The Rangers scored 3 fewer runs than the Mustangs. How many runs did the Rangers get?

   $m - 3$

3. During the softball season, the Rangers won y games. They lost 4 more games than they won. How many games did the Rangers lose during the season?

   $y + 4$

Enrich

Explore Addition and Subtraction Expressions
Expression Magic

1. Evaluate each expression for $n = 2.35$.

$31.95 - n$	$1.35 + n$	$19.85 + n$
29.6	3.7	22.2
$8.75 + n$	$20.85 - n$	$28.25 - n$
11.1	18.5	25.9
$12.45 + n$	$35.65 - n$	$5.05 + n$
14.8	33.3	7.4

What is the sum of each row, column, and diagonal? 55.5

2. Let n equal 10. Write the new value of each expression from above in the table below.

21.95	11.35	29.85
18.75	10.85	18.25
22.45	25.65	15.05

Check the sum of each row, column, and diagonal. What do you notice?

The sums are different.

3. Rewrite each expression above so that, when $n = 10$, each row, column, and diagonal has the sum of 55.5.

$39.6 - n$	$n - 6.3$	$12.2 + n$
$1.1 + n$	$28.5 - n$	$35.9 - n$
$4.8 + n$	$43.3 - n$	$n - 2.6$

How did you decide how to rewrite the expressions? Answers may vary. Possible answer: Work backward; for each expression, use the value in exercise 1. Then add or subtract to find the number that, when combined with 10, has that value.

Daily Homework

 10-1   Explore Addition and Subtraction Expressions

Write an expression for each situation.

1. There are c cars in a parking lot. Then 7 more cars drive into the lot. How many cars are in the lot now?

   $c + 7$

2. Diane has f oranges. She gives 3 of her oranges to Ben. How many oranges does she have now?

   $f - 3$

3. Julio talks to his grandmother for t minutes. He talks to her for another $5\frac{1}{2}$ minutes. How long does he talk to her in all?

   $t + 5\frac{1}{2}$

4. Alison's family orders a pizza. After everyone takes a slice, there are p slices left. Alison takes $1\frac{1}{2}$ more slices. How many slices are left?

   $p - 1\frac{1}{2}$

Evaluate each expression for the value given.

5. $b + 15$ for $b = 6$ ____ 21

6. $w - 9$ for $w = 13$ ____ 4

7. $14 + j$ for $j = 18.3$ ____ 32.3

8. $19.7 - s$ for $s = 12.1$ ____ 7.6

Solve.

9. Kim has run r meters. She runs 13 more meters. If $r = 87$, how many meters does Kim run in all? ____ 100 meters

10. Gary has been studying for s minutes. He studies for $21\frac{1}{2}$ more minutes. If $s = 32$ minutes, how long does Gary study in all? ____ $53\frac{1}{2}$ minutes

Spiral Review

Find the GCF for each pair of numbers.

11. 9 and 24 ____ 3

12. 20 and 36 ____ 4

13. 15 and 18 ____ 3

14. 30 and 36 ____ 6

Chapter 10 ~ Lesson 2

Practice

Explore Multiplication and Division Expressions

P 10-2 PRACTICE

1. At a nature preserve, visitors are divided into groups of 3 to go on bird watches. How many groups are there?

   Draw □ to show the number of groups when there are certain numbers of visitors. Let each □ represent one group.

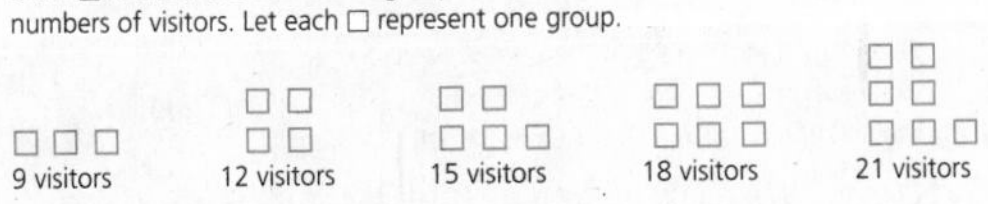

   Use your drawings to complete the table.

Number of visitors	9	12	15	18	21
Number of groups	3	4	5	6	7

2. Write an algebraic expression for the relationship between the number of groups and the number of visitors. Use the variable v to represent the number of visitors.

   $v \div 3$

3. Suppose there were 36 visitors. How many groups are there? Evaluate the expression you wrote for $v = 36$. Show your work.

   $36 \div 3 = 12$

Write an expression for each situation.

4. Every year the school's Science Club builds 2 bird feeders. How many bird feeders will the club build in x years?

   $2x$

5. The nature preserve expects 500 geese to stop at it during their 90-day migration. On the average, how many geese will stop in x days?

   $\frac{500}{90}x$

6. Volunteers clean up the nature trail at the nature preserve. The trail is x miles long. Each volunteer is to clean up 0.3 mile of the trail. How many volunteers are needed to clean up the whole trail?

   $\frac{x}{0.3}$

7. Each day a naturalist puts $1\frac{1}{2}$ pounds of birdseed in each feeder. There are x feeders. How many pounds of seed are needed for one day?

   $1\frac{1}{2}x$

Use with Grade 5, Chapter 10, Lesson 2, pages 436–437. (301)

Reteach

Explore Multiplication and Division Expressions

R 10-2 RETEACH

Joe takes a bag containing 3 cookies to eat with his lunch at school. How many cookies are needed for lunch for one week?

You can draw models to show the total number of cookies needed.

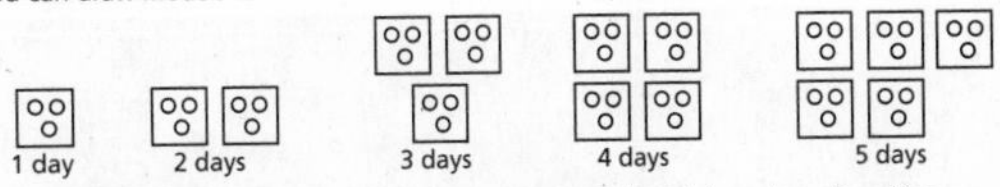

You can also write an algebraic expression to represent the total number of cookies.

- The number of cookies in each bag stays the same: 3.
- The number of bags of cookies changes, so represent it with the variable c.
- Multiply the number of cookies in the bag by the number of bags to find the total number of cookies.

So, $3 \times c$, or $3c$ represents the total number of cookies.

Suppose Joe needs cookies for lunch for 9 days. You can find the number of cookies he needs by evaluating the expression.

$c = 9$
$3c$
$3 \times 9 = 27$ cookies

Complete the steps to write and evaluate an expression for the situation.

1. Mrs. Cook bought some sliced turkey. She puts 3 slices of turkey on each sandwich. How many sandwiches could she make?

   What number changes in this situation? slices of turkey bought

   Write a variable to represent the number that changes. t

   What number stays the same? slices on each sandwich

   Write the number that stays the same. 3

   Write an expression to represent the sandwiches Mrs. Cook could make. $t \div 3$

Write an expression for each situation.

2. Sandy uses 6 slices of bread to make sandwiches for lunch. How many slices does she need for s lunches?

   $6s$

3. Sam drinks 8 ounces of juice everyday. How many servings can he get from a container with j ounces?

   $j \div 8$

Use with Grade 5, Chapter 10, Lesson 2, pages 436–437. (302)

Enrich

Explore Multiplication and Division Expressions

E 10-2 ENRICH

Expression Match

Match each phrase in Column A to a phrase in Column B to make a true sentence. Then write the letters above each exercise number to solve the riddle in the box.

Column A	Column B
1. If $n = 12$, then	O. $n \div 4 = 0.8$.
2. If $n = 20$, then	I. $1\frac{1}{4}n = 3\frac{1}{8}$.
3. If $n = 14$, then	E. $\frac{n}{7} = 0.7$.
4. If $n = 6$, then	O. $3n = 36$.
5. If $n = 3.5$, then	W. $\frac{n}{12} = 7$.
6. If $n = 2\frac{1}{2}$, then	A. $1\frac{1}{2}n = 9$.
7. If $n = 3.2$, then	V. $n \div 1\frac{3}{4} = 12$.
8. If $n = 84$, then	N. $\frac{n}{0.5} = 40$.
9. If $n = 2.1$, then	A. $6n = 12.6$.
10. If $n = 21$, then	R. $n \div \frac{7}{8} = 16$.
11. If $n = 4.9$, then	S. $\frac{3}{4}n = 12$.
12. If $n = 16$, then	D. $2.4n = 8.4$.

Where do disc jockeys surf?

O	N	R	A	D	I	O	W	A	V	E	S
1	2	3	4	5	6	7	8	9	10	11	12

What strategy did you use to help you match the phrases?

Answers may vary. Possible answer: I looked at the phrases in Column B and used guess, test, and revise. Sometimes I worked until I figured out what n had to be. When I could make a good guess for n, I looked in Column A to see if there was a value close to my guess.

Use with Grade 5, Chapter 10, Lesson 2, pages 436–437. (303)

Daily Homework

10-2 Explore Multiplication and Division Expressions

Write an expression for each situation.

1. Roberto eats t oranges each week. How many oranges will he eat in 5 weeks?

   $5t$

2. Leah has d ounces of juice in a glass. She drinks $\frac{1}{3}$ of the juice. How many ounces of juice does she drink?

   $\frac{d}{3}$

Evaluate each expression for the value given.

3. $4g$ for $g = 29$ 116
4. $\frac{z}{6}$ for $z = 96$ 16
5. $\frac{k}{5}$ for $k = 225$ 45
6. $\frac{3}{4}a$ for $a = 28$ 21
7. $7f$ for $f = 9$ 63
8. $5.2n$ for $n = 7$ 36.4
9. $\frac{3}{8}h$ for $h = 48$ 18
10. $\frac{u}{4}$ for $u = \frac{4}{9}$ $\frac{1}{9}$
11. $\frac{2}{3}c$ for $c = \frac{6}{5}$ $\frac{4}{5}$
12. $6.25x$ for $x = 7$ 43.75
13. $\frac{b}{8}$ for $b = 72$ 9
14. $0.2y$ for $y = 7.5$ 1.5

Solve.

15. Alicen has chosen a 250-page book for her book report. If she reads t pages a day, how long will it take her to read the book? $\frac{250}{t}$

16. Angel is helping pack grapefruits for the historical society fund-raiser. If Angel can pack n grapefruits in each box, how many grapefruits will he pack into 8 boxes? $8n$

Spiral Review

Add or subtract.

17. $4 - 2\frac{1}{3} =$ $1\frac{2}{3}$
18. $3\frac{2}{5} + 4\frac{4}{5} =$ $8\frac{1}{5}$
19. $2\frac{1}{4} + \frac{2}{3} =$ $2\frac{11}{12}$
20. $1\frac{5}{6} - \frac{1}{2} =$ $1\frac{1}{3}$

92 Grade 5, Chapter 10, Lesson 2, Cluster A

Chapter 10 ~ Lesson 3

Practice

Order of Operations

P 10-3 PRACTICE

Simplify. Use the order of operations.

1. $44 + 7 \times 3$	65	2. $48 \div (8 - 2)$	8
3. $(3 + 4) \times 8 \div 2$	28	4. $18 + 12 \div 2 + 3$	27
5. $4^2 \times 2 - 10$	22	6. $(3.6 \div 3) + (8 \times 5)$	41.2
7. $(3 + 2) \times 3^2$	45	8. $24 \div 6 \times 3 + 52$	64
9. $(2\frac{1}{2} \times 2) - (3 \times \frac{1}{3})$	4	10. $96 \div (3 \times 4) \div 2$	4
11. $100 - 8^2 + 4 \div 4$	37	12. $(200 - 50) \div (12 - 9)$	50
13. $47 + 3 \times 11 - 36 \div 3$	68	14. $(3.7 + 6.3) \times (7.2 - 3.1)$	41
15. $50 - (^-4 + 1)^2 \div 9$	49	16. $6^2 - 9 \times 4 + (\frac{1}{3})^2$	$\frac{1}{9}$

Evaluate the expression for the value given.

17. $37 + 2p$ for $p = 6$	49	18. $\frac{45}{a} - 2$ for $a = 5$	7
19. $7 + s - 12$ for $s = 23$	18	20. $3c - 15$ for $c = 21$	48
21. $\frac{m}{4} + 3.9$ for $m = 40$	13.9	22. $29 - h + 13$ for $h = 8$	34
23. $(18 + 9) \div 3d$ for $d = 3$	3	24. $8 + 24 \div 4k$ for $k = 2$	11
25. $\frac{e}{3} - 2 \times 3$ for $e = 41.4$	7.8	26. $(z^2 + 7) - 5 \times 10$ for $z = 9$	38
27. $4d + 30$ for $d = 10$	70	28. $\frac{k}{3} - 6.4$ for $k = 12$	5.6

Problem Solving

29. Tickets to the school play cost \$4.50 for adults and \$2.00 for students. If 255 adults and 382 students attended the play, write an expression that shows the total amount of money made on ticket sales. Then simplify the expression.
(255 × \$4.50) + (382 × \$2.00); \$1,911.50

30. At the school play, popcorn costs \$1 and juice costs \$0.75. Suppose 235 people buy popcorn and 140 people buy juice. Write an expression that shows the total amount of money made by selling refreshments. Then simplify the expression.
(235 × \$1) + (140 × \$0.75); \$340

Use with Grade 5, Chapter 10, Lesson 3, pages 438–439. (304)

Reteach

Order of Operations

R 10-3 RETEACH

You can use a phrase to help you remember the order of operations.

Please	Excuse	My	Dear	Aunt	Sally
Parentheses	Exponents	Multiply	Divide	Add	Subtract

Simplify: $8^2 + (6 - 2) \times 5 - 10 \div 2$

Step 1 Parentheses — $8^2 + \mathbf{4} \times 5 - 10 \div 2$

Step 2 Exponents — $\mathbf{64} + 4 \times 5 - 10 \div 2$

Step 3 Multiply and divide from left to right. — $64 + \mathbf{20} - \mathbf{5}$

Step 4 Add and subtract from left to right. — **79**

Simplify. Follow the steps in the order of operations.

1. $6^2 - 10 + 5 \times (2 - 1)$
$6^2 - 10 + 5 \times$ 1
36 $- 10 + 5 \times$ 1
36 $- 10 +$ 5 $=$ 31

2. $6 \times (9 - 4) + 3^2$
$6 \times$ 5 $+ 3^2$
$6 \times$ 5 $+$ 9
30 $+$ 9 $=$ 39

Simplify. Use the order of operations.

3. $7 \times (3 + 9) =$ 84	4. $(12 + 3) - 2 + 3 \times 7 =$ 34
5. $3 \times 4^2 + 8 - 5 =$ 51	6. $100 + 10^2 \times (6 - 3) =$ 400
7. $36 \times 3 - 10 =$ 98	8. $5^2 \times 2 + 4 =$ 54
9. $1.2 \times (4 + 3) - 7 =$ 1.4	10. $25 - 2 \times 6 + 4^2 =$ 29
11. $9 \times (14 - 3) \div 3 =$ 33	12. $63 \div 9 + 2 \times 5 =$ 17
13. $15.4 + 2 \times 5.3 =$ 26	14. $6^2 \div (9 - 5) + 7 =$ 16
15. $(^-4 + 8) \times 6 \div 2 =$ 12	16. $(\frac{1}{4})^2 + 6 \times 2 - 24 \div 2 =$ $\frac{1}{16}$

Use with Grade 5, Chapter 10, Lesson 3, pages 438–439. (305)

Enrich

Order of Operations

Four in a Row

E 10-3 ENRICH

Write a numerical expression that has a value equal to each number from 1 through 30. In each expression, use each of four consecutive digits exactly once. You may use any operation, parentheses, exponents, or 2-digit numbers.

Here are some examples.

Numbers used: 1, 2, 3, 4
$1 = 3^1 - (4 - 2)$

Numbers used: 3, 4, 5, 6
$4 = 36 \div (4 + 5)$

Numbers used: 2, 3, 4, 5
$5 = 4 + (3 - 2)$

Answers may vary. Possible answers are given.

$1 = 3 - 1 - 2^0$	$11 = (5 + 6) \times (8 - 7)$	$21 = 5 \times 7 - (8 + 6)$
$2 = (3 + 4 + 5) \div 6$	$12 = 6 + 7 - (9 - 8)$	$22 = 78 - 56$
$3 = 2 \times 5 - (3 + 4)$	$13 = 3^2 + (1 \times 4)$	$23 = (2 \times 4) + (3 \times 5)$
$4 = 6 + 7 - (4 + 5)$	$14 = 6 + 7 + 9 - 8$	$24 = 1 \times 2 \times 3 \times 4$
$5 = 4 \times 2 - (3 \times 1)$	$15 = 10 + 2 + 3$	$25 = 4 \times 5 + 2 + 3$
$6 = 3 \times 2 \times 1^0$	$16 = 6 \times 4 - (3 + 5)$	$26 = 5 + 6 + 7 + 8$
$7 = (3 + 4) \times 1^2$	$17 = 5 \times 3 + 4 - 2$	$27 = (4 + 5) \times (6 - 3)$
$8 = (3 + 1) \times 4 \div 2$	$18 = 65 - 47$	$28 = (9 - 7) \times (6 + 8)$
$9 = (4 + 5) \div 3 + 6$	$19 = 8 \times 9 \div 6 + 7$	$29 = 7 \times 4 + 6 - 5$
$10 = (3 \times 4 \times 5) \div 6$	$20 = (6 + 4) \times (7 - 5)$	$30 = 5 \times 4 \times 3 \div 2$

Use with Grade 5, Chapter 10, Lesson 3, pages 438–439. (306)

Daily Homework

10-3 Order of Operations

Simplify. Use the order of operations.

1. $8 \times 3 - (9 + 4) =$ 11	2. $18 \div 2 - 3 \times 2 =$ 3
3. $(5.2 + 7) \times 4 =$ 48.8	4. $67 - 7 \times 5 + 24 \div 3 =$ 40
5. $(26 + 14) \div 4 + 7 =$ 17	6. $5^2 + 12 \div 2 =$ 31

Evaluate the expression for the value given.

7. $27 + h - 18$ for $h = 14$ 23	8. $55 - k \div 6$ for $k = 30$ 50
9. $401 + 18 \times z$ for $z = 10$ 581	10. $32 + 55 \times b \div 11$ for $b = 2$ 42

Place parentheses to make the sentence true.

11. $10 \times 8 - 5 + 7 = 37$ $10 \times (8 - 5) + 7$

12. $55 - 15 \div 3 + 2 = 8$ $55 - 15 \div (3 + 2)$

Problem Solving

13. Antoine orders 4 boxes of daffodil bulbs and 7 boxes of tulip bulbs to plant in his garden. Each box of daffodil bulbs contains 12 bulbs, and each box of tulip bulbs contains 10 bulbs. Write an expression to find out how many more tulips than daffodils Antoine ordered. Then evaluate the expression.
(7×10) – (4 × 12) = 22 more tulips

14. Elena goes to the bank and gets 17 rolls of quarters and 12 rolls of dimes. If each roll of quarters contains 40 coins, and each roll of dimes contains 50 coins, write an expression for the total number of coins that Elena gets. Then evaluate the expression.
(17 × 40) + (12× 50) = 1,280 coins

Spiral Review

Complete the equivalent fraction.

15. $\frac{3}{4} = \frac{9}{12}$ 16. $\frac{14}{20} = \frac{7}{10}$ 17. $\frac{1}{2} = \frac{42}{84}$ 18. $\frac{6}{7} = \frac{30}{35}$

Grade 5, Chapter 10, Lesson 3, Cluster A 93

Practice

Functions

10-4 PRACTICE

Write an equation to describe each situation.
Tell what each variable represents.

Answers may vary. Possible answers are given.

1. Marie is sending some paperback books to her cousin. Each book weighs 4 ounces. She is mailing them in a box that weighs 6 ounces.

   Variables: b = number of books

   w = total weight of package

   Equation: $w = 4b + 6$

2. A mailing service charges $3 plus $2 a pound to wrap and send a package.

   Variables: p = weight of package in pounds

   c = total of cost

   Equation: $c = 2p + 3$

Complete the table. Then write an equation to describe the situation.
Tell what each variable represents.

3. **Cost of Ordering Puzzles from a Catalog**
   Cost of Each Puzzle: $7.50

Number of Puzzles	1	2	3	4	5
Total Cost	$12.50	$20.00	$27.50	$35.00	$42.50

Variables: p = number of puzzles

c = total cost

Equation: $c = 7.50p + 5$

Use data from the information below to solve problems 4–5.

It takes Beth 20 minutes to drive to and from a mailing service and 2 minutes to fill out a mailing label and have each package weighed.

4. Write an equation to describe the situation. Tell what the variables represent.

   p = number of packages, t = total time in minutes, $t = 2p + 20$

5. How long will it take Beth to mail 3 packages? Use the equation you wrote to solve the problem.

   26 minutes

Use with Grade 5, Chapter 10, Lesson 4, pages 440–441. (307)

Reteach

Functions

10-4 RETEACH

A function is a relationship in which one quantity depends on another quantity. You can use a table, words, graph, or an equation to represent a function.

Mr. Sharp bought some paint and a brush. Each can of paint cost $8, and the brush cost $4.

The total amount Mr. Sharp spent depends on the number of cans of paint he bought.

You can make a table to show the function.

Number of Cans of Paint	1	2	3	4	5
Total Spent	$12	$20	$28	$36	$44

← Each number is 1 greater than the previous number.
← Each amount is $8 greater than the previous amount.

Describing a function in words can help you write an equation.
Let t = total spent, in dollars.
Let c = number of cans of paint.

Total amount Mr. Sharp spent	equals	the number of cans of paint times the cost of each can	plus	the cost of the brush.
t	=	$8c$	+	$4

You can evaluate this equation if Mr. Sharp bought 5 cans of paint.

$t = 8c + 4$, $c = 5$
$t = 8 \times 5 + 4$
$t = 40 + 4$
$t = 44$
Mr. Sharp spent $44.

Write an equation to describe each situation.
Tell what each variable represents.

Variables may vary. Sample answers are given.

1. Luann is going to paint some shelves. It takes her 15 minutes to gather the materials and to clean up when she is done. It takes her 10 minutes to paint each shelf.

   Variables: s = number of shelves

   m = total number of minutes

   Equation: $m = 10s + 15$

2. A long distance telephone call costs 10 cents per minute and there is a 30-cent connection charge.

   Variables: m = total number of minutes of call

   c = total cost of phone call, in dollars

   Equation: $c = 0.10m + 0.30$

Use with Grade 5, Chapter 10, Lesson 4, pages 440–441. (308)

Enrich

Functions

10-4 ENRICH

Polygon Functions

All the figures are made of toothpicks. For each exercise, draw the next two figures in the sequence. Record the number of polygons and the number of toothpicks in each figure. Then write an equation that describes the relationship between the number of toothpicks and the number of polygons.

1. 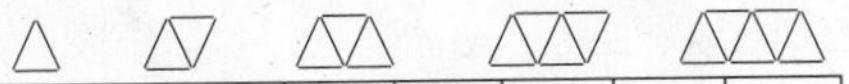

Number of triangles (t)	1	2	3	4	5
Number of toothpicks (n)	3	5	7	9	11

Equation: $n = 2t + 1$

2. 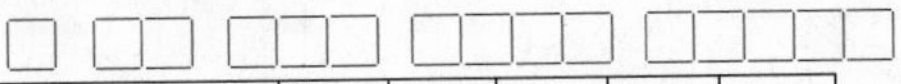

Number of squares (s)	1	2	3	4	5
Number of toothpicks (n)	4	7	10	13	16

Equation: $n = 3s + 1$

3. 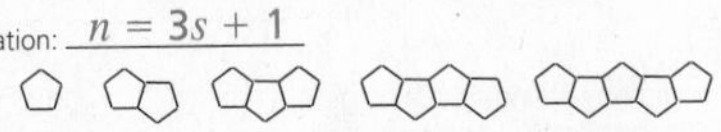

Number of pentagons (p)	1	2	3	4	5
Number of toothpicks (n)	5	9	13	17	21

Equation: $n = 4p + 1$

Suppose a sequence of figures like those above was made using octagons. What equation do you think would describe the relationship between the number of toothpicks (n) and the number of octagons (o)? Explain your thinking.

$n = 7o + 1$; I looked at the equations I wrote for problems 1–3 and saw a pattern. The number of polygons was always multiplied by 1 fewer than the number of sides of one polygon. Then 1 was added to that product.

Use with Grade 5, Chapter 10, Lesson 4, pages 440–441. (309)

Daily Homework

10-4 Functions

Write an equation to describe the situation. Tell what each variable represents.

1. Victor is sending an express package to his father through a delivery service. The service charges $2.50 per pound, plus a $10.00 fee for express delivery.

   p = weight of Victor's package in pounds, q = cost of sending the package; $q = \$10.00 + \$2.50p$

Complete the table. Write an equation to describe the situation.

2. Calculating Taxi Fare

   Cost to hire a taxi: $1.50

Number of miles	1	2	3	4	5
Total Fare	$3.50	$5.50	$7.50	$9.50	$11.50

Possible answer: f = total fare, m = number of miles; $f = \$2.00m + \$1.50$

Problem Solving

3. Gina is ordering CDs over the Internet. There is a $6 shipping charge, and each CD costs $12. Gina orders 4 CDs. Write an equation to describe the situation. Tell what the variables represent. Use your equation to solve the problem.

   Possible answer: $c = \$12d + \$6$; c = cost of Gina's order, d = the number of CDs that Gina orders; It will cost Gina $54.

4. Juan is going to ride his bicycle 12 blocks to his grandmother's house. It takes him 5 minutes to get ready and leave his house. It then takes him $\frac{1}{2}$ a minute to ride each block. Write an equation to describe the situation. Tell what the variables represent. Use your equation to solve the problem.

   Possible answer: $k = 12j + 5$; k = time it takes Juan to get to his grandmother's; j = time it takes Juan to ride a block; It will take 11 minutes.

Spiral Review

5. 330 min = 5.5 h 6. 10,560 ft = 2 mi 7. 56 oz = 3.5 lb

94 Grade 5, Chapter 10, Lesson 4, Cluster A

Practice

Graphing a Function

10-5 PRACTICE

Write the coordinates for each point.

1. A (5, 9) 2. I (7, 2) 3. F (0, 4)
4. L (9, 8) 5. G (0, 7) 6. D (6, 6)

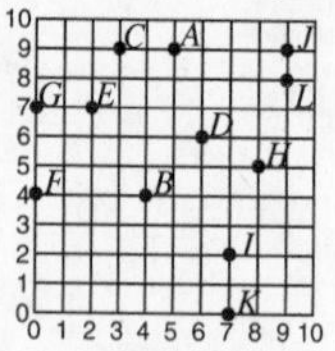

Name the point for the ordered pair.

7. (8, 5) H 8. (4, 4) B 9. (2, 7) E
10. (7, 0) K 11. (3, 9) C 12. (9, 9) J

Complete each table using the function represented in the equation. Then graph the function. Sample graphs are given.

13. $h = 3c$

c	h
0	0
1	3
2	6
3	9

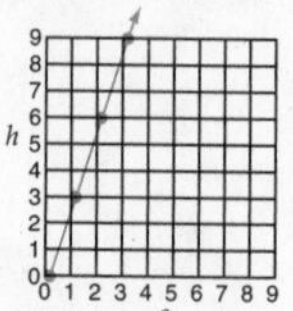

14. $b = 4a - 1$

a	b
1	3
2	7
3	11
4	15

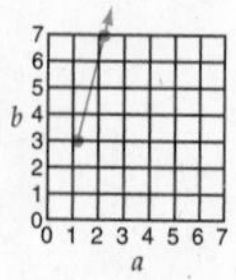

15. $s = 2t + 6$

t	s
0	6
1	8
2	10
3	12

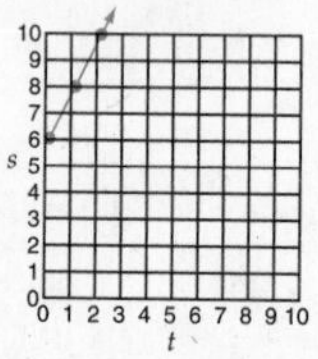

16. $q = 2m$

m	q
0	0
1	2
2	4
3	6

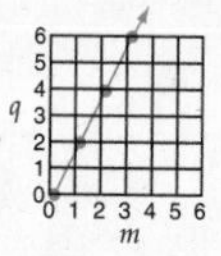

A fifth-grade class checks the pond water in the school's nature center. Each day they collect some 4-ounce samples of water and one 8-ounce sample of water.

17. Write an equation that describes the relationship between the total ounces of water collected, w, and the number of 4-ounce samples, s.

$w = 4s + 8$

18. What is the total amount of water that will be collected if students collect three 4-ounce samples?

20 ounces

Use with Grade 5, Chapter 10, Lesson 5, pages 442–445. (310)

Reteach

Graphing a Function

10-5 RETEACH

Another way to represent a function is to use a graph.

Graph the function represented in the following equation.

$b = 2a + 1$

Make a table to find ordered pairs. Choose several values for a. For each value, evaluate the expression $2a + 1$ to find the corresponding value of b.

a	$2a + 1$	b	Ordered Pair (a, b)
0	$2 \times 0 + 1$	1	(0, 1)
1	$2 \times 1 + 1$	3	(1, 3)
2	$2 \times 2 + 1$	5	(2, 5)
3	$2 \times 3 + 1$	7	(3, 7)

Graph the ordered pairs and connect them with a line.

Remember, the first coordinate tells the number of units to the right of the origin. The second coordinate tells the number of units above the origin.

(3, 7) is (3 units right, 7 units up).

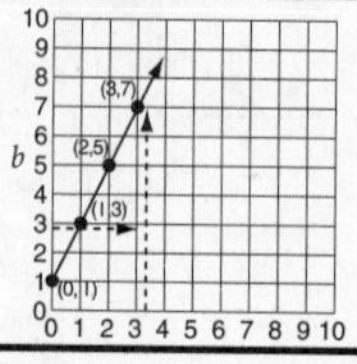

Complete the table for the function represented in each equation. Then graph the function.

1. $n = m + 3$

m	$m + 3$	n	Ordered Pair (m, n)
0	0 + 3	3	(0, 3)
1	1 + 3	4	(1, 4)
2	2 + 3	5	(2, 5)

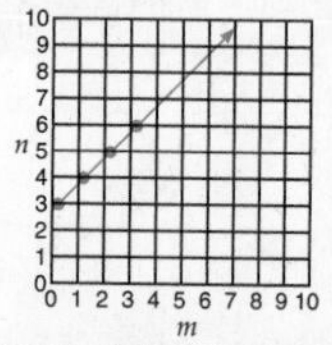

2. $t = 3s - 1$

s	$3s - 1$	t	Ordered Pair (s, t)
1	$3 \times 1 - 1$	2	(1, 2)
2	$3 \times 2 - 1$	5	(2, 5)
3	$3 \times 3 - 1$	8	(3, 8)
4	$3 \times 4 - 1$	11	(4, 11)

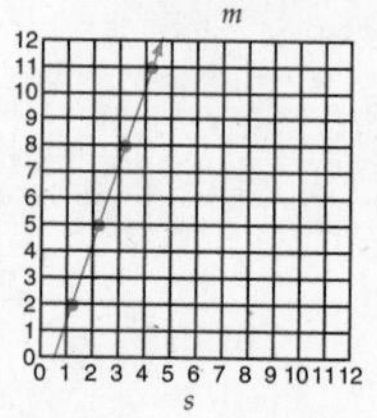

Use with Grade 5, Chapter 10, Lesson 5, pages 442–445. (311)

Enrich

Graphing a Function
Patterns in Reversing Coordinates

10-5 ENRICH

1. Graph the ordered pairs (2, 2), (0, 4), (2, 6), and (4, 4). Connect the points in the order given.

Then reverse the x- and y-coordinates in the ordered pairs. Graph the new set of points and connect them in the order given.

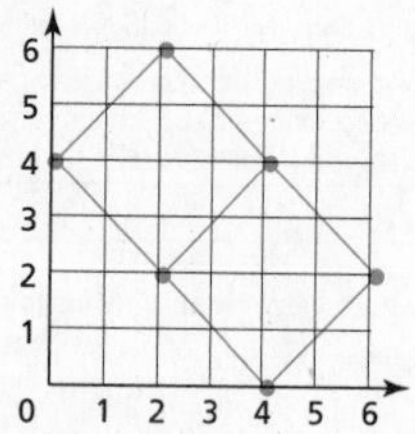

2. Graph the ordered pairs (0, 0), (0, 3), (3, 3), (3, 5), and (4, 4). Connect the points in the order given.

Then reverse the x- and y-coordinates in the ordered pairs. Graph the new set of points and connect them in the order given.

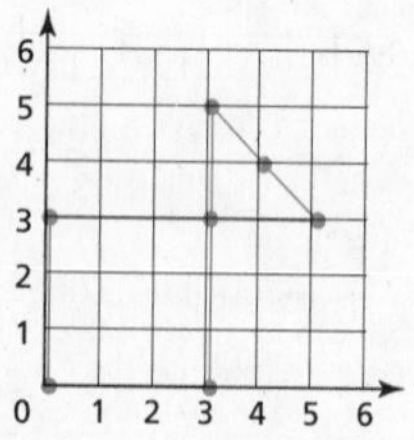

3. Graph the ordered pairs (1, 1), (3, 0), (3, 2), (3, 5), and (6, 6). Connect the points in the order given.

Then reverse the x- and y-coordinates in the ordered pairs. Graph the new set of points and connect them in the order given.

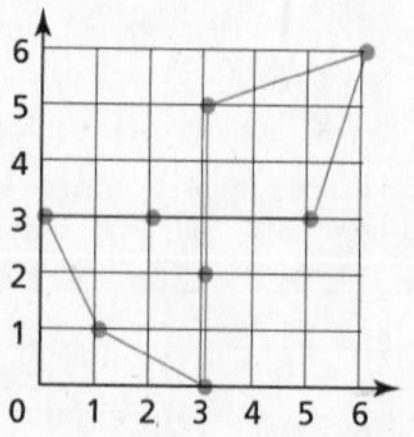

Use with Grade 5, Chapter 10, Lesson 5, pages 442–445. (312)

Daily Homework

10-5 Graphing a Function

Write the coordinates for each point.

1. C (2, 1) 2. D (1, 4) 3. G (3, 3)

Name the point for each ordered pair.

4. (1, 6) R 5. (6, 3) S 6. (2, 5) T

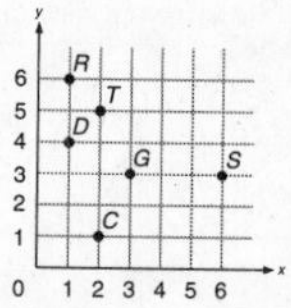

Complete the table. Then graph the function. Check students' graphs.

7. $m = 2n + 1$

n	m
0	1
1	3
2	5
3	7

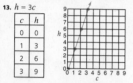

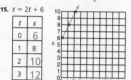

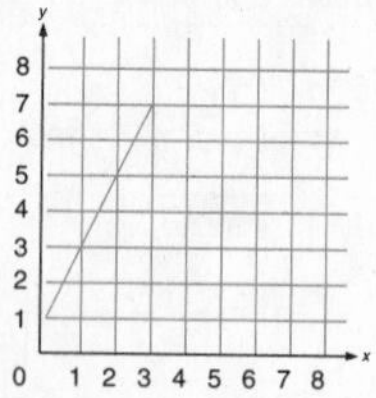

Problem Solving

8. Debra makes $3 an hour baby-sitting. She also gets a $2 tip each time she baby-sits. Write an expression that describes the relationship between the number of hours that she baby-sits, h, and the amount of money she earns, m.

$m = \$3h + \$2$

9. The taxi to the airport charges $1.35 per mile plus the cost of tolls. If the parkway toll is $0.25 and the bridge toll is $3.50, what is the cost of a trip to the airport? Write your answer as an expression describing the relationship between miles and total cost.

$c = \$1.35m + \$3.75$

Spiral Review

10. $\frac{2}{7} \times \frac{2}{5} = \frac{4}{35}$ 11. $\frac{4}{9} \div \frac{1}{6} = 2\frac{2}{3}$ 12. $\frac{5}{8} \times \frac{7}{10} = \frac{7}{16}$

Grade 5, Chapter 10, Lesson 5, Cluster A 95

Chapter 10 ~ Lesson 6

Practice

P 10-6 PRACTICE

Graph in Four Quadrants and Solve Problems Using Graphs

Use data from the coordinate graph for exercises 1–8.

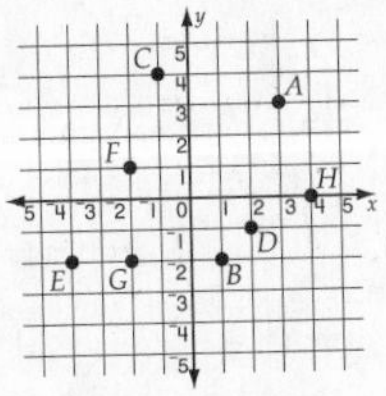

Give the coordinates of the point.

1. A (3, 3)
2. E (-4, -2)
3. C (-1, 4)
4. H (4, 0)

Name the point for each ordered pair.

5. (2, -1) D
6. (-2, 1) F
7. (1, -2) B
8. (-2, -2) G

Complete the tables. Then graph the function. Check students' graphs. Sample graphs are given.

9.

y = x + 3	
x	y
-3	0
-2	1
-1	2
0	3

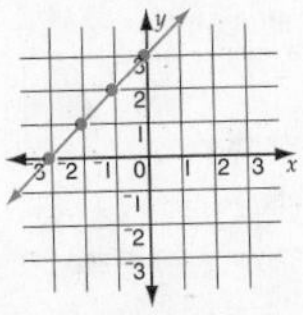

10.

y = x − 2	
x	y
-2	-4
-1	-3
0	-2
1	-1

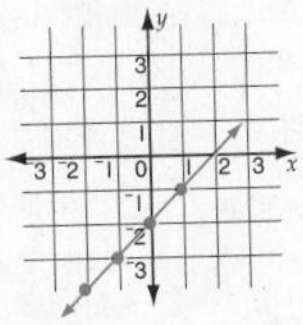

11.

y = 1 − x	
x	y
-2	3
0	1
2	-1
4	-3

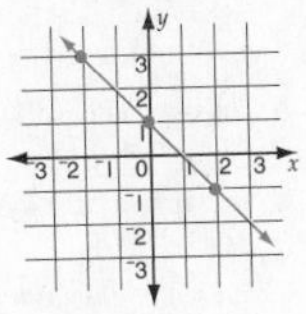

Problem Solving

12. A meteorologist discovered that a storm is following a path determined by the equation $y = x + 5$. Will the storm pass over the point (1, 4) on the graph? Explain.
No, the point (1, 4) is not on the graph.

13. Another storm is following the path $y = 5 - x$. Will this storm pass over the point (1, 4) on the graph? Explain.
Yes, the point (1, 4) is on the graph.

Use with Grade 5, Chapter 10, Lesson 6, pages 446–449. (313)

Reteach

R 10-6 RETEACH

Graph in Four Quadrants and Solve Problems Using Graphs

The **coordinate grid** is made by crossing two number lines. The number lines are called **axes**.

The point where the axes cross is called the **origin**. It is labeled (0, 0).
The horizontal axis is called the ***x*-axis**. It goes from left to right.
The vertical axis is called the ***y*-axis**. It goes up and down.

To plot an ordered pair on a coordinate grid:

- Start at the origin.
- If the first number is positive, move right. If it is negative, move left.
- If the second number is positive, move up. If it is negative, move down.

Point ***A*** has coordinates (5, -4).
To get there, start at (0, 0).
Move 5 right, then 4 down.

Point ***B*** has coordinates (-3, 5).
To get there, start at (0, 0).
Move 3 left, then 5 up.

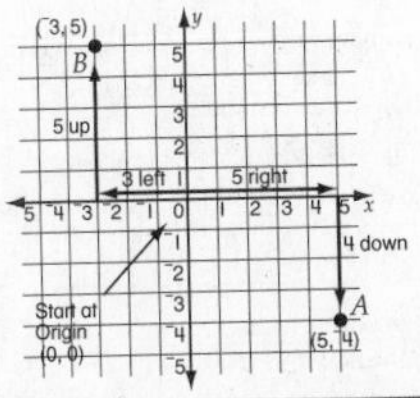

Write the ordered pair for the point described.

1. Move 3 left, then 1 up. (-3, 1)
2. Move 5 right, then 1 down. (5, -1)
3. Move 1 left, then 2 down. (-1, -2)

Give the coordinates of the point.

4. C (4, 1)
5. D (-3, -2)
6. E (-1, 3)
7. F (2, -2)

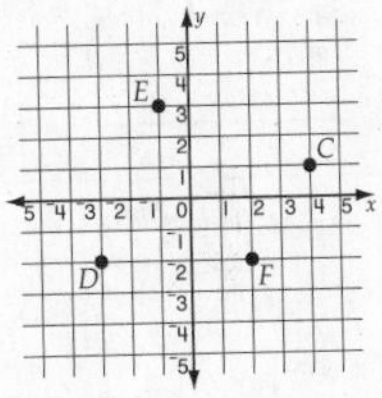

Use with Grade 5, Chapter 10, Lesson 6, pages 446–449. (314)

Enrich

E 10-6 ENRICH

Graph in Four Quadrants and Solve Problems Using Graphs

Rectangle Search

Play this game with a partner. Throughout the game, keep your paper hidden from your partner.

- Draw a rectangle on Grid A below. Place each vertex of the rectangle on an intersection of grid lines.
- Take turns guessing points to figure out the location of your partner's rectangle.
- When your partner guesses a point, tell whether it is a vertex of the rectangle, inside the rectangle, outside the rectangle, or on a side of the rectangle.
- Mark what you find out about your partner's rectangle on Grid B. To help, mark points inside, outside, and on the rectangle with different colors or with different letters.

The winner is the first player to correctly guess the location of his or her partner's rectangle.

Grid A

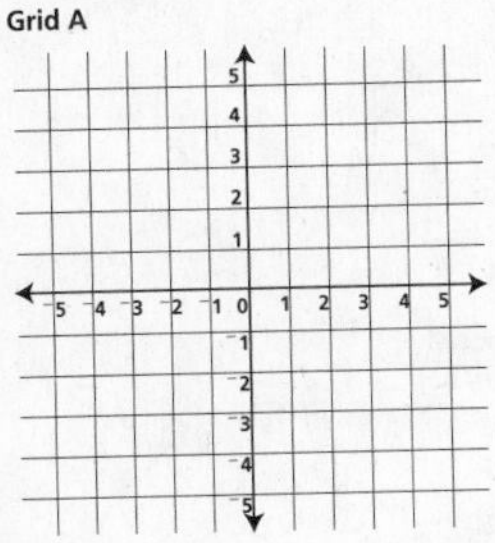

Grid B

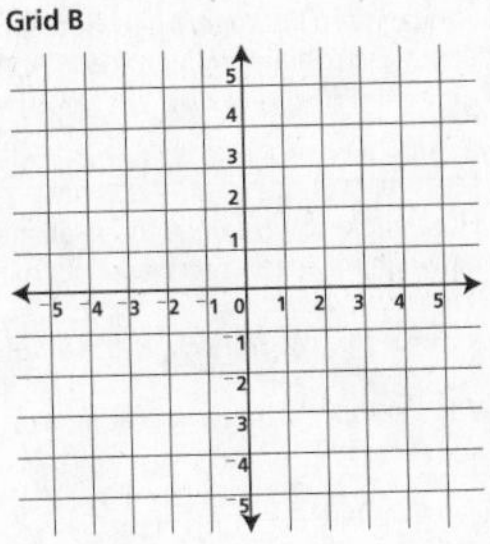

Name one strategy you used to play this game.
Answers may vary. Possible answer: Once I discovered one vertex of the rectangle, I guessed points having one of the same coordinates.

Use with Grade 5, Chapter 10, Lesson 6, pages 446–449. (315)

Daily Homework

10-6 Graph in Four Quadrants and Solve Problems Using Graphs

Write the ordered pair for each point described.

1. 3 units to the right of the origin; 2 units below the origin (3, -2)
2. 5 units above the origin; 1 unit to the left of the origin (-1, 5)

Give the coordinates of the point.

3. R (1, 3)
4. T (-2, -5)
5. V (-4, 2)

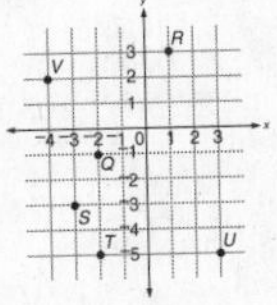

Name the point for the ordered pair.

6. (3, -5) U
7. (-2, -1) Q
8. (-3, 3) S

Complete the table. Then graph the function.
Check students' graphs.

9. $y = 3 - x$

x	y
-2	5
0	3
2	1
4	-1

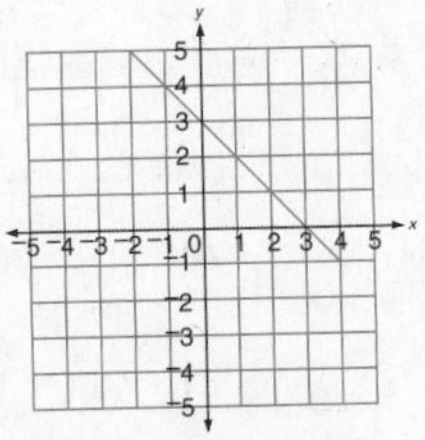

Problem Solving

10. Linda is graphing the equation $y = x + 4$. Will the coordinates (1, 5) show up on her graph? Yes.

11. John's graph of a straight line function begins at point (-3, -3) and ends at point (4, 2). Through how many quadrants of the graph does his line run? 3

Spiral Review

Find the LCD.

12. 4 and 5 20
13. 6 and 8 24
14. 4 and 15 60

96 Grade 5, Chapter 10, Lesson 6, Cluster A

Chapter 10 ~ Lesson 7

Practice

Problem Solving: Reading for Math
Use Graphs to Identify Relationships

P 10-7 PRACTICE — Reading Skill

Use data from the graph for exercises 1–7.

The graph shows the air temperature in Jackson for a 24-hour period.

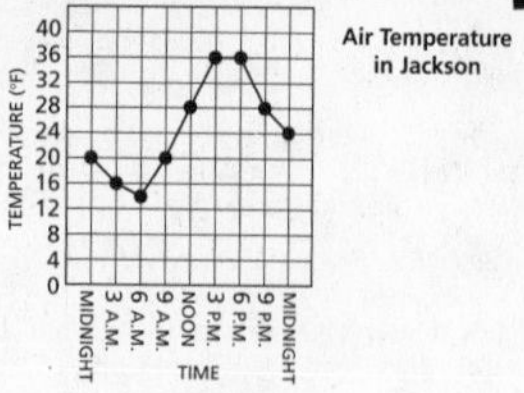

1. Describe how the temperature was changing from midnight to 6 A.M.
   Temperature was decreasing.
2. During what time period was the temperature constant? Explain.
   From 3 P.M. to 6 P.M. the temperature did not change, indicated by the horizontal line on the graph.
3. Describe the relationship in the temperatures from 6 A.M. to 3 P.M. How does the graph show this change?
   The temperature is increasing; the line rises.
4. By about how many degrees did the temperature change from 9 A.M. to 3 P.M.? Did the temperature increase or decrease?
   Temperature increased 16°F.
5. During what part of the 24-hour period shown in the graph did the temperature decrease in Jackson?
   The temperature decreased between 12 midnight and 6 A.M. and again between 6 P.M. and 12 midnight.
6. Between what times did the temperature fall about 2°F?
   between 3 A.M. and 6 A.M.
7. What was the temperature difference from midnight to noon? From midnight to midnight?

Use with Grade 5, Chapter 10, Lesson 7, pages 450–451. (316)

Practice

Problem Solving: Reading for Math
Use Graphs to Identify Relationships

P 10-7 PRACTICE — Math Skills Test Prep

Choose the best answer.

During a five-day period, the daily low temperature dropped 3°F each day. At the beginning of the period, the daily low temperature was 25°F. At the end of the period, the daily low temperature was 10°F.

1. Which of the following statements is true?
   - A The daily low temperature remained the same as time passed.
   - (B) The daily low temperature decreased as time passed.
   - C The daily low temperature increased as time passed.
   - D The daily low temperature changed by 10°F from the first day to the last day.
2. Suppose a horizontal line connects two points representing temperature on a line graph. What relationship does the line indicate?
   - F The temperature is rising.
   - G The temperature is falling.
   - (H) The temperature is the same.
   - J No relationship is indicated.

During a 12-hour period, the temperature increased 2°F every hour for the first eight hours. Then the temperature decreased 1°F every hour. The first hour the temperature was 68°F.

3. Which of the following statements is true?
   - A The temperature only increased as time passed.
   - B The temperature only decreased as time passed.
   - C The temperature did not change as time passed.
   - (D) The temperature was greater at the end of the 12-hour period than at the beginning of the 12-hour period.
4. What does a rising line in a line graph tell you?
   - (F) The quantity is increasing.
   - G The quantity is decreasing.
   - H The quantity is not changing.
   - J The quantity is either increasing or decreasing.

Use with Grade 5, Chapter 10, Lesson 7, pages 450–451. (317)

Practice

Problem Solving: Reading for Math
Use Graphs to Identify Relationships

P 10-7 PRACTICE — Math Skills Test Prep

Choose the best answer.

A severe winter storm hit Yellowstone in March. The temperature dropped 6°F every hour for four hours. Then the temperature dropped 2°F every hour for three hours.

5. Which of the following statements is true?
   - A The temperature at the end of the first four hours was less than the temperature at the end of the second three hours.
   - B A graph of the temperatures would show a falling line and then a horizontal line.
   - (C) The lowest temperature was recorded at the end of seven hours.
   - D The temperature decreased and then increased.
6. What does a falling line in a line graph tell you?
   - F The quantity is increasing.
   - (G) The quantity is decreasing.
   - H The quantity is not changing.
   - J The quantity is either increasing or decreasing.

Solve.

Use data from the graph for problems 7–10. The graph shows the water temperature recorded at a mountain lake.

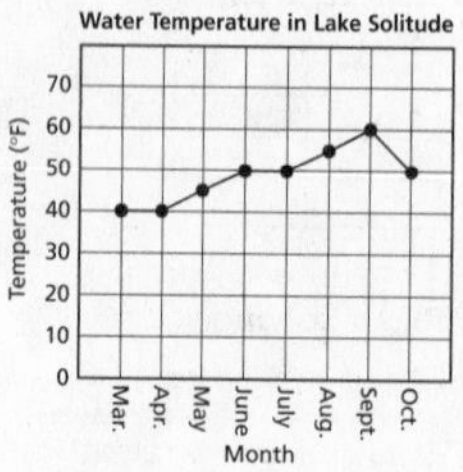

7. Between which two months did the temperature decrease?
   September and October
8. How would you describe the relationship between month and lake temperature between the months of April and June?
   Between each month, temperature increases.
9. What change occurred in the lake temperature between May and June? Between May and August?
   Temperature increased about 5°F; about 10°F
10. Describe the relationship between lake temperatures from March to April. Does any other period show a similar relationship? How do you know?
    The water temperature did not change. From June to July the temperature did not change. The line on the graph is horizontal.

Use with Grade 5, Chapter 10, Lesson 7, pages 450–451. (318)

Daily Homework

10-7 Problem Solving: Reading for Math

Use Graphs to Identify Relationships

1. The graph shows the air temperature at the top of Mount McMillan from 5 A.M. to 10 A.M. on March 13. How would you describe the relationship between time and air temperature as shown in this graph?
   Air temperature increased as time passed.

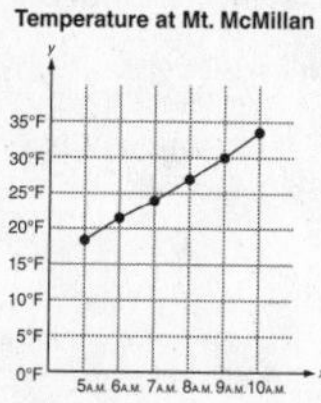

2. From 10 A.M. on, the air temperature stayed at 34°F. How would this be shown on a graph?
   (horizontal) straight line

Use data from the graph for problems 3–5.

3. The graph at the right shows the average monthly precipitation in Seattle, Washington, for each month of the year. What change occurs in the average precipitation between January and February? between February and March? between March and April?
   decrease of 1.4 inches; decrease of 0.2 inches; decrease of 1.3 inches

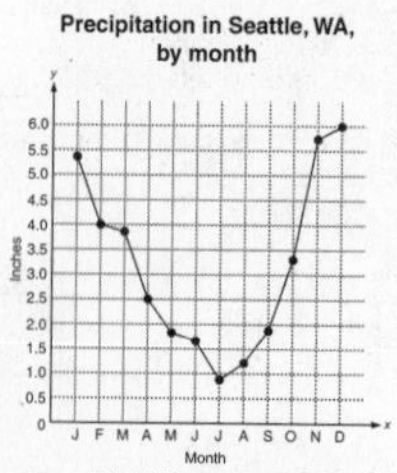

source: *World Almanac and Book of Facts 2000*

4. How would you describe the relationship between month and precipitation from January to July?
   Precipitation decreases as the months pass.
5. What is the difference in precipitation between the wettest month and the driest month?
   5.1 inches

Spiral Review

6. $1.4 \times 2.3 =$ 3.22
7. $9.54 \div 0.6 =$ 15.9
8. $191.4 \div 3.3 =$ 58

Grade 5, Chapter 10, Lesson 7, Cluster A 97

Chapter 10 ~ Lesson 8

Practice

Explore Addition Equations

10-8 PRACTICE

Each sheet of paper represents one side of the equation. The counters represent the numbers and the cups stand for the variables. Write the equation represented by each model. Then solve it.

1.
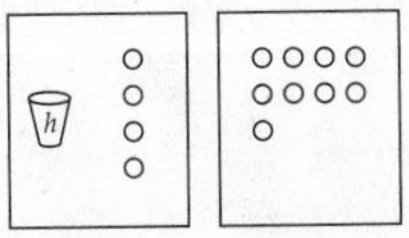

$h + 4 = 9$; 5

2.
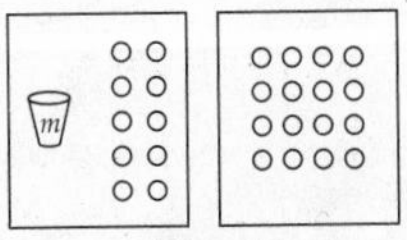

$m + 10 = 16$; 6

3.

$7 + s = 14$; 7

4.

$3 + w = 20$; 17

Solve.

5. $q + 4 = 10$ 6
6. $2 + v = 17$ 15
7. $t + 6 = 13$ 7
8. $b + 9 = 19$ 10
9. $12 + r = 15$ 3
10. $16 + c = 24$ 8
11. $10 = a + 3$ 7
12. $18 = k + 7$ 11
13. $14 = 5 + d$ 9
14. $19 = 8 + f$ 11
15. $25 = n + 10$ 15
16. $28 = 15 + p$ 13

Use the data in the information below to solve problems 17–18.

A box contains 4 pounds of sculpting clay and some painting supplies. The contents of the box weighs 7 pounds in all.

17. Draw a model to represent the situation.

18. Write an equation represented by the model you drew. Solve it to find the weight of the painting supplies.

$4 + p = 7$; 3 pounds

Use with Grade 5, Chapter 10, Lesson 8, pages 454–455. (319)

Reteach

Explore Addition Equations

10-8 RETEACH

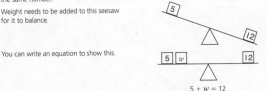

This seesaw is balanced. Each side has 12 pounds.

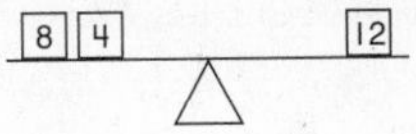

You can think of an equation as a balanced seesaw. Both sides of an equation must represent the same number.

Weight needs to be added to this seesaw for it to balance.

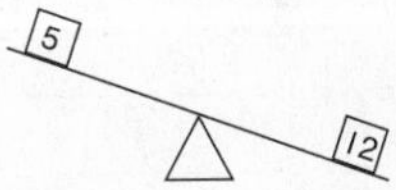

You can write an equation to show this.

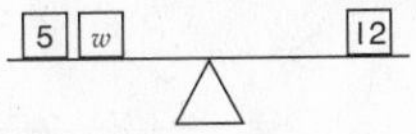

$5 + w = 12$

Think: 5 plus what number equals 12?

$5 + 7 = 12$, so $w = 7$.

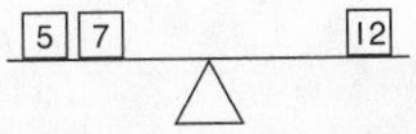

$w = 7$

Write the equation represented by each seesaw. Then solve it.

1.
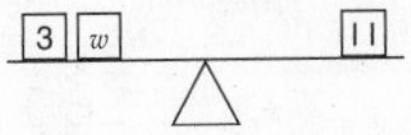

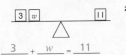

3 + w = 11

Think: 3 plus what number equals 11?

$w =$ 8

2.
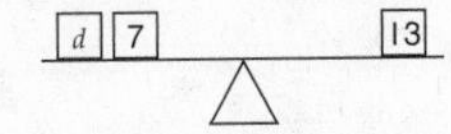

$d + 7 = 13$

Think: What number plus 7 equals 13?

$d =$ 6

3.
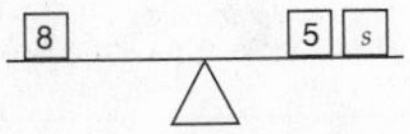

$8 = 5 + s$

$s =$ 3

4.
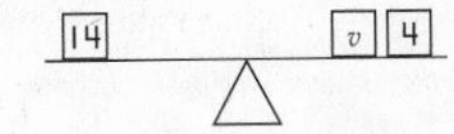

$14 = v + 4$

$v =$ 10

Use with Grade 5, Chapter 10, Lesson 8, pages 454–455. (320)

Enrich

Explore Addition Equations

10-8 ENRICH

Equation Writing Equations may vary. Possible equations are given.

Follow the directions to write other addition equations. For each new equation, change only one number. Look at the example if you need help. Record the solution of each equation you write.

Directions	Equations	Solutions
Example Write an equation that has a solution that is 3 more than the solution of $x + 12 = 40$.	$x + 12 = 43$ or $x + 9 = 40$	$x = 31$
1. Write an equation that has a solution that is 1 more than the solution of $30 = b + 20$.	$30 = b + 19$ or $31 = b + 20$	$b = 11$
2. Write an equation that has a solution that is twice the solution of $9 + d = 10$.	$9 + d = 11$ or $8 + d = 10$	$d = 2$
3. Write an equation that has a solution that is 5 less than the solution of $n + 2 = 30$.	$n + 2 = 25$ or $n + 7 = 30$	$n = 23$
4. Write an equation that has a solution that is half the solution of $16 = p + 6$.	$11 = p + 6$ or $16 = p + 11$	$p = 5$
5. Write an equation that has a solution that is 3 less than the solution of $h + 4 = 24$.	$h + 4 = 21$ or $h + 7 = 24$	$h = 17$
6. Write an equation that has a solution that is 3 times the solution of $17 = k + 16$.	$17 = k + 14$ or $19 = k + 16$	$k = 3$
7. Write an equation that has a solution that is 20 more than the solution of $7 + s = 16$.	$7 + s = 36$	$s = 29$
8. Write an equation that has a solution that is one fourth the solution of $29 = r + 1$.	$29 = r + 22$ or $8 = r + 1$	$r = 7$
9. Write an equation that has a solution that is 6 less than the solution of $7 + z = 26$.	$7 + z = 20$ or $13 + z = 26$	$z = 13$
10. Write an equation that has a solution that is 7 more than the solution of $17 = 5 + c$.	$24 = 5 + c$	$c = 19$

What do the solutions of all the equations you wrote have in common?

They are prime numbers.

Use with Grade 5, Chapter 10, Lesson 8, pages 454–455. (321)

Daily Homework

10-8 Explore Addition Equations

Solve each equation. Check your answer.

1. $c + 5 = 11$ $c = 6$
2. $j + 4 = 22$ $j = 18$
3. $p + 2 = 19$ $p = 17$
4. $n + 9 = 34$ $n = 25$
5. $15 + g = 23$ $g = 8$
6. $23 + b = 36$ $b = 13$
7. $19 + t = 38$ $t = 19$
8. $12 + f = 26$ $f = 14$
9. $17 = d + 9$ $d = 8$
10. $28 = e + 12$ $e = 16$
11. $34 = 19 + w$ $w = 15$
12. $41 = 34 + q$ $q = 7$
13. $29 + r = 46$ $r = 17$
14. $z + 12 = 23$ $z = 11$
15. $22 = h + 9$ $h = 13$
16. $51 = a + 18$ $a = 33$

Solve.

17. Susan has to look up 12 vocabulary words for school. She has looked up 3 vocabulary words, but still has *w* words to look up, as expressed in the equation $3 + w = 12$. How many words does she still have to look up?

9 words

18. Edgar and Don agree to bring 23 cans of fruit juice to a picnic. Don brings 10. As expressed in the equation $23 = 10 + e$, how many cans does Edgar have to bring?

13 cans

19. The baby has spilled Julia's crayons all over the floor, and Julia must pick them up and put them back into the box. The box contains 48 crayons, and Julia has already picked up 22. As expressed in the equation $22 + c = 48$, how many more crayons must Julia pick up?

26 crayons

Spiral Review

20. $120 \times \frac{2}{3} =$ 80
21. $600 \div \frac{2}{5} =$ 1,500
22. $360 \div \frac{3}{4} =$ 480

98 Grade 5, Chapter 10, Lesson 8, Cluster B

Practice

Addition and Subtraction Equations

P 10-9 PRACTICE

Solve each equation. Check your answer.

1. $a + 8 = 23$ $a = 15$
2. $s - 9 = 26$ $s = 35$
3. $f - 36 = 17$ $f = 5$
4. $z + 16 = 59$ $z = 43$
5. $v - 14 = 162$ $v = 176$
6. $h - 2.7 = 3.8$ $h = 6.5$
7. $k - 60 = 84$ $k = 144$
8. $t + 30 = 94$ $t = 64$
9. $r + \frac{3}{4} = 17$ $r = 16\frac{1}{4}$
10. $96 = d + 78$ $d = 18$
11. $s - 14.9 = 31.6$ $s = 46.5$
12. $100 = c - 42$ $c = 142$
13. $4.5 = e + 0.4$ $e = 4.1$
14. $z + 2\frac{1}{2} = 6\frac{3}{4}$ $z = 4\frac{1}{4}$
15. $29 = g - 300$ $g = 329$
16. $c + 200 = 473$ $c = 273$
17. $w + 356 = 500$ $w = 144$
18. $p - \frac{2}{3} = 7$ $p = 7\frac{2}{3}$
19. $e - 211 = 481.6$ $e = 692.6$
20. $923 = y + 127$ $y = 796$
21. $h + 41.8 = 48.2$ $h = 6.4$
22. $3\frac{1}{4} = q - 1\frac{5}{8}$ $q = 4\frac{7}{8}$
23. $m + 4 = 1$ $m = -5$
24. $d - 6 = -7$ $d = -1$

Problem Solving

25. The low temperature in Nashville, TN, one day was 26°F. The difference between the high and low temperatures that day was 14°F. Write an equation to describe the situation. Solve it to find the high temperature in degrees Fahrenheit, t, that day.

    Equations may vary.
    Possible equation:
    $t - 26 = 14$; $t = 40$

26. One year Chicago, IL, received 39.2 inches of snow. That was 9.8 inches more than the previous year. Write an equation to describe the situation. Solve it to find last year's snowfall in inches, s.

    Equations may vary.
    Possible equation:
    $s + 9.8 = 39.2$; $s = 29.4$

Use with Grade 5, Chapter 10, Lesson 9, pages 456–459. (322)

Reteach

Addition and Subtraction Equations

R 10-9 RETEACH

You can use subtraction to solve addition equations.

Solve: $c + 25 = 39$

To find the value of c, subtract 25 from both sides of the equation.

$$\begin{aligned} c + 25 &= 39 \\ -25 &\quad -25 \\ c &= 14 \end{aligned}$$

Check your answer by substituting 14 for c in the original equation.

$$\begin{aligned} c + 25 &= 39 \\ 14 + 25 &= 39 \\ 39 &= 39 \leftarrow \text{It checks.} \end{aligned}$$

You can use addition to solve subtraction equations.

Solve: $f - 2.4 = 13.8$

To find the value of f, add 2.4 to both sides of the equation.

$$\begin{aligned} f - 2.4 &= 13.8 \\ +2.4 &\quad +2.4 \\ f &= 16.2 \end{aligned}$$

Check your answer by substituting 16.2 for f in the original equation.

$$\begin{aligned} f - 2.4 &= 13.8 \\ 16.2 - 2.4 &= 13.8 \\ 13.8 &= 13.8 \leftarrow \text{It checks.} \end{aligned}$$

Solve each equation. Show your work. Check your answer.

1. $n + 36 = 75$
   $-\boxed{36} \quad -\boxed{36}$
   $n =$ 39
2. $b - 4.6 = 15.9$
   $+\boxed{4.6} \quad +\boxed{4.6}$
   $b =$ 20.5
3. $w + \frac{1}{8} = \frac{7}{8}$
   $-\boxed{\frac{1}{8}} \quad -\boxed{\frac{1}{8}}$
   $w =$ $\frac{6}{8}$, or $\frac{3}{4}$
4. $p - 7 = 83$
   $p =$ 90
5. $c + 46 = 213$
   $c =$ 167
6. $s + 0.9 = 12.5$
   $s =$ 11.6
7. $x - 3.2 = 32.4$
   $x =$ 35.6
8. $m - 1\frac{1}{5} = 3\frac{4}{5}$
   $m =$ 5
9. $d + 0.7 = 52$
   $d =$ 51.3
10. $a + 9 = 7$
    $a =$ $^-2$
11. $z - 6 = {^-12}$
    $z =$ $^-6$
12. $y + ({^-10}) = {^-10}$
    $y =$ 0

Use with Grade 5, Chapter 10, Lesson 9, pages 456–459. (323)

Enrich

Addition and Subtraction Equations

E 10-9 ENRICH

Equation Race

- Write a whole number or a decimal less than 100, a fraction, or a mixed number in each square of the grid at the right.
- Trace a path from any square in the left column to any square in the right column.
- For each square in your path, write an addition or subtraction equation with the number in the square as the solution. Write the equations in order on the lines below.
- Fold your paper in half along the dotted line so your partner can see the equations but not the grid. Trade papers with your partner.

- Solve each other's equations. Then unfold the papers to check the solutions.
- The winner is the first player to have solved all the equations correctly or the player who solved more equations correctly.

Use with Grade 5, Chapter 10, Lesson 9, pages 456–459. (324)

Daily Homework

10-9 Addition and Subtraction Equations

Solve each equation. Check your answer.

1. $h + 9 = 21$ $h = 12$
2. $k + 34 = 71$ $k = 37$
3. $u - 8 = 72$ $u = 80$
4. $a - 7.3 = 15.6$ $a = 22.9$
5. $131 + m = 147$ $m = 16$
6. $f - 19 = 92$ $f = 111$
7. $y + \frac{3}{5} = 35\frac{1}{5}$ $y = 34\frac{3}{5}$
8. $326.7 - s = 297.4$ $s = 29.3$
9. $m + 5 = {^-1}$ $m = {^-6}$
10. $u + ({^-3}) = 7$ $u = 10$

Without solving each equation, tell whether the solution is greater than 44, less than 44, or equal to 44.

11. $r + 10 = 44$ $r < 44$
12. $x - 56 = 44$ $x > 44$

Problem Solving

13. The gas tank in Maria's mother's car can hold 14 gallons of gas. If her mother fills the tank by putting in 9 gallons of gas, how much gas was already in the tank? Write an equation and solve it.

    Possible answer: $9 + g = 14$; 5 gallons

14. The road from Chicago to Minneapolis goes through Madison, Wisconsin. It is 409 miles from Chicago to Minneapolis, and 146 miles from Chicago to Madison. How far is it from Madison to Minneapolis? Write an equation and solve it.

    Possible answer: $146 + x = 409$; 263 miles

Spiral Review

Identify each property.

15. $(2{,}903 + 4{,}255) + 860 = 2{,}903 + (4{,}255 + 860)$

    Associative Property of Addition

16. $92{,}754 \times 0 = 0$

    Zero Property of Multiplication

Grade 5, Chapter 10, Lesson 9, Cluster B 99

Chapter 10 ~ Lesson 10

Practice

Multiplication and Division Equations

P 10-10 PRACTICE

Solve each equation. Check your answer.

1. $7w = 28$ $w = 4$
2. $q \div 6 = 108$ $q = 648$
3. $d \times 20 = 180$ $d = 9$
4. $\frac{q}{9} = 7.2$ $q = 64.8$
5. $e \times 4 = 276$ $e = 69$
6. $15y = 48$ $y = 3.2$
7. $k \div 40 = 8$ $k = 320$
8. $0.4 \times p = 16$ $p = 40$
9. $\frac{j}{52} = 13$ $j = 676$
10. $s \div 12 = 60$ $s = 720$
11. $30h = 15$ $h = 0.5$ or $\frac{1}{2}$
12. $w \div 0.8 = 64$ $w = 51.2$
13. $b \div \frac{5}{8} = 8$ $b = 5$
14. $2.4c = 120$ $c = 50$
15. $1\frac{1}{2} \times n = 15$ $n = 10$
16. $\frac{s}{0.7} = 21$ $s = 14.7$
17. $\frac{x}{1.2} = 1.2$ $x = 1.44$
18. $f \times 32 = 6.4$ $f = 0.2$
19. $0.6t = 60$ $t = 100$
20. $w \div \frac{1}{4} = 24$ $w = 6$
21. $\frac{z}{60} = 20$ $z = 1{,}200$
22. $\frac{3}{5}b = 12$ $b = 20$
23. $4.1 \times v = 20.5$ $v = 5$
24. $w \div 1.6 = 8$ $w = 12.8$
25. $r \times 8.6 = 21.5$ $r = 2.5$
26. $0.5x = 4.2$ $x = 8.4$
27. $9.5 \div s = 0.95$ $s = 10$
28. $d \div \frac{1}{3} = 225$ $d = 75$
29. $2\frac{1}{2} \times b = 50$ $b = 20$
30. $\frac{2}{3}a = 24$ $a = 36$

Problem Solving

31. The Martinez family paid $37.50 for 5 movie passes. Write a multiplication equation to describe the situation. Solve it to find the cost in dollars, c, of each movie pass.
$5c = 37.50;\ c = 7.50$

32. Three friends split the cost of a gift equally. Each paid $4.19. Write a division equation to describe the situation. Solve it to find the total cost in dollars, t, of the gift.
$\frac{t}{3} = 4.19;\ t = 12.57$

Use with Grade 5, Chapter 10, Lesson 10, pages 460–463. (325)

Reteach

Multiplication and Division Equations

R 10-10 RETEACH

You can use division to solve multiplication equations.

Solve: $12s = 240$

To find the value of s, divide both sides of the equation by 12.

$$12s = 240$$
$$\div 12 \quad \div 12$$
$$s = 20$$

Check your answer by substituting 20 for s in the original equation.

$$12s = 240$$
$$12 \times 20 = 240$$
$$240 = 240 \leftarrow \text{It checks.}$$

You can use multiplication to solve division equations.

Solve: $\frac{t}{3} = 4.8$

To find the value of t, multiply both sides of the equation by 3.

$$\frac{t}{3} = 4.8$$
$$\frac{t}{3} \times 3 = 4.8 \times 3$$
$$t = 14.4$$

Check your answer by substituting 14.4 for t in the original equation.

$$\frac{t}{3} = 4.8$$
$$\frac{14.4}{3} = 4.8$$
$$4.8 = 4.8 \leftarrow \text{It checks.}$$

Solve each equation. Show your work. Check your answer.

1. $8d = 96$ $d =$ 12
2. $2.5m = 75$ $m =$ 30
3. $\frac{1}{2}k = 3.2$ $k =$ 6.4
4. $0.7y = 42$ $y =$ 60
5. $n \div 15 = 60$ $n =$ 900
6. $w \div 7 = 56$ $w =$ 392
7. $a \div \frac{3}{4} = \frac{1}{2}$ $a =$ $\frac{3}{8}$
8. $v \div 0.8 = 72$ $v =$ 57.6
9. $30b = 600$ $b =$ 20

Use with Grade 5, Chapter 10, Lesson 10, pages 460–463. (326)

Enrich

Multiplication and Division Equations

E 10-10 ENRICH

Equation A-maze-ment

Solve each equation. Circle each solution in the maze below. Then trace the path through the maze from Start to Finish.

1. $5.2 = 4m$ $m = 1.3$
2. $500 = b \div 5$ $b = 2{,}500$
3. $36n = 72$ $n = 2$
4. $g \div 0.2 = 50$ $g = 10$
5. $h \times \frac{3}{4} = 12$ $h = 16$
6. $30 = p \div \frac{2}{5}$ $p = 12$
7. $96 = 12t$ $t = 8$
8. $\frac{k}{3} = 0.5$ $k = 1.5$
9. $d \div \frac{1}{4} = 18$ $d = 4\frac{1}{2}$
10. $7.5 = 1.5a$ $a = 5$
11. $\frac{r}{12} = 3$ $r = 36$
12. $25 = 1\frac{1}{4}c$ $c = 20$

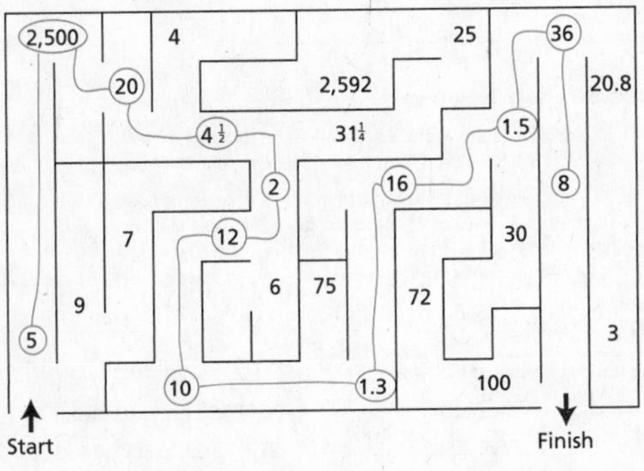

Use with Grade 5, Chapter 10, Lesson 10, pages 460–463. (327)

Daily Homework

10-10 Multiplication and Division Equations

For each equation, decide if you should multiply or divide both sides to solve.

1. $7y = 21$ divide
2. $f \div 2 = 19$ multiply
3. $15x = 125$ divide
4. $\frac{s}{3} = 51$ multiply

Solve each equation. Check your answer.

5. $u \times 6 = 618$ $u = 103$
6. $\frac{y}{7} = 32$ $y = 224$
7. $t \times 4.2 = 21$ $t = 5$
8. $\frac{p}{3.5} = 3$ $p = 10.5$
9. $12n = 1{,}440$ $n = 120$
10. $125 \div t = 25$ $t = 5$
11. $w \times 8 = 680$ $w = 85$
12. $336 \div g = 96$ $g = 3.5$

Choose the equation for which the value of n is a solution. Circle your answer.

13. $n = 5$
A. $n + 2 = 9$ (B. $2n = 10$) C. $\frac{n}{2} = 3$

14. $n = 3.2$
(A. $7.7 - n = 4.5$) B. $10n = 35$ C. $n \div 0.5 = 6$

Problem Solving

15. At the grocery store, 16 oz of apples costs $2.40, 24 oz costs $3.60, and 32 oz costs $4.80. Write an equation that relates the price of the apples to their weight. $p = \$0.15w$

16. According to the equation from problem 13, how much will 132 oz of apples cost? $19.80

Spiral Review

Describe each number as prime or composite.

17. 17 prime
18. 49 composite
19. 230 composite

100 Grade 5, Chapter 10, Lesson 10, Cluster B

Chapter 10 ~ Lesson 11

Practice

Problem Solving: Strategy
Make a Graph

P 10-11 PRACTICE

Solve. Use a graph.

1. The average surface temperature on Venus is 870°F. Use the equation $F = 1.8°C + 32$ to estimate the average surface temperature on Venus in degrees Celsius.
   Check students' graphs; temperature is about 465°C.
2. The surface temperature on Venus can reach 900°F. Use the graph from problem 1 to find this surface temperature in degrees Celsius.
   about 480°C
3. A botanist finds that the height of a tree, in centimeters, is related to its age, in weeks, by the equation $y = 3x + 1$. Graph this equation.
   Check students' graphs.
4. If a tree measures to be 16 centimeters, how many weeks old is the tree? If the tree is 1 month old, how tall is the tree? Use the graph from problem 3 to solve.
   5 weeks; 13 cm

Mixed Strategy Review Strategies may vary. Possible strategies are given.
Solve. Use any strategy.

5. **Career** A jeweler has 3 necklaces and 7 pairs of earrings. How many different combinations of necklaces and earrings can he put together in a display?
   21
   Strategy: Make an Organized List
6. Ana Maria gave 5 flowers to her sister and twice as many to her mother. If she has a half dozen flowers left, how many flowers did she have to start with?
   21 flowers
   Strategy: Write an Equation
7. **Literature** Jeremy has four times as many books by K.A. Applegate as by Lynne Reid Banks. If he has 30 books by the two authors, how many does he have by each one?
   K.A. Applegate: 24 books; Lynne Reid Banks: 6 books
   Strategy: Guess and Check
8. **Create a problem** in which you must use a graph to solve the problem. Share it with others.
   Check students' problems.

Use with Grade 5, Chapter 10, Lesson 11, pages 464–465. (328)

Reteach

Problem Solving: Strategy
Make a Graph

R 10-11 RETEACH

Page 465, Problem 1

If the average temperature of Earth rises to 62°F, about what is the new temperature in Celsius?

Step 1 Read

Be sure you understand the problem.
Read carefully.

What do you know?

- The average temperature of Earth in degrees Fahrenheit

What do you need to find?

- The average temperature of Earth in degrees Celsius

Step 2 Plan

- Find a Pattern
- Guess and Check
- Work Backward
- Make a Graph
- Make a Table
- Write an Equation
- Make an Organized List
- Draw a Diagram
- Solve a Simpler Problem
- Logical Reasoning

Make a plan.
Choose a strategy.

Use a Graph will help you solve the problem.

The equation $F = 1.8°C + 32$ relates degrees Fahrenheit and degrees Celsius. Use the equation to graph the function.

Use the graph to find a solution.

Use with Grade 5, Chapter 10, Lesson 11, pages 464–465. (329)

Reteach

Problem Solving: Strategy
Make a Graph

R 10-11 RETEACH

Step 3 Solve

Carry out your plan.

Make a table of values. Pick values for °C and use the equation to find values for °F. Graph the results.

$F = 1.8C + 32$

°C	°F
0	32
5	41
10	50
15	59
20	68
30	86

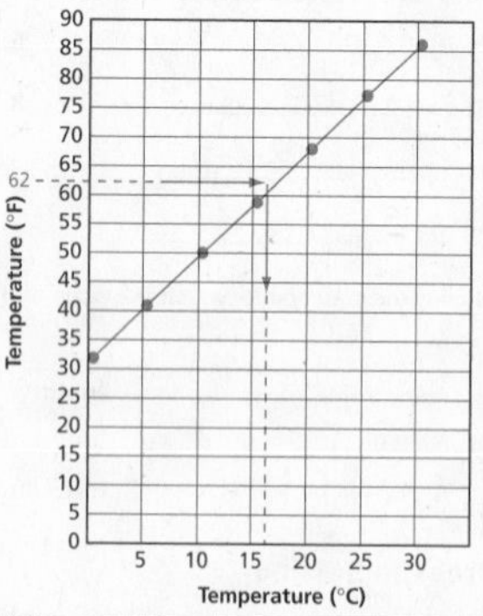

Find 62° on the vertical axis.

Move across to the graphed line.

Move down to find the value on the horizontal axis.

62°F is equal to about 16°C.

Step 4 Look Back

Is the solution reasonable?
Reread the problem.

Is your answer reasonable? Yes, from the table 68°F is about 20°C

What other way could you solve this problem?
Substitute F = 62 into the equation and solve for C.

Practice

1. If the temperature at 5 P.M. is 25°C, what is the temperature in Fahrenheit?
   about 77°F
2. The high temperature for the day is 80°F. What is the temperature in Celsius?
   about 26°C

Use with Grade 5, Chapter 10, Lesson 11, pages 464–465. (330)

Daily Homework

10-11 Problem Solving: Strategy
Make a Graph

Use the graph to solve.

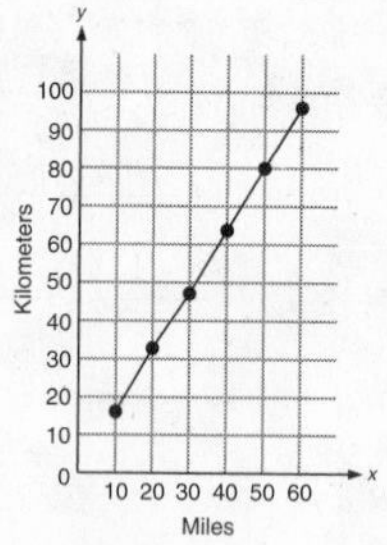

1. It is 44 miles from San Francisco to San Jose. About what is this distance in kilometers?
   about 70 kilometers
2. It is 48 kilometers from Dallas to Fort Worth. About what is this distance in miles?
   about 30 miles
3. Steve travels 50 miles to visit his grandmother, and decides to check the graph to see how far he has traveled in kilometers. He estimates that he has traveled about 30 kilometers. Is he reading the graph correctly?
   No.
4. Pam drives 15 miles to the beach. Going home, she takes a different route, and drives 18 miles. About how far does she drive in kilometers?
   about 53 kilometers

Mixed Strategy Review

5. Electra owns 4 skirts. If she wants to wear a different outfit every day for a full month, how many blouses must she have? 8 blouses
6. Harry would like to surprise his mother with a bouquet of flowers for her birthday. The flowers cost $38 plus a 6% sales tax. The delivery charge is $5. Harry has one $20 bill, one $10 bill, and eight $1 bills. How much more money does Harry need? $7.28

Spiral Review

Name the place-value of the 6 in each problem.

7. 41.68 tenths
8. 62,993.3 ten-thousands
9. 2,910.96 hundredths
10. 56.207 ones

Grade 5, Chapter 10, Lesson 11, Cluster B 101

Chapter 10 ~ Lesson 12

Practice

Two-Step Equations

10-12 PRACTICE

Solve.

1. $2c + 9 = 35$ $c = 13$
2. $\frac{v}{5} - 13 = 37$ $v = 250$
3. $7t - 3 = 60$ $t = 9$
4. $\frac{h}{4} + 7 = 12$ $h = 20$
5. $\frac{w}{20} - 1 = 15$ $w = 320$
6. $24 + 3a = 36$ $a = 4$
7. $73 = 12s - 23$ $s = 8$
8. $11y - 14 = 173$ $y = 17$
9. $8 + 1.3d = 36.6$ $d = 22$
10. $23 + \frac{b}{10} = 26$ $b = 30$
11. $18 = \frac{y}{2.5} - 2$ $y = 50$
12. $10 = \frac{3}{4}e + 7$ $e = 4$
13. $16m - 2 = 46$ $m = 3$
14. $\frac{s}{18} - \frac{1}{2} = 3\frac{1}{2}$ $s = 72$
15. $20 = \frac{z}{5} + 16$ $z = 20$
16. $5 = \frac{a}{3.1} - 1$ $a = 18.6$
17. $4 + \frac{p}{15} = 11$ $p = 105$
18. $\frac{5}{6} = \frac{2}{3}d - \frac{1}{6}$ $d = 1\frac{1}{2}$
19. $25y + 7 = 157$ $y = 6$
20. $\frac{b}{12} - 2 = 10$ $b = 144$
21. $\frac{f}{0.4} + 1.6 = 9.6$ $f = 3.2$
22. $15 = 7.5 + 3u$ $u = 2.5$
23. $1\frac{5}{12} = \frac{3}{4} + 2w$ $w = \frac{1}{3}$
24. $30t - 120 = 180$ $t = 10$

Problem Solving

25. A large pizza with cheese costs $8.00. Each additional topping costs $0.75. Glenn ordered a large pizza with toppings that cost $10.25. Write a two-step equation to represent this situation. Solve it to find the number of additional toppings, t, on the pizza.

$8 + 0.75t = 10.25;$

$t = 3$

26. With a $2-off coupon, 4 sandwiches at a restaurant cost $5.16. Write a two-step equation to represent this situation. Solve it to find the original cost in dollars, c, of each sandwich.

$4c - 2 = 5.16;$

$c = 1.79$

Reteach

Two-Step Equations

10-12 RETEACH

When you solve two-step equations, first undo the addition or subtraction step. Then undo the multiplication or division step.

Solve: $5w - 13 = 42$

To undo the subtraction, add 13 to both sides of the equation.

$5w - 13 = 42$
$\quad + 13 \quad + 13$
$\frac{5w}{5} = \frac{55}{5}$

To undo the multiplication, divide both sides the equation by 5.

$w = 11$

Check your answer by substituting 11 for w in the original equation.

$5w - 13 = 42$
$5 \times 11 - 13 = 42$
$55 - 13 = 42$
$42 = 42$ ← It checks.

Complete. Solve.

1. $4d + 10 = 22$
   $-\boxed{10} \quad -\boxed{10}$
   $\frac{\boxed{4d}}{4} = \frac{\boxed{12}}{4}$
   $d =$ 3
2. $\frac{s}{2} + 3.2 = 8.6$
   $-\boxed{3.2} \quad -\boxed{3.2}$
   $\boxed{\frac{s}{2}} = \boxed{5.4}$
   $\times\boxed{2} \quad \times\boxed{2}$
   $s =$ 10.8
3. $\frac{t}{6} - 4 = 1$
   $\boxed{+4} \quad \boxed{+4}$
   $\frac{t}{6} = \boxed{5}$
   $\boxed{\times 6} \quad \boxed{\times 6}$
   $t =$ 30
4. $7r - 4.9 = 56$ $r =$ 8.7
5. $3.4w + 12.8 = 114.8$ $w =$ 30
6. $\frac{b}{9} + 14 = 21$ $b =$ 63
7. $\frac{1}{3}z - \frac{1}{8} = \frac{1}{8}$ $z = \frac{3}{4}$
8. $0.7c + 2.4 = 5.9$ $c =$ 5
9. $\frac{a}{4} - 15 = 65$ $a =$ 320
10. $29 = 12x - 7$ $x =$ 3
11. $15 = \frac{n}{5} - 5$ $n =$ 100
12. $31.4 = 2.7m + 1.7$ $m =$ 11

Enrich

Two-Step Equations
A Famous Equation

10-12 ENRICH

Find each solution.

A. $2a + 9 = 37;\ a =$ 14
D. $51 = 6d - 21;\ d =$ 12
E. $4e + 6.5 = 12.1;\ e =$ 1.4
F. $\frac{f}{2} - 3 = 2;\ f =$ 10
G. $5g + \frac{1}{2} = 3;\ g =$ $\frac{1}{2}$
H. $194 = 10h - 6;\ h =$ 20
I. $\frac{i}{6} + 25 = 28;\ i =$ 18
L. $0.5 = \frac{l}{4} - 0.2;\ l =$ 2.8
M. $3m - 42 = 15;\ m =$ 19
N. $6.2 = 0.5n + 3.2;\ n =$ 6
O. $7o - 40 = 170;\ o =$ 30
P. $\frac{p}{3} - \frac{5}{8} = 2\frac{3}{8};\ p =$ 9
Q. $167 = 67 + 4q;\ q =$ 25
R. $\frac{7}{8}r + 6 = 20;\ r =$ 16
S. $1.2s - 4 = 14;\ s =$ 15
T. $233 = 17 + 9t;\ t =$ 24
U. $\frac{u}{0.3} - 15 = 55;\ u =$ 21
Y. $5 = \frac{y}{10} + 1\frac{1}{2};\ y =$ 35

One of the most famous equations is $E = mc^2$. Find each solution below. Write the letter of the exercise above the matching solution to find out what $E = mc^2$ means.

E	N	E	R	G	Y		E	Q	U	A	L	S		M	A	S	S
1.4	6	1.4	16	$\frac{1}{2}$	35		1.4	25	21	14	2.8	15		19	14	15	15

T	I	M	E	S		T	H	E		S	Q	U	A	R	E		O	F
24	18	19	1.4	15		24	20	1.4		15	25	21	14	16	1.4		30	10

T	H	E		S	P	E	E	D		O	F		L	I	G	H	T
24	20	1.4		15	9	1.4	1.4	12		30	10		2.8	18	$\frac{1}{2}$	20	24

Daily Homework

10•12 Two-Step Equations

Solve.

1. $2y + 7 = 79$ $y = 36$
2. $4u - 9 = 91$ $u = 25$
3. $9t + 45 = 243$ $t = 22$
4. $551 = 6f - 19$ $f = 95$
5. $12.3e + 17 = 140$ $e = 10$
6. $11r - 19 = 102$ $r = 11$
7. $67.1 = 4.8h + 9.5$ $h = 12$
8. $\frac{p}{4} + 4 = 19$ $p = 60$
9. $240 = 6m + 18$ $m = 37$
10. $\frac{38}{s} - 7 = 12$ $s = 2$
11. $7.1q + 2.9 = 81$ $q = 11$
12. $\frac{w}{3} - \frac{5}{6} = \frac{1}{2}$ $w = 4$
13. $3k - \frac{2}{3} = \frac{1}{3}$ $k = \frac{1}{3}$
14. $4v + 7 = {}^{-}9$ $w = {}^{-}4$

Problem Solving

15. Candice has 23 plums. She bought 8 of these at the grocery store and was given the rest by her neighbor. Her neighbor gave Candice exactly $\frac{1}{4}$ of the plums he got from his plum tree. How many plums did her neighbor get from his tree? 60 plums

16. The fifth grade at Pierce Elementary School is going on a field trip to the art museum. There are 119 students and teachers going in all. Of these, 7 students are being driven to the museum by their parents. Everyone else will go in 4 school buses. How many people will be on each bus if each bus has the same number of people on it? 28 people

Spiral Review

Compare. Write >, <, or =.

17. $\frac{1}{8}$ < $\frac{2}{9}$
18. $\frac{3}{4}$ > 0.7
19. 4.6 = $4\frac{3}{5}$

Chapter 10 ~ Lesson 13

Part A Worksheet

Problem Solving: Application

Applying Algebra

Part A 10-13 WORKSHEET Decision Making

Use the table below to help you record the data. Then use the information to help you make your decision.

	Tanya's Idea	Andrew's Idea	Steve's Idea	Dena's idea
Total costs				
Total time				

Your Decision

What is your recommendation for which two projects the Save the Earth Committee should do this spring? Explain.

Answers may vary.

Use with Grade 5, Chapter 10, Lesson 13, pages 468–469. (334)

Part B Worksheet

Problem Solving: Application

How long can you make a string phone?

Part B 10-13 WORKSHEET Math & Science

Work with a partner.

Decide how you will rate the sound quality as you take turns sending a message. Discuss what each sound quality score should sound like.

Do you think it will be easier to hear through a string phone that is 3 meters long or 15 meters long?

Answers may vary.

Record your data in the table.

Length of String	Sound Quality (1 = perfect, 2 = good, 3 = OK, 4 = fair, 5 = terrible)
15 meters	
12 meters	
9 meters	
6 meters	
3 meters	

1. How did your hypothesis compare with the results of the experiment? Were you surprised?

   Answers may vary.

Use with Grade 5, Chapter 10, Lesson 13, pages 470–471. (335)

Part B Worksheet

Problem Solving: Application

How long can you make a string phone?

Part B 10-13 WORKSHEET Math & Science

2. Did you notice much of a difference in the sound quality between different lengths of string phones? Explain.

   Answers may vary.

3. Compare your data with the data of some of your classmates. How does the data compare?

   Answers may vary.

4. What type of graph would be most appropriate to show the data?

   bar graph

5. In the space below, make a graph to show your data.

   Check students' graphs.

6. Compare your graphs with the graphs of some of your classmates. How do the graphs compare?

   Answers may vary.

7. Describe how the graphs reflect the data.

   Answers may vary.

8. What are some other materials that you could use to investigate how sound travels through string phones?

   Answers may vary. Possible answers: cord, rope, plastic cups

Use with Grade 5, Chapter 10, Lesson 13, pages 470–471. (336)

Chapter 11 ~ Lesson 1

Practice

Basic Geometric Ideas

P 11-1 PRACTICE

Identify the figure. Then name it using symbols.

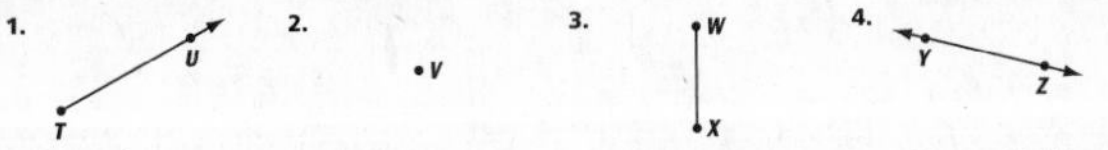

1. ray; $\overrightarrow{TU}$
2. point; V
3. line segment; $\overline{WX}$ or $\overline{XW}$
4. line; $\overleftrightarrow{YZ}$ or $\overleftrightarrow{YZ}$

Use the diagram for exercises 5–8.

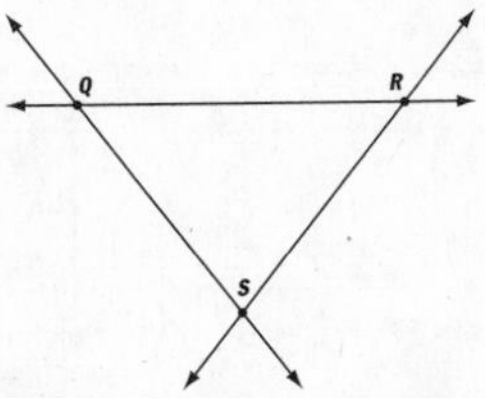

5. Name all the points. Q, R, S
6. Name a line segment. Any of the following: $\overline{QR}$ or $\overline{RQ}$; $\overline{QS}$ or $\overline{SQ}$; $\overline{RS}$ or $\overline{SR}$
7. Name a ray with endpoint R. Either of the following: $\overrightarrow{RQ}$; $\overrightarrow{RS}$
8. Name a line. Any of the following: $\overleftrightarrow{QR}$ or $\overleftrightarrow{RQ}$; $\overleftrightarrow{QS}$ or $\overleftrightarrow{SQ}$; $\overleftrightarrow{RS}$ or $\overleftrightarrow{SR}$

Name the polygon. Then tell if the sides are congruent line segments. Use a ruler to measure.

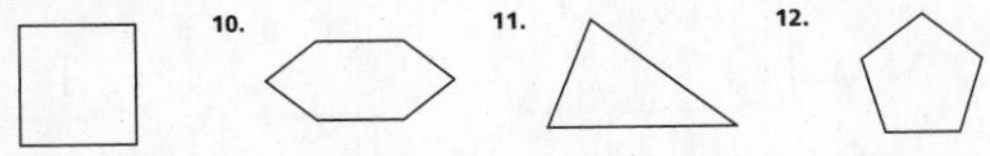

9. Accept quadrilateral or square; congruent
10. hexagon; not congruent
11. triangle; not congruent
12. pentagon; congruent

Problem Solving

13. In the dark, Veronica turned on a flashlight. What geometric figure is suggested by the beam of light? ray
14. Drivers know that, when they see an 8-sided red sign, they are to stop. What geometric figure is used for this sign? octagon

Use with Grade 5, Chapter 11, Lesson 1, pages 486–489. (337)

Reteach

Basic Geometric Ideas

R 11-1 RETEACH

This table describes some basic geometric figures.

Figure	Example	Name Using Symbols
Point	• A	A
Line	B ⟷ C	$\overleftrightarrow{BC}$ or $\overleftrightarrow{CB}$
Line segment	D —— E	$\overline{DE}$ or $\overline{ED}$
Ray	F ⟶ G	$\overrightarrow{FG}$

In the figures above, line segment DE has two endpoints, D and E. Ray FG has one endpoint, F. Line BC has no endpoints.

Identify the figure. Then name it using symbols.

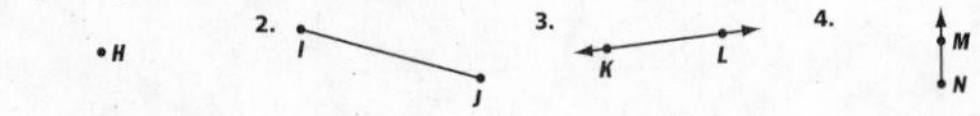

1. point; H
2. line segment; $\overline{IJ}$ or $\overline{JI}$
3. line $\overleftrightarrow{KL}$ or $\overleftrightarrow{LK}$
4. ray; $\overrightarrow{NM}$

Use data from the diagram for problems 5–10.

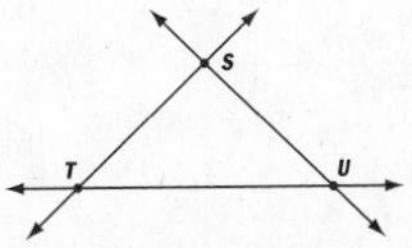

5. Name a line segment. Any of the following: $\overline{ST}$ or $\overline{TS}$; $\overline{SU}$ or $\overline{US}$; $\overline{TU}$ or $\overline{UT}$
6. Name the endpoint(s), if any, of the line segment you named in problem 5. depending upon the line segment named in exercise 5, S & T, S & U, or T & U
7. Name a line. any of the following: $\overleftrightarrow{ST}$ or $\overleftrightarrow{TS}$; $\overleftrightarrow{SU}$ or $\overleftrightarrow{US}$; $\overleftrightarrow{TU}$ or $\overleftrightarrow{UT}$
8. Name the endpoint(s), if any, of the line you named in exercise 7. no endpoints
9. Name a ray with endpoint T. either of the following: $\overrightarrow{TS}$ or $\overrightarrow{TU}$
10. Name two rays with endpoint S. $\overrightarrow{ST}$; $\overrightarrow{SU}$

Use with Grade 5, Chapter 11, Lesson 1, pages 486–489. (338)

Enrich

Basic Geometric Ideas

When Is It True?

E 11-1 ENRICH

Tell whether each statement is *always*, *sometimes*, or *never* true.

A. To draw a polygon, you must draw at least three line segments. always

E. Lines are part of a ray. never

I. A line segment that connects two vertices of a polygon is a side. sometimes

I. A polygon has more vertices than sides. never

L. A line segment has one more point than a ray. never

N. Vertical line segments have the same length. sometimes

N. You can measure the length of a line. never

O. A closed figure is a polygon. sometimes

P. An octagon is larger than a pentagon. sometimes

R. A hexagon has fewer sides than an octagon. always

T. Congruent line segments have a common endpoint. sometimes

Y. A point on a line is the endpoint of two rays. always

Write the letters of the exercises whose answer is *always*, *sometimes*, or *never*. Unscramble each group of letters to form a math word.

Answers		
always	ARY	RAY
sometimes	INOPT	POINT
never	EILN	LINE

Choose one statement above that is never true. Rewrite it so that it is always true.

Answers may vary. Possible answers: E. Line segments and rays are part of a line. I. A polygon has an equal number of vertices and sides. L. A line segment has one more endpoint than a ray. N. You can measure the length of a line segment.

Use with Grade 5, Chapter 11, Lesson 1, pages 486–489. (339)

Daily Homework

11-1 Basic Geometric Ideas

Identify the figure. Then name it using symbols.

1. F ⟶ G ray; FG
2. M —— N line segment; MN

Use data from the diagram for problems 3–4.

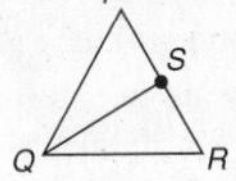

3. Name all the points. P, Q, R, S
4. Name a line segment. Any of the following: PQ, QP, QR, RQ, QS, SQ, PR, RP, PS, SP, RS, SR

Tell which line segments are congruent. Use a ruler to measure.

5. H —— I; J —— K Yes.
6. W —— X; Y —— Z No.

Write if the figure is a polygon. If not, explain why.

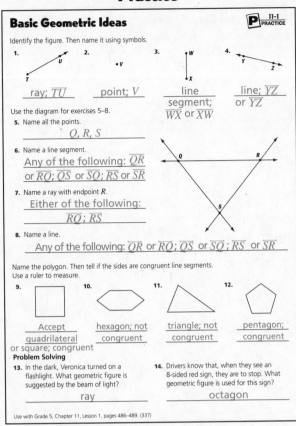

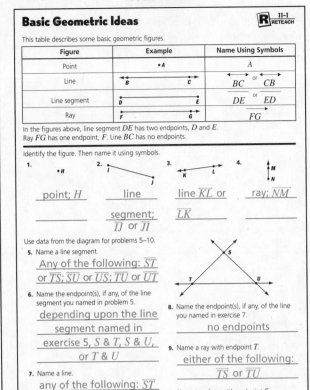

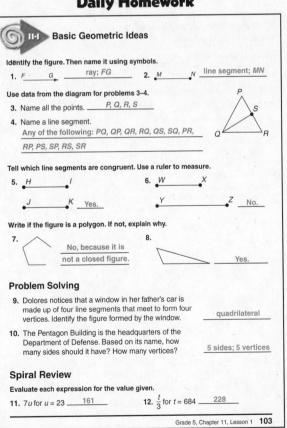

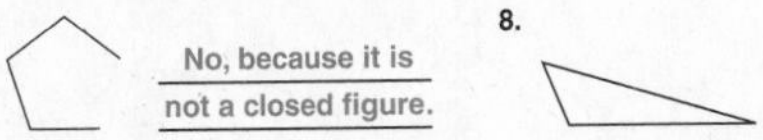

7. No, because it is not a closed figure.
8. Yes.

Problem Solving

9. Dolores notices that a window in her father's car is made up of four line segments that meet to form four vertices. Identify the figure formed by the window. quadrilateral
10. The Pentagon Building is the headquarters of the Department of Defense. Based on its name, how many sides should it have? How many vertices? 5 sides; 5 vertices

Spiral Review

Evaluate each expression for the value given.

11. $7u$ for $u = 23$ 161
12. $\frac{t}{3}$ for $t = 684$ 228

Practice

Measure and Classify Angles

P 11-2 PRACTICE

Use a protractor to measure each angle. Classify the angle as acute, right, or obtuse.

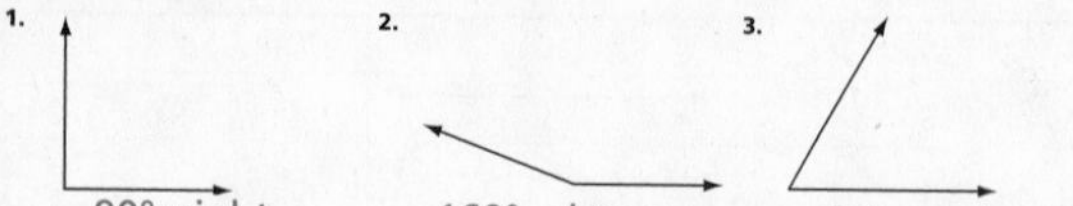

1. 90°; right
2. 160°; obtuse
3. 60°; acute

Name the pair of lines as intersecting, parallel, or perpendicular.

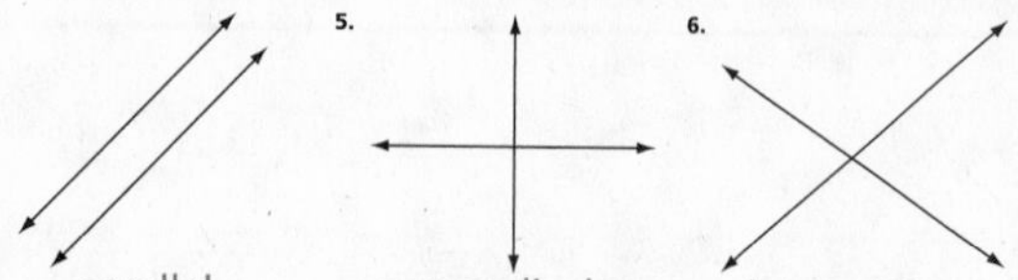

4. parallel
5. perpendicular
6. intersecting

Draw the figure. Drawings may vary. Sample drawings are given.

7. angle *MNO* with a measure of 50°
8. obtuse angle *DEF*
9. line *GH* parallel to line *KL*

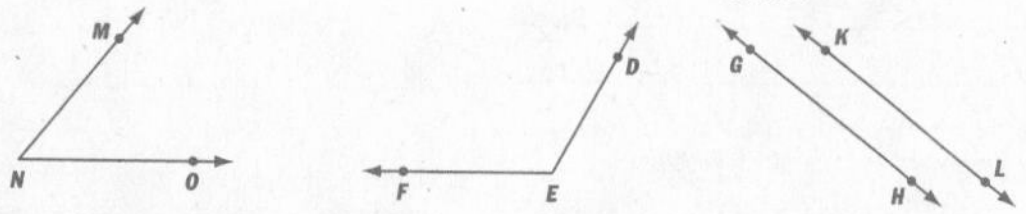

Problem Solving

10. First Avenue and Main Street cross each other, making angles of 75° and 105°. What type of lines are suggested by these streets? intersecting lines
11. First Avenue and Park Drive are perpendicular to each other. What type of angles are formed where these streets meet? right angles

Use with Grade 5, Chapter 11, Lesson 2, pages 490–493. (340)

Reteach

Measure and Classify Angles

R 11-2 RETEACH

You can think about a sheet of paper to help you classify an angle by its measure.

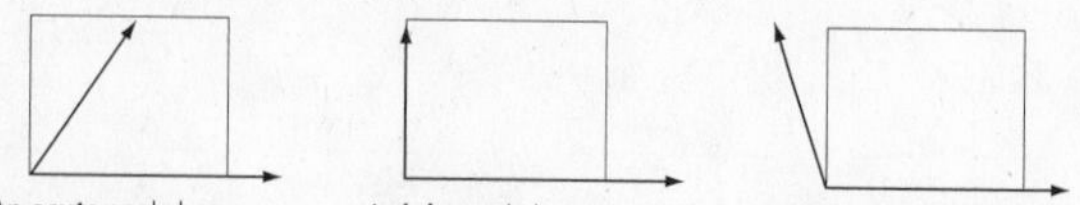

An **acute** angle has a measure less than the square corner of a sheet of paper.

A **right** angle has a measure the same as the square corner of a sheet of paper.

An **obtuse** angle has a measure greater than the square corner of a sheet of paper.

You can also think about a sheet of paper to help you classify a pair of lines.

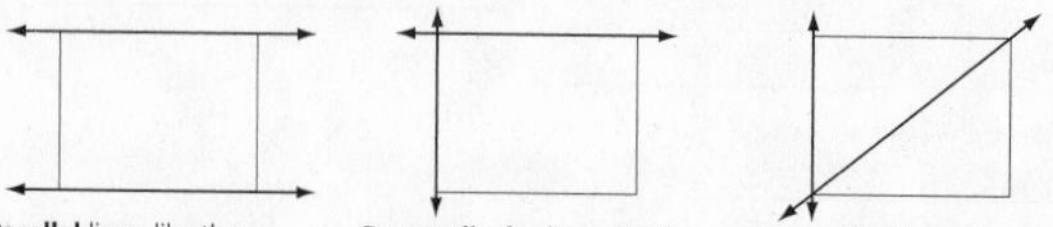

Parallel lines, like the opposite sides of a sheet of paper, never intersect.

Perpendicular lines, like the conjunct sides of a sheet of paper, cross at right angles.

Intersecting lines, like the side of a sheet of paper and its diagonal, cross.

Classify the angle as acute, right, or obtuse. You may use a square corner to help.

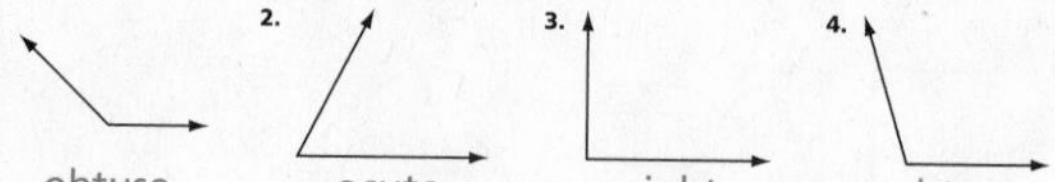

1. obtuse
2. acute
3. right
4. obtuse

Name the pair of lines as intersecting, parallel, or perpendicular.

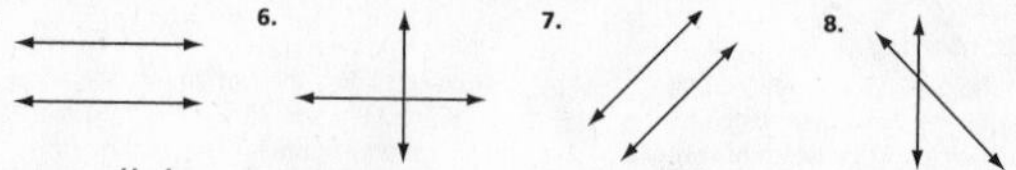

5. parallel
6. perpen-dicular
7. parallel
8. intersecting

Use with Grade 5, Chapter 11, Lesson 2, pages 490–493. (341)

Enrich

Measure and Classify Angles

E 11-2 ENRICH

Welcome to Treetown!

Use the clues to draw a map of downtown Treetown. Label the streets, the library, post office, and school.

Clues

- Oak Street and Pine Street are parallel to each other.
- Cherry Street is perpendicular to Oak Street.
- The library, located at the southeast corner of Cherry and Oak Streets, is north of the post office, located at the northeast corner of Cherry and Pine Streets.
- Elm Street starts east of Cherry Street and intersects Oak Street, Pine Street, and Cherry Street.
- The school, located on the northwest corner of Elm and Oak Streets, is east of Cherry Street.
- Maple Street starts west of Cherry Street. It intersects Oak Street and ends at Cherry Street.

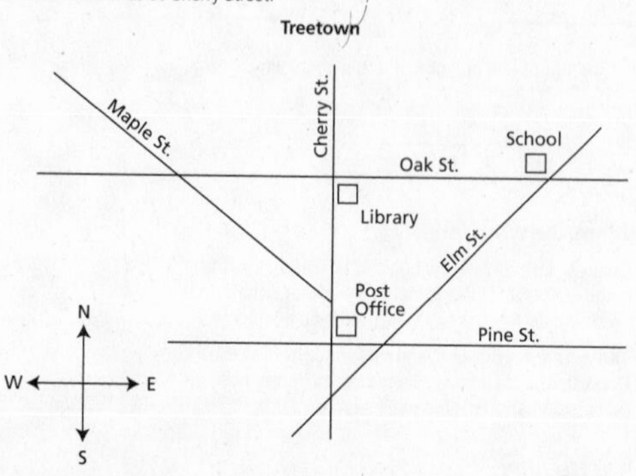

Identify right angles, acute angles, and obtuse angles on your map.

Check students' work.

Use with Grade 5, Chapter 11, Lesson 2, pages 490–493. (342)

Daily Homework

11-2 Measure and Classify Angles

Use a protractor to measure each angle. Classify the angle as acute, right, or obtuse.

1. 150°, obtuse
2. 90°, right
3. 45°, acute

Name the pair of lines as intersecting, parallel, or perpendicular.

4. intersecting
5. parallel
6. perpendicular

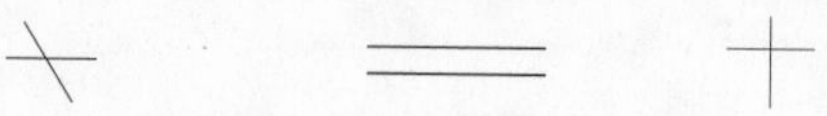

Find the measure of the following angles in the diagram. Classify each angle as acute, right, or obtuse.

7. *DCF* 60°, acute
8. *ECF* 120°, obtuse

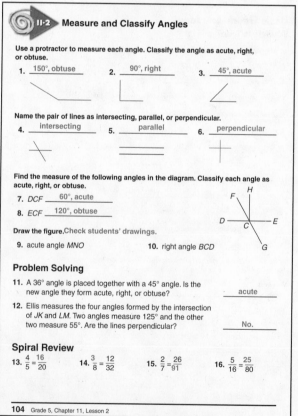

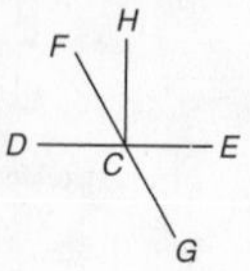

Draw the figure. Check students' drawings.

9. acute angle *MNO*
10. right angle *BCD*

Problem Solving

11. A 36° angle is placed together with a 45° angle. Is the new angle they form acute, right, or obtuse? acute
12. Ellis measures the four angles formed by the intersection of *JK* and *LM*. Two angles measure 125° and the other two measure 55°. Are the lines perpendicular? No.

Spiral Review

13. $\frac{4}{5} = \frac{16}{20}$
14. $\frac{3}{8} = \frac{12}{32}$
15. $\frac{2}{7} = \frac{26}{91}$
16. $\frac{5}{16} = \frac{25}{80}$

104 Grade 5, Chapter 11, Lesson 2

Chapter 11 ~ Lesson 3

Practice

Triangles

P 11-3 PRACTICE

Classify each triangle as equilateral, isosceles, or scalene and right, acute, or obtuse.

1. 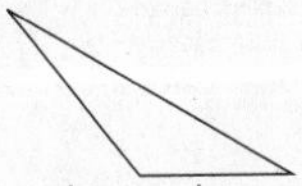
scalene; obtuse

2. 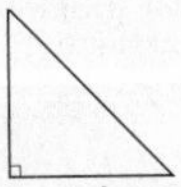
isosceles; right

3. 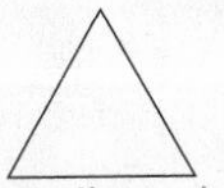
equilateral; acute

4. 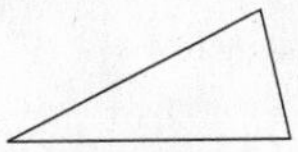
isosceles; acute

5. 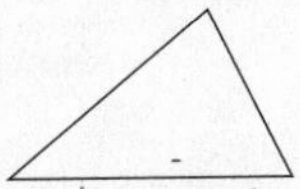
scalene; acute

6. 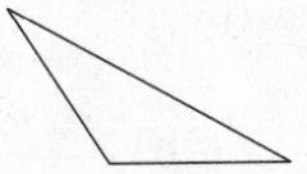
isosceles; obtuse

Use a ruler and protractor to draw these triangles and then classify them.
Drawings may vary. Sample drawings are given.

7. All angles equal, all sides congruent

acute; equilateral

8. One angle greater than 90 degrees, no congruent sides
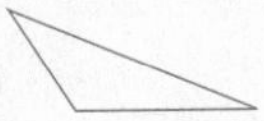
obtuse; scalene

9. All angles less than 90 degrees, two sides congruent
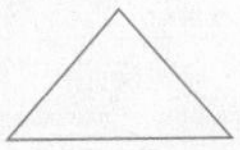
acute; isosceles

Problem Solving

10. Tyler drew a triangle with a 35° angle and an 85° angle. What is the measure of the third angle?
60°

11. Amber drew an obtuse, isosceles triangle with a 110° angle. What are the measures of the other two angles?
35° and 35°

Use with Grade 5, Chapter 11, Lesson 3, pages 494–497. (343)

Reteach

Triangles

R 11-3 RETEACH

You can classify triangles by the lengths of their sides.

equilateral
3 sides the same length
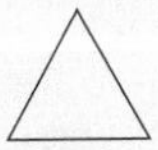

isosceles
2 sides the same length

scalene
no sides the same length
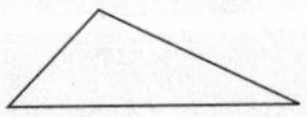

You can also classify triangles by the measures of their angles.

right
1 right angle
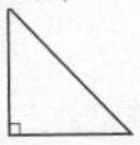

acute
3 acute angles

obtuse
1 obtuse angle
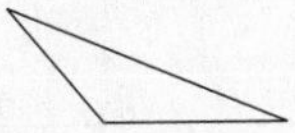

The sum of the measures of the angles of any triangle is 180 degrees. If you know the measures of two angles of a triangle, you can figure out the measure of the third angle.

Circle the characteristics of each triangle. Then classify the triangle as equilateral, isosceles, or scalene and right, acute, or obtuse.

1. 3 sides the same length
2 sides the same length
(no sides the same length)
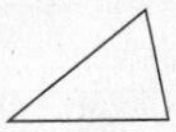
1 right angle
(3 acute angles)
1 obtuse angle
scalene; acute

2. (3 sides the same length)
2 sides the same length
no sides the same length
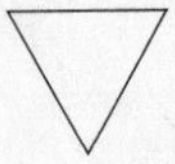
1 right angle
(3 acute angles)
1 obtuse angle
equilateral; acute

Find the measure of the unknown angle.

3. 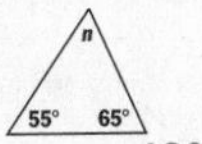

55° + 65° + n = 180°
n = 60°

4. 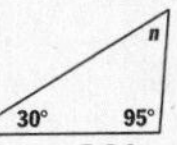

95° + 30° + n = 180°
n = 55°

Use with Grade 5, Chapter 11, Lesson 3, pages 494–497. (344)

Enrich

Triangles

E 11-3 ENRICH

Angle Patterns

∠*ABC* is an interior angle. ∠*HAB* is an exterior angle. Use a protractor to measure all of the interior and exterior angles of this figure. Record the measures on the figure. Then look for patterns.

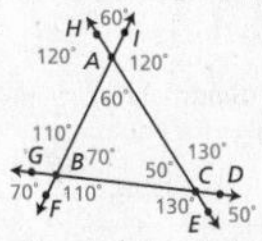

1. ∠*BAC* and ∠*HAI* are vertical angles. They have the same vertex, but they have no common sides. One angle is an interior angle, and one angle is an exterior angle. Name the other pairs of vertical angles that are interior and exterior angles.
∠*ABC* and ∠*GBF*; ∠*ACB* and ∠*DCE*

What do you notice about the measures of the angles in each pair?
The measures are equal.

2. ∠*BAC* and ∠*IAC* are adjacent angles because they are next to each other. One angle is an interior angle, and one angle is an exterior angle. Name two other pairs of adjacent angles that are interior and exterior angles.
Answers may vary. Possible answers: ∠*ABC* and ∠*ABG*; ∠*ACB* and ∠*ACD*

What do you notice about the measures of the angles in each pair?
The sum of the measures is 180°.

3. Besides the pairs of angles you listed in exercise 1, what other pairs of angles have equal measures?
Vertical obtuse exterior angles, or ∠*HAB* and ∠*IAC*, ∠*ACD* and ∠*BCE*, and ∠*CBF* and ∠*ABG*

4. For each exterior angle, find two interior angles whose measures together equal the measure of the exterior angle.
∠*HAB* ∠*ABC* and ∠*ACB*   ∠*CBF* ∠*BCA* and ∠*BAC*
∠*ACD* ∠*ABC* and ∠*CAB*

What do you notice about these groups of interior and exterior angles?
The sum of the measures of two interior angles of the triangle equals the measure of an exterior angle at the other vertex.

Use with Grade 5, Chapter 11, Lesson 3, pages 494–497. (345)

Daily Homework

11-3 Triangles

Classify each triangle as equilateral, isosceles, or scalene and right, acute, or obtuse.

1. isosceles, acute

2. isosceles, right

3. scalene, obtuse
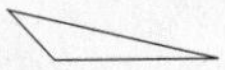

4. equilateral, acute

5. isosceles, right

6. scalene, obtuse

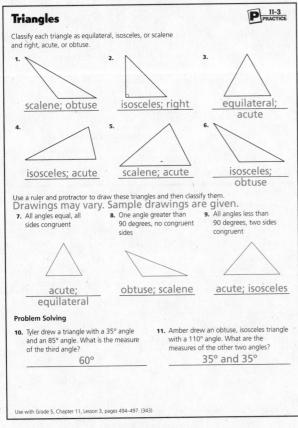

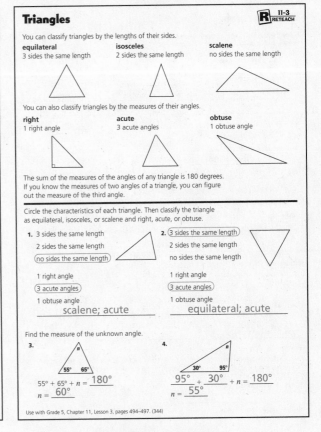

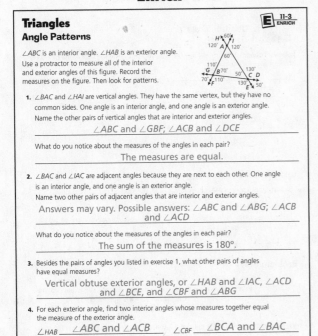

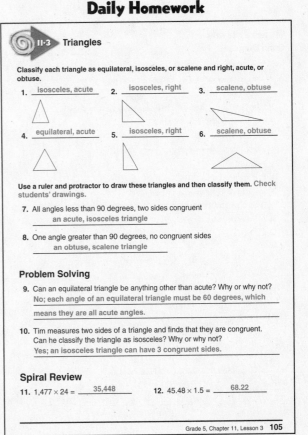

Use a ruler and protractor to draw these triangles and then classify them. Check students' drawings.

7. All angles less than 90 degrees, two sides congruent
an acute, isosceles triangle

8. One angle greater than 90 degrees, no congruent sides
an obtuse, scalene triangle

Problem Solving

9. Can an equilateral triangle be anything other than acute? Why or why not?
No; each angle of an equilateral triangle must be 60 degrees, which means they are all acute angles.

10. Tim measures two sides of a triangle and finds that they are congruent. Can he classify the triangle as isosceles? Why or why not?
Yes; an isosceles triangle can have 3 congruent sides.

Spiral Review

11. 1,477 × 24 = 35,448

12. 45.48 × 1.5 = 68.22

Grade 5, Chapter 11, Lesson 3 105

Chapter 11 ~ Lesson 4

Practice

Quadrilaterals

P 11-4 PRACTICE

Name the quadrilateral in as many ways as you can.
Write the sum of the measure of the angles.

1. 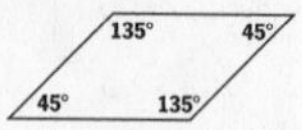

parallelogram; 360°

2. 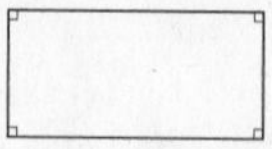

rectangle, rhombus, parallelogram; 360°

3. 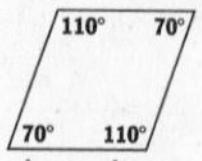

rhombus, parallelogram; 360°

Write *true* or *false*. Explain your reasoning.

4. All squares are rhombuses.
True; the opposite sides of a square are congruent and parallel; all sides of a square are the same length.
5. All trapezoids have exactly one pair of congruent sides.
False; some trapezoids have four different-length sides.
6. All rhombuses are parallelograms.
True; the opposite sides of a rhombus are congruent and parallel.

Draw each quadrilateral with a ruler and protractor. Tell what kind of quadrilateral you drew. Check students' drawings.

7. two pairs of congruent sides
Students should have drawn a rectangle or parallelogram.
8. two pairs of parallel sides
Students should have drawn a rectangle, square, parallelogram, or rhombus.
9. no right angles
Students should have drawn a rhombus, parallelogram, or trapezoid.

Problem Solving

10. Lee drew a quadrilateral with three angles that measure 120 degrees, 110 degrees, and 70 degrees. What is the measure of the fourth angle?
60°
11. Robert drew a parallelogram with two 55-degree angles. What are the measures of the other two angles?
125° and 125°

Use with Grade 5, Chapter 11, Lesson 4, pages 498–501. (346)

Reteach

Quadrilaterals

R 11-4 RETEACH

You can classify quadrilaterals by their sides and angles.

parallelogram
opposite sides congruent
opposite sides parallel

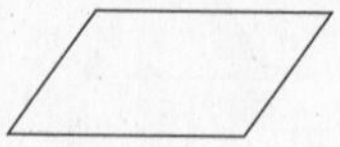

rectangle
opposite sides congruent
opposite sides parallel
4 right angles

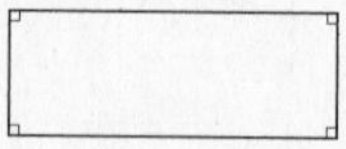

square
all sides congruent
opposite sides parallel
4 right angles

rhombus
all sides congruent opposite sides parallel

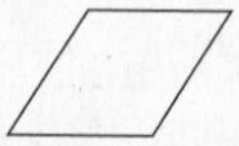

trapezoid
exactly one pair of parallel sides

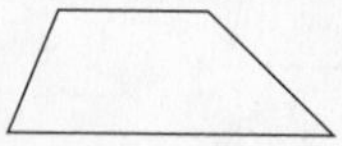

Circle the characteristics of each quadrilateral. Then classify the quadrilateral in as many ways as possible.

1. 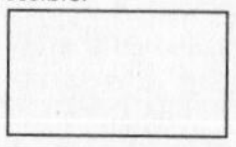

(opposite sides congruent)
all sides congruent
(opposite sides parallel)
exactly one pair of parallel sides
(4 right angles)

parallelogram; rectangle

2. 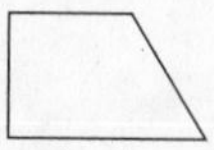

opposite sides congruent
all sides congruent
opposite sides parallel
(exactly one pair of parallel sides)
4 right angles

trapezoid

Find the measure of the unknown angle.

3. 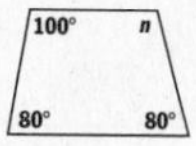

$100° + 80° + 80° + n = 360°$

$n =$ 100°

4. 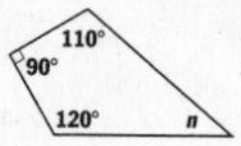

$120° + 90° + 110° + n = 360°$

$n =$ 40°

Use with Grade 5, Chapter 11, Lesson 4, pages 498–501. (347)

Enrich

Quadrilaterals

Quad Diagram

E 11-4 ENRICH

Follow these steps to complete the diagram below.

1. Write each of these names of quadrilaterals in the appropriate circle.

Parallelograms   Trapezoids   Rectangles

2. Write the letter of each property in the appropriate part(s) of the diagram.
   - **A.** sum of the measures of the angles is 360°
   - **B.** four right angles
   - **C.** exactly one pair of parallel sides
   - **D.** four sides
   - **E.** four congruent sides
   - **F.** four congruent sides and four congruent angles
   - **G.** opposite sides parallel
   - **H.** opposite sides congruent

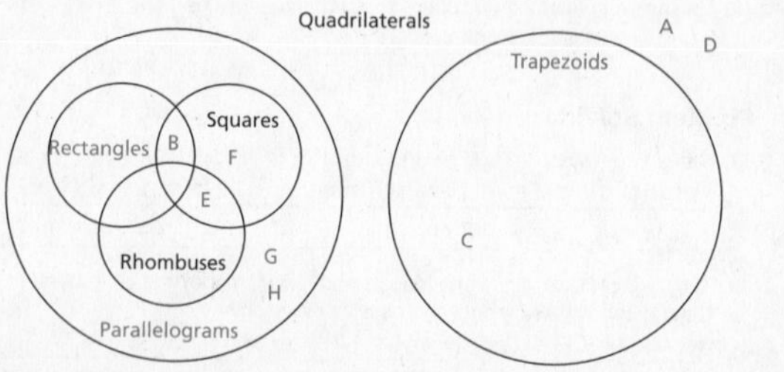

How did you decide where to write the letter E in the diagram?
All squares and all rhombuses have four congruent sides, so I wrote an E where the circle representing squares and the circle representing rhombuses overlap.

Use with Grade 5, Chapter 11, Lesson 4, pages 498–501. (348)

Daily Homework

11-4 Quadrilaterals

Name the quadrilateral in as many ways as you can. Write the sum of the measure of the angles for each one.

1. parallelogram; 360°

2. rectangle, parallelogram; 360°

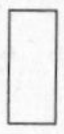

3. trapezoid; 360°

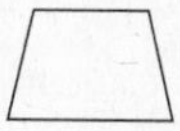

4. rhombus, parallelogram; 360°

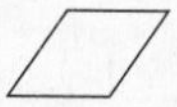

Write true or false.

5. All parallelograms are squares.
False.
6. All squares are parallelograms.
True.
7. The sum of the angles of a trapezoid is less than 360°.
False.
8. All squares are rhombuses.
True.

Problem Solving

9. Bob notices a quadrilateral in a mural. The quadrilateral has two angles of 75° and two angles of 105°. It also has two pairs of congruent sides that are parallel with one another. What is the name of the quadrilateral?
parallelogram
10. Vera is measuring the angles of a trapezoid. She measures the first three to be 100°, 65°, and 75°. What is the measure of the fourth angle?
120°

Spiral Review

Find the LCD.

11. 4 and 10 20
12. 6 and 10 30
13. 8 and 9 72

106 Grade 5, Chapter 11, Lesson 4

Chapter 11 ~ Lesson 5

Practice

Problem Solving: Reading for Math
Draw a Diagram

P 11-5 PRACTICE — Reading Skill

Draw a diagram to solve each problem. Check students' drawings.

1. Rita wants to send two pictures to her grandmother. One is a rectangular picture 25 centimeters by 40 centimeters. The other is a square picture that is 35 centimeters on each side. She places the square picture on top of the rectangular picture. What is the smallest size rectangular box she can use?
   40 cm by 35 cm

2. Manuel wants to send two mosaics that he made to his father. One is a rectangular mosaic 50 centimeters by 30 centimeters. The other is a circular mosaic with a 40-centimeter diameter. He places the circular mosaic on top of the rectangular mosaic to send them. What is the smallest size rectangular box he can use?
   50 cm by 40 cm

3. Lily is sending a picture frame to her cousin. The frame measures 12 inches by 18 inches. The shipping store only sells square boxes. What size must she buy?
   18 in. by 18 in.

4. Austin has two stained glass pictures that he wants to send to his grandparents. One is a rectangular picture that measures 30 centimeters by 20 centimeters. The other is a circular picture with a diameter of 24 centimeters. He puts the circular picture on top of the rectangular picture to send them. What is the smallest size rectangular box he can use?
   30 cm by 24 cm

5. Max has two paintings to ship. One is a rectangular painting that is 70 centimeters by 90 centimeters. The other is shaped like an equilateral triangle with sides that are 80 centimeters long. He stacks the triangular painting on top of the rectangular painting for shipping. What size and shape box can he use?
   rectangle; 80 cm by 90 cm

Use with Grade 5, Chapter 11, Lesson 5, pages 502–503. (349)

Practice

Problem Solving: Reading for Math
Draw a Diagram

P 11-5 PRACTICE — Math Skills Test Prep

Choose the correct answer.

Emma works in a stationery store. She has a sheet of paper that is 4 inches wide and 2 feet long. She cuts the paper into six 4-inch strips.

1. Which of the following statements is true?
   - A The strips are rectangles.
   - (B) The strips are squares.
   - C The total length of the strips is 28 inches.
   - D The strips can be used to form a circle.

2. A diagram
   - F makes solving problems harder.
   - G should always include a date.
   - (H) can help you identify important details to solve a problem.
   - J takes the place of the solution when solving a problem.

Lars has a piece of plywood that is 2 feet wide and 3 yards long. He cuts the wood into nine 1-foot sections.

3. Which of the following statements is true?
   - A The sections are triangles.
   - B The sections are squares.
   - (C) The sections are rectangles.
   - D Each section is 1 yard long.

4. A diagram can help you
   - F organize data in a table.
   - G identify separate parts of a problem.
   - H take less space to solve a problem.
   - (J) see how different items can be combined.

Elena has a piece of fabric that is 6 inches wide and 3 feet long. She cuts the fabric into nine 4-inch long pieces.

5. Which of the following statements is NOT true?
   - A The sections are rectangles.
   - (B) The sections are 4 inches by 9 inches.
   - C The sections are the same size.
   - D The sections are 6 inches wide.

6. Drawing a diagram can help you solve problems that
   - F involve many calculations.
   - (G) involve shapes and sizes.
   - H use data from a table.
   - J use fractions.

Use with Grade 5, Chapter 11, Lesson 5, pages 502–503. (350)

Practice

Problem Solving: Reading for Math
Draw a Diagram

P 11-5 PRACTICE — Math Skills Test Prep

Choose the correct answer.

Timothy has a piece of wood that is 3 inches wide and 3 feet long. He cuts the wood into six 6-inch sections.

7. Which of the following statements is true?
   - A The total length of the wood is less than 1 yard.
   - B The sections are squares.
   - C The sections are triangles.
   - (D) The length of each section is twice the width of each section.

8. Using a diagram can
   - (F) help you see how different shapes can be combined.
   - G make it possible for you to ignore the numbers in a problem.
   - H make the problem more difficult.
   - J change the meaning of a problem.

Draw a diagram to solve each problem. Check students' drawings.

9. Margo has two rectangular paintings that she wants to ship. One painting is 70 centimeters by 45 centimeters. The other is 55 centimeters by 60 centimeters. She stacks one painting on top of the other. What is the smallest size rectangular box she can use?
   70 cm by 55 cm

10. A portrait studio is mailing out two photographs. One is a square with 16-inch sides. The other is rectangular with sides that are 18 inches by 12 inches. What is the smallest size rectangular photo mailer they can use to send both pictures?
   16 in. by 18 in.

11. Larry made two ceramic trays that he wants to send to his aunt. One is a rectangular tray that is 15 inches by 6 inches. The other is circular with a diameter of 8 inches. What is the smallest size rectangular box he can use?
   15 in. by 8 in.

12. Gregory wants to send a book to a friend. The book is 14 inches by 10 inches. The packaging store only has square boxes available. What is the smallest box Gregory could buy?
   14 in. by 14 in.

Use with Grade 5, Chapter 11, Lesson 5, pages 502–503. (351)

Daily Homework

11-5 Problem Solving: Reading for Math

Draw a Diagram

Draw a diagram to solve each problem.

1. Jorge plays the triangle in a band. He orders a new triangle by mail. The triangle is equilateral, with sides of 10 inches. What is the smallest rectangular box the triangle can be shipped in?
   10 inches by 10 inches.

2. Renata orders a poster that is 11 inches by 13 inches, and music that is 10 inches by 15 inches. In what size and shape box will her order be sent?
   11 inches by 15 inches, rectangular

3. Tom orders a music stand. The stand is made up of a square easel that is 17 inches by 17 inches, and a 3-foot rod that attaches to the top of the easel. What is the smallest size rectangular box that the stand can be shipped in?
   17 inches by 3 feet

Use data from the diagrams for problems 4–6.

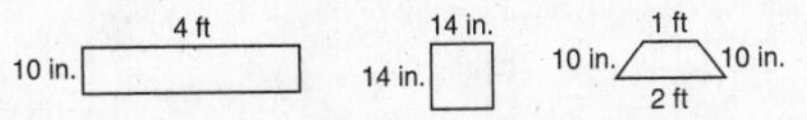

4. The figures above show choices available at Board World, a lumber store. Can a trapezoid be shipped in a box that measures 2 feet by 2 feet?
   Yes.

5. Hal orders a square. Which of the following boxes could possibly contain Hal's shipment? 3 feet by 1 foot; 2 feet by 15 inches; 10 inches by 20 inches
   2 feet by 15 inches

6. What is the smallest rectangular box that an order for a rectangle and a square could be shipped in?
   4 feet by 14 inches

Spiral Review

7. $\frac{4}{5} \times \frac{6}{7} = \frac{24}{35}$

8. $\frac{9}{4} \div \frac{3}{8} = 6$

9. $\frac{11}{2} \times \frac{5}{3} = 9\frac{1}{6}$

Grade 5, Chapter 11, Lesson 5 107

Chapter 11 ~ Lesson 6

Practice

Congruence and Similarity

P 11-6 PRACTICE

Tell whether the figures are congruent, similar, or neither.

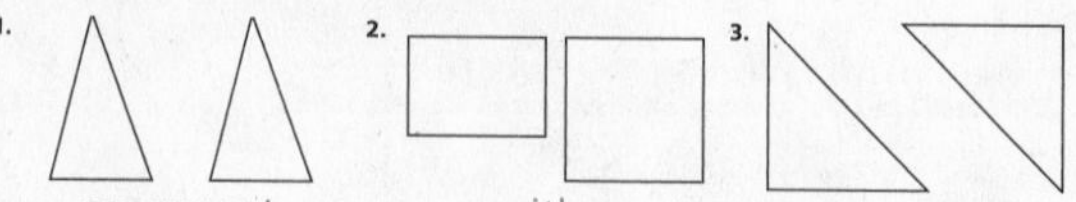

1. congruent
2. neither
3. congruent

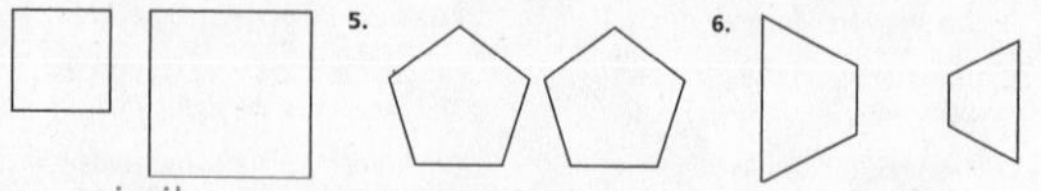

4. similar
5. congruent
6. similar

Find the measure of the missing angle in each pair of similar figures.

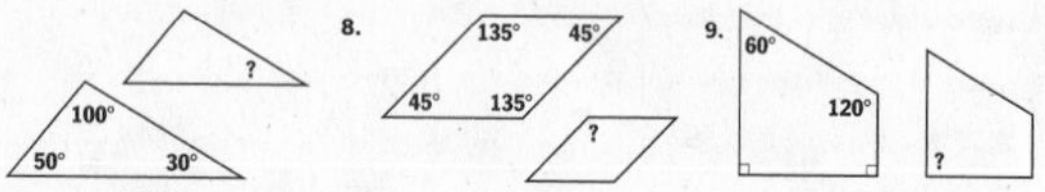

7. 30°
8. 135°
9. 90°

Identify the corresponding side or angle.

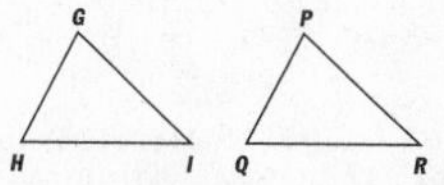

10. $\overline{GI}$ $\overline{PR}$
11. $\angle P$ $\angle G$
12. $\overline{PQ}$ $\overline{GH}$
13. $\angle R$ $\angle I$
14. $\overline{HI}$ $\overline{QR}$
15. $\angle H$ $\angle Q$

Problem Solving

16. A poster is in a rectangular frame 16 inches long and 12 inches wide. What is the shape and size of a congruent frame?
rectangle; 16 inches long and 12 inches wide

17. A painting is in a square frame with 18-inch sides. What is the shape and size of a similar frame?
square; sizes will vary but all sides of the frame should be the same length.

Use with Grade 5, Chapter 11, Lesson 6, pages 506–507. (352)

Reteach

Congruence and Similarity

R 11-6 RETEACH

Figures that are the same shape are congruent or similar.

Two figures with the **same angle measures** and **same side lengths** are **congruent**.

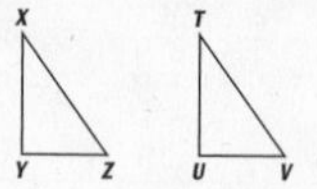

$\angle X \cong \angle T$ $\overline{XY} \cong \overline{TU}$
$\angle Y \cong \angle U$ $\overline{XZ} \cong \overline{TV}$
$\angle Z \cong \angle V$ $\overline{YZ} \cong \overline{UV}$
$\triangle XYZ$ and $\triangle TUV$ are congruent.

Two figures with the **same angle measures** and **different side lengths** are **similar**.

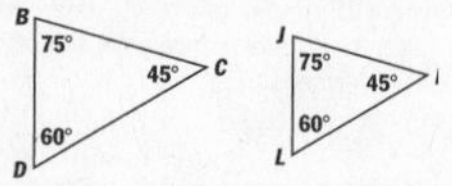

$\angle B \cong \angle J$ $\angle C \cong \angle K$ $\angle D \cong \angle L$
The corresponding line segments are not congruent.
$\triangle BCD$ and $\triangle JKL$ are similar.

Tell whether the figures in each pair are congruent or not. If they are, for each angle and side write the corresponding congruent part.

1.

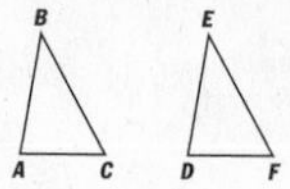

Congruent shapes? yes

$\angle A \cong \angle D$ $\overline{AB} \cong \overline{DE}$
$\angle B \cong$ $\angle E$ $\overline{BC} \cong$ $\overline{EF}$
$\angle C \cong$ $\angle F$ $\overline{AC} \cong$ $\overline{DF}$
Congruent

2.

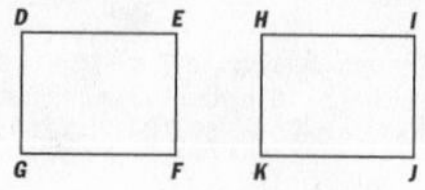

Congruent shapes? yes

$\angle D \cong$ $\overline{DE} \cong$ $\overline{HI}$
$\angle E \cong$ $\overline{EF} \cong$ $\overline{IJ}$
$\angle F \cong$ $\angle J$ $\overline{FG} \cong$ $\overline{JK}$
$\angle G \cong$ $\overline{DG} \cong$ $\overline{HK}$
Congruent

Find the measure of the missing angle in each pair of similar figures.

3.

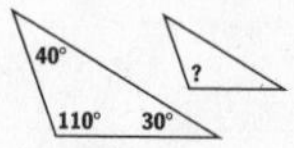

110°

4.

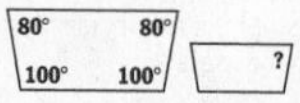

80°

Use with Grade 5, Chapter 11, Lesson 6, pages 506–507. (353)

Enrich

Congruence and Similarity

E 11-6 ENRICH

Similar Drawings

For each figure, draw another figure that is similar but not congruent. Use a ruler and a protractor to help you. Explain how you used your knowledge of polygons and similar figures to make each drawing. Check students' drawings.

1.

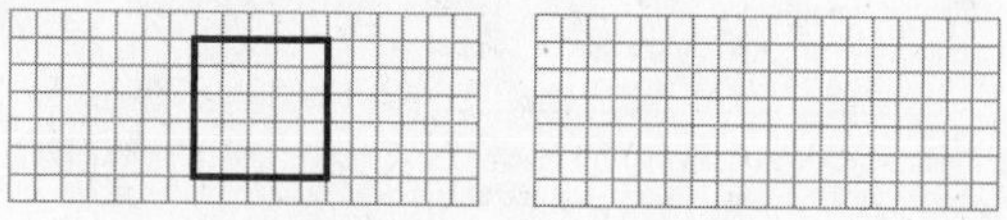

Explanations may vary. Possible explanation: All squares are the same shape, so I drew a square with shorter sides.

2.

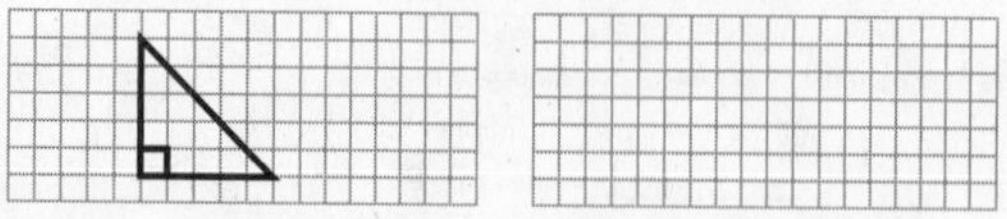

Explanations may vary. Possible explanation: Two triangles have the same shape if the measures of their angles are the same. I drew a longer side for the bottom. Then I drew the other sides so they formed the same size angles where they intersected the bottom side.

3.

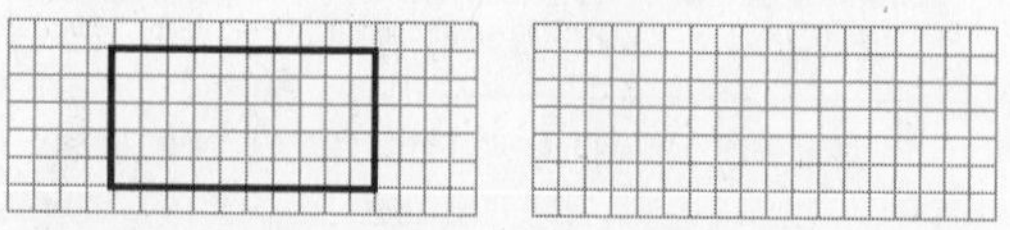

Explanations may vary. Possible explanation: All rectangles have four right angles, but they are not all the same shape. I noticed that the length of the given rectangle is twice its width. I drew a shorter width. Then I made my rectangle twice as long as the new width.

Use with Grade 5, Chapter 11, Lesson 6, pages 506–507. (354)

Daily Homework

11-6 Congruence and Similarity

Tell whether the figures are congruent, similar, or neither.

1.

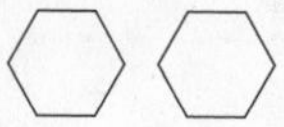

congruent and similar

2.

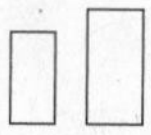

similar

3.

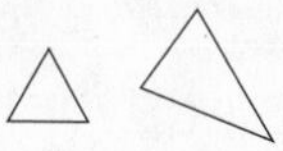

neither

4.

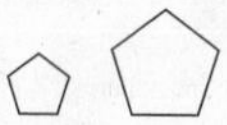

similar

Find the measure of the missing angle in each pair of similar figures.

5.

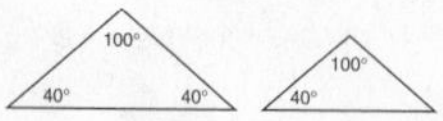

40°

6.

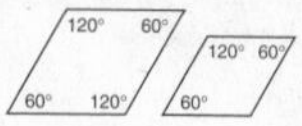

120°

Identify the corresponding side or angle.

7. $\overline{BC}$ $\overline{EF}$
8. $\overline{TU}$, $\overline{HI}$

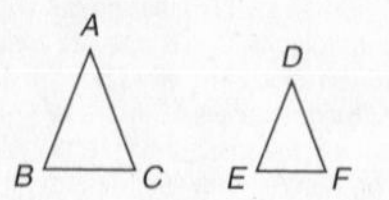

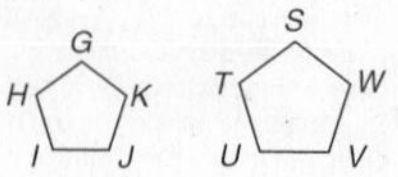

Problem Solving

9. There are two large windows in Ms. Fehler's classroom. Both measure 6 feet wide by 4 feet tall. Are the two windows congruent? Yes.

Spiral Review

Solve.

10. $n + 17 = 39$ $n = 22$
11. $u - 48 = 101$ $u = 149$

108 Grade 5, Chapter 11, Lesson 6

Chapter 11 ~ Lesson 7

Practice

Transformations

P 11-7 PRACTICE

Write whether a translation, reflection, or rotation was made.

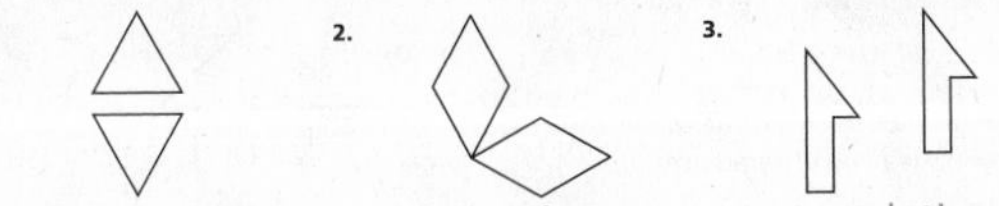

1. reflection
2. rotation
3. translation

4. translation, reflection, glide reflection
5. rotation, reflection
6. translation, rotation

Write the combination of transformations used.

Draw each figure after the transformation described. Check students' drawings. Sample drawings are given.

7. rotation
8. translation
9. reflection

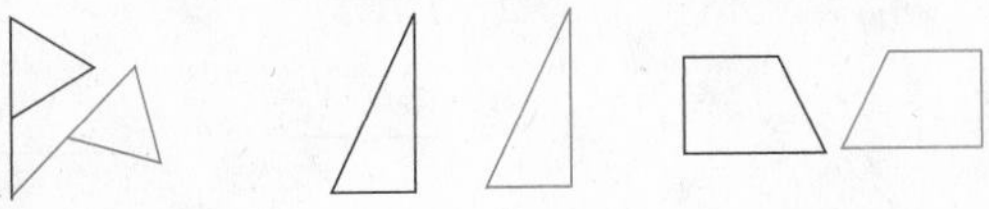

Problem Solving

10. Which uppercase letters look like different uppercase letters when they are reflected over a horizontal line? M and W

11. You can transform a lowercase *v* in two different ways so that the *v* and its transformations form other lowercase letters. Describe the transformations and tell what letters you would form. Reflect *v* over a horizontal line to form *x*; translate *v* horizontally to form *w*.

Reteach

Transformations

R 11-7 RETEACH

You can transform figures by using translations, reflections, or rotations.

In a **translation**, a figure **slides** along a line. In a **reflection**, a figure **flips** over a line. In a **rotation**, a figure **turns** around a point.

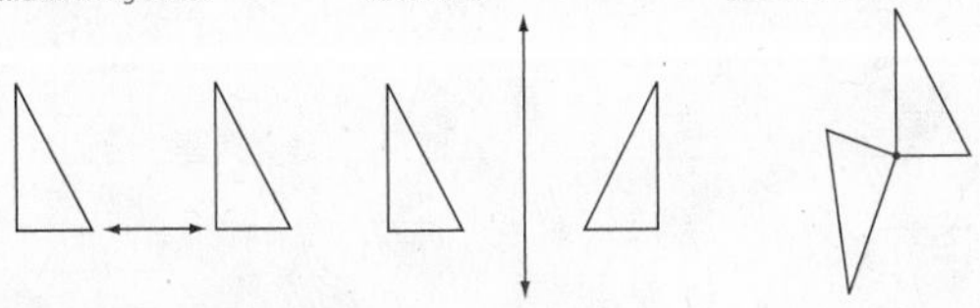

A **glide reflection** is a transformation that combines a reflection and a translation. Figure 2 is a reflection of Figure 1. Figure 3 is a translation of Figure 2.

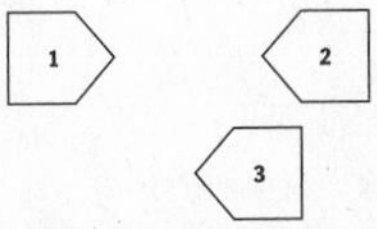

Complete the statement about each transformation that was made.

1. 

The figure was flipped over an imaginary line, so a reflection was made.

2. 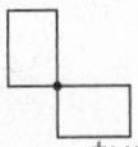

The figure was turned around a point, so a rotation was made.

Write whether a translation, a reflection, a rotation, or a glide reflection was made.

3. translation
4. rotation
5. reflection

6. glide reflection
7. translation
8. rotation

Enrich

Transformations

E 11-7 ENRICH

Transform to the Center

Play this game with a partner.

Cut out the triangles. Take turns. Each player places a triangle on the game board.

- Toss a number cube.
- Move the triangle following the rules in the table.

The first player to reach the center of the game board wins.

Number Tossed	Number of Spaces	Kind of Movement
1 or 4	1 or 4	Translation
2 or 5	2 or 5	Rotation
3 or 6	3 or 6	Flip

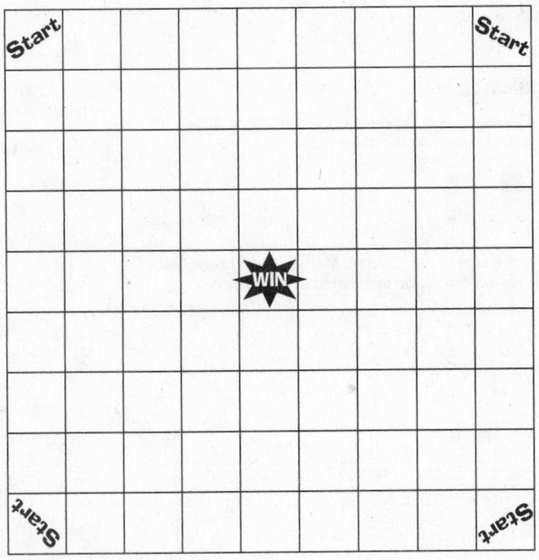

Daily Homework

11-7 Transformations

Write whether a translation, reflection, or rotation was made.

1. 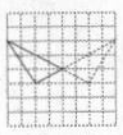 reflection
2. 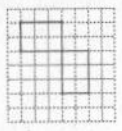 rotation
3. 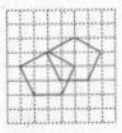 translation

Choose the figure that is made by the transformation described.

4. Rotation B

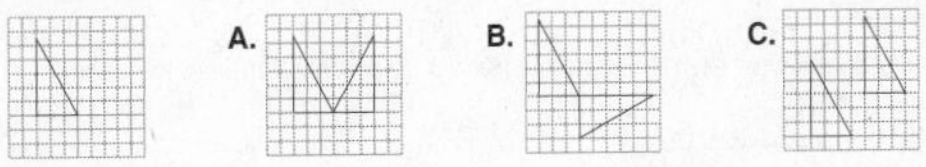

5. Translation A

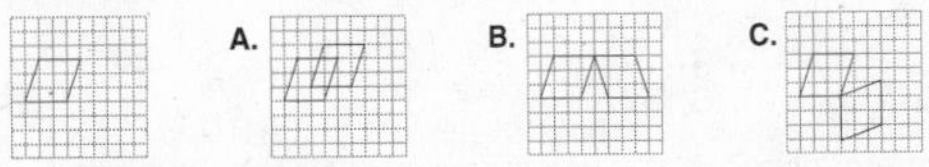

Problem Solving

6. The flag of Iceland is shown. If the flag is reflected, will it look the same? No.

7. In an abstract painting, two congruent squares sit next to one another as shown. What are two possible ways to describe the transformation that these squares show? reflection, translation

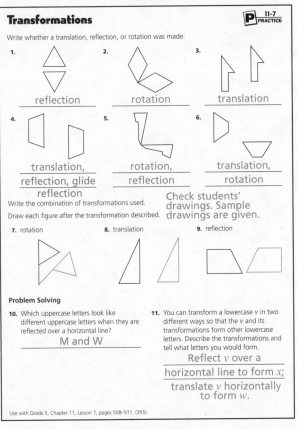

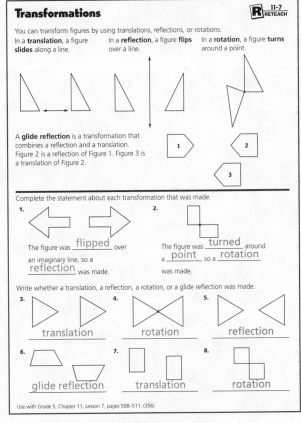

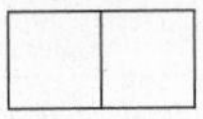

Spiral Review

Simplify. Use the order of operations.

8. $51 + 17 \times 8 =$ 187

9. $228 \div 2^2 - 15 =$ 42

Chapter 11 ~ Lesson 8

Practice

Symmetry

P 11-8 PRACTICE

Tell which figures are symmetric about a line.

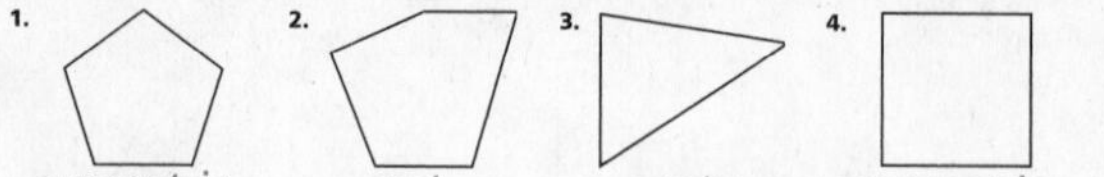

1. symmetric
2. not symmetric
3. not symmetric
4. symmetric

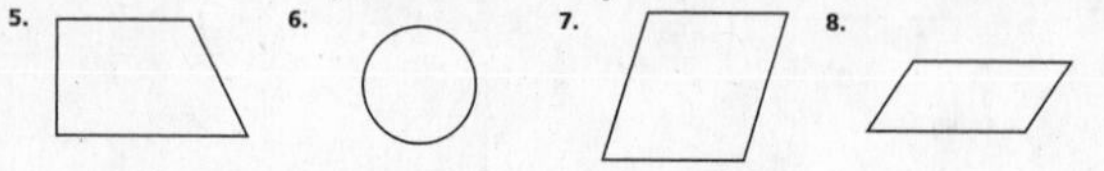

5. not symmetric
6. symmetric
7. symmetric
8. not symmetric

Draw all the lines of symmetry.

9. 10. 11. 12.

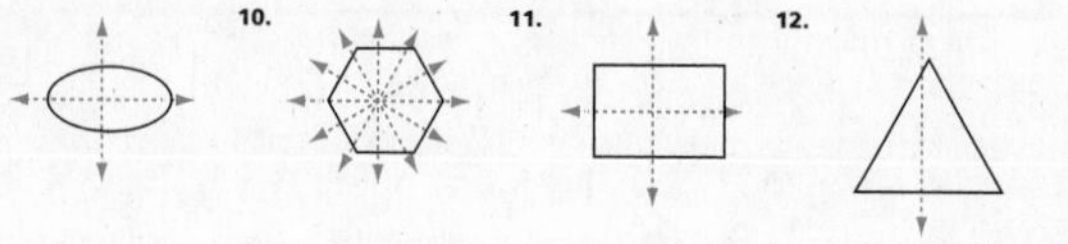

13. 14. 15. 16.

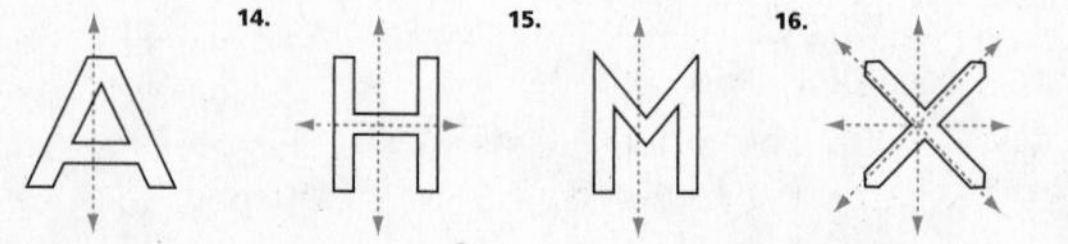

Problem Solving

17. Print your name in uppercase letters. Then print your name in lowercase letters. Show which letters are symmetric.

Check students' work.

18. Draw a polygon with more than four sides that has a least one line of symmetry. Name the polygon you draw.

Check students' drawings.

Use with Grade 5, Chapter 11, Lesson 8, pages 512–513. (358)

Reteach

Symmetry

R 11-8 RETEACH

A figure is **symmetric** if it can be folded along a line so that the two halves match exactly.

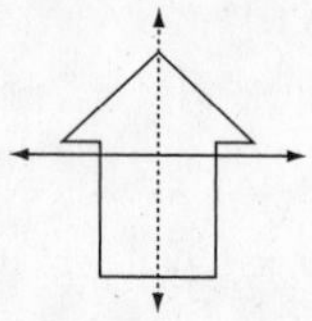

If you cut out the figure at the right and fold it in half along the dotted line, the halves will match. The figure is symmetric, and the dotted line is a **line of symmetry**.

If you fold the figure along the solid line, the halves will not match. The solid line is not a line of symmetry.

Figures may have zero lines of symmetry, one line of symmetry, two lines of symmetry, or more than two lines of symmetry.

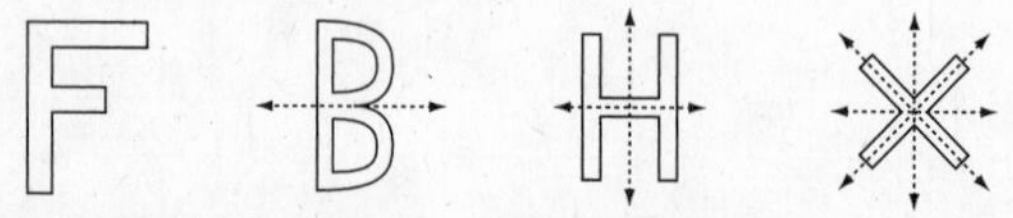

0 lines of symmetry | 1 line of symmetry | 2 lines of symmetry | 4 lines of symmetry

Tell whether each figure is symmetric or not symmetric. If it is symmetric, draw all the lines of symmetry. To help, you may trace the figure, cut it out, and try folding it in half.

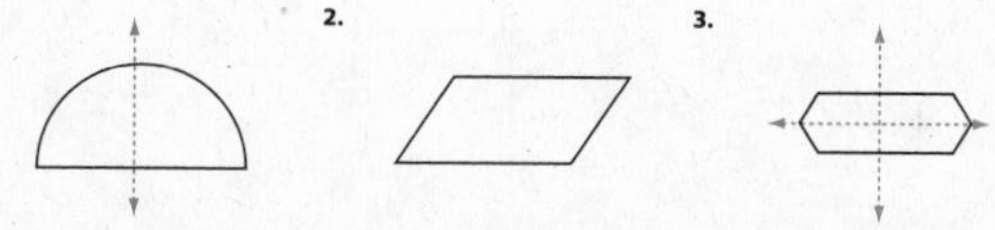

1. symmetric
2. not symmetric
3. symmetric

4. not symmetric
5. symmetric
6. symmetric

Use with Grade 5, Chapter 11, Lesson 8, pages 512–513. (359)

Enrich

Symmetry

Cut It Out!

E 11-8 ENRICH

Suppose each shape is cut from a piece of paper that has been folded once. When the cut-out shape is unfolded, what shape will you see? Check your answers by cutting each shape from a folded piece of paper.

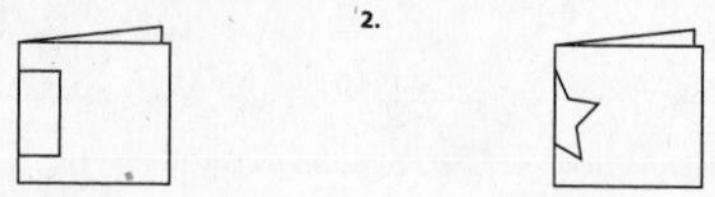

1. rectangle
2. star

Show how you could cut each shape from a piece of paper that has been folded once.

Check students' work.

3. 4.

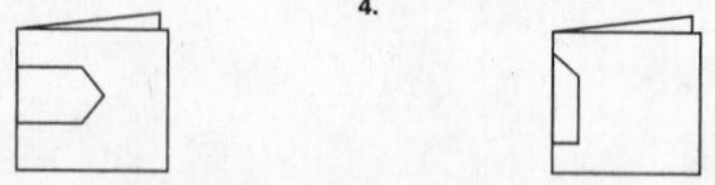

Suppose each of these shapes is cut from a piece of paper that has been folded twice. When the cut-out shape is unfolded, what shape will you see? Check your answers by cutting each shape from a folded piece of paper.

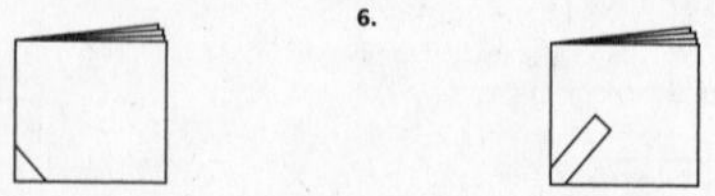

5. square
6. letter X

Show how you could cut each shape from a piece of paper that has been folded twice.

Check students' work.

7. 8.

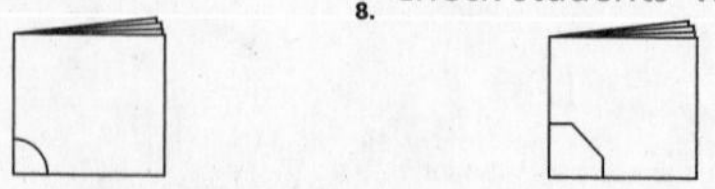

Use with Grade 5, Chapter 11, Lesson 8, pages 512–513. (360)

Daily Homework

11-8 Symmetry

Tell which figures are symmetric about a line.

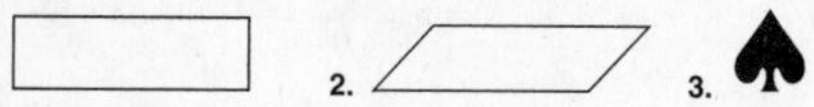

1. symmetric
2. not symmetric
3. symmetric

Draw all the lines of symmetry for each figure. Check students' lines.

4. 5.

Problem Solving

6. The flag of Mali, a nation in West Africa, is shown below. Is the flag symmetric about a line? Yes.

7. The shape of the nation of Mali is shown below. Is the shape of the nation symmetric about a line? No.

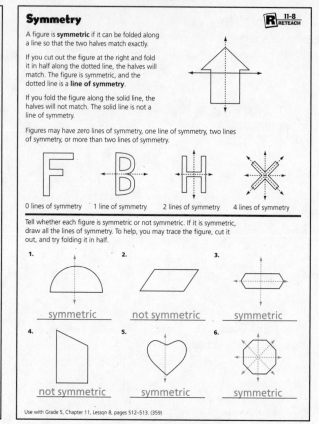

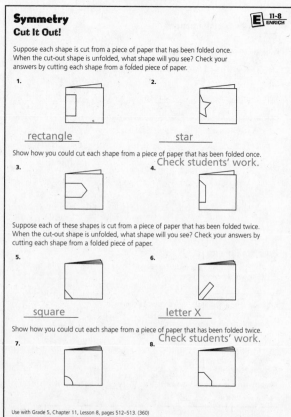

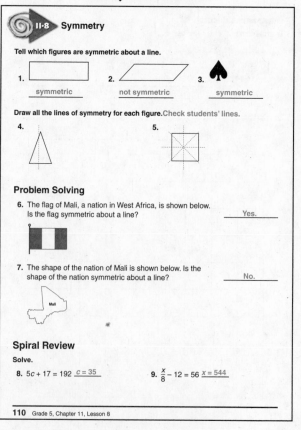

Spiral Review

Solve.

8. $5c + 17 = 192$ $c = 35$

9. $\frac{x}{8} - 12 = 56$ $x = 544$

110 Grade 5, Chapter 11, Lesson 8

Chapter 11 ~ Lesson 9

Practice

Problem Solving: Strategy
Find a Pattern

P 11-9 PRACTICE

Find a pattern to solve each problem. State the pattern you followed.

1. Martina is designing chains. The diagram shows the number of rings she uses in each chain. If she continues the pattern, how many rings will be in the next chain?

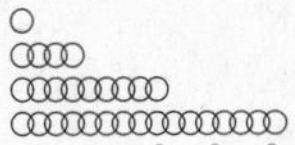

25 rings; $1^2, 2^2, 3^2, 4^2, 5^2$

2. **Art** A sculptor is using a pattern of different sized cubes to create a sculpture with four sections. The first section has 1 cube, the second section has 16 cubes, and the third section has 81 cubes. How many cubes are in the fourth section?

256 cubes; $1^4, 2^4, 3^4, 4^4$

3. Mika is making a pattern of circles. The smallest circle has a diameter of 8 centimeters. The next circle has a diameter of 12 centimeters and the circle after that has a diameter of 16 centimeters. What is the diameter of the sixth circle?

28 cm; add 4 cm to the previous diameter

4. The bottom layer of a pyramid has 216 blocks. The layer above the bottom has 125 blocks. The third layer from the bottom has 64 blocks. If the pattern continues, how many blocks will be in the next two layers?

27 cubes, 8 cubes; $6^3, 5^3, 4^3, 3^3, 2^3$

Mixed Strategy Review

Solve. Use any strategy.

5. **Number Sense** In a set of bowls, the difference in the diameter between one bowl and the next size is 5 centimeters. The largest bowl has a diameter of 40 centimeters. If the smallest bowl has a diameter of 15 centimeters, how many bowls are in the set?

6 bowls

Strategy: make an organized list

6. Jessica buys a combination of 8 erasers and pencils. Pencils cost $0.18 each and erasers cost $0.35 each. The total cost of the pencils and the erasers is $1.78. How many of each did she buy?

6 pencils, 2 erasers

Strategy: guess and check

7. **Create a problem** for which you could find a pattern to solve. Share it with others.

Check students' problems.

Use with Grade 5, Chapter 11, Lesson 9, pages 514–515. (361)

Reteach

Problem Solving: Strategy
Find a Pattern

R 11-9 RETEACH

Page 515, Problem 1

Measure the length of the sides of the four squares. If you were going to add another square after the largest one, what would the length of the side be?

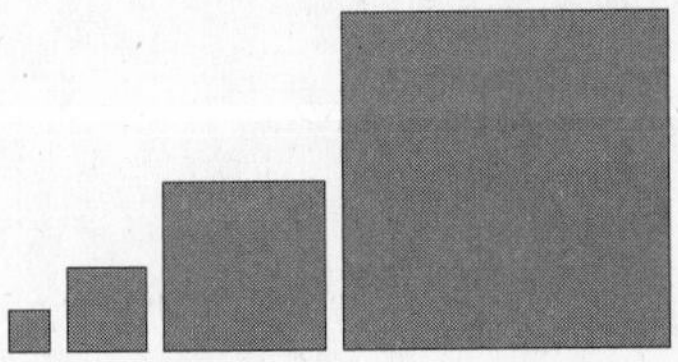

Step 1 Read

Be sure you understand the problem.
Read carefully.

What do you know?

- The lengths of the sides of the 4 squares.

What do you need to find?

- The length of the side of the next largest square.

Step 2 Plan

- Find a Pattern
- Guess and Check
- Work Backward
- Make a Graph
- Make a Table
- Write an Equation
- Make an Organized List
- Draw a Diagram
- Solve a Simpler Problem
- Logical Reasoning

Make a plan.
Choose a strategy.

You can find a pattern to solve the problem.

Find the pattern between the lengths of the sides of the squares. Then extend the pattern to find the length of a side of the next largest square.

Use with Grade 5, Chapter 11, Lesson 9, pages 514–515. (362)

Reteach

Problem Solving: Strategy
Find a Pattern The answers in the table will depend on the size of the reproduction, but the side length doubles each time.

R 11-9 RETEACH

Step 3 Solve

Carry out your plan.

Measure the length of each side of the squares in the painting. Record the data in a table to help you see the pattern.

Square	1	2	3	4
Side length				

Look at the data in the table. What pattern do you see?

The length of the side doubles from the previous square as the squares increase in size.

Use the pattern to find the length of the next square.

The answer will depend on the size of the reproduction, but the side length doubles each time.

Step 4 Look Back

Is the solution reasonable?
Reread the problem.

Have you answered the question? Yes

Is your answer reasonable? Explain. Possible answer: Yes, because the side of the square is longer.

How can you check your answer? Possible answer: Make a diagram

Practice

1. Paige uses different size squares to make a quilt. The smallest square is 2 inches on a side. The next three squares have sides of 5, 8, and 11 inches. If the pattern continues, what are the lengths of the sides of the next two squares?

14 in., 17 in.

2. There are 64 cans used in the first row of a display. The second row uses 49 cans and the third row uses 36 cans. If the pattern continues, how many cans are used in the fifth row of the display? What is the pattern?

16 cans; $8^2, 7^2, 6^2, 5^2, 4^2$

Use with Grade 5, Chapter 11, Lesson 9, pages 514–515. (363)

Daily Homework

11-9 **Problem Solving: Strategy**
Find a Pattern

Solve.

1. Jody is drawing the pattern shown above. Use a ruler to measure the dimensions of the rectangles in the pattern. If Jody continues the pattern in the same way, what will be the dimensions of the sixth rectangle she draws?

1 cm × 6 cm

2. Instead of continuing, Jody begins to count back down, so that the fifth rectangle is 1 × 3. What will the dimensions of the seventh rectangle be?

1 cm × 1 cm

3. Luke draws a pattern that also starts with a 1 cm × 1 cm square. The second figure in his pattern is a 4 cm × 4 cm square, and the third figure is a 7 cm × 7 cm square. What will the dimensions of the seventh figure be?

19 cm × 19 cm

4. Sarah is making a pyramid out of blocks. She begins with a base of 15 blocks × 15 blocks. She then gives the second level dimensions of 13 blocks × 13 blocks, and the third level dimensions of 11 blocks × 11 blocks. How many blocks will it take to construct the fifth level?

49 blocks

5. Sarah decides to make a pyramid that follows the same pattern as the first one but is one level taller. How many levels will the second pyramid have?

9 levels

6. What will the dimensions of the base of the second pyramid be?

17 blocks × 17 blocks

Spiral Review

Find the GCF.

7. 15 and 40 5
8. 16 and 56 8
9. 148 and 100 4
10. 72 and 108 36

Grade 5, Chapter 11, Lesson 9 111

Chapter 11 ~ Lesson 10

Practice

Circles

P 11-10 PRACTICE

Identify the parts of circle H.

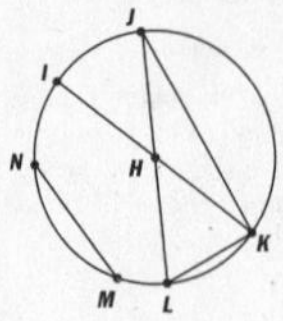

J
I
N
H
K
M
L

1. center *H*
2. diameters $\overline{IK}$; $\overline{JL}$
3. radii $\overline{HI}$; $\overline{HK}$; $\overline{HJ}$; $\overline{HL}$
4. chords $\overline{MN}$; $\overline{JK}$; $\overline{KL}$
5. central angles ____ ; ____ ; ____ ; ____
6. points on the circle *I, J, K, L, M, N*

Solve. Use circle H above.

7. If $\overline{HK}$ = 7 inches, how long is $\overline{IK}$? 14 inches
8. If $\overline{JL}$ = 10 cm, how long is $\overline{HL}$? 5 cm
9. If $\overline{HI}$ = 6 feet, how long is $\overline{HK}$? 6 feet
10. If the sum of the measures of $\angle IHJ$, $\angle JHK$, and $\angle KHL$ equals 240 degrees, what is the measure of $\angle IHL$? 120°
11. If the measure of $\angle IHJ$ equals 50 degrees, what is the measure of $\angle JHK$? 130°

On a seperate piece of parer, draw circles with the given measurements.

12. radius = $1\frac{1}{2}$ inches
13. diameter = 4 inches

Check students' drawings.

Problem Solving

14. At 3:00 A.M., what is the measure of the central angle of the hands on an analog clock? 45°
15. At 9:00 A.M., what is the measure of the central angle of the hands on an analog clock? 270°
16. At 4:00 P.M., what is the measure of the central angle of the hands on an analog clock? 120°
17. A clock has a diameter of 12 inches. To the nearest inch, what is the longest the minute hand can be? 6 inches

Use with Grade 5, Chapter 11, Lesson 10, pages 516–519. (364)

Reteach

Circles

R 11-10 RETEACH

A circle is named by its center. The circle below is circle L. M, N, O, P, and Q are points on the circle.

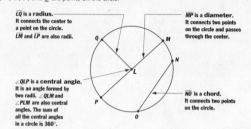

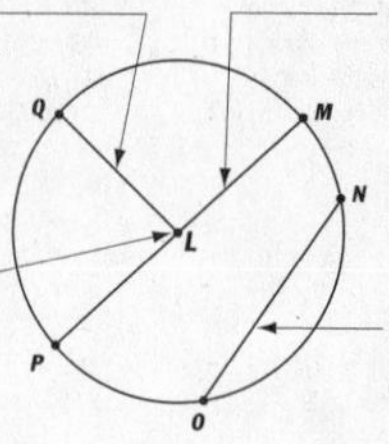

$\overline{LQ}$ is a radius. It connects the center to a point on the circle. $\overline{LM}$ and $\overline{LP}$ are also radii.
$\overline{MP}$ is a diameter. It connects two points on the circle and passes through the center.
$\angle QLP$ is a central angle. It is an angle formed by two radii. $\angle QLM$ and $\angle PLM$ are also central angles. The sum of all the central angles in a circle is 360°.
$\overline{NO}$ is a chord. It connects two points on the circle.
Q
M
N
L
P
O

The diameter of a circle is twice the length of a radius.

If the radius of a circle is 10 inches, its diameter is 20 inches.

2 × 10 in. = 20 in.

If the diameter of a circle is 10 inches, its radius is 5 inches.

10 in. ÷ 2 = 5 in.

Identify the parts of circle S.

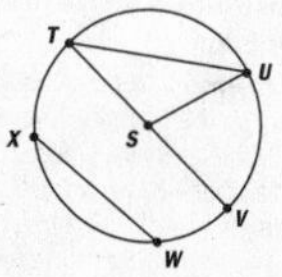

T
U
X
S
V
W

1. Diameter $\overline{TV}$
2. Radii $\overline{ST}$, $\overline{SV}$, $\overline{SU}$
3. Chords $\overline{TU}$, $\overline{WX}$
4. Central angles $\angle TSU$, $\angle USV$, $\angle TSV$

Complete each statement about circle S above.

5. The sum of the measures of $\angle TSU$, $\angle SUV$, and $\angle TSV$ is 360 degrees.
6. If $\overline{TV}$ is 18 inches, then $\overline{ST}$ is 9 inches.

Use with Grade 5, Chapter 11, Lesson 10, pages 516–519. (365)

Enrich

Circles

E 11-10 ENRICH

Angle Investigation

Follow these steps to learn more about circles and angles.

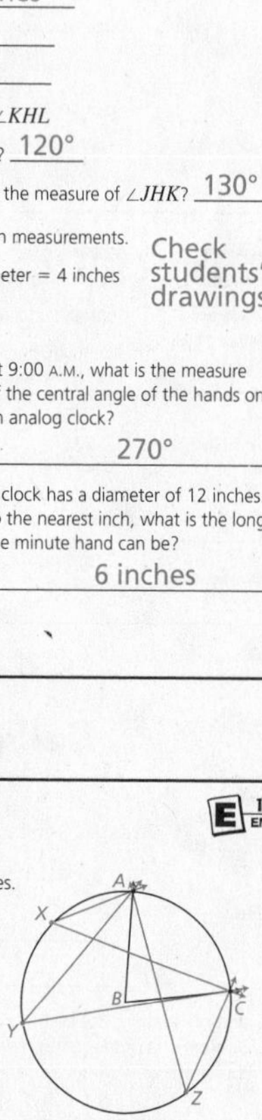

A
X
B
C
Y
Z

1. Label the central angle ABC.
2. Use a protractor to measure $\angle ABC$. Record its measure in the table at the right.
3. An inscribed angle is an angle whose vertex is a point on the circle. Each ray of an inscribed angle passes through a point on the circle.
   a. Pick three points on the circle outside $\angle ABC$. Label them X, Y, and Z.
   b. Draw three inscribed angles having vertices X, Y, and Z. The rays of each angle should pass through A and C.
   c. Measure each inscribed angle. Record your findings in the table at the right.
4. Draw a central angle in the circle below. Repeat steps 1–3. Record your findings in the tables below.

Central Angle

Name	Measure
$\angle ABC$	80°

Check students' drawings.

Inscribed Angles

Name	Measure
$\angle AXC$	40°
$\angle AYC$	40°
$\angle AZC$	40°

Check students' drawings. Angle measures will vary depending on central angle drawn.

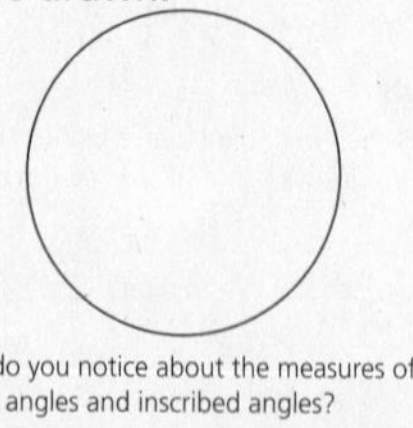

Central Angle

Name	Measure
$\angle ABC$	80°

Inscribed Angles

Name	Measure
$\angle AXC$	40°
$\angle AYC$	40°
$\angle AZC$	40°

What do you notice about the measures of central angles and inscribed angles?

The measures of inscribed angles whose rays pass through the same points on a circle as a central angle are half the measure of the central angle.

Use with Grade 5, Chapter 11, Lesson 10, pages 516–519. (366)

Daily Homework

11-10 Circles

Identify the parts of circle *E*.

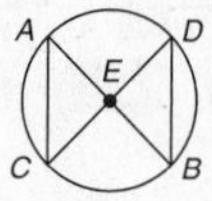

A
D
E
C
B

1. Center E
2. Chords AC, BD, AB, CD
3. Radii EA, EB, EC, ED
4. Diameters AB, CD

Solve. Use circle *E*.

5. If *CD* = 7 feet, how long is *AB*? 7 feet
6. A new chord *BC* is drawn on the circle. Is this chord a diameter? No.

Draw circles with the given measurements. Check students' drawings and measurements.

7. diameter = 2 inches
8. radius = 2 inches

Problem Solving

9. Tamara has a circular wall clock. She imagines the following line segment running through the clock. What part of a circle is she imagining? diameter
10. A basketball hoop has a radius of 9 inches. What is its diameter? 18 inches

Spiral Review

11. $3\frac{1}{2} - 1\frac{4}{5} = 1\frac{7}{10}$
12. $2\frac{2}{3} + 4\frac{3}{4} = 7\frac{5}{12}$

112 Grade 5, Chapter 11, Lesson 10

Chapter 11 ~ Lesson 11

Practice

Explore Tessellations

P 11-11 PRACTICE

Tell whether each shape tessellates. Record your work.
Check students' drawings.

1. 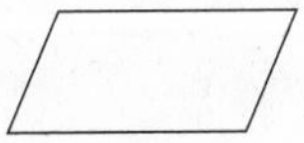 yes

2. 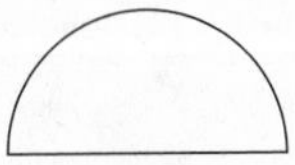 no

3. 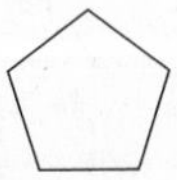 no

4. 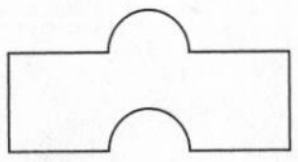 yes

5.  no

6. 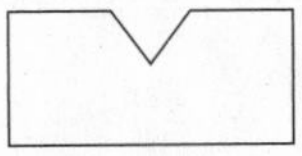 no

7. 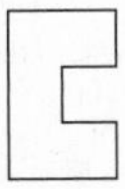 yes

8. 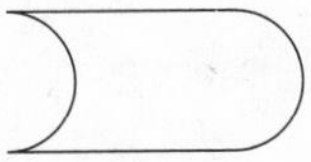 yes

9. 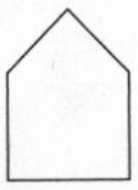 yes

10. 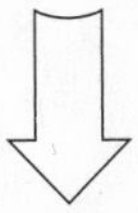 no

11. 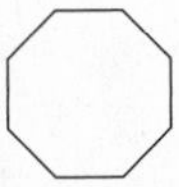 no

12. 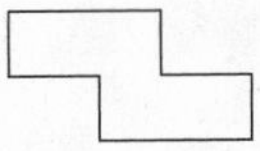 yes

Use with Grade 5, Chapter 11, Lesson 11, pages 520–521. (367)

Reteach

Explore Tessellations

R 11-11 RETEACH

A tessellation is an arrangement of shapes that covers an area without any gaps or overlaps. A shape tessellates if you can use it to make a tessellation.

This hexagon tessellates.

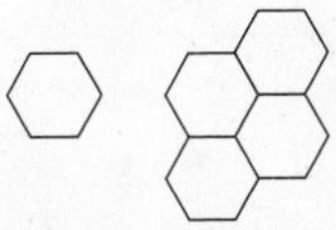

This pentagon does not tessellate.

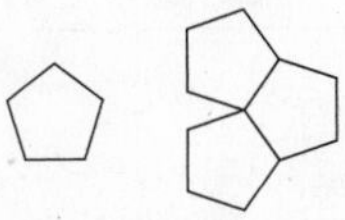

Tell whether each is an example of a tessellation.

1. 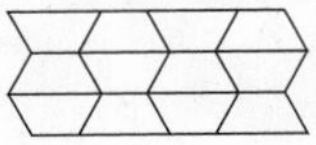 yes

2. 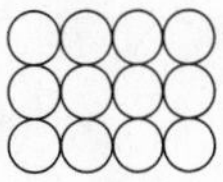 no

3. 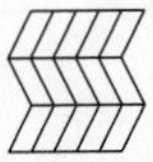 yes

Tell whether each shape tessellates. Record your work. Check students' drawings.

4. 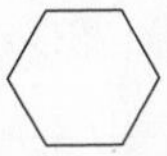 yes

5.  yes

6.  no

7. 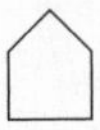 yes

8. 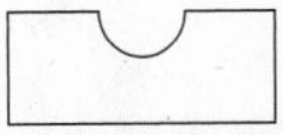 no

9. 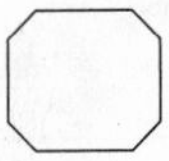 no

Use with Grade 5, Chapter 11, Lesson 11, pages 520–521. (368)

Enrich

Explore Tessellations

E 11-11 ENRICH

Pentominoes

A pentomino is a figure made of five congruent squares. Each square in a pentomino must share at least one complete side with a neighboring square.

Pentominoes **Not Pentominoes**

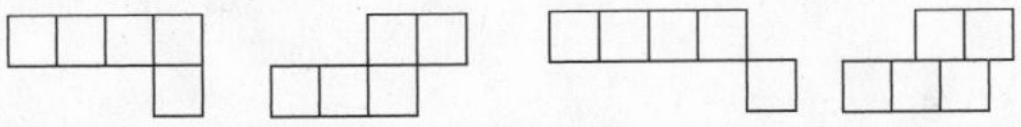

There are 12 different pentominoes. Draw each one on the grids below. Do not draw a pentomino that is only a reflection or a rotation of a pentomino you have already drawn.

Do all pentominos tesselate? yes

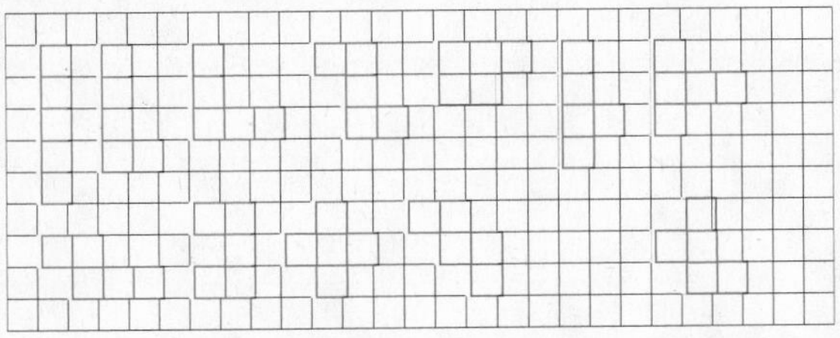

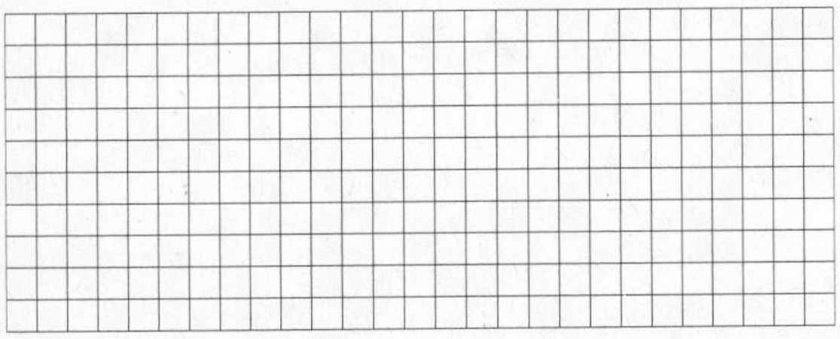

Use with Grade 5, Chapter 11, Lesson 11, pages 520–521. (369)

Daily Homework

11-11 Explore Tessellations

Tell whether the shapes tessellate. Show your work. Check students' drawings.

1. Yes.
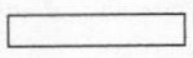

2. Yes.

3. No.
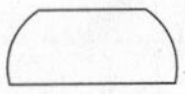

4. Yes.
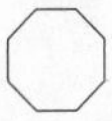

5. No.

6. Yes.

Solve.

7. A rectangular window in Hiram's house is made up of square panes as shown. Do the panes in the window tessellate? Yes.

8. Elaine is making a pattern with oak leaves like the one shown here. Will the oak leaves in her pattern tessellate? No.

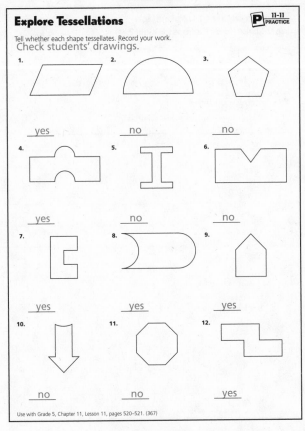

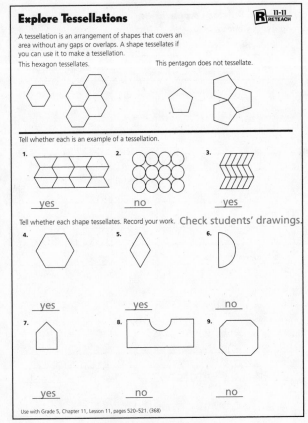

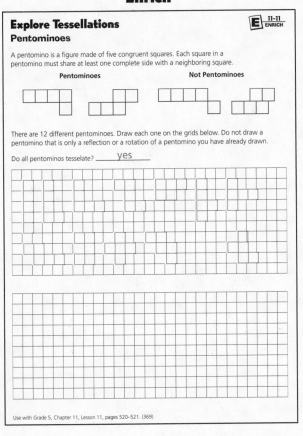

Spiral Review

Evaluate each expression for the value given.

9. $\frac{s}{3}$ for $s = {}^-12$ $^-4$

10. $8k$ for $k = {}^-2$ $^-16$

Grade 5, Chapter 11, Lesson 11 **113**

Chapter 11 ~ Lesson 12

Part A Worksheet

Problem Solving: Application

Part A 11-12 WORKSHEET Decision Making

Applying Geometry

Use the table to help you determine which tiles you will choose.

Tile	Number of Tiles Needed	Number of Tiles per Box	Number of Boxes Needed	Cost per Box	Total Cost

Your Decision

Which tile would you choose? Explain your decision.

Answers may vary. Possible answer: I would choose the 4 in. square tiles because the cost fits the budget, they tessellate, and I like the patterns I can make with them.

Use with Grade 5, Chapter 11, Lesson 12, pages 522–523. (370)

Part B Worksheet

Problem Solving: Application

Part B 11-12 WORKSHEET Math & Science

What shape holds the most weight?

Remember to be careful when you work with scissors.

Work in a small group. Discuss some of the structures you would like to build. Decide if they will be possible to make.

Compare structures to try to improve the design of other structures you build.

Use the table below to sketch or describe each platform you built. Record the number of books each platform was able to hold.

Shape	Number of Books

Use with Grade 5, Chapter 11, Lesson 12, pages 524–525. (371)

Part B Worksheet

Problem Solving: Application

Part B 11-12 WORKSHEET Math & Science

What shape holds the most weight?

1. Which structure held the most weight? Explain why you think it was able to hold the most weight.

   Answers may vary.

2. How did you decide which designs to try?

   Answers may vary.

3. Were you able to successfully improve a design and make a stronger structure? Explain how you were able to do this.

   Answers may vary.

4. Compare your structures and the number of books they were able to hold with the results of your classmates. Make a bar graph to display the data.

   Check students' graphs.

5. Discuss similarities and differences in the data from the entire class.

   Answers may vary.

Use with Grade 5, Chapter 11, Lesson 12, pages 524–525. (372)

Chapter 12 ~ Lesson 1

Practice

Perimeter of Polygons

P 12-1 PRACTICE

Find the perimeter of each figure.

1. 14 ft, 9 ft — P = 46 ft
2. 13 ft, 13 ft — P = 52 ft
3. 15.8 cm, 6.3 cm — P = 44.2 cm
4. 4.8 m, 4.8 m — P = 19.2 m
5. $2\frac{1}{2}$ ft, 11 ft — P = 27 ft
6. 1.93 m, 4.76 m — P = 13.38 m

Find each missing measurement.

7. a, 3 in. — P = 24 in. — a = 9 in.
8. s, s — P = 48 cm — s = 12 cm
9. 18 ft, r — P = 50 ft — r = 7 ft

Problem Solving

10. A square patio is 18 feet on each side. What is the perimeter of the patio? 72 feet
11. A rectangular garden is 9.7 meters long and 6 meters wide. How many meters of fencing are needed to enclose the garden? 31.4 meters

Use with Grade 5, Chapter 12, Lesson 1, pages 540–541. (373)

Reteach

Perimeter of Polygons

R 12-1 RETEACH

Perimeter is the distance around a closed figure. To find the perimeter of a rectangle or square, you can add the lengths of all four sides. You can also use a formula.

Find the perimeter of the rectangle. Use the formula $P = 2l + 2w$, where P = perimeter, l = length, and w = width.

4.5 cm, 2.3 cm

$P = 2l + 2w$
$P = (2 \times 4.5) + (2 \times 2.3)$
$P = 9 + 4.6$
$P = 13.6$ cm

Find the perimeter of the square. Use the formula $P = 4s$, where P = perimeter and s = length of a side.

17 cm, 17 cm

$P = 4s$
$P = 4 \times 17$
$P = 68$ cm

Find the perimeter of each figure.

1. 15 ft, 7 ft
   $P = 2l + 2w$
   $P = (2 \times$ 15$) + (2 \times$ 7$)$
   $P =$ 30 + 14
   $P =$ 44 ft
2. 2.9 m, 1.3 m
   $P = 2l + 2w$
   $P = (2 \times$ 2.9$) + (2 \times$ 1.3$)$
   $P =$ 5.8 + 2.6
   $P =$ 8.4 m
3. 12 cm, 12 cm
   $P = 4s$
   $P = 4 \times$ 12
   $P =$ 48 cm
4. 90 in., 40 in. — P = 260 in.
5. 3.5 cm, 4.2 cm — P = 15.4 cm
6. 27 ft, 14 ft — P = 82 ft

Use with Grade 5, Chapter 12, Lesson 1, pages 540–541. (374)

Enrich

Perimeter of Polygons
Coordinate Rectangles

E 12-1 ENRICH

Graph the ordered pairs. Connect the points.
Record the length, width, and perimeter of the rectangle.

1. (3, 2), (3, 8), (7, 8), (7, 2)

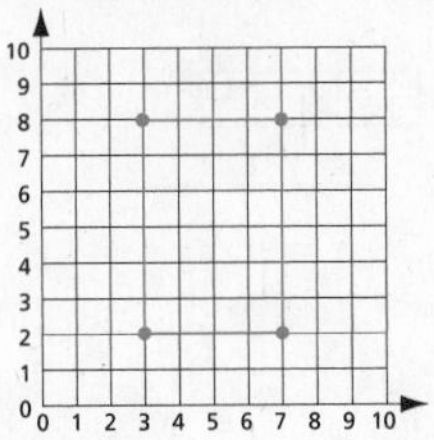

l = 4 w = 6 P = 20

2. (7, 1), (4, 1), (4, 10), (7, 10)

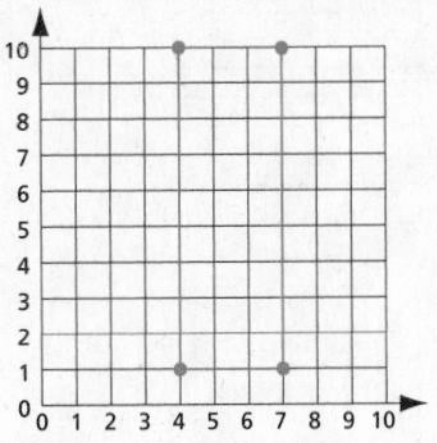

l = 3 w = 9 P = 24

3. (9, 9), (9, 2), (2, 2), (2, 9)

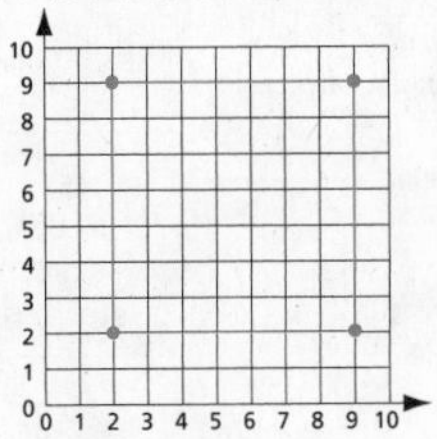

l = 7 w = 7 P = 28

4. (7, 9), (7, 1), (1, 1), (1, 9)

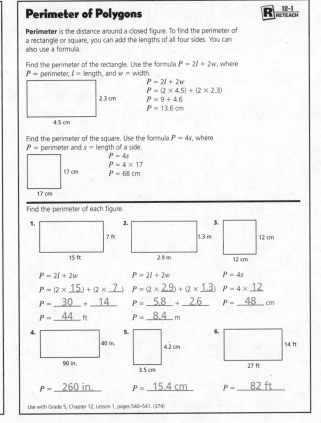

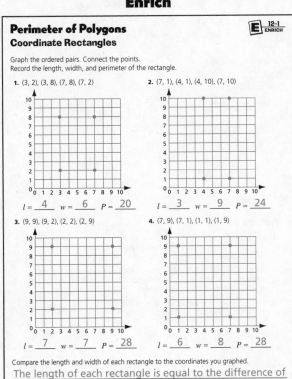

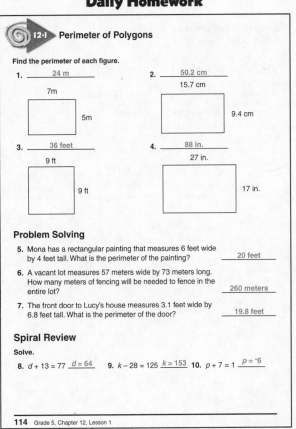

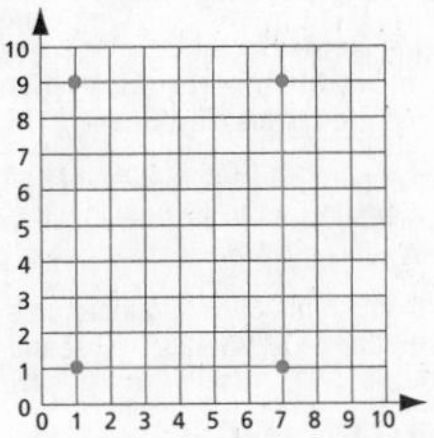

l = 6 w = 8 P = 28

Compare the length and width of each rectangle to the coordinates you graphed.
The length of each rectangle is equal to the difference of the second (y) coordinates. The width of each rectangle is equal to the difference of the first (x) coordinates.

Use with Grade 5, Chapter 12, Lesson 1, pages 540–541. (375)

Daily Homework

12-1 Perimeter of Polygons

Find the perimeter of each figure.

1. 24 m — 7m, 5m
2. 50.2 cm — 15.7 cm, 9.4 cm
3. 36 feet — 9 ft, 9 ft
4. 88 in. — 27 in., 17 in.

Problem Solving

5. Mona has a rectangular painting that measures 6 feet wide by 4 feet tall. What is the perimeter of the painting? 20 feet
6. A vacant lot measures 57 meters wide by 73 meters long. How many meters of fencing will be needed to fence in the entire lot? 260 meters
7. The front door to Lucy's house measures 3.1 feet wide by 6.8 feet tall. What is the perimeter of the door? 19.8 feet

Spiral Review

Solve.

8. $d + 13 = 77$ $d = 64$
9. $k - 28 = 125$ $k = 153$
10. $p + 7 = 1$ $p = {}^{-}6$

114 Grade 5, Chapter 12, Lesson 1

Chapter 12 ~ Lesson 2

Practice

Area of Rectangles

Find the area of each figure.

1.

4 in.
8 in.

$A = \underline{32 \text{ in.}^2}$

2.
16 cm
21 cm

$A = \underline{336 \text{ cm}^2}$

3.
9 ft
9 ft

$A = \underline{81 \text{ ft}^2}$

4.
3.5 m
3.5 m

$A = \underline{12.25 \text{ m}^2}$

5.
6.3 cm
1.7 cm

$A = \underline{10.71 \text{ cm}^2}$

6.
25 in.
25 in.

$A = \underline{625 \text{ in.}^2}$

Find each missing measurement.

7.

z
12 cm

$A = 48 \text{ cm}^2$
$z = \underline{4 \text{ cm}}$

8.
b
b

$A = 16 \text{ ft}^2$
$b = \underline{4 \text{ ft}}$

9.
4 in.
p

$A = 72 \text{ in.}^2$
$p = \underline{18 \text{ in.}}$

Problem Solving

10. A family room is 24 feet long and 18 feet wide. What is the area of the family room?

$\underline{432 \text{ ft}^2}$

11. A square carpet is 3.6 meters on each side. What area will the carpet cover?

$\underline{12.96 \text{ m}^2}$

Reteach

Area of Rectangles

Area is the number of square units needed to cover a figure. To find the area of a rectangle or square, you can multiply its length times its width. This can be shown by a formula.

Find the area of the rectangle. Use the formula $A = lw$, where A = area, l = length, and w = width.

4 in.
13 in.

$A = lw$
$A = 13 \times 4$
$A = 52 \text{ in.}^2$

Find the area of the square. Use the formula $A = s^2$, where A = area and s = length of a side.

2.9 m
2.9 m

$A = s^2$
$A = 2.9 \times 2.9$
$A = 8.41 \text{ m}^2$

Find the area of each figure.

1.
5 in.
7 in.

$A = lw$
$A = \underline{7} \times \underline{5}$
$A = \underline{35} \text{ in.}^2$

2.
5 ft
5 ft

$A = s^2$
$A = \underline{5} \times \underline{5}$
$A = \underline{25} \text{ ft}^2$

3.
1.8 cm
3.6 cm

$A = lw$
$A = \underline{3.6} \times \underline{1.8}$
$A = \underline{6.48} \text{ cm}^2$

4.
10 in.
25 in.

$A = \underline{250 \text{ in.}^2}$

5.
0.8 m
0.8 m

$A = \underline{0.64 \text{ m}^2}$

6.
76 ft
49 ft

$A = \underline{3,724 \text{ ft}^2}$

Enrich

Area of Rectangles
Roll an Area Game

Play this game with a partner. Take turns.

- Toss two 1–6 number cubes. Use the two numbers rolled to form a 2-digit number.
- If possible, draw and shade a rectangle on the grid below that has as many square units in its area as the two-digit number rolled. Write your initials in it. Your rectangle may not overlap another rectangle.
- When the number cubes have been rolled four consecutive times without a rectangle being drawn, the game is over.
- The player who drew more rectangles wins.

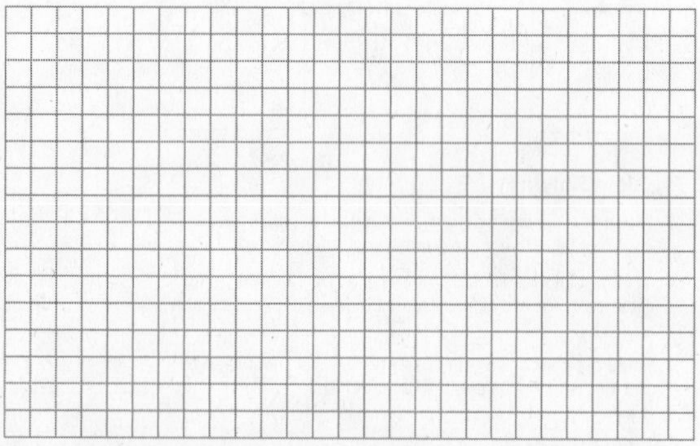

Describe a strategy you and your partner used to play this game.

Answers may vary. Possible answer: First we drew narrow rectangles scattered throughout the game board to leave places that would be too small for each other to draw rectangles in as the game progressed.

Daily Homework

Area of Rectangles

Find the area of each figure.

1. $\underline{45 \text{ square units}}$

2. $\underline{16 \text{ square units}}$

3. $\underline{58.1 \text{ ft}^2}$
8.3 ft
7 ft

4. $\underline{27.04 \text{ m}^2}$
5.2 m

Problem Solving

5. Ms. Newton's classroom is a rectangle that measures 7 meters wide by 12 meters long. What is the area of the classroom?

84 m^2

6. Anna notices that a sheet of notebook paper measures 11 inches tall and 8.5 inches wide. What is the area of the sheet of paper?

93.5 in.^2

7. Demetrius's backyard measures 60 feet long by 45 feet wide. What is the area of the backyard?

$2,700 \text{ ft}^2$

Spiral Review

Compare. Write >, <, or =.

8. $\frac{4}{5} \underline{=} 0.8$

9. $\frac{4}{3} \underline{>} \frac{5}{4}$

10. $\frac{8}{7} \underline{<} 1.2$

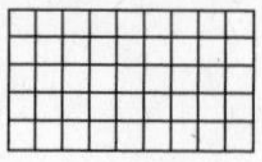

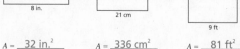

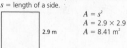

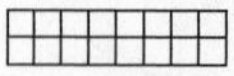

Chapter 12 ~ Lesson 3

Practice

Problem Solving: Reading for Math

Distinguish Between Perimeter and Area

P 12-3 PRACTICE — Reading Skill

State whether perimeter or area is needed. Then solve the problem.

1. Hayden wants to make a rectangular herb garden that is 4 feet long and 3 feet wide. She wants to plant lavender in half of the garden. How can she decide how much of the garden will be covered with lavender?
   area of half of the garden; 6 square feet of lavender

2. Daniel wants to plant a row of marigolds along the border of his vegetable garden. The garden is 6 feet long and 4 feet wide. How can he decide how much of the garden will need to be covered with marigolds?
   perimeter; the border is 20 feet long

3. Ms. Carmichael is building a deck with two levels. The lower level is a square. The length of each side is 5 feet. The upper level is rectangular in shape, 12 feet long and 8 feet wide. How can she decide how much wood she will need to construct each level? area of each level; area of the lower level is 25 square feet, area of the upper level is 96 square feet, total area is 121 square feet.

4. Ms. Carmichael wants to put railing around the sides of the lower level. How can she decide how much railing she will need?
   perimeter; 20 feet

5. Jamison has 70 square feet of plywood to make a floor for a two-room clubhouse he is building. The floor of one room is 8 feet long and 6 feet wide. The floor of the other room is 5 feet long and 4 feet wide. How can he decide if he has enough plywood?
   area of both rooms; total area is 68 square feet which is less than 70 square feet; he has enough plywood.

6. Amy wants to make a frame for a painting that is 24 inches long and 18 inches wide. She found a wood molding she would like to use. How can she decide how much molding she needs to make the frame?
   perimeter; 84 inches

Use with Grade 5, Chapter 12, Lesson 3, pages 544–545. (379)

Practice

Problem Solving: Reading for Math

Distinguish Between Perimeter and Area

P 12-3 PRACTICE — Math Skills Test Prep

Choose the best answer.

Tami's birds need a birdcage with a base that is at least 12 square feet. She plans to build a rectangular birdcage that is 4 feet long and 3 feet wide. Will the birdcage be large enough for the birds?

1. Which of the following statements is false?
   - A The area of the base of the birdcage is 12 square feet.
   - B Tami's birdcage will be large enough for her birds.
   - C A birdcage with a square base that is 3 feet long on each side would not be large enough.
   - (D) A birdcage with a base that is 5 feet long and 2 feet wide will be large enough for the birds.

2. When you need to find the area of a rectangle, you need to know
   - F the length of one side.
   - G the width of one side.
   - (H) the length of one side and the width of one side.
   - J the perimeter.

Mr. Gonzalez wants to enclose a field for his horse. The field is 20 feet wide and 35 feet long. He has 100 feet of fence available to use. Does he have enough fence?

3. When you need to find the perimeter of a rectangle, you need to know
   - A the area.
   - B the length of one side.
   - (C) the length and width of the sides.
   - D the square is a rectangle.

4. Which of the following statements is true?
   - F Mr. Gonzalez needs 55 feet of fence.
   - G Mr. Gonzalez needs 100 feet of fence.
   - H Mr. Gonzalez needs 700 feet of fence.
   - (J) Mr. Gonzalez needs 10 more feet of fence.

Nicole has 18 square feet of corkboard to make 2 bulletin boards. She wants to make each bulletin board 4 feet long and 2 feet wide. Does she have enough corkboard to make both bulletin boards?

5. Which of the following statements is true?
   - A She needs 2 more feet of corkboard.
   - (B) She will have 2 extra square feet of corkboard.
   - C She needs 16 feet of corkboard.
   - D She can only make one bulletin board.

6. When you need to find the perimeter of a rectangle, you need to know
   - F the length of one side.
   - G the width of one side.
   - (H) the length of one side and the width of one side.
   - J the area.

Use with Grade 5, Chapter 12, Lesson 3, pages 544–545. (380)

Practice

Problem Solving: Reading for Math

Distinguish Between Perimeter and Area

P 12-3 PRACTICE — Math Skills Test Prep

Choose the best answer.

An artisan wants to decorate the base of a jewelry box with a ribbon border around the box. The box is 18 inches long and 6 inches wide. He has 45 inches of the ribbon. Does he have enough ribbon?

7. Which of the following statements is true?
   - (A) The artisan needs 3 more inches of ribbon.
   - B The artisan will have 2 extra inches of ribbon left.
   - C The artisan needs 108 inches of ribbon.
   - D The artisan has enough ribbon.

8. When you find the area of a triangle, you need to know
   - F the length of each side.
   - G the length of the base.
   - H the length of the height.
   - (J) the length of the base and the height.

Solve.

9. Taylor wants to build a fort in a spot that is 45 square feet. The fort is a square and each side is 6 feet long. How can Taylor decide if the fort will fit? Will it fit?
   Taylor should find the area of the fort. Yes, it will fit. It is 36 square feet.

10. A field is 25 feet wide and 65 feet long. Karin wants to find out how much alfalfa seed is needed to cover the field. Explain what Karin needs to find. Then find it.
    Karin should find the area of the field. It is 1,625 square feet.

11. A rectangular banner is 4 feet wide and 8 feet long. A square banner is 3 feet wide. How much ribbon is needed to trim the borders of both banners?
    36 feet

12. The floors of two rectangular rooms need new carpet. One room is 10 feet wide and 12 feet long. The other room is 16 feet wide and 18 feet long. How much carpet is needed to cover both floors?
    408 square feet

13. Brad has a 50 square inch piece of glass. He wants to use it to make a window in a rectangular opening that is 9 inches long and 5 inches wide. Does he have enough glass? Explain.
    Yes, he needs 45 square inches of glass.

14. Mr. Clark wants to put railing around his deck. He has 75 feet of railing to put around a deck that is 24 feet long and 8 feet wide. Does he have enough railing? Explain.
    Yes, he needs 64 feet of railing.

Use with Grade 5, Chapter 12, Lesson 3, pages 544–545. (381)

Daily Homework

12-3 Problem Solving: Reading for Math

Distinguish Between Perimeter and Area

State whether perimeter or area is needed. Then solve the problem.

1. A construction company is building a new house. The house will be rectangular, and it will measure 50 feet long by 32 feet wide. The builders are using string to mark where the house will be. How much string do they use?
   perimeter; 164 feet

2. The lot on which the house is being built measures 90 feet by 100 feet. How large is the lot? area; 9,000 ft^2

3. The owner of the house wants to have at least 5,000 ft^2 of space for a lawn. If the house is built as planned, will there be enough lawn? Yes.

Use data from the table for problems 4–7.

Posters for Sale at Dave's Poster Shop

Poster	Dimensions
Basketball Players	40 in. × 30 in.
Grizzly Bear	2.5 ft × 2 ft
Snowy Mountains	5 ft × 4 ft
Skyscraper	10 in. × 50 in.

4. Scott wants to buy the Snowy Mountains poster but is not sure how much space it will take up on the wall in his room. How can he determine the space? How much space will that be?
   Scott should calculate area; 20 ft^2

5. Scott buys the Basketball Players poster and has it framed. How can he determine the total length of framing needed? What is that length?
   Scott should calculate perimeter; 140 inches

6. Dina has a square space totaling 9 ft^2 for a poster. Will the Grizzly Bear poster fit in the space? area, yes

7. Tyra buys the Skyscraper poster. She places the poster on a piece of cardboard and traces its outline. What is the length of the line she traces? 120 inches

Spiral Review

Solve.

8. $4x = 164$ $x = 41$ 9. $\frac{y}{4} = 164$ $y = 656$ 10. $\frac{333}{z} = 9$ $z = 37$

116 Grade 5, Chapter 12, Lesson 3

Chapter 12 ~ Lesson 4

Practice

Explore Area of Parallelograms

P 12-4 PRACTICE

Find the area of each figure.

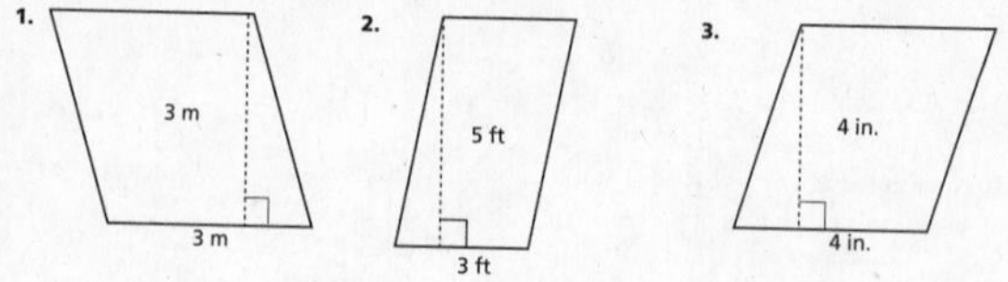

1. A = 9 m² 2. A = 15 ft² 3. A = 16 in.²

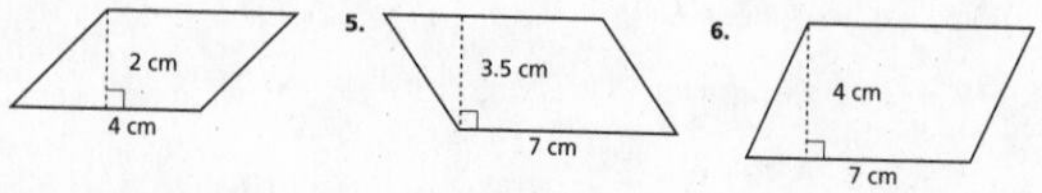

4. A = 8 cm² 5. A = 24.5 cm² 6. A = 28 cm²

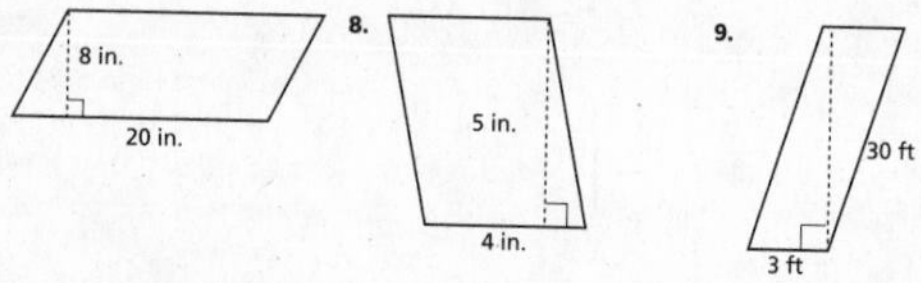

7. A = 160 in.² 8. A = 20 in.² 9. A = 90 ft²

Problem Solving

10. A garden in the shape of a parallelogram has a base of 14 meters and a height of 3 meters. What is the area of the garden?

42 m²

11. Another garden in the shape of a parallelogram covers 76 square feet. Its height is 4 feet. What is its base?

19 ft

Use with Grade 5, Chapter 12, Lesson 4, pages 546–547. (382)

Reteach

Explore Area of Parallelograms

R 12-4 RETEACH

You can use a formula to find the area of a parallelogram.

Find the area of the parallelogram. Use the formula $A = b \times h$, where A = area, b = base, and h = height. The height of a parallelogram is the vertical distance from its base to the opposite side.

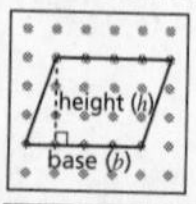

$A = b \times h$
$A = 4 \times 3$
$A = 12$ square units

On each figure, label the base, b, and label the height, h. Then find the area of each figure.

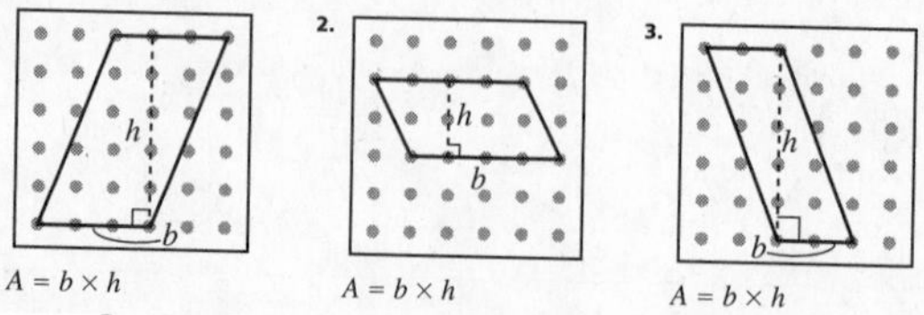

1. $A = b \times h$
A = 3 × 5
A = 15 square units

2. $A = b \times h$
A = 4 × 2
A = 8 square units

3. $A = b \times h$
A = 2 × 5
A = 10 square units

Find the area of each figure.

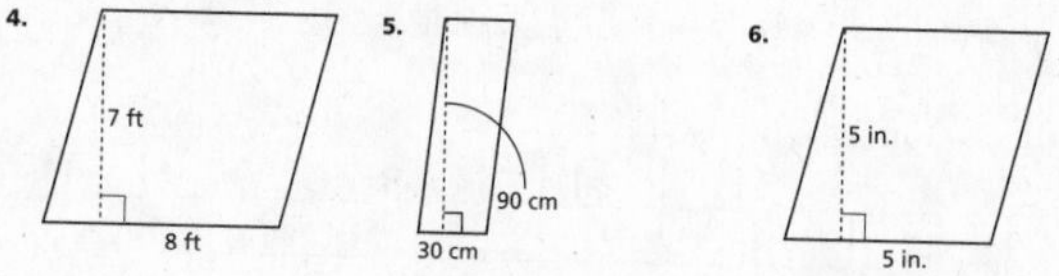

4. $A = b \times h$
A = 8 × 7
A = 56 ft²

5. $A = b \times h$
A = 30 × 90
A = 2,700 cm²

6. $A = b \times h$
A = 5 × 5
A = 25 in.²

Use with Grade 5, Chapter 12, Lesson 4, pages 546–547. (383)

Enrich

Explore Area of Parallelograms
Pick's Formula

E 12-4 ENRICH

You can use Pick's Formula to find the area of a figure on a geoboard or dot paper.

- Count the number of nails or dots that form the perimeter of the polygon. 6
- Divide by 2. 3
- Add the number of nails or dots inside the polygon. 3 + 4 = 7
- Subtract 1. This is the area. 6

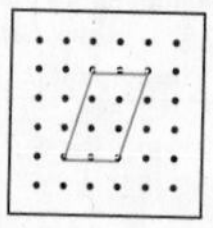

Use Pick's Formula to find the area of each figure.

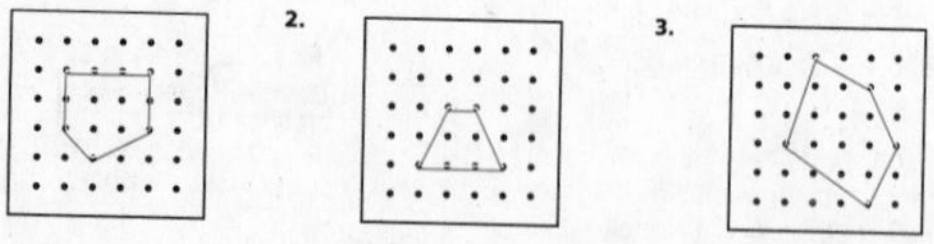

1. 7.5 square units 2. 4 square units 3. 11.5 square units

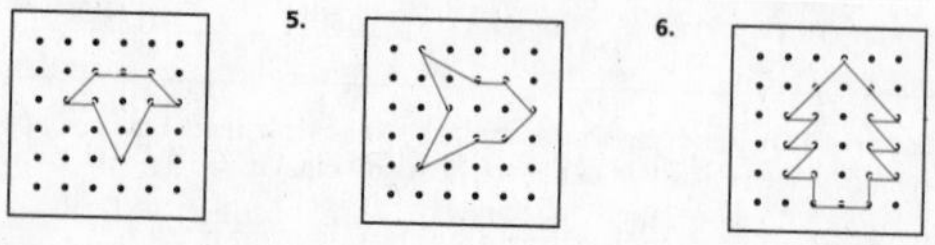

4. 5 square units 5. 7 square units 6. 12 square units

Suppose the area of a polygon on a geoboard is 5 square units and there are 4 nails inside the polygon. How many nails form the perimeter? Explain your work.

Answers may vary. Possible answer: 4; I worked backward by adding 1, subtracting the 4 nails inside, and then multiplying by 2.

Use with Grade 5, Chapter 12, Lesson 4, pages 546–547. (384)

Daily Homework

12·4 Explore Area of Parallelograms

Find the area of each figure.

1. 28 m² 2. 144 ft²

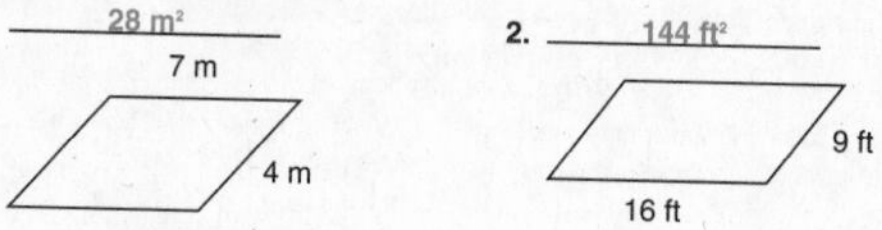

3. 136 m² 4. 252 in.²

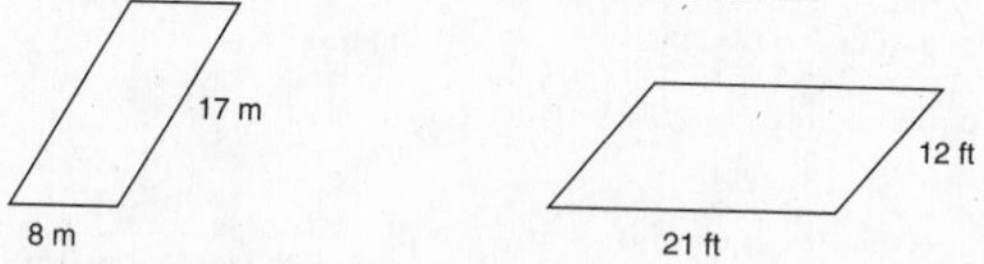

5. 20.4 in.² 6. 18.75 m²

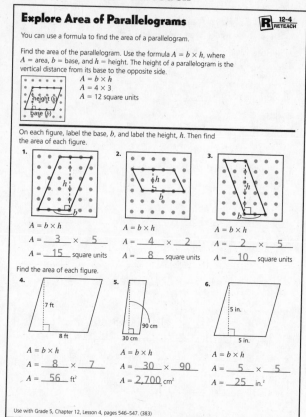

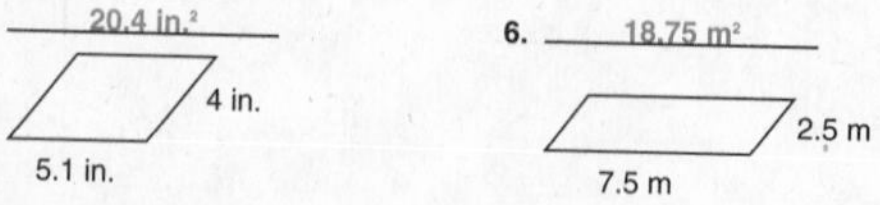

Solve.

7. While riding the bus, José notices that one of the windows is a parallelogram. If the base of the parallelogram is 14 inches and its height is 9 inches, what is its area? 126 in.²

8. The lot on which Kelly's house is built has the shape of a parallelogram. The base of the lot is 35 meters, and its height is 20 meters. What is the area of the lot? 700 m²

Spiral Review

9. $7c - 29 = 209$ $c = 34$

10. $\frac{p}{4} + 8 = 44$ $p = 144$

Grade 5, Chapter 12, Lesson 4 117

Practice

Explore Area of Triangles

P 12-5 PRACTICE

Find the area of each triangle.

1. 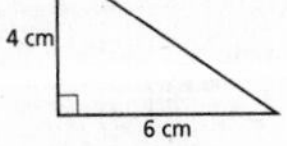

$A =$ 12 cm²

2. 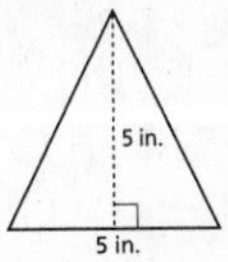

$A =$ 12.5 in.²

3. 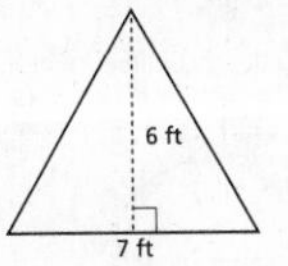

$A =$ 21 ft²

4. 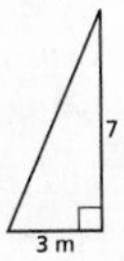

$A =$ 10.5 m²

5. 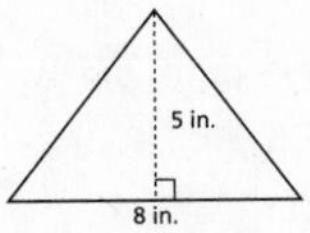

$A =$ 20 in.²

6. 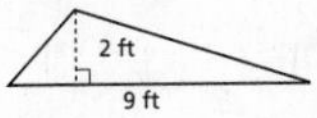

$A =$ 9 ft²

7. 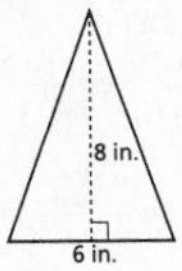

$A =$ 24 in.²

8. 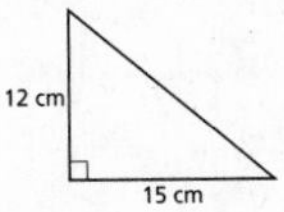

$A =$ 90 cm²

9. 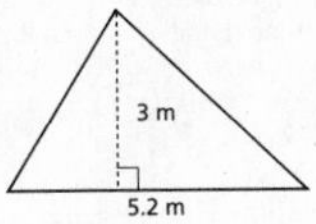

$A =$ 7.8 m²

Problem Solving

10. The triangular sail on a boat has a base of 8 feet and a height of 12 feet. What is the area of the sail?

48 ft²

11. A triangular flag has a base of 18 centimeters and a height of 30 centimeters. What is the area of the flag?

270 cm²

Use with Grade 5, Chapter 12, Lesson 5, pages 548–549. (385)

Reteach

Explore Area of Triangles

R 12-5 RETEACH

You can use a formula to find the area of a triangle.

Find the area of the triangle. Use the formula $A = \frac{1}{2} \times b \times h$, where A = area, b = base, and h = height.

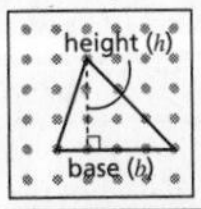

$A = \frac{1}{2} \times b \times h$

$A = \frac{1}{2} \times 4 \times 3$

$A = 6$ square units

On each figure, label the base, b, and label the height, h. Then find the area of each figure.

1. 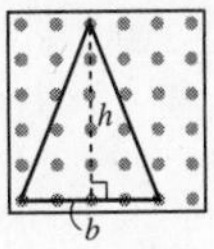

$A = \frac{1}{2} \times b \times h$

$A = \frac{1}{2} \times$ 4 $\times$ 5

$A =$ 10 square units

2. 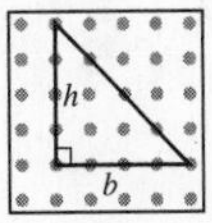

$A = \frac{1}{2} \times b \times h$

$A = \frac{1}{2} \times 4 \times 4$

$A =$ 8 square units

3. 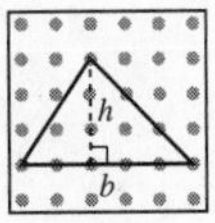

$A = \frac{1}{2} \times b \times h$

$A = \frac{1}{2} \times 5 \times 3$

$A = 7\frac{1}{2}$ square units

Find the area of each figure.

4. 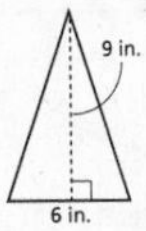

$A = \frac{1}{2} \times b \times h$

$A = \frac{1}{2} \times 6 \times 9$

$A =$ 27 in.²

5. 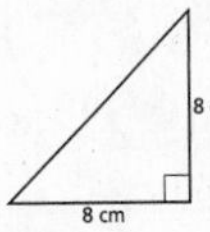

$A = \frac{1}{2} \times b \times h$

$A = \frac{1}{2} \times 8 \times 8$

$A =$ 32 cm²

6. 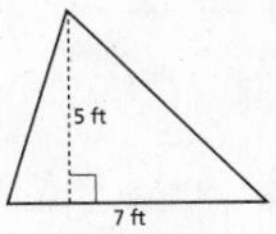

$A = \frac{1}{2} \times b \times h$

$A = \frac{1}{2} \times 7 \times 5$

$A = 17\frac{1}{2}$ ft²

Use with Grade 5, Chapter 12, Lesson 5, pages 548–549. (386)

Enrich

Explore Area of Triangles

E 12-5 ENRICH

Triangles, Triangles, and More Triangles

Within this figure there are many triangles with different areas. Find as many triangles with different areas as you can. Record each different area in the table below. Then count and record the number of triangles in the figure that have that area. Each small triangle has an area of 8 square units.

Area (in square units)	Number of Triangles
8	25
32	13
72	6
128	3
200	1

Use with Grade 5, Chapter 12, Lesson 5, pages 548–549. (387)

Daily Homework

12-5 Explore Area of Triangles

Find the area of each triangle.

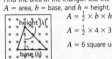

1. 9 in.²

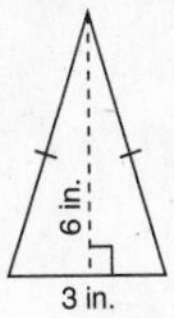

2. 14.2 m²

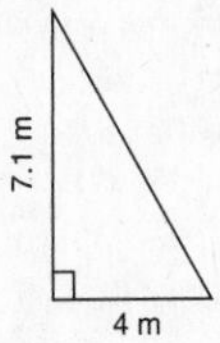

3. 6 ft²

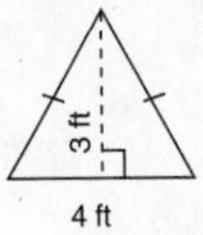

4. 7 in.²

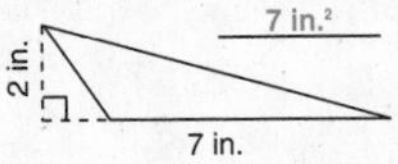

Solve.

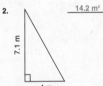

5. At the museum, Julia sees a painting on a triangular canvas. The triangle's base is 4 feet, and its height is 2.5 feet. What is the area of the painting?

5 ft²

6. A park near Tyler's house has the shape of a right triangle with a base of 160 meters and a height of 200 meters. What is the area of the park?

16,000 m²

Spiral Review

Tell whether the figures are congruent, similar, or neither.

7. similar and congruent

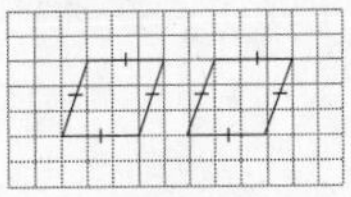

8. neither

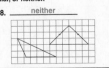

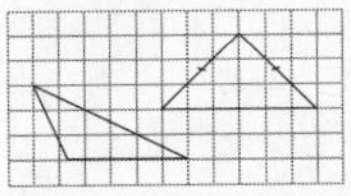

118 Grade 5, Chapter 12, Lesson 5

Chapter 12 ~ Lesson 6

Practice

Explore Circumference of Circles

P 12-6 PRACTICE

Find the approximate circumference of each circle. Use $\pi \approx 3.14$. Round to the nearest tenth, if necessary.

1.
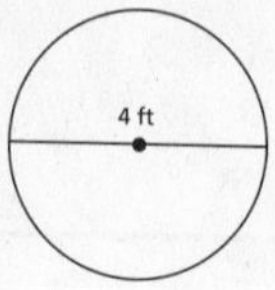

C = 12.6 ft

2.
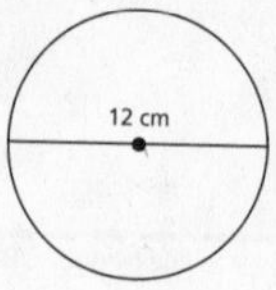

C = 37.7 cm

3.
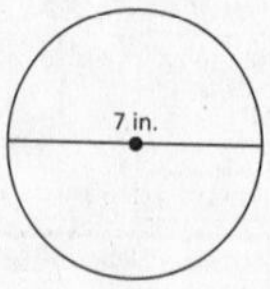

C = 22 in.

4.
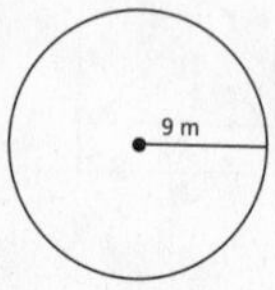

C = 56.5 m

5.
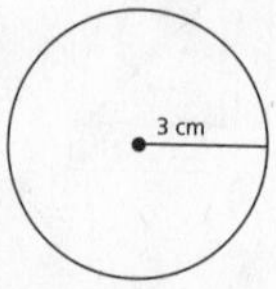

C = 18.8 cm

6.
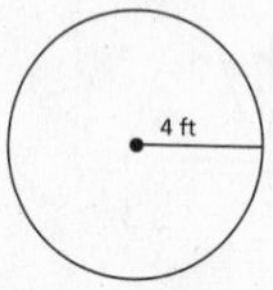

C = 25.1 ft

7.
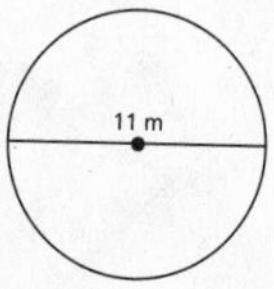

C = 34.5 m

8.
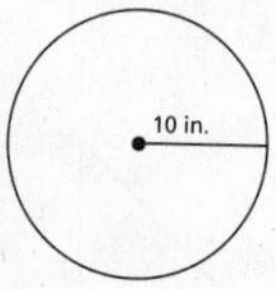

C = 62.8 in.

9.
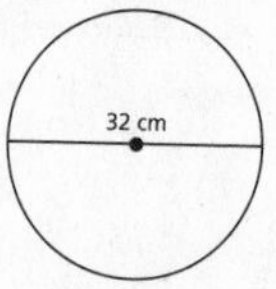

C = 100.5 cm

Problem Solving

10. A swimming pool has a diameter of 22 feet. To the nearest tenth of a foot, what is the circumference of the pool?

69.1 ft

11. A fountain is directly in the center of a circular pool. It is 8 meters from the wall surrounding the pool. To the nearest tenth of a meter, what is the length of the wall of the pool?

50.2 m

Use with Grade 5, Chapter 12, Lesson 6, pages 550–551. (388)

Reteach

Explore Circumference of Circles

R 12-6 RETEACH

The **circumference** is the distance around a circle. You can use a formula to find the circumference of a circle.

Find the circumference of the circle. When you are given the diameter of the circle, use the formula $C = \pi \times d$, where C = circumference and d = diameter. The value of π is approximately 3.14.

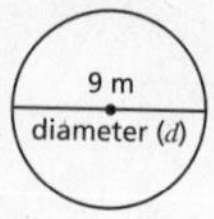

$C = \pi \times d$
$C = 3.14 \times 9$
$C = 28.26$ m, or about 28.3 m

When you are given the radius of the circle, first multiply it by 2 because 2 times the radius is the diameter. Then use the formula.

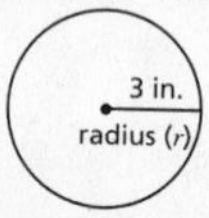

The radius is 3 in., so the diameter is 2×3 in., or 6 in.
$C = \pi \times d$
$C = 3.14 \times 6$
$C = 18.84$ in., or about 18.8 in.

Find the circumference of each circle.
Round to the nearest tenth, if necessary.

1.
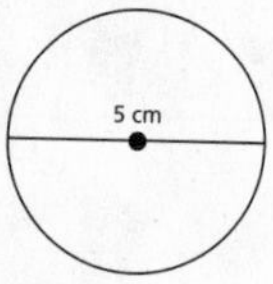

d = 5 cm
$C = \pi \times d$
C = 3.14 × 5
C = 15.7 cm

2.
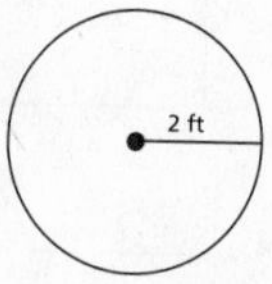

d = 4 ft
$C = \pi \times d$
C = 3.14 × 4
C = 12.6 ft

3.
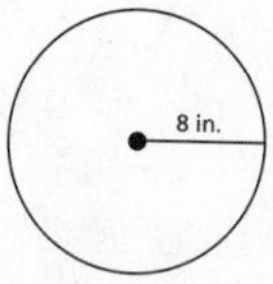

d = 16 in.
$C = \pi \times d$
C = 3.14 × 16
C = 50.2 in.

Use with Grade 5, Chapter 12, Lesson 6, pages 550–551. (389)

Enrich

Explore Circumference of Circles
Riddle Around

E 12-6 ENRICH

Each set of measurements is supposed to include the radius, the diameter, and the circumference (rounded to the nearest tenth) of one circle. Cross out the measurement that does not belong.

1. E. 20 ft	**L.** 15 ft X	**F.** 62.8 ft	**D.** 10 ft
2. N. 1 km	**U.** 6.3 km	**L.** 2 km	**O.** 3.1 km X
3. R. 3.1 mi	**D.** 1 mi	**A.** 0.8 mi X	**E.** $\frac{1}{2}$ mi
4. F. 3.3 m X	**U.** 47.1 m	**O.** 7.5 m	**R.** 15 m
5. A. 16 mm	**N.** 50.2 mm	**E.** 4 mm X	**L.** 8 mm
6. U. 31.4 in.	**F.** 10 in.	**O.** 5 in.	**D.** 2.5 in. X
7. N. $\frac{3}{4}$ yd	**A.** $\frac{1}{2}$ yd X	**R.** 4.7 yd	**O.** $1\frac{1}{2}$ yd
8. R. 7.2 m X	**D.** 2.4 m	**E.** 15.1 m	**N.** 4.8 m
9. O. 13.2 ft X	**U.** 4.5 ft	**F.** 14.1 ft	**L.** $2\frac{1}{4}$ ft
10. A. 7.4 cm	**F.** 23.2 cm	**E.** 3.7 cm	**U.** 21.0 cm X
11. R. 9.4 in.	**A.** 3 in.	**N.** $2\frac{1}{2}$ in. X	**D.** $1\frac{1}{2}$ in.
12. L. 4.2 cm	**D.** 13.2 cm X	**U.** 26.4 cm	**N.** 8.4 cm

Write the crossed-out letter above each problem number to find out what the bread did on vacation.

L	O	A	F	E	D	A	R	O	U	N	D
1	2	3	4	5	6	7	8	9	10	11	12

What strategy or strategies did you use to find out which number did not belong in each set?

Answers may vary. Possible answer: I checked if one of the two smaller measurements was the radius by doubling it and looking for that diameter. When I identified the diameter, I multiplied it by 3 to estimate the circumference.

Use with Grade 5, Chapter 12, Lesson 6, pages 550–551. (390)

Daily Homework

12-6 Explore Circumference of Circles

Find the approximate circumference of each circle. Use × ≈ 3.14. Round to the nearest tenth, if necessary.

1. 28.3 cm
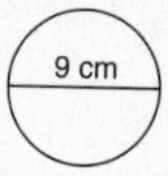

2. 18.8 ft
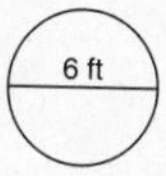

3. 44 m
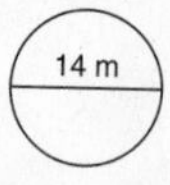

4. 14.1 in.
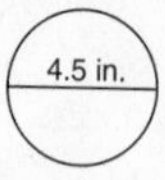

5. 23.2 m
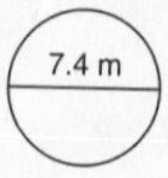

6. 9.1 in.
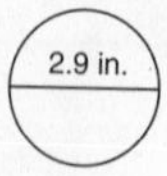

Solve.

7. Manuel and Fern order a large pizza from Cabot's Pizza. The pizza has a diameter of 16 inches. What is its approximate circumference? 50.2 inches

8. The largest pie ever baked was a pecan pie 40 feet in diameter baked in Okmulgee, Oklahoma, in 1989. What was the pie's approximate circumference? 125.6 feet

Spiral Review

Evaluate the expression for the value given.

9. $91 \times (h + 4)$ for $h = 5$ 819

10. $a + 625 \div 5$ for $a = 14$ 139

Grade 5, Chapter 12, Lesson 6 119

Chapter 12 ~ Lesson 7

Practice

Explore Area of Circles

P 12-7 PRACTICE

Find the approximate area of each circle. Use $\pi \approx 3.14$. Round to the nearest tenth, if necessary.

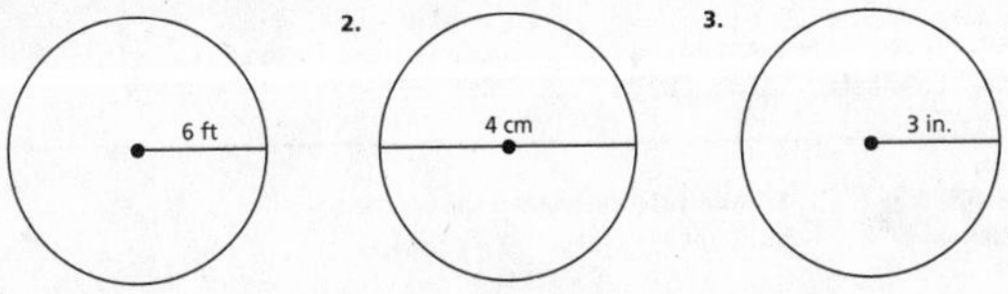

1. $A =$ 113.0 ft^2
2. $A =$ 12.6 cm^2
3. $A =$ 28.3 in.^{2}

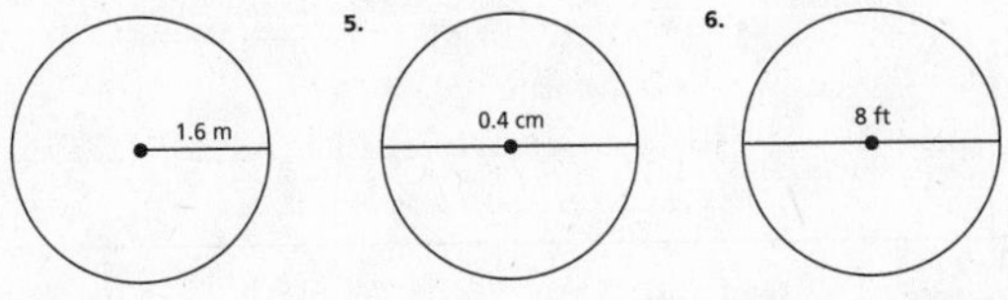

4. $A =$ 8.0 m^2
5. $A =$ 0.1 cm^2
6. $A =$ 50.2 ft^2

7. $r = 12$ in. $A =$ 452.2 in.^{2}
8. $r = 3.5$ m $A =$ 38.5 m^2
9. $d = 2$ ft $A =$ 3.1 ft^2
10. $d = 9$ cm $A =$ 63.6 cm^2
11. $r = 7$ in. $A =$ 153.9 in.^{2}
12. $d = 16$ ft $A =$ 201.0 ft^2

Problem Solving

13. A flagpole stands in the center of a circular grassy area. It is 10 meters from the flagpole to the edge of the grass. How many square meters does the grassy area cover?
314 m^2

14. A circle in the center of a flag has a diameter of 15 inches. What is the area of that circle?
176.6 in.^{2}

Use with Grade 5, Chapter 12, Lesson 7, pages 552–553. (391)

Reteach

Explore Area of Circles

R 12-7 RETEACH

You can use a formula to find the area of a circle.

When you are given the radius of the circle, use the formula $A = \pi r^2$, where A = area and r = radius. The value of π is approximately 3.14.

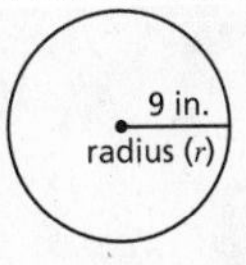

$A = \pi r^2$
$A = 3.14 \times 9^2$
$A = 3.14 \times 81$
$A = 254.34$ in.^{2}, or about 254.3 in.^{2}

When you are given the diameter of the circle, first divide it by 2 because the radius is half the diameter. Then use the formula.

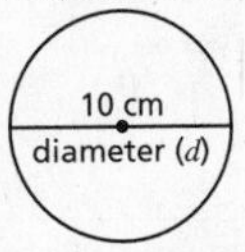

The diameter is 10 cm, so the radius, r, is 5 cm.
$A = \pi r^2$
$A = 3.14 \times 5^2$
$A = 3.14 \times 25$
$A = 78.5$ cm^2

Find the area of each circle. Round to the nearest tenth, if necessary.

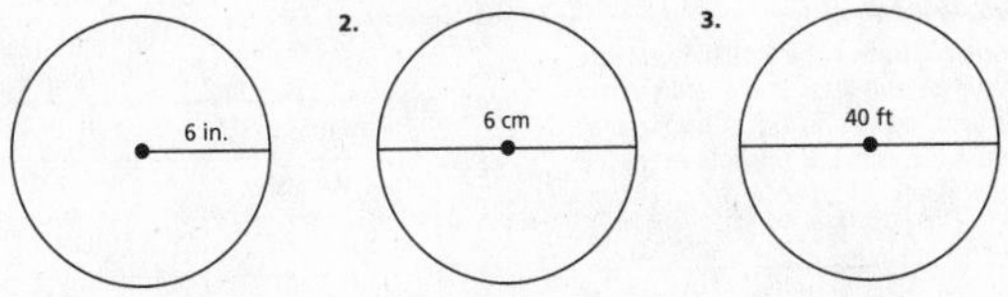

1.	2.	3.
$r =$ 6 in.	$r =$ 3 cm	$r =$ 20 ft
$A = \pi r^2$	$A = \pi r^2$	$A = \pi r^2$
$A =$ 3.14 × 6^2	$A =$ 3.14 × 3^2	$A =$ 3.14 × 20^2
$A =$ 3.14 × 36	$A =$ 3.14 × 9	$A =$ 3.14 × 400
$A =$ 113.0 in.^{2}	$A =$ 28.3 cm^2	$A =$ 1,256 ft^2

Use with Grade 5, Chapter 12, Lesson 7, pages 552–553. (392)

Enrich

Explore Area of Circles

E 12-7 ENRICH

Area Approximation

You can use the perimeter and area of squares to estimate the area of circles.

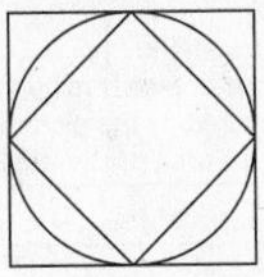

Measure the side of each square to the nearest centimeter.
Each side of the small square is about 3 cm.
Each side of the large square is about 4 cm.

The area of the small square is about 9 cm^2.
The area of the large square is about 16 cm^2.
The area of the circle is between 9 cm^2 and 16 cm^2.

Measure the side of each square to the nearest centimeter.
Use your measurements to estimate the area of each circle.

1.

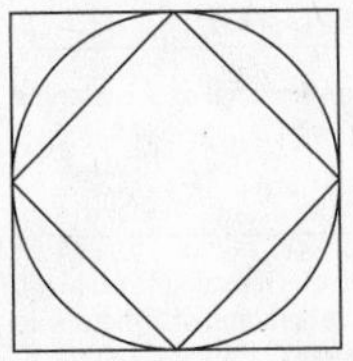

The area of the circle is between 16 cm^2 and 25 cm^2

2.

The area of the circle is between 4 cm^2 and 9 cm^2

Suppose you want to use a square to draw a circle that has an area of about 60 cm^2. You plan to draw the circle inside a large square so that it touches the four sides of the square. About how many centimeters long should you make each side of the square? Explain.

8 cm; the area of the square would be 64 cm^2, and the area of the circle would be less than this.

Use with Grade 5, Chapter 12, Lesson 7, pages 552–553. (393)

Daily Homework

12-7 Explore Area of Circles

Find the approximate area of each circle. Use $\pi \approx 3.14$. Round to the nearest tenth, if necessary.

1. 78.5 in.^{2}
2. 615.4 m^2
3. 201 ft^2

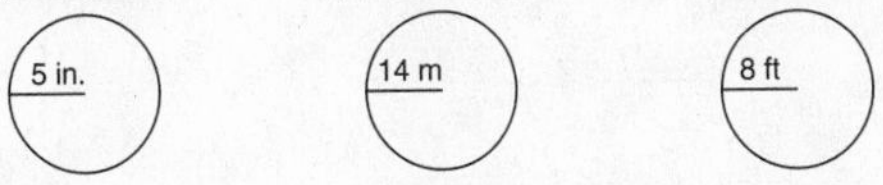

4. 38.5 cm^2
5. 191 in.^{2}
6. 339.6 ft^2

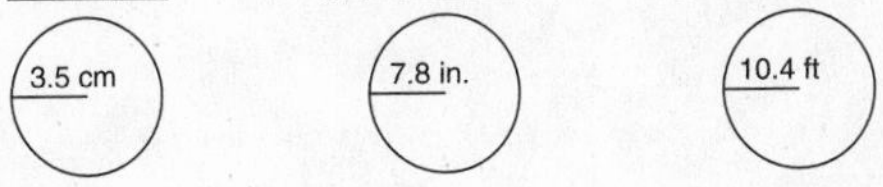

Solve.

7. Mary eats her dinner off a plate that has a radius of 4 inches. What is the approximate area of the plate? 50.2 in.^{2}
8. Roberto's parents have a circular table. The diameter of the table is 5 feet. What is its approximate area? 19.6 ft^2

Spiral Review

Write whether a translation, reflection, or rotation was made.

9. reflection

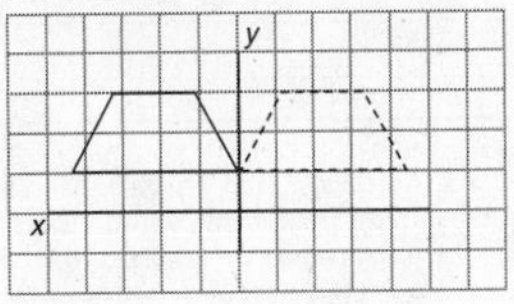

10. translation

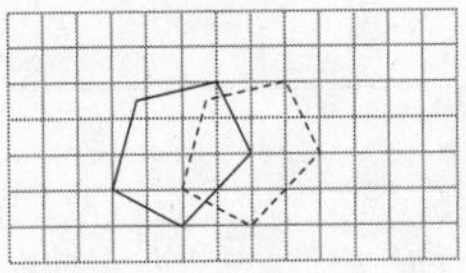

Chapter 12 ~ Lesson 8

Practice

Problem Solving: Strategy
Solve a Simpler Problem

P 12-8 PRACTICE

Solve. Explain how you simplified each problem.

1. What is the area of the garden shown in the plan below?

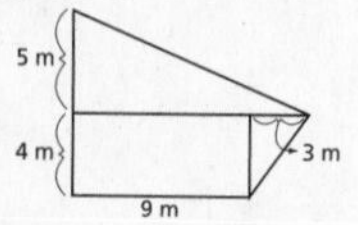

72 m²; Find the area of each figure and add.

2. How much wood is needed to make the deck shown in the plan below?

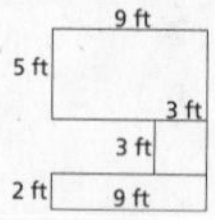

72 ft²; Find the area of each figure and add.

3. A field measures 80 feet by 90 feet. A barn will be built that covers 30 feet by 45 feet. How many square feet of the field will be left after the barn is built?
5,850 ft²; Find the area of each figure and subtract.

4. A window is designed with two panels that are each 12 inches by 8 inches. How many square inches of glass are needed to construct the window?
192 in.²; Find the area of each panel and add.

Mixed Strategy Review
Solve. Use any strategy.

5. **Social Studies** The total land area of four states is listed in the table. What type of graph would best display the data? Explain. Use the data to make the graph. Answers may vary. Possible answer: bar graph; check students' graphs.

Strategy: make a graph

State	Total Land Area (in mi²)
Delaware	1,955
New Hampshire	8,969
Rhode Island	1,045
Connecticut	4,845

6. **Health** Leo increases the number of push-ups he does each week by 8. The first week he did 10 push-ups. He is now doing 42 push-ups. How many weeks has he been doing push-ups?
5 weeks

Strategy: find a pattern

7. **Create a problem** for which you could solve a simpler problem to solve. Share it with others.
Check students' problems.

Use with Grade 5, Chapter 12, Lesson 8, pages 556–557. (394)

Reteach

Problem Solving: Strategy
Solve a Simpler Problem

R 12-8 RETEACH

Page 557, Problem 1

A backyard measures 50 feet by 60 feet and is covered with grass. A pool will be installed that covers 30 feet by 20 feet. How many square feet of grass will be left after the pool is built?

Step 1
Read

Be sure you understand the problem.
Read carefully.

What do you know?

- The dimensions of the backyard are 50 feet by 60 feet.
- The dimensions of the pool are 30 feet by 20 feet.

What do you need to find?

- You need to find how many square feet of grass will be left after the pool is built.

Step 2
Plan

- Find a Pattern
- Guess and Check
- Work Backward
- Make a Graph
- Make a Table
- Write an Equation
- Make an Organized List
- Draw a Diagram
- Solve a Simpler Problem
- Logical Reasoning

Make a plan.
Choose a strategy.

Think of the problem in simpler parts to help solve it. It is easier to solve the problem in pieces instead of all at once.

Find the area of the backyard.

Find the area of the pool.

Then you can subtract to find the area that will be left.

Use with Grade 5, Chapter 12, Lesson 8, pages 556–557. (395)

Reteach

Problem Solving: Strategy
Solve a Simpler Problem

R 12-8 RETEACH

Step 3
Solve

Carry out your plan.

Find the area of the backyard:
$A = lw$
$= 50 \times 60$
$= 3{,}000$ ft²

Find the area of the pool:
$A = lw$
$= 30 \times 20$
$= 600$ ft²

What must you do to find how many square feet of grass are left after the pool is built?
Subtract the area of the pool from the area of the backyard.
$3{,}000 - 600 = 2{,}400$

How many square feet of grass will be left? 2,400 ft²

Step 4
Look Back

Is the solution reasonable?
Reread the problem.

Does your answer make sense?
Yes, the area of the grass that is left is less than the original area of the grass in the backyard.

Practice

1. A rectangular park is 80 meters by 70 meters. A square piece of land next to the park is purchased to enlarge the park. The land is 30 meters on each side. What will the total area of the enlarged park be?
6,500 m²

2. A rectangular rock garden is 18 feet by 15 feet. Ms. Smithson wants to put a triangular pond with a base of 6 feet and a height of 4 feet in one corner of the garden. How many square feet of the rock garden will not be covered by the pond?
258 ft²

Use with Grade 5, Chapter 12, Lesson 8, pages 556–557. (396)

Daily Homework

12-8 **Problem Solving: Strategy**
Solve a Simpler Problem

Solve. Explain how you simplified each problem.

1. In the middle of a square park there is a picnic shelter. The park is 80 meters on each side, and the picnic shelter has dimensions of 5 meters by 12 meters. What is the area of the park that is not covered by the picnic shelter?
6,340 m²; Find the area of the park. Then find the area of the shelter. Then subtract the area of the shelter from the area of the park.

2. The city decides to fence in the park completely except for an entrance that is 4 meters wide. How much fencing is needed?
316 feet; Find the perimeter of the park and subtract the width of the entrance.

3. The city buys a lot next to the park. The lot has the shape of a triangle with a base of 70 meters and a height of 40 meters. The city adds the lot to the park to create a larger park. What is the area of the larger park?
7,800 m²; Find the areas of the park and the new lot. Then add them together.

4. Tina is making a lowercase "i" out of colored paper. She makes a rectangle that measures 18 inches by 6 inches, and a circle with a radius of 3 inches. How much paper does she use in all?
136.3 in.²; Find the areas of the rectangle and the circle, and then add them.

5. Daniel's backyard measures 10 meters by 20 meters. He wants to build a circular patio in the backyard. The patio would have a radius of 3 meters. If he builds the patio, how much room will be left in the yard?
171.7 m²; Find the area of the backyard. Then find the area of the patio. Then subtract the area of the patio from the area of the yard.

Spiral Review

6. $\frac{3}{7} = \frac{18}{42}$ 7. $\frac{4}{9} = \frac{48}{108}$ 8. $\frac{10}{11} = \frac{220}{242}$ 9. $\frac{2}{15} = \frac{10}{75}$

Chapter 12 ~ Lesson 9

Practice

3-Dimensional Figures and Nets

P 12-9 PRACTICE

Write the number of faces, edges, and vertices for each figure.

1. 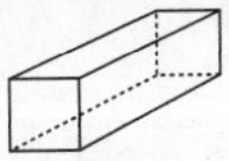 Faces: 6 Edges: 12 Vertices: 8

2. 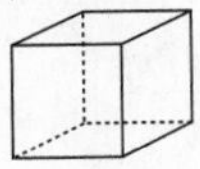 Faces: 6 Edges: 12 Vertices: 8

3. 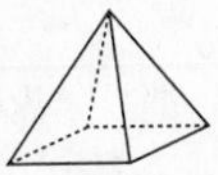 Faces: 5 Edges: 8 Vertices: 5

4. 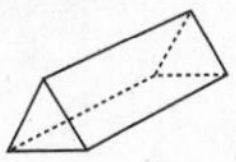 Faces: 5 Edges: 9 Vertices: 6

What 3-dimensional figure does each net make when cut and folded?

5. 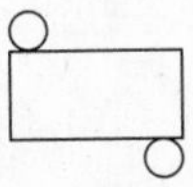
cylinder

6. 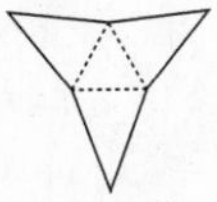
triangular pyramid

Problem Solving Use data from the art for exercises 7–8.

7. What shape was used for the bottom part of the building?
rectangular prism

8. What shape was used for the top part of the building?
triangular prism

Use with Grade 5, Chapter 12, Lesson 9, pages 558–561. (397)

Reteach

3-Dimensional Figures and Nets

R 12-9 RETEACH

Compare these two figures.

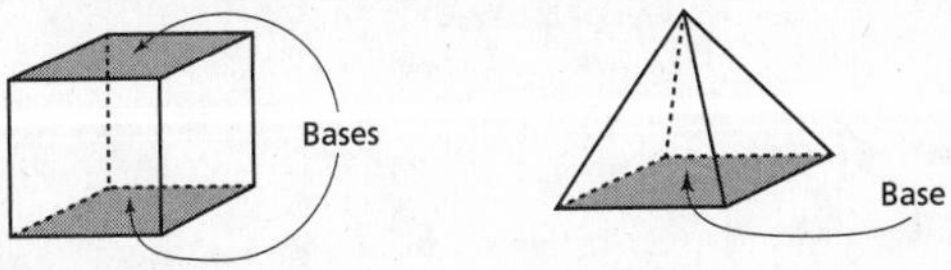

Prisms have:
- two congruent bases
- rectangular side faces

Pyramids have:
- one base
- triangular faces that meet at a vertex

Prisms and pyramids are named by the shape of their bases. They both have:
- faces—flat sides
- edges—line segments where two faces meet
- vertices—common points where three or more edges meet

Shade the base(s) of each figure. Then identify the figure. Tell how many faces, edges, and vertices each figure has.

1. 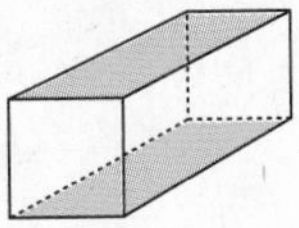
rectangular prism
6 faces
12 edges
8 vertices

2. 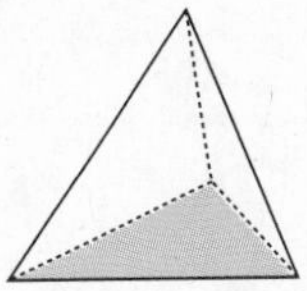
triangular pyramid
4 faces
6 edges
4 vertices

3. 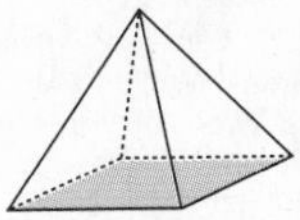
rectangular pyramid
5 faces
8 edges
5 vertices

Use with Grade 5, Chapter 12, Lesson 9, pages 558–561. (398)

Enrich

3-Dimensional Figures and Nets
A 3-Dimensional Pattern

E 12-9 ENRICH

Complete the table for these 3-dimensional shapes.

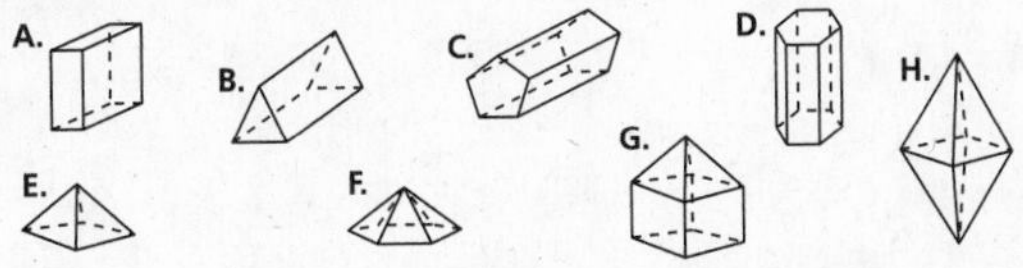

Figure	Number of Faces	Number of Vertices	Total Faces and Vertices	Number of Edges
A	6	8	14	12
B	5	6	11	9
C	7	10	17	15
D	8	12	20	18
E	5	5	10	8
F	7	7	14	12
G	9	9	18	16
H	8	6	14	12

Look for a pattern in the table above. Then complete this statement.

The sum of the number of faces and vertices is equal to the number of edges plus 2.

Let f = number of faces, v = number of vertices, and e = number of edges. Write the statement you completed above as an equation.

$f + v = e + 2$

Write a formula for the number of edges.

$e = f + v - 2$

Use with Grade 5, Chapter 12, Lesson 9, pages 558–561. (399)

Daily Homework

12-9 3-Dimensional Figures and Nets

Write the number of faces, edges, and vertices for each figure.

1. 6, 12, 8 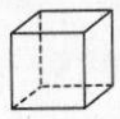

2. 4, 6, 4 

3. 7, 15, 10 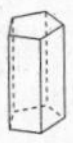

What 3-dimensional figure does each net make when cut and folded?

4. triangular prism 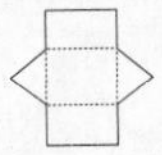

5. rectangular prism 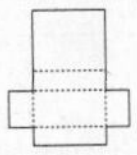

6. cone 

Draw the net for each 3-dimensional figure. Check that students' net drawings match each 3-dimensional figure.

7. 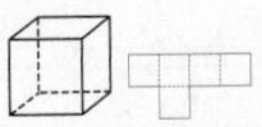

8. 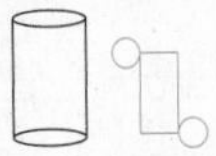

9. 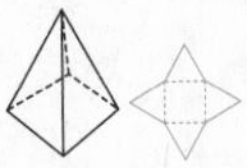

Problem Solving

10. Lou receives a package that is a cube with sides of 11 inches. What is the area of one of its faces?
121 in.^{2}

11. Michael says that the net shown is for a sphere. Is he correct? 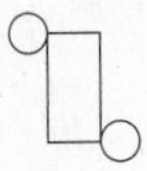
No

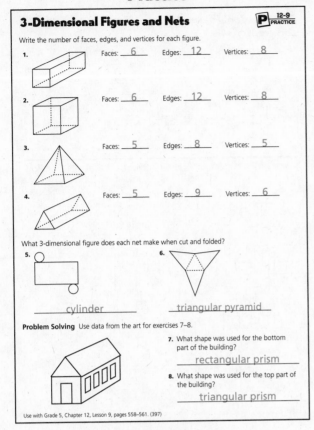

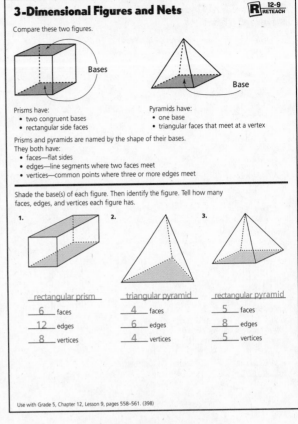

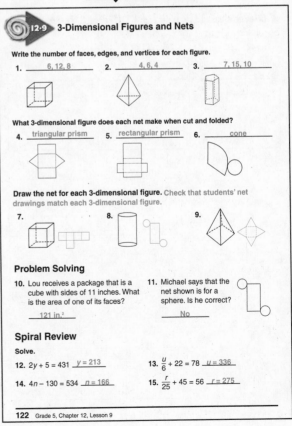

Spiral Review

Solve.

12. $2y + 5 = 431$ $y = 213$

13. $\frac{u}{6} + 22 = 78$ $u = 336$

14. $4n - 130 = 534$ $n = 166$

15. $\frac{r}{25} + 45 = 56$ $r = 275$

122 Grade 5, Chapter 12, Lesson 9

Chapter 12 ~ Lesson 10

Practice

3-Dimensional Figures from Different Views

P 12-10 PRACTICE

Draw the top view, front view, and a side view of the shape.

Top | Front | Side

1.
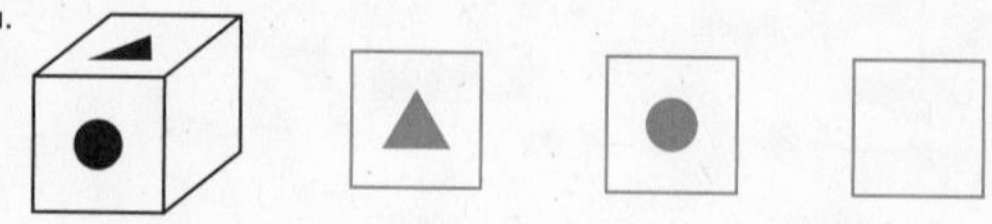

2.
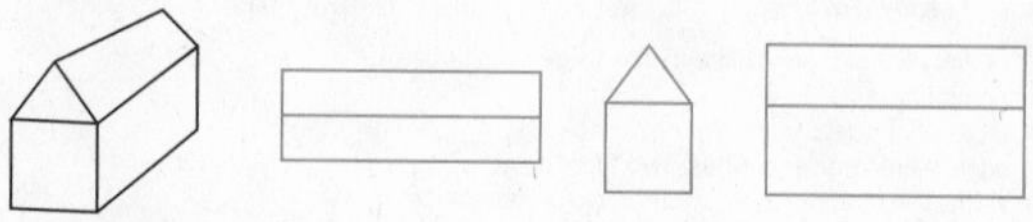

3.

4.
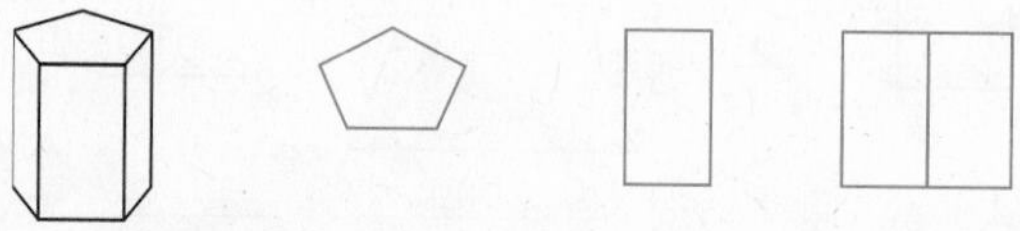

Problem Solving

5. This staircase is made from cubes. Draw the top view, front view, and side view of the staircase.

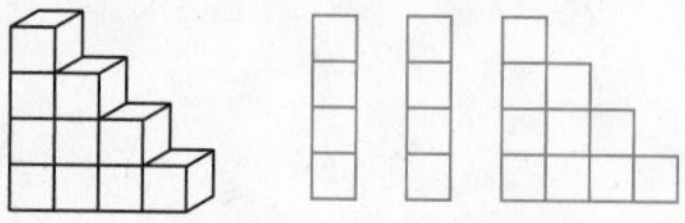

Use with Grade 5, Chapter 12, Lesson 10, pages 562–563. (400)

Reteach

3-Dimensional Figures from Different Views

R 12-10 RETEACH

You can view this 3-dimensional figure in different ways.

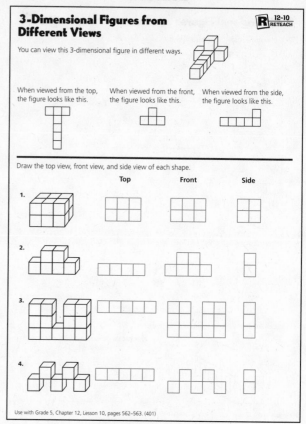

When viewed from the top, the figure looks like this. | When viewed from the front, the figure looks like this. | When viewed from the side, the figure looks like this.

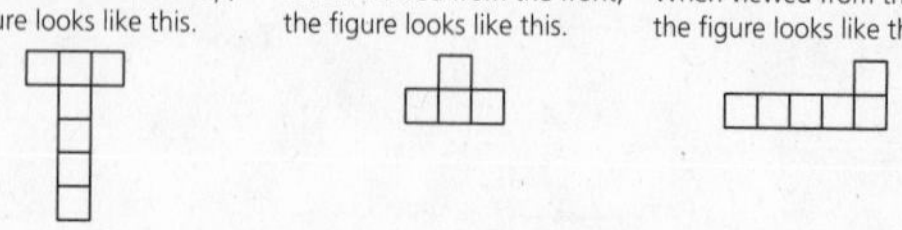

Draw the top view, front view, and side view of each shape.

Top | Front | Side

1.
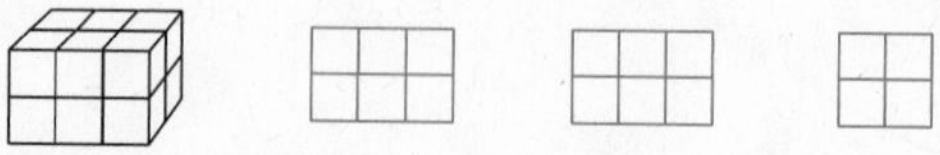

2.

3.
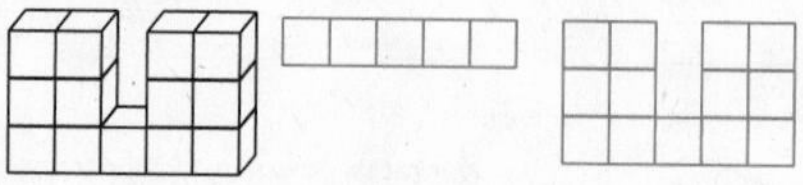

4.
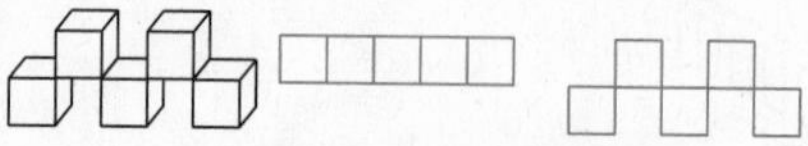

Use with Grade 5, Chapter 12, Lesson 10, pages 562–563. (401)

Enrich

3-Dimensional Figures from Different Views

E 12-10 ENRICH

Numbered Views

The 3-dimensional figure at the right can be viewed in different ways.

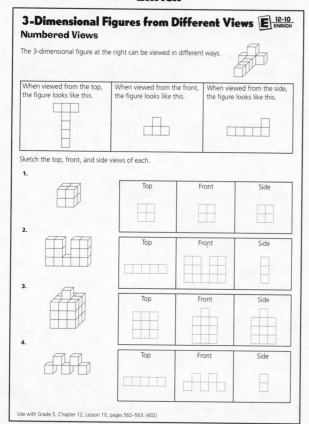

When viewed from the top, the figure looks like this.	When viewed from the front, the figure looks like this.	When viewed from the side, the figure looks like this.
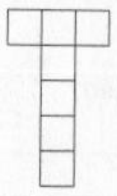	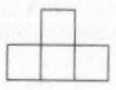	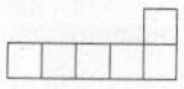

Sketch the top, front, and side views of each.

1.
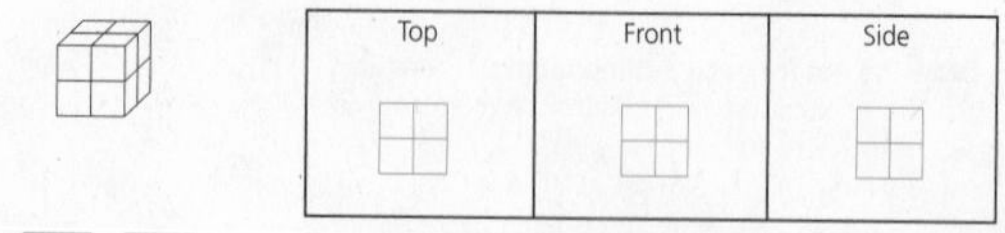

2.
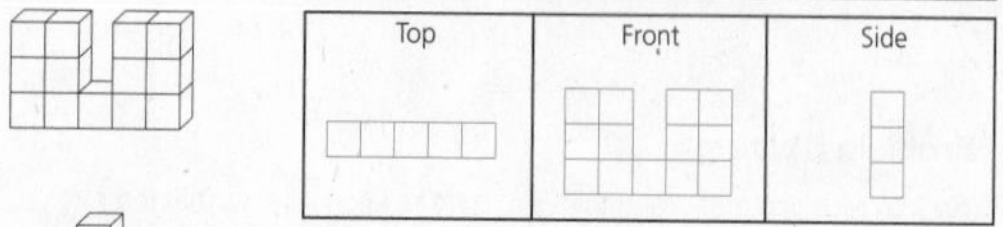

3.
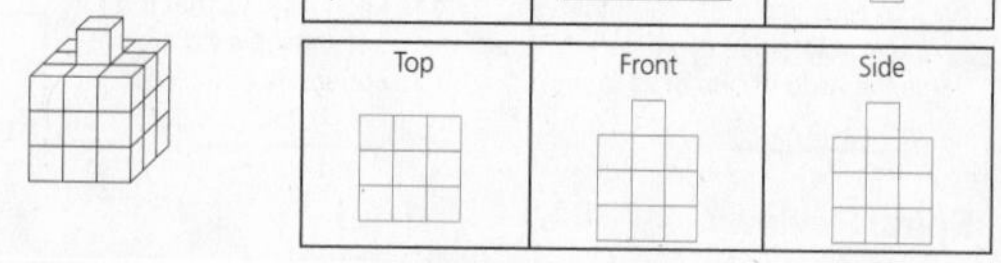

4.
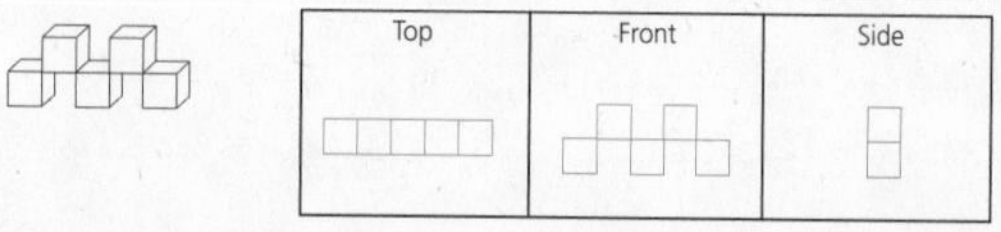

Use with Grade 5, Chapter 12, Lesson 10, pages 562–563. (402)

Daily Homework

12-10 3-Dimensional Figures from Different Views

Draw the top view, the front view, and one side view of the shape. Check students' drawings.

1.
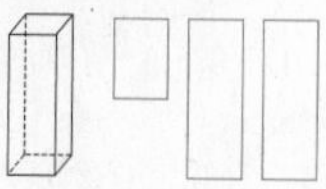

2.
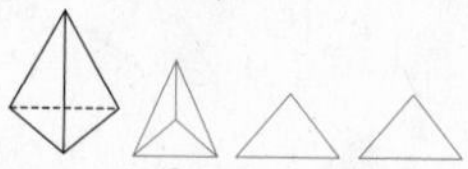

Problem Solving

3. Edna's Ice Cream uses cones like the one shown below. Is this view of the cone a side view or a top view? side view

4. With one eye closed, Elise is looking at a 3-dimensional figure. All she can see of the figure is one square. Name at least one 3-dimensional figure that she could be looking at.
Possible answers: cube, rectangular prism, rectangular pyramid

Spiral Review

Complete the table. Then graph the function.

5. $y = x - 2$

x	y
-2	-4
0	-2
2	0
4	2

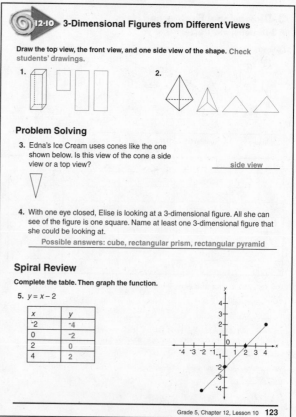

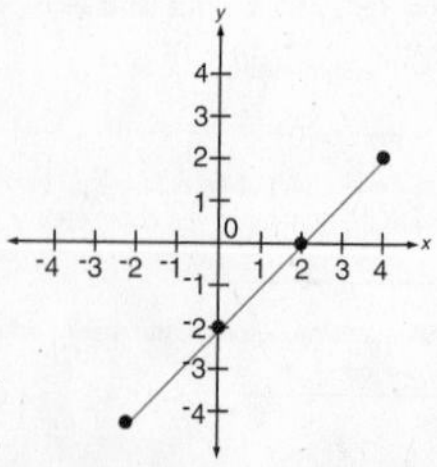

Grade 5, Chapter 12, Lesson 10 123

Chapter 12 ~ Lesson 11

Practice

Explore Surface Area of Rectangular Prisms

P 12-11 PRACTICE

Find the surface area of each rectangular prism.

1.

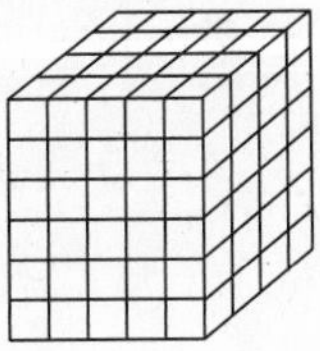

148 square units

2.

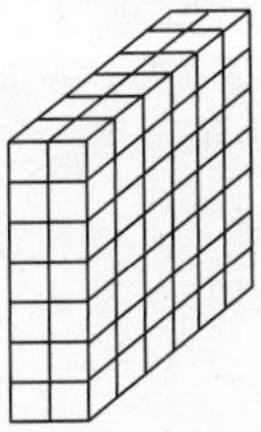

136 square units

3.

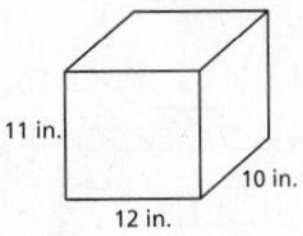

724 in.^2

4.

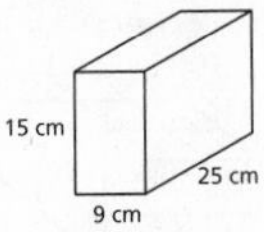

$1{,}470 \text{ cm}^2$

5.

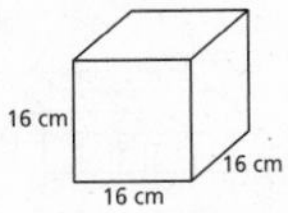

$1{,}536 \text{ cm}^2$

6.

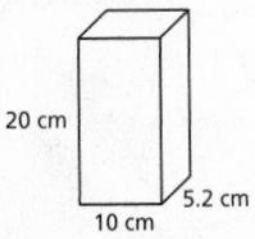

712 cm^2

7.

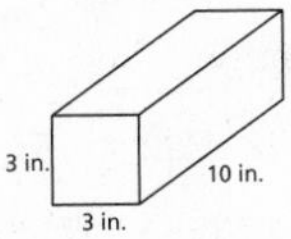

138 in.^2

8.

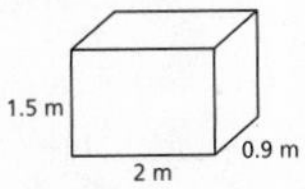

12.3 m^2

Problem Solving

9. What is the surface area of a cardboard shipping box that is 26 inches long, 26 inches wide, and 18 inches high?

$3{,}224 \text{ in.}^2$

10. What is the surface area of a 9-centimeter cube?

486 cm^2

Use with Grade 5, Chapter 12, Lesson 11, pages 564–565. (403)

Reteach

Explore Surface Area of Rectangular Prisms

R 12-11 RETEACH

You can find the **surface area** of a rectangular prism by finding the total area of all its faces. Each face is a rectangle, so use the formula $A = lw$ to find the area of each face.

Find the surface area of this rectangular prism.

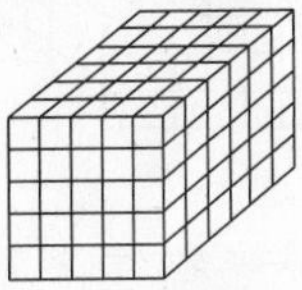

Front face:	$5 \times 5 = 25$ square units
Back face:	$5 \times 5 = 25$ square units
Top face:	$5 \times 6 = 30$ square units
Bottom face:	$5 \times 6 = 30$ square units
Right face:	$5 \times 6 = 30$ square units
Left face:	$5 \times 6 = 30$ square units
Total surface area:	170 square units

Find the surface area of each rectangular prism.

1.

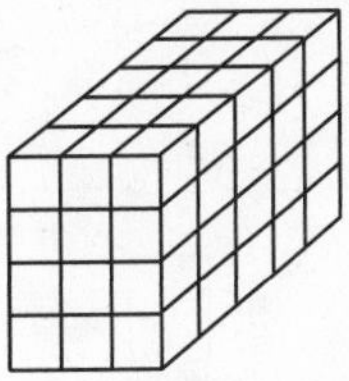

Front face:	$3 \times 4 = 12$ square units
Back face:	$3 \times 4 = 12$ square units
Top face:	$3 \times 5 = 15$ square units
Bottom face:	$3 \times 5 = 15$ square units
Right face:	$5 \times 4 = 20$ square units
Left face:	$5 \times 4 = 20$ square units
Total surface area:	94 square units

2.

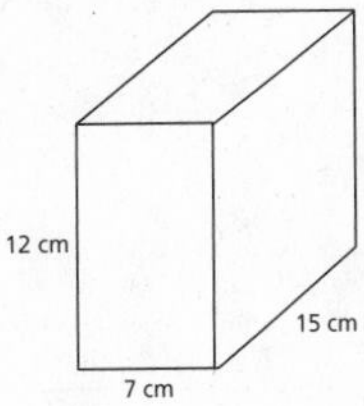

Front face:	$7 \times 12 = 84 \text{ cm}^2$
Back face:	$7 \times 12 = 84 \text{ cm}^2$
Top face:	$7 \times 15 = 105 \text{ cm}^2$
Bottom face:	$7 \times 15 = 105 \text{ cm}^2$
Right face:	$15 \times 12 = 180 \text{ cm}^2$
Left face:	$15 \times 12 = 180 \text{ cm}^2$
Total surface area:	738 cm^2

Use with Grade 5, Chapter 12, Lesson 11, pages 564–565. (404)

Enrich

Explore Surface Area of Rectangular Prisms

E 12-11 ENRICH

Package Design

Suppose that your job is to design boxes for a gift manufacturer. You know the name of an item and its dimensions. Your job is to draw a box to fit the item. Then you have to draw its corresponding net. You need to label the dimensions on the box and net and tell the surface area of the box. When designing a box, you also need to follow these guidelines:

- Boxes must be rectangular prisms.
- Boxes should be as small as possible.
- The dimensions of each box must be in whole numbers of inches to allow room for packing materials.
- You do not have to be concerned about sides of the boxes overlapping.

Design a box for each item.

Check students' work. Orientation of boxes and nets may vary, but dimensions and surface area should be as shown.

Item 1: A pottery giraffe that is $11\frac{1}{2}$ in. tall, $5\frac{1}{4}$ in. long, and $2\frac{5}{8}$ in. wide

Box

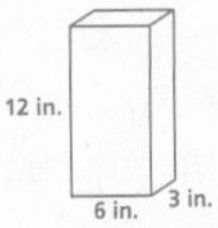

Net

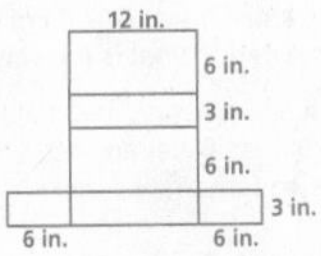

Surface area: 252 in.^2

Item 2: A pyramid-shaped paperweight $4\frac{5}{8}$ in. tall with a $3\frac{3}{4}$ in. square base

Box

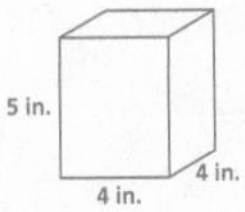

Net

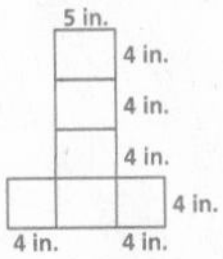

Surface area: 112 in.^2

Use with Grade 5, Chapter 12, Lesson 11, pages 564–565. (405)

Daily Homework

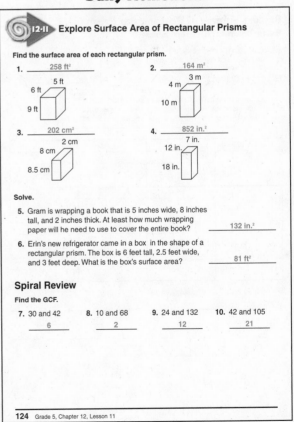

12-11 Explore Surface Area of Rectangular Prisms

Find the surface area of each rectangular prism.

1. 258 ft^2

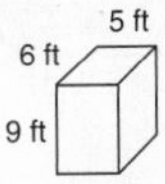

2. 164 m^2

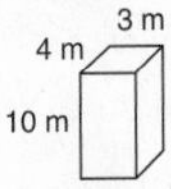

3. 202 cm^2

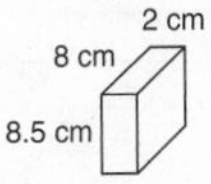

4. 852 in.^2

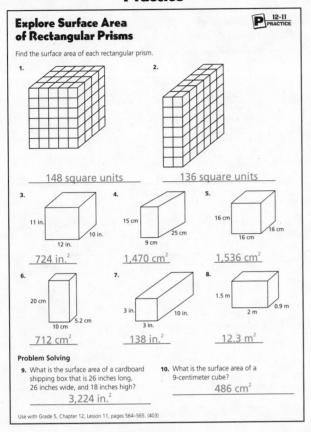

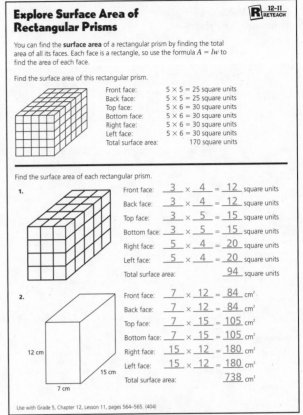

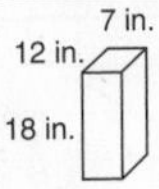

Solve.

5. Gram is wrapping a book that is 5 inches wide, 8 inches tall, and 2 inches thick. At least how much wrapping paper will he need to use to cover the entire book? 132 in.^2

6. Erin's new refrigerator came in a box in the shape of a rectangular prism. The box is 6 feet tall, 2.5 feet wide, and 3 feet deep. What is the box's surface area? 81 ft^2

Spiral Review

Find the GCF.

7. 30 and 42 — 6

8. 10 and 68 — 2

9. 24 and 132 — 12

10. 42 and 105 — 21

124 Grade 5, Chapter 12, Lesson 11

Chapter 12 ~ Lesson 12

Practice

Explore Volume of Rectangular Prisms

P 12-12 PRACTICE

Find the volume of each rectangular prism.
Round to the nearest tenth, if necessary.

1. 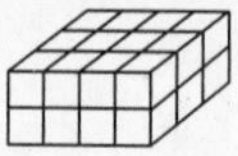

$V =$ 24 cubic units

2. 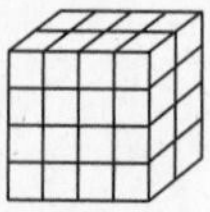

$V =$ 32 cubic units

3. 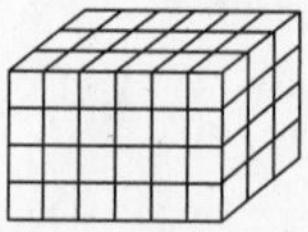

$V =$ 72 cubic units

4. 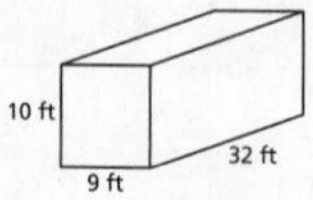

$V =$ 2,880 ft³

5. 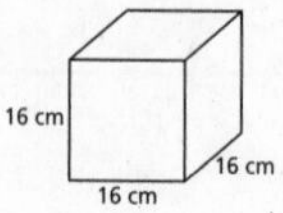

$V =$ 4,096 cm³

6. 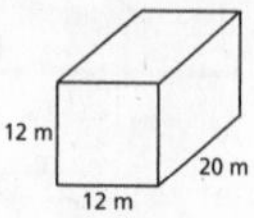

$V =$ 2,880 m³

7. 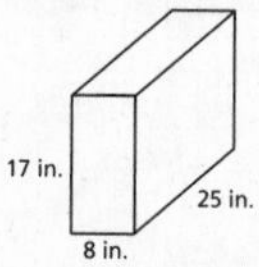

$V =$ 3,400 in.³

8. 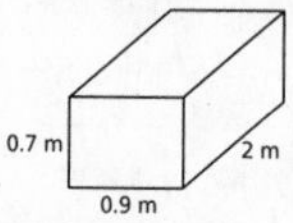

$V =$ 1.3 m³

9. 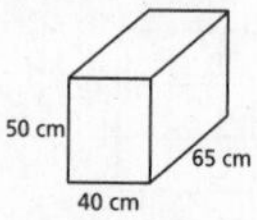

$V =$ 130,000 cm³

Problem Solving

10. The dimensions of a gift box for jewelry are 6 inches by 3 inches by 2 inches. What is the volume of the gift box?

36 in.³

11. The dimensions of a shoe box are 13 inches by 9 inches by 4 inches. What is the volume of the shoe box?

468 in.³

Use with Grade 5, Chapter 12, Lesson 12, pages 566–567. (406)

Reteach

Explore Volume of Rectangular Prisms

R 12-12 RETEACH

Volume is the amount of space a 3-dimensional figure encloses. To find the volume of a rectangular prism, you can use a formula.

Find the volume of the rectangular prism. Use the formula $V = l \times w \times h$, where V = volume, l = length, w = width, and h = height.

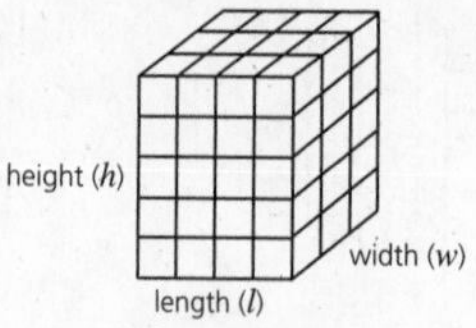

$V = l \times w \times h$
$V = 4 \times 3 \times 5$
$V = 60$ cubic units

Find the length, width, height, and volume of each figure.

1. 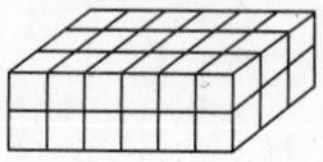

$l =$ 6 units
$w =$ 3 units
$h =$ 2 units
$V = l \times w \times h$
$V =$ 6 × 3 × 2
$V =$ 36 cubic units

2. 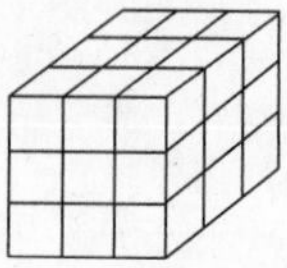

$l =$ 3 units
$w =$ 3 units
$h =$ 3 units
$V = l \times w \times h$
$V =$ 3 × 3 × 3
$V =$ 27 cubic units

3. 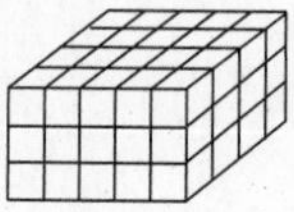

$l =$ 5 units
$w =$ 4 units
$h =$ 3 units
$V = l \times w \times h$
$V =$ 5 × 4 × 3
$V =$ 60 cubic units

Use with Grade 5, Chapter 12, Lesson 12, pages 566–567. (407)

Enrich

Explore Volume of Rectangular Prisms

E 12-12 ENRICH

Same Volume, Different Shape

Rectangular prisms of different shapes can have the same volume. These rectangular prisms have different shapes, but the volume of both prisms is 24 cm³.

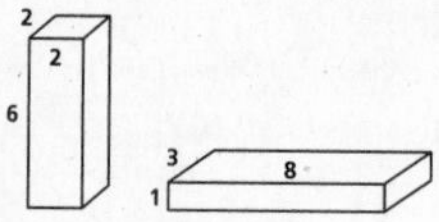

The table below shows the volumes of different rectangular prisms. For each volume, write as many different sets of three numbers that could represent a rectangular prism with that volume. One has been started for you.

32 in.³	40 m³	60 cm³	72 mm³
1, 1, 32	1, 1, 40	1, 1, 60	1, 1, 72
1, 2, 16	1, 2, 20	1, 2, 30	1, 2, 36
1, 4, 8	1, 4, 10	1, 3, 20	1, 3, 24
2, 2, 8	1, 5, 8	1, 4, 15	1, 4, 18
2, 4, 4	2, 2, 10	1, 5, 12	1, 6, 12
	2, 4, 5	1, 6, 10	1, 8, 9
		2, 2, 15	2, 2, 18
		2, 3, 10	2, 3, 12
		2, 5, 6	2, 4, 9
		3, 4, 5	2, 6, 6
			3, 3, 8
			3, 4, 6

What strategy did you use to complete the table?

Possible answer: I made an organized list for each prism. First I thought of all the different numbers of units that could be a dimension of the prism. For each number, I thought of all the different numbers that could be another dimension of the prism. Then I thought of the number of units that would have to be the third dimension. I did not record any set that had the same numbers in any order as another set.

Use with Grade 5, Chapter 12, Lesson 12, pages 566–567. (408)

Daily Homework

12-12 Explore Volume of Rectangular Prisms

Find the volume of each rectangular prism. Round to the nearest tenth, if necessary.

1. 720 ft³

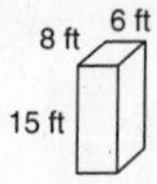

2. 445.2 m³

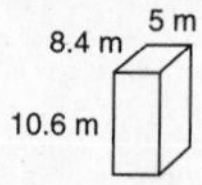

3. 5,184 cm³

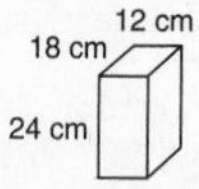

4. 2849.1 in.³

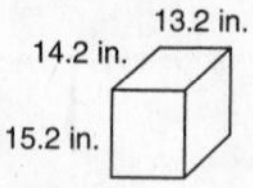

Solve.

5. Kyle is sending a package to his grandmother in a small box that is 8 cm wide, 6 cm tall, and 6 cm deep. What is the volume of the box?

288 cm³

6. Teri has an aquarium that is 10 inches tall, 25 inches wide, and 12 inches deep. What is the aquarium's volume?

3,000 in³

Spiral Review

7. 241 × 1.6 = 385.6

8. 560 × 7.2 = 4032

9. 1.56 × 4.4 = 6.864

10. 314 × 822 = 258,108

Chapter 12 ~ Lesson 13

Part A Worksheet

Problem Solving: Application
Applying Perimeter, Area, and Volume

Part A 12-13 WORKSHEET
Decision Making

Use the table to record your different ideas for the pool design.

Shape of Pool	Total Area	Total Perimeter	Number of Tiles Needed	Cover	Pump Filter

Your Decision

What is your decision for the shape and size of your pool? How did you arrive at your decision? Which tiles, cover, and pump filter did you choose?

Answers may vary.

Use with Grade 5, Chapter 12, Lesson 13, pages 568–569. (409)

Part B Worksheet

Problem Solving: Application
Elbow Room: How close is too close?

Part B 12-13 WORKSHEET
Math & Science

Hypothesis How close do you think you can be to another person before you feel *really* uncomfortable? Estimate the distance below.

Answers may vary.

Use the following scale to rate your comfort next to another person:

3 = I feel fine, 2 = I feel a little crowded, 1 = I can't stand it!

Record the area of the room, the estimated difference between you and the nearest student, and your level of comfort (1, 2, or 3) in the table below.

Room Size	Area	Distance	Comfort Level
Full			
$\frac{1}{2}$			
$\frac{1}{4}$			
$\frac{1}{8}$			
$\frac{1}{16}$			
$\frac{1}{32}$			

1. How did your actual comfort level compare to your original estimate? Were you surprised? Explain.

   Answers may vary.

2. What reactions did you notice from your classmates as you all got closer to each other?

   Answers may vary. Possible answer: At first students were friendly. Then they got increasingly uncomfortable.

Use with Grade 5, Chapter 12, Lesson 13, pages 570–571. (410)

Part B Worksheet

Problem Solving: Application
Elbow Room: How close is too close?

Part B 12-13 WORKSHEET
Math & Science

3. Do you think your results would be different in a room full of strangers? Explain.

   Answers may vary. Possible answer: I think I would start to feel uncomfortable with strangers when they were farther away than with people I know.

4. Compare your data with your classmates. Were distances and comfort levels similar or very different? Why do you think this is so?

   Answers may vary.

5. Use the space below to create a graph comparing distances and comfort levels for you and some of your classmates.

   Check students' graphs.

6. Do you think you would react differently if you were crowded by objects instead of people? Would it make a difference if the objects were large or small? Explain.

   Answers may vary.

Use with Grade 5, Chapter 12, Lesson 13, pages 570–571. (411)

Chapter 13 ~ Lesson 1

Practice

Explore Ratio

P 13-1 PRACTICE

Write each ratio in three ways.

1. circles to rectangles
6 to 7; 6:7; $\frac{6}{7}$

2. total to circles
13 to 6; 13:6; $\frac{13}{6}$

3. rectangles to total
7 to 13; 7:13; $\frac{7}{13}$

4. rectangles to circles
7 to 6; 7:6; $\frac{7}{6}$

5. total to rectangles
13 to 7; 13:7; $\frac{13}{7}$

6. circles to total
6 to 13; 6:13; $\frac{6}{13}$

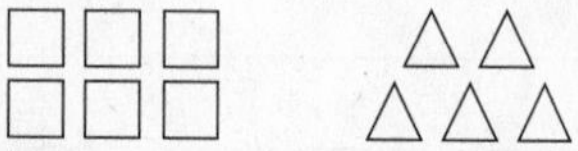

7. squares to triangles
6 to 5; 6:5; $\frac{6}{5}$

8. squares to total
6 to 11; 6:11; $\frac{6}{11}$

9. triangles to squares
5 to 6; 5:6; $\frac{5}{6}$

10. total to triangles
11 to 5; 11:5; $\frac{11}{5}$

11. total to squares
11 to 6; 11:6; $\frac{11}{6}$

12. triangles to total
5 to 11; 5:11; $\frac{5}{11}$

Problem Solving Accept any form of the given ratios.

13. There are 12 boys and 11 girls in a fifth-grade class. Write a ratio to describe the number of boys to the number of girls in the class.
12:11

14. There are 19 students in another fifth-grade class. Of these, 11 are girls. Write a ratio to describe the number of girls to the number of boys in this class.
11:8

Use with Grade 5, Chapter 13, Lesson 1, pages 586–587. (412)

Reteach

Explore Ratio

R 13-1 RETEACH

A ratio is used to compare two quantities. You can write different ratios to compare these circles and squares in different ways. You can also write each ratio in different ways.

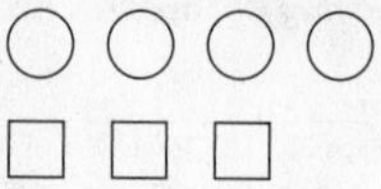

4 circles
3 squares
7 total shapes

	Part to Part circles to squares	Part to Total circles to total shapes	Total to Part total shapes to squares
In Words	4 to 3	4 to 7	7 to 3
Using:	4:3	4:7	7:3
As a Fraction	$\frac{4}{3}$	$\frac{4}{7}$	$\frac{7}{3}$
Read as:	four to three	four to seven	seven to three

Write each ratio in three ways.

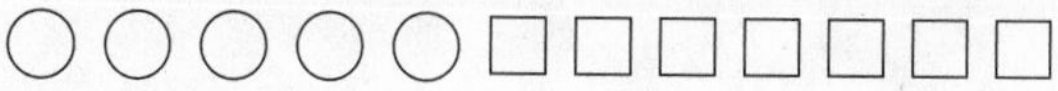

1. circles to squares
5 to 7; 5:7; $\frac{5}{7}$

2. circles to total shapes
5 to 12; 5:12; $\frac{5}{12}$

3. total shapes to circles
12 to 5; 12:5; $\frac{12}{5}$

4. squares to total shapes
7 to 12; 7:12; $\frac{7}{12}$

5. squares to circles
7 to 5; 7:5; $\frac{7}{5}$

6. total shapes to squares
12 to 7; 12:7; $\frac{12}{7}$

Use with Grade 5, Chapter 13, Lesson 1, pages 586–587. (413)

Enrich

Explore Ratio
Picture the Ratios

E 13-1 ENRICH

Look at the objects pictured below. Describe all the different ways you could use the objects to model each ratio.

1. 2 to 5
2 tapes to 5 bows,
2 pens to 5 bows,
2 scissors to 5 bows

2. 3:1
3 bows to 1 box, 3 bows to 1 tape, 3 bows to 1 pen, 3 bows to 1 scissor, 3 pens to 1 box, 3 pens to 1 tape, 3 pens to 1 bow, 3 pens to 1 scissor, 3 scissors to 1 box, 3 scissors to 1 tape, 3 scissors to 1 bow, 3 scissors to 1 pen

3. $\frac{4}{3}$
4 bows to 3 pens, 4 bows to 3 scissors,
4 pens to 3 bows,
4 pens to 3 scissors

4. 1 to 4
1 box to 4 bows, 1 box to 4 pens, 1 tape to 4 bows,
1 tape to 4 pens, 1 bow to 4 pens, 1 pen to 4 bows,
1 scissor to 4 bows, 1 scissor to 4 pens

Use with Grade 5, Chapter 13, Lesson 1, pages 586–587. (414)

Daily Homework

13-1 Explore Ratio

Write each ratio in three ways.

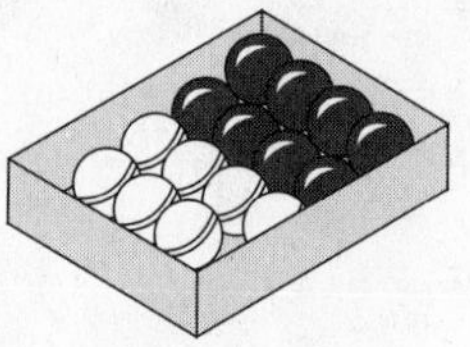

1. white marbles to black marbles
7 to 8; 7:8; $\frac{7}{8}$

2. black marbles to white marbles
8 to 7; 8:7; $\frac{8}{7}$

3. total marbles to white marbles
15 to 7; 15:7; $\frac{15}{7}$

4. black marbles to total marbles
8 to 15; 8:15; $\frac{8}{15}$

Solve.

5. Maia notices that there are 3 hot dogs and 5 hamburgers on the grill. What is the ratio of hamburgers to hot dogs?
Possible answers: 5 to 3; 5:3; $\frac{5}{3}$

6. Greg buys 4 peach yogurts and 6 plain yogurts. Is the ratio 10 to 4 the ratio of total yogurts to peach yogurts, peach yogurts to plain yogurts, or peach yogurts to total yogurts?
total yogurts to peach yogurts

Spiral Review

Find the area.

7.
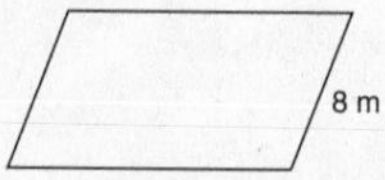

112 m²

8.
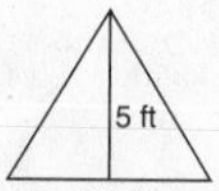

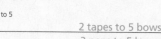

15.5 ft²

126 Grade 5, Chapter 13, Lesson 1, Cluster A

Chapter 13 ~ Lesson 2

Practice

Equivalent Ratios

P 13-2 PRACTICE

Complete each ratio table.

1.

1	2	3	4	5
4	8	12	16	20

2.

5	10	15	20	25
7	14	21	28	35

3.

9	18	27	36	45
4	8	12	16	20

4.

10	20	30	40	50
3	6	9	12	15

Tell whether the ratios are equivalent.

5. $\frac{2}{5}, \frac{8}{20}$ yes **6.** $\frac{6}{7}, \frac{30}{42}$ no **7.** $\frac{20}{12}, \frac{4}{3}$ no

8. 15:9, 5:3 yes **9.** 4:10, 30:12 no **10.** 5:8; 25:40 yes

Name four ratios equivalent to each given ratio. Answers may vary. Possible answers are given.

11. $\frac{1}{3}$ $\frac{2}{6}, \frac{3}{9}, \frac{4}{12}, \frac{5}{15}$ **12.** $\frac{4}{5}$ $\frac{8}{10}, \frac{12}{15}, \frac{16}{20}, \frac{20}{25}$

13. $\frac{7}{2}$ $\frac{14}{4}, \frac{21}{6}, \frac{28}{8}, \frac{35}{10}$ **14.** $\frac{9}{8}$ $\frac{18}{16}, \frac{27}{24}, \frac{36}{32}, \frac{45}{40}$

15. $\frac{80}{20}$ $\frac{4}{1}, \frac{8}{2}, \frac{16}{4}, \frac{20}{5}$ **16.** $\frac{25}{75}$ $\frac{1}{3}, \frac{5}{15}, \frac{10}{30}, \frac{20}{60}$

Find each missing number.

17. 4:7 = c:35 c = 20 **18.** 3:8 = 27:s s = 72 **19.** 32:12 = h:3 h = 8

20. 7 to 2 = 42 to d d = 12 **21.** 65 to 25 = k:5 k = 13 **22.** 5 to 11 = 40 to m m = 88

Problem Solving

23. One store has 3 managers and 12 salespeople. Another store has 4 managers and 15 salespeople. Do both stores have equivalent ratios of managers to salespeople? Explain.

no; 3 × 15 = 45 and 4 × 12 = 48, so the cross products are not the same.

24. A store uses the ratio 1 to 5 as a guide for managers to salespeople. Suppose the store has 30 salespeople. How many managers should it have?

6 managers

Use with Grade 5, Chapter 13, Lesson 2, pages 588–591. (415)

Reteach

Equivalent Ratios

R 13-2 RETEACH

You can use the phrase *for every* to help you think about equivalent ratios.
The picture shows that there are 3 batteries *for every* 1 calculator.
This means that there will be 6 batteries *for every* 2 calculators.
There will be 9 batteries *for every* 3 calculators.
There will be 12 batteries *for every* 4 calculators.
There will be 15 batteries *for every* 5 calculators.
You can show this information in a ratio table.

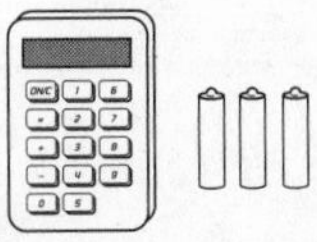

Number of Batteries	3	6	9	12	15
Number of Calculators	1	2	3	4	5

$\frac{3}{1}, \frac{6}{2}, \frac{9}{3}, \frac{12}{4}$, and $\frac{15}{5}$ are **equivalent ratios**.

You can also write a ratio equivalent to $\frac{3}{1}$ by multiplying the numerator and the denominator by the same number.

$\frac{3}{1} = \frac{3 \times 5}{1 \times 5} = \frac{15}{5}$ $\frac{3}{1}$ and $\frac{15}{5}$ are equivalent ratios.

Complete the ratio table. Then write the equivalent ratios shown in the table.

1. There are 4 shoes for every 1 horse.

$\frac{4}{1}$, $\frac{8}{2}, \frac{12}{3}, \frac{16}{4}$

Number of Shoes	4	8	12	16
Number of Horses	1	2	3	4

2. There are 5 weekdays for every 2 weekend days.

$\frac{5}{2}, \frac{10}{4}, \frac{15}{6}, \frac{20}{8}$

Number of Weekdays	5	10	15	20
Number of Weekend Days	2	4	6	8

Use multiplication to write an equivalent ratio. Show your work.

Answers may vary in exercise 4. Possible answers are shown.

3. $\frac{3}{7} = \frac{3 \times 2}{7 \times \boxed{2}} = \frac{\boxed{6}}{\boxed{14}}$ **4.** $\frac{1}{8} = \frac{1 \times \boxed{4}}{8 \times \boxed{4}} = \frac{\boxed{4}}{\boxed{32}}$

Find the missing number.

5. $\frac{6}{4} = \frac{18}{x}$ 12 **6.** $\frac{9}{7} = \frac{n}{35}$ 45 **7.** $\frac{3}{y} = \frac{15}{20}$ 4 **8.** $\frac{a}{3} = \frac{14}{21}$ 2

Use with Grade 5, Chapter 13, Lesson 2, pages 588–591. (416)

Enrich

Equivalent Ratios
Equivalent Ratio Game

E 13-2 ENRICH

Play this game with a partner. Take turns.

- Drop six counters on the number chart below. Record the six numbers your counters land on. If a counter lands on more than one number, record the number in the square that contains more of the counter. Cross out each recorded number.
- Use the six recorded numbers to write equivalent ratios. If you can write two equivalent ratios, give yourself 1 point. If you can write three equivalent ratios, give yourself 2 points. Remember, ratios that contain exactly the same numbers are also equivalent.
- If a counter lands on a crossed-out number, you may choose any number that is not crossed out in its place.

Play until all the numbers have been crossed out.
The player with more points is the winner.

1	2	3	4	6	8	9	12
1	2	3	4	6	8	9	12
1	2	3	4	6	8	9	12
1	2	3	4	6	8	9	12
1	2	3	4	6	8	9	12
1	2	3	4	6	8	9	12

Score

Player 1	
Player 2	

Use with Grade 5, Chapter 13, Lesson 2, pages 588–591. (417)

Daily Homework

13-2 Equivalent Ratios

Complete each ratio table.

1.

4	8	12	16	20
9	18	27	36	45

2.

12	24	36	48	60
7	14	21	28	35

Tell whether the ratios are equivalent. Write *Yes* or *No*.

3. $\frac{4}{5}, \frac{24}{30}$ Yes. **4.** $\frac{7}{4}, \frac{42}{24}$ Yes. **5.** $\frac{27}{3}, \frac{9}{2}$ No. **6.** $\frac{5}{11}, \frac{25}{55}$ Yes.

7. 9:10, 19:20 No. **8.** 36:81, 4:9 Yes. **9.** 3:8, 36:96 Yes. **10.** 24:12, 8:3 No.

Name three ratios equivalent to the given ratio. Answers may vary. Possible answers are given.

11. $\frac{3}{4}$ $\frac{6}{8}, \frac{9}{12}, \frac{12}{16}$ **12.** $\frac{7}{2}$ $\frac{14}{4}, \frac{21}{6}, \frac{28}{8}$ **13.** $\frac{25}{30}$ $\frac{5}{6}, \frac{10}{12}, \frac{15}{18}$

Find the missing number.

14. 3:5 = x:25 15 **15.** 8:1 = u:9 72 **16.** 35 to 21 = r to 3 5

Problem Solving

17. The ratio of girls to boys in Ms. Needham's class is 4:5. Find an equivalent ratio. Possible answer: 12:15

18. There are two fruit baskets for sale at the grocery store. One has 3 bananas and 7 kiwi fruit. The other has 9 bananas and 14 kiwi fruit. Are the ratios of bananas to kiwi fruit in the baskets equivalent? No.

Spiral Review

19. $1\frac{1}{4} \times 1\frac{1}{5} =$ $1\frac{1}{2}$ **20.** $6\frac{2}{3} \div \frac{5}{6} =$ 8 **21.** $2\frac{1}{9} \div 1\frac{1}{3} =$ $1\frac{7}{12}$

Grade 5, Chapter 13, Lesson 2, Cluster A 127

Chapter 13 ~ Lesson 3

Practice

Rates

P 13-3 PRACTICE

Complete.

1. 120 mi in 3 h = 360 mi in 9 h
2. 27 pages in 2 d = 135 pages in 10 d
3. 7 problems in 10 min = 42 problems in 60 min
4. 10 oz for 3 people = 40 oz for 12 people
5. 3 books in 2 wk = 24 books in 16 wk
6. 16 people in 1 van = 48 people in 3 vans
7. $15 for 2 tickets = $150 for 20 tickets
8. 5 for $1.99 = 20 for $7.96

Find each unit rate.

9. 35 people in 7 cars = 5 people per 1 car
10. 175 words in 5 min = 35 words in 1 min
11. $4.96 for 16 oz = $0.31 per 1 oz
12. 210 mi in 4 h = 52.5 mi per 1 h
13. 192 mi on 8 gal = 24 mi per 1 gal
14. 15 in. of rain in 30 d = 0.5 in. per 1 d
15. $40.50 for 9 tickets = $4.50 for 1 ticket
16. $49.50 for 6 h = $8.25 for 1 h

Decide which is the better buy.

17. 20 disks for $5
50 disks for $12
50 disks for $12
18. 10 pens for $4.50
3 pens for $1.47
10 pens for $4.50
19. 5 pounds of apples for $2.75
8 pounds of apples for $4.00
8 pounds of apples/$4.00
20. 6 eggs for $0.84
1 dozen eggs for $1.80
6 eggs for $0.84
21. 12 granola bars for $5.76
8 granola bars for $3.60
8 bars for $3.60
22. 2 rolls of film for $5.38
3 rolls of film for $8.37
2 rolls for $5.38

Problem Solving

23. A $3.36 box of cereal contains 14 servings. What is the cost per serving?
$0.24
24. Enough bread for 10 sandwiches costs $1.89. How much will enough bread for 80 sandwiches cost?
$15.12

Use with Grade 5, Chapter 13, Lesson 3, pages 592–595. (418)

Reteach

Rates

R 13-3 RETEACH

A **rate** is a ratio that compares measurements or amounts such as miles and hours. When the second measurement in a rate is 1 unit, the rate is a unit rate.

Rate: 100 miles in 2 hours
Unit rate: 50 miles in 1 hour, or 50 miles per hour

To find a unit rate, simplify the rate.

$$\frac{100 \text{ miles}}{2 \text{ hours}} \xrightarrow{\div 2} \frac{50 \text{ miles}}{1 \text{ hour}} = 50 \text{ miles per hour}$$

Find each unit rate.

1. 240 miles in 4 hours

$$\frac{240 \text{ miles}}{4 \text{ hours}} \xrightarrow{\div 4} \frac{60 \text{ miles}}{1 \text{ hour}} = 60 \text{ miles per hour}$$

2. 161 miles on 7 gallons

$$\frac{161 \text{ miles}}{7 \text{ gallons}} \xrightarrow{\div 7} \frac{23 \text{ miles}}{1 \text{ gallon}} = 23 \text{ miles per gallon}$$

3. 72 students in 3 classes = 24 students in 1 class
4. $4.00 for 5 bus tokens = $0.80 for 1 bus token
5. 60 minutes for 12 problems = 5 minutes per problem
6. 10 cups for 20 servings = $\frac{1}{2}$, or 0.5 cup per serving
7. $3.84 for 16 oz = $0.24 for 1 oz

Use with Grade 5, Chapter 13, Lesson 3, pages 592–595. (419)

Enrich

Rates
Better Buys

E 13-3 ENRICH

Circle the letter of the better buy in each row.

1. G. 4 books for $17.00 — (A.) 3 books for $12.00
2. S. 2 tickets for $9.50 — (D.) 5 tickets for $22.00
3. (O.) 30 ounces of cereal for $3.30 — K. 48 ounces of cereal for $5.76
4. (E.) 4 rides for $1.60 — H. 10 rides for $5.00
5. (A.) 3 chicken strips for $2.55 — C. 8 chicken strips for $6.96
6. (E.) 16 ounces of milk for $0.96 — P. 12 ounces of milk for $0.84
7. L. box of 8 popsicles for $1.84 — (N.) box of 12 popsicles for $2.40
8. (W.) 8 hamburgers for $3.76 — I. 5 hamburgers for $2.45
9. (B.) 1 dozen pens for $3.48 — U. 5 pens for $1.55
10. F. 40 ounces of grapes for $4.40 — (T.) 2 pounds of grapes for $3.20
11. (R.) 3 yards of ribbon for $3.87 — M. 10 feet of ribbon for $4.50

Write the letter you circled in each problem above the problem number to solve this riddle.

Where does a mermaid sleep?

O	N	A	W	A	T	E	R	B	E	D
3	7	5	8	1	10	4	11	9	6	2

Use with Grade 5, Chapter 13, Lesson 3, pages 592–595. (420)

Daily Homework

13-3 **Rates**

Complete.

1. 175 km in 2 h = 700 km in 8 h
2. 16 oz in 3 min = 80 oz in 15 min
3. 13 people at 2 tables = 104 people at 16 tables
4. $81.35 in 8 hours = $406.75 in 40 hours

Find each unit rate.

5. $4.50 for 5 lb = $0.90 for 1 lb
6. 640 pages in 8 notebooks = 80 pages in 1 notebook
7. 504 tissues in 9 boxes = 56 tissues in 1 box
8. 384 mi on 12 gal = 32 mi on 1 gal

Decide which is the better buy.

9. 4 shirts for $24
5 shirts for $35
4 shirts for $24
10. 7 CDs for $77
11 CDs for $99
11 CDs for $99
11. 9 bicycles for $2,700
6 bicycles for $2,000
9 bicycles for $2,700

Problem Solving.

12. It costs $6.40 to add 4 toppings to a large pizza from Rick's Pizza House. What is the rate per topping? $1.60
13. During a storm, 1.5 inches of rain falls in one minute. If rain continues to fall at this rate for 10 minutes, how much rain will fall? 15 inches

Spiral Review

Find the approximate circumference. Round to the nearest tenth. Use $\pi = 3.14$.

14. 25.1

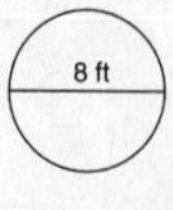

15. 34.5

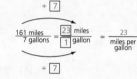

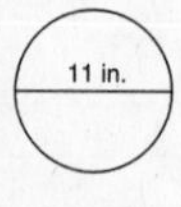

128 Grade 5, Chapter 13, Lesson 3, Cluster A

Chapter 13 ~ Lesson 4

Practice

Problem Solving: Reading for Math

P 13-4 PRACTICE Reading Skill

Check the reasonableness of an answer

Read the details in each problem. Check whether each solution is reasonable. Explain.

1. Cynthia and Marcy are starting a pet-sitting business. While pet owners are out of town, Cynthia and Marcy will take care of each pet for $5.00 a day. This week, they will watch 3 pets for 4 days. They decide they will make $30 for the week. Is their estimate reasonable?
   No. Answers may vary. Possible answer: They will make $15 each day, so for 4 days $30 is not a reasonable estimate.
2. Tasha earns extra money by babysitting on weekends. For each child she watches, she charges $4.50 per evening. On Friday evening she watches 4 children and on Saturday evening she watches 5 children. She thinks she will earn about $40. Is her estimate reasonable?
   Yes. Answers may vary. Possible answer: $4 + 5 = 9$ and $40 is between $9 \times \$4 = \$36$ and $9 \times \$5 = \$45$.
3. Chandler charges $10.00 to mow a lawn. This week, he is scheduled to mow 2 lawns each day from Monday through Saturday. He decides that he will make $70. Is his estimate reasonable?
   No. Answers may vary. Possible answer: He will earn $60 for mowing one lawn a day for 6 days. So, for 2 lawns each day he will make $120.
4. Ricky hangs sale advertisements in a grocery store window. He earns $2.25 for each advertisement that he hangs up. On Monday, he hangs up 6 advertisements. On Friday, he hangs up 3 advertisements with the weekend specials. On Saturday, he hangs up 2 more advertisements. He thinks he will earn $16. Is his estimate reasonable?
   No. Answers may vary. Possible answer: Since he hangs up 11 advertisements and gets $2.25 for each one, he will earn at least $22.
5. To raise money for her school, Amy sells gift-wrapping paper. She thinks she can sell 8 rolls per day. She can only sell the gift-wrapping paper from Thursday through Saturday. The paper costs $3 per roll. She decides she will raise about $70. Is her estimate reasonable?
   Yes. Answers may vary. Possible answer: She will raise $24 for each of 3 days, so she will raise about $70.

Use with Grade 5, Chapter 13, Lesson 4, pages 596–597. (421)

Practice

Problem Solving: Reading for Math

P 13-4 PRACTICE Math Skills Test Prep

Check the reasonableness of an answer

Choose the correct answer.

Marianna wants to buy 9 craft sets for the students in her crafts class. Each set costs $3.25. She estimates her total cost will be about $27.

1. Which of the following statements is true?
   - A Since the sum of $3 and $27 is $30, the calculation is not reasonable.
   - B Since the difference between $9 and $3 is $6, the calculation is not reasonable.
   - C Since the quotient of $27 and $3 is 9, the calculation is not reasonable.
   - (D) Since the product of $3 and 9 is $27, the calculation is reasonable.
2. When you check the reasonableness of an answer, you
   - F do all the calculations twice.
   - (G) use the details in the problem to make sure the answer makes sense.
   - H try another strategy to solve the problem.
   - J reverse the order of operations to check the answer.

Jamal uses 15 gallons of gas each week in his lawn-mowing business. The cost of gas is $1.25 per gallon. He estimates that his total cost for gas will be about $30.

3. Which of the following statements is true?
   - (A) Since the product of 15 and $1 is $15, the estimate is not reasonable.
   - B Since the product of 15 and $2 is $30, the estimate is reasonable.
   - C Since the sum of $30 and $1.25 is $31.25, the estimate is not reasonable.
   - D Since the difference between $30 and $1 is $29, the estimate is reasonable.
4. When you check the reasonableness of an answer, you
   - F use a calculator to redo all the calculations.
   - G draw a diagram.
   - (H) check that the answer fits with the facts you know.
   - J guess the answer.

Austin and six of his friends plan to go skating. Admission costs $4.80 per person and for every 6 people, the seventh person gets free admission. He estimates the total admission cost will be about $30.

5. Which of the following statements is true?
   - A Since the product of $4 and 6 is $24, the estimate is not reasonable.
   - (B) Since the product of $5 and 6 is $30, the estimate is reasonable.
   - C Since the difference between $30 and 4 is $26, the estimate is not reasonable.
   - D Since the product of $5 and 7 is $35, the estimate is not reasonable.
6. Which of the following should you do to check that an answer is reasonable?
   - (F) Notice the important details in the problem and decide if the answer fits with the facts.
   - G Make a table.
   - H Use a calculator to check each calculation.
   - J Solve the problem two different ways.

Use with Grade 5, Chapter 13, Lesson 4, pages 596–597. (422)

Practice

Problem Solving: Reading for Math

P 13-4 PRACTICE Math Skills Test Prep

Check the reasonableness of an answer

Choose the correct answer.

Alicia wants to buy 4 packages of trading cards. Each package costs $6.78. She has $24 and estimates that it will be enough to buy the cards.

7. Which of the following statements is true?
   - A Since the difference of $24 and $7 is $17, the estimate is not reasonable.
   - B Since the sum of $24 and $6 is $30, the estimate is not reasonable.
   - C Since the product of $6 and 4 is $24, the estimate is reasonable.
   - (D) Since the product of $7 and 4 is $28, the estimate is not reasonable.
8. When you check the reasonableness of an answer, you
   - F work through the problem from the beginning a second time.
   - (G) determine if the answer makes sense.
   - H do all the calculations twice with a calculator.
   - J guess whether the answer makes sense.

Solve. Explain your answer.

9. Emily is watching her neighbor's house while they are gone. They are paying her $5.25 per day. She will be watching the house for 14 days. She calculates that she will earn $70. Is her calculation reasonable?
   Yes. Answers may vary. Possible answer: In 7 days she will earn about $35, so in 14 days she will earn about $70.
10. Ben is babysitting twin brothers for 5 hours. He charges $2.25 per child per hour. He calculates that he will earn a total of $11.25. Is his calculation reasonable?
    No. Answers may vary. Possible answer: He will earn about $10 for each child, so he will earn more than $11.25.
11. A youth group washes 28 cars on Saturday. They charge $8.50 per car. They say that they have raised about $240. Is their statement reasonable?
    Yes. Answers may vary. Possible answer: The product of 30 and $8 is $240.
12. Kathleen earns $6.25 per hour weeding flowerbeds. She wants to earn $35. She told a friend that she could earn the money working for 5 hours. Is this statement correct?
    No. Answers may vary. Possible answer: $6.25 is close to $6, so the total will be closer to $30 than $35.

Use with Grade 5, Chapter 13, Lesson 4, pages 596–597. (423)

Daily Homework

13-4 Problem Solving: Reading for Math

Check the Reasonableness of an Answer

Use data from the table for problems 1–4. Explain your answer.

Chore	Time
Taking out Trash	3 min
Cleaning Bathroom	45 min
Sorting Recycling	20 min
Vacuuming	1 h
Unloading Dishwasher	10 min
Weeding	2 h

1. The table shows how long it takes Marisa and David to do different chores. On Saturday, Marisa is supposed to clean both bathrooms in her family's house. She calculates that it will take her about an hour and a half. Is her calculation reasonable?
   Yes; she will work for 90 minutes, which is an hour and a half.
2. On the same Saturday, David is supposed to take out the trash, vacuum, and unload the dishwasher. He calculates that he has to work longer than Marisa. Is his calculation reasonable?
   No; David's 3 chores combined still take less than an hour and a half.
3. Marisa weeds the garden twice a month during June, July, and August. She calculates that in all, she spends about half a day of her summer vacation weeding. Is her calculation reasonable?
   Yes; she weeds a total of 6 times, each of which takes 2 hours, and $6 \times 2 = 12$ hours, which is half a day.
4. David decides to start a neighborhood recycling service. He plans to charge each neighbor $3.00 for sorting his or her recycling once a week. He calculates that if each neighbor's recycling takes him as long as his family's recycling, he will make about $9.00 an hour. Is his calculation reasonable?
   Yes; there are 3 twenty-minute periods in an hour, and 3 times $3.00 is $9.00.

Spiral Review

5. $312 \times 4.5 = 1{,}404$
6. $7.54 \times 80 = 603.2$
7. $1.65 \times 6.4 = 10.56$
8. $10.933 \times 28 = 306.124$

Grade 5, Chapter 13, Lesson 4, Cluster A 129

Chapter 13 ~ Lesson 5

Practice

Scale Drawings

P 13-5 PRACTICE

Use data from the floor plan. Find each actual size.

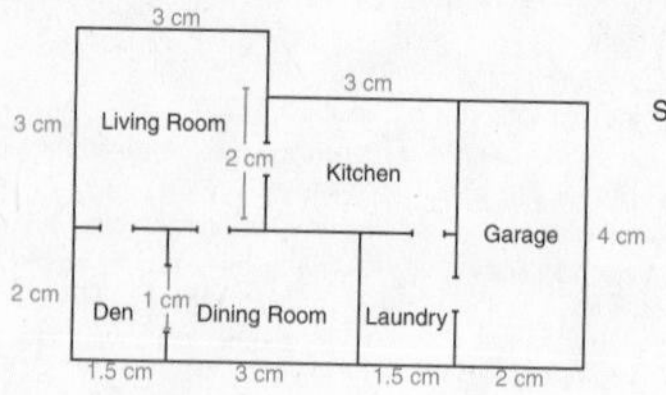

Scale: 1 cm = 3 m

1. length of garage 12 m
2. width of garage 6 m
3. width of doorway from den to dining room 3 m
4. perimeter of kitchen 30 m
5. width of the house 24 m
6. length of living room and den together 15 m

Find the scale.

7. An actual family room that is 8 meters long is 4 centimeters on a drawing.
   2 m = 1 cm
8. An actual closet that is 6 feet long is 2 inches on a drawing.
   3 ft = 1 in.
9. An actual bedroom that is 15 feet long is 3 inches on a drawing.
   5 ft = 1 in.
10. An actual house that is 16 meters wide is 4 centimeters on a drawing.
   4 m = 1 cm

Problem Solving

11. A map has a scale of 1 inch = 4 miles. The map distance from Jacob's house to his school is $2\frac{1}{2}$ inches. How far does Jacob actually live from his school?
   10 miles
12. Shannon lives 15 kilometers from her school. She plans to draw a map using the scale 1 centimeter = 5 kilometers to show this. How far will her house be from the school on her map?
   3 cm

Reteach

Scale Drawings

R 13-5 RETEACH

A scale drawing shows the actual shape of something, but not the actual size. The rectangle at the right is a scale drawing of a playground. The length of the rectangle is 2 inches.

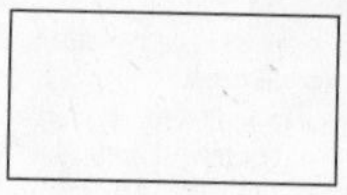

The scale is a ratio of the distance on the drawing to the actual distance.

Scale: 1 in. = 50 ft

You can find the actual length of the playground. Write two equivalent ratios.

Scale ↓

distance on drawing → / actual distance → $\frac{1 \text{ in.}}{50 \text{ ft}} = \frac{2 \text{ in.}}{w}$ ← distance on drawing / ← actual distance

Find the missing number.

× 2

distance on drawing → / actual distance → $\frac{1 \text{ in.}}{50 \text{ ft}} = \frac{2 \text{ in.}}{\textbf{100 ft}}$ ← distance on drawing / ← actual distance

× 2

The playground is actually 100 feet long.

Use a ruler to measure the distance on the drawing.

Then find the actual diameter of the bicycle wheel.

Scale ↓

distance on drawing → / actual distance → $\frac{1 \text{ in.}}{10 \text{ in.}} = \frac{2 \text{ in.}}{w}$ ← distance on drawing / ← actual distance

Find the missing number. × 2

distance on drawing → / actual distance → $\frac{1 \text{ in.}}{10 \text{ in.}} = \frac{2 \text{ in.}}{20 \text{ in.}}$ ← distance on drawing / ← actual distance

× 2

Scale: 1 in. = 10 in.

Enrich

Scale Drawings

Scaling the Solar System

E 13-5 ENRICH

As part of a museum display, the solar system was drawn to scale to show the positions of the planets in relation to each other and to the Sun. A scale of 1 inch = 50 million miles was used to make the display.

Complete this table to find the actual distances, according to the display, of the planets from the Sun.

Planet	Scale Distance (nearest tenth inch)	Actual Average Distance from Sun (nearest million miles)
Mercury	0.7	35
Venus	1.3	65
Earth	1.9	95
Mars	2.8	140
Jupiter	9.7	485
Saturn	17.7	885
Uranus	35.7	1,785
Neptune	55.9	2,795
Pluto	73.5	3,675

Use the table to answer these questions.

1. Write the average distance from the Sun to Mercury in standard form.
   35,000,000 miles
2. Write the average distance from the Sun to Neptune in standard form.
   2,795,000,000 miles
3. Which planets are closest to each other?
   Mercury and Venus, and Venus and Earth
4. Which two planets are farthest apart?
   Uranus and Neptune

Daily Homework

13-5 Scale Drawings

Use data from the map for problems 1–3. Find each actual size.

1. perimeter of the school building
   400 m
2. length of the sidewalk from the parking lot to the school
   30 m
3. dimensions of the basketball courts
   50 meters by 20 meters

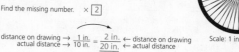

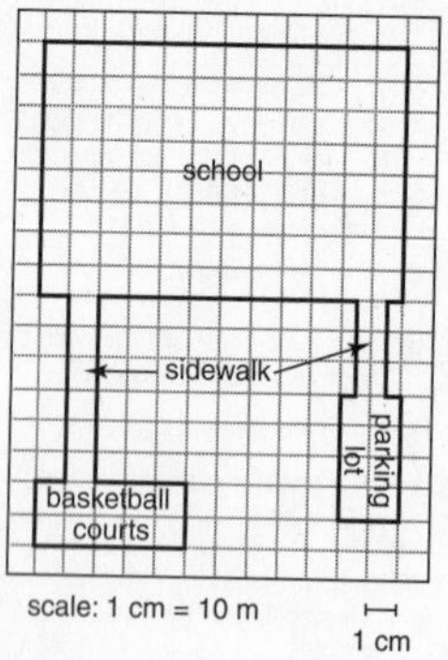

Find the scale.

4. A classroom that is 36 feet long is 3 inches long on a drawing.
   12 ft = 1 in.
5. A playground that is 45 meters wide is 5 cm wide on a drawing.
   9 m = 1 cm

Problem Solving

6. Debbie is looking at a map of Minnesota with a scale of 1 inch = 50 miles. She measures 3 inches on the map from her home town to the border between the United States and Canada. What is the actual distance?
   about 150 miles
7. A wall map shows an area of 4 kilometers by 6 kilometers in a space 2 meters by 3 meters. What is the map's scale?
   2 kilometers = 1 meter

Spiral Review

Solve.

8. $p - 314 = 315$ $p = 629$ 9. $\frac{x}{3} - 12 = 10$ $x = 66$ 10. $4c + 14 = 258$ $c = 61$

Chapter 13 ~ Lesson 6

Practice

Explore Probability

P 13-6 PRACTICE

Use the spinner for exercises 1–6.

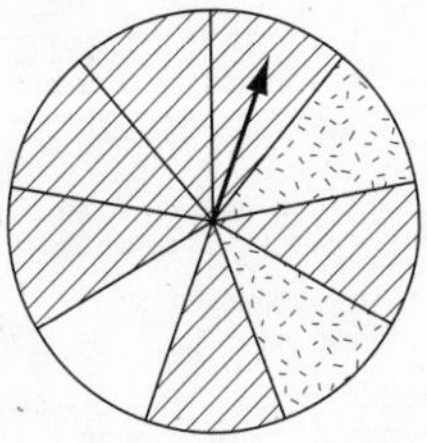

1. What are the possible outcomes? striped, speckled, white
2. Which outcome is likely? striped
3. Which outcome is unlikely? white
4. If you spin the spinner 30 times, what outcome do you think you will get most often? striped
5. If you spin the spinner 30 times, what outcome do you think you will get least often? white
6. What if you make 3 of the striped sections dotted. Which outcome will be likely? unlikely? speckled; white

Use the bag of cubes for exercises 7–12.

7. How many possible outcomes are there if you pick a cube out of the bag with your eyes closed? What are they? 3 outcomes; striped, stars, dots
8. Which outcome is likely? stars
9. Which outcome is unlikely? striped
10. If you pick a cube out of the bag 40 times, what cube do you think you will get most often? stars
11. If you pick a cube out of the bag 40 times, what cube do you think you will get least often? striped
12. What cubes could you add to the bag to make picking a striped cube very likely? Accept 3 or more striped cubes.

Use with Grade 5, Chapter 13, Lesson 6, pages 602–603. (427)

Reteach

Explore Probability

R 13-6 RETEACH

If you were to spin this spinner, it could land on A, B, or C. A, B, and C are the possible outcomes.

The likelihood of landing on a particular outcome depends on how many of that outcome are on the spinner.

4 A sections — Landing on A is likely.

1 C section — Landing on C is unlikely.

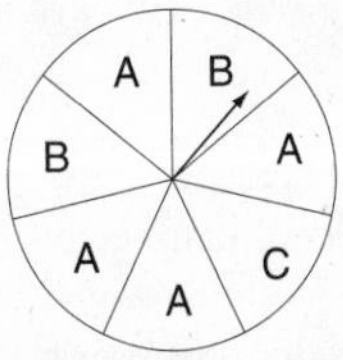

Use the spinner at the right for exercises 1–3.

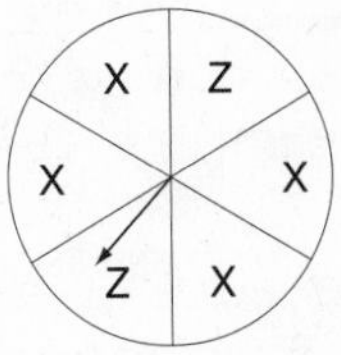

1. There are 2 outcomes, X and Z.
2. Landing on X is likely, because 4 sections are X.
3. Landing on Z is unlikely, because 2 sections are Z.

Use the spinner at the right for exercises 4–7.

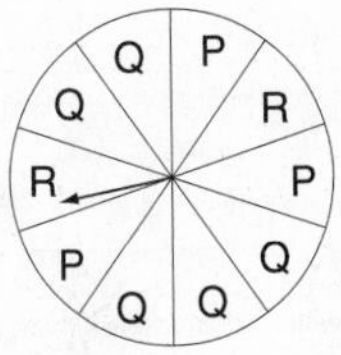

4. What are the possible outcomes? P, Q, and R
5. Which outcome is unlikely? R
6. Which outcome is likely? Q
7. If you spin the spinner 50 times, which letter do you think you will get most often? Q

Use with Grade 5, Chapter 13, Lesson 6, pages 602–603. (428)

Enrich

Explore Probability
Experiment with Number Cubes

E 13-6 ENRICH

1. Suppose you were to toss two number cubes and find their sum. Complete the table to show all the possible outcomes.

	1	2	3	4	5	6
1	2	3	4	5	6	7
2	3	4	5	6	7	8
3	4	5	6	7	8	9
4	5	6	7	8	9	10
5	6	7	8	9	10	11
6	7	8	9	10	11	12

2. How many different outcomes are possible? 11 outcomes
3. Is each outcome equally likely to happen? Explain. No; some sums occur only once, and other sums occur more than once.
4. Which sum is least likely to happen? 2 or 12
5. Which sum is most likely to happen? 7
6. Conduct an experiment. Toss two number cubes and record their sum in the table below. Repeat 25 times. Results will vary.

Sum	2	3	4	5	6	7	8	9	10	11	12
Tally											
Frequency											

7. Do the results of your experiment match the results of exercises 4 and 5? Why or why not? Results may or may not match.

Use with Grade 5, Chapter 13, Lesson 6, pages 602–603. (429)

Daily Homework

13-6 Explore Probability

Use the spinner for problems 1–4.

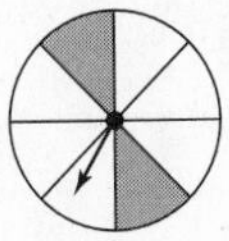

1. What are the possible outcomes? white and gray
2. Which outcome is unlikely? gray
   Which outcome is likely? white
3. If you spin the spinner 60 times, which outcome do you think you will get more often? white
4. Suppose you change 4 of the white sections to gray. Now which outcome is unlikely? white

Solve.

5. Caleb has a spinner with 9 orange sections and 1 blue section. If he changes 1 of the orange sections to blue, which outcome will be likely? orange
6. Laura makes a spinner with 12 sections. One of the sections is red, a second is yellow, and a third is green. The rest are blue. When she spins, is it likely or unlikely that the outcome will be a color other than blue? unlikely

Spiral Review

Find the approximate area of each circle. Round to the nearest tenth if necessary. Use $\pi = 3.14$.

7.

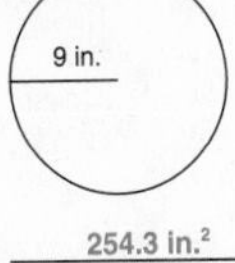

254.3 in.^{2}

8.

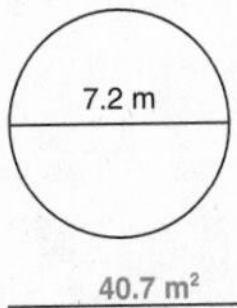

40.7 m^2

Grade 5, Chapter 13, Lesson 6, Cluster B 131

Chapter 13 ~ Lesson 7

Practice

Probability

P 13-7 PRACTICE

If you spin this spinner, what is the probability of each event?

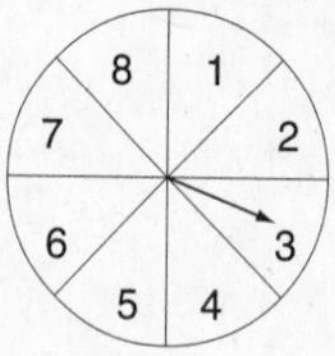

1. spinning a 3 $\frac{1}{8}$
2. spinning a 7 $\frac{1}{8}$
3. spinning a 4 or 6 $\frac{2}{8}$, or $\frac{1}{4}$
4. spinning an even number $\frac{4}{8}$, or $\frac{1}{2}$
5. spinning a number less than 9 1
6. spinning a number greater than 20 0

If you pick a card, what is the probability of each event? Write *certain* or *impossible* for each event.

G T C M S

7. picking an R impossible
8. picking C, G, M, T, or S certain
9. picking a consonant certain
10. picking a number impossible

If you pick a card, what is the probability of each event? Write *more likely than, less likely than,* or *equally likely as* to complete each sentence.

△ △ □ ○ △ □ △ ○ □ □ △ ○ ○ □

11. Picking a circle is less likely than picking a triangle.
12. Picking a square is equally likely as picking a triangle.
13. Picking a square is more likely than picking a circle.

Problem Solving

14. You and three friends are trying to decide what video to rent. You each write a different movie name on a card. If you pick a card at random, what is the probability that the movie name you wrote will be chosen? $\frac{1}{4}$

15. Two girls and three boys want to borrow the same book from the school library. Each writes his or her name on a card. If the librarian picks a card at random, what is the probability that a girl will be chosen to borrow the book? $\frac{2}{5}$

Use with Grade 5, Chapter 13, Lesson 7, pages 604–607. (430)

Reteach

Probability

R 13-7 RETEACH

These seven cards are going to be mixed and placed facedown on a table. One will be picked.

1 2 3 4 5 6 7

You can write a fraction to express the probability of picking a particular card—an event such as picking a number less than 4.

Favorable outcomes: 1, 2, 3 ← numbers less than 4

Possible outcomes: 1, 2, 3, 4, 5, 6, 7 ← all possible outcomes

Probability of picking a number less than 4 $= \frac{\text{number of favorable outcomes}}{\text{number of possible coutcomes}} = \frac{3}{7}$

The probability of picking a card with a number less than 4 is $\frac{3}{7}$.
You can write $P(\text{number less than } 4) = \frac{3}{7}$.

Use the cards above. Find each probability.

1. $P(6)$ Favorable outcome(s): 6
   Possible outcome(s): 1, 2, 3, 4, 5, 6, 7
   $P(6) = \frac{\text{number of favorable outcomes}}{\text{number of possible coutcomes}} = \frac{1}{7}$
2. $P(3 \text{ or } 5)$ Favorable outcome(s): 3, 5
   Possible outcome(s): 1, 2, 3, 4, 5, 6, 7
   $P(3 \text{ or } 5) = \frac{\text{number of favorable outcomes}}{\text{number of possible coutcomes}} = \frac{2}{7}$
3. $P(9) =$ $\frac{0}{7}$, or 0
4. $P(\text{number less than } 7) =$ $\frac{6}{7}$
5. $P(\text{odd number}) =$ $\frac{4}{7}$
6. $P(\text{number greater than zero}) =$ $\frac{7}{7}$, or 1
7. An event that has a probability of 0 is an impossible event. Which event named in exercises 1–6 is an impossible event? picking a 9
8. An event that has a probability of 1 is a certain event. Which event named in exercises 1–6 is a certain event? picking a number greater than zero

Use with Grade 5, Chapter 13, Lesson 7, pages 604–607. (431)

Enrich

Probability
Spinner Designs

E 13-7 ENRICH

Design a spinner for each set of clues. Divide each spinner into as few sections as possible. Write a color word, letter, or number in each section.

1. The probability of spinning yellow is $\frac{3}{8}$. Spinning red is equally likely as spinning yellow. The event spinning red, yellow, or blue is certain.

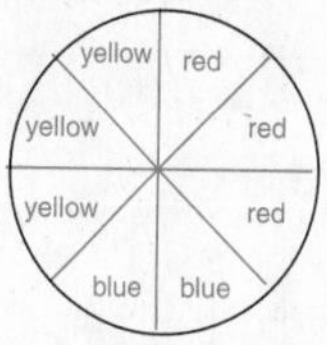

2. The probability of spinning a letter in the word *certain* is $\frac{7}{10}$. The probability of spinning a vowel is $\frac{1}{2}$. Spinning an o is more likely than spinning an e. The probability of spinning a letter in the word *record* is $\frac{6}{10}$.

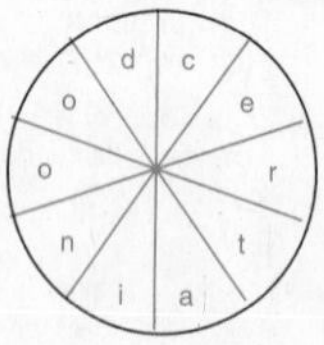

3. The probability of spinning a factor of 12 is certain. The probability of spinning a number that is neither prime nor composite is $\frac{1}{3}$. The probability of spinning a prime number is $\frac{4}{9}$. Spinning an odd number is twice as likely as spinning an even number. The probability of spinning a multiple of 3 is $\frac{5}{9}$.

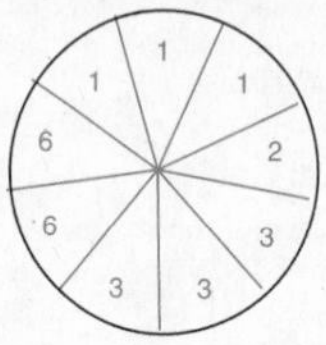

Use with Grade 5, Chapter 13, Lesson 7, pages 604–607. (432)

Daily Homework

13-7 **Probability**

If you pick a counter without looking, what is the probability of each event?

1. picking a black counter $\frac{7}{12}$
2. picking a counter with an "X" $\frac{2}{12}$ or $\frac{1}{6}$

If you pick a ball without looking, what is the probability of each event? Write *certain* or *impossible* for each event.

3. picking a volleyball impossible
4. picking a ball certain

If you spin the spinner, what is the probability of each event? Write *more likely than, less likely than,* or *equally likely* to complete each sentence.

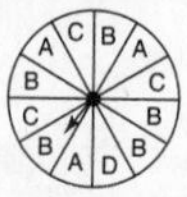

5. Spinning a D is less likely than spinning a B.
6. Spinning a C is equally likely as spinning an A.

Problem Solving

7. In a cooler are 4 bottles of juice, 3 bottles of water, and 5 bottles of lemonade. If Christine picks without looking, what is the probability that she will pick lemonade? $\frac{5}{12}$
8. Before Christine picks, someone puts 3 cartons of milk into the cooler. What is the probability that Christine will now pick a carton of milk? $\frac{3}{15}$ or $\frac{1}{5}$

Spiral Review

Simplify each expression.

9. $4 \times 13 + 12 \div 3 =$ 56
10. $126 + 14 \div 7 =$ 128
11. $6 \times 5 \times 2^2 =$ 120
11. $140 - (3^2 + 3 \times 7) =$ 110

132 Grade 5, Chapter 13, Lesson 7, Cluster B

Chapter 13 ~ Lesson 8

Practice

Problem Solving: Strategy 13-8 PRACTICE

Do an Experiment Check students' frequency tables.

Do an experiment to solve. Record the results in a frequency table.

1. **Language Arts** Which consonant is used most often in writing: N, R, S, or T? First, make a prediction. Then choose 20 lines of text from a book and count the number of each consonant to solve.
   Answers may vary.

2. **Language Arts** Which vowel (A, E, I, O, or U) is used most often to start a sentence? Predict which vowel you think is used the most. Then choose 50 sentences from a book and record the number of times each vowel starts a sentence to solve.
   Answers may vary.

3. What is the probability that a dropped dollar bill will land faceup or facedown? First, make a prediction, and then record the results of dropping a dollar bill 50 times.
   Answers may vary.

4. **Literature** How often does the title of a novel include the word *the*? First, make a prediction. Then gather the titles of 20 novels and record the number of times each title includes the word *the*.
   Answers may vary.

Mixed Strategy Review

Solve. Use any strategy.

5. A music store sells new CDs for \$12.75 and used CDs for \$5.25 each. Blake buys 2 new CDs. He spends a total of \$41.25. How many used CDs did he buy?
   3 used CDs
   Strategy: Work Backward

6. Cindy has 500 coupons to hand out. She hands out about 125 coupons per hour. If she starts at 9 A.M., what time can she expect to be finished?
   1 P.M.
   Strategy: Make a Table

7. **Literature** *The Box Car Children,* a book by Gertrude Chandler Warner, has 153 pages. The book is being reprinted with a smaller type size. The new book will have $\frac{2}{3}$ the number of pages. How many pages will the new book have?
   102 pages
   Strategy: Write an Equation

8. **Create a problem** for which you could do an experiment to solve. Share it with others.
   Check students' problems.

Use with Grade 5, Chapter 13, Lesson 8, pages 608–609. (433)

Reteach

Problem Solving: Strategy 13-8 RETEACH

Do an Experiment

Page 609, Problem 2

Lauren wants to know which vowel is used the most in writing–A, E, I, O, or U. Predict which vowel you think is used the most. Then choose 20 lines of text from a book and count the number of each vowel to solve.

Step 1 Read

Be sure you understand the problem.
Read carefully.

What do you know?

- The letters that are vowels.
- They are A, E, I, O, and U.

What do you need to find?

- The vowel used most in writing.

Step 2 Plan

- Find a Pattern
- Guess and Check
- Work Backward
- Make a Graph
- Make a Table
- Write an Equation
- Make an Organized List
- Draw a Diagram
- Solve a Simpler Problem
- Logical Reasoning

Make a plan.
Choose a strategy.

Some problems can be solved by doing an experiment.

You may have no idea how often each vowel is used, so you can do an experiment to get an idea of which vowel is used most often.

Select a book. Count 20 lines of text in the book. Then count the number of vowels in each line of text.

Use with Grade 5, Chapter 13, Lesson 8, pages 608–609. (434)

Reteach

Problem Solving: Strategy 13-8 RETEACH

Do an Experiment

Step 3 Solve

Carry out your plan.
First, predict the vowel you think will be used most often.
Answers may vary.

Choose 20 lines of text from a book.

Count the number of times each vowel occurs.

Record your results in the frequency table below.

Vowel	Tally	Frequency
A		
E		
I	Answers may vary.	
O		
U		

Which vowel is used the most? Answers may vary.

Step 4 Look Back

Is the solution reasonable?
Reread the problem.

Have you answered the question? Yes

How can you decide if your results are reasonable?

Answers may vary. Possible answer: Conduct the experiment again or compare results with other students.

Practice

1. Fifty envelopes are dropped out of a box. What is the probability of the envelopes landing with the flap facing down?
   Answers may vary. Possible answer: 25 out of 50, or $\frac{1}{2}$

2. Which consonant is used least often in writing: W, Q, X, or J? First, make a prediction. Then choose 20 lines of text from a book and count the number of each consonant to solve.
   Answers may vary.

Use with Grade 5, Chapter 13, Lesson 8, pages 608–609. (435)

Daily Homework

13-8 Problem Solving: Strategy

Do an Experiment

Do an experiment to solve. Record the results in the frequency table below.

Check students' frequency tables.

1. A dollar bill is dropped face-up from a height of 3 feet. What is the probability that it will land face down? First make and record a prediction. Then record the results of dropping a dollar bill 50 times. Answers may vary.

Prediction: ____

How It Lands	Tally	Frequency
Faceup		
Facedown		

2. Which punctuation mark is the most commonly used? First make and record a prediction. Then choose 40 sentences from a book and record the occurrence of punctuation. Answers may vary.

Prediction: ____

Punctuation Mark	Tally	Frequency
Period		
Question Mark		
Exclamation Point		
Comma		

Mixed Strategy Review

3. Angela wants to order a tool set that costs \$44.95 plus \$2.25 for shipping. She has 160 quarters in her bank. Does she have enough money? Explain.
   No; \$44.95 + \$2.25 = \$47.20; 160 × \$0.25 = \$40.00.

4. Ralph has a $6\frac{1}{4}$-ounce jar of metallic paint. He uses $1\frac{3}{4}$ ounces to paint one model and $2\frac{1}{2}$ ounces to paint another. How much paint is left? 2 oz

Spiral Review

5. $\frac{7}{2} \times 6 =$ 21
6. $\frac{3}{4} + \frac{5}{3} =$ $2\frac{5}{12}$
7. $1.5 \times 4.2 =$ 6.3
8. $3\frac{3}{4} \times 7\frac{1}{3} =$ $27\frac{1}{2}$
9. $\frac{8}{9} \div \frac{12}{5} =$ $\frac{10}{27}$
10. $3\frac{3}{5} - \frac{2}{3} =$ $2\frac{14}{15}$

Grade 5, Chapter 13, Lesson 8, Cluster B 133

Chapter 13 ~ Lesson 9

Part A Worksheet

Problem Solving: Application
Applying Probability

Part A 13-9 WORKSHEET Decision Making

Use the tables to record the outcomes for each spinner and the number cube.

Spinner A and Number Cube			
Number Spun	Number Rolled	Product	Add 15 if odd.

Sum = ______

Spinner B and Number Cube			
Number Spun	Number Rolled	Product	Add 15 if odd.

Sum = ______

Spinner C and Number Cube			
Number Spun	Number Rolled	Product	Add 15 if odd.

Sum = ______

Spinner D and Number Cube			
Number Spun	Number Rolled	Product	Add 15 if odd.

Sum = ______

Your Decision

Which spinner should you choose if you want the greatest chance of winning the game? Explain. Answers may vary. Possible answer: Spinner D because you can get the highest possible product and highest possible odd-number product; Spinner A because you have the greatest chance of getting an odd-number product and earning bonus points.

Use with Grade 5, Chapter 13, Lesson 9, pages 610–611. (436)

Part B Worksheet

Problem Solving: Application
Which solution makes the biggest bubbles?

Part B 13-9 WORKSHEET Math & Science

Which ratio of soap to water do you think will make the biggest soap bubble solution: 1:1, 1:5, 1:10, or 1:20? Explain. Answers may vary. Possible answer: 1:1 because it has the most soap.

Work with a partner.

Decide how you will estimate the diameter of the soap bubble. Discuss how you can keep conditions the same for each soap bubble.

Record your data and observations for each solution in the tables.

1:1 Solution	Diameter	Lifetime	Observations
Trial 1			
Trial 2			
Trial 3			
Trial 4			
Trial 5			
Average diameter:			
Average lifetime:			

1:5 Solution	Diameter	Lifetime	Observations
Trial 1			
Trial 2			
Trial 3			
Trial 4			
Trial 5			
Average diameter:			
Average lifetime:			

Use with Grade 5, Chapter 13, Lesson 9, pages 612–613. (437)

Part B Worksheet

Problem Solving: Application
Which solution makes the biggest bubbles?

Part B 13-9 WORKSHEET Math & Science

1:10 Solution	Diameter	Lifetime	Observations
Trial 1			
Trial 2			
Trial 3			
Trial 4			
Trial 5			
Average diameter:			
Average lifetime:			

1:20 Solution	Diameter	Lifetime	Observations
Trial 1			
Trial 2			
Trial 3			
Trial 4			
Trial 5			
Average diameter:			
Average lifetime:			

1. Which solution made the biggest bubbles? Explain.
   Answers may vary.
2. How do your results compare with your hypothesis? Were you surprised? Explain.
   Answers may vary.
3. Compare your results with the results of some of your classmates. How do the results compare?
   Answers may vary.

Use with Grade 5, Chapter 13, Lesson 9, pages 612–613. (438)

Chapter 14 ~ Lesson 1

Practice

Explore the Meaning of Percent

P 14-1 PRACTICE

Write a fraction, a decimal, a ratio, and a percent to show the shaded part of each grid. For each fraction, use simplest form.

1. 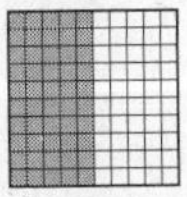
$\frac{1}{2}$, 0.50, 50:100, 50%

2. 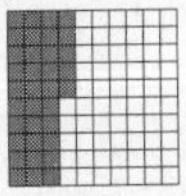
$\frac{7}{20}$, 0.35, 35:100, 35%

3. 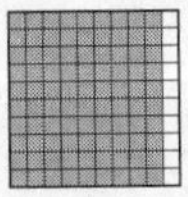
$\frac{9}{10}$, 0.90, 90:100, 90%

4. 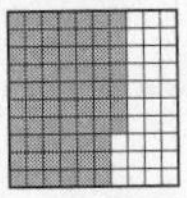
$\frac{67}{100}$, 0.67, 67:100, 67%

5. 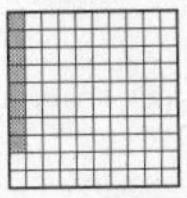
$\frac{2}{25}$, 0.08, 8:100, 8%

6. 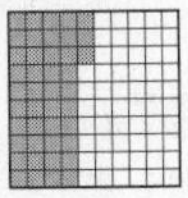
$\frac{43}{100}$, 0.43, 43:100, 43%

Write each fraction, decimal, or ratio as a percent.

7. $\frac{1}{4}$ 25%
8. $\frac{17}{100}$ 17%
9. $\frac{3}{10}$ 30%
10. $\frac{1}{2}$ 50%
11. 0.40 40%
12. 0.35 35%
13. 0.12 12%
14. 0.46 46%
15. 70:100 70%
16. 65:100 65%
17. 6:100 6%
18. 23:100 23%
19. $\frac{1}{10}$ 10%
20. 0.19 19%
21. 99:100 99%
22. $\frac{9}{100}$ 9%
23. 0.08 8%
24. $\frac{7}{10}$ 70%
25. 0.77 77%
26. 10:100 10%

Problem Solving

27. Three fourths of the shirts a store stocks are extra large. What percent of the shirts are extra large?
75%

28. Of the 100 shirts a store sold on Saturday, 82 had a sports-team logo on them. What percent of the shirts had a sports-team logo?
82%

Use with Grade 5, Chapter 14, Lesson 1, pages 628–629. (439)

Reteach

Explore the Meaning of Percent

R 14-1 RETEACH

You can think of a percent as:
- the numerator of a fraction with 100 as the denominator
- a hundredths decimal
- the ratio of a number to 100

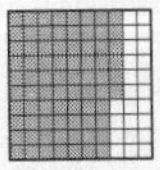

This grid contains 100 small squares, so each square represents 1%. 76 small squares are shaded.

Percent: 76 parts of 100, or 76%
Fraction: 76 parts of 100, or $\frac{76}{100}$. In simplest form, that's $\frac{19}{25}$.
Decimal: 76 hundredths, or 0.76
Ratio: 76 shaded squares to 100 total squares, or 76:100

Write a percent, a fraction, a decimal, and a ratio to show the shaded part of each grid. For each fraction, use simplest form.

1. 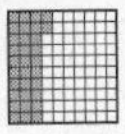
32 shaded parts / 100 total parts
Percent: 32%
Fraction: $\frac{8}{25}$
Decimal: 0.32
Ratio: 32:100

2. 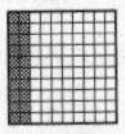
20 shaded parts / 100 total parts
Percent: 20%
Fraction: $\frac{1}{5}$
Decimal: 0.20 or 0.2
Ratio: 20:100

3. 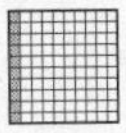
Percent: 10%
Fraction: $\frac{1}{10}$
Decimal: 0.10 or 0.1
Ratio: 10:100

4. 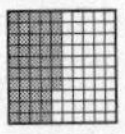
Percent: 47%
Fraction: $\frac{47}{100}$
Decimal: 0.47
Ratio: 47:100

Use with Grade 5, Chapter 14, Lesson 1, pages 628–629. (440)

Enrich

Explore the Meaning of Percent
Sporty Percents

E 14-1 ENRICH

One hundred fifth graders at Washington School participate in swimming, baseball, or soccer. Some students participate in more than one of these sports. The diagram below shows the number of students in each.

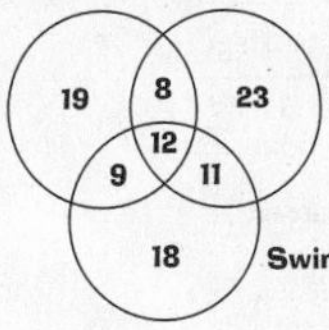

What percent of the 100 fifth graders participate in each of the following?

1. swimming
50%; 18 + 11 + 12 + 9 = 50; $\frac{50}{100}$ = 50%

2. baseball
48%; 19 + 12 + 9 + 8 = 48; $\frac{48}{100}$ = 48%

3. soccer
54%; 23 + 11 + 12 + 8 = 54; $\frac{54}{100}$ = 54%

4. swimming and baseball
21%; 12 + 9 = 21; $\frac{21}{100}$ = 21%

5. swimming and soccer
23%; 12 + 11 = 23; $\frac{23}{100}$ = 23%

6. exactly one sport
60%; 19 + 23 + 18 = 60; $\frac{60}{100}$ = 60%

7. soccer and baseball
20%; 8 + 12 = 20; $\frac{20}{100}$ = 20%

8. exactly two sports
28%; 8 + 9 + 11 = 28; $\frac{28}{100}$ = 28%

9. all three sports
12%; $\frac{12}{100}$ = 12%

10. baseball or soccer or both
82%; 19 + 23 + 8 + 12 + 9 + 11 = 82; $\frac{82}{100}$ = 82%

11. either baseball or swimming, but not both
56%; 19 + 18 + 8 + 11 = 56; $\frac{56}{100}$ = 56%

12. soccer or swimming or both
81%; 18 + 23 + 12 + 9 + 11 + 8 = 81; $\frac{81}{100}$ = 81%

Why isn't the sum of the percents of students for exercises 1–3 equal to 100%?
Some students participate in more than one sport, so they are included more than once in exercises 1–3.

Use with Grade 5, Chapter 14, Lesson 1, pages 628–629. (441)

Daily Homework

14-1 Explore the Meaning of Percent

Write each fraction, decimal, or ratio as a percent.

1. $\frac{1}{4}$ 25%
2. 0.40 40%
3. 50:100 50%
4. $\frac{36}{100}$ 36%
5. $\frac{6}{10}$ 60%
6. 0.73 73%
7. $\frac{2}{5}$ 40%
8. 0.14 14%
9. $\frac{9}{10}$ 90%

Solve.

10. A 10 × 10 grid has 54 squares shaded blue. What is the percent of squares that are shaded blue? 54%

11. In a survey, 5 out of 10 residents of Silo City say they are happy with the job that their mayor is doing. What is the percent of residents surveyed who are happy with the mayor? 50%

12. In a basket of 5 apples, 3 are red and 2 are yellow. What is the percent of apples that are red? 60%

Spiral Review

Find the area.

13. 

18 ft²

14. 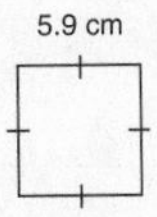

34.81 cm²

15. 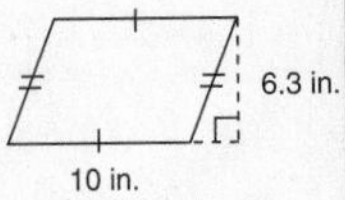

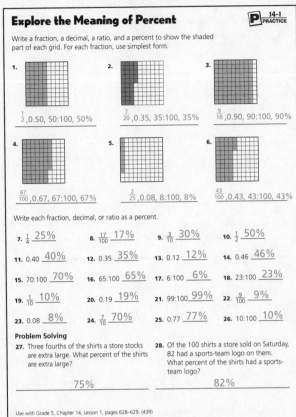

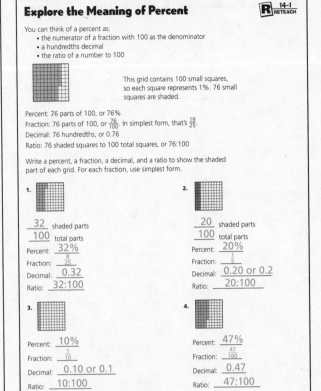

63 in.²

134 Grade 5, Chapter 14, Lesson 1, Cluster A

Chapter 14 ~ Lesson 2

Practice

Percents, Fractions, and Decimals

P 14-2 PRACTICE

Write each percent as a decimal and as a fraction in simplest form.

1. 34% 0.34, $\frac{17}{50}$
2. 70% 0.7, $\frac{7}{10}$
3. 48% 0.48, $\frac{12}{25}$
4. 25% 0.25, $\frac{1}{4}$
5. 7% 0.07, $\frac{7}{100}$
6. 45% 0.45, $\frac{9}{20}$
7. 12% 0.12, $\frac{3}{25}$
8. 54% 0.54, $\frac{27}{50}$
9. 91% 0.91, $\frac{91}{100}$
10. 95% 0.95, $\frac{19}{20}$
11. 32% 0.32, $\frac{8}{25}$
12. 82% 0.82, $\frac{41}{50}$
13. 57% 0.57, $\frac{57}{100}$
14. 24% 0.24, $\frac{6}{25}$
15. 30% 0.3, $\frac{3}{10}$
16. 18% 0.18, $\frac{9}{50}$
17. 72% 0.72, $\frac{18}{25}$
18. 88% 0.88, $\frac{22}{25}$
19. 60% 0.6, $\frac{3}{5}$
20. 22% 0.22, $\frac{11}{50}$
21. 96% 0.96, $\frac{24}{25}$
22. 9% 0.09, $\frac{9}{100}$
23. 35% 0.35, $\frac{7}{20}$
24. 61% 0.61, $\frac{61}{100}$

Write each fraction or decimal as a percent.

25. $\frac{3}{4}$ 75%
26. $\frac{2}{5}$ 40%
27. $\frac{1}{2}$ 50%
28. $\frac{7}{25}$ 28%
29. $\frac{11}{50}$ 22%
30. $\frac{1}{10}$ 10%
31. $\frac{17}{20}$ 85%
32. $\frac{3}{5}$ 60%
33. 0.75 75%
34. 0.2 20%
35. 0.88 88%
36. 0.03 3%
37. 0.16 16%
38. 0.99 99%
39. 0.85 85%
40. 0.4 40%

Find each missing number.

41. $29\% = \frac{s}{100}$ $s =$ 29
42. $80\% = \frac{w}{5}$ $w =$ 4
43. $44\% = \frac{c}{25}$ $c =$ 11
44. $90\% = \frac{a}{10}$ $a =$ 9

Problem Solving

45. A basketball team won 0.8 of its games. What percent of its games did the team win? 80%

46. A basketball player made 23 out of 25 free throws. What percent of his free throws did the player make? 92%

Use with Grade 5, Chapter 14, Lesson 2, pages 630–633. (442)

Reteach

Percents, Fractions, and Decimals

R 14-2 RETEACH

You can write percents as fractions and decimals. Write 35% as a fraction in simplest form.
Write a fraction with a denominator of 100. Simplify the fraction.

$35\% = \frac{35}{100}$ $\qquad \frac{35}{100} = \frac{35 \div 5}{100 \div 5} = \frac{7}{20}$

$35\% = \frac{7}{20}$

Write 35% as a decimal.
Write a fraction with a denominator of 100. Read the fraction. Then write the decimal.

$35\% = \frac{35}{100}$ $\qquad \frac{35}{100}$ = 35 hundredths = 0.35

35% = 0.35

You can also write fractions and decimals as percents.
Write $\frac{12}{25}$ as a percent.

Write an equivalent fraction with a denominator of 100.

$\frac{12}{25} = \frac{12 \times 4}{25 \times 4} = \frac{48}{100}$

$\frac{12}{25} = 48\%$

Write the numerator of the fraction with a percent sign.

$\frac{48}{100} = 48\%$

Write 0.64 as a percent.

Read the decimal. Write the fraction.

0.64 = 64 hundredths = $\frac{64}{100}$

0.64 = 64%

Write the numerator of the fraction with a percent sign.

$\frac{64}{100} = 64\%$

Write the percent as a fraction in simplest form.

1. $25\% = \frac{25}{100} = \frac{1}{4}$
2. $40\% = \frac{40}{100} = \frac{2}{5}$
3. $56\% = \frac{56}{100} = \frac{14}{25}$

Write the percent as a decimal.

4. $70\% = \frac{70}{100} =$ 0.70, or 0.7
5. $93\% = \frac{93}{100} =$ 0.93
6. $3\% = \frac{3}{100} =$ 0.03

Write the fraction as a percent.

7. $\frac{1}{4} = \frac{25}{100} =$ 25%
8. $\frac{9}{10} = \frac{90}{100} =$ 90%
9. $\frac{11}{20} = \frac{55}{100} =$ 55%

Write the decimal as a percent.

10. $0.95 = \frac{95}{100} =$ 95%
11. $0.51 = \frac{51}{100} =$ 51%
12. $0.04 = \frac{4}{100} =$ 4%

Use with Grade 5, Chapter 14, Lesson 2, pages 630–633. (443)

Enrich

Percents, Fractions, and Decimals

E 14-2 ENRICH

Mixed-Up Triplet

Each set of three numbers includes a fraction, a decimal, and a percent.
Circle the letter of the number that is not equal to the other two.

1. K. $\frac{11}{20}$ (I.) 0.5 D. 55%
2. A. 0.25 G. $\frac{1}{4}$ (T.) 40%
3. (A.) 76% W. 0.95 S. $\frac{19}{20}$
4. T. 0.05 P. 5% (C.) $\frac{1}{5}$
5. T. $\frac{2}{5}$ (O.) 0.04 Z. 40%
6. (C.) $\frac{18}{50}$ L. 0.18 H. 18%
7. I. 8% E. 0.08 (N.) $\frac{4}{5}$
8. S. 0.5 (M.) 5% B. $\frac{1}{2}$
9. (M.) 0.03 O. $\frac{3}{10}$ X. 30%
10. Q. $\frac{12}{25}$ D. 0.48 (U.) 24%
11. (T.) 0.41 C. 82% W. $\frac{41}{50}$
12. (S.) $\frac{3}{5}$ F. 75% Y. 0.75
13. (E.) 1.0% B. 0.1 V. $\frac{1}{10}$
14. U. 66% A. 0.66 (H.) $\frac{3}{5}$
15. N. 68% R. $\frac{17}{25}$ (S.) 0.85
16. (T.) 0.28 M. $\frac{7}{20}$ C. 35%
17. J. 0.7 (A.) $\frac{1}{7}$ E. 70%

Write each circled letter above the problem number to find an important message.

M	A	T	H	E	M	A	T	I	C	S
8	17	2	14	13	9	3	11	1	4	15

C	O	U	N	T	S	!
6	5	10	7	16	12	

Use with Grade 5, Chapter 14, Lesson 2, pages 630–633. (444)

Daily Homework

14-2 Percents, Fractions, and Decimals

Write each percent as a decimal and as a fraction in simplest form.

1. 20% 0.2; $\frac{1}{5}$
2. 70% 0.7; $\frac{7}{10}$
3. 35% 0.35; $\frac{7}{20}$
4. 55% 0.55; $\frac{11}{20}$
5. 25% 0.25; $\frac{1}{4}$
6. 30% 0.3; $\frac{3}{10}$
7. 90% 0.9; $\frac{9}{10}$
8. 47% 0.47; $\frac{47}{100}$
9. 63 % 0.63; $\frac{63}{100}$

Write each fraction or decimal as a percent.

10. $\frac{2}{5}$ 40%
11. 0.24 24%
12. $\frac{6}{10}$ 60%
13. 0.76 76%
14. $\frac{1}{2}$ 50%
15. 0.51 51%
16. $\frac{3}{4}$ 75%
17. $\frac{81}{100}$ 81%
18. 0.93 93%

Problem Solving

19. Colin takes 10 of his paintings to an art show and sells 2 of them. How can you write this number as a percent? 20%

20. Greta takes 20 shots during a basketball game and makes 11 of them. How can you write this number as a percent? 55%

Spiral Review

Find each unit rate.

21. \$3.60 for 5 lb = \$0.72 for 1 lb
22. 264 seats in 8 rows = 33 seats in 1 row
23. \$34.95 for 5 books = \$6.99 for 1 book
24. 110 mi in 2 hours = 55 in 1 hour
25. 176 mi on 8 gal = 22 mi on 1 gal

Grade 5, Chapter 14, Lesson 2, Cluster A 135

Chapter 14 ~ Lesson 3

Practice

More About Percents

P 14-3 PRACTICE

Write each percent as a decimal and as a mixed number in simplest form, or as a whole number.

1. 450% 4.5, $4\frac{1}{2}$
2. 225% 2.25, $2\frac{1}{4}$
3. 300% 3
4. 140% 1.4, $1\frac{2}{5}$
5. 590% 5.9, $5\frac{9}{10}$
6. 420% 4.2, $4\frac{1}{5}$
7. 260% 2.6, $2\frac{3}{5}$
8. 950% 9.5, $9\frac{1}{2}$
9. 175% 1.75, $1\frac{3}{4}$
10. 525% 5.25, $5\frac{1}{4}$
11. 280% 2.8, $2\frac{4}{5}$
12. 340% 3.4, $3\frac{2}{5}$
13. 800% 8
14. 110% 1.1, $1\frac{1}{10}$
15. 650% 6.5, $6\frac{1}{2}$
16. 775% 7.75, $7\frac{3}{4}$
17. 365% 3.65, $3\frac{13}{20}$
18. 980% 9.8, $9\frac{4}{5}$

Write each percent as a decimal and as a fraction in simplest form.

19. 37.5% 0.375, $\frac{3}{8}$
20. 49.6% 0.496, $\frac{62}{125}$
21. 12.5% 0.125, $\frac{1}{8}$
22. 6.5% 0.065, $\frac{13}{200}$
23. 45% 0.45, $\frac{9}{20}$
24. 31.5% 0.315, $\frac{63}{200}$
25. 35.5% 0.355, $\frac{71}{200}$
26. 29.6% 0.296, $\frac{37}{125}$
27. 57% 0.57, $\frac{57}{100}$
28. 43.5% 0.435, $\frac{87}{200}$
29. 87.5% 0.875, $\frac{7}{8}$
30. 43.2% 0.432, $\frac{54}{125}$
31. 14.5% 0.145, $\frac{29}{200}$
32. 38.4% 0.384, $\frac{48}{125}$
33. 64% 0.64, $\frac{16}{25}$

Find each missing number.

34. 245% = 2.[4]5
35. 30% = 0.[3]
36. 94.5% = [0].945
37. 67% = 0.6[7]
38. 52.5% = 0.[5]25
39. 880% = 8.[8]
40. 20.2% = 0.2[0]2
41. 500% = [5]
42. 71.3% = 0.71[3]

Problem Solving

43. A softball player got hits in 37.5% of her at bats. Write a decimal to represent her batting average.
0.375

44. This year a baseball team increased its wins by 130% over last year. Write a decimal to show how many times more wins the team had this year than last.
1.3

Use with Grade 5, Chapter 14, Lesson 3, pages 634–637. (445)

Reteach

More About Percents

R 14-3 RETEACH

You can write percents greater than 100% as decimals and mixed numbers. Write 620% as a decimal.

Write a fraction with a denominator of 100. Rewrite as a mixed number.

$620\% = \frac{620}{100} = 6\frac{20}{100}$

620% = 6.20, or 6.2

Read the mixed number. Then write the decimal.

$\frac{620}{100}$ = 6 and 20 hundredths =

6.20, or 6.2

Write 620% as a mixed number in simplest form. Write a fraction with a denominator of 100.

$620\% = \frac{620}{100}$

Simplify the fraction.

$620 = 6\frac{20}{100} = 6\frac{20 \div 20}{100 \div 20} = 6\frac{1}{5}$

You can write percents that include decimals as decimals and fractions. Write 76.5% as a decimal.

Write a fraction with a denominator of 100. Write an equivalent fraction with a whole number numerator.

$76.5\% = \frac{76.5}{100} = \frac{76.5 \times 10}{100 \times 10} = \frac{765}{1{,}000}$

76.5% = 0.765

Read the fraction. Then write the decimal.

$\frac{765}{1{,}000}$ = 765 thousandths = 0.765

Write 76.5% as a fraction with a whole number numerator.

$76.5\% = \frac{76.5}{100} = \frac{76.5 \times 10}{100 \times 10} = \frac{765}{1{,}000}$

$76.5\% = \frac{153}{200}$

Simplify the fraction.

$\frac{765}{1{,}000} = \frac{765 \div 5}{1{,}000 \div 5} = \frac{153}{200}$

Write the percent as a fraction or mixed number and as a decimal.

1. 625% = $6\frac{25}{100}$ = 6.25
2. 850% = $8\frac{50}{100}$ = 8.5
3. 23.5% = $\frac{235}{1{,}000}$ = 0.235
4. 46.8% = $\frac{468}{1{,}000}$ = 0.468

Write the percent as a mixed number or fraction in simplest form.

5. 540% = $5\frac{40}{100}$ = $5\frac{2}{5}$
6. 145% = $1\frac{45}{100}$ = $1\frac{9}{20}$
7. 63.5% = $\frac{635}{1{,}000}$ = $\frac{127}{200}$
8. 16.2% = $\frac{162}{1{,}000}$ = $\frac{81}{500}$

Use with Grade 5, Chapter 14, Lesson 3, pages 634–637. (446)

Enrich

More About Percents

E 14-3 ENRICH

Greater Percent Game

Play this game with a partner. Take turns.

Materials: two number cubes

You are each writing a book.

- Toss both number cubes.
- Find the product of the numbers tossed. This represents the percent of the book that you have written.
- Record this percent with its equivalent fraction and decimal in the table.
- Repeat. Keep a running total of your percents, fractions, and decimals.
- The first player to reach 100 percent has completed writing the book and is the winner.

Player 1

Product	Percent	Fraction	Decimal
TOTAL			

Player 2

Product	Percent	Fraction	Decimal
TOTAL			

Use with Grade 5, Chapter 14, Lesson 3, pages 634–637. (447)

Daily Homework

14-3 More About Percents

Write each percent as a decimal and as a mixed number in simplest form, or as a whole number.

1. 125% 1.25; $1\frac{1}{4}$
2. 300% 3
3. 240% 2.4; $2\frac{2}{5}$
4. 500% 5
5. 370% 3.7; $3\frac{7}{10}$
6. 425% 4.25; $4\frac{1}{4}$
7. 950% 9.5; $9\frac{1}{2}$
8. 800% 8
9. 680% 6.8; $6\frac{4}{5}$

Write each percent as a decimal and as a fraction in simplest form.

10. 32% 0.32; $\frac{8}{25}$
11. 60% 0.6; $\frac{3}{5}$
12. 36% 0.36; $\frac{18}{50}$
13. 21% 0.21; $\frac{21}{100}$
14. 56% 0.56; $\frac{14}{25}$
15. 84% 0.84; $\frac{21}{25}$
16. 37.5% 0.375; $\frac{3}{8}$
17. 74% 0.74; $\frac{37}{50}$
18. 15% 0.15; $\frac{3}{20}$

Problem Solving

19. Of the 8 houses on Danny's street, only 1 is painted blue, for a ratio of 1:8. Write this ratio as a percent and as a fraction in simplest form.
12.5%; $\frac{1}{8}$

20. Over the last 20 years, the population of Cactusville has grown by 225%. Write this percent as a decimal and as a mixed number in simplest form.
2.25; $2\frac{1}{4}$

Spiral Review

Solve.

21. $\frac{q}{8} + 13 = 120$ $q = 856$
22. $2r + 4 = {}^-10$ $r = {}^-7$
23. $3s - 50 = {}^-5$ $s = 15$
24. $\frac{t}{10} + 8 = 11$ $t = 30$

Chapter 14 ~ Lesson 4

Practice

Problem Solving: Reading for Math

Represent Numbers

P 14-4 PRACTICE — Reading Skill

Explain which numbers you would compare to solve each problem. Then solve the problem.

1. Monica plays forward on her soccer team. Last year, 0.30 of her shots scored goals. This year, she made 16 goals out of 40. Did Monica improve her record this year? Explain.
   Yes; 16 out of 40 is 0.40 and 0.40 is better than 0.30.
2. Brian plays tournament Ping-Pong. Last year, he won 72 percent of his games. This year, he has won 15 of his 20 games. Has Brian improved his record? Explain.
   Yes; $\frac{15}{20}$ = 75% and 75% is better than 72%.
3. Jessica swam on a swim team last year. She placed first 12 times out of 20 in the breaststroke. This year, she has placed first 55 percent of the time. Was Jessica's record of winning better last year or this year? Explain.
   Last year; 12 out of 20 = 60% and 60% > 55%, so Jessica's record was better last year.
4. Anja competes in chess tournaments. Last year, she won 12 of her 15 tournament games. This year, she has won 68% of her games. Was her record better this year or last year? Explain.
   Last year; 12 out of 15 = 80%, so her record was better last year.
5. Elisa's family got a pool table two months ago. The first month, 0.12 of the shots she tried went in. This month, she made 120 out of 500 shots. Is Elisa's game improving? Explain.
   Yes; 120 out of 500 = 0.24, so her game is improving.
6. Peter's class is doing timed division tests. Last month, Peter was able to correctly complete 66 percent of the problems. This month, he is able to correctly complete 60 out of 80 problems. Has Peter improved his score? Explain.
   Yes; 60 out of 80 = 75%, so his score is improving.

Use with Grade 5, Chapter 14, Lesson 4, pages 638–639. (448)

Practice

Problem Solving: Reading for Math

Represent Numbers

P 14-4 PRACTICE — Math Skills Test Prep

Choose the correct answer.

Of the students on the swim team, 0.68 were able to finish their practice laps in 15 minutes. So, 32 percent of the team took more than 15 minutes to complete their practice laps.

1. Which of the following statements is true?
   - A Only half of the students completed the practice laps in 15 minutes.
   - (B) Of the students on the team, $\frac{8}{25}$ did not complete the practice laps in 15 minutes.
   - C Only students who swim the laps in 15 minutes can be on the swim team.
   - D About 40% of the team could not swim the laps in 15 minutes.
2. When comparing a decimal and a percent
   - F never use fractions.
   - G always use percents.
   - H you should not compare a decimal and a percent.
   - (J) use the same representation for both.

Of the actors trying out for a community theater play, 24 percent were from out of town. So, $\frac{19}{25}$ of the actors were local actors.

3. Which of the following statements is true?
   - A Of the actors trying out for the play, $\frac{2}{3}$ were local actors.
   - B There were fewer local actors than out-of-town actors.
   - (C) Of the actors, 0.76 were local actors.
   - D All of the actors got roles in the play.
4. Which of the following is an example of using the same representation to compare amounts?
   - F Compare decimals with fractions.
   - G Compare percents with decimals.
   - (H) Compare fractions with fractions.
   - J Never compare amounts.

Of the students in the band, 92 percent come to practice regularly. So, 0.08 do not come to practice regularly.

5. Which of the following statements is NOT true?
   - A More students come to practice regularly than do not.
   - B Of the band members, $\frac{23}{25}$ come to practice regularly.
   - (C) Of the band members, $\frac{8}{10}$ do not come to practice regularly.
   - D Of the band members, $\frac{46}{50}$ come to practice regularly.
6. When comparing a fraction and a decimal
   - (F) write both amounts using the same representation.
   - G never use fractions.
   - H never use percents.
   - J always use percents.

Use with Grade 5, Chapter 14, Lesson 4, pages 638–639. (449)

Practice

Problem Solving: Reading for Math

Represent Numbers

P 14-4 PRACTICE — Math Skills Test Prep

Choose the correct answer.

In Bill's class, 82 percent of the students finished a timed test. So, $\frac{18}{100}$ did not finish the test on time.

7. Which of the following statements is true?
   - A There are 100 students in Bill's class.
   - B Of the students in the class, about $\frac{1}{4}$ did not finish the test.
   - C Of the students in the class, $\frac{9}{10}$ did not finish the test.
   - (D) Of the students in the class, 0.82 finished the test.
8. When comparing a percent and a fraction
   - F you cannot compare a fraction and a percent.
   - G always use percents.
   - H do not change the percent to a fraction.
   - (J) write both the fraction and the percent using the same representation.

Solve.

9. A survey at Albion Elementary School asked fifth graders to select their favorite kind of pizza. Of the students surveyed, 42 percent chose cheese, 0.23 chose sausage, and $\frac{7}{20}$ chose pepperoni. How would you list the favorite kinds of pizza from greatest to least number of responses?
   cheese, pepperoni, sausage
10. In Ms. Williams class, 24 percent of the students have lived in the same town all their lives, 0.46 have moved within the state, and $\frac{9}{30}$ have moved from out of the state. Which category has the greatest number of students? the least?
    greatest: 0.46, within the state; least: 24%, same town
11. Last year, a pediatrician vaccinated 47 percent of his patients to prevent chicken pox. This year, he vaccinated 33 out of 75 patients. Did he vaccinate a greater percent of patients this year or last year? Explain.
    last year; 33 out of 75 is 44% and 44% < 47%.
12. Last year, Jefferson made 21% of his free throws in basketball. This year, he has made 12 out of 48 of his free throws. Did Jefferson improve his record? Explain.
    Yes; this year he made 25% of his free throws.

Use with Grade 5, Chapter 14, Lesson 4, pages 638–639. (450)

Daily Homework

14-4 Problem Solving: Reading for Math

Represent Numbers

Solve.

1. A survey asks customers of the Super Grocery Center what their favorite fruits are. Of the people surveyed, $\frac{1}{4}$ say apples, 28% say bananas, 0.29 say oranges, and 18% say mangoes. How would you list these fruits from least to greatest number of responses?
   mangoes, apples, bananas, oranges
2. Did more than $\frac{1}{8}$ of those surveyed say mangoes are their favorite fruit?
   Yes
3. Charles is working to improve his free-throw shooting in basketball. In the first game of the season, he shoots 40% from the free-throw line. By the last game of the season, he makes 8 of the 10 free throws he attempts. Does he improve his shooting?
   Yes; by the end of the season, he makes 80% of his free throws.

Use data from the table for problems 4–7.

1860 Presidential Election Results

Candidate	Percent of Popular Vote
Stephen Douglas	29%
John Breckinridge	18%
Abraham Lincoln	40%
John Bell	13%

4. Of the four candidates listed, which one received the most popular votes?
   Abraham Lincoln
5. Who received more popular votes, John Breckinridge or John Bell?
   John Breckinridge
6. List the candidates from most popular votes to least.
   Abraham Lincoln, Stephen Douglas, John Breckinridge, John Bell
7. Write Lincoln's percent of the popular vote as a decimal and as a fraction in its simplest form.
   0.4; $\frac{2}{5}$

Spiral Review

8. 6.27 − 0.88 = 5.39
9. 1.45 + 17.2 = 18.65
10. 4.68 × 3.1 = 14.508

Grade 5, Chapter 14, Lesson 4, Cluster A 137

Chapter 14 ~ Lesson 5

Practice

Percent of a Number

P 14-5 PRACTICE

Find the percent of each number.

1. 25% of 48 __12__
2. 30% of 50 __15__
3. 10% of 50 __5__
4. 45% of 40 __18__
5. 50% of 64 __32__
6. 20% of 85 __17__
7. 40% of 60 __24__
8. 95% of 80 __76__
9. 65% of 60 __39__
10. 10% of $12.00 __$1.20__
11. 60% of $4.00 __$2.40__
12. 35% of $20.00 __$7.00__
13. 75% of $6.00 __$4.50__
14. 30% of $15.00 __$4.50__
15. 80% of $10.00 __$8.00__
16. 15% of $30.00 __$4.50__
17. 85% of $16.00 __$13.60__
18. 5% of $30.00 __$1.50__
19. 120% of 50 __60__
20. 150% of 64 __96__
21. 125% of 60 __75__
22. 190% of 70 __133__
23. 130% of 60 __78__
24. 225% of 40 __90__
25. 140% of $8.00 __$11.20__
26. 120% of $7.00 __$8.40__
27. 180% of $5.00 __$9.00__
28. 225% of 84 __189__
29. 55% of $7.00 __$3.85__
30. 150% of $15.00 __$22.50__

Find each missing number.

31. [10]% of 90 = 9
32. 20% of [25] = 5
33. [25]% of 40 = 10
34. 10% of [70] = 7
35. [20]% of 60 = 12
36. [50]% of 80 = 40

Problem Solving

37. Students at Rockhill School pay 25% of the adult ticket price to attend ball games. An adult ticket costs $3.00. How much does each student pay?
__$0.75__

38. The Rockhill School football team won 80% of its 10 games. The basketball team won 45% of its 20 games. Which team won more games? Explain.
__The basketball team; 80% of 10 = 8; 45% of 20 = 9__

Use with Grade 5, Chapter 14, Lesson 5, pages 642–645. (451)

Reteach

Percent of a Number

R 14-5 RETEACH

To find the percent of a number, write the percent as a fraction or decimal and multiply. Remember, "of" means "times."

Find 40% of 20.
$40\% = \frac{40}{100} = \frac{2}{5}$
$\frac{2}{5} \times 20 = 8$
40% of 20 = 8

Find 60% of $9.00.
$60\% = \frac{60}{100} = 0.60$, or 0.6
$0.6 \times \$9.00 = \$5.40$
60% of $9.00 = $5.40

Find 140% of 20.
$140\% = \frac{140}{100} = \frac{7}{5}$
$\frac{7}{5} \times 20 = 28$
140% of 20 = 28

Find 160% of $9.00.
$160\% = \frac{160}{100} = 1\frac{60}{100} = 1.60$, or 1.6
$1.6 \times \$9.00 = \$14.40$
160% of $9.00 = $14.40

Find the percent of each number.

1. 25% of 24
$25\% = \frac{25}{100} = \frac{1}{4}$
$\frac{1}{4} \times 24 =$ __6__

2. 30% of 70
$30\% = \frac{30}{100} = \frac{3}{10}$
$\frac{3}{10} \times 70 =$ __21__

3. 150% of 38
$150\% = \frac{150}{100} = \frac{3}{2}$
$\frac{3}{2} \times 38 =$ __57__

4. 140% of 40 __56__
5. 75% of 84 __63__
6. 110% of 90 __99__

7. 50% of $8.00
$50\% = \frac{50}{100} =$ __0.50, or 0.5__
0.__5__ × $8.00 = __$4.00__

8. 120% of $20.00
$120\% = \frac{120}{100} =$ __1.2__
__1.2__ × $20.00 = __$24.00__

9. 25% of $11.00
$25\% = \frac{25}{100} =$ __0.25__
__0.25__ × $11.00 = __$2.75__

10. 80% of $14.00 __$11.20__
11. 250% of $16.00 = __$40.00__
12. 175% of $10.00 __$17.50__

Use with Grade 5, Chapter 14, Lesson 5, pages 642–645. (452)

Enrich

Percent of a Number
Percent Maze

E 14-5 ENRICH

Find your way from Start to Finish by moving to a neighboring space with the next greater value.

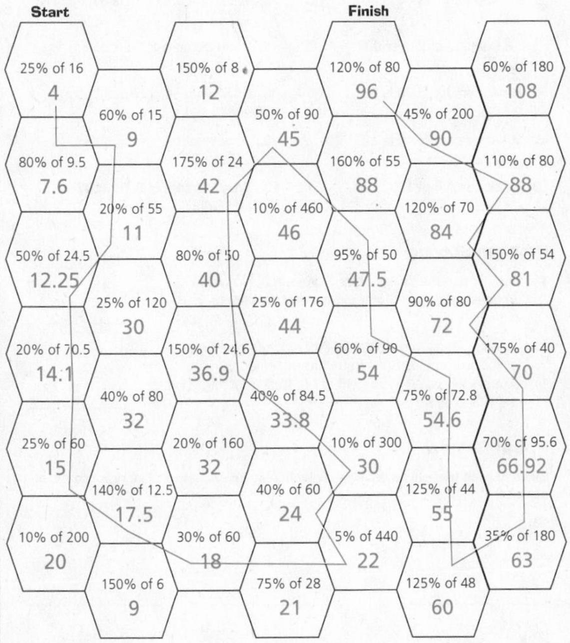

Use with Grade 5, Chapter 14, Lesson 5, pages 642–645. (453)

Daily Homework

14-5 Percent of a Number

Find the percent of each number.

1. 40% of 60 __24__
2. 50% of 90 __45__
3. 10% of 50 __5__
4. 300% of 40 __120__
5. 20% of 20 __4__
6. 80% of 70 __56__
7. 25% of 64 __16__
8. 150% of 50 __75__
9. 210% of 80 __168__
10. 35% of 60 __21__
11. 75% of 120 __90__
12. 40% of 70 __28__
13. 40% of $7.00 __$2.80__
14. 15% of $4.00 __$0.60__
15. 35% of $6.00 __$2.10__
16. 250% of $3.00 __$7.50__
17. 20% of $6.00 __$1.20__
18. 200% of $0.40 __$0.80__
19. 80% of $1.00 __$0.80__
20. 110% of $0.70 __$0.77__

Problem Solving

21. Of the 60 students who sign up for basketball, 65% say that they have played the game before. How many students say that they have played basketball before? __39 students__
22. Of the 28 students who sign up for softball, 25% want to be pitchers. How many want to be pitchers? __7 students__

Spiral Review

23. 43 students in 2 buses = __172__ students in 8 buses
24. 15 mi in 12 min = __75__ mi in 1 h
25. 6 pies for $21.60 = __15__ pies for $54.00
26. 32 oz in 2 qt = __256__ oz in 4 gal
27. 17 rabbits in 3 cages = __68__ rabbits in 12 cages
28. 5 doz egg whites in 6 cakes = __80__ egg whites in 8 cakes

138 Grade 5, Chapter 14, Lesson 5, Cluster B

Chapter 14 ~ Lesson 6

Practice

Percent One Number Is of Another

P 14-6 PRACTICE

Find the percent each number is of another. Round to the nearest whole percent, if necessary.

1. What percent of 60 is 48? 80%
2. 24 is what percent of 40? 60%
3. What percent of 32 is 16? 50%
4. 15 is what percent of 20? 75%
5. 33 is what % of 60? 55%
6. What percent of 96 is 64? 67%
7. 24 is what percent of 80? 30%
8. What percent of 65 is 52? 80%
9. 21 is what percent of 60? 35%
10. 45 is what percent of 81? 56%
11. What percent of 18 is 6? 33%
12. What percent of 85 is 13? 15%
13. 60 is what percent of 40? 150%
14. 100 is what percent of 50? 200%
15. What percent of 60 is 72? 120%
16. 50 is what percent of 40? 125%
17. What percent of 80 is 200? 250%
18. What percent of 30 is 48? 160%
19. 35 is what percent of 20? 175%
20. What percent of 50 is 90? 180%
21. 56 is what percent of 40? 140%
22. What percent of 36 is 81? 225%
23. What percent of 70 is 77? 110%
24. 75 is what percent of 50? 150%
25. 15 is what percent of 300? 5%
26. What percent of 80 is 100? 125%

Compare. Use <, >, or =

27. 30% of 40 (<) 40% of 40
28. 100% of 30 (=) 50% of 60
29. 75% of 36 (>) 75% of 32
30. 7% of 50 (<) 8% of 50

Problem Solving

31. A football team won 12 of its 16 games one season. What percent of its games did it win? 75%

32. Last year a football team won 10 games. This year it won 15 games. What percent of last year's games did it win this year? 150%

Use with Grade 5, Chapter 14, Lesson 6, pages 646–649. (454)

Reteach

Percent One Number Is of Another

R 14-6 RETEACH

You can use models and fractions to help you think about what percent one number is of another.

What percent of 30 is 12?

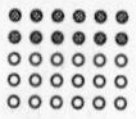

The part of this model that is shaded is 12 counters.

The whole model contains 30 counters.

Write a fraction to describe the shaded part of the model. part → 12 / whole → 30

Write the fraction as a percent. $\frac{12}{30} = \frac{4}{10} = \frac{40}{100} = 40\%$

12 is 40% of 30.

Find the percent each number is of the other. Shade the model to help you solve each problem.

1. What percent of 18 is 9?

part → 9 / whole → 18 = 50%

2. 6 is what percent of 20?

part → 6 / whole → 20 = 30%

3. 24 is what percent of 32?

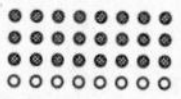

part → 24 / whole → 32 = 75%

4. What percent of 25 is 12?

part → 12 / whole → 25 = 48%

Find the percent each number is of the other.

5. What percent of 60 is 15? 25%
6. 32 is what percent of 40? 80%
7. 3 is what percent of 30? 10%
8. What percent of 50 is 30? 60%

Use with Grade 5, Chapter 14, Lesson 6, pages 646–649. (455)

Enrich

Percent One Number Is of Another
Shaded Grids

E 14-6 ENRICH

Find the percent of each area that is shaded.

1. 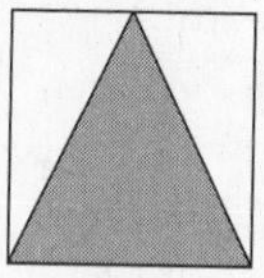 50%
2.  75%
3. 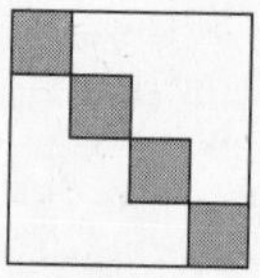 25%
4. 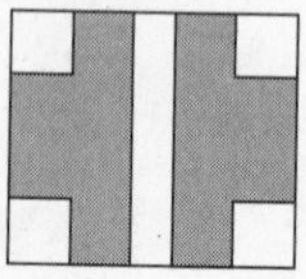 60%
5. 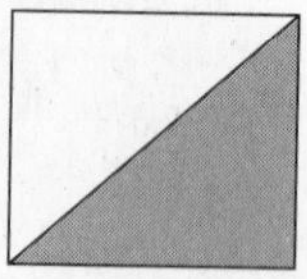 50%
6. 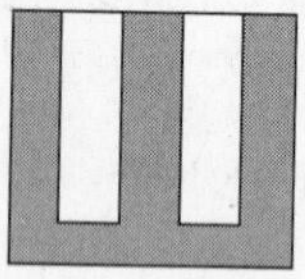 70%
7. 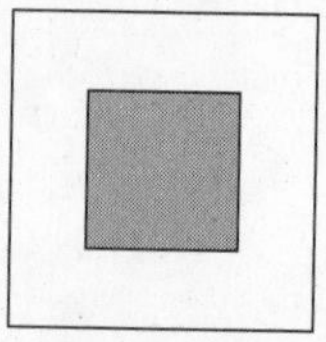 36%
8. 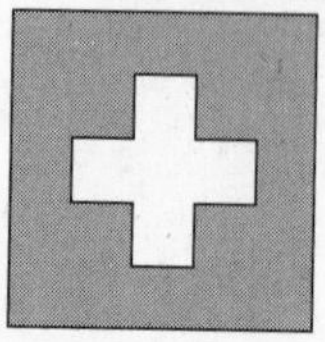 80%
9. 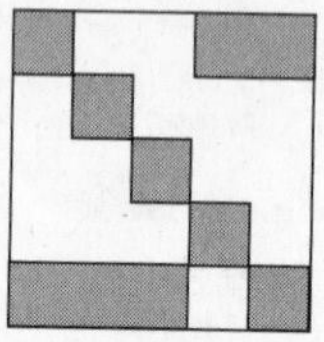 40%

Find the percent.

10. There are 36 squares in a grid. 18 of the squares are shaded. What percent of the squares are not shaded? 50%

11. There are 64 squares in a grid. 16 of the squares are shaded. What percent of the squares are not shaded? 75%

Use with Grade 5, Chapter 14, Lesson 6, pages 646–649. (456)

Daily Homework

14-6 Percent That One Number Is of Another

Find the percent each number is of the other. Round to the nearest whole number percent, if necessary.

1. What percent of 80 is 20? 25%
2. What percent of 30 is 9? 30%
3. 18 is what percent of 90? 20%
4. What percent of 50 is 35? 70%
5. What percent of 70 is 56? 80%
6. 81 is what percent of 90? 90%
7. What percent of 40 is 22? 55%
8. 90 is what percent of 60? 150%
9. What percent of 120 is 30? 25%
10. What percent of 80 is 160? 200%

Problem Solving

11. Asa goes to the store to buy 5 grapefruit. He winds up buying a bag of 6 grapefruit. What percent of 5 is 6? 120%

12. Celeste needs to collect 40 different kinds of leaves for a class project. So far, she has collected 32 different kinds. What percent of her total goal has she collected so far? 80%

Spiral Review

Classify each triangle as equilateral, isosceles, or scalene and as right, acute, or obtuse.

13. 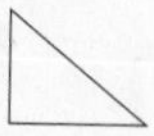 right isosceles
14. 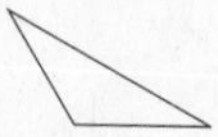 obtuse isosceles
15. 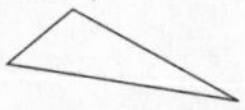 acute scalene

Grade 5, Chapter 14, Lesson 6, Cluster B 139

Chapter 14 ~ Lesson 7

Practice

Problem Solving: Strategy
Logical Reasoning

P 14-7 PRACTICE

Use a Venn diagram to solve each problem.

1. Of 26 people surveyed, 19 said they go to basketball games and 12 said they go to football games. Five of the people said they go to both. How many people said they go to basketball games, but not football games?

   14 people

2. **Music** Of 40 teachers surveyed, 34 said they listen to classical music and 17 said they listen to opera. Eleven of the teachers said they listen to both classical music and opera. How many teachers listen to classical music, but not opera?

   23 teachers

3. Of 24 students surveyed, 17 students said they liked board games and 12 said they like card games. Five students said they liked both. How many students said they like board games, but not card games?

   12 students

4. **Health** Of the 50 people surveyed at a recreation center, 32 said they used the basketball courts and 24 said they used the racquetball courts. Six of the people said they used both courts. How many people said they use the racquetball courts, but not the basketball courts?

   18 people

Mixed Strategy Review

Solve. Use any strategy.

5. Nathan wants to buy trading cards. Superstar packages cost $3.23 each and mixed packages cost $1.78 each. Nathan buys 7 packages and spends a total of $15.36. How many of each type of package did he buy?

   5 mixed and 2 superstar

   Strategy: Make a Table

6. An after-school club is building a clubhouse that is 8 feet by 6 feet. They are also including a trampoline with a radius of 4 feet. What is the total area of the clubhouse and the trampoline, to the nearest square foot?

   98 square feet

   Strategy: Solve a Simpler Problem

7. A band is performing on a rectangular stage that is 36 feet by 24 feet. They want to set up lights every 4 feet around the stage, including the corners. How many lights will they need?

   30 lights

   Strategy: Draw a Diagram

8. **Create a problem** for which you could use logical reasoning to solve. Share it with others.

   Check students' problems.

Use with Grade 5, Chapter 14, Lesson 7, pages 650–651. (457)

Reteach

Problem Solving: Strategy
Logical Reasoning

R 14-7 RETEACH

Page 651, Problem 1

Of 35 people surveyed, 28 said they go to baseball games and 14 said they go to hockey games. Seven of the people said they go to both. How many people said they go to hockey games, but not baseball games?

Step 1 Read

Be sure you understand the problem.
Read carefully.

What do you know?

- A total of 35 people were surveyed.
- Of those surveyed, 28 go to basketball games, 14 go to hockey games, and 7 go to both types of games.

What do you need to find?

- The number of people who go to hockey games, but not baseball games.

Step 2 Plan

- Find a Pattern
- Guess and Check
- Work Backward
- Make a Graph
- Make a Table
- Write an Equation
- Make an Organized List
- Draw a Diagram
- Solve a Simpler Problem
- Logical Reasoning

Make a plan.
Choose a strategy.

You can draw a Venn diagram to solve the problem.

One circle shows the number of people who go to baseball games. The other circle shows the number of people who go to hockey games. The overlapping part of the circles shows the number of people who go to both.

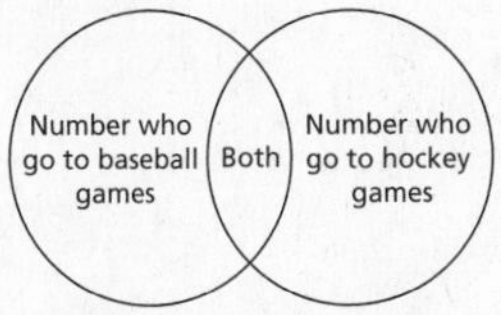

Use with Grade 5, Chapter 14, Lesson 7, pages 650–651. (458)

Reteach

Problem Solving: Strategy
Logical Reasoning

R 14-7 RETEACH

Step 3 Solve

Carry out your plan.

How many people go to both types of games? Write the number in the overlapping section of the Venn diagram.

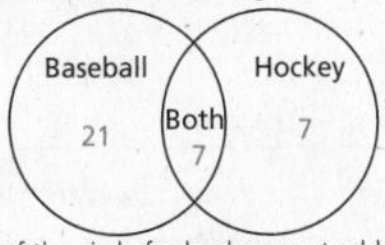

The two sections of the circle for hockey must add to 14. You can write and solve an equation to find the number of people who only go to hockey games.

Let x = the number of people who only go to hockey games

Use the Venn diagram. So, $x + 7 = 14$

Solve the equation and complete the Venn diagram. $x = 7$

How many people go to hockey games, but not baseball games? 7 people

Step 4 Look Back

Is the solution reasonable?
Reread the problem.

Have you answered the question? Yes

How can you check your answer?

Possible answer: Work backwards

Practice

1. Of 25 pet owners surveyed, 16 have a dog and 12 have a cat. Three people have both a cat and a dog. How many pet owners have only dogs?

   13 pet owners

2. Of 50 people surveyed at a movie theater, 38 buy popcorn and 24 buy a beverage. Twelve people said they buy both popcorn and a beverage. How many people buy popcorn only?

   26 people

Use with Grade 5, Chapter 14, Lesson 7, pages 650–651. (459)

Daily Homework

14-7 Problem Solving: Strategy
Use Logical Reasoning

Use a Venn diagram to solve each problem.

1. Of 28 students in Jean's class, 19 have signed up for volleyball and 12 have signed up for basketball. Three have signed up for both sports. How many students have signed up for volleyball but not basketball?

   16 students

2. Of 15 children in a neighborhood, 10 like to ride bicycles and 8 like to rollerblade. Three children like to do both. How many children like to rollerblade but don't like to ride bicycles?

   5 children

3. Of 55 students in the fifth grade, 43 are fans of the local basketball team and 35 are fans of the local hockey team. Twenty-three students are fans of both teams. How many students are fans of the hockey team but not the basketball team?

   12 students

4. Of 30 runners surveyed, 22 go running in the morning and 15 go running in the evening. Seven of the runners surveyed go running in both the morning and the evening. How many runners go running in the morning but not the evening?

   15 runners

Spiral Review

Complete the table. Then graph the function.
Check students' graphs.

5. $y = x + 3$

x	y
-4	-1
-2	1
0	3
2	5

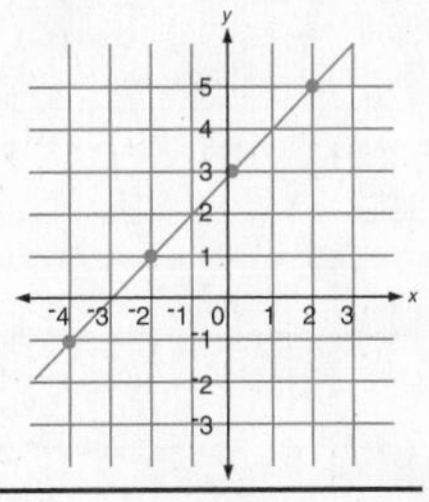

140 Grade 5, Chapter 14, Lesson 7, Cluster B

Chapter 14 ~ Lesson 8

Practice

Circle Graphs

P 14-8 PRACTICE

Use Data from the circle graph for problems 1–5.

1. List the activities from favorite to least favorite.
rollerblading, basketball, cycling, jumping rope

2. What fraction of the total votes did in-line skating get?
$\frac{2}{5}$ or equivalent

3. If 200 people were surveyed, how many people chose jumping rope?
30 people

4. If 140 people were surveyed, how many people chose basketball?
35 people

Favorite After-School Activity

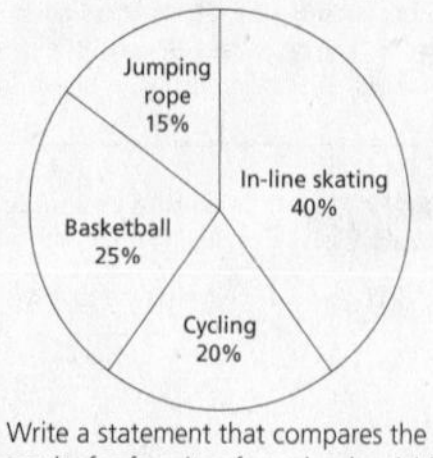

5. Write a statement that compares the results for favorite after-school activities.
Possible answer: Basketball received more votes than cycling.

Use data from the table for problems 6–8.

6. List the number of degrees you would use to make each part of a circle graph to show the data.

Baseball: 126°
Basketball: 108°
Football: 54°
Soccer: 72°

Sport	Percent of Total Responses
Baseball	35%
Basketball	30%
Football	15%
Soccer	20%

7. Make a circle graph at the right to show the data.

Favorite Spectator Sport

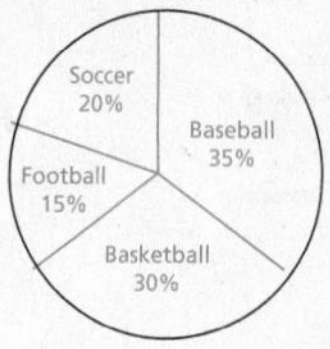

8. If 120 people were surveyed, how many named baseball as their favorite spectator sport?
42 people

Use with Grade 5, Chapter 14, Lesson 8, pages 652–655. (460)

Reteach

Circle Graphs

R 14-8 RETEACH

The table shows the results of a survey of 160 students. You can also display this data in a circle graph. Circle graphs are used to compare parts of a whole.

Favorite Family Activity	
Sport	Percent of Total Responses
Cycling	25%
Bowling	40%
In-line skating	35%

Find the measure of each angle to be drawn in the circle.

Percent written as a decimal ↓ — Degrees in a circle ↓

Cycling: 0.25 × 360° = 90°
Bowling: 0.40 × 360° = 144°
Rollerblading: 0.35 × 360° = 126°

Draw the angles in the circle. Then label the sections.

Favorite Family Sport

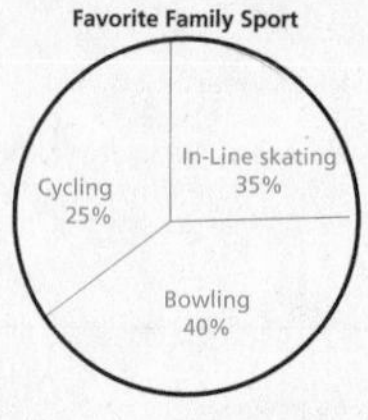

Find how many students named cycling.

Percent written as a decimal ↓ — Students surveyed ↓

0.25 × 160 = 40

40 students named cycling.

Use data from the table for problems 1–3.

Favorite Team Sport	
Sport	Percent of Total Responses
Basketball	35%
Baseball	40%
Soccer	25%

1. List the number of degrees in the measure of each angle you would draw in a circle graph to show the data.

Percent written as a decimal ↓ — Degrees in a circle ↓

Basketball: 0.35 × 360° = 126°
Baseball: 0.40 × 360° = 144°
Soccer: 0.25 × 360° = 90°

2. Draw the angles in the circle at the right to show the data. Label the sections of the graph.

Favorite Team Sport

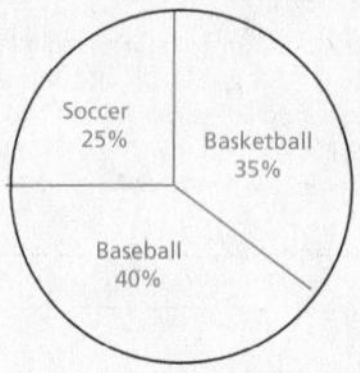

3. Suppose the table shows the results of a survey of 180 students. How many named soccer as their favorite team sport?

Percent written as a decimal ↓ — Students surveyed ↓

0.25 × 180 = 45

Use with Grade 5, Chapter 14, Lesson 8, pages 652–655. (461)

Enrich

Circle Graphs

E 14-8 ENRICH

Vacation Surveys

Two groups of people were asked to name their favorite place to go for vacation. The survey results are shown in the table.

Place	Group A	Group B
Beach	40	24
Theme Park	64	48
Museum	16	60
Campgrounds	32	36
Foreign Country	8	72

Make circle graphs to show the survey results from both groups.

Group A

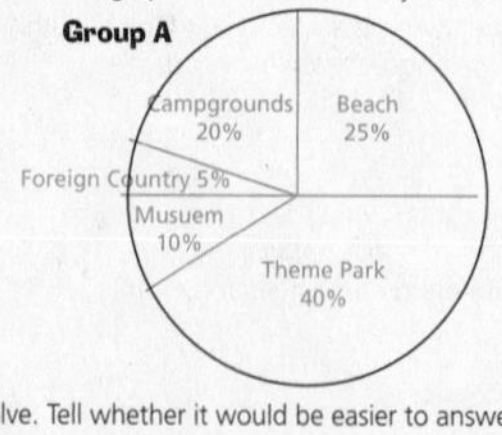

Group B

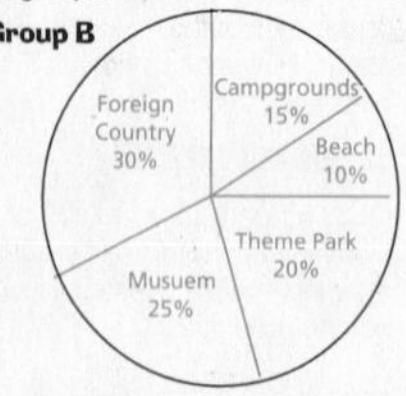

Solve. Tell whether it would be easier to answer each question by using the table or the circle graphs.

1. Did more people in Group A or in Group B name a theme park?
Group A; table

2. Which place(s) did more than 25% of Group B name?
Foreign Country; circle graph

3. Which place(s) did fewer than 20 people in Group A name?
Museum and Foreign Country; table

4. Did a greater part of Group A or of Group B name campgrounds?
Group A; circle graphs

Use with Grade 5, Chapter 14, Lesson 8, pages 652–655. (462)

Daily Homework

14-8 Circle Graphs

Use data from the circle graph for problems 1–4.

1. List the sports from least favorite to favorite.
tennis, football, soccer, basketball

2. What fraction of the total votes did football receive?
$\frac{1}{5}$ or equivalent

3. If 150 people were surveyed, how many voted for basketball? 60

Votes for Favorite Sport

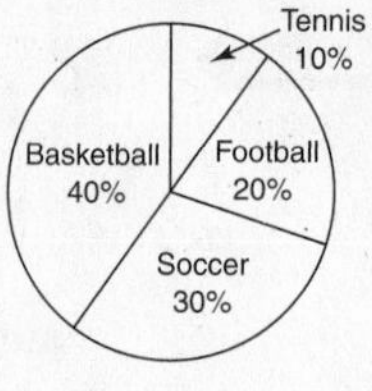

Problem Solving

Use data from the table for problems 4–6.

4. List the number of degrees that each answer will occupy on a circle graph.
Walking, 72°; Swimming, 180°; Volleyball 36°; Reading 72°

Favorite Beach Activity	Percent of Responses
Walking	20%
Swimming	50%
Volleyball	10%
Reading	20%

5. Make a circle graph to show the data.
Check students' graphs.

6. If 320 people were surveyed, how many people said swimming was their favorite beach activity? 160 people

Spiral Review

Tell whether the ratios are equivalent.

7. 4:5, 48:60 Yes
8. 120:45, 8:3 Yes
9. 6:7, 25:28 No

Grade 5, Chapter 14, Lesson 8, Cluster B 141

Chapter 14 ~ Lesson 9

Part A Worksheet

Problem Solving: Application
Applying Percents

Part A 14-9 WORKSHEET — Decision Making

Use the table to determine and record each price for a bicycle.

Store	Original Price	Sale Price	Price with assembly	Price with delivery	Price with assembly and delivery

Your Decision

Where will you buy your bicycle? Explain.

Answers may vary. Possible answer: I will buy the bicycle at Hilltop because I prefer to have the bicycle assembled and

Use with Grade 5, Chapter 14, Lesson 9, pages 656–657. (463)

Part B Worksheet

Problem Solving: Application
Which paper towel would you buy?

Part B 14-9 WORKSHEET — Math & Science

Examine the three types of paper towels. Which one do you think is the best paper towel? Explain.

Answers may vary.

Work in a group of three. You will need several sheets of each type of paper towel.

Decide how you will measure how much water each paper towel will hold.

Record in the table your data and observations for each paper towel.

Brand	Observations	Area	Water	Cubes	Price/Towel
A					
B					
C					

Use with Grade 5, Chapter 14, Lesson 9, pages 658–659. (464)

Part B Worksheet

Problem Solving: Application
Which paper towel would you buy?

Part B 14-9 WORKSHEET — Math & Science

1. Look back at the different categories in the table. Which one do you think is most important when deciding to buy a paper towel?

   Answers may vary.

2. Explain why you might be interested in the paper-towel data in each of the categories.

   Answers may vary. Possible answers: You may use paper towels to clean up spills, so you want to know which holds the most water. You may want the least expensive paper towels, so you need to know the price per towel. You may want the paper towel least likely to tear. You may want the largest paper towel.

3. Which paper towel would you choose? Explain.

   Answers may vary.

4. Did you and your partners agree on which paper towel is the best? Explain.

   Answers may vary.

5. Compare your choice of the best paper towel with the choices of your classmates. Did most students select the same paper towel as the best one?

   Answers may vary.

6. Is one of the paper towels better than the others? Explain.

   Answers may vary.

Use with Grade 5, Chapter 14, Lesson 9, pages 658–659. (465)